RESEARCH METHODS IN PSYCHOLOGY

RESEARCH METHODS IN PSYCHOLOGY

SECOND EDITION

John J. Shaughnessy
Hope College

Eugene B. Zechmeister
Loyola University of Chicago

McGRAW-HILL PUBLISHING COMPANY

New York St. Louis San Francisco Auckland Bogotá Caracas Hamburg
Lisbon London Madrid Mexico Milan Montreal New Delhi
Oklahoma City Paris San Juan São Paulo Singapore Sydney Tokyo Toronto

This book was set in Palatino by the College Composition Unit
in cooperation with Ruttle, Shaw & Wetherill, Inc.
The editors were Susan Badger and Ira C. Roberts;
the production supervisor was Denise L. Puryear.
The cover was designed by Rafael Hernandez.
R. R. Donnelley & Sons Company was printer and binder.

RESEARCH METHODS IN PSYCHOLOGY

2 3 4 5 6 7 8 9 0 DOC DOC 9 5 4 3 2 1 0

ISBN 0-07-072859-3

Library of Congress Cataloging-in-Publication Data is Available: LC Card Number 89-49176.

About the Authors

JOHN J. SHAUGHNESSY is Associate Professor of Psychology at Hope College, a relatively small, select, undergraduate liberal arts college in Holland, Michigan. After completing the B.S. degree from Loyola University of Chicago in 1969, he received the Ph.D. in 1972 from Northwestern University. He has been a frequent contributor of research on human memory, a consulting editor for the *American Journal of Psychology*, and coauthor, with Benton J. Underwood, of *Experimentation in Psychology* (Wiley, 1975), and his teaching expertise has been recognized by his colleagues' selection of him as a campus teaching consultant. At Hope College and during visiting faculty appointments at the University of California at Berkeley (1974–75, 1977–78), student responses to his problem-solving approach to teaching the research methods course have been enthusiastic.

EUGENE B. ZECHMEISTER is a Professor of Psychology at Loyola University of Chicago, a large metropolitan university where he has taught both undergraduate and graduate courses since 1970. Professor Zechmeister completed his B.A. in 1966 at the University of New Mexico. He later received both the M.S. (1968) and Ph.D. (1970) from Northwestern University. A specialist in the field of human cognition, Professor Zechmeister is the author of numerous articles and paper presentations, and is frequently called on to review manuscripts for major research journals, as well as proposals for granting agencies. He authored, with S. E. Nyberg, *Human Memory: An Introduction to Research and Theory* (Brooks/Cole, 1982). While at Loyola, Professor Zechmeister has held several administrative positions, including Director of the Experimental Psychology Program, Chairperson of the Institutional Review Board for Protection of Human Subjects, and Social Sciences Dean. In 1986 he was elected a Fellow in Division 3 (Experimental Psychology) of the American Psychological Association.

Contents

PART II   EXPERIMENTAL METHODS

5   Independent Groups: Design and Analysis   158

Preface

We have written a broad-based introduction to research methods in psychology. Various methodological approaches in psychology (naturalistic observation, survey research, and experimentation, for example) are viewed as complementary. In short, we have emphasized a multimethod approach to hypothesis testing.

Most students who take research methodology will be research consumers rather than research producers. For many students, the psychology research methods course will be their only opportunity to study the processes by which conclusions emerge from research. This book attempts to teach students to be discerning research consumers. At the same time, it provides the necessary background for students who will do research as part of their undergraduate or professional careers. Rather than emphasize specific content areas, we have illustrated concepts and methods with research from many areas of psychology. Students who use this book will find it an introduction to many contemporary and historical problems in psychology, ranging from cognitive interpretations of depression, to social attribution theory, to clinical treatment of maladaptive behavior, to program evaluation of crime deterrence programs using helicopter patrols. As students progress, they will find that they have learned much about psychology in general while coming to understand psychological research methods. Of course, by using a variety of examples from the psychology literature, we also hoped to make this introduction to research methods inherently interesting.

We also have emphasized the problem-solving nature of research. We believe that, by taking this problem-solving approach, a research methods course can develop students' critical thinking abilities. We believe that these critical thinking skills generalize well to actual problem-solving situations.

The success of the first edition prompted many instructors and students to suggest how to make the book even better. We are indebted to the many individuals who contributed ideas for improving this second edition, and we have tried to incorporate as many of these suggestions as possible. Our goal in this revised edition has been to include the best of the old and the new.

CHANGES IN THE NEW EDITION

The pedagogy and organization of the book have been improved in several ways. A major change suggested by both instructors and students was the addition of a glossary of key terms. The glossary itself appears at the end of the text, but it is integrated with the text in two ways. Key terms appear in boldface type in the body of the text and they appear again at the end of the chapter in a list of Key Concepts. In this edition we have also tried to show even greater sensitivity to the needs of beginning students with respect to the use of technical vocabulary. We have tried whenever possible to use a single term for a given concept to simplify and clarify the presentation.

The Challenge Questions that represent a distinctive pedagogical feature of our book have been retained. In response to suggestions from adopters, however, we present fewer questions in each chapter and we have provided the answer in the text to some of the questions. The Challenge Questions are an important tool for helping students develop a problem-solving attitude toward research. There are at least four questions with each chapter, including the best of those from the first edition along with ones newly written for this edition. For those instructors who do want more Challenge Questions for use in class discussion or for testing, we have included supplementary ones in the Instructor's Manual, along with answers to all of the questions.

The organization of several chapters has been changed to make it easier for instructors to adapt the book to their course structures and their own preferences for covering certain topics. In Chapter 3 we have set off the section on questionnaire construction from that of survey methodology. This allows the instructor to delete the section on constructing questionnaires unless the use of them was specifically planned as part of a course project.

A second type of reorganization took place in Chapters 5, 6, and 7 (experimental methods). We separated the material dealing with the methodological issues from the discussion of the conceptual issues of statistical analysis. By making this change we hope to put the instructor in a better position to make his or her own decision about when and to what degree the statistical issues will be covered. Our own view is that undergraduates are rarely exposed sufficiently to statistical matters and built-in redundancy is an important pedagogical technique. We recognize, however, that either the lack of background on the part of the students or the constraints of the course structure may mitigate against covering the statistical material. We hope the new organization will make the choices easier.

Another change was made in Chapter 6. Originally, we had included a Special Applications section in this chapter covering psychophysics, signal detection, and scaling. We were encouraged to delete this section by several reviewers because they thought that the chapter would be more effective if it tried to cover less material. These special topics may now be found in a new Appendix D. This keeps the material available for instructors who wish to use it.

One further bit of reorganization (and non-reorganization): Several reviewers suggested that Chapter 8 contained too much coverage of methods of behavioral conditioning prior to the coverage of $N = 1$ designs. We continue to believe that these few pages are not intrusive and that they provide an important, albeit sketchy, background for understanding single-case research. Nevertheless, in this edition we provide clear road markers to both students and instructors who want to find a detour around this part of Chapter 8. We also have adopted the more straightforward title of "$N = 1$ Designs" in this edition.

Another important pedagogical feature of this text is the four appendixes. Appendix A includes computational formulae for most standard statistics tests needed to analyze data from class research projects involving observation, survey research, or experiments. Appendix B treats ethical issues in the conduct of psychological research. Abstracts of published studies taken from the psychology literature serve as the basis for discussion of many of the ethical principles. Instructors can determine at what point in the course they wish to introduce this material. Appendix C is a writing guide. It introduces library research, including computerized bibliographic searches, along with a discussion of oral presentations and proposal writing. The major topics of Appendix C are instruction in techniques of effective writing and the stylistic requirements of the American Psychological Association for preparing a research manuscript. In this edition annotated comments are included on a sample APA paper to make it easier for students to type their research reports in accordance with the APA guidelines. As already indicated, Appendix D covers psychophysics, signal detection, and scaling.

As in the first edition, we have tried to structure the text to give instructors maximum flexibility in planning their courses. We hesitate to give many specific suggestions lest we disturb the creative juices that flow when many instructors make up a course syllabus. However, we see the following chapters as a "Basic Course": Chapters 1, 2, 5, 6, 7, and 9. The remaining chapters and appendixes can be used to expand on this core material with the choices guided by what the instructor thinks is most important and by other constraints.

Throughout the text we have sought to convey to students the excitement of psychological research.

SOME WORDS OF THANKS

There is no second edition without a first, and we owe a debt of appreciation to many people who helped us to take our first steps. They are acknowledged in the Preface to our first edition. With the second edition our debt increases and we wish to thank those people who made this new edition possible.

The book has been improved largely due to the help we received from comments on the first edition provided by students and colleagues who used the book. Although it is not possible to list everyone who talked to us about the book in the last few years, we hope that the new edition is evidence that we were listening. Thanks.

We do want to make special mention of the individuals who provided formal reviews of the earlier edition: Darryl Beale, Cerritos College; Paul Foos, Florida International University; John Jahnke, Miami University of Ohio; and Jean Volckmann, Pasedena City College.

A number of people worked very hard on specific parts of the new edition. We particulary want to thank Kathy Adamski, departmental assistant in the psychology department of Hope College, for typing a picture perfect draft of the Instructor's Manual and for encouraging us throughout the project. When preparing an extensive index, it pays to have a large and helpful family. Elizabeth, Katherine, and Peter Zechmeister all pitched in to type, proofread, and edit.

Finally, many fine professionals both at Random House/Alfred A. Knopf and then at McGraw-Hill carried us along. We especially want to acknowledge Rochelle Diogenes who helped us get the revision started and Susan Badger who guided us to its completion. Renee Shively Leonard facilitated communication between "us and them" in many ways. We were very fortunate to work with a careful and caring editor, Ira Roberts.

John J. Shaughnessy
Eugene B. Zechmeister

Permissions/Acknowledgments

CHAPTER 1

Box 1.1 Photos courtesy of The Bettman Archive and Culver Pictures. Figure 1.1. Photos courtesy of the Research Center for Language and Semiotic Studies, Indiana University, Bloomington. Figure 1.2. Photo courtesy of Eric Roth/The Picture Cube. Figure 1.3. From T. Millon, *Modern Psychopathology* (1969). Philadelphia: W. B. Saunders. Figure 3.5, page 106. Copyright Theodore Millon. Reprinted by permission of author.

CHAPTER 2

Excerpt, pages 50–51. From narrative record is from pages 769–771 of work by R. G. Barker, M. F. Schoggen, and L. S. Barker, "Hemerography of Mary Ennis." In A. Burton and R. E. Harris (Eds.), *Clinical studies of personality* (1955), pp. 768–807. New York: Harper & Row. Copyright 1955 by Harper & Row, Publishers, Inc. Reprinted by permission of publisher. Figure 2.1. From D. A. Jenni and M. A. Jenni, "Carrying behavior in humans: Analysis of sex differences." *Science* (1976), *194*, 859–860. Figure 1, page 859. Copyright 1976 by the American Association for the Advancement of Science. Reprinted by permission of publisher and author. Figure 2.2. From J. V. Becker, S. M. Turner, and T. E. Sajwag, "Multiple behavioral effects of the use of lemon juice with a ruminating toddler-age child." *Behavior Modification* (1978), *2*, 267–268. Figure 1, page 272. Copyright 1978 by Sage Publications, Inc. Reprinted by permission of Sage Publications, Inc., and author. Table 2.2. From J. R. Dickie, and S. C. Gerber, "Training in social competence: The effect on mothers, fathers, and infants." *Child Development* (1980), *51*, 1248–1251. Materials from Jane Dickie, Psychology Department, Hope College, Holland, MI. 49423. Table 2.3. From M. LaFrance and C. Mayo, "Racial differences in gaze behavior during conversations: Two systematic observational studies." *Journal of Personality and Social Psychology* (1976), *33*, 547–552. Table 2, page 550. Copyright 1976 by the American Psychological Association. Reprinted by permission of the publisher and author.

CHAPTER 3

Tables 3.1, 3.2, and 3.3. From A. Campbell, *The sense of well-being in America* (1981). New York: McGraw-Hill. Appendix Table 5, Appendix Table 2, Appendix Table 8, respectively. Copyright 1981 by McGraw–Hill, Inc. Reprinted by permission of publisher. Table 3.4. From D. D. Barron and D. Yankelovich, "Today's American woman: How the public sees her" (1980). Report prepared for President's Advisory Committee for Women by the Public Agenda Foundation. Table 5, page 69. Reprinted by permission of Daniel Yankelovich. Table 3.5. From R. A. Hicks and J. Kilcourse, "Habitual sleep duration and the incidence of headaches in college students." *Bulletin of the Psychonomic Society* (1983). *21*, 119. Table 1, page 119. Copyright 1983 by the Psychonomic Society. Reprinted by permission of publisher and author. Table 3.9. Questionnaire used in a survey conducted by researchers at the Institute for Social Research (ISR), University of Michigan. Reprinted by permission of Philip E. Converse and Willard Rodgers, ISR, Ann Arbor, MI 48106. Table 3.10. Questionnaire given to authors, who were passengers on Amtrak's Chicago–St. Louis train, by representatives of the Illinois Department of Transportation.

CHAPTER 4

Table 4.1. Based on material from E. J. Webb, D. T. Campbell, R. D. Schwartz, L. Sechrest, and J. B. Grove, *Nonreactive measures in the social sciences*, 2nd ed. (1981). Boston: Houghton Mifflin. Copyright 1981 by Harper & Row, Publishers, Inc. Used with permission of publisher. Figure 4.1. From D. P. Phillips, "Motor vehicle fatalities increase just after publicized suicide stories." *Science* (1977), *196*, 1464–1465. Figure 1, page 1465. Copyright 1977 by the American Association for the Advancement of Science. Reprinted by permission of publisher and author. Table 4.2. Adapted from material in R. M. Brandt, *Studying behavior in natural settings* (1972). New York: Holt, Rinehart & Winston. (Republished 1981 by University Press of America, Washington, D.C.). Pages 203–206. Used by permission of author. Box 4.3. From I. Kirsch, "Teaching clients to be their own therapists: A case study illustration." *Psychotherapy: Theory, Research and Practice* (1978), *15*, 302–05. Reprinted by permission of Donald K. Freedheim, Editor.

CHAPTER 5

Figure 5.1. Photo by Harry F. Harlow, courtesy of the University of Wisconsin Primate Laboratory.

CHAPTER 6

Figure 6.1. From H. A. Sackheim, R. C. Gur, and M. C. Saucy, *Science* (1978), *202*, 434–436. Figure 1, page 434. Copyright 1978 by the American Association for the Advancement of Science. Reprinted by permission of publisher and authors. Quotation in Box 6.1 and Figure 6.2. From P. Rozin and J. Jonides, "Mass reaction time: Measurement of the speed of the nerve impulse and duration of mental processes in class." *Teaching of Psychology* (1977), *4*, 91–94. Quote, page 91; Figure 1, page 91. Reprinted by permission of Robert S. Daniel. Figure 6.3. From G. S. Klein, "Semantic power measured through the interference of words with color naming." *American Journal of Psychology* (1964), *77*, 576–588. Figure 1, page 57. Copyright 1963 by the Board of Trustees of the University of Illinois. Reprinted by permission of publisher.

CHAPTER 7

Table 7.1. From G. L. Wells, R. C. L. Lindsay, and T. J. Ferguson, "Accuracy, confidence, and prior perceptions in eyewitness identification." *Journal of Applied Psychology* (1979), *64*, 440–448. Based on Table 2, page 444. Copyright 1979 by the American Psychological Association. Adapted by permission of the publisher and author. Page 247. Data for 2×2 illustration from J. E. Johnson, T. P. Petzel, L. M. Hartney, and R. A. Morgan, "Recall and importance ratings of completed and uncompleted tasks as a function of depression." *Cognitive Therapy and Research* (1983), *7*, 51–56. Copyright 1983 by Plenum Publishing Corporation. Adapted by permission of publisher and author. Figure 7.5. From J. V. Hinrichs and L. R. Novik, "Memory for numbers: Nominal versus magnitude information." *Memory & Cognition* (1982), *10*, 479–486. Figure 1, page 484. Copyright 1982 by the Psychonomic Society. Reprinted by permission of publisher and author. Figure 7.6. From W. P. Wallace and B. J. Underwood, "Implicit responses and the role of intralist similarity in verbal learning by normal and retarded subjects." *Journal of Educational Psychology* (1964) *55*, 362–370. Figures 1 and 2, page 361. Copyright 1964 by the American Psychological Association. Adapted by permission of publisher and author. Table 7.4 and Figure 7.9. From M. L. Dittmar, D. B. Berch, and J. S. Warm, "Sustained visual attention in deaf and hearing adults." *Bulletin of the Psychonomic Society* (1982), *19*, 339-342. Figure 1, page 341. Copyright 1982 by the Psychonomic Society. Adapted by permission of publisher and author. Table 7.5. From J. L. Rodman and J. M. Burger, "The influence of depression on the attribution of responsibility for an accident." *Cognitive Therapy and Research* (1985) *9*, 651–657. Used with permission of publisher and author.

CHAPTER 8

Figure 8.1. From C. B. Ferster and B. F. Skinner, *Schedules of reinforcement* (1957). New York: Appleton-Century-Crofts. Figure 1, page 14; Figure 2, page 15; Figure 6, page 24; Figure 7, page 25. Copyright by B. F. Skinner. Adapted by permission of author. Figure 8.2. Photos by E. B. Zechmeister. Used by permission of Brookfield Zoo and Chicago Zoological Society. Our thanks to Randy Brill, Director of Marine Mammal Training, and dolphin trainer, Tim Sullivan, for the opportunity to see "up close" the dolphin behavior. Figure 8.3. From S. V. Horton, "Reduction of disruptive mealtime behavior by facial screenings." *Behavior Modification* (1987), *11*, 53–64. Figure 1, page 60. Copyright 1987 by Sage Publications, Inc. Adapted by permission of Sage Publications, Inc., and author. Reprinted by permission of publisher and author. Figure 8.4. From M. G. Allison and T. Ayllon, "Behavioral coaching in the development of skills in football, gymnastics, and tennis." *Journal of Applied Behavioral Analysis* (1980), *13*, 297–304. Figure 1, page 301. Copyright 1980 by the Experimental Analysis of Behavior, Inc. Reprinted by permission of publisher and author.

CHAPTER 9

Figure 9.2. From D. T. Campbell, "Reforms as experiments." *American Psychologist* (1969), *24*, 409–429. Figure 5 and Figure 6, page 416. Copyright 1969 by the American Psychological Association. Reprinted by permission of publisher and author. Figure 9.3. From A. S. Ross and S. White, "Shoplifting, impaired driving, and refusing the breathalyzer." *Evaluation Review* (1987), *11*, 254–260. Figure 1, page 257. Copyright 1987 by Sage Publications, Inc. Reprinted by permission of Sage Publications, Inc. and author. Figure 9.4. From A. J. McSweeney, "Effects of response cost on the behavior of a million persons: Charging for directory assistance in Cincinnati." *Journal of Applied Behavior Analysis* (1978), *11*, 47–51. Copyright 1978 by the Society for the Experimental Analysis of Behavior, Inc. Reprinted by permission of publisher and author. Figure 9.5. From J. F. Schnelle, R. E. Kirchner, J. W. Macrae, M. P. McNees, R. H. Eck, S. Snodgrass, J. D. Casey, and P. H. Uselton, Jr., "Police evaluation research: An experimental and cost benefit analysis of a helicopter patrol in a high-crime area." *Journal of Applied Behavior Analysis* (1979), *11*, 11–21. Copyright 1978 by the Society for the Experimental Analysis of Behavior, Inc. Reprinted by permission of publisher and author. Box 9.3. Figure from G. Salomon, "Basic and applied research in psychology: Reciprocity between two worlds." *International Journal of Psychology* (1987), *22*, 441–446. Figure 2, page 444. Reprinted by permission of Elsevier Science Publishers, Physical Sciences and Engineering Division, and author.

APPENDIX A

Permission to use statistical tables in Appendix A is acknowledged with tables in Appendix A.

APPENDIX B

APA Principles governing research with human participants. Pages 5–7 of American Psychological Association, *Ethical principles in the conduct of research with human participants* (1982). Washington, D.C. Copyright 1982 by the American Psychological Association. Reprinted by permission of publisher. Ethical principles for "Care and Use of Animals." Principle 10, on page 638 of American Psychological Association, "Ethical principles of psychologists," *American Psychologist* (1981), *36,* 633–638. Copyright 1981 by the American Psychological Association. Reprinted by permission of publisher.

APPENDIX C

Table C.1. From the G. L. Trigg, "In your own write." *Physical Review Letters* (1979), *42,* 748. Copyright 1979 by the American Physical Society. Reprinted by permission of publisher. Table C.3 and C.3a. "Guidelines for Nonsexist Language" and extensive quotations from APA *Publication Manual* from American Psychological Association. *Publication Manual of the American Psychological Association,* 3rd ed. (1983). Washington, D.C. Copyright 1983 by the American Psychological Association. Reprinted by permission of publisher. Table C.4. From M. Anisfeld, "A course to develop competence in critical reading of empirical research in psychology." *Teaching of Psychology* (1987), *14,* 224–227. Table 1, page 225. Adapted by permission of author. Figure C.4. Courtesy of Eastman Kodak Company.

RESEARCH METHODS IN PSYCHOLOGY

CHAPTER

1

Introduction

OUTLINE

PSYCHOLOGY AS A SCIENCE

There is no record of who first observed behavior carefully and systematically, or of who conducted the first public opinion survey, or even of who performed the first psychology experiment. We don't really know exactly when psychology first became an independent discipline. Psychology emerged gradually, with its roots in the thinking of Aristotle (the "father" of all psychology; Keller, 1937), in the writings of later philosophers such as Descartes and Locke, and, more recently, in the work of early nineteenth-century physiologists and physicists. The date usually taken to mark psychology's official beginning is 1879. In that year Wilhelm Wundt established a formal psychology laboratory at Leipzig, Germany. Although there is some disagreement about whether his was actually the first psychology laboratory, the weight of historical evidence favors Wundt as the founder of scientific psychology (see Box 1.1). We can see, therefore, that psychology as a science is little more than one hundred years old.

Psychology has changed significantly since its beginnings. Wundt and his colleagues were interested primarily in questions dealing with sensation and perception—for instance, visual illusions and imagery. Experiments on reaction time also were conducted with the goal of measuring the time necessary for various cognitive processes, such as those involved in making a choice (Boring, 1950). Psychologists continue to be interested in sensation-perception, and Wundt's procedures were the basis of some of the experimental methods that are used today. However, research on sensation-perception represents but a fraction of the research undertaken in

BOX 1.1

WHO WAS FIRST, WUNDT OR JAMES?

Wilhelm Wundt
(1832–1920)

William James
(1842–1910)

In 1979 the American Psychological Association celebrated the 100th anniversary of the beginning of a "scientific" psychology. The year chosen for the centennial event was based on the founding by Wilhelm Wundt, in 1879, of an experimental psy-chology laboratory at Leipzig, Germany. The histo-rian E. G. Boring calls Wundt the "first man who without reservation is properly called a psycholo-gist" (Boring, 1950, p. 316). Although there were philosophers, physiologists, physicists, and others

contemporary psychology. Today psychologists are interested in a myriad of topics, including those in such general areas as clinical, social, industrial, experimental, counseling, physiological, cognitive, educational, and developmental psychology. At present there are more than 60,000 members of the American Psychological Association (Spielberger, 1988). Another important association of psychologists, which was formed recently to emphasize scientific issues in psychology, is the American Psychological Society.

Psychology has also not developed strictly as a laboratory science. Although laboratory investigation remains at the heart of psychological inquiry, psychologists and other behavioral scientists do research in schools, clinics, businesses, hospitals, and other nonlaboratory settings. Many research psychologists are engaged in program evaluation, a type of research in which the impact of large-scale interventions on groups or institutions is evaluated. Program evaluators confront such questions as whether a new management-labor relations program will lead to increased employee morale and company productivity, or whether the nationwide Head Start program has significantly raised the IQ of hundreds of thousands of preschoolers (see Chapter 9).

who had considered many of the problems that later were to become the province of psychology, no one promoted psychology as an independent discipline until Wundt.

In 1856, like many scientists in those days, Wundt took a doctorate degree in medicine, having earlier studied under Johannes Müller (at the time Müller was perhaps the world's foremost physiologist). After receiving his degree, Wundt published in the fields of anatomy and physiology but he soon developed a "physiological psychology" that was the basis for his idea of an experimental psychology (Boring, 1950).

There is no question that Wundt founded a formal psychology laboratory in 1879. Soon dozens of researchers flocked to Germany to study with Wundt and to work in his modest laboratory. James McKeen Cattell and G. Stanley Hall from the United States were but two of the individuals to study with Wundt and later become prominent psychologists (Benjamin, 1979). Cattell pioneered the use of mental tests and statistical methods. G. Stanley Hall founded the first psychology journal in the United States, the *American Journal of Psychology,* and helped plan the American Psychological

Association, which was organized in 1892 with Hall as its first president (Boring, 1950). From Wundt's laboratory the new psychology spread quickly to the intellectual centers of the world.

It has been pointed out, however, that the American philosopher and psychologist William James also established a psychology laboratory, at Harvard University in 1875 or 1876 (Lippman, 1979). It was a small room (apparently under a stairway in one of the Harvard buildings) set aside for psychology experimentation. Should Wundt or James get credit for establishing the first psychology laboratory? The argument against James is that he really did not "found" a psychology laboratory. As Boring (1950) notes, there were other demonstration laboratories known to exist prior to 1879, but such laboratories were "not 'founded'; they simply occurred and existed" (p. 324). Also, James apparently never saw himself as an experimental psychologist and even disliked the "tedium" of laboratory pursuits (Bringmann, 1979; Jacobson, 1979). We might consider, therefore, James' lab an "anticipation" (Boring, 1950) of the laboratory that was officially "founded" by Wundt and from which sprang a scientific psychology.

THE SCIENTIFIC METHOD

There is one way in which psychology has not changed in the one hundred years or so of its existence: the **scientific method** is still emphasized as the basis for investigation. The founding of Wundt's laboratory marked the beginning of the formal application of the scientific method to problems in psychology. This method is not identified with particular kinds of equipment nor is it associated exclusively with specific research procedures. The scientific method is something abstract. It is an approach to knowledge that is best described by distinguishing it from what might be called nonscientific or everyday approaches to knowledge.

SCIENTIFIC AND NONSCIENTIFIC APPROACHES TO KNOWLEDGE

The major differences between a scientific and a nonscientific approach to knowledge are outlined in Table 1.1. Collectively, the characteristics listed under the scientific approach in Table 1.1 define what is called the *scientific method.* The distinctions made there between a scientific and a nonscientific approach are intended to highlight differences that frequently exist between

TABLE 1.1 CHARACTERISTICS OF SCIENTIFIC AND NONSCIENTIFIC (EVERYDAY) APPROACHES TO KNOWLEDGE*

	Nonscientific (everyday)	Scientific
General Approach:	Intuitive	Empirical
Observation:	Casual, uncontrolled	Systematic, controlled
Reporting:	Biased, subjective	Unbiased, objective
Concepts:	Ambiguous, with surplus meanings	Clear definitions, operational specificity
Instruments:	Inaccurate, imprecise	Accurate, precise
Measurement:	Not valid or reliable	Valid and reliable
Hypotheses:	Untestable	Testable
Attitude:	Uncritical, accepting	Critical, skeptical

*Based in part on distinctions suggested by Marx (1963).

"everyday" or informal kinds of thinking and thinking that is characteristic of the scientist's approach to knowledge. These distinctions are briefly summarized as follows.

General Approach   Many everyday judgments are made intuitively. This usually means that we act on the basis of what "feels right" or what "seems reasonable." Intuition is not based on a formal decision process, such as that of deductive logic, nor is it based on information that was taught to us or that was acquired through direct experience. The many everyday inferences and conclusions reached intuitively are the product of insight and of what we quickly perceive as true.

Intuition is a valuable cognitive process. We frequently have little to go on other than what intuition suggests is the right answer or the proper course to follow. Intuition also can help us make decisions in situations that we have not encountered before. Consider, for example, what intuition might suggest as the answer to a question based on the following situation:

Assume that on two different occasions you are the victim of a street crime. Let us say that you are walking down the street and someone tries to grab your wallet or purse. The thief begins to wrestle with you in order to get it. You find yourself in need of assistance. On one occasion there is a crowd of bystanders who witness the attempted robbery. On the other occasion there is only one person who sees the event.

The question is: In which situation would you be more likely to receive help, when many people are present or when only one bystander is present?

Intuition would suggest that, the more people who are present, the greater the chances are that you will receive help. Surprisingly, social psychologists have determined that just the opposite is true. A bystander is more likely to act in an emergency when alone than when a group of people is present (Latané and Darley, 1970; see also Chapter 2 in this book).

Our intuition about what is true does not always agree with what is actually true because we fail to recognize that our perceptions may be distorted by what are called cognitive biases or because we neglect to weigh available evidence appropriately (Kahneman and Tversky, 1973; Tversky and Kahneman, 1974). One such cognitive bias, called *illusory correlation,* is our tendency to perceive a relationship between events when none exists. Ward and Jenkins (1965) showed their subjects the results of a hypothetical 50-day cloud seeding experiment. For each of the 50 days, subjects were told whether cloud seeding had been done and whether it had rained on that day. Ward and Jenkins constructed the results such that there was actually no relationship between cloud seeding and the likelihood of rain—rain was equally likely on days when seeding had and had not been done. Nonetheless, subjects were convinced that the evidence supported their intuitive supposition that cloud seeding and rain varied together. One possible basis for the illusory correlation bias is that we are more likely to notice events that are consistent with our beliefs than those that violate them. Thus, subjects in the cloud seeding experiment may have been more likely to notice and remember the days on which cloud seeding was followed by rain than the days on which clouds were seeded in vain.

The scientific approach to knowledge is empirical rather than intuitive. An **empirical approach** emphasizes direct observation and experimentation as a way of answering questions. This does not mean that intuition plays no role in science. Any scientist can probably recount tales of getting empirical outcomes or experimental results that intuition had suggested would emerge. On the other hand, the same scientist is also likely to have come up with just as many findings that were counterintuitive. Research at first may be guided by what the scientist's intuition suggests is the proper direction to take. Eventually, however, the scientist strives to be guided by what direct observation and experimentation reveal to be true.

Observation   We can learn a great deal about behavior by simply observing the actions of others. However, everyday observations are not always made carefully or systematically. Most people do not attempt to control or eliminate factors that might influence the events that they are observing. As a consequence, erroneous conclusions are often drawn. Consider, for instance, the classic case of Clever Hans. Hans was a horse who was said by his owner, a German mathematics teacher, to have amazing talents. Hans could count, do simple addition and subtraction problems (even involving fractions), read German, answer simple questions ("What is the lady holding in her hands?"), and give the date and tell time (Watson, 1914/1967). Hans answered questions by tapping with his forefoot or by pointing with his nose at different alternatives shown to him. His owner considered Hans to be truly intelligent and denied using any tricks to guide his horse's behavior. And, in fact, Clever Hans was clever even when the questioner was someone other than his owner.

Newspapers carried accounts of Hans' performances, and hundreds of people came to view this amazing horse (see Figure 1.1). In 1904 a scientific commission was established with the goal of discovering the basis for Hans' abilities. The scientists found that Hans was no longer clever if either of two circumstances obtained. First, Hans did not know the answers to questions if

FIGURE 1.1 *Top*: Clever Hans performing before onlookers. *Bottom*: Hans being tested under more controlled conditions. Note the presence of a blindfold during testing.

the questioner also did not know the answers. Second, Hans was not very clever if he could not see his questioner. It was discovered that Hans was responding to very slight movements of the questioner. A slight bending forward by the questioner would start Hans tapping and any movement upward or backward would cause Hans to stop tapping. The commission demonstrated that questioners were unintentionally cueing Hans in this way.

This famous account of Clever Hans illustrates the fact that scientific observation (unlike casual observation) is systematic and controlled. Indeed, it has been suggested that "control" is the essential ingredient of science, distinguishing it from nonscientific procedures (Boring, 1954; Marx, 1963). In the case of Clever Hans, investigators exercised control by manipulating *one at a time* such conditions as whether the questioner knew the answer to questions asked of Clever Hans and whether Hans could see the questioner (see Figure 1.1). By exercising **control,** taking care to investigate the effect of various factors one by one, the scientist seeks to gain a clearer picture of those factors that actually produce a phenomenon.

The factors that the researcher controls or manipulates in order to determine their effect on behavior are called the **independent variables.** In the simplest of studies, the independent variable has two levels. These two levels often represent the presence and the absence of some treatment, respectively. The condition in which the treatment is present is commonly called the *experimental condition;* the condition in which the treatment is absent is called the *control condition.* If we wanted to study the effect of drinking alcohol on the ability to process complex information quickly and accurately, the independent variable would involve the presence or absence of alcohol in a drink that subjects were given. Subjects in the experimental condition would receive alcohol, while subjects in the control condition would receive the same drink without alcohol. Sometimes the levels of the independent variable are selected by a researcher rather than manipulated. This is typically the case when a **subject variable** serves as an independent variable. A subject variable is a characteristic or trait that varies consistently across subjects. For example, a researcher may be interested in the effect of age on the ability to process complex information. Do older adults, for instance, process verbatim and inferential information differently from younger adults (see Till, 1985). Age would be the independent variable in this study. Age is a subject variable and necessarily would not be manipulated by a researcher; rather, the researcher controls this independent variable by systematically selecting individuals of particular ages or within specific age groups. Intelligence, aggressiveness, and fraternity or sorority membership are other examples of subject variables.

The term *independent variable* is used for both subject variables when levels of the variable are selected and for nonsubject variables when levels can be manipulated. There are important differences, however, between these kinds of independent variables. As we will see later in this chapter and in Chapter 5, manipulating the levels of an independent variable has considerable advantages over selecting the levels of a subject variable. Studying the effects of subject variables poses additional challenges of control. Nonetheless, subject variables are of significant interest in many research areas of psychology.

The measures of behavior that are used to assess the effect (if any) of the independent variables are called **dependent variables.** In our example of a study which investigates the effects of alcohol on processing complex information, the researcher might measure the number of errors made by control and experimental subjects when playing a difficult video game. Errors, then, would be the dependent variable. When Till (1985) investigated the ability of young and elderly adults to process verbatim and inferential messages appearing in a list of unrelated sentences, he recorded subjects' answers to twenty-four questions based on the information in the sentences. Number of questions answered correctly was the dependent variable. Most studies in psychology are done in order to discover the nature of the relationship between particular independent and dependent variables.

If changes in the dependent variable are to be interpreted as a result of the effects of the independent variable, control techniques must be used properly. The control techniques available to scientists can be divided into three types: manipulation, holding conditions constant, and balancing. We have already seen how *manipulation* of the levels of an independent variable can be used as a control technique. The second type of control, holding conditions constant, is probably the one that is most commonly associated with the word "control." If we were studying the effect of drinking alcohol on errors made while playing a video game, we would *not* want to test the experimental subjects using a large, color screen and the control subjects using a small, black-and-white screen. Instead, we would want to make sure that the same screen was used for all subjects, thereby *holding constant* the potentially significant variable of type of display screen.

When an independent variable is manipulated, at least one set of factors typically cannot be held constant—the characteristics of the subjects tested. Just as the researcher would not want experimental and control subjects in the alcohol study to use different screens, the researcher also would not want control and experimental subjects to differ systematically in terms of some subject characteristic that affects video game performance. People are likely to differ in the amount of experience they have had playing video games. It would be important that control and experimental subjects have similar amounts of experience playing video games. Researchers control factors that are not manipulated and that cannot be held constant by *balancing* the influence of these factors across the conditions. The most common technique used to avoid imbalance is to assign subjects randomly to the different groups being tested. Without random assignment, we might find that one group had more younger people, more women, more overweight people, and so on—all differences that might distort the results of the study. Of course, even groups whose members are randomly assigned are not all perfectly equivalent in all characteristics, but any imbalance is likely to be minor, and very unlikely to affect research results. Throughout this text, we will be describing specific procedures for the use of each of the three types of control (see especially Chapters 5 and 6).

When the independent variable is a subject variable, such as age, and levels of the independent variable must be selected rather than manipulated, it should be apparent that balancing subject characteristics through random assignment is not feasible. Young and elderly adults, for example, are selected from natural groups to represent levels of an age variable; thus, it is not possible to assign subjects randomly to different levels of the independent variable. The process of selecting subjects to represent different levels of a subject variable serves to define the levels of the independent variable. However, subject characteristics other than the one which is explicitly defined also may differentiate the groups. If a researcher set out to investigate the effect of age on ability to play video games, it must be acknowledged that subjects are likely to differ in ways other than age. In other words, elderly adults are not only "older" (by definition) than younger adults but also likely to have had less experience playing video games than are younger adults. Video games simply were not around when today's elderly were adolescents. Elderly adults also may differ from younger adults in their motivation to play video games, or in terms of many other relevant characteristics. Because it is not possible to balance these factors between young and elderly groups through randomization, the researcher must deal with the fact that differences in performance associated with age need not be (nor are they even likely to be) due to differences in "age" per se.

One solution to this methodological dilemma is to select subjects for each level who are similar with respect to certain important characteristics such as, for instance, amount of experience with video games. Till (1985) gave young and elderly adults a vocabulary test prior to their participation in his information processing experiment and selected young and old subjects who were similar in verbal ability. This procedure matches the groups of subjects with respect to the characteristic of verbal ability. Matching as a procedure for holding a variable constant across groups presents problems of its own and is discussed at length in Chapter 5. For now it is sufficient to understand that when a difference in a dependent variable is found corresponding to the levels of a subject variable, it is difficult to know to what exactly this difference should be attributed. Is it age or motivation? Age or amount of education? Suggestions for dealing with the interpretation of differences across levels of a subject variable are presented in Chapter 7.

Reporting   If we ask someone to *report* to us about events that occurred in our absence, we probably want the report to be unbiased and objective. Otherwise we will be unable to determine exactly what happened. As you might imagine, personal biases and subjective impressions often enter into everyday reports that we receive. Ask anyone to describe an event to you and you are likely to receive not merely details of the event but personal impressions as well. You may also find that the details reported to you are not the ones that *you* would have reported. We often report events in terms of our own interests and attitudes. Obviously, these interests and attitudes do not always coincide with those of others. The next time you take a class examination, poll several classmates on their impressions of the test. Their reports are likely to vary dramatically, depending on such factors as how well prepared they were, what they concentrated on when they studied, and their expectations about what the instructor was going to emphasize on the test.

When scientists report their findings, they seek to separate what they have observed from what they conclude or infer on the basis of these observations. For example, consider the photograph shown in Figure 1.2. How would you describe to someone what you see there? One way to describe this scene is to say that two people are running along the street with one person in front of the other. You might also describe this scene as one person *chasing* the other. If you use this second description, you are reporting an inference drawn from what you have seen and not just reporting what you

FIGURE 1.2   How would you describe this scene?

have observed. The description of two people running would be preferred in a scientific report.

This distinction between description and inference in reporting can be carried to extremes. For example, describing what is shown in Figure 1.2 as running could be considered an inference, the actual observation being that two people are moving their legs up and down and forward in rapid, long strides. Such a literal description also would not be appropriate. The point is that, in scientific reporting, observers must guard against a tendency to draw inferences too quickly. Further, events should be described in sufficient detail without including trivial and unnecessary minutiae. We will discuss proper methods for making observations and reporting them in Chapter 2.

Scientific reporting also seeks to be unbiased and objective. For instance, one accepted check on whether a report is unbiased is whether it can be verified by more than one independent observer. For example, a measure of interobserver agreement is usually found in observational studies (see Chapter 2). Unfortunately, many biases are subtle and are not always detected even in scientific reporting. There is, for example, a species of fish in which the eggs are incubated in the mouth of the male parent until they hatch. The first scientist to observe the eggs disappear into their father's mouth could certainly be forgiven for assuming, momentarily, that he was eating them. That's simply what we expect organisms to do with their mouths! But the careful observer waits, watches for unexpected results, and takes *nothing* for granted.

Furthermore, occasional instances of intentional biasing have been discovered (see Appendix B, on ethics). Although unbiased and objective reporting is a goal of science, we must acknowledge that that goal is not always achieved. Avoiding biased reporting and detecting its presence in scientific reports are two lessons you will be asked to learn.

Ironically, Wundt himself was criticized because of possible bias in the reports he used in the first systematic investigation of cognitive processes. A major research method used by Wundt and his colleagues was **introspection.** The subjects in Wundt's lab whose cognitive processes were being probed were asked to describe their feelings and sensations when presented with various kinds of stimuli. To be sure, these reports were not given carelessly; the subjects completed thousands of practice trials before they were permitted to contribute real data. Nevertheless, introspection as a methodology was severely criticized because observers viewing the same stimulus could not always agree on what they had observed. Critics questioned whether a science of psychology could be based on such a subjective method of reporting. Eventually, problems with introspection turned many psychologists toward a science of strictly observable behavior (see, for example, Watson, 1913).

Concepts   We use the term *concepts* to refer to things (both living and inanimate), to events (things in action), and to relationships among things or events, as well as to their characteristics (Marx, 1963). *Dog* is a concept, as is *barking,* and so is *obedience.* Concepts are the symbols by which we ordinarily communicate. Clear, unambiguous communication of ideas requires that we use concepts that are clearly defined. This means that the concepts we use should be free of unwarranted or surplus meaning. That is, a concept should not convey more meaning than was intended.

In everyday conversation we can often get by without having to worry too much about how we define a concept. Many words, for instance, are commonly used and apparently understood even though neither party to the communication knows *exactly* what the words mean. We are suggesting that people frequently communicate with one another without being fully aware of what they are talking about. This may sound ridiculous but, to prove our point, try the following.

Ask a few people whether they believe that intelligence is mostly inherited or that intelligence is mostly acquired. You might try arguing a point of view opposite to theirs just for the fun of it. After having engaged them in a discussion about the roots of intelligence, ask them what they mean by "intelligence." You will probably find that most people have a difficult time defining this concept. Yet people are frequently willing to debate an important point regarding intelligence, and even take a definite stand on the issue, without being able to say exactly what intelligence is. When someone does provide a definition, it is unlikely to be exactly the same as that given by another person. That is, intelligence means one thing to one person and something else to another. Clearly, in order to attempt actually to answer the question of whether intelligence is mainly inherited or mainly acquired, we must provide an exact definition that all parties involved can accept. On the other hand, to merely talk about this issue, even to argue about it, we can get by in everyday conversation without knowing exactly what it is that we are talking about!

Just as the average layperson may not know exactly what intelligence is, experts who do research in this area are also not always in complete agreement about what constitutes intelligence (see Detterman and Sternberg, 1982). Interestingly, the views held by nonscientists about the nature of intelligence are not all that different from the ideas developed by experts who do research and publish books and articles about intelligence (Sternberg, 1982). What, then, is the role of the scientist who studies intelligence (or any other psychological concept)? As Sternberg (1982, pp. 35–36) points out, the nonscientist's ideas of intelligence represent only a starting point—a base— from which this important topic can be investigated:

> Why, if we know people's informal theories of intelligence, do we need formal scientific theories at all? A careful examination of the kinds of behaviors people have listed will show why we do. Consider some examples of such behaviors: "reasons logically and well," "makes good decisions," "is verbally fluent," and "reads with high comprehension." One might well ask just what it means to do any of these things. These descriptions label behaviors without really explaining them or even

defining what goes into them. What does it mean, psychologically, to reason logically and well, or to read with high comprehension? What makes some people reason or read better than others? These are the kinds of questions psychologists must address in their scientific theories. Thus, the informal theories of laymen can be seen as setting up a framework within which scientists can work; the detailed contents falling within that framework can be filled in only by scientific research.

One way in which a scientist gives meaning to a concept is by defining it operationally. An **operational definition** explains a concept solely in terms of the operations used to produce and measure it. Intelligence, for instance, can be defined operationally by specifying a paper-and-pencil test emphasizing understanding of logical relationships, short-term memory, and acquaintance with the meaning of words. Some may not like this operational definition of intelligence, but once a particular test has been identified, there can be no argument about what intelligence means according to this definition. Operational definitions facilitate communication, at least among those who know how and why they are used.

Although exact meaning is conveyed via operational definitions, this approach to communication has not escaped criticism. One problem has been alluded to already. That is, if we don't like one operational definition of intelligence, there is nothing to prevent us from giving intelligence another operational definition. Does this mean that there are as many kinds of intelligence as there are operational definitions? Each time a new set of questions is added to a paper-and-pencil test of intelligence do we have a new definition of intelligence? The answer, unfortunately, is that we don't really know. To determine whether a different procedure yields a new definition of intelligence, we would have to seek additional evidence. For example, do people who score high on one test also score high on the second test? If they do, the new test may be measuring the same thing as the old one.

Another criticism of using operational definitions is that the definitions are not always meaningful. For example, defining intelligence in terms of how long one can balance a ball on one's nose is an operational definition that most people would not find very meaningful. How do we decide whether a concept has been meaningfully defined? Once again, the solution is to appeal to other forms of evidence. How does performance on a balancing task compare to performance on other tasks that *are* commonly accepted as measures of intelligence? We must also be willing to apply common sense to the situation. Do people usually consider balancing a ball evidence of intelligence? Scientists are generally aware of the limitations of operational definitions; however, the clarity of communication that derives from this approach is assumed to outweigh the problems it raises.

Instruments   You depend on instruments to measure events more than you probably realize. The speedometer in the car, the clock in the bedroom, and the thermometer used to measure body temperature are all instruments that we would find it difficult to do without. And you can appreciate the problems that arise if one of these instruments is inaccurate. *Accuracy* refers to the difference between what an instrument says is true and what is known to be true. A clock that is consistently 5 minutes slow is not very accurate. Inaccurate clocks can make us late, inaccurate speedometers can earn us traffic tickets, and inaccurate thermometers can lead us to believe that we are ill when we are not. Accuracy of an instrument is determined by calibrating or checking it with another instrument known to be true. Thus, we periodically call the telephone company to check the accuracy of our clocks based on the recorded messages telling us "the time at the tone," which we assume represents the true time. Accuracy of speedometers can be checked using a combination of observations of roadside distance markers and the seconds ticking off on an accurate watch.

Measurements can be made at varying levels of *precision*. A measure of time in tenths of a second is not as precise as one that is in hundredths of a second. One instrument that yields imprecise measures is the gas gauge in most cars. Although reasonably accurate, gas gauges do not give very precise readings. Most of us have wished at one time or another that the gas gauge would permit us to determine whether we had that extra half gallon of gas that would get us to the next service station.

To measure behavior we also need instruments. Wundt used reaction time apparatus to measure the time required for cognitive processing. You can be assured that the precision, and even the accuracy, of instruments of this kind have improved significantly in the last one hundred years. Today electronic counters provide precise measures of reaction time in milliseconds (thousandths of a second). Many other instruments are employed in contemporary psychology. To perform a biofeedback experiment requires instruments that give accurate feedback to a participant regarding such internal states as heart rate and blood pressure. Tests of anxiety sometimes employ instruments to measure galvanic skin response (GSR). Other behavioral instruments are of the paper-and-pencil variety. Questionnaires are a popular instrument used by psychologists to measure behavior (see especially Chapter 3). So, too, are the rating scales used by human observers (see Chapter 2). For instance, rating aggression in children on a 7-point scale ranging from not at all aggressive (1) to very aggressive (7) can yield relatively accurate (although perhaps not too precise) measures of aggression. It is the responsibility of the behavioral scientist to use instruments that are as precise and as accurate as possible.

Measurement   Even an instrument that is both accurate and precise is of little value if the measure it provides is not valid. In general, **validity** refers to the "truthfulness" of a measure. A valid measure of a concept is one that measures what it claims to measure. We discussed this aspect of measurement when we mentioned possible operational definitions of intelligence. Intelligence, it was suggested, could be defined in terms of performance on a task requiring one to balance a ball on one's nose. According to the principle of operationalism, this is a perfectly permissible definition. However, we would be led to ask whether this is really a measure of intelligence; we would want to question the validity of this measure. Is intelligence actually being measured by how long we can keep a ball twirling on our nose? As we indicated earlier, evidence bearing on the validity of this definition would have to come from other sources. The validity of a measure is supported to the extent that subjects do as well on *it* as they do on independent measures that are presumed to measure the same concept. For example, if time spent balancing a ball is a valid measure of intelligence, then a person who does well on the balancing task should also do well on such measures as size of vocabulary, reasoning ability, and other accepted measures of intelligence. Note that an instrument, such as a stopwatch, may be very accurate and precise, yet not provide a valid measure of the concept of intelligence. We need to be concerned with not only the accuracy and precision of our instruments when measuring an event but also the validity of the measurement when defining a concept.

Another important aspect of measurement is **reliability.** Measurement is reliable when it is consistent. Several different kinds of reliability can be distinguished. When we speak of instrument reliability, we are discussing whether an instrument works consistently. The car that sometimes starts and sometimes doesn't when we engage the ignition is not very reliable. Observations made by two or more independent observers are said to be reliable if they show agreement—that is, if the observations are consistent from one observer to another. In the context of psychological testing, researchers need to be concerned with test reliability. Are the results obtained on a test consistent from one administration of the test to another? In subsequent chapters of this book we will discuss these various kinds of reliability and introduce various methods for measuring reliability.

In one sense validity and reliability are independent. A measure can be highly reliable but not valid. For instance, subjects whose intelligence was being tested might be able to perform consistently (reliably) on a balancing task, but there are serious questions about the validity of this measure of intelligence. Similarly, the rate of firing of an individual neuron in the brain might be a valid measure of a person's mental alertness, but with present instruments such a measure would probably prove unreliable. It is generally easier to confirm that a measure is reliable than it is to confirm its validity, but both are essential to successful measurement.

Psychologists must deal with two types of measurement. The first type, physical measurement, involves dimensions for which there is an agreed-upon standard and an instrument for doing the measuring. Length is a dimension that can be scaled with physical measurement, and there are agreed-upon standards for units of length. For instance, 1 meter was at one time defined as 1/10,000,000 of the distance between the North Pole and the equator. This proved impossible to measure precisely, so the definition of 1 meter was changed to the distance between two points on a platinumiridium bar kept under controlled conditions near Paris, France. Although this provided accuracy to one part in a million, greater precision was sought. In 1960 the meter was defined as 1,650,763.73 wavelengths of the red-orange radiation of the inert gas krypton-86. But even this proved not precise enough for scientists. (When using it to measure the distance from the earth to the moon, scientists found themselves in error by more than 1.5 meters.) Recently, the definition of the meter was changed to the length of the path traveled by light in a vacuum in 1/299,792,458 of a second.

In most research in psychology, however, the dimensions to be measured do not involve physical measurement. Rulers do not exist for measuring beauty, aggression, or intelligence. For these dimensions we must use a second type of measurement: psychological measurement. Agreement among a certain number of observers provides the basis for psychological measurement. If several independent observers agree that a certain action warrants a rating of 3 on a 7-point rating scale of aggression, we can say that we have a psychological measurement of the aggressiveness of the action. Of course, many dimensions that can be scaled physically can also be measured using psychological measurement. Observers can be asked to judge which of two lines is longer, and, if they consistently select the longer one, we know the observers can "measure" length. This type of measurement is called psychophysical measurement and it represents one of the earliest areas of experimental investigation in psychology. The methods of psychophysics are discussed in considerably greater detail in Appendix D.

There are four levels of measurement, called **measurement scales,** that apply to both physical and psychological measurement. The lowest level or scale is called a *nominal scale*, and it involves simply categorizing the stimulus to be measured into one of a number of discrete categories. For instance, we could measure the color of people's eyes by categorizing them as brown-eyed or blue-eyed. In terms of the arithmetic operations that we can perform on data recorded on a nominal scale, we can use only the relationships "equal" and "not equal." A common way of summarizing nominal data is to report the frequency or proportion of instances in each of the several categories. Sometimes nominal scales involve the use of numbers, and we must be careful to remember that these numbers serve only as labels for categories. For example, telephone numbers and the numbers seen on the jerseys of competing athletes are used only to distinguish one from another.

The second level or scale is called an *ordinal scale*, and it involves ordering or ranking the stimuli to be measured. Ordinal scales add the arithmetic relationships "greater than" and "less than" to the measurement process. One common example of an ordinal scale is class rank. We can order students in a class from highest to lowest, but if we know only their ranks we have no information about how far apart the students were in academic performance. When we know that an Olympic distance runner won a silver medal, we do not know whether she finished second in a photo finish with the first-place contestant or trailed 200 meters behind the gold medal winner.

The third level or scale is called an *interval scale,* and it involves being able to specify how far apart two stimuli are on a given dimension. On an ordinal scale, the difference between the stimulus ranked first and the stimulus ranked third does not necessarily equal the distance between the stimuli ranked third and fifth. On an interval scale, however, differences of the same numerical size in scale values *are* equal. For example, the difference between fifty and seventy correct answers on an aptitude test is equal to the difference between seventy and ninety correct answers, and thus the ratio of scale intervals is meaningful. What is missing from an interval scale is a meaningful zero point. For instance, if your score were zero on a verbal aptitude test you would not necessarily have absolutely zero verbal ability. On the other hand, the standard arithmetic operations of addition, multiplication, subtraction, and division can be performed on data that are measured on an interval scale. Whenever possible, therefore, psychologists try to measure psychological dimensions using interval scales.

The fourth level of measurement is a *ratio scale.* A ratio scale has all the properties of an interval scale with the important additional quality of an absolute zero point. In terms of arithmetic operations, a zero point makes the ratio of scale values meaningful. For example, temperature as expressed on the Celsius scale represents an interval scale of measurement. A reading of zero degrees Celsius does not really mean absolutely no temperature. Therefore it is not meaningful to say that 100 degrees Celsius is twice as hot as 50 degrees, or that 40 degrees is half as cold as 20 degrees. On the other hand, the Kelvin scale of temperature does have an absolute zero, and the ratio of scale values can be meaningfully calculated. Physical scales measuring time, weight, and distance can usually be treated as ratio scales.

Table 1.2 summarizes the characteristics of levels of measurement that we have discussed. You will need to keep these four types of scales in mind as you select statistical procedures for analyzing the results of the research you will be doing (see Appendix A).

Hypotheses An **hypothesis** is a tentative explanation for something. It frequently attempts to answer the questions "How?" and "Why?" At one

TABLE 1.2 CHARACTERISTICS OF MEASUREMENT SCALES

Type of Scale	Operations	Objective
Nominal	Equal/not equal	Sort stimuli into discrete categories
Ordinal	Greater than/less than	Rank-order stimuli on a single dimension
Interval	Addition/multiplication/subtraction/ division	Specify the distance between stimuli in a given dimension
Ratio	Addition/multiplication/subtraction/ division/formation of ratios of values	Specify the distance between stimuli in a given dimension and express ratios of scale values

level, an hypothesis may simply suggest how particular variables are related. For example, a researcher may hypothesize that elderly adults will remember less of inferential information than will young adults. At a more theoretical level, an hypothesis may offer a reason (the "why") for the way that particular variables are related. For example, Till (1985) hypothesized that older adults remember less inferential information because they are less able to encode (register) and retrieve (recall) such information than are younger adults.

Nearly everyone has proposed hypotheses to explain some human behavior at one time or another. Why do people commit apparently senseless acts of violence? What causes people to smoke cigarettes? Why are some students academically more successful than others? One characteristic often distinguishes the hypotheses proposed by the nonscientist from those offered by the scientist: testability. As attractive as it might be, if an hypothesis cannot be tested, it is of no immediate use to science (Marx, 1963).

Hypotheses are not testable if *the concepts to which they refer are not adequately defined.* To say that a would-be assassin shoots a U.S. president or other prominent figure because he was mentally disturbed is not a testable hypothesis unless a definition of "mentally disturbed" can be agreed upon. Unfortunately, psychologists and psychiatrists cannot always agree on what such terms as "mentally disturbed" and "insane" mean. Often this occurs because an acceptable operational definition is not available for these concepts. As one prominent researcher has commented, "a criterion of whether or not a so-called empirical concept is a scientific concept is whether or not it has been operationally defined" (Underwood, 1957, p. 52). Therefore, in addition to facilitating clarity in communication, operational definitions offer a means of evaluating whether our hypotheses contain scientifically acceptable concepts.

Hypotheses are also untestable if they are *circular,* in which case the event itself becomes an explanation for the event. Consider the hypothesis that people like to smoke cigarettes because they enjoy smoking. When it is read another way, this hypothesis claims that people enjoy something that they like. But isn't liking something the same as enjoying it? This hypothesis is untestable because it leads nowhere except back to its own beginning.

Finally, an hypothesis may be untestable if it *appeals to ideas or forces that are not recognized by science.* As we have shown, science deals with the observable, the demonstrable, the empirical. To suggest that people who commit horrendous acts of violence are under orders from the Devil is not testable because it invokes a principle (the Devil) that is not in the province of science. Such hypotheses might be of value to philosophers or theologians but not to the scientist.

Hypotheses in scientific research often are derived from a **theory.** A scientific theory, generally speaking, is a logically organized set of propositions which serves to define events, describe relationships among these events, and explain the occurrence of these events. The major functions of a theory are to *guide* research and to *organize* empirical knowledge (Marx, 1963). In the early 1960s, Rotter (1966) developed a theory of internal versus external locus of control. In this theory Rotter differentiates individuals who perceive a contingency between their behavior and what happens to them (internal locus of control) and those who perceive that their behavior has little consequence for what happens to them (external locus of control). Rotter developed a questionnaire to define this concept on the the basis of the idea that individuals differ in locus of control because of the way that they have been rewarded developmentally. The theory suggests a relationship between perceived locus of control and anxiety, with greater anxiety associated with greater perceived external locus of control. The theory has guided researchers for many years and has served to organize a body of empirical literature regarding self-efficacy, or the feeling of being able to cope with the environment (see, for example, Tedeschi et al., 1985). The success of a psychological theory such as the locus of control theory can be measured by the degree to which it achieves the two important goals of guiding research and organizing empirical findings.

Attitude   More than anything else, scientists are skeptical. Not only do they want to "see it before believing it," but they are also likely to want to see it again, and again, perhaps under conditions of their own choosing. Behavioral scientists come to this skepticism by recognizing two important facts. First, behavior is complex and often many factors interact to give rise to a psychological phenomenon. Discovering these factors is often a difficult task. Explanations that are proposed are sometimes premature, not enough factors having been considered or the existence of one or more factors having gone unnoticed. Second, the behavioral scientist recognizes that science is a human endeavor. People make mistakes. Human inference, as we have suggested, is not always to be trusted. Therefore scientists are often skeptical about "new discoveries" and extraordinary claims.

The skepticism of scientists produces a cautiousness that is often lacking in those without scientific training. Too many people are apparently all too ready to accept explanations that are based on insufficient or inadequate evidence. This is illustrated by the widespread belief in the occult (see Box 1.2). Rather than approach cautiously the claims of those who promote belief in the paranormal, many people are uncritical in their acceptance. Of course, scientists also do not automatically assume that unconventional interpretations of unexplained phenomena could not possibly be true. They simply insist on being allowed to test all claims and to reject those that are inherently untestable.

GOALS OF THE SCIENTIFIC METHOD

The scientific method is intended to meet three goals: description, prediction, and understanding.

BOX 1.2

BELIEF IN THE INCREDIBLE

Belief in the occult and the paranormal is widespread. According to public opinion surveys, a large majority of Americans believe in ESP (extrasensory perception) and many people apparently are convinced that beings from outer space have visited earth, as was suggested in the best-selling book *Chariots of the Gods*. About two in five Americans give some scientific credibility to astrology reports, and as many as 12 million adults report changes in their behavior due to astrology reports (Miller, 1986). Such beliefs are held despite minimal evidence of their validity and even despite contradictory evidence. This tendency to ignore certain kinds of evidence is not peculiar to the present generation. When scientists successfully demonstrated the means by which Clever Hans was so clever, many people dismissed these observations and continued to believe in his superior reasoning ability and in that of other horses who performed similar feats (Watson, 1914/1967). Such obstinate belief in the face of apparent contradiction may at times be the basis of true conviction, but all too often it leads people to credit the incredible.

Several social psychologists demonstrated just how strong college students' belief in the occult and paranormal is (Benassi, Singer, and Reynolds, 1980). They presented a magic show to students in several large introductory psychology classes. The magician performed several standard magic tricks, including bending a bar, "teleportation" of ashes, and "mental telepathy." To some of the students the magician was introduced as a person alleged to be "psychic"; to others he was introduced as a "magician." After the performance students were asked to give written feedback about their reactions to the demonstration. When the performer was introduced as a "psychic," approximately three-fourths of the students indicated that they thought he indeed had psychic abilities. When he was introduced as the magician that he really was, more than half of the students also indicated that they thought he was actually a psychic! Written comments made by the students suggested that many believed the performer to have supernatural powers. Following the "psychic" performance, some students even rushed forward to learn how they could develop these abilities. The scientists speculated that, had the magician desired to found a cult, he could have done so right on the spot!

Description *Description* refers to the procedures by which events and their relationships are defined, classified, cataloged, or categorized. Millon (1969), for instance, described eight basic personality patterns representing mild pathology. These patterns are diagramed in Figure 1.3. Characteristics in the center of the circle refer to the patient's self-image; those toward the edge of the circle describe an individual's interpersonal attitudes and coping strategies. Classifying various personality patterns in this way serves to focus the clinician's attention on those characteristics that are most important in diagnosis and treatment (Millon, 1969).

Psychology (like science in general) develops descriptions of phenomena using the *nomothetic approach*. The objective of the nomothetic approach is to establish broad generalizations and universal "laws" that apply to a wide population of organisms. As a consequence, psychological research frequently consists of studies involving large numbers of participants with the purpose being to determine the "average" or typical performance of a group. This average may or

What is responsible for this tendency to propose explanations based on the occult and even to resist evidence to the contrary? Singer and Benassi (1981) propose several reasons for the uncritical attitude that many take toward these events. First, there are many distortions in the media. The public is constantly exposed to television shows, newspaper accounts, and other reports that describe events presumably based on occult or supernatural forces. These reports are often presented with little critical evaluation, and scientific evidence for alternative explanations is frequently absent. The sheer pervasiveness of such reports may lend credibility to them. Some colleges and universities are also guilty of allowing uncritical courses to be offered on the occult. People tend to respect courses offered by a university as legitimate subject matter, and a teacher's affiliation with a university may be interpreted as evidence of the validity of occult phenomena.

Another reason for the widespread acceptance of the occult may be known deficiencies in human reasoning. Everyday inferences are susceptible to many biases, including the tendency to seek only confirmatory evidence, to jump to conclusions, and to perceive order or causality in events when none is actually present. The researchers also point out that occult beliefs are likely to increase in times of environmental uncertainty, which they define as a situation that cannot be controlled or predicted. Astrology, for instance, may be a popular belief because people find that nothing else seems to predict events any better. In times of economic uncertainty these kinds of beliefs increase.

Finally, in trying to account for why people propose explanations based on the occult rather than seeking scientific explanations, Singer and Benassi (1981) find fault with science education. Too often, they suggest, science is taught as a set of facts rather than as a way of approaching knowledge systematically. They also find that the general public exhibits woefully little general scientific knowledge. Many people believe that islands float on the ocean surface, for instance, and that the moon is fixed in the sky but only visible at night. Belief in astrology reports and "lucky numbers," for example, is stronger among people with little formal education than it is among college-educated individuals (Miller, 1986). Unfortunately, others also believe that science is subjective—that, because scientists change their minds, scientific arguments are weakened. The fact that a few scientists are duped by the fraudulent performance of "psychics" and support their claims must be an additional source of confusion for the individual who is trying to determine what is true.

What do you believe?

may not represent the performance of any one individual in the group. At times, research psychology's emphasis on aggregate performance is taken as a denial of individuality, but this need not be the case. The nomothetic approach does not deny that there are important differences among individuals; it simply seeks to identify the similarities that exist among these differences. For example, a person's individuality is not threatened by our knowledge that that person's heart, like the hearts of other human beings, is located in the upper left chest cavity. Similarly, we do not deny a person's individuality when we state that that person's behavior is influenced by patterns of reinforcement. Researchers merely seek to describe what organisms are like "in general" on the basis of the average performance of a group of different organisms.

Although the nomothetic approach predominates in psychological research, there is an alternative. Some psychologists, notably Allport (1961), argue that the nomothetic approach is inadequate—that the individual cannot be represented by an average value. Allport argues that the individual both is unique and exhibits behavior that conforms to general laws, or principles. He maintains

CLINICAL ANALYSIS

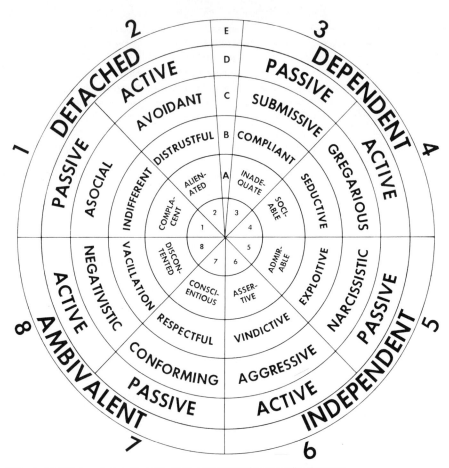

FIGURE 1.3   Millon's (1969) description of eight mildly pathological personality patterns.

that study built on the individual, called *idiographic* research, is important. A major form of idiographic research is the case study method, which we will describe in detail in Chapter 4.

Prediction   A description of events and their relationships often provides a basis for *prediction*, the second goal of the scientific method. There are important questions in psychology that call for predictions. For example: Does the early loss of a parent make a child especially vulnerable to depression? Are children who are overly aggressive likely to have emotional problems as adults? Do stressful life events lead to increased physical illness? Research findings suggest an affirmative answer to all these questions. This information not only adds valuable knowledge to the discipline of psychology but is also helpful in both the treatment and the prevention of emotional disorders.

An important occupation of many psychologists is the prediction of later performance (for example, on the job, in school, or in specific vocations) on the basis of earlier performance on various standardized tests. For instance, a student's scores on the Graduate Record Exam (GRE), as well as undergraduate grade point average (GPA), can be used to predict how well the student will do in graduate school. Interestingly, research has shown that faculty recommendations, which are usually required for graduate school admittance, are a rather poor predictor of whether a student will successfully complete a doctorate degree (Willingham, 1974). On the other hand, there is research showing that amount of undergraduate research activity and ratings by peers of a student's commitment to psychology are better predictors of later success in psychology (as indicated, for example, by number of scientific publications) than are the more traditional measures such as GRE scores and GPA (Hirschberg and Itkin, 1978).

When scores on one variable can be used to predict scores on a second variable, we say that the two variables are correlated. A **correlation** exists when two different measures of the same people, events, or things vary together. That is, particular scores on one variable tend to be associated with particular scores on another variable. For example, typically there is a correlation between first and last test scores in a large introductory psychology class. Test performance is correlated in that students who have high scores on the first test tend to have high scores on the last test, while students who score low on the first test tend to score low on the last test. Thus, if we know students' scores on the first test we are able to predict to some degree students' scores on the final test.

It is possible to determine quantitatively how well two measures vary together by computing a **correlation coefficient.** (See Appendix A for details on computing a correlation coefficient.) We can, therefore, obtain a quantitative index of how well we are able to predict one set of scores, for example, final test scores, based on another set of scores, for example, first test scores. A correlation coefficient expresses the degree of relationship between two variables in terms of both the direction and the magnitude of that relationship.

The *direction* of a correlation coefficient can be either positive or negative. A *positive correlation* indicates that, as the value of one measure increases, the value of the other measure also increases. Scores on the first and final tests in a large psychology class should be positively correlated. Similarly, Scholastic Aptitude Test (SAT) scores and the first-semester GPAs of college students are positively correlated. In a *negative correlation*, as the value of one measure increases, the value of the other measure decreases. We would expect time spent studying to correlate negatively with the number of errors made on a classroom examination. Thus, it is perhaps not surprising to learn that data from a national survey of high school seniors showed that the amount of time spent watching TV and the number of correct answers on an academic achievement test were negatively correlated (Keith et al., 1986). Interestingly, the higher a person's social class, the *less* likely that person is to be admitted to a mental hospital; social class and likelihood of admission to a mental hospital are negatively correlated.

The *magnitude* of the correlation coefficient can range from 0 to 1.00. A value of 0 indicates that we have no ability to predict one measure on the basis of knowing a value on another measure. The relationship between intelligence and mental illness exhibits a zero correlation; we cannot predict the likelihood that a person will become mentally ill by knowing the person's intelligence quotient (IQ). A value of + 1.00 indicates a perfect positive correlation, and a value of − 1.00 indicates a perfect negative correlation. Values between 0 and 1.00 indicate predictive relationships of intermediate strength. Remember, the sign of the correlation signifies only its direction; a correlation coefficient of − .46 indicates a stronger relationship than one of + .20. Degree of correlation can be assessed when data are presented in the form of a *scatterplot*. A scatterplot shows the intersecting points for each pair of scores in the data set. Hypothetical examples of scatterplots showing strong positive, practically zero, and strong negative correlations are shown in Figure 1.4.

Successful prediction doesn't always depend on knowing *why* a relationship exists between related events. For example, Reimanis and Green (1971) reported larger declines in IQ test performances for elderly subjects who died within one year of taking the test than for those who lived for two or more years after taking the test. If these results should prove reliable, they could be used to identify elderly people at risk. This prediction would not, however, require that we understand *why* IQ test scores decline more rapidly during the year or so before death.

As a second illustration of successful prediction without understanding, consider the report that the Chinese rely on observing animals to help them predict earthquakes. Certain animals apparently behave unusually just before an earthquake. In other words, the dog that barks and runs in circles

FIGURE 1.4 Three scatterplots illustrating a strong positive (*a*), a zero (*b*), and a strong negative (*c*) correlation between scores on two variables: X and Y.

(a) Positive relationship   (b) Zero relationship   (c) Negative relationship and the snake seen fleeing its hole may be reliable predictors of earthquakes. If so, they could be used to warn people of forthcoming disasters. We might even imagine that, in areas where earthquakes are likely, residents would be asked to keep certain animals under observation (as miners once kept canaries) to warn them of conditions of which they are not aware. Once again, however, this would not require that we understand why certain animals behave strangely before an earthquake, or even why earthquakes occur.

Understanding   Although they are important goals in themselves, description and prediction are only the first steps in understanding a phenomenon. *Understanding* is the third and most important goal of the scientific method. It is achieved when the cause or causes of a phenomenon are identified. The scientist sets three important conditions on the demonstration of causality and, hence, of understanding: *covariation of events; a time-order relationship;* and the *elimination of plausible alternative causes.* If one event is the cause of another, the two events must vary together; that is, when one changes, the other must also change. This is the principle of covariation. Further, the presumed cause must occur before the presumed effect. This is the second condition, a time-order relationship. Finally, causal explanations are accepted only when other possible causes of the effect have been ruled out— when plausible alternative causes have been eliminated.

Unfortunately, people have a tendency to conclude that all three conditions for a *causal inference* have been met when really only the first condition is satisfied. For example, research has shown that parents who are stern disciplinarians and who use physical punishment are more likely to have aggressive children than are those parents who are less stern and use other forms of discipline. Parental discipline and children's aggressiveness obviously covary. Moreover, the fact that parents are typically assumed to influence how their children behave might lead us to think that the time-order condition has been met—parents use physical discipline and children's aggressiveness results. More recent research has shown, however, that infants vary in how active and aggressive they are and that the infant's behavior has a strong influence on the *parents'* responses in trying to exercise control. In other words, some children may be naturally aggressive and require stern discipline rather than stern discipline producing aggressive children. Therefore, the direction of the causal relationship may be opposite to what we thought at first.

It is important to recognize, however, that the causes of events cannot be identified unless covariation has been demonstrated. The first objective of the scientific method, description, can be met by describing events under a single set of circumstances. The goal of understanding, however, requires more than this. For example, a teacher who emphasized active learning strategies could accurately describe the performance of a group of students who received instruction in this particular way. But before the teacher could claim that this performance was *caused* by the particular method of instruction, she would have to compare this method with some other reasonable approach that did not employ active learning strategies. Without showing that teaching strategy and performance covary, it is not possible to demonstrate conclusively that the strategy is the cause of any subsequent performance that is measured. This is why manipulation is such an important method of control for scientists. By manipulating independent variables, the investigator can determine whether any subsequent covariation occurs in the dependent variable. If it does, a bonus results from using manipulation: the time-order condition has also been met, because the researcher changes the independent variable and *subsequently* measures the changes, if any, in subjects' behavior.

By far the most challenging condition to be met in making a causal inference is eliminating other plausible alternative causes. The methods of control we mentioned earlier—manipulation, holding conditions constant, and balancing—are intended primarily to allow the researcher to eliminate alternative causes of an observed effect. For example, consider a study in which the effect of two different teaching approaches (active and passive) is to be assessed. You can see that one way *not* to assign students to teaching conditions in this study would be to have all men in one group and all women in the other. If this were done, the independent variable of teaching method would be "confounded" with the independent variable of gender. **Confounding** occurs when two potentially effective variables are allowed to covary simultaneously. When research is confounded, it is impossible to determine what variable is responsible for any obtained difference in performance. When no confoundings are present a research study is said to have **internal validity.** Much of the discussion in this book will focus on developing skills in performing internally valid research by learning to identify and eliminate confoundings.

The internal validity of a study, which relates to our ability to make causal inferences, must be distinguished from the study's **external validity.** External validity involves the extent to which research results can be generalized to different populations, settings, and conditions. A research finding may be internally valid but have little external validity. Although free of confoundings, the study may not be able to be generalized. Questions of external validity in science often arise when results obtained with animal subjects are claimed to apply to human subjects as well. Researchers frequently depend on experiments with animals to obtain information about human psychopathology. In one series of experiments, uncontrollable electric shock was used in an attempt to investigate in animal subjects the kinds of stressful experiences that are thought to cause ulcers and depression in humans (Weiss, 1977). Animal models have also been used to study drug addiction, minimal brain dysfunction, and various forms of mild to severe psychopathology (Maser and Seligman, 1977). Joffe et al. (1973) tested Rotter's theory of locus of control using rats as subjects (see Chapter 5 for more information about this experiment).

A major standard by which these laboratory models are evaluated is the degree to which they apply to real-life phenomena. Is the reaction of rats to uncontrollable electric shock the same as that observed in humans who experience unavoidable traumatic events (such as the death of a spouse or the loss of a job)? Validation of a laboratory model of psychopathology must be made in terms of its similarity to the course, symptoms, prevention, and cure of naturally occurring disorders (Abramson and Seligman, 1977). This problem of external validity is an extremely complex one. For instance, as Abramson and Seligman (1977) have pointed out, although specific symptoms can be produced in the laboratory, this does not mean that naturally occurring symptoms are necessarily caused in the same way.

Because laboratory research, in general, is often conducted under more controlled conditions than are found in natural settings, an important task of the scientist is to determine whether laboratory findings generalize to "the real world." This is often the goal of what is called *field research*. By performing "in the field" (outside the laboratory) an experiment that is similar to an experiment carried out in the laboratory, a researcher can provide evidence bearing on the external validity of laboratory results. Research outside the laboratory often requires methods and procedures that are specifically designed to be used in this less well-controlled environment. Later in this book we will introduce some of the methods used by psychologists to conduct field research (see especially Chapters 2 and 9).

THE GOALS OF THIS BOOK

This book provides an introduction to the way in which the scientific method is applied in psychology. As you probably are aware, the scope of psychology is quite large, encompassing many problem areas. Moreover, no single research methodology can be said to answer all the questions raised in a particular area. Therefore there is much ground to cover. In the first part of the book we introduce you to what are called descriptive methods. Naturalistic observation, for instance, is an important tool of psychologists who want to describe behavior in a natural context (see Chapter 2). Questionnaires are one of the most commonly used instruments in psychology. The nature of questionnaires and how they are prepared are discussed in Chapter 3. Several less commonly used measures of behavior—those based on the examination of archival records and those deriving from the study of physical traces—are treated in Chapter 4. In that chapter we also discuss the important case study method.

In the second part of the book we deal with experimental approaches to the study of behavior. The emphasis is on experiments done with groups of subjects (see Chapters 5–7). Experimental approaches are aimed chiefly at discovering cause-and-effect relationships. However, experimental methods used in the laboratory are not necessarily the same as those used outside the laboratory.

In the third part of the book we introduce you to methods used in applied research. In Chapter 8 is a discussion of experiments conducted with a single subject ($N = 1$). The last chapter deals with quasi-experimental designs and with the important topic of program evaluation, which, as we have seen, is concerned with assessing the effects of "treatments" applied in natural settings (see Chapter 9).

This book is not just about research methods in psychology. We have attempted to incorporate many of the interesting facts and ideas in psychology that have been associated with particular research methods. For instance, the problem of bystander intervention, which was mentioned briefly in this chapter, will be used to illustrate concepts introduced in Chapters 2 and 3. We have avoided hypothetical examples describing situations that no one is likely to encounter. Instead, we have drawn on the rich field of psychology for examples. Accordingly, reading this book will increase your general knowledge of psychology. In this chapter, you have already learned something about the historical basis for a scientific psychology and about scientists' concern regarding the public's uncritical acceptance of the occult. It is now time to get on with the study of specific research methods so that you can learn more about what psychologists have discovered and how they have gone about making these discoveries.

SUMMARY

Psychology's official beginning is marked by the establishment, in 1879, of a formal psychology laboratory in Leipzig, Germany, under the direction of Wilhelm Wundt. With this beginning came the first applications of the scientific method to problems of psychology. As an approach to knowledge, the scientific method is characterized by a reliance on empirical procedures, rather than intuition, and by an attempt to control (through manipulation, holding conditions constant, and balancing) the investigation of those factors believed responsible for a phenomenon. Those factors that are systematically controlled in an attempt to determine their effect on behavior are called independent variables. The measures of behavior used to assess the effect (if any) of the independent variable are called dependent variables. It is important to recognize when levels of an independent variable have been manipulated and when, as is the case for a subject variable, the levels have been selected.

Scientists seek to report results in an unbiased and objective manner. This goal is enhanced by giving operational meaning to concepts. Scientists also seek to measure phenomena as accurately and precisely as possible. Both the validity and the reliability of measures are important. How data that are collected can be analyzed depends largely on the level of measurement used. Measurement scales are characterized as nominal, ordinal, interval, or ratio scales.

Hypotheses are tentative explanations of events. To be useful to the scientist, however, hypotheses must be testable. Hypotheses that lack adequate definition, that are circular, or that appeal to ideas or forces outside the province of science are not testable. Hypotheses often are derived from theories, which have the important functions of guiding research and organizing empirical knowledge. More than anything else, scientists are skeptical. A skeptical attitude is not always found among nonscientists, who may rush to accept "new discoveries" and extraordinary claims.

The goals of the scientific method are description, prediction, and understanding. Observation is the principal basis of scientific description. When two measures correlate, we can predict the value of one measure by knowing the value of the other. A quantitative measure of our predictive ability is the correlation coefficient, which has both a direction (positive or negative) and a magnitude (0 to 1.00). Understanding is achieved when the causes of a phenomenon are discovered. This requires that evidence be provided for covariation of events, that a time-order relationship exist, and that alternative causes be eliminated. When two potentially effective variables covary such that the independent effect of each on behavior cannot be determined, we say that our research is confounded. Confounding must be avoided to produce a study with internal validity. The external validity of a study involves the extent to which research results can be generalized to different populations, settings, and conditions.

KEY CONCEPTS

scientific method

empirical approach

control

independent variable

subject variable

dependent variable

introspection

operational definition

validity

reliability

measurement scale

hypothesis

theory

correlation

correlation coefficient

causal inference

confounding

internal validity

external validity

REVIEW QUESTIONS

1 For each of the following characteristics, indicate how the scientific approach differs from nonscientific (everyday) approaches to knowledge: general approach, observation, reporting, concepts, instruments, measurement, hypotheses, and attitudes.

2 Under what two circumstances did scientists demonstrate that Clever Hans was not too clever? To what conclusion did this lead the scientists?

3 Why is it important to distinguish between nonsubject variables, with levels that are manipulated, and subject variables, with levels that are selected?

4 Name and give an example of each of the three types of control used by scientists.

5 What is the major advantage of using operational definitions in psychology? What disadvantages are there in using operational definitions?

6 Distinguish between the accuracy of a measuring instrument and its precision.

7 What distinguishes physical measurement from psychological measurement?

8 Name the four scales of measurement and give an example of each scale.

9 What three shortcomings often keep hypotheses from being testable?

10 Describe how a scientific theory can be used to guide and organize empirical research. (Use Rotter's locus of control theory as an example.)

11 Why do behavioral scientists always seek to maintain a skeptical attitude?

12 What are the three goals of the scientific method?

13 What do we mean by saying that the nomothetic approach is used in science? How is the nomothetic approach different from the idiographic approach?

14 Name and briefly describe the two characteristics of a correlation coefficient.

15 What three conditions must be met if one event is to be considered the cause of another event?

16 Distinguish between the internal validity and the external validity of a research study.

CHALLENGE QUESTIONS

1 In each of the following descriptions of research studies, you are to identify the independent variable(s). You should also be able to identify at least one dependent variable in each study.

A A psychologist was interested in the effect of food deprivation on motor activity. She assigned each of sixty rats to one of four conditions differing in the length of time for which the animals were deprived of food: 0 hours, 8 hours, 16 hours, 24 hours. She then measured the amount of time the animals spent in the activity wheel in their cages.

B A physical education instructor was interested in specifying the changes in motor coordination with increasing age in young children. He selected six groups of children and gave each child a test of motor coordination. The groups of children differed in age; that is, one group was made up of all 5-year-olds, the next group was all 6-year-olds, and so on up to the sixth group, which was all 10-year-olds.

C A developmental psychologist was interested in the amount of verbal behavior very young children displayed depending on who else was present. The study he did involved selecting children who were either 2, 3, or 4 years old. These children were observed in a laboratory setting for a 30-minute period. Half of the children of each age were assigned to a condition in which an adult was present with the child during the session. The other half of the children were assigned to a condition in which another young child was present during the session with the child being observed. The psychologist measured the number, duration, and complexity of the verbal utterances of each observed child.

2 A student employee in the college dining hall had many opportunities to observe his fellow students during the dinner hour. On the basis of these nonsystematic observations he became convinced of two things. He decided that women were more health-conscious than men and that men were less likely to obey rules than were women. Both of these ideas express an hypothesis about behavior, but they are not stated in a testable form. How might this student go about testing each of them? He has little research experience, so you will have to begin by helping him to define concepts using operational definitions and to state his hypotheses in testable form. Further, he will need help identifying which independent variables will need

to be controlled in each study and how this control can best be done (manipulation, holding conditions constant, balancing). You might find it interesting to save your answer to this question. You can then return to this problem after you complete your study of the book to see how, if at all, the approach you propose will change.

3 In the following description the independent variable of interest is confounded with a potentially relevant independent variable. Identify the confounding variable and explain clearly how the confounding occurred. Also state exactly what conclusion can be supported on the basis of the evidence presented. Finally, suggest ways in which the study could be done so that it would be internally valid.

A physiological psychologist developed a drug that she thought would revolutionize the world of horse racing. She named the drug Speedo, and it was her contention that this drug would lead horses to run much faster than they do now. (Forget, for the sake of this problem, that it is illegal to give drugs to race horses.) She selected two groups of horses and gave one of the groups injections of Speedo once a week for 4 weeks. Because Speedo was known to have some negative effects on the horses' digestive systems, those horses given the Speedo had to be placed on a special high-protein diet. Those horses not given the Speedo were maintained on their regular diet. After the 4-week period, all the horses were timed in a 2-mile race and the mean times for the horses given Speedo were significantly faster than the mean times for those not given Speedo. The psychologist concluded that her drug was effective.

4 When presented with only correlational evidence, the investigator can only hypothesize about possible causal factors underlying a relationship between variables. A stage wherein the investigator thinks about possible causal factors and "tries them out" as explanations, perhaps during discussions with other researchers, is often a preliminary step to doing research which may provide evidence for the factors responsible for the reported relationship. For each of the following reports of covariation, identify a possible causal factor; that is, speculate on "why" these events are correlated.

A A study of nearly 5,000 Swedish women (20 to 44 years old) revealed that couples who live together before marriage have an 80 percent higher probability of getting divorced than do married couples who do not live together before marriage (*Behavior Today,* December 21, 1987).

B Dual-income couples now outnumber those with single incomes and questions have been raised about how career demands affect relationships. One study reported that among dual-income couples the greater the amount of togetherness, the more satisfactory was the relationship (*Psychology Today,* January, 1988).

C Married women are found to suffer from depression more than men. However, the greater is marital compatibility the less the risk of depression among women (*Behavior Today Newsletter,* July 28, 1986).

D In the late 1980s the National Institutes of Health sponsored a conference to assess available data regarding the "healing power of pets." The idea is that having pets is good for you. One investigator reported that among ninety-two coronary patients, pet owners were more likely to be alive one year after discharge from a coronary heart unit than were people who do not own a pet (*Science,* September 25, 1987).

ANSWER TO CHALLENGE QUESTION 1

1 **A** IV: hours of food deprivation with four levels; DV: time (in minutes) animals spent in activity wheel

B IV: age of children with six levels (distinguish selection of levels from manipulation in part A); DV: scores on test of motor coordination

C IV: age at three levels and additional person present with two levels (again, distinguish selection and manipulation); DV: number, duration, and complexity of child's verbal utterances

Descriptive Methods

2

Observation

OUTLINE

As was mentioned in Chapter 1, scientists and nonscientists alike rely on observation to learn about behavior. What distinguishes scientific observation from nonscientific observation is the manner in which observations are made. Nonscientists are likely to observe casually and are often unaware of personal and situational biases that may influence the observational process. Nonscientists rarely keep formal records of what they observe and consequently depend on memory for information about an event. Unfortunately, what one remembers about an event is not likely to be a literal record of what one experienced, and memory can be affected by information added after an event is observed (Bartlett, 1932; Loftus, 1979b). Scientific observation, on the other hand, is made under precisely defined conditions, in a systematic and objective manner, and with careful record keeping. When observations are made in this manner, valuable behavioral information and its antecedents can be obtained.

An important task of the psychologist is to describe behavior in its natural context and to identify relationships among variables that are present. Changes in behavior are frequently observed to result from the context in which behavior occurs. For example, Schaller (1963) observed that mountain gorillas regularly eat meat when in captivity, but he found no evidence of meat eating by gorillas in the wild. Moderately obese people eating in a cafeteria were observed to purchase less food and to consume fewer calories when eating with others than when eating alone (Krantz, 1979). By describing behavior in natural settings, the psychologist seeks to establish a basis for predicting future behavior.

Often, observation is also the first step in discovering the reasons why organisms behave the way they do. For example, both animals and humans are known to display distinctive reactions to novel or unfamiliar situations. By observing 2- and 3-year-old children in the presence of an unfamiliar person or object, Kagan et al. (1988) identified children who were consistently shy, quiet, and timid in contrast to those who were consistently sociable, talkative, and affectively spontaneous. When the same children were observed at 7 years of age, a majority of the children in each group exhibited similar behaviors. The researchers speculated that a cause of shyness in childhood, as well as of extreme social anxiety in adulthood, is the result of temperamental differences present at birth.

Systematic observation is an important tool not only of psychologists but also of anthropologists, sociologists, and ethologists. In this chapter we examine observational methods used to investigate behavior—especially, but not exclusively, in natural settings. As you will see, the scientist-observer is not always passive, being present merely to record behavior. Researchers sometimes intervene in the situation in which they are observing behavior. Scientists' reasons for intervening in natural settings are discussed. Methods for recording data and techniques for analyzing data are also illustrated, and some limitations and problems associated with the observation of behavior are explained.

CLASSIFICATION OF OBSERVATIONAL METHODS

Observational methods can be classified according to the degree to which an observer intervenes in an observational setting, as well as according to the way in which that behavior is recorded (see Willems, 1969). Hence we make an important distinction between observation with intervention and observation without intervention. Methods of recording behavior also generally differ in terms of whether all (or nearly all) of the behavior exhibited in a given setting is recorded or only particular units of behavior are recorded. In some situations an observer may seek a comprehensive description of behavior. This may be accomplished by the use of film, tapes, or lengthy verbal descriptions. More often, a researcher records specific units of behavior that are seen as related to the goals of a particular study. An investigator, for instance, who is interested in prosocial behavior likely will concentrate on specific behaviors which define this type of behavior. Chambers and Ascione (1987) observed that children who played an aggressive video game put less money in a donation box and volunteered to help sharpen pencils significantly less than did those who played a video game with prosocial content.

We will discuss observational methods first in terms of the extent of observer intervention and then in terms of methods of recording behavior.

OBSERVATION WITHOUT INTERVENTION

Observation of behavior in a more or less natural setting without any attempt by the observer to intervene is frequently called **naturalistic observation,** a *naturalistic field study,* or, more formally, *systematic observation in a natural setting.* An observer using this method of observation acts as a passive recorder of what occurs. The events witnessed are those that occur naturally and have not been manipulated or in any way controlled by the observer. What exactly constitutes a natural setting is not easily defined (see Bickman, 1976; Willems and Raush, 1969). In general, we can consider a natural setting as one in which behavior ordinarily occurs and one that has not been arranged specifically for the purpose of recording behavior. Observing people in a psychology laboratory would not, for instance, be considered naturalistic observation. The laboratory situation has been created purposely to study behavior and, in a manner of speaking, is an artificial rather than a natural setting. In fact, an important reason for doing naturalistic observation is to verify relationships between variables that have been identified in the psychology laboratory. Observation in natural settings serves, among other functions, as a way of establishing the external validity of laboratory findings.

The major goals of observation in natural settings are to describe behavior as it ordinarily occurs and to investigate the relationship among variables that are present. Hartup (1974) chose naturalistic observation to investigate the frequency and types of aggression exhibited by preschoolers in a St. Paul, Minnesota, children's center. He distinguished hostile aggression (person-oriented) from instrumental aggression (aimed at the retrieval of an object, territory, or privilege). Although he observed boys to be more aggressive overall than girls, his observations provided no evidence that the types of aggression differed between the sexes. Thus Hartup was able to conclude that, with respect to hostile and instrumental aggression, there was no evidence that boys and girls were "wired" differently.

Hartup's study of children's aggression illustrates why a researcher may choose to use naturalistic observation rather than to manipulate conditions related to behavior. There are certain aspects of human behavior that moral or ethical considerations prevent us from controlling. Researchers may be interested in the relationship between early childhood isolation and later emotional and psychological development. However, we would object strenuously if they tried to take children from their parents in order to raise them in isolation. Alternative methods of data collection must be considered if this problem is to be investigated. For example, the effect of early isolation on later development has been studied through experimentation on animal subjects (Harlow and Harlow, 1966), case studies of children subjected to unusual conditions of isolation by their parents (Curtiss, 1977), and systematic observation of institutionalized children (Spitz, 1965). The nature of children's aggression is another aspect of behavior the investigation of which is subject to moral and ethical limitations. We would not want to see children intentionally harassed and picked on simply to record their reactions. However, as anyone knows who has observed children, there is plenty of naturally occurring aggression. Hartup's study shows how observation without intervention can be a useful alternative to methods of data collection that attempt to manipulate the behavior of interest.

Psychologists are not the only researchers who observe behavior in natural settings. Observation is a fundamental method of ethologists. Although related to psychology, **ethology** is generally considered a branch of biology (Eibl-Eibesfeldt, 1975). Ethologists study the behavior of organisms in relation to their natural environment. A major question they seek to answer is how natural selection has worked to produce particular behavior patterns in an animal species. The focus of an ethological investigation is often the development of an **ethogram.** This is nothing less than a complete catalog of all the behavior patterns of an organism, including information on frequency, duration, and context of occurrence.

Ethologists adopt a comparative approach to understanding behavior and often seek to explain behavior in one animal species on the basis of innate patterns of behavior observed in species lower on the phylogenetic scale. Speculations about the role of innate mechanisms in determining human behavior are not uncommon among ethologists. For instance, Barash (1977) observed whether male and female human pedestrians visually scanned both directions before crossing a dangerous intersection in Seattle, Washington. When a male adult and a female adult were together, adult males scanned more than females. This was true regardless of whether children were also present. The ethologist-observer suggested an evolutionary explanation: adult male monkeys and baboons in the wild generally function as lookouts to warn the rest of the group of approaching danger. An ethological perspective has proved important for the understanding of both normal and abnormal human behavior. An interesting example is the ethological analysis of psychiatric problems based on comprehensive descriptions of facial behavior of schizophrenic patients (see Pitman et al., 1987).

OBSERVATION WITH INTERVENTION

It is characteristic of the scientist to "tamper" with nature, to intervene, in order to make a point or to test a theory (see Box 2.1). Intervention rather than nonintervention characterizes most psychological research. Kinds of intervention vary widely in psychological studies, depending on such things as the purpose for investigating behavior, the nature of the behavior under observation, and the ingenuity of the researcher.

Although the types of intervention employed by psychologists are too numerous and diverse to classify, their reasons for intervening are generally one or more of the following:

1 To precipitate or cause an event that occurs infrequently in nature or that normally occurs under conditions that make it difficult to observe.

2 To investigate the limits of an organism's response by varying systematically the qualities of a stimulus event.

3 To gain access to a situation or event that is generally not open to scientific observation.

BOX 2.1

PSYCHOLOGISTS TAKING TERNS

In 1913, the same year he launched psychology on a new course with his remarks entitled "Psychology as the Behaviorist Views It," John B. Watson set sail for the Tortugas Islands off the coast of Florida. He had been to the islands before when he had begun observations of noddy and sooty terns in their natural habitat. This year fellow psychologist Karl Lashley went with Watson to help him make his observations and to help test the homing abilities of these birds. At one point during the summer Lashley took 30 birds with him on a boat trip to Mobile, Alabama, where he released 15 of them. Traveling more than 100 miles farther to Galveston, Texas, Lashley set free the remaining 15 birds. Watson waited on the island to record the arrival of the birds if, indeed, they were able to make it back as popular stories of the time suggested. Four days after Lashley released them, the birds began returning to the island. Watson and Lashley had demonstrated that the terns could safely navigate across an open sea with no obvious landmarks from a distance of 1000 miles. They were at a loss to explain how the birds managed their remarkable feat, and, as events transpired, Watson did not have the opportunity to carry out any more tests of the birds' homing abilities (Cohen, 1979).

4 To arrange conditions so that important antecedent events are controlled and consequent behaviors can be readily observed.

5 To establish a comparison by manipulating one or more independent variables to determine their effect on behavior.

These reasons for intervening are illustrated in three methods of observation: participant observation, structured observation, and the field experiment. As we review these major observational techniques, the investigator's reasons for intervening will become clear.

PARTICIPANT OBSERVATION

Observation of behavior by someone who also plays an active and significant role in the situation or context in which behavior is recorded is called **participant observation.** In *undisguised* participant observation, the individuals who are being observed know that the observer is present for the purpose of collecting information about their behavior. This method is frequently used by anthropologists who seek to understand the culture and behavior of groups by living and working with members of the group.

When the observer's role is not known to those who are being observed, we speak of *disguised* participant observation. As you might imagine, people do not always behave in the way they ordinarily would when they know their behavior is being recorded. Politicians, for instance, often make different statements when speaking to the press, depending on whether their comments are "for" or "off" the record. Our own behavior is likely to be affected by knowing that we are being watched. This problem associated with observational methods will be discussed more fully later in the chapter. For now, let us simply say that researchers may decide to disguise their role as observers if they believe that subjects will not act as they ordinarily would if they know their activities are being recorded.

Disguised participant observation was used by Rosenhan (1973) to investigate the basis of psychiatric diagnosis in the context of a mental institution. Eight individuals (including psychologists, a pediatrician, and a housewife) misrepresented their names and occupations and sought admission to twelve different mental hospitals. Each complained of similar symptoms: that he or she was hearing voices. Rosenhan (1973, p. 251) described these symptoms and the rationale for their selection by the observers as follows:

> Asked what the voices said, he replied that they were often unclear, but as far as he could tell they said "empty," "hollow," and "thud." The voices were unfamiliar and were of the same sex as the pseudopatient. The choice of these symptoms was occasioned by their apparent similarity to existential symptoms. Such symptoms are alleged to arise from painful concerns about the perceived meaninglessness of one's life. It is as if the hallucinating person were saying, "My life is empty and hollow." The choice of these symptoms was also determined by the *absence* of a single report of existential psychoses in the literature. Beyond alleging the symptoms and falsifying name, vocation, and employment, no further alterations of person, history, or circumstances were made.

Immediately after being put in the mental ward, the researchers stopped complaining of any symptoms and refrained from acting abnormal. In addition to observing patient-staff interactions, the observers were interested in how long it took for a "sane" person to be released from the hospital. Length of hospitalization ranged from seven to fifty-two days. The researchers were never detected as sane and, when they were discharged, their schizophrenia was said only to be "in remission." Apparently, once the pseudopatients were labeled schizophrenic, they were stuck with that label no matter what the nature of their subsequent behavior.

Participant observation allows an observer to gain access to a situation that is not usually open to scientific observation. In addition, the participant observer is often in a position to have the same experiences as the subjects under study. This may provide important insights and understanding of individuals or groups. The pseudopatients in the Rosenhan study, for instance, felt what it was like to be labeled schizophrenic and not to know how long it would be before they could return to society. In the fall of 1959, John Howard Griffin set out to research "what it was like to be a Negro in a land where we keep the Negro down." Griffin, a white man, darkened his skin using medication and stain in order to pass himself off as black. For more than a month he traveled (walking, hitchhiking, riding buses) through Mississippi, Alabama, and Georgia. He described his experiences as a participant observer in his book *Black Like Me* (1960), which was an important precursor of the civil rights movement of the 1960s.

A participant observer's role in a situation can produce certain methodological problems. By identifying with the individuals under study, it is possible for an observer to lose the scientific objectivity that accurate and valid observation requires. Changes in a participant observer are sometimes dramatic and are not easily anticipated. Witness the experiences of a criminologist who used undisguised participant observation to study police officers at work. Kirkham (1975) went through police academy training like any recruit and became a uniformed patrol officer assigned to a high-crime area in a city of about half a million. His immersion in the daily activities of an officer on the beat led to marked changes in his attitudes and personality. As Kirkham (1975, p. 19) himself noted:

> As the weeks and months of my new career as a slum policeman went by, I slowly but inexorably began to become indistinguishable in attitudes and behavior from the policemen with whom I worked. . . . According to the accounts of my family, colleagues and friends, I began to increasingly display attitudinal and behavioral elements that were entirely foreign to my previous personality—punitiveness, pervasive cynicism and mistrust of others, chronic irritability and free-floating hostility, racism, a diffuse personal anxiety over the menace of crime and criminals that seemed at times to border on the obsessive. A former opponent of capital punishment, I became its vociferous advocate in cases involving felony murder, kidnapping and the homicide of police officers—even though as a criminologist I continued to recognize its ineffectiveness as a deterrent to crime.

Participant observers must be aware of the threat to objective reporting that arises due to their involvement in the situation wherein they are recording behavior. This threat necessarily increases as degree of involvement increases.

Another problem with observer involvement is the effect the observer has on the behavior of those being studied. It is more than likely that the participant observer will have to interact with other people, make decisions, initiate activities, assume responsibilities, and otherwise act like everyone else in that situation. Whenever observers intervene in a natural setting, they must ask to what degree subjects and events are affected by the intervention. Is what is being observed the same as it would have been if the observer had never appeared? It is difficult to generalize results to other situations if intervention produces behavior that is specific to the conditions and events created by the observer.

In the case of participant observation, the extent of an observer's influence on behavior under observation is not easily assessed. Several factors must be considered, such as whether participation is disguised or undisguised, the size of the group entered, and the role of the observer in the group. Griffin, for example, was not known to be a white man even by most of the blacks he associated with, and his entry into a subculture of literally thousands of disadvantaged blacks could not reasonably be expected to influence the nature of black-white interactions that he observed. Similarly, it does not appear

that Rosenhan and his associates significantly affected the natural environment of the mental ward by assuming the role of mental patients. (However,
some of the patients—though none of the staff—apparently detected the sanity of the pseudopatients, suggesting to the observers that they were there to
check up on the hospital.)

When the group under observation is small or the activities of the participant are prominent, the observer is more likely to have a significant effect on
subjects' behavior. This problem confronted several social psychologists who
infiltrated a group of people who claimed to be in contact with beings from
outer space (Festinger et al., 1956). A leader of the group had received a message from the aliens predicting a cataclysmic flood on a specific date. The
flood was to stretch from the Arctic Circle to the Gulf of Mexico. The prophecy was reported in the newspapers, and certain psychologists who read the
account saw an opportunity to test a theory of group cohesion and reaction
in the face of unfulfilled prophecy. (The psychologists evidently assumed
that the flood was not going to occur.) Because of the attitudes of members of
the group toward "nonbelievers," the researchers were forced to make up
bizarre stories in order to gain access to the group. This tactic worked too
well. Not only were the disguised participant observers welcomed into the
group, which never consisted of more than a dozen hard-core believers, but
their stories were taken as signs from the extraterrestrial beings. One of the
observers was even thought to be a spaceman bringing a message. The researchers had inadvertently reinforced the group's beliefs and influenced in
an undetermined way the course of events that followed. By the way, the
flood never occurred, but at least some of the group members came to use
this disconfirmation as a means of strengthening their initial belief. They began to seek new members by arguing that their faith had prevented the
prophesied flood.

STRUCTURED OBSERVATION

There are a variety of observational methods using intervention that are not
easily categorized. Because researchers exert some control over events, these
procedures differ from naturalistic observation without intervention. However, the degree of control is often less than that seen in field experiments,
which we will consider later. We have labeled these procedures **structured
observations.** Often the observer intervenes in order to cause an event to occur or to "set up" a situation so that events can be more easily recorded than
they would be without intervention. The intervention might be quite simple,
as was Watson and Lashley's removal of the terns from their nests in order to
study homing behavior. In other cases the observer may create quite elaborate procedures to investigate a particular behavior more fully.

Structured observations can be arranged in either a natural setting or a laboratory setting. Structured laboratory observations are often used by clinical
psychologists when making behavioral assessments of parent-child interac-

tions (see, for example, Hughes and Haynes, 1978). A parent and child who are seeking some sort of help come to a diagnostic clinic or laboratory and are asked to engage in specific tasks while they are being observed (often from behind a one-way window). Observations are made of various specific behaviors (for instance, tantrums or other emotional outbursts by the child) and of the general nature of the parent-child interactions. Partly on the basis of the results of this structured observation, the therapist plans a strategy to address the behavioral problems that exist. A group of educational psychologists observed elementary and junior-high school students while they worked on class assignments in a private room containing various kinds of furniture, as well as a television set and radio (Patton et al., 1986). Results confirmed what had been reported previously for descriptions of study at home: a majority of the children preferred to study with the television set or radio turned on.

Structured observations are also frequently used by developmental psychologists. Perhaps most notable are the methods of the famous Swiss psychologist Jean Piaget. In many of Piaget's studies a child is first given a problem to solve, and then several variations on the problem are presented to test the limits of the child's understanding. The observer acquaints the child with the nature of the problem and then usually asks questions to probe the child's reasoning processes. These structured observations have provided a wealth of information regarding children's cognition and are the basis for Piaget's stage theory of intellectual development. The methods have not escaped criticism, however. The fact that Piaget did not always follow exactly the same procedure from one observation to another, and the fact that his observations were frequently based on only a few (and sometimes very select) individuals, are viewed as problems with his observational techniques (see Brainerd, 1978).

In spite of these criticisms many researchers, including Piaget, see structured observations as a compromise between the passive nonintervention of naturalistic observation and the systematic manipulation of independent variables and precise control that characterize laboratory methods. Such a compromise permits observations to be made under conditions that are more natural than those imposed in a laboratory, but there may be a price to pay. The failure to follow similar procedures each time an observation is made may make it difficult for other observers to obtain the same results when investigating a problem. Uncontrolled, and perhaps unknown, variables may play an important part in producing the behavior under observation. As described in Box 2.1, Watson and Lashley took terns from their nests and carried them away on board a ship in order to study homing behavior. Suppose that this procedure caused some of the birds to become ill (something that actually happened on a previous occasion when the birds died in transit) and that their illness affected their homing behavior. When no birds returned to their nests after being released, the observers might have wrongly concluded that these animals had no homing instinct. This possibility does not seem that farfetched when you consider that more recent observations of bird navigation have revealed that homing pigeons make use of airborne odors to recognize the location of their lofts (see Wallraff and Sinsch, 1988). Birds who were allowed to smell only filtered air before being released did not show any tendency to return home. Although structured observations are often important for gathering information about behavior, and even for testing specific hypotheses, researchers must be aware of the limitations they impose when they allow some variables to remain uncontrolled and when procedures differ with the circumstances or the behavior of the subject under observation.

Ethologists frequently use structured observations to study the limits of an organism's response by varying systematically the characteristics of a stimulus event. For example, observations by Nobel Prize-winning ethologist Konrad Lorenz led to the discovery of imprinting (see Eibl-Eibesfeldt, 1975). Imprinting is an attachment shown by certain animal species to an object encountered during a critical or sensitive period in their lives. Immediately after hatching, for example, the young graylag gosling will imprint on almost any moving object in its environment and follow that object for some time afterwards. Under ordinary conditions, the object of the bird's imprinting is its parent and the innately triggered response is important for the young bird's survival. To better understand the imprinting response, ethologists have sometimes created models of both male and female parents and tested the young animal's response when the models were moving, when they made a noise, or when the imprinting response was punished (see Eibl-Eibesfeldt, 1975). Lorenz himself served as a model; many students of psychology have been introduced to ethology by scenes of the famous ethologist being energetically pursued over land and water by the young birds who attached themselves to him.

FIELD EXPERIMENTS

When an observer manipulates one or more independent variables in a natural setting in order to determine their effect on behavior, the procedure is called a **field experiment.** Although experimental methods will be discussed extensively in later chapters of this book, we mention the field experiment here because it represents one end of the nonintervention-intervention dimension that characterizes observational methods. In conducting a field experiment, the observer (now usually called the experimenter) seeks to control the antecedents of an event in order to measure systematically the effect of a variable on behavior. Control or comparison groups are included, and the experimenter usually dictates the assignment of subjects to conditions. The field experiment is probably the most frequently used field observational technique in social psychology (Bickman, 1976). In most cases subjects are unaware that they are participating in an experiment. In a field experiment a researcher also typically makes use of **confederates.** A confederate is someone in the research situation who is instructed to behave in a certain way in order to produce an experimental treatment. Confederates, for example, have been employed by social psychologists to pose as robbers when bystander reaction to a crime has been investigated (Latané and Darley, 1970), and to mimic the behavior of individuals cutting into a waiting line in order to study the reactions of those in line (Milgram et al., 1986).

Field experiments sometimes yield valuable practical knowledge. For example, research by Latané and Darley (1970) and others has helped us to understand those variables that affect a bystander's willingness to come to the aid of a victim. Interestingly, many studies show that a bystander is more likely to aid a victim when the bystander is alone than when other bystanders are present. In a less serious, but also in a potentially practical vein, Crusco and Wetzel (1984) investigated the effect of touching on diners in a restaurant. Waitresses working as confederates touched restaurant customers on either the hand or the shoulder while returning change. The researchers speculated that the touch on the hand would produce positive affect toward the waitress, whereas a touch on the shoulder, which may be seen as a sign of dominance, would not be viewed positively, especially by male diners. The subjects were 114 diners from two restaurants who were randomly assigned to three levels of the independent variable: Fleeting Touch, when the waitress twice touched the diner's palm for one-half second when returning change; Shoulder Touch, when she placed her hand for one to one and one-half seconds on the diner's shoulder as she gave back change; and No Touch, when no physical contact was made with the customers. The major dependent variable was the size of the gratuity. Results showed that males tipped overall more than females, but that both male and female diners gave a significantly larger tip after being touched than when not touched. The results did not show, as the researchers had expected, that the nature of the touch made a difference; male and female diners were affected equally by both kinds of touches.

RECORDING BEHAVIOR

We have mentioned two important characteristics of observational methods. One is the degree of observer intervention, the other the method of recording behavior. Intervention is a dimension anchored at one end by the absence of any intervention (as is associated with passive observation in a natural setting) and at the other end by the active and systematic manipulation of antecedent events that characterizes field experiments. Observational methods also differ in the manner in which behavior is recorded, particularly the degree to which behavior is abstracted from the situation in which it is observed (see Willems, 1969, for a thorough discussion of this aspect of observational methods).

In general, methods of recording behavior can be classified as those that seek a comprehensive description of behavior and the situation in which it occurs and those that record only behavior and events that fall into pre-defined categories. Whether *all* behavior in a given setting or only selected aspects are to be observed depends on the purpose or goals of an observational study. But it is also important to understand that how the results of a study can later be summarized or analyzed statistically hinges on the way in which behavior is recorded.

NARRATIVE RECORDS

Narrative records are intended to provide a more or less faithful reproduction of behavior as it originally occurred. Written descriptions of behavior made by an observer are one major type of narrative record. So are the spoken records produced by using a tape recorder and the visual records obtained with videotape or movie cameras. Ethologists are often interested in every detail of a behavioral event, so motion picture film turns out to be one of their most important means of recording behavior (Eibl-Eibesfeldt, 1975). To study the function of the "eyebrow flash" in social interactions, ethologists made use of 67 hours of film showing individuals in naturally occurring social situations (Grammer et al., 1988). Across three different cultures, the eyebrow flash was found, usually accompanied by a smile, to be a universal social signal, for example, as a sign of factual "yes."

Once narrative records are obtained, the observer can study, classify, and organize the records at leisure. Particular hypotheses or expectations about the behaviors under observation can be tested by examining the data. This constitutes an important difference between narrative records and other forms of behavior measurement wherein the classification or coding of behaviors is done at the time of observation. Thus, it is critical that narrative records capture the particular information that is critical for evaluating a study's goals or hypotheses. Henderson and Dias (1987) prepared narrative records of approximately 75 hours of infant problem-solving behavior. The goal of the study was to examine how children less than a year and a half old adapted to situations that blocked ongoing behavior, for example, as might occur when a baby swing becomes stuck or a door won't open. Observers were instructed to "make a running account of who and what the infant was attending to, the environmental conditions, and responses to stimuli" (p. 207), and to note apparent instances of blocks and responses to them. Observers were, however, told not to initiate interaction and to ignore initiation by the infant. Results showed that the infants encountered a problem on the average once every 3 minutes, and that about two thirds of the problems were solved.

Illustrations   One of the prominent psychologists to rely heavily on narrative records was Piaget. We have already mentioned how Piaget used structured observations to study the cognitive development of children. Having selected a problem to present to the child, Piaget then made a rather literal record of the child's attempts to solve the problem. The following narrative record was obtained by Piaget when investigating a child's understanding of quantity.

> The child is given two containers A and L of equal height, A being wide and L narrow. A is filled to a certain height (one-quarter or one-fifth) and the child is asked to pour the same quantity of liquid into L. The dimensions are such that the level will be four times as high in L as in A for the same amount of liquid. In spite of this striking difference in the proportions, the child at this stage proves incapable of grasping that the smaller diameter of L will require a higher level of liquid. Those children who are clearly still at this stage are satisfied that there is "the same amount to drink" in L when they have filled it to the same level as A.
>
> Blas (4.0): "Look, your mummy has poured out a glass of lemonade for herself (A) and she gives you this glass (L). We want you to pour into your glass as much lemonade as your mummy has in hers.—(She poured rather quickly and exceeded the level equal to that in A that she was trying to achieve.)—Will you both have the same like that?—*No.*—Who will have more?—*Me.*—Show me where you must pour to so that you both have the same.—(She poured up to the same level.)—Will you and mummy have the same amount to drink like that?—*Yes.*—Are you sure?—*Yes.*" (Piaget, J. *The Child's Conception of Number.* New York: Norton, 1965, pp. 11–12. First published in French in 1941 under the title *La Genèse du nombre chez l'enfant.*)

The narrative begins with the observer's comments to the child, Blas, who is age 4. The observer says, "Look, your mummy has poured out a glass of lemonade...." After that follows an exact reproduction of what the observer said, what the child said, and what happened in this situation. The narrative is free of observer inference and the exact sequence of behaviors is recorded. His many observations of children's behavior led Piaget to a number of important conclusions about human cognitive development. As you can see, Piaget used the narrative record to illustrate that the child of 4 had not yet mastered the principle of "conservation of volume." The two containers, which were of equal height but different width, were perceived by the child to hold the same amount of liquid when the level of the liquid was the same.

Hartup (1974) obtained narrative records as part of his naturalistic study of children's aggression. He investigated a number of different aspects of children's aggression, including the relationship between particular kinds of antecedent events and the nature of the aggressive episodes that followed. Here is a sample narrative record from Hartup's (1974, p. 339) study:

> Marian [a seven-year-old]...is complaining to all that David [who is also present] had squirted her on the pants she has to wear tonight. She says, "I'm gonna do it to him to see how he likes it." She fills a can with water and David runs to the teacher and tells of her threat. The teacher takes the can from Marian. Marian attacks David and pulls his hair very hard. He cries and swings at Marian as the teacher tries to restrain him; then she takes him upstairs....Later, Marian and Elaine go upstairs and into the room where David is seated with a teacher. He throws a book at Marian. The teacher asks Marian to leave. Marian kicks David, then leaves. David cries and screams, "Get out of here, they're just gonna tease me."

Hartup (1974) instructed his observers to avoid making any inferences about the intentions, motives, or feelings of the subjects and to use precise language in describing behavior. We are not told why David might want to throw a book at Marian or how Marian feels about being attacked. Hartup believed that certain antecedent behaviors were related to specific types of aggression. Because any inferences or impressions of the observers were strictly excluded, the content of the narrative records could be classified and coded in an objective manner. Individuals doing the coding would not be influenced by what the observer inferred was going on.

The narrative records obtained by Piaget and by Hartup are similar in that both are rather literal descriptions of behavior in a particular context. They are devoid of observer inference, and nearly everything that occurs in a relatively brief period of time is recorded. As many details of the setting, context, and characteristics of the subjects are recorded as is necessary to give a meaningful description of what happened. The narratives focus on particular aspects of children's behavior. Piaget observed the problem-solving abilities of children, whereas Hartup focused on children's aggression.

An example of a narrative record that does not focus on particular behaviors, and one that does include inferences and impressions of the observer, is drawn from a study of "a day in the life" of a midwestern schoolgirl (Barker, Wright, Schoggen, and Barker, 1978, pp. 56–58). Eight different observers took turns observing an 8-year-old girl from the time she awoke in the morning until she went to sleep at night. In reproducing her day, the researchers wanted to include information about motives, feelings, and perceptions that were part of her daily activities. This required that the observers make a number of inferences. Generally, only those inferences that two or more independent observers agreed on were included. For example, people can often agree when someone is sad or happy or excited or calm. By recording their impressions of the girl's feelings and moods, the observers hoped to provide a record that was true to real life and might yield important information to those who seek to understand these more subjective aspects of human behavior. Personality and social psychologists might be able to learn from this record about the kinds of frustrations, anxieties, and feelings an 8-year-old experiences in the context of her activities during one day in a small midwestern town. A comprehensive description of individuals in everyday contexts is an important goal of **ecological psychology.**

The narrative record of this little girl's day was made on May 12, 1949. The complete record was about 100,000 words in length and was later determined to contain 969 different behavior episodes. The beginning of this record is as follows:

> I went to the back door and knocked. Mrs. Ennis opened the door and asked me in. She said that Mary had awakened about ten minutes after six, but she had put her back to bed and she thought that Mary had gone to sleep. She said, "I'll go in first and see if Mary is awake." Mrs. Ennis did this; when she returned she said "She is sitting up in bed, and it is OK to go ahead."

I went to Mary's room, which opened off the dining room. Timothy's crib was in the dining room opposite the door to Mary's room.

7:00. Mary was sitting up in bed and Timothy was standing in his crib crowing and talking.

I smiled at Mary and she smiled at me.

Mary immediately started to talk to Timothy. From her bed, she called gaily, "Hi, Timothy."

Timothy crowed in response.

This verbal play was repeated four or five times. Both children enjoyed it greatly.

Timothy's footing was none too secure; he fell over and started to cry rather hard.

Mary immediately jumped off the bed and ran to him. I think she genuinely wanted to help.

Mrs. Ennis came in from the kitchen and said, "Well, what is the trouble, what happened?" and "You're all right, Timothy, you're all right." She was matter-of-factly reassuring, showing little concern. As she said this, she sort of pushed Mary aside. The mother picked Timothy up and told him he was all right; she looked around and said, "Where is your bottle?" She saw the bottle on the floor, put Timothy back in his crib, and took the bottle back to the kitchen for more milk.

While her mother went for the milk, Mary returned quickly and eagerly to her own room.

Before her mother got back, Mary brought a big Teddy bear, which I presume was hers, and laid it in the crib beside Timothy. She seemed to want to contribute to comforting him.

When Mrs. Ennis brought the milk, she left the Teddy bear in the crib; she pushed it over so there was room for both Timothy and the Teddy bear. Mrs. Ennis patted the Teddy bear as she settled Timothy with his bottle.

7:01. Mary went again from the crib to her own room.

Unlike the previous illustrations, this narrative record contains the subjective impressions of the observers. Mary's younger brother is "crowing" in his bed and Mary calls "gaily." As for the verbal play between the two youngsters, the observer recorded that "both children enjoyed it greatly." In recording Mary's response to her brother's fall, the observer suggests that "she genuinely wanted to help." In planning an observational study using narrative records, an important decision one must make is to what degree observer inferences are to be included in the verbal description of behavior.

Although the narrative records we have discussed so far have differed in their focus, as well as in the degree of observer inference allowed, each has been a rather complete description of behavior in a particular setting or context. Not all narrative records are as detailed as those we have examined. Often the narrative records of an observer are merely running descriptions of participants, events, settings, and behaviors. These records are generally called **field notes.** Field notes are nothing more than the verbal records of a trained observer. Used by journalists, social workers, anthropologists, ethologists, and others, they do not always contain an exact record of everything that occurred. Events and behaviors that especially interest the observer are recorded and are likely to be interpreted in terms of the observer's specialized knowledge or field of expertise. In making notes about a particular patient, a psychiatrist might compare the client's symptoms with those of other patients or with a textbook definition. An ethologist might record how behavior of one species appears to parallel that of another.

Field notes tend to be highly personalized (Brandt, 1972), but they are probably used more frequently than any other kind of narrative record. Field notes have generated numerous revelations about behavior; they are the basis of Darwin's theory of evolution as well as Rosenhan's description of being sane in insane places. Their usefulness as scientific records depends on the accuracy and precision of their content. These in turn are related to the training of the observer and the extent to which the observations that are recorded can be verified by independent observers and through other means of investigation.

Considerations Practical, as well as methodological, considerations dictate the manner in which narrative records are made. As a general rule, records should be made as soon as possible after behavior is observed. The passage of time blurs details and makes it harder to reproduce the original sequence of actions. Adjang (1986) used a portable cassette recorder to make narrative records of his spoken observations of teasing behavior of young chimpanzees; however, he then transcribed these spoken reports onto paper "as soon as possible" (p. 139). This rule is sometimes not easy to follow when observations are made in natural settings. An ethologist who is trying to record the behavior of animals in the wild is sometimes hampered by bad weather, animal migration, dwindling daylight, and so forth. Notes may have to be made quickly—even while the observer is quite literally on the run. At other times observers may have to wait until they return to camp to make written records of behavior. When Festinger and his colleagues infiltrated the group of people waiting for spacemen to rescue them from a cataclysmic flood, the participant observers sometimes found it difficult to take notes without being seen by members of the group. Excuses had to be made to leave the group (to go to the bathroom, for example) in order to make written records of the group's activities.

Decisions regarding the content of a narrative record must be made prior to observing behavior. We have seen that verbal narratives may differ according to the degree of observer inference or how literal the record of behavior is. Table 2.1 contains suggestions for improving the quality of narrative records (see also Brandt, 1972). Once the content of narrative records is decided, observers must be trained to record behavior according to the criteria that have been set up. Practice observations may have to be conducted and

TABLE 2.1 SUGGESTIONS FOR IMPROVING THE QUALITY OF NARRATIVE RECORDS*

---

1 Record what you observe as soon as possible after you observe it.
2 Decide whether observer inferences and interpretations of behavior are to be included. If they are, only those inferences should be included on which two independent observers could reasonably be expected to agree.
3 When a particular behavior or event is the focus of the observation, provide observers with a precise operational definition of what is to be observed.
4 Judge how literal and complete a record is needed. Exact reproductions of behavior sequences are difficult to record accurately, so you must decide what is and what is not to be recorded. Generally speaking, exact reproductions are possible only when the observation interval is relatively short. Always record enough details of the setting or context to indicate the "who, what, and where" of the behavior episode.
5 Decide on the key subjects or the major events and focus on these. The responses or reactions of minor subjects should be included only to the extent that they complement the activities of the main participants.
6 When observing particular sequences of behaviors or when focusing on specific behavior episodes (such as aggression or helping), decide what events mark the beginning of the episode and what events mark the end. Significant variations in observer reports can be expected unless all observers begin and end their observations at the same points.
7 Use language that is precise and unambiguous.
8 When conversations are to be recorded, decide whether direct quotations are necessary or summaries of what is said are sufficient. Be sure to distinguish (for example, by quotation marks) what is a direct quote from what is an indirect quote.
9 When possible use a tape recorder to record initial descriptions of behavior. Recorded material can be transcribed to written form later and additional details (such as information about the context or setting) can be added.
10 In planning the content of the narrative, keep in mind how it will be analyzed. For example, if narratives are to be coded according to whether certain expressions are used in conversations, then direct quotes of what was said should be recorded.

---

*Based to a large extent on recommendations made by Brandt (1972).

records critiqued by more than one investigator before "real" data are collected.

RECORDING UNITS OF BEHAVIOR

When only certain behaviors or specific aspects of individuals and settings are of interest, it is often possible to define them prior to observing and to record only certain characteristics of their occurrence. This allows the researcher to make observations of only behavior and events that fit predefined categories.

Checklists The simplest category system is a **checklist.** A checklist is used to record the presence or absence of something in the situation under observation (Brandt, 1972). A distinction can be made between static and action checklists. A *static checklist* contains descriptions of relatively permanent aspects of subjects or settings. Age, race, and sex are examples of subject characteristics that are often noted. Features of the setting—such as time of day, location, and whether other people are present—also may be part of a static checklist. An *action checklist* is used to record the presence or absence of specific behaviors. A classroom observer may note whether children are talking or are quiet. An environmental psychologist may be interested in whether people use seat belts or do not use seat belts or in whether people dispose of litter or do not dispose of litter.

As you might expect, static and action checklists are often combined. Specific characteristics of subjects as well as their behavior are likely to be of interest. For example, it is often informative to observe behavior as a function of certain static characteristics. Do males use seat belts more than females? Are people who drive inexpensive automobiles more likely to share a ride than people who drive expensive automobiles? These questions can be answered by observing the presence or absence of certain behaviors (seat belt use, car-pooling) for different categories of subjects and events (male and female, expensive and inexpensive automobiles).

Jenni (1976; also Jenni and Jenni, 1976) used a checklist to study book-carrying behavior of male and female college students. Three types of book-carrying behaviors were defined: two major types and an "other" category. Figure 2.1 illustrates the two major types of carrying behavior. Students using Type I wrap one or both arms around the books, with the short edges of the books resting on the hip or in front of the body. Students using Type II support the books by one arm and hand at the side of the body, with the long edges of the books approximately horizontal to the ground. The "other" category included a variety of book-carrying methods that did not fit either Type I or Type II. For example, students occasionally hold books by the edges with both hands in front of the body (for instance, when reading while walking).

FIGURE 2.1 Two methods that students were observed to use to carry books. In the Type I method, the short edges of the book rest on the hip or in front of the body. In the Type II method, the books are either pinched from above or supported from below by the hand or by both the hand and the arm. (*From Jenni and Jenni, 1976.*)

Type I   Type II

Observations were made of 2,626 individuals on six college campuses (three in the United States, one in Canada, and two in Central America). Individuals were observed as they passed a certain point on campus. Type of carrying behavior and sex of the subject were noted. Across the six college campuses, 82 percent of the females were observed to use the Type I method, whereas only 3 percent of the males used this method. On the other hand, the observers found that 96 percent of the males used the Type II carrying method compared with 16 percent of the females. The "other" methods were used 2 percent of the time or less by both male and female students. It appears that book-carrying behavior among college students is almost totally sex-specific.

Measures: Frequency, Duration, and Ratings In observing book-carrying behavior, Jenni (1976) made only one observation of each individual. Frequency of book-carrying behavior, therefore, was described in terms of the number (or percentage) of *different* individuals who used one method or another. Checklists also can be used to obtain information about the frequency of particular behaviors in the *same* individual or group of individuals. In this case, repeated observations of the same individual or group are made over a period of time. The presence or absence of specific behaviors is noted at the time of each observation. For instance, the Schedule for Classroom Activity Norms (SCAN) is a checklist that divides classroom behavior into twenty-seven discrete categories (McKinney et al., 1975). At repeated intervals of time, an observer records what each child in the classroom is doing. Many observations of the same child show which categories of behavior are most frequent for that child. In one study using the SCAN checklist, researchers looked for relationships between the frequency of certain classroom behaviors and performance on standard tests of academic achievement. Combining information obtained from observing the children's behavior with information obtained from IQ tests yielded a more accurate prediction of school achievement than could be obtained by either using observation or IQ information alone (McKinney et al., 1975).

Checklists have been used to document the social behavioral environment of psychiatric treatment centers as well as of nursing homes for the elderly (see Alevizos et al., 1978; Powell et al., 1984). For instance, in one study twenty-five residents of a Veterans Administration nursing home were observed for a minimum of 2 hours each day for 30 days (see Powell et al., 1984). Trained observers used a twenty-five-item checklist of behaviors divided into three categories: social behaviors (for example, talking with others); nonsocial, active behaviors (for example, walking alone); and solitary, inactive behaviors (for example, watching TV alone). The presence or absence of these behaviors was noted every 15 minutes during a 2-hour observation period. A measure of social activity based on these observations was positively correlated with performance on a learning task administered to the residents. The researchers pointed to the difficulty of drawing conclusions about causation based on correlational data; however, they indicated that the results are consistent with an activity theory of aging, which posits a relationship between amount of social activity and quality of cognitive functioning. If premature decline of functioning in the elderly is at least in part produced by psychosocial factors, then a method of direct observation could serve to identify possible avenues for behavioral interventions aimed at slowing this decline.

Frequency of occurrence of behaviors from one or more categories is generally recorded as part of a behavior modification program. Once the behavior that is to be modified has been identified (the target behavior), its frequency of occurrence per some unit of time (minute, hour, or day) is observed. This initial observation period, prior to the application of treatment, is called the *baseline* observational period. When the frequency of the behavior has stabilized in the baseline period, the behavioral treatment is introduced. The effectiveness of the treatment can be judged by observing the change in frequency of the target behavior from the baseline to the treatment periods. Box 2.2 contains a description of a behavior modification study involving the treatment of chronic rumination in a profoundly retarded youngster. In this particular study the effectiveness of a treatment was measured in one individual. (Experimental designs involving only one subject are a major topic of Chapter 8. At this point, it is sufficient for you to note the important role that observation plays in behavior modification programs.)

Although frequency of occurrence is a common response measure, other measures may be used in the context of an observational study. *Duration* of a behavioral event is another important measure. LaFrance and Mayo (1976) investigated racial differences in amount of eye contact between individuals of the same race engaged in conversation. Pairs of black individuals and pairs of white individuals were observed in natural settings. The amount of time each member of the pair spent looking into the face of the other member was recorded. The researchers found that blacks gazed less at another person while listening to conversation than did whites. LaFrance and Mayo suggest that subtle differences in eye contact may be a source of social misunderstandings. White speakers may feel that lack of eye contact by a black listener indicates untrustworthiness or lack of interest when it may merely be a manifestation of a cultural difference between the races.

Observers are also sometimes called on to make *ratings* of behaviors and events. Rather than record whether an event from a predefined category did or did not occur, or how frequently an event occurred, or its duration, such observers must make subjective judgments about the degree or quantity of some trait or condition (see Brandt, 1972). Generally a rating system requires an observer to evaluate some characteristic of an individual or situation on a psychological dimension.

Dickie (1987) asked observers to rate parent-infant interactions in the context of a study designed to assess the effects of a parent training program.

BOX 2.2

BEHAVIORAL TREATMENT OF CHRONIC RUMINATION

Rumination involves the regurgitation of food in the absence of nausea or retching. The vomited food is either ejected from the mouth or reswallowed. At the time of the observation, the child was 36 months old and had been ruminating since she was 3 months old. She had been hospitalized on more than one occasion and various treatments by medical personnel had been tried without success. Prior to treatment, a baseline period of observation was scheduled. During 20-minute observation sessions conducted over several days, a check was made on the occurrence of rumination during 10-second intervals. The number of intervals in which rumination occurred was expressed as a percentage of the total number of 10-second intervals. Following

eleven baseline observation sessions the treatment was initiated. Each time the child ruminated, unsweetened lemon juice was squirted in her mouth. The treatment was carried out by the teacher in a daycare program and later by the mother when the child was at home.

The percentages of times the child ruminated during the baseline and treatment periods are shown in Figure 2.2. The lemon juice therapy quickly reduced the frequency of this behavior. In addition, the therapists reported that the child began to gain weight and that the frequency of other behaviors, such as smiling, babbling, and spontaneous interaction with adults, increased during the treatment period. (Becker et al., 1978.)

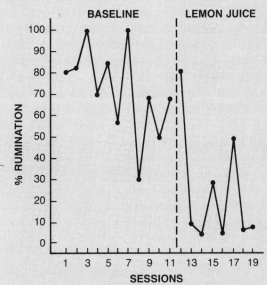

FIGURE 2.2   The percentages of times the child was observed to ruminate during baseline and treatment (lemon juice) periods. (*From Becker et al., 1978.*)

The observers visited the home and rated both the mother and the father while the parents interacted with their infant child. During most of the observation period, the observers sat in the room with the infant and asked the parents to "act as normal as possible—just as if we [the observers] weren't here." Structured observations involving assigned play with each parent were also used. Parent-infant interactions were rated on thirteen different dimensions, including degree of verbal, physical, and emotional interaction. For each dimension a continuum was defined that represented different degrees of this variable. A 7-point scale was used, whereon 1 represented the absence or very little of the characteristic and larger numbers represented increasingly more of this trait. Table 2.2 outlines one of the dimensions used by the observers in this study: warmth and affection directed toward the child. Note that precise verbal descriptions are given with the scale numbers to help observers define different degrees of this trait. The investigators found that parents who had taken part in a program aimed at developing competency in dealing with an infant were rated higher than untrained parents on many of the variables.

Recording behavior as part of an observational study has been aided by the development of hand-held microcomputers which permit an observer to record complex information rapidly. In an observational study of family interactions of depressed women, the observers used microcomputers to record both static and active categories of relevant behavior (see Hops et al., 1987). Family members were given codes, as were various behaviors and characteristics of the family interaction, and these were recorded using hand-held high-technology devices. Kirmeyer and Biggers (1988) used a similar

TABLE 2.2 EXAMPLE OF RATING SCALE USED TO MEASURE PARENT'S WARMTH AND AFFECTION TOWARD AN INFANT CHILD*

Scale Value	Description
1	There is an absence of warmth, affection, and pleasure. Excessive hostility, coldness, distance, and isolation from the child are predominant. Relationship is on an attacking level.
2	
3	There is occasional warmth and pleasure in interaction. Parent shows little evidence of pride in the child. Or pride is shown in relation to deviant or bizarre behavior by the child. Parent's manner of relating is contrived, intellectual, not genuine.
4	
5	There is moderate pleasure and warmth in the interaction. Parent shows pleasure in some areas but not in others.
6	
7	Warmth and pleasure are characteristic of the interaction with the child. There is evidence of pleasure and pride in the child. Pleasure response is appropriate to the child's behavior.

*From materials provided by Jane Dickie.

electronic recording device to record the duration and characteristics of activities of seventy-two police radio dispatchers as part of an observational study investigating Type A behavior (that is, "behavior characterized by ambitiousness, hostility, impatience, and competitiveness," p. 997). As in the previously mentioned study, codes were developed for both static and active aspects of behavior and observers were practiced prior to actual data collection in the use of the microcomputer recording system. Type A individuals were observed to place demands on themselves by initiating work tasks and by attending to multiple tasks.

SAMPLING TECHNIQUES

Before conducting an observational study, a researcher must make a number of important decisions about the times when observations will be made and the conditions under which they will be made. In some cases, it might be possible to observe *all* the behavior of interest—for instance, the behavior patterns of certain short-lived organisms. In the vast majority of observational studies, however, the investigator must be satisfied with something considerably less than a complete record of behavior. Only certain behaviors occurring at particular times and in specific settings can generally be observed. In other words, behavior and settings must be sampled. The nature of these samples determines to what extent generalizations are possible. Observations made of classroom behavior at the beginning of a school year, for instance, may not yield results that are typical of behavior seen at the end of the school year. Nor, for that matter, do observations made in the morning necessarily reveal the same pattern of classroom behavior as observations made in the afternoon. The frequency and type of aggression observed in children living in lower socioeconomic areas may not be representative of the aggression found in children from upper socioeconomic neighborhoods. As we saw in Chapter 1, our ability to generalize research findings is a question of the study's external validity. Results can reasonably be generalized only to subjects, conditions, and situations that are similar to those included in the study in which the results were actually observed. Behavior sampling (including both time and event sampling) and situation sampling are techniques used to lend external validity to observational findings.

BEHAVIOR SAMPLING

Behavior sampling is generally accomplished by either time sampling or event sampling. Hartup (1974) used a combination of time and event sampling when studying children's aggression. In **time sampling,** the intervals at which observations are made are chosen either systematically or randomly with the goal of obtaining a representative sample of behavior. As examples, we might consider the application of these techniques in the context of observing a child's classroom behavior.

Suppose that observations are to be made for a total of 2 hours each day. As we indicated, restricting observations to certain times of the day (say, in the mornings only) would not necessarily permit us to generalize our findings to the rest of the school day. One approach to obtaining a representative sample is to schedule observation periods *systematically* throughout the school day. Observations might be made during four 30-minute periods beginning every two hours. The first observation period could begin at 9:00 A.M., the second at 11:00 A.M., and so forth. Another possibility would be to schedule 10-minute observation periods every half hour during the school day. A *random* time-sampling technique could be used in the same situation by distributing four 30-minute periods (or twelve 10-minute periods) randomly over the course of the day. A different random schedule would be determined each day on which observations are made. Times would vary from day to day but, over the long run, behavior would be sampled equally from all times of the school day.

Systematic and random time-sampling procedures are often combined, as when observation intervals are scheduled systematically but observations within an interval are made at random times. For example, having scheduled four 30-minute observation periods at the same time each day, an observer might then decide to observe only during 20-second intervals that are randomly distributed within each half-hour period. Or observation periods might be scheduled randomly during certain weeks of the school year but the weeks selected systematically from the early, middle, and late parts of the year. Whatever method is used, the observer must carefully scrutinize the schedule, noting both its limitations and its advantages in terms of yielding a representative record of behavior. Sampling plays a central role in conducting surveys. Many issues related to the topic of sampling will be discussed in Chapter 3 when survey methods are introduced.

Event sampling may be a more efficient method of sampling behavior than time sampling when the event of interest occurs infrequently. In this case researchers want to maximize their opportunities to observe an event in order to get enough information about its occurrence to make investigating it worthwhile. Not only may time sampling cause precious instances of an event to be missed, but if the event is of significant duration, time sampling may not permit an observer to be present at the beginning of an event or to witness an event in its entirety. In event sampling the observer records each event that meets a predetermined definition. Researchers interested in children's reactions to special events in school such as a Christmas play would want to use event sampling. The special event defines when the observations are to be made. Researchers would certainly *not* want to use time sampling in this situation in the hope that a special event might occur during one of their randomly selected observation periods.

In many situations in which event sampling is used, a formally scheduled event like a school play is not the event of interest. Instead, researchers are often interested in events that occur unpredictably. Researchers interested in victims' reactions to violent crimes are dependent on event sampling in selecting the occasions for making their observations. Whenever possible, observers try to be present in those situations and at those times when an event of interest has occurred or is likely to occur. Thus, in an ethological study of children's "rough-and-tumble" play, an observer positioned herself in the corner of a playground to observe members of a nursery school class (Smith and Lewis, 1985). Event sampling was the method of choice due to the relatively low frequency of this behavior. However, this manner of observing behavior can easily introduce biases into the behavioral record—as when, for instance, an observer samples at the times that are most "convenient" or only when an event is certain to occur. Characterization of events at these times may not be the same as at other times. In most situations, only through some form of time sampling is an observer likely to guarantee a representative sample of behavior.

SITUATION SAMPLING

The external validity of observational findings can be significantly increased through **situation sampling.** Whenever possible—and when it is in keeping with the goals of a study—behavior should be observed under many different circumstances, locations, and conditions. By sampling different situations researchers reduce the chance that their results are peculiar to a certain set of circumstances or conditions. It is clear that behavior often changes as a function of the context in which it is observed. Animals in zoos do not behave the same way as they do in the wild. Children do not always behave the same when one parent is present as they do when the other is present. By sampling different situations, a researcher can also increase the diversity of the subject sample and hence achieve greater generality than could be claimed if only particular types of individuals were observed. As part of a naturalistic observation of beer drinking among college students, investigators purposely sampled behavior in various settings where beer was served, including five town bars, a student center, and a fraternity party (see Geller et al., 1986). When LaFrance and Mayo (1976) investigated racial differences in eye contact, they sampled many different situations. Pairs of individuals were observed in college cafeterias, business-district fast-food outlets, hospital and airport waiting rooms, and restaurants. By using situation sampling the investigators included subjects who differed in age, socioeconomic class, sex, and race in their sample. Their observations of an apparent cultural difference in eye contact behavior have considerably greater external validity than if only certain types of subjects, or behavior in only a specific situation, had been studied.

ANALYSIS OF OBSERVATIONAL DATA

DATA REDUCTION

Analysis of Narrative Records   Once they have been collected, narrative records can provide a wealth of information about behavior in natural settings. However, for meaningful information to emerge, data relevant to the goals of an observational study must be abstracted from the lengthy behavioral descriptions included in most narrative records. Results must be organized and statements summarizing important findings have to be prepared. This process of abstracting and summarizing in the analysis of behavioral data is called **data reduction.**

The first step in analyzing the content of narrative records often consists of identifying units of behavior or particular events. This stage of data reduction involves **coding** behavioral records according to specific criteria. For instance, we previously noted that a narrative record describing a day in the life of a schoolgirl was found to contain 969 different behavior episodes. Hartup's (1974) 10-week observation of children's aggression yielded information about 758 units of aggression. As part of an ethological study of preschool children, McGrew (1972) identified 115 different behavior patterns. Patterns of behavior were classified according to the body part involved, ranging from facial expressions such as bared teeth, grin face, and pucker face, to locomotion behaviors such as gallop, crawl, run, skip, and step. Coders classified these behavioral patterns while watching videotape records showing interactions of children attending nursery school.

Relevant units of behavior or events are often classified in terms of their apparent function or their particular antecedents. For instance, Hartup used nine categories to classify the nature of aggressive episodes. Antecedents of aggression were described using eighteen different categories. Relationships between antecedent events and types of aggression were then summarized, and comparisons were made between different age groups. When derogation ("put-down") elicited aggression, more younger children than older children retaliated via some form of physical aggression (such as hitting). McGrew (1972) found that children exhibit a "pout face" after losing a fight over a toy. This ethologist-observer noted that young chimpanzees show a similar expression when seeking reunion with their mother. A "pucker face" was observed in children particularly after being frustrated (and often just prior to weeping). Interestingly, there seems to be no record of a pucker face in nonhuman primates.

Descriptive Measures   When events are classified into mutually exclusive categories, the most common descriptive measure is one of relative frequency. The proportion or percentage of times that various behaviors occur is expressed in terms of the total frequency of events observed. We have already seen several examples of this type of descriptive measure. Jenni (1976), for instance, reported the percentage of times that male and female students were observed to use three different book-carrying methods. Barash (1977) summarized his observations of pedestrian behavior in terms of the percentage of people in various social groupings who looked both ways.

When behavior is recorded on at least an interval scale of measurement, as when measures of time (duration, latency) are used or when ratings are made, one or more measures of central tendency are generally reported. The most common measure is the *arithmetic mean,* or *average.* The mean describes the "typical" score in a group of scores and is an important summary measure of group performance. Measures of variability or dispersion of scores around the mean are necessary to describe group performance completely. The *standard deviation* approximates the average distance of a score from the mean. (Computational procedures for measures of central tendency and variability, as well as confidence intervals for the mean, are found in Appendix A.)

The mean and standard deviation as descriptive measures are illustrated in the results of the study by LaFrance and Mayo (1976). You may remember that these investigators observed other-directed looking behavior in pairs of black and white conversants. The number of seconds that each listener in a pair spent looking into the speaker's face was recorded. Table 2.3 (LaFrance and Mayo, 1976, p. 58) gives the means and standard deviations that summarize the results of this study. As we noted previously, white listeners spent more time looking into the face of a white speaker than black listeners spent looking into the face of a black speaker. This was found for same-sex pairs as well as mixed-sex pairs.

OBSERVER RELIABILITY

In assessing the results of an observational study, we need to inquire about observer reliability. Would another observer viewing the same events obtain the same results?

Interobserver Reliability   The degree to which two independent observers are in agreement is referred to as **interobserver reliability.** Lack of agreement prevents us from generalizing research results, because our findings apparently vary from one observer to another. Low interobserver reliability is sometimes due to characteristics of the observers or to the procedures and

TABLE 2.3   MEANS AND STANDARD DEVIATIONS DESCRIBING THE TIME (IN SECONDS) THAT LISTENERS SPENT LOOKING INTO THE FACE OF A SPEAKER PER ONE-MINUTE OBSERVATION UNIT*

Group	Mean	Standard deviation
Black conversants		
Male pairs	19.3	6.9
Female pairs	28.4	10.2
Male-female pairs	24.9	11.6
White conversants		
Male pairs	35.8	8.6
Female pairs	39.9	10.7
Male-female pairs	29.9	11.2

*From LaFrance and Mayo (1976).

methods of observing. The eighteenth-century royal astronomer Maskelyne (see Box 2.3) attributed the lack of agreement between himself and his assistant to confusion on the part of his less experienced associate (Boring, 1950) and there was only one solution: the assistant had to go. Hindsight makes it clear that the differences between the two astronomers were due to relatively fundamental individual differences in perception and reaction time.

In the context of a behavioral study, differences between observers in terms of experience, attitude, fatigue, boredom, and outcome expectancies are possible reasons for low interobserver reliability. Observer reliability is generally increased by training observers and giving them specific feedback regarding any discrepancies between their observations and those of other observers (Kidder and Judd, 1986).

Low interobserver reliability may also result when the event to be recorded is not clearly defined. Imagine Hartup (1974) asking his observers to record aggressive episodes among children without giving them an exact definition of aggression. What exactly is aggression? Some observers might decide to define aggression as exhibited only in one child's physical attack on another; other observers may include verbal assaults in their definition of aggression. What is a playful push and what is an angry shove? Without a clear definition of behavior or of the events to be recorded, observers do not always agree—and hence show low interobserver reliability. In addition to providing precise verbal definitions, giving concrete examples of a phenomenon generally helps increase reliability among observers. Showing observers the pictures of book-carrying methods in Figure 2.1, for example, could

---

BOX 2.3

A MATTER OF A SECOND

In the eighteenth century, astronomers recorded the times of stellar events using the "eye-and-ear" method (Boring, 1950). This was a complex task requiring an observer to listen to the second beats of a clock while simultaneously watching the movement of a star through a telescope the field of which was divided by parallel cross wires. By making a series of precise judgments of time and distance, astronomers obtained estimates of stellar movement that were considered to be accurate within one or two tenths of a second. Therefore it was difficult for Maskelyne, the royal astronomer in 1796 at the Greenwich Observatory, to understand why the observations of his assistant, Kinnebrook, differed from his own by nearly a whole second. Although Kinnebrook was advised of the problem, the difference persisted and Kinnebrook was fired. Some years later it was discovered that the eye-and-ear method did not guard against individual differences in perception among observers. The method was called into question and astronomers sought ways to adjust for differences in observers through the use of a "personal equation." These events in astronomy were important antecedents to the study in psychology of sensory processes and individual differences in reaction time (Boring, 1950).

be assumed to improve their ability to classify behavior according to this characteristic.

The story of Maskelyne and Kinnebrook suggests yet another conclusion regarding observer reliability: high observer reliability is not sufficient evidence that observations are accurate. Suppose Maskelyne and Kinnebrook had both been in error by the same amount. Agreement between these two observers would be very good, but neither observer's observations would reflect true stellar transit times. We can also imagine two observers of behavior who are both "in error" to the same degree. For instance, both might be influenced in a similar way by what they expect the outcome of the observational study to be. It is conceivable that the two observers would agree about what they saw but that, as in the case of the two astronomers, neither observer would provide a valid record of behavior. Instances are occasionally reported in the media of several observers claiming to see the same thing [for instance, an unidentified flying object (UFO)], only to have the event or object turn out to be something other than what observers claimed it to be (for instance, a weather balloon). Nevertheless, when two independent observers agree, we are generally more inclined to believe that observations are valid than when data are based on the observations of a single observer. The chance of both observers being influenced to the same degree by outcome expectancies, fatigue, or boredom is generally so small that we can feel confident that what was reported actually occurred. Of course, the more independent observers who agree, the more confident we become.

Measures of Reliability   How observer reliability is measured depends on the way in which behavior is measured. When events are classified according to mutually exclusive categories, such as when individuals are classified in terms of whether they show a certain behavior, observer reliability is generally assessed via a percentage agreement measure.

A standard formula for calculating percentage agreement between observers is

$$\frac{\text{Number of times two observers agree}}{\text{Number of opportunities to agree}} \times 100$$

Barash (1977) reported that observers were 100 percent reliable when classifying pedestrians as to the type of social group that was present (adult male and female, female with children, etc.) and in agreement 97 percent of the time when deciding whether pedestrians scanned both directions before crossing the street. Hartup (1974) reported measures of reliability that ranged from 83 to 94 percent for judges who coded narrative records according to type of aggression and nature of antecedent events. Although there is no hard-and-fast percentage of agreement that defines low interobserver reliability, a perusal of the literature reveals that researchers generally report estimates of reliability that exceed 85 percent, suggesting that agreement much lower than that is unacceptable.

Because in many observational studies most of the data are collected by one observer, or by several observers who collect data at different times, measures of reliability are often based only on a sample of observations for any one observer. Two observers might be asked to record the same behavior according to some time-sampling procedure. Amount of agreement for these times can be used to indicate the degree of reliability for the study as a whole. For example, when studying beer drinking among college students, investigators reported the percent agreement for two independent observers who were present at slightly fewer than half of the 243 total observation periods; during the remaining periods only one observer was present (Geller et al., 1986). Observer reliability for home observations of family interactions involving depressed women was based on 86 of the 520 (17 percent) sessions (see Hops et al., 1987).

When observational data are of at least an interval nature, as when ratings are made or when some variable such as time is measured, observer reliability can be measured using what is called the Pearson correlation coefficient. (The formula for the Pearson r is found in Appendix A.) LaFrance and Mayo (1976) obtained measures of reliability when observers recorded how much of the time a listener gazed into the speaker's face during a conversation. The average correlation for observer reliability between pairs of observers was .92 in their study.

PROBLEMS IN THE CONDUCT OF OBSERVATIONAL RESEARCH

INFLUENCE OF THE OBSERVER

Reactivity The influence that an observer has on the behavior under observation is referred to as **reactivity.** Generally, we can think of reactive research situations as situations in which subjects "react" to the presence of an observer. Behavior in these situations may not be representative of behavior when an observer is not present. Underwood and Shaughnessy (1975) relate how a student, as part of a class assignment, set out to observe whether drivers came to a complete stop at an intersection with a stop sign. The student had hypothesized that drivers of high-priced cars would be less likely than drivers of low-priced cars to stop at the sign. The observer located himself on the street corner with clipboard in hand. However, he soon observed that *all* cars were stopping at the stop sign. He then realized that his presence was influencing the driver's behavior. When he concealed himself near the intersection, he found that drivers' behavior changed and he was able to gather data regarding his hypothesis.

Although human subjects may not exhibit innate reactions to an observer, as is the case with certain animals (for example, see Moore and Stuttard, 1979), they can respond in very subtle ways when they are aware that their behavior is being observed (see Box 2.4). For instance, subjects are sometimes apprehensive and more than a little anxious about participating in psychological research. Measures of arousal, such as heart rate and galvanic skin

BOX 2.4

AN EFFECT OF MERE PRESENCE

Consider having to perform a task under two different conditions. In the first condition, after being given instructions by a researcher, you are left alone in a room to work on the task. In the second condition, once again after delivering instructions, the researcher leaves, but when working on the task you now find that another person is in the room with you. Will your performance on the task be affected by the presence of another person?

This question has been addressed by social psychologists for many years and the answer is clear: behavior is affected by the presence of another person. Research reveals that performance on simple tasks can be facilitated by the presence of another person, a so-called social facilitation effect, whereas performance on more complex tasks is often inhibited, a so-called social impairment effect (see, for example, Bond and Titus, 1983).

As you might suspect, whether social facilitation and impairment effects are found depends not only on the complexity of the task, but on who is present. For example, if the other person present is someone whose job it is to evaluate performance, as would be the case if an experimenter or observer were present, then effects due to another's presence are rather robust (see Guerin, 1986). In this case, social facilitation is usually attributed to increased arousal brought about by anticipation of being evaluated or to an increased desire on the part of the subject to gain approval and do what is socially acceptable. Social impairment would be produced if increased arousal interfered with performance, as sometimes happens when an individual facing tough competition "chokes," or if the presence of an observer distracts a subject and

brings about poorer performance than that found when the subject is alone. Although of interest as social psychological phenomena, these effects, of course, also help to define reactivity in a research situation and must be guarded against by the researcher.

Moreover, it is interesting to note that effects also have been found when another person is present who does not watch or evaluate (Guerin, 1986). In other words, behavior may differ when performed alone and when performed in the passive presence of another human. A possible explanation for an effect on behavior due simply to another human's presence is that the subject is reacting defensively because there is some uncertainty associated with the behavior of the person who is present. For example, the subject may perceive either a personal threat or a threat to personal space (Guerin, 1986). It is unclear to what extent these defensive reactions are natural or are environmentally conditioned; however, the fact that similar effects are found regularly with animal subjects indicates that reactions to the mere presence of a conspecific are widespread among living organisms. Thus, a researcher must be alert to the fact that subtle differences in behavior may arise if behavior is investigated when a subject is performing alone and when a subject is performing in the presence of others. A decision, for example, to observe individuals in a research project who will participate in pairs or in small groups, as opposed to participating alone, implies an additional concern. In addition to the possible effects that an observer has on behavior, there are possible effects due to the fact that the subject is participating in the presence of others.

response (GSR), may show changes simply as a function of an observer being present.

Subjects may also attempt to behave in the way they think the researcher wants them to behave. Knowing that they are part of a scientific investigation, subjects usually want to cooperate and to be good subjects. "Being a good subject" may be seen by the participant in a psychological study as doing what is expected by the observer. Orne (1962) has referred to the cues and other information used by subjects to guide their behavior in a psychological study as the **demand characteristics** of the research situation. Orne suggests that subjects generally ask themselves the question "What am I supposed to be doing here?" By paying attention to cues present in the setting, including those that are part of the research procedure itself, or even by attending to implicit cues given by the researcher, the subjects can perhaps figure out what is "expected" of them and attempt to modify their behavior accordingly. Subject reactions to the demand characteristics of a research situation pose threats to both the external and the internal validity of psychological research. When subjects behave in a manner that is not representative of their behavior outside the psychological research setting, our ability to generalize the results is restricted. Also, by behaving in a manner that they think is expected of them, subjects may unintentionally make a research variable look more effective than it actually is or even nullify the effects of an otherwise significant variable.

Controlling Reactivity   Problems of reactivity can be approached in several ways. Reactivity can be eliminated if observations are made in such a way that the presence of the observer is not detected by subjects. Measures of behavior in such circumstances are referred to as **unobtrusive** or **nonreactive measures.** Obtaining nonreactive measures may involve concealing the observer or hiding mechanical recording devices such as tape recorders and videotape cameras. LaFrance and Mayo (1976) observed people in conversation without their knowledge. Observations were made in a variety of natural settings, such as restaurants and waiting rooms, so we can imagine that observers had to keep their stopwatches and data sheets hidden behind menus and potted plants in order to obtain unobtrusive measures of behavior. Yet another approach is for a researcher to adopt a role in the situation other than that of observer. Subjects do not know that an observer is present, so we assume that they act as they ordinarily would. To investigate honesty, Hays (1980) worked as a clerk in a college student union. When patrons asked for change for a dollar bill, he gave them a nickel extra. Only 45 percent of the subjects (those patrons who were judged by the observer to be aware of the extra nickel) returned the extra money.

Whenever individuals are observed without their knowledge, important ethical issues arise. In many circumstances, observing people without their consent can represent a serious invasion of privacy. And when subjects are involved in situations that are deliberately arranged by an investigator, as might happen in a field experiment, ethical problems associated with placing subjects at risk may arise. Ethical issues in psychological research are discussed at length in Appendix B.

Another way of dealing with reactivity is to adapt subjects to the presence of an observer. It can be assumed that, as subjects get used to an observer being present, they will come to behave normally in that person's presence. Adaptation can be accomplished through either habituation or desensitization.

In a *habituation* procedure observers simply introduce themselves into the situation on many different occasions until subjects cease to react to their presence. In order to film a documentary entitled "An American Family," which was shown on public television in the early 1970s, the observers (with their cameras) literally moved into a California home and recorded activities of the family over a 7-month period. Although it is impossible to tell how much of their behavior was influenced by the observers' presence, events that unfolded and remarks by family members gave evidence of a habituation process. During filming the family broke up, the mother asking the father to move out of the house. When interviewed later about having the divorce announced to millions of television viewers, the father admitted that they might have asked the camera crew to get out but that, by this time, "we had gotten used to it" (*Newsweek*, 1973, p. 49). Habituation may also set in when undisguised participant observers spend a great deal of time with the subjects they are observing. Although they are still aware that an observer is present, subjects may begin to behave as though the observer were not present. As part of a study of agonistic (aggressive) behavior in preschool children, Addison (1986) reported that before actual data were collected a 5-day adaptation period was used to adapt the children to the presence of both the observer and the videotape equipment. Because the children often experienced classroom observers in the form of student teachers and other adults there appeared to be no effect due to the presence of the researcher. Moreover, Addison (1986) stated that the children's interest in the videotape equipment diminished after a few days.

Desensitization as a means of dealing with reactivity is similar to the desensitization used in the behavioral treatment of phobias. In a therapy situation an individual with a specific fear (say, an irrational fear of spiders) is first exposed to the fear stimulus at a very low intensity. The patient might be asked to think of things that are related to spiders, such as dusty rooms and cobwebs. At the same time the therapist helps the patient practice relaxing. Gradually the intensity of the stimulus is increased until the patient can tolerate the actual fear stimulus itself.

Desensitization is often used by ethologists to adapt animal subjects to the presence of an observer. Prior to a violent death in the land of her beloved subjects, Fossey (1981, 1983) conducted fascinating observational studies of the mountain gorilla in Africa. Over a period of time she moved closer and closer to the gorillas so that they would get used to her presence. She found that by imitating their movements—for instance, by munching the foliage they ate and by scratching herself—she could put the gorillas at ease. Eventually she was able to sit among the gorillas and observe them as they touched her and explored the research equipment she was using.

Finally, nonreactive measures of behavior can be obtained by observing behavior indirectly (see Webb et al., 1981). This may involve examining physical traces left behind or examining archival information, which consists of the records kept by society about individuals and events. One researcher investigated the drinking behavior of people living in a town that was officially "dry" by counting empty liquor bottles in their trash cans. Another researcher used the records kept by a library to assess the effect on a community of the introduction of television. Withdrawals of fiction titles dropped, but the demand for nonfiction was not affected (see Webb et al., 1981). Physical traces and archival data are important unobtrusive measures that can be valuable sources of information about behavior. In Chapter 4 we will discuss more fully these indirect methods of observation.

OBSERVER BIAS

You may remember that, when Rosenhan (1973) and his colleagues observed the interaction between staff members and patients in mental hospitals, they found a serious bias on the part of the staff. Once patients were labeled schizophrenic, their behavior was interpreted solely in light of this label. Behaviors that might have been considered normal when performed by sane individuals were interpreted by the staff as evidence of the patients' insanity. For instance, note taking by the participant observers, which was done openly, was later discovered to have been cited by members of the staff as an example of the pseudopatients' pathological state. As a result of the staff's tendency to interpret patients' behavior in terms of the label that had been given them, the sanity of the pseudopatients was not detected. This example clearly illustrates the danger of **observer bias,** the systematic errors in observation that result from the observer's expectations.

Expectancy Effects   Although we might hope that scientific observations are free from the kind of observer bias documented by Rosenhan, we know that this is not always the case. In many scientific studies the observer has some expectancy about what behavior should be like in a particular situation or should result from a specific psychological treatment. This expectancy may be created by knowledge of the results of past investigations or perhaps by the observer's own hypothesis about behavior in this situation. Expectancies can be a source of observer bias—*expectancy effects*—if they lead to systematic errors in observation (Rosenthal, 1966, 1976).

An example of a study designed to document observer bias will illustrate this problem (see Cordaro and Ison, 1963). The study required college student observers to record the number of head turns and body contractions made by two groups of planarians (flatworms). The observers were led to expect different rates of turning and contracting in the two groups. The worms in the groups were, however, essentially identical. What differed was the observers' expectations about what they would see. Results showed that the observers reported twice as many head turns and three times as many body contractions when a high rate of movement was expected than when a low rate was expected. Apparently, the students interpreted the actions of the worms differently depending on what they expected to observe.

Other Biases An observer's expectancies regarding the outcome of a study may not be the only source of observer bias. You might think that using automated equipment such as movie cameras would eliminate observer bias. Although automation reduces the opportunity for observer bias, it does not necessarily eliminate it. Consider the fact that, in order to record behavior on film, the observer must determine the angle, location, and time of filming. To the extent that they are influenced by personal biases of the observer, decisions about these aspects of the study can introduce systematic errors into the results. Altmann (1974) describes an observational study of animal behavior in which the observers biased the results by taking a midday break whenever the animals were inactive. Observations of the animals during this period of inactivity were conspicuously absent from the observational records. Furthermore, using automated equipment generally only postpones the process of classification and interpretation, and it is perfectly possible for the effects of observer bias to be introduced when narrative records are coded and analyzed.

Controlling Observer Bias Observer bias cannot be eliminated, but it can be controlled in several ways. As we mentioned, the use of automatic recording equipment can help, although the potential for bias is still present. Probably the most important control over observer bias is the awareness that it might be present.

Observer bias can be reduced by limiting the information provided to observers. When Hartup (1974) analyzed the results of his observational study of children's aggression, the individuals who performed the analysis were not permitted to see all the narrative record. When the nature of the aggressive act was classified, the antecedent events were blacked out, and when antecedent events were coded, the nature of the aggressive act was blacked out. Therefore, in making their classifications, the coders could not be influenced by information related to the event that they were coding. In a manner of speaking the coders were "blind" to certain aspects of the study. Observers are *blind* when they do not know the reason why the observations are being made or the goals of a study. When Burns et al. (1987) observed problem-solving strategies of children from two different socioeconomic groups, they first videotaped children while they worked on five tasks selected from standardized intelligence tests. When task strategies were observed and coded from the videotape records, however, the observer-coder was blind as to which group the child was from. When LaFrance and Mayo (1976) investigated eye contact between individuals conversing in natural settings, their observers did not know that possible differences along racial lines were being probed. Using "blind" observers greatly reduces the possibility of introducing systematic errors due to observer expectancies.

SUMMARY

Observational methods can be characterized in terms of both the degree of observer intervention and the manner in which behavior is recorded. Observation in a natural setting without observer intervention is called naturalistic observation. On the other hand, both structured observations (frequently used by the developmental psychologist Piaget) and field experiments (often used by social psychologists) depend on some degree of observer intervention. The manner of record keeping in an observational study varies according to whether a comprehensive description of behavior is sought or the observer seeks to describe only certain predefined units of behavior. Whereas narrative records, including field notes, are used to provide comprehensive descriptions of behavior, checklists (action and static) are typically used when it is simply of interest whether a specific behavior has occurred. The frequency and duration of behaviors also may be recorded, and observers are sometimes called on to make subjective judgments, in the form of ratings, about the quality or degree of a characteristic of the subject or situation.

Observations rarely can be made of all behavior that occurs. Consequently some form of behavior sampling (time and event) or situation sampling must be used. An important goal of sampling is to achieve a representative sample of behavior. When narrative records are made, some type of coding system is generally used as one step in the process of data reduction. Measures of frequency and duration, as well as ratings, are typically summarized using descriptive statistics such as the mean and standard deviation.

It is essential to provide measures of observer reliability when reporting the results of an observational study. Depending on the level of measurement that has been used, either a percentage agreement measure or a correlation coefficient can be used to assess reliability. Finally, it is important to control for the possible influence of both reactivity and observer bias in any observational study.

KEY CONCEPTS

naturalistic observation	time sampling
ethology	event sampling
ethogram	situation sampling
participant observation	data reduction
structured observation	coding
field experiment	interobserver reliability
confederate	reactivity
narrative records	demand characteristics
ecological psychology	unobtrusive (nonreactive) measures
field notes	observer bias
checklist	

REVIEW QUESTIONS

1 What three characteristics distinguish scientific observation from nonscientific observation?
2 What critical characteristics distinguish among naturalistic observation, participant observation, structured observation, and a field experiment?
3 What two dimensions can be used to classify observational methods?
4 What is meant by a comparative approach to understanding behavior?
5 There are five general reasons for intervening in conducting an observational study. Identify a study illustrating each reason—either from the studies cited in this chapter or from research you have studied in other psychology courses.
6 What two methodological problems arise in participant observation?
7 What factors in participant observation can be expected to influence the extent of the observer's influence on the behavior being observed?
8 What is the principal advantage of the structured observation method?
9 Describe the role of a confederate in a field experiment.
10 In what ways does the sample narrative record from the study of a day in the life of a midwestern schoolgirl differ from that taken from Hartup's study of children's aggression?
11 What factors determine the usefulness of field notes as scientific records, and what determines the likelihood that these factors will be present?
12 How can the quality of narrative records be improved?
13 Define and give an example of a static checklist and an action checklist.
14 Give an example of each of the three measures most commonly used in observational studies to record units of behavior?
15 What aspect of an observational study is the proper use of behavior sampling and situation sampling intended to ensure?
16 What are the most common descriptive measures (1) when events are classified into mutually exclusive categories and (2) when behavior is recorded on at least an interval scale?
17 What factors contribute to low interobserver reliability and how can interobserver reliability be increased?
18 Does high interobserver reliability ensure the validity of observations? Why or why not?
19 Why are subjects' reactions to demand characteristics a threat to both the internal and the external validity of psychological research?
20 What ethical issues must one address when using unobtrusive measures?
21 Give an example of each of the two general procedures investigators use to deal with the problem of reactivity by adapting subjects to the presence of the observer.
22 What is the best procedure to control observer bias?

CHALLENGE QUESTIONS

1 Students in a developmental psychology lab course conducted an observational study of parent-infant interactions in the home. When they first entered the home on each of the 4 days they did the observation of a given family, they greeted both the parents and the infant (and any other children at home). They instructed the family to follow its daily routine and they asked a series of questions about the ac-

tivities of that day to determine whether it was a "normal" day or something unusual had happened. The students tried to make the family feel comfortable, but they also tried to minimize their interactions with the family and with each other. For any given 2-hour observation period there were always two student observers present in the home, and the two observers recorded their notes independently of each other. There were six pairs of students who were randomly assigned to carry out the 8 hours of observation on each of the twelve families who volunteered to serve in the study. The same pair of observers always observed a given family, and two families were assigned to each pair of observers. The observers used checklists to record behaviors on a number of different dimensions, such as mutual warmth and affection of the parent-infant interaction. They key-punched the data they obtained into the computer and used statistical programs to analyze their results.

A Cite *two* specific procedures used by the students to ensure the *reliability* of their findings.

B Cite one possible threat to the generality of the findings of this study; once again, cite a specific example from the description provided.

C Cite one specific aspect of their procedure that indicated that the students were sensitive to the possibility that their measurements might be reactive. What other methods might they have used to deal with this problem of reactivity?

2 A student hypothesized that men were much more serious about their studies than were women. As a preliminary test of this hypothesis she decided to do a simple observation on the study habits of men versus women.

The investigator's method was to go to the library and watch a student for a period of 15 minutes. During that period, whenever the student appeared to be reading, the investigator would keep the time with a stop watch. When the student appeared to be daydreaming, was talking to someone else, or was just looking away from his or her books, the investigator turned off her stopwatch. Thus her measure of how serious a student she was observing was simply the time, expressed as a percentage of the 15-minute period, that was spent reading.

To do an adequate job of observing, the woman spent an entire day in the library. From 8:00 A.M. until 11:00 A.M. she observed twelve men. On the same day from 1:00 P.M. until 4:00 P.M. she observed twelve women. Her results were clear. The men spent an average of 82 percent of their time in the library actually reading. The women spent an average of only 58 percent of their time reading.

The student concluded that the data supported her hypothesis. State clearly why you agree or disagree with her conclusion.

3 A friend of yours is absolutely convinced that he has a positive influence on the friendliness of conversations in which he is a participant. He has reached this conclusion on the basis of his everyday observations. You convince him that a systematic study is needed to confirm his hypothesis. Your friend (still smiling) carefully develops an operational definition of the friendliness of a conversation and records a rating for each of the next fifty conversations in which he is a participant. His results show that 75 percent of these conversations are rated "very friendly," 20 percent are rated "friendly" and 5 percent are rated neutral. Your friend returns to you—now convinced beyond a shadow of a doubt that he has a positive effect on the friendliness of a conversation. Although your friend won't be pleased with you, explain to him why the results of his study are essentially useless as a means of confirming his hypothesis. While you have this chance to lecture your friend on research methods, explain to him why it would be better for you or someone else to

rate the friendliness of the conversations in a proper study testing your friend's hypothesis.

4 A recent carefully controlled observational study was undertaken to determine whether differences in student-teacher ratings correspond to genuine instructional differences among teachers. The subjects were forty-eight full-time social science faculty (thirty-nine males and nine females) at a major university. Ten were full professors, eighteen were associate professors, and twenty were assistant professors. A number of undergraduate students were carefully trained as observers. They used a checklist including 100 specific observable classroom behaviors, and their visits to the classrooms were unnoticed by the professors. Six to eight observers visited three separate 1-hour class periods taught by these instructors over a 3-month period. The results of the study showed that teachers who receive high ratings from students do in fact teach differently from instructors who receive average or poor ratings.

Use the above description to answer the following questions.

A Suggest what specific procedure was used in this study to avoid reactivity?

B What factor in this study is likely to have affected the reliability of the results?

C What factor in this study affected the external validity of the findings?

D Given the final conclusion, which goal of the scientific method (description, prediction, causal inference) was the basis for this study?

ANSWER TO CHALLENGE QUESTION 1

1 A The students' procedures that enhanced reliability were as follows: observing each family for 8 hours, using two independent observers, and using checklists to provide operational definitions.

B One possible threat to generality of the findings was that the twelve families volunteered for the study and such families may differ from typical families.

C The students' efforts to minimize interactions with the family and with each other suggested that they were sensitive to the problem of reactivity. Two other methods they might have used are habituation and desensitization.

CHAPTER

3

Surveys and Questionnaires

OUTLINE

In Chapter 2 we discussed how psychologists use observational methods in their study of human and animal behavior. You have seen how these methods can be used to describe behavior and its context. Results of these observations can be used to infer how people must have been thinking or feeling to have behaved in a certain way. We now turn our attention to a method designed to deal more directly with the nature of people's thoughts, opinions, and feelings. The method is called *survey research*. On the surface, survey research is deceptively simple. If you want to know what people are thinking, ask them! In a similar vein one could suggest that, if you want to know what people are doing, observe them! As we have seen, however, observation from which we hope to infer general principles of behavior requires considerably more sophistication. So, too, the proper use of the survey research method requires more than simply asking people questions.

The deceptive ease of conducting a survey is illustrated in a recent report by a young girl named Bridgette that was published in a suburban grammar school's newsletter. The report read, "I surveyed fifty people on which candy bar they liked best. Here are my results in order of preference: Hershey bar—35, Snickers—10, Whachamacallit—5." These results may please the manufacturers of Hershey bars, but the operator of the school's vending machine should be wary of stocking it on the basis of these findings. Who were the "fifty people" surveyed and how were they selected? How was the survey conducted? Was each child interviewed separately? If other children were present during the interview, were they eating candy bars? If so, what brands? Do the children who claim to like Hershey bars best really eat them most often? These and many other questions must be answered before we can confidently interpret the results of this survey. You may be thinking at this point that we are taking Bridgette's survey more seriously than she intended, and you are probably right. Nonetheless, these questions are typical of those that should be asked when we read or hear a report of a nationwide survey indicating that, for example, a majority of Americans oppose gun control. After reading this chapter you should be better able to formulate such questions and to evaluate responses to them.

The first part of this chapter includes a description of the basic logic and techniques of sampling—that is, the process of selecting a subset of a population to represent the population as a whole. The advantages and disadvantages of the various survey methods and designs are then discussed. Procedures for summarizing and analyzing survey results are described. The correspondence between people's reported behavior and their actual behavior also is briefly discussed.

In the final major section of this chapter, general and specific guidelines are provided for the construction of the most typical survey instrument, the questionnaire. Should you decide to use a questionnaire as part of a psychology research project, it is important that you know how to prepare an actual questionnaire. In this final section of Chapter 3 you will find important information that will aid you when you begin the process of preparing a questionnaire.

USES AND CHARACTERISTICS OF SURVEYS

Surveys are used in research by social scientists such as political scientists, psychologists, and sociologists for a variety of reasons. For example, Jessor, Chase, and Donovan (1980) conducted a national survey to determine the extent of, and possible reasons for, drug and alcohol use by adolescents. Mulder (1979) surveyed voters on two occasions to determine the effectiveness of TV advertising in a Chicago mayoral election. Campbell (1981) used surveys to study changes in people's sense of satisfaction in various domains of their lives during the turbulent 1970s. The specific survey research techniques used in these studies and the major results of each study will be described later in this chapter.

Surveys are also used to meet the more pragmatic needs of political candidates, public health officials, and advertising and marketing directors. The scope and purpose of such surveys can be limited and specific, or they can be truly global. A very specific application occurred in connection with a personal injury suit in Chicago. The lawyer for the injured party hired a market research team to conduct a survey of registered voters to determine what sort of person would identify with the victim and, therefore, be most likely to award a multi-million-dollar settlement. The lawyer used this information to screen prospective jurors. Gallup (1976), on the other hand, reported the results of surveys sampling two-thirds of the world's population to measure human needs and satisfactions. One objective was to establish an international data bank that would make it possible to measure and chart trends in global attitudes and behavior.

Though they differ in scope and purpose, most surveys have certain characteristics in common. Surveys generally involve sampling, a concept that was introduced in our discussion of observational methods (Chapter 2) and about which we will have more to say in the next section of this chapter. Surveys are also characterized by their use of a set of predetermined questions for all respondents. Oral or written responses to these questions constitute the principal data obtained in a survey. By using the same phrasing and ordering of questions, it is possible to summarize the views of all respondents succinctly. For example, a 1967 survey showed that over 80 percent of Americans condemned premarital sex as morally wrong, whereas just under 40 percent of respondents held that view in 1979 (Yankelovich, 1981).

Another advantage of asking questions systematically is that doing so makes it possible to describe relationships among variables. As an illustration, consider two surveys concerning the relationship between educational level and perceived happiness. Table 3.1 shows the results of these surveys. In 1957, 44 percent of college graduates but only 23 percent of those with no high school education said they were "very happy." In the same year only 4 percent of college graduates reported being "not too happy," whereas 20 percent of those who spent no time in high school were in this category. Apparently, the more education people have, the happier they are. These differences were in the same direction but were much smaller in 1978. The usefulness of this descriptive function of surveys has even led to efforts to develop indicators of national well-being comparable to economic indicators such as the consumer price index (see Sheldon and Freeman, 1972). The media may soon be reporting reasons for the changes in the "consumer satisfaction index."

As these examples illustrate, properly conducted surveys are an excellent basis for describing people's attitudes and opinions. They are not, however, without their limitations. The consistent ordering and phrasing of questions is ill

TABLE 3.1 PERCEIVED HAPPINESS IN EDUCATIONAL GROUPS

Educational level	Percent "very happy"		Percent "not too happy"	
	1957	1978	1957	1978
No high school	23	28	20	13
Some high school	30	25	9	9
High school graduate	46	28	6	8
Some college	43	33	6	5
College graduate	44	33	4	6

*From Campbell (1981).

suited for in-depth examination of the thoughts or feelings of individual respondents. And, because questionnaires must be constructed prior to data collection and adhered to closely during data collection, surveys do not provide a good vehicle for exploratory studies. Observation is the preferred method for such ground-breaking studies, in which the research question and the method of attack take shape during the process of conducting the study.

Another potential limitation in survey research involves interpretation of causal relationships. For instance, the relationship between educational level and happiness shown in Table 3.1 is both strong and reliable. We could not, however, use these data alone to argue convincingly that increasing education causes increasing happiness. Increasing education *may* result in increasing happiness, but it is also possible that happier people do better in school and thus are more likely to continue. Another possibility is that those who are more financially well off are *both* happier *and* more likely to obtain more education. There is a technique for causal analysis of survey data that we will describe later in this chapter. Even more sophisticated statistical procedures are available, but discussion of these techniques used in the causal analysis of survey data goes beyond the scope of the present text (see Babbie, 1979; Kenny, 1979; Kidder and Judd, 1986). For now, let us assume that you are interested in doing a survey to describe characteristics of a population of interest. In the following sections we will discuss the procedures necessary to carry out that survey successfully.

SAMPLING TECHNIQUES

Assuming that you have determined the population of interest for your survey, the next step is to decide whom to interview. This involves selecting a sample of respondents to represent the population. The power and efficiency of sampling are aptly summarized by the noted survey researcher Angus Campbell (1981, p. 17):

> The method of choice for portraying all the variety of a large heterogeneous population is clearly that of the sample survey. Ever since statisticians and social scientists learned how to draw a sample from a large universe in such a way that every member of the universe has an equal chance of being chosen, it has been possible to describe the national population accurately by obtaining information from a few thousand carefully selected individuals.

Whether we are describing a national population or a much smaller one, such as the employees of a certain company, the procedures are the same. This section explains how to make that careful selection of individuals which Campbell describes.

BASIC TERMINOLOGY OF SAMPLING

In discussing sampling techniques, it is essential that we clearly understand the definitions of four terms: population, sampling frame, sample, and element. A **population** is the set of *all* the cases of interest. If you were interested in the attitudes of students on your campus toward the services provided by the library, your population would be all students on your campus. If we were conducting a census, we would attempt to obtain information from every member of the population; in a survey, for the sake of efficiency, we select a subset of the population to represent the population as a whole.

Most often a population is a hypothetical entity, and we need to develop a specific list of the members of the population. This specific list is called a **sampling frame** and is, in a sense, an operational definition of the population of interest. In a survey assessing the attitudes of students toward library services, the sampling frame might be a list obtained from the registrar's office of all currently enrolled students. It is easy to see that the extent to which the sampling frame reflects the population of interest determines the adequacy of the subset we ultimately select. The list provided by the registrar should provide a good sampling frame, but it is still possible that some students may be excluded, such as those who have just recently been processed for admission. An inadequate sampling frame can pose a much more serious problem, as pollsters in the 1936 presidential election found out (see Box 3.1).

The subset of the population actually drawn from the sampling frame is called the **sample.** We might select 100 students from the registrar's list to serve as the sample in our library survey. How closely the attitudes of this sample of students will correspond to those of all the students depends critically on how the sample is chosen. Each member of the population is called an **element,** and the identification and selection of those elements that will serve as a sample are the basis of all sampling techniques. The relationships among the four critical sampling terms are summarized in Figure 3.1 on page 83.

Remember that samples are of little or no interest in themselves. Library policy would not be changed solely for the 100 students surveyed. Similarly, the social psychologist is not interested solely in the racial attitudes of the 50 people he surveyed, nor is the marketing director interested only in the preferences of the 200 consumers she surveyed. The "power" of descriptions derived from an analysis of the sample stems from the fact that they are assumed to be applicable to the population from which the sample was drawn. Populations, not samples, are of primary interest.

The ability to generalize from a sample to the population depends critically on the **representativeness** of the sample. Characteristics of individuals in the population are distributed in various ways. That is, the relative frequencies with which the characteristics appear in the population vary. For example, in one population there might be 40 percent males and 60 percent females, whereas in another the distribution might be 75 percent female and 25 percent male. A sample is representative to the extent that it exhibits the same distribution of characteristics as the population from which it was selected. If 30 percent of the students on your campus are sophomores, then your library survey sample of 100 students should include approximately 30 sophomores if it is to be representative.

BOX 3.1

THE NOT-ALWAYS-VAULTED HISTORY OF POLLING

In 1936 a *Literary Digest* poll involving a mail survey of almost 2 million voters predicted incorrectly that Alfred M. Landon would beat Franklin D. Roosevelt by a landslide. The sample of voters was drawn from telephone directories, magazine subscription lists, and automobile registration lists. Using this same technique, pollsters had correctly predicted the outcome of the previous four elections. Spurred by the Depression, however, increasing numbers of the poor voted in 1936 and they were not adequately represented on such lists. In the same election George Gallup used a different technique to predict Roosevelt's 1936 victory. Even so, in 1948 Gallup (and many other pollsters) confidently and incorrectly predicted that Dewey would defeat Truman.

These early polling failures were partly responsible for the development of probability sampling, the most respected survey research method in use today. [This method is described in detail later in this chapter.] The 1976 election provided what is perhaps the high point in the successful use of this method. The *Times*-CBS poll predicted 51.1 percent for Carter and 48.9 percent for Ford (ignoring undecideds)—the same as the actual vote totals! What makes this feat even more impressive is that samples of 2,000 voters were used to predict the voting of 80 million people.

The 1980 campaign was a sobering one for pollsters. President Reagan's landslide victory followed weeks of public opinion polling in which survey after survey reported that the race was "too close to call." A *Time* magazine piece entitled "Where the Polls Went Wrong" (Dec. 1, 1980) cited negative voting, large numbers of undecideds, and low voter turnout as factors contributing to the inaccuracy of the polls. What the 1980 campaign made clear is that polls based on carefully selected samples are accurate reflections of people's voting preferences *at the time the poll is taken.* Polls do not necessarily predict the future.

On the other hand, polls sometimes can reveal important reasons why people did what they did, as is evidenced by results of "exit polling." An exit poll involves asking voters after they have voted (that is, while exiting the voting area) why they voted as they did. Of course, it is unlikely that random selection will be used in choosing the voters to interview, and not everyone who is chosen will volunteer to take the time to talk to an exit pollster. Thus, we must be concerned about possible selection and response biases. Nonetheless, information gathered from exit polls can identify critical concerns of the voter at the actual time of voting. This information may prove useful to leaders of political parties as they plot a strategy for the next election. For example, in the 1988 presidential election between George Bush and Michael Dukakis, exit polls showed that major factors in Bush's victory were voters' "general sense of well-being" and Bush's experience in government (see "The Issues that Mattered," *Time,* Nov. 21, 1988).

The major threat to representativeness is bias. A **biased sample** is one in which the distribution of characteristics is *systematically* different from that of the target population. There are two sources of bias: *selection bias* and *response bias.* (We will discuss selection bias now and deal with response bias when we discuss response rates associated with various survey methods.) Selection bias occurs when the procedures used to select the sample result in the over-representation of some segment of the population or, conversely, in the exclusion or underrepresentation of a significant segment. A particularly salient case of selection bias once led to some serious errors in estimating the public health needs of the elderly (see Box 3.2).

FIGURE 3.1   Diagram illustrating relationships among basic sampling terms.

BOX 3.2

AN UNHEALTHY LOOK AT THE HEALTH OF THE ELDERLY

In the late 1950s a survey research project was funded by the Foundation for Voluntary Welfare. This foundation was generally acknowledged to be opposed to public welfare programs. The intended purpose of the study was to determine the needs and resources of the elderly by conducting a nationwide survey. The sample was selected in such a way that upper-class respondents were overrepresented. In addition, the sample excluded nonwhite persons over 65, individuals in nursing homes, and those receiving old-age assistance. The exclusion of these groups was par-ticularly troublesome because the problems of aging are relatively severe in each of them. Not surprisingly, given this serious selection bias, the results showed that older people were more healthy and more satisfied with existing programs than earlier studies had indicated. As often happens, this survey had an impact beyond the confines of the research community. These findings were part of the basis of a national campaign mounted by the American Medical Association against federal programs for medical care for the elderly (Warwick and Lininger, 1975, p. 41).

A more subtle example of selection bias was described by Lewin (1981). Two research reports are summarized, both of which make the point that the obesity charts that doctors and insurance companies had used for 20 years include "desired" weights that are at least 15 pounds too low. Thus some people who considered themselves overweight were in fact not overweight. The charts were originally prepared by the Metropolitan Life Insurance Company in 1959 on the basis of information supplied by policyholders. The underestimation of desired weights was attributable, at least in part, to the fact that the charts were based only on data regarding people who were accepted for insurance coverage. Because these people tend to be healthier than average, their weights would probably be lower than those of the general population. The need to adjust for this selection bias and for other factors influencing the accuracy of the desired weights led Metropolitan Life to publish a 1983 chart to replace the 1959 chart.

Survey researchers must be constantly alert to the threat of selection bias in sampling. Fortunately, as we will see, they have developed techniques that can minimize the risk.

APPROACHES TO SAMPLING

There are two basic approaches to sampling, nonprobability sampling and probability sampling. In **nonprobability sampling** there is no way to estimate the probability of each element's being included in the sample and no guarantee that each element has some chance of being included. If a researcher were to interview the first 10 students she met after she walked out of her office, she would be using nonprobability sampling. Clearly, not all students on campus would be equally likely to be outside the researcher's office at that particular time, and some students would have essentially no chance of being included in the sample.

By contrast, if the researcher were to select ten students randomly from the registrar's list of enrolled students, she would be using **probability sampling.** All students would have an equal chance of being included in such a sample. Only when probability sampling is used is it possible to estimate the likelihood that sample findings differ from the findings that would have emerged from studying the whole population. Hence probability sampling is far superior to nonprobability sampling in ensuring that selected samples will be representative samples. The principal advantages of nonprobability sampling are convenience and economy. In order to choose appropriately between nonprobability sampling and probability sampling, you will need to learn more about specific types of sampling plans.

Types of Nonprobability Samples Two types of nonprobability sampling are accidental samples and purposive samples. **Accidental samples** are those that result when availability and willingness to respond are the overriding factors used in selecting respondents. If an instructor who is interested in the attitudes of college students uses the students who happen to be en-rolled in his classes that semester as his sample, he is using an accidental sample. On a Saturday afternoon at the beginning of the 1981 major league baseball strike, NBC surveyed its viewers about their attitudes toward the strike. Periodically during the program substituted for the scheduled telecast of a baseball game, an announcer asked those who favored the owners to call one telephone number and those who favored the players to call a different number. Clearly the respondents in this survey constituted an accidental sample: those who happened to be watching at that time.

Shere Hite's book *Women and Love: A Cultural Revolution in Progress* (1987) illustrates an extreme case of accidental sampling. She mailed 100,000 questionnaires to women who belonged to a variety of women's groups in forty-three states. These groups ranged from feminist organizations to church groups to garden clubs. Her questionnaires included 127 essay questions on topics ranging from hobbies to communication between spouses. Only 4.5 percent of the original sample responded to the survey. The problem is not the size of the sample; Shere Hite herself said, "It's 4,500 people. That's enough for me." The problem is whether these respondents can be considered representative of the intended population, women in the United States. Without additional information about the population it is impossible to confirm that an accidental sample is not representative. In this case, however, one can be quite certain that the survey respondents do not fairly represent the whole population. Even the initial 100,000 selected were not representative of women in general because they all belonged to some organization. It is also reasonable to expect that discontented women might be more likely to respond and therefore be overrepresented in the final sample. For example, Hite reported that 95 percent of women feel emotionally harassed by the men they love. This contrasts sharply with other national surveys with random samples in which half or more of women report being completely satisfied with their marriage and only 3 percent say they are "not at all happy" (Peplau and Gordon, 1985). As a general rule, accidental samples should be considered biased unless there is strong evidence corroborating their representativeness.

In the second type of nonprobability sampling, **purposive sampling,** the investigator handpicks the elements to be included in the sample on the basis of expert judgment. The individuals selected may be either those judged to have certain special characteristics or (more commonly) those who are likely to provide the most useful information for the purposes for which the study is being done. A small number of election districts are sometimes used as a purposive sample. These "key" districts are selected for polling because in previous years their election results have approximated overall state or national voting patterns. Goleman (1981) describes the use of purposive sampling in a survey for which respondents who were most likely to prove informative were selected. In developing new tests for use in personnel selection, psychologist David C. McClelland asked top management people to nominate "water walkers"—people who were so outstanding they could do no wrong. The managers were also asked to nominate employees who simply did their jobs well enough not to get fired. McClelland and his colleagues then conducted intensive interviews of the nominees from both groups and, from these interviews, developed a list of competencies that set the water walkers apart from the more typical employees. Job applicants were then screened on the basis of these competency-based tests to try to detect potential water walkers. In this situation the characteristics of workers in general were not McClelland's primary interest, so purposive sampling was ideally suited to the task at hand. When representative samples *are* essential, the method of choice is probability sampling.

Types of Probability Samples The distinguishing characteristic of probability sampling is that the researcher can specify, for each element of the population, the probability that it will be included in the sample. Three types of probability samples are used most often: simple random samples, stratified samples, and cluster samples. **Simple random sampling** is the basic technique of probability sampling, and it is incorporated in the other two types of probability sampling. In a simple random sample, each possible sample of a specified size in the population has an equal chance of being chosen. Because samples are usually drawn from large populations, it is not common practice to list all possible samples and then select one randomly. Instead, the most common definition of a random sample is that every element has an equal chance of being included in it. The procedures for selecting such a sample are outlined in Box 3.3.

One critical decision that must be made in selecting a random sample is how large it should be. For now, we will simply note that the size of a random sample needed to ensure representativeness varies with the homogeneity of the population. College students in Ivy League schools represent a more homogeneous population than college students in all U.S. colleges. In the extreme case of homogeneity, where all members of the population are identical, a sample of one is representative regardless of the size of the population. At the other extreme, if the population were so heterogeneous that each member was completely different from all other members on all characteristics, then *no* sample, regardless of its size, could be representative. Every individual would have to be included to describe such a heterogeneous population. Fortunately, the populations with which survey researchers work fall somewhere between these two extremes. Thus the representativeness of samples, like the joy of eating a piece of chocolate cake, increases with increasing size—up to a point.

The representativeness of the obtained sample can often be increased by using **stratified random sampling.** In this procedure, the population is divided into subpopulations called strata (singular, *stratum*) and random samples are drawn from each of these strata. Two general approaches are fol-

BOX 3.3

SAMPLES OF RANDOM SAMPLES

The following names represent a scaled-down version of a sampling frame obtained from the registrar's office of a small college campus. Pro- cedures for drawing both a random sample and a stratified random sample from this list are described below.

Adamski	F	Jr	Hedlund	F	So
Alderink	F	Sr	Hoogland	F	Sr
Baxter	M	Sr	Johnson	F	Fr
Bowen	M	Fr	Knecht	F	Jr
Broder	M	So	Mason	F	Sr
Brown	M	Jr	Nowaczyk	M	Jr
Bufford	M	So	O'Keane	F	Sr
Campbell	F	Fr	Osgood	M	So
Carnahan	F	So	Owens	F	So
Cowan	F	Fr	Penzien	M	Jr
Cushman	M	Sr	Powers	M	Sr
Dawes	M	Jr	Rogers	M	Fr
Dennis	M	Sr	Sawyer	M	Jr
Douglas	F	Fr	Shaw	M	Sr
Dunne	M	So	Sonders	F	Sr
Fahey	M	Fr	Suffolk	F	So
Fedder	M	Fr	Taylor	F	Fr
Foley	F	So	Thompson	M	Fr
Grossman	F	Jr	Watterson	F	Jr
Harris	F	Jr	Zimmerman	M	So

Drawing a random sample

Step 1. Number each element in the sampling frame: Adamski would be number 1, Harris number 20, and Zimmerman number 40.

Step 2. Decide on the sample size you want to use. This is just an illustration, so we will use a sample size of 5.

Step 3. Choose a starting point in the Table of Random Numbers in Appendix A (a finger stab with your eyes closed works just fine—our stab came down at column 8, row 22 at the entry 26384). Because our sampling frame ranges only from 1 to 40, we had decided *prior* to entering the table to use the left two numbers in each set of five and to go across the table from left to right. We could just as easily have decided to go up, down, or from right to left. We could also have used the middle two or the last two digits of each set of five, but one should make these decisions before entering the table.

Step 4. Identify the numbers to be included in your sample by moving across the table. We got the numbers 26, 06, 21, 15, and 32. Notice that numbers over 40 are ignored. The same would be true if we had come across a repetition of a number we had already selected.

Step 5. List the names corresponding to the selected numbers: In our case the sample will include Nowaczyk, Brown, Hedlund, Dunne, and Rogers.

An even easier system, called *systematic sampling,* can be used to obtain a random sample. In this procedure you divide the sample size you want into the size of the sampling frame to obtain the value *k*. Then you select every *k*th element after choosing the first one randomly. In our example we want a sample size of 5 from a sampling frame of 40, so *k* would be 8. Thus we would choose one of the first eight people randomly and then take every eighth person thereafter. If Alderink were chosen from among the first 8, the remaining members of the sample would be Cowan, Foley, Nowaczyk, and Shaw. Note: This system should *not* be used if the sampling frame has a periodic organization—if, for example, you had a list of dormitory residents arranged by room and every tenth pair listed occupied a corner room. You can readily see that, in such a list, if your sampling interval was 10 you could end up with all people from corner rooms or no people from corner rooms.

Drawing a stratified random sample

Step 1. Arrange the sampling frame in strata. For our example we will stratify by class standing, so our sampling frame now looks like this:

Freshmen	Sophomores	Juniors	Seniors
1 Bowen	1 Broder	1 Adamski	1 Alderink
2 Campbell	2 Bufford	2 Brown	2 Baxter
3 Cowan	3 Carnahan	3 Dawes	3 Cushman
4 Douglas	4 Dunne	4 Grossman	4 Dennis
5 Fahey	5 Foley	5 Harris	5 Hoogland
6 Fedder	6 Hedlund	6 Knecht	6 Mason
7 Johnson	7 Osgood	7 Nowaczyk	7 O'Keane
8 Rogers	8 Owens	8 Penzien	8 Powers
9 Taylor	9 Suffolk	9 Sawyer	9 Shaw
10 Thompson	10 Zimmerman	10 Watterson	10 Sonders

In our example the strata are equal in size, but this need not be the case.

Step 2. Number each element within each stratum, as has been done in the foregoing list.

Step 3. Decide on the overall sample size you want to use. For our example we will draw a sample of 8.

Step 4. Draw an equal-sized sample from each stratum such that you obtain the desired overall sample size. For our example this would mean drawing 2 from each stratum.

Step 5. Follow the steps for drawing a random sample and repeat for each stratum. We used the previously determined starting point (column 8, line 22) in the Table of Random Numbers, but this time we used the last digit in each set of five. The numbers identified for each stratum were: Freshmen (4 and 1), Sophomores (6 and 4), Juniors (7 and 9), and Seniors (2 and 9).

Step 6. List the names corresponding to the selected numbers. Our stratified random sample would include Douglas, Bowen, Hedlund, Dunne, Nowaczyk, Sawyer, Baxter, and Shaw.

lowed in determining how many elements should be drawn from each stratum. One approach (illustrated in the last example of Box 3.3) is to draw equal-sized samples from each stratum. The second approach is to draw elements for the sample on a proportional basis. For example, if there are three strata representing 40 percent, 40 percent, and 20 percent of the population, respectively, then a stratified sample of 200 would include 80 individuals from each of the first two strata and 40 from the third stratum.

Stratified random sampling is especially beneficial when the strata represent relatively homogeneous segments of the population. In addition to increasing the representativeness of samples, stratified random sampling is a useful technique when you want to make general statements about portions of the population you have sampled. For example, a simple random sample of 100 students would be sufficient to survey students' attitudes on a campus of 2,000 students. It would be risky, however, to use views of the two chemistry students who happened to be included in this sample to represent those of the 40 chemistry majors on campus. If the investigators knew in advance that they wanted to describe the views of students majoring in various departments, a simple random sample of the students on campus would not be the method of choice. Instead, a stratified random sample according to majors could be constructed without drastically increasing the overall sample size.

As the previous examples demonstrate, simple random sampling and stratified sampling involve the use of a sampling frame. Unfortunately, survey researchers are often faced with the task of sampling from populations for which sampling frames are not readily available. When this problem arises, they use **cluster sampling.** In this technique the sampling unit is some aggregate or cluster of elements in the population for which an appropriate sampling frame can be found. This technique can best be defined by giving an example of its use.

Jessor et al. (1980) were confronted with the task of developing a national sample of adolescents. Needless to say, they did not have a sampling frame listing all adolescents presently living in the United States. They solved this problem by using multistage cluster sampling. In the first stage they used a sampling frame of all counties within the forty-eight contiguous states and the District of Columbia. They then drew a stratified random sample of fifty counties from this list. The counties were stratified by census region, county population, and ethnic makeup. In the second stage they used a sampling frame of junior- and senior-high school home rooms from schools in the fifty counties they had selected. The home rooms were stratified by grade level. Each home room represents a *cluster* of adolescents. The researchers randomly selected approximately 700 home rooms from the sampling frame. These 700 clusters provided an overall sample of approximately 16,000 adolescents. As this illustration shows, cluster sampling is somewhat more complex than simple random sampling or stratified sampling. But the objective is still the same: to obtain a representative sample of the population of interest, in this case all adolescents residing in the continental United States.

SURVEY METHODS

In this section we describe the alternatives from which the survey researcher may choose in deciding *how* to conduct the interview. There are three general survey methods: mail surveys, personal interviews, and telephone interviews. As was true of sampling techniques, there is no one best method for all circumstances; each survey method has its own advantages and disadvantages. The challenge facing the survey researcher is to select the method that best fits the problem under study.

MAIL SURVEYS

Mail surveys represent the most common means of distributing self-administered questionnaires. A principal advantage of mail surveys is that they can be done relatively quickly. Because they are self-administered, mail surveys avoid the problems of interviewer bias (to be defined more completely in the next section). And among the three types of surveys, mail surveys are the best for dealing with highly personal or embarrassing topics, especially when the anonymity of respondents is preserved.

Unfortunately, there are as many disadvantages to mail surveys as there are advantages. For instance, because the respondent will not be able to ask questions if a portion of the questionnaire is unclear, the questionnaire must be completely self-explanatory. A second disadvantage is that the researcher has little control over the order in which the respondent proceeds through the questionnaire. Different respondents may follow different sequences, and the order of questions may affect the way respondents answer certain of them. It is reasonable to expect that, when all respondents do not follow the same sequence, the variability among their responses to a given question is likely to increase.

The most serious problem with mail surveys, however, is one of bias—namely, *response bias*. Mail surveys exclude respondents with literacy problems and are generally intimidating to those of low educational background. Those with problems with their vision, such as many of the elderly, are also excluded. The major factor leading to response bias in mail surveys is the generally low response rate. Quite often people included in a sample are too busy or not interested enough in the study to return a completed questionnaire. Low response rates necessarily produce smaller samples. Generally, however, the size of the sample is not the most serious concern. The problem is that low response rates make it likely that the resultant sample is biased. For example, if 200 store managers are included in a survey about store security, but only 50 respond, the results may be biased because only those stores that are the least busy are represented. Unless the return rate is 100 percent, the potential for bias exists regardless of how carefully the *initial* sample was selected. Nonetheless, the bias problem decreases with increasing response rate. A 50 percent response rate is considered adequate, 60 percent is good, and 70 percent is very good (Babbie, 1979). These are demanding standards in light of the fact that a typical return rate for a mail survey is around 30 percent.

Certain procedures should be followed in a mail survey to enhance response rate. For instance, the initial mailing should include a letter summarizing the purpose of the survey, explaining the basis on which the respondents were selected, and assuring the respondents of confidentiality. A postage-paid return envelope should also be included along with the questionnaire. As questionnaires are returned, the researcher should plot a cumulative response rate graph like that shown in Figure 3.2. Numbering the returned questionnaires in the order received allows researchers to make

FIGURE 3.2 Sample graph showing cumulative response rate for a mail survey. Five hundred surveys were mailed on Wednesday, September 16.

comparisons such as that between early and late respondents. Plateaus in the cumulative response rate graph indicate that a follow-up mailing should be sent. To obtain a 70 percent response rate, it is often necessary to send three mailings. These should be spaced about 2 to 3 weeks apart or when a plateau appears on the cumulative response rate graph. Because the original copy is likely to have been lost, a new copy of the questionnaire should be sent with each mailing.

Several factors contribute to higher than usual return rates. Return rates will be highest when the questionnaire has a "personal touch," when it requires a minimum of effort for the respondent, when the topic of the survey is of intrinsic interest to the respondent, and when the respondent identifies in some way with the organization or researcher sponsoring the survey. Warwick and Lininger (1975) describe a survey that met these requirements. About 100,000 members of women's religious congregations in the United States were surveyed. The study was sponsored by, and had the support of, the religious congregations. It was done by a visible and respected member of one of the religious orders and the subject matter was of great interest to the respondents. The result was an almost perfect response rate. Warwick and Lininger note, however, that most mail surveys fall far short of this ideal. Fortunately, survey researchers have available other survey methods that generate much higher response rates than mail surveys.

PERSONAL INTERVIEWS

When personal interviews are used to collect survey data, respondents are usually contacted in their homes and trained interviewers administer the questionnaire. The personal interview allows much greater flexibility in asking questions than the mail survey. In a personal interview the respondent can obtain clarification of unclear questions, and the trained interviewer can pursue incomplete or ambiguous answers to open-ended questions. Respondents are also much less likely to fail to respond to an item on the questionnaire, and they are less likely to use "don't know" as a response. The interviewer controls the sequencing of questions and can ensure that all respondents complete the questionnaire in the same order. Traditionally, the response rate to personal interviews has been much higher than that to mail surveys; the commonly accepted response rate is 80 to 85 percent. In recent years, however, increasing fear of urban crime and an increasing number of households with no one home during the day have tended to reduce the attractiveness of using personal interviews.

This impressive list of the advantages of personal interviews is offset by two disadvantages. The first disadvantage, high cost, results because the use of trained interviewers is expensive in terms of both money and time. The second, perhaps more critical disadvantage involves the potential for **interviewer bias.** The interviewer should be a neutral medium through which questions and answers are transmitted. Interviewer bias occurs when the interviewer tries to adjust the wording of a question to "fit" the respondent or records only selected portions of the respondent's answers. Most often, however, interviewer bias results from the use of probes. *Probes* are follow-up questions used by interviewers to get respondents to elaborate on ambiguous or incomplete answers. In trying to clarify the respondent's answers, the interviewer must be careful not to introduce ideas that may then become part of the respondent's subsequent answer. For example, if a respondent in a survey of television viewing said that the major problem with current TV programming was excessive violence, the probe "Could you elaborate on what you mean by violence?" would be better than the probe "By violence do you mean murders, muggings, and rapes?" Interviewers must also be mindful of the feedback their verbal and nonverbal responses give to respondents. Smiling and nodding approvingly when a respondent fails to answer a question may lead the respondents to withhold responses to later questions.

The best protection against interviewer bias is highly motivated, well-paid interviewers who are trained to follow question wording exactly, to record responses accurately, and to use probes judiciously. Interviewers should also be given a detailed list of specifications—that is, instructions about how difficult or confusing situations are to be handled. Finally, interviewers should be closely supervised by the survey research director. It should now be clear that the decision to use personal interviews is not one that survey researchers take lightly.

TELEPHONE INTERVIEWS

Prohibitive travel costs and the difficulties involved in supervising interviewers when personal interviews are used have led many survey researchers to turn to telephone interviews. This method met with considerable criticism when it was first used because of serious limitations on the sampling frame of potential respondents. Many people have unlisted numbers, and the poor and those in rural areas were unlikely to have a phone. By 1979, however, more than 95 percent of all households had telephones, and techniques such as random-digit dialing have been developed to reach households with unlisted numbers. Telephone interviewing also provides access to dangerous neighborhoods, locked buildings, and respondents available only during evening hours. Interviews can be completed more quickly when contacts are made by phone, and interviewers can be better supervised when all interviews are conducted from one central location.

Of course, the telephone survey is not without its drawbacks. There is still a selection bias when respondents are limited to those people who have telephones, and the problem of interviewer bias remains. There is a limit to how long respondents are willing to stay on the phone, and the fact that responses are being given to a "faceless voice" may influence how people respond. In spite of these limitations, the high response rate and flexibility of the telephone interview make it the method of choice for nearly all brief surveys.

SURVEY RESEARCH DESIGNS

After investigators have decided who the respondents will be (sampling) and how to conduct the survey (survey method), one critical decision remains. This decision involves the selection of a research design, the overall plan by which the survey is administered. In making this decision, the survey researcher chooses among three general survey research designs: the one-shot or cross-sectional study, the successive independent samples study, and the panel or longitudinal study. As you probably suspect, there is no all-purpose research design to meet every survey need; the choice of design must be tailored to the objectives of the study.

ONE-SHOT OR CROSS-SECTIONAL STUDY

The most commonly used survey research design is the **one-shot** or **cross-sectional study.** In this design a sample of the population is selected and information is collected from this sample at one time. This design is not limited to the use of one sample, however, and the data collection period is not necessarily short. Jessor et al. (1980) used the cross-sectional design in their nationwide survey of drinking and marijuana use among teenagers. They made comparisons among different samples defined by age, gender, and ethnic group. The survey took each respondent 45 minutes to complete, but the overall testing of respondents took over a month. In some studies it can be even longer.

The focus in a one-shot survey is on description—describing the characteristics of a population or the differences among two or more populations. Cross-sectional studies can also be used to assess interrelationships among variables within a population. This is what Jessor et al. (1980) did when they tried to determine what personality, social, and behavioral characteristics were most strongly related to marijuana use. They found that increased marijuana use was associated with several factors, such as lower expectations for academic achievement, greater tolerance of deviance, less compatibility between friends and parents, and a greater value placed on independence than on academic achievement. The three strongest predictors of marijuana use, however, were friends as models of marijuana use, the number of times drunk in the past year, and involvement in general deviant behavior. Thus marijuana use can be understood as a component of a larger behavior pattern and not as an isolated issue.

One-shot surveys can be especially useful in epidemiology, the study of the incidence and prevalence of disease in a population. *Incidence* refers to the number of new cases of a disorder reported during a specific time period—a year, for example. *Prevalence* is the frequency of a disorder in a particular population. Seligman (1988) used such epidemiological studies to make a provocative argument about factors contributing to an increase in the occurrence of unipolar depression. The first step in his investigation was to determine whether there had, in fact, been a change in the occurrence of depression. Seligman used the lifetime prevalence of depression—the percentage of the population that has had the disorder at least once in their lifetime. In general, this is a cumulative statistic; if you look at the prevalence of broken legs, you find that it increases with age. As expected, the prevalence of depression increased from about 5 percent for those born around 1960 to about 9 percent for those born around 1945. For those born around 1925, however, the lifetime prevalence went down to 4 percent, and for those born around 1910 it went down to only 1 percent. After carefully tracking through possible artifacts in these results, Seligman concluded that there had been a genuine tenfold increase in the prevalence of unipolar depression since World War II. He went on to argue that the increase was attributable to an increasing emphasis on individualism and a decreasing emphasis on commitment to common values such as family and religion. Seligman's interpretation is one well worth considering, but the methodological point his study illustrates is that surveys can play a critical role in describing important epidemiological findings. Such findings can not only be used to test theoretical explanations of disorders such as unipolar depression but can also be helpful in identifying individuals or groups at risk for certain disorders.

One-shot or cross-sectional studies are ideally suited to the descriptive and predictive functions we have been discussing so far. Surveys are also used to assess changes in attitudes or behaviors over time and to determine the effect of some naturally occurring event, such as the passage of a law to raise the drinking age. For these purposes the cross-sectional survey is not the method of choice. Rather, research designs are needed that systematically sample respondents across time. Two such designs are discussed in the next two sections.

SUCCESSIVE INDEPENDENT SAMPLES STUDY

The **successive independent samples** design can be understood as a series of cross-sectional surveys in which the same questions are asked of each succeeding sample of respondents. This design is most appropriate when the major aim of the study is to describe changes over time in the attitudes or behaviors of members of a population. Campbell (1981) used the successive independent samples design in a series of national surveys that were done to assess changes in Americans' sense of well-being over a 20-year period. The studies were massive in scale. In each of five different years, over 2,000 people were interviewed in their homes and each interview lasted about an hour.

Studies of this kind are invaluable when discussion turns to the topics of the "good old days" or "the wonders of modern times." For instance, you may have heard someone say that people aren't so satisfied with life as they used to be. The data summarized in Table 3.2 show that people's reported satisfaction with a variety of areas of their lives changed little during the 1970s. This lack of change is remarkable, given the many changes in American society that occurred during this turbulent period. Consider, for example, the results of another survey measuring people's trust in government. Surveys were done in 1972 and 1978; the results are shown in Table 3.3. As these data suggest, Americans' attitudes clearly changed in at least one area—more were cynical in 1978 than in 1972. Such dramatic changes in attitude make it all the more surprising that Campbell's (1981) survey showed that people simply don't seem to be either more or less satisfied with their lives as a whole. Findings of this kind are typical of the provocative in-

TABLE 3.2   MEAN SATISFACTION RATINGS IN VARIOUS DOMAINS OF LIFE*

Domain	1971	1978
Marriage	1.73	1.77
Family life	2.08	2.22
Health	2.22	2.28
Neighborhood	2.24	2.29
Friendships	2.26	2.33
Housework	2.29	2.65
Work	2.33	2.42
Life in the United States	2.39	2.38
Community	2.40	2.41
Housing	2.43	2.34
Standard of living	2.69	2.78
Amount of education	3.31	3.57
Savings	3.73	3.78
Life as a whole	2.45	2.46
Number of cases	(2146)	(3692)

*The mean values are based on a 7-point scale whereon 1 represents "completely satisfied" and 7 represents "completely dissatisfied." Data taken from Campbell (1981), Appendix Table 2.

TABLE 3.3   TRUST IN GOVERNMENT, 1972–1978*

	1972	1978
Cynical	36%	52%
Mixed	24%	26%
Trusting	38%	19%
Not answered	2%	3%
Number of cases	(2285)	(2304)

*Data taken from Campbell (1981), Appendix Table 8.

formation that becomes available when the successive independent samples design is used.

The successive independent samples design has several limitations. The data given in Table 3.3 can be used to illustrate one of these limitations. Consider the change from 36 percent to 52 percent in the "cynical" category from 1972 to 1978. It is tempting to conclude that 16 percent of the population was added between 1972 and 1978 to the original 36 percent of Americans who were already cynical about government in 1972. We also might try to say that, of the 19 percent who were no longer "trusting," 16 percent were now cynical, 2 percent had mixed feelings, and 1 percent failed to answer. What we must remember, however, is that the people surveyed in 1978 were *not* the same people surveyed in 1972. It is possible (though unlikely) that all of them could have changed their views between 1972 and 1978. That is, the formerly cynical may now be mixed or trusting, the formerly trusting may now be mixed or cynical, and the formerly mixed may now be cynical or trusting. The extent to which individuals change categories can be determined only by testing the same individuals on both occasions. Given that you cannot determine who has changed or by how much, it is not surprising that it is difficult to use successive independent samples to ferret out the reasons for the changes you record.

A second problem with the successive independent samples design arises when samples are not representative of the *same* population. If Campbell had sampled affluent Americans in 1957 and poor Americans in 1978, his comparisons of the well-being of Americans over this time period would be meaningless. Changes in the population across time can be described accurately only when the characteristics of the samples representing that population are the same.

This problem of *noncomparable successive samples* has recently been the focus of debate between representatives of the chemical industry and environmentalists. The issue involved is the incidence of cancer in the United States. The chemical industry has consistently pointed to findings showing a relatively stable incidence of cancer. This is taken as evidence that increasing exposure to chemicals is not endangering the public. However, a survey carried out by the National Cancer Institute (Pollack and Horm, 1980) showed evidence of increasing cancer incidence from 1969 to 1976, and some environmentalists point to chemical use as a major factor contributing to the increase. Unfortunately, the results of this most recent survey were based on samples that varied considerably from year to year. Only four out of eleven geographic regions were common to the survey populations in 1969 and 1976. There is also some question about how representative either sample is of the total U.S. population. Sophisticated statistical procedures are being used to try to unravel the problems of interpretation introduced by noncomparable successive samples, but it is not clear that these efforts will lead to a definitive answer about the effect of exposures to chemicals on cancer incidence.

One final problem with surveys based on successive independent samples arises when they are used to determine the effect of some naturally occurring or researcher-manipulated event. For example, a survey of attitudes toward teenage drinking might be done before and after the passage of a law raising the legal drinking age, or a campus fraternity might sample students' attitudes toward the organization before and after a campaign publicizing the fraternity's activities. The major problem in this type of study is the high risk of confounding. We have already discussed one possible source of confounding: if the samples drawn before and after the event are not comparable, there is no way to attribute any obtained differences to the intervening event. Even when the samples *are* comparable, the threat of confounding is not eliminated. A dramatic accident involving teenage drunken driving may have been publicized at the same time as the new drinking law was passed. There would be no way to tell whether publicity surrounding this accident or the change in the drinking law caused any subsequent change in the respondents' attitudes toward teenage drinking. Fortunately, the problems of confounding by extraneous factors are not insurmountable; we discuss possible solutions to these problems in much greater detail in Chapter 9. Nonetheless, it is important to be on the alert for such problems whenever successive independent samples are used and conclusions are reached about the cause of changes over time.

PANEL OR LONGITUDINAL STUDY

The distinguishing characteristic of the **panel** or **longitudinal study** is that the same sample of respondents is interviewed more than once. There are two principal advantages of this design. First, the investigator can determine the direction and extent of change for individual respondents. This obviously makes it easier to answer questions about the reasons for attitude or behavior changes. Second, the panel study is the best available survey research design when the effect of some experimental manipulation needs to be assessed. Mulder (1979) used this design to determine the effects of television advertising in a Chicago mayoral election. The same individuals were interviewed before and after the TV political ads were broadcast. Thus it was possible to study the influence of the ads on changes in voters' preferences. Mulder found that, the more relative exposure a voter had to ads for Alderman Singer, the challenger in the election, the more likely that person was to favor Singer. Somewhat surprisingly, the TV ads were as effective for voters who were actively involved in the campaign as they were for inactive voters.

One problem in a panel study is that it can be difficult to obtain a sample of respondents who will agree to participate in a longitudinal study, which more often than not means a long-term study. In Mulder's study only two brief phone calls to each respondent were required. In other studies, however, the respondents may be asked to complete several lengthy surveys at regular intervals over a number of years. People are often hesitant to make the commitment of time necessary to complete such an extensive project.

Even when the respondents do agree to participate, there are further problems. You might think that this design solves the problem of noncomparable samples that can occur when successive independent samples are used. After all, how much more comparable can a sample be than one that is identical to the original sample? Unfortunately, successive samples in a panel study are identical only if *all* members of the original sample are retained throughout the study. This is not likely to be the case. Mulder's (1979) study is typical; he was able to complete a second interview with 80 percent of his original sample. A respondent's failure to complete all phases of a panel study is referred to as **respondent mortality** (sometimes literal, but most often figurative). Respondent mortality is probably the most serious disadvantage of the panel study. It is usually possible, however, to determine whether the final sample is comparable to the original sample in a panel study, because the characteristics of nonrespondents in the follow-up phase are known (they were included in the original sample).

Problems also arise in a panel study because the same respondents are interviewed more than once. One problem is that respondents may strive heroically to be consistent across interviews. This can be particularly troublesome if the study is designed to assess changes in respondents' attitudes. Although their attitudes have actually changed, people may report their original attitudes in an effort to appear consistent. Another problem is that the initial interview may sensitize respondents to the issue under investigation and make them more likely or less likely than they would otherwise have been to respond to the manipulation under investigation. For example, consider again Mulder's (1979) election study. Those people interviewed prior to the broadcast of the TV ads may have paid more attention to the ads because participating in the survey piqued their interest in election issues. You might recognize that this is another illustration of reactive measurement—people reacting differently because they know they are being observed (see Chapter 2).

QUESTIONNAIRE CONSTRUCTION

Throughout this chapter we have been discussing procedures for administering a survey without describing in detail the nature of the most common survey research instrument, the questionnaire. Even if the sample is perfectly representative, the response rate is 100 percent, and the research design is elegantly planned and perfectly executed, the survey results will be useless if the questionnaire has been poorly constructed. How questions are worded, for instance, can seriously affect the results (see, for example, Box 3.4). As in many other areas, there is no substitute for experience when it comes to preparing a good

BOX 3.4

AN OPEN AND CLOSED CASE

Schuman and Scott (1987) have documented the inherent limitations and liabilities of both open and closed survey questions. They demonstrated that significant differences to the same question can be obtained depending on whether the question was asked in an open or closed format. Consider a frequently asked question in national surveys: What is the most important problem facing this country today? Schuman and Scott found that when respondents were asked this question using an open-ended or free-response format, the issues mentioned most often were unemployment, general economic problems, threat of nuclear war, and foreign affairs. When asked the same question in a closed format the most frequently mentioned problem in the open format, namely, unemployment, was now mentioned much less frequently.

Why the difference? In the closed format four specific problems were identified, but respondents were also given an opportunity to name a different problem in an "other" category. The four specific problems appearing in the closed question were chosen by the researchers from those that were rarely spontaneously mentioned in the open format. These included, for example, the energy shortage and the quality of public schools. Given that these alternatives were known to be infrequent responses when using an open-ended question, Schuman and Scott wanted to find out how many people would use the "other" category to name a problem. Only 40 percent of the respondents took the opportunity to list a different problem, and unemployment, previously named as important by 17 percent of the respondents, was mentioned by fewer than 7 percent of the respondents. Using the closed format the most important problem facing this country was the quality of public schools. This particular problem had been identified by fewer than 2 percent of the respondents when asked an open-ended question!

In a subsequent investigation, Schuman and Scott showed that responses to an open-ended question about the most significant national or world event or change in the last 50 years were not the same as those to a closed question. This time, alternatives to the closed question included the most frequent responses given to the open-ended question. Schuman and Scott, however, felt that the wording of the question likely focused people on responses in the political domain. For instance, the most frequent response using the open format was "World War II." They included as one of the alternatives in the closed question "the invention of the computer." Although mentioned by fewer than 2 percent of people responding to the open-ended question, it was selected by nearly 30 percent of people when the very same question was asked using the closed format.

The problem, if not the solution, is clear. How a question is worded can drastically influence people's responses and what alternatives appear as choices to a closed-ended question can just as dramatically affect results. It is not surprising, therefore, that differences in the way questions are worded is seen as one of the major reasons for discrepancies in public opinion polls which supposedly focus on the same or similar issues (see Converse and Traugott, 1986). A solution, according to Schuman and Scott, is for investigators to realize the limitations on assessing, in an absolute sense, people's opinions or attitudes based on any one set of questions, and, perhaps consider emphasizing subjects' responses to the same set of questions over time. Researchers should also, of course, consider emphasizing a multimethod approach to investigating behavior.

questionnaire. Nonetheless, there are a few general principles of sound questionnaire construction with which you should be familiar before you set out to get that first bit of experience. In the final major section of this chapter, we describe six basic steps in preparing a questionnaire and then offer some more specific guidelines for writing and administering individual questions. It will be important for you to review this section of the chapter should you decide to make use of a questionnaire as part of a research project you are doing.

In the immediately following section we turn to problems of data analysis when a survey is conducted. Results of surveys are often reported in terms of descriptive statistics, such as the mean or standard deviation, and in the form of correlations. Understanding how data obtained from a questionnaire are correctly analyzed is essential if results of a questionnaire study are to be interpreted meaningfully. Moreover, should you plan to construct a questionnaire using the guidelines given later in this chapter, you will find that it is important to plan how the data will be analyzed before you actually construct the questionnaire.

ANALYSIS OF SURVEY RESULTS

So far we have described the procedures necessary to conduct a good survey. The purpose of these procedures has been mentioned several times. The goal of a good survey is to ask a carefully selected sample of individuals the same set of questions, so that their answers can be used as a basis for describing the characteristics of the population from which the sample was drawn. Worthwhile general descriptions of the population cannot be obtained, however, by simply enumerating all the responses of all the respondents to all the questions. The process of data reduction must be applied to survey results before general descriptive statements can be made. In this section we discuss the most common data reduction techniques in survey research.

Before describing the measures themselves, however, let us briefly comment on the role of computers in survey research. By their very nature, surveys often involve collecting large amounts of information from large numbers of people. When you consider the task of thoroughly analyzing the results of a 100-item questionnaire administered to 300 respondents, it is easy to see why survey researchers make extensive use of computers. Many packaged programs are available, such as the *Statistical Package for the Social Sciences* (SPSS), and their use increases both the ease and the accuracy of survey analysis. We will not describe the specific procedures for using such programs efficiently and effectively, but we encourage you, regardless of your level of experience and expertise, to explore using the computer for data analysis.

DESCRIPTIVE MEASURES

Data reduction procedures differ for open-ended and closed questions. The first step in analyzing open-ended questions is to code the responses and to ensure that this coding is done reliably. The procedures for this are the same as those described for coding narrative records (see Chapter 2). When closed questions have been used, scoring the responses presents little problem. The next step in data reduction is to prepare a frequency distribution for each questionnaire item, listing the number of respondents who used each response category. To allow for easier comparison of results across surveys with different sample sizes, proportions or percentages of respondents in each category are typically reported. For example, in a 1976 Gallup survey, respondents were asked for each of thirteen occupations whether they would prefer to deal with a man or a woman. The results for those respondents who expressed a preference for a given occupation are summarized in Table 3.4. Besides illustrating the use of percentages in data reduction, the results of this survey show that strong work stereotypes exist. One word of caution about percentages: They should not be used when small sample sizes are involved. If you report that 75 percent of those surveyed agreed with your position, few of us would suspect that you meant that three of the four people you asked agreed with you. As a general rule, the sample size should always be reported when percentages or proportions are used.

When rating scales or other interval scale data are involved in a survey, it is possible to summarize responses to these items succinctly by using measures of central tendency such as the *mean, median,* or *mode.* Measures of central tendency should always be accompanied by measures of dispersion such as the *standard deviation* or *range.* The use of these descriptive measures was discussed in Chapter 2, and the procedures for computing them are described in Appendix A.

A given sample is just one of an infinite number of possible samples that could have been drawn from the population. Therefore it is unlikely that the

TABLE 3.4 GENDER PREFERENCES FOR VARIOUS OCCUPATIONS*

Occupation	Preference, %	
	Men	Women
Police officer	59	2
Physician	53	7
Lawyer	45	5
Dentist	45	5
Banker	34	5
Insurance agent	32	5
Stockbroker	30	4
Real estate agent	25	12
Physician specializing in female problems	20	26
Door-to-door salesperson	12	21
Salesperson in a store	8	36
Hairdresser	7	45
Nurse	2	66

*From Barron and Yankelovich (1980).

sample mean is exactly equal to the population mean. It is possible, however (when probability sampling techniques have been used), to estimate intervals for which we can have varying degrees of confidence that they contain the population mean. Appropriately enough, these are called **confidence intervals.** More details about computing confidence intervals are provided in Appendix A. For now, it is sufficient for you to understand that there is a specifiable margin of error involved in estimating population values on the basis of sample statistics and that this margin of error is used to establish confidence intervals.

At some time in reporting your survey results, it will be necessary to summarize them in verbal form. Great care must be taken in choosing among such terms as "few," "most," "many," and "some" in order to communicate your findings clearly and fairly. The safest route to follow is not to use general summary terms unless the exact values on which they were based have been reported. Similarly, as consumers of research findings, we should demand that the quantitative information be provided along with the verbal summaries. When we are told that a majority of Americans favor a certain policy, it is certainly helpful to know whether the exact percentage favoring the position is 50.1 or 99.9 percent.

CORRELATIONAL STUDIES

Surveys often are conducted with the goal of describing relationships between variables. Because these studies typically do not involve the manipulation of independent variables and merely assess covariation between different variables, they are frequently referred to as *correlational studies*. Describing relationships between variables often provides, of course, a basis for prediction.

When responses to a survey constitute an interval or ratio level of measurement, a Pearson Product-Moment Correlation Coefficient r is appropriately used to assess the degree of relationship (see Appendix A for computational formula). A common type of correlational study is one in which responses obtained as part of the survey are correlated. For example, in one recent study investigating the relationship between measures of physical and mental health, investigators personally interviewed 1,543 adults living in the United States (Lubin et al., 1988). They asked the respondents to provide self-ratings of physical health as well as to give information about such health-related factors as frequency of visits to a physician and the nature and frequency of any medications they were taking. The interviewers also collected demographic data (for example, occupation and religious affiliation of respondents) and data regarding the frequency of volunteer and social activities. Each of the respondents also was asked to complete a paper-and-pencil test measuring both positive affect (for example, happiness) and negative affect (for example, depression). Measures of affect and measures of physical health were found to be correlated. For instance, positive affect was directly correlated with self-ratings of health; frequency of volunteer activities correlated negatively with a measure of depression. In addition to providing data on the prevalence of psychological disorders, such as depression, in the United States, the investigators suggest that correlational studies of this type can prove useful in the prediction of physical and psychological health-related problems.

Other types of correlational studies seek evidence for a relationship between responses to a questionnaire and specific measures of behavior. Nowaczyk (1984) administered a questionnaire to students in various computer programming courses. Questions included in the survey instrument requested information about such things as previous computer experience and expected grade in the course. One page of the questionnaire contained eighteen statements measuring attitudes toward computer science. Students also were asked to take a test assessing internal versus external locus of control. In general, an internalizer perceives a high degree of personal control over the environment, whereas an externalizer perceives luck or chance determining what occurs in one's life (locus of control was discussed briefly in Chapter 1). Amount of previous computer experience correlated with final grades in an introductory computer course, and thus could be used to predict performance in the course. Interestingly, neither attitude toward computer science nor perceived locus of control was correlated with final grades in the courses; therefore, there was no evidence that course grades could be predicted by these measures.

When an ordinal level of measurement is used in a correlational study (for example, when respondents are asked to rank stimuli according to preference), a Spearman Rank-Order Correlation Coefficient r_S should be substituted for the Pearson r (see Appendix A for computational formula). However, analysis of relationships between variables that are measured on a nominal scale typically takes a different form than that used when ordinal and interval or ratio levels of measurement are used. Examples of statistical procedures commonly used in this situation are described in the following sections.

CROSS TABULATIONS

The most common format used in reporting relationships between variables is the *cross tabulation*. As the name implies, cross tabulations involve the preparation of tables describing results relating two or more variables. An example of a cross tabulation is presented in Table 3.5. Hicks and Kilcourse (1983) used this table to summarize the results of their survey of 176 students. They asked the students to indicate (1) the hours of sleep they typically got and (2) how often they had tension or migraine headaches. The question of interest in cross tabulations is whether a relationship exists between the two variables. That is, is there a relationship between the number of hours of sleep a person typically gets and the frequency of headaches? Sixty-six percent (38 of 58) of the students

TABLE 3.5   FREQUENCY OF HEADACHES AS A FUNCTION OF TYPICAL SLEEP DURATION*

Hours of sleep	Frequency of headaches		
	Never	**Sometimes**	**Often**
> 8	38	17	3
7	37	21	5
< 6	19	31	5

Taken from Hicks and Kilcourse (1983).

who reported 8 or more hours of sleep never had headaches. Only 35 percent of those reporting fewer than 6 hours of sleep were headache-free (19 of 55). These findings suggest that habitual sleep duration and tension headaches may be related. (The statistical technique used to answer this question more definitely is the chi-square (χ^2) test, and the computational procedures for this test are found in Appendix A.)

CONTROL VARIABLES AND EXPLANATION

In the last section we discussed the use of cross tabulations in describing relationships among variables. Cross tabulations can also be used in developing or testing proposed explanations for obtained relationships. We can provide only a brief introduction to the technique here; a much more complete introduction and description is available in Babbie (1979). The basic application of the technique is to begin with a relationship and to use additional variables, called *control variables*, to determine whether the original relationship changes as a function of the control variables. Let's consider an example.

National surveys have consistently shown that men earn higher incomes than women. A typical set of data illustrating this relationship is presented in the top half of Table 3.6. The data are clear; men are more than twice as likely as women to earn over $8,000 (64 percent versus 27 percent). You may be able to think of several reasons for this relationship, but for now we will consider only one. Women may earn less if, as has been true traditionally, they obtain less formal education than men do. We know that the amount of education one has affects one's income. In this case we have identified amount of education as a possible control variable. That is, we could argue that the relationship between gender and income changes when we control for amount of education. For this example, we will look at only one "level" of the control variable; that is, we will examine the relationship between gender and income only for those individuals who have attended college.

The three hypothetical outcomes when a control variable is used are illustrated in the bottom half of Table 3.6. In Outcome I, the control variable has had no effect; the relationship between gender and income is just as strong when only those with a college education are considered. In a sense, our

TABLE 3.6 ILLUSTRATION OF THE USE OF CONTROL VARIABLES IN THE ANALYSIS OF SURVEY DATA

Overall survey results		
	Male	**Female**
Income < 8,000	36%	73%
Income > 8,000	64%	27%
N	495	330

College student data only								
Outcome I			**Outcome II**			**Outcome III**		
	Male	**Female**		**Male**	**Female**		**Male**	**Female**
< 8,000	22%	67%	< 8,000	22%	39%	< 8,000	22%	22%
> 8,000	78%	33%	> 8,000	78%	61%	> 8,000	78%	78%
N	110	59	N	110	59	N	110	59

Note: The top half of the table shows the relationship between gender and income. The percentage of men earning above and below $8,000 is shown along with the corresponding breakdown for women. In the bottom half of the table, three possible outcomes are shown when the control variable, amount of education, is held constant. These data represent the findings when only those who have attended college are included.

overall results are replicated for the particular sample defined by the control variable. In this case, obviously, the control variable does not explain why the original relationship was obtained, but we have identified one factor that does *not* affect the relationship of interest. In Outcome II, the relationship has changed somewhat, but men are still more likely than women to earn more than $8,000. With this outcome, the control variable of amount of education helps us to see at least part of the reason for the original relationship. That is, at least some of the difference between men's and women's incomes can be accounted for by differences in education.

Outcome III is the most dramatic. Here the relationship between gender and income has disappeared! Once we control for amount of education, there are no income differences to explain. Thus the control variable completely accounts for the relationship we originally observed. Note that this analysis does not explain why women may have less formal education than men; it simply shows that male-female income differences can be attributed to differences in education. (By the way, the most realistic of the three outcomes for this sample relationship is Outcome II. Some, but not all, of women's lower earning power can be attributed to differences in education.)

This one illustration barely suffices as an introduction to the use of control variables in survey analysis; full appreciation of the power of the technique will come only when you have applied it to a data set of your own. Remember, the trick is to select for examination variables that might reasonably be expected to affect the relationship you are trying to explain, and this is one instance where random selection is *not* a recommended procedure.

VALIDITY OF SURVEY RESULTS

An important issue involves a question that may have been in the back of your mind as you read about the procedures for conducting and analyzing a survey. Regardless of how carefully survey data are collected and analyzed, the value of these data depends on the veracity of the respondents' answers to the survey questions. How willing should we be to believe that the survey responses validly reflect people's true thoughts, opinions, feelings, and behavior?

The question of the validity of verbal reports has been debated extensively and no clear-cut conclusion has emerged. Kidder and Judd (1986) note, however, that in everyday life we regularly accept the verbal reports of others as valid. If a friend tells us that he enjoyed reading a certain novel, we may ask why, but we do not usually question whether the statement accurately reflects our friend's feelings. However, in everyday life we also come across situations in which we *do* have reason to suspect the validity of someone's statements. Generally we accept people's remarks at their face value unless we have reason to do otherwise. We should apply the same standards to the information we obtain from survey responses.

By its very nature, survey research involves reactive measurement. Respondents not only know that their responses are being recorded, but they may also suspect that their responses may serve as the basis for some social or political action. Hence the pressures are strong for people to respond as they "should" and not as they actually do believe. The term that is often used to describe these pressures is **social desirability.** For example, if respondents are asked whether they favor giving help to the needy, they may respond affirmatively because they believe that this is the most socially acceptable attitude to have. As suggested in Chapter 2, the best protection against reactive measurement is to be aware of its existence.

Sometimes it is possible to examine the validity of verbal reports directly. Kidder and Judd (1986) describe research by Parry and Crossley (1950) wherein responses obtained by experienced interviewers were subsequently compared with the records of respondents kept by various agencies. Forty percent of respondents gave inaccurate reports to a question concerning contributions to United Fund (a charitable organization), 25 percent erred when reporting whether they had registered and voted in a recent election, and 17 percent misrepresented their age. A pessimist might find these figures disturbingly high, but an optimist would note that a majority of respondents' reports were accurate even when social desirability pressures were high, as in the question pertaining to charitable contributions.

Another source of evidence against which to compare the accuracy of verbal reports is direct observation of the respondents' behavior. The field experiment done by Latané and Darley (1970) that was described in Chapter 2 illustrates the problem. They found that bystanders are more likely to help a victim when the bystander is alone than when other witnesses are present. Subsequently, a second group of subjects was asked whether the presence of others would influence the likelihood that they would help a victim. They uniformly said that it would not. Research findings such as these should make us extremely cautious of reaching conclusions about people's behavior solely on the basis of verbal reports. Of course, we should be equally cautious of reaching conclusions about what people think solely on the basis of direct observation of their behavior.

Petzel et al. (1973) used a more subtle method of testing the validity of respondents' answers. As part of a drug survey among high school students, they included a question about the students' use of a fictitious drug. Some respondents said they used this drug. Interestingly, admitted users of the bogus drug were different from the other respondents on almost every question concerning drug use. As might be expected, those reporting using the bogus drug consistently reported more drug use than other respondents. The results also showed that the percentage of admitted users of the drug was small (less than 4 percent). Including these respondents did not significantly alter the proportion of respondents admitting or denying the use of various drugs.

One final point needs to be made about the validity of survey results. The process of doing a survey has much in common with the process of writing an essay. You often begin with a grand topic that must be focused so that it can be covered manageably. As you narrow your focus, you may sometimes have the feeling that your original topic has been lost or at least made trivial. No essay can capture all of the aspects of a given topic, and no 20-item or even 200-item questionnaire can do so, either. Survey research, like the rest of the scientific enterprise, is built on faith that compiling reliable findings in a series of limited studies will eventually lead to increased understanding of the important broader issues we face.

PREPARING THE QUESTIONNAIRE

STEPS IN PREPARING A QUESTIONNAIRE

The six basic steps in preparing a questionnaire are listed in Table 3.7. The warning "Watch out for that first step!" is appropriate here. The first step in questionnaire construction, deciding what information is to be sought, should actually be the first step in planning the survey as a whole. This de-

TABLE 3.7 SIX BASIC STEPS IN PREPARING A QUESTIONNAIRE

Step 1. Decide what information should be sought.
Step 2. Decide what type of questionnaire should be used.
Step 3. Write a first draft of the questionnaire.
Step 4. Reexamine and revise the questionnaire.
Step 5. Pretest the questionnaire.
Step 6. Edit the questionnaire and specify procedures for its use.

cision, of course, determines the nature of the questions included in the questionnaire. It is important to project what the results are likely to be if the proposed questionnaire is used and then to decide whether these "findings" answer the questions that the study is intended to address. Surveys are frequently done under considerable time pressure, and inexperienced researchers are especially prone to being impatient. Just remember that a poorly conceived questionnaire takes just as much time and effort to administer and to analyze as a well-conceived questionnaire. The difference is that a well-constructed questionnaire leads to interpretable results. The best that can be said for a poorly designed one is that it is a good way to learn how important careful deliberation is in the planning stages.

Once the information to be sought from respondents has been clearly specified, the next step is to decide what type of questionnaire should be used. For example, will the questionnaire be self-administered or will trained interviewers be using it? This decision is determined primarily by the survey method that has been selected. For instance, if a telephone survey is to be done, trained interviewers will be needed. In designing the questionnaire, one should also consider using items that have been prepared by other researchers. There is no reason to develop your own instrument to assess racial prejudice if a reliable and valid one is already available. Besides, if you use items from a questionnaire that has already been used, you can compare your results directly to those obtained in earlier studies.

If you decide that no available instrument suits your needs, you will have to take the third step and write a first draft of your own questionnaire. Guidelines concerning the format and ordering of questions, as well as suggestions for wording questions effectively, will be presented in later sections of this chapter.

The fourth step in questionnaire construction, reexamining and rewriting, is an essential one. Questions that appear objective and unambiguous to you may strike others as slanted and ambiguous. It is most helpful to have your questionnaire reviewed by experts, both those who have knowledge of survey research methods and those with expertise in the area on which your study is focused. For example, if you are doing a survey of students' attitudes toward the campus food service, it would be advisable to have your questionnaire reviewed by the campus food service director. When you are dealing with a controversial topic, it is especially important to have representatives of both sides of the issue screen your questions for possible bias. Sometimes no one particular wording can be agreed on by all. In such cases, the *split-ballot technique* is helpful. In this technique different wordings of the same questions are used for equivalent samples of respondents. The effect of the wording can be directly examined by comparing responses made in these two (or more) samples.

By far the most critical step in the development of a sound questionnaire is Step 5, the pretest. A pretest involves actually administering the questionnaire to a small sample of respondents under conditions as much as possible like those to be used in the final administration of the survey. Pretest respondents must also be typical of those to be included in the final sample; it makes little sense to pretest a survey of nursing home residents by administering the questionnaire to college students. There is one way, however, in which a pretest does differ from the final administration of the survey. Respondents should be interviewed at length regarding their reactions to individual questions and to the questionnaire as a whole. This provides information about potentially ambiguous or offensive items.

The pretest should also serve as a "dress rehearsal" for interviewers, who should be closely supervised during this stage to ensure that they understand and adhere to the proper procedures for administering the questionnaire. If major changes have to be made as a result of problems arising during the pretest, a second pretest may be needed to determine whether these changes solved the problems originally encountered. After pretesting is complete, the final step is to edit the questionnaire and specify the procedures to be followed in its final administration. Before turning our attention to procedures used in analyzing the results of the completed questionnaire, we need to address a few additional issues involved in questionnaire construction. In the next two sections we will consider two sets of guidelines: one for writing questions and one for the general format of a questionnaire.

GUIDELINES FOR EFFECTIVE WORDING OF QUESTIONS

Lawyers have long known that how a question is phrased has great impact on how that question is answered. Survey researchers need to be equally conscious of this principle. This point is illustrated in a survey Loftus (1979a) conducted for the manufacturer of a leading headache remedy. She found that people reported having more headaches when they were asked "Do you get headaches frequently and, if so, how often?" than when they were asked "Do you get headaches occasionally and, if so, how often?" Unfortunately, the extent of the influence of the wording of questions in a given survey can almost never be determined precisely. Therefore the exact wording of critical questions should always be reported along with the data describing respondents' answers (see Box 3.4).

There are certain guidelines to follow to minimize problems arising from the phrasing of survey questions. These guidelines can be applied to **open-ended** or **free-response** questions and to **closed** or **multiple-choice** questions. *Free-response* questions, like the essay questions on a classroom test, merely specify the area to be addressed in a response. For example, the question "What are your views on the legalizing of abortion?" is a free-response question. By contrast, *closed questions* provide specific response alternatives. "Is police protection very good, fairly good, neither good nor bad, not very good, or not good at all?" is a closed question about the quality of police protection in a community.

The advantages of free-response questions are that they can be written more quickly and that they offer the respondent greater flexibility. However, these advantages are often more than offset by the difficulties that arise in recording and scoring responses to open-ended questions. For example, extensive coding is frequently necessary before rambling responses to open-ended questions can be summarized succinctly. Closed questions, on the other hand, are more difficult to write, but they can be answered more easily and quickly and fewer scoring problems arise. It is also much easier to summarize responses to multiple-choice questions, because answers are readily comparable across respondents. A major disadvantage of closed questions is that they reduce expressiveness and spontaneity. Further, the possibility exists that the respondent will have to choose a less than preferred response because no presented alternative really captures his or her views. Hence, the responses obtained may not accurately reflect the respondent's opinion.

Newcomb et al., (1967) used both open-ended and closed questions in a survey of students' attitudes. Their survey was done in two stages. In the first stage, student respondents were asked a series of open-ended questions about how their lives had changed as a result of having attended college. The trained interviewers used probes extensively and effectively in this stage. A self-administered questionnaire was then developed for the second stage of the survey. During this phase, a second sample of students rated how much they had changed in each of a number of areas. Using the answers to the original set of open-ended questions, the researchers identified specific areas of change for these closed questions. The survey revealed that one area in which change did occur was students' political views. What is more, these changes were shown to persist well after the students left college.

Several characteristics of good questionnaire items are listed in Table 3.8. For instance, regardless of the type of question used, the vocabulary should be simple, direct, and familiar to all respondents. Questions should be as clear and specific as possible. "Double-barreled" questions should be avoided. An example of a double-barreled question is: "Have you suffered from headaches and nausea recently?" A person may respond "no" if both symptoms have not occurred at exactly the same time or may respond "yes" if either symptom has occurred. The solution to the problem of double-barreled questions is a simple one—rewrite them as separate questions. Survey questions should be as short as possible without sacrificing the clarity of the question's meaning; twenty or fewer words should suffice for most sur-

TABLE 3.8   GOOD QUESTIONNAIRE ITEMS SHOULD...

1 Include vocabulary that is simple, direct, and familiar to all respondents
2 Be clear and specific
3 *Not* involve leading, loaded, and double-barreled questions
4 Be as short as possible (twenty or fewer words)
5 Include all conditional information prior to the key idea
6 Be edited for readability

vey questions. Each question should be carefully edited for readability and should be phrased in such a way that all conditional information precedes the key idea. For example, it would be better to ask, "If you were forced to leave your present job, what type of work would you seek?" than to ask, "What type of work would you seek if you were forced to leave your present job?"

Leading or loaded questions should also be avoided in a questionnaire. *Leading questions* take the form "Most people favor the use of nuclear energy. What do you think?" To avoid bias, it is better to mention all possible perspectives or to mention none. A survey question about attitudes toward nuclear energy could read either: "Some people favor the use of nuclear energy, some people oppose the use of nuclear energy, and some people have no opinion one way or the other. What do you think?" or "What do you think about the use of nuclear energy?" *Loaded questions* are those that contain emotion-laden words. For example, terms such as "radical" and "racist" should be avoided. To guard against loaded questions, it is best to have your questionnaire reviewed by individuals representing a range of social and political perspectives.

GUIDELINES FOR GENERAL FORMAT OF THE QUESTIONNAIRE

Two aspects of the general format should be considered in constructing the final copy of a questionnaire: the design or layout of the questionnaire and the ordering of questions. An effort should be made to make the design of the questionnaire attractive, but the emphasis should be on making it as easy as possible to use. A section of a well-designed questionnaire is shown in Table 3.9. This questionnaire was used by trained interviewers in a survey done by the Institute for Social Research at the University of Michigan. The aim of the survey was to examine the quality of American life (Campbell et al., 1975). Several characteristics of this questionnaire are noteworthy. Each question is identified with a letter indicating the section of the questionnaire and a number specifying the individual question. This is done to facilitate later scoring and analysis of responses. The arrangement of the questions on each page is compact, but the structure is designed to make it easy to read the questions and to record responses. Whenever possible, questions with the same response format appear together. When multiple-choice questions are asked, a note is included to remind the interviewer to give the respondent a card listing the response alternatives so that the respondent can concentrate on the question and not on remembering the alternatives. At the beginning of the first question the respondent is given a brief rationale for the study as a whole, but this preamble is kept short so as to require as little of the respondent's time as possible.

The format of a questionnaire changes somewhat when it is to be self-administered. The first section of a self-administered questionnaire distributed to passengers on Amtrak trains is shown in Table 3.10. The items are

TABLE 3.9 SAMPLE QUESTIONNAIRE FORMAT FOR PERSONAL OR PHONE INTERVIEW

Section A: City and Neighborhood

A1 In this study we are interested in measuring the quality of life of people in this country—that is, the things people like and dislike about their homes, cities, neighborhoods, jobs, and so on. The first question is: How long have you lived in (INSERT NAME OF COMMUNITY, OR OF COUNTY IF RURAL)? _____. (IF LESS THAN TWO YEARS, GET NUMBER OF MONTHS.)

_____ YEARS _____ MONTHS, OR SINCE: _____

A2 And how long have you lived here in this (house/apartment)? (IF *LESS* THAN TWO YEARS, GET NUMBER OF MONTHS.)

_____ YEARS _____ MONTHS, OR SINCE: _____

A3 I'd like to ask how satisfied you are with some of the main public services you are supposed to receive. (HAND R CARD 1, YELLOW) Please tell me how you feel about each thing I mention, using one of the answers on this card. First, how about the way streets and roads are kept up around here. Would you say this service is *very good, fairly good, neither good nor bad, not very good, or not good at all?*

1. VERY GOOD	2. FAIRLY GOOD	3. NEITHER GOOD NOR BAD	4. NOT VERY GOOD	5. NOT GOOD AT ALL

A4 How do you feel about the quality of the *public* schools that the children from around here go to—would you say it is *very good, fairly good, neither good nor bad, not very good, or not good at all?*

1. VERY GOOD	2. FAIRLY GOOD	3. NEITHER GOOD NOR BAD	4. NOT VERY GOOD	5. NOT GOOD AT ALL	8. DK

IF R LIVES IN A CITY, TOWN, OR VILLAGE, ASK A5 AND A6: IF RURAL, TURN TO A7

A5 How good is garbage collection in this neighborhood? Is it *very good, fairly good, neither good nor bad, not very good, or not good at all?*

1. VERY GOOD	2. FAIRLY GOOD	3. NEITHER GOOD NOR BAD	4. NOT VERY GOOD	5. NOT GOOD AT ALL	8. DK

A6 What about the parks and playgrounds for children in this neighborhood? Are they *very good, fairly good, neither good nor bad, not very good, or not good at all?*

1. VERY GOOD	2. FAIRLY GOOD	3. NEITHER GOOD NOR BAD	4. NOT VERY GOOD	5. NOT GOOD AT ALL	8. DK

ASK EVERYBODY:

A7 How about police protection around here. Is it *very good, fairly good, neither good nor bad, not very good, or not good at all?*

1. VERY GOOD	2. FAIRLY GOOD	3. NEITHER GOOD NOR BAD	4. NOT VERY GOOD	5. NOT GOOD AT ALL	8. DK

A8 How good do you think relations are between the police and the people around here? Are they *very good, fairly good, neither good nor bad, not very good, or not good at all?*

| 1. VERY GOOD | 2. FAIRLY GOOD | 3. NEITHER GOOD NOR BAD | 4. NOT VERY GOOD | 5. NOT GOOD AT ALL | 8. DK |

A9 Another way people judge a place to live is what the weather throughout the year is like—as far as you are concerned, how good is the climate here? Is it *very good, fairly good, neither good nor bad, not very good, or not good at all?*

| 1. VERY GOOD | 2. FAIRLY GOOD | 3. NEITHER GOOD NOR BAD | 4. NOT VERY GOOD | 5. NOT GOOD AT ALL | 8. DK |

A10 (HAND R CARD 2, GREEN) Would you say that the local taxes in (NAME CITY OR COUNTY) are *very low, low, moderate, high, or very high?*

| 1. VERY LOW | 2. LOW | 3. MODERATE | 4. HIGH | 5. VERY HIGH | 8. DK |

A11 Have you ever lived in a place where life is much different from what it is here?

| 1. YES | 5. NO | —GO TO A12

A11a Where was that? _____
(COUNTRY OR STATE AND CITY)

A12 Now I have some questions about this neighborhood. First, thinking about the kinds of things you would like to have near where you live—places you go fairly often—how convenient would you say this location is: is it *very convenient, convenient enough, not very convenient, or not convenient at all?*

| 1. VERY CONVENIENT | 2. CONVENIENT ENOUGH | 3. NOT VERY CONVENIENT | 4. NOT CONVENIENT AT ALL |

arranged in a clear and uncluttered manner, and the order of the questions is clearly indicated by the large boldface numbers. Each item is short and direct and the instructions for each question are simple. The small numbers next to each blank are used to computer-code the responses. The numbers in parentheses indicate column numbers on a computer card, and the other numbers are the ones to be entered if the respondent checks that blank. Such prior coding saves time when the data are to be analyzed and helps reduce the number of errors in data entry. In designing a self-administered questionnaire, one should spare no effort to make it visually appealing; visual appeal increases the response rate. It is most important that the questions be self-explanatory and that respondents be able to complete the questionnaire quickly and correctly.

A crucial issue in deciding the order of the questions in a survey is which question or questions to ask first. The first few questions set the tone for the rest of the questionnaire and determine how willingly and conscientiously

TABLE 3.10 SAMPLE FORMAT FOR SELF-ADMINISTERED QUESTIONNAIRE

Illinois Department of Transportation
Survey of Amtrak Passengers

Dear Amtrak Passenger:

The Illinois Department of Transportation is conducting a study of rail passenger service on the Chicago–St. Louis corridor to determine what improvements should be made to upgrade service on this route. This survey is designed to identify the preferences and travel needs of passengers on Amtrak trains. Your cooperation in filling out this questionnaire will be greatly appreciated.

A Department representative will collect the survey when you have finished. If you leave your seat before the representative returns, kindly leave the questionnaire on your seat. If you have filled out this survey previously, please take a few minutes to answer questions 1 through 7 and 21 through 26.

Have an enjoyable trip and thank you for your cooperation.

---

1 Please check the station where you boarded this train and the station where you will get off.

Station	Boarded	Will Get Off
Chicago	_____ 01 (6–6)	_____ 01 (7–8)
Joliet	_____ 02	_____ 02
Pontiac	_____ 03	_____ 03
Bloomington	_____ 04	_____ 04
Lincoln	_____ 05	_____ 05
Springfield	_____ 06	_____ 06
Carlinville	_____ 07	_____ 07
Alton	_____ 08	_____ 08
St. Louis	_____ 09	_____ 09
Points in Missouri	_____ 10	_____ 10
Points in Arkansas	_____ 11	_____ 11
Points in Texas	_____ 12	_____ 12

2 Please indicate how you reached the station to board this train and how you will reach your next destination after you get off this train. (Check as many as apply.)

	To Station Where You Got On	From Station Where You Will Get off
Automobile	_____ 01 (6–11)	_____ 01 (12–14)
Taxi	_____ 02	_____ 02
City Bus	_____ 03	_____ 03
Airline	_____ 04	_____ 04
Commuter Train	_____ 05	_____ 05
Amtrak Train	_____ 06	_____ 06
Amtrak Shuttle	_____ 07	_____ 07
Intercity Bus	_____ 08	_____ 08
Walker	_____ 09	_____ 09
Other	_____ 10	_____ 10

3 Is your car parked at or near an Amtrak Station during this trip?
Yes _____ 15.1   No _____ 15.2

4 What is the zip code of the place you left to get to this train? (If zip code is unknown, the city and a nearby major street intersection will be sufficient.)

Zip Code _____
$\quad$ 16 17 18 19 20
OR: City _____

$\quad$ Street
$\quad$ Intersection _____
$\quad$ _____

5 What is the zip code (or city and nearby street intersection) of the place where you will be going upon leaving this train?

Zip Code _____
$\quad$ 21 22 23 24 25
OR: City _____

$\quad$ Street
$\quad$ Intersection _____
$\quad$ _____

6 Which one of the following best describes the main purpose of this trip? (Mark only one)

26-1 _____ Business or work
$\quad$ 2 _____ Vacation or recreation
$\quad$ 3 _____ Travel to or from school
$\quad$ 4 _____ Personal business
$\quad$ 5 _____ Shopping
$\quad$ 6 _____ Visit family or friends
$\quad$ 7 _____ Entertainment/Spectator sport
$\quad$ 8 _____ Other (Please specify) _____

7 How long before the departure time of this train did you leave for the station?

27-1 _____ $\quad$ 10–15 minutes
$\quad$ 2 _____ $\quad$ 16–30 minutes
$\quad$ 3 _____ $\quad$ 31–45 minutes
$\quad$ 4 _____ $\quad$ 46–60 minutes
$\quad$ 5 _____ $\quad$ more than 1 hour

respondents will work on subsequent questions. For self-administered questionnaires, it is best to begin with the most interesting set of questions in order to capture the respondent's attention. For example, demographic data should be obtained at the end of a self-administered questionnaire. However, in surveys involving personal or telephone interviews, demographic questions are frequently asked at the beginning because they are easy for the respondent to answer, thus bolstering the respondent's confidence. They also allow time for the interviewer to establish rapport before asking questions about more sensitive matters.

The order of asking particular questions can have dramatic effects, as illustrated in a study by Schuman et al. (1981). They found differential responding depending on the order of two questions concerning abortion, one general and one specific. The general question was "Do you think it should be possible for a pregnant woman to obtain a legal abortion if she is married and does not want any more children?" The more specific question was "Do you think it should be possible for a pregnant woman to obtain a legal abortion if there is a strong chance of a serious defect in the baby?" When the general question was asked first, 60.7 percent of respondents said "yes," but when the general question followed the specific question, only 48.1 percent of respondents said "yes." The corresponding values for the specific question were 84 percent and 83 percent agreement in the first and second positions, respectively. The generally accepted method for dealing with this problem is to use *funnel questions*, which means proceeding from the most general to the most specific when ordering the questions pertaining to a given topic.[1]

Problems resulting from the order of questions can also arise when several questions on a topic are asked and they are all at the same level of specificity. For example, we might ask a series of questions regarding a person's views about several minority groups. Effects due to the order in which such questions are asked can be handled in one of two ways. The first technique is to use exactly the same order for all samples to be compared, thus holding the effect of order constant. This technique does not allow us to determine what the effects of order were. Alternatively, many different orders of the questions can be used within each of the samples to be compared so as to neutralize the effect of order. This problem of dealing with order effects is discussed much more fully in Chapter 6.

The final aspect of the ordering of survey questions that we will consider is the use of *filter questions*—general questions asked of respondents to find out whether they need to be asked more specific questions. For example, the question "Do you own a car?" might precede a series of questions about the

---

[1]Oppenheim (1966) describes in detail the question-wording plan developed by Gallup called the Quintamensional Plan of Question Design. The first step is to ask the respondent whether he or she has thought about the issue at all. This is followed by open-ended questions about general feelings and closed questions about specific aspects of the issue. The fourth step involves asking for the respondent's reasons for the views he or she holds. Finally, the interviewer inquires how strongly the respondent's views are held.

costs of maintaining a car. In this instance the respondent would answer the specific questions only if her or his response to the general question was "yes." If that answer was "no," the interviewer would not ask the specific questions (in a self-administered questionnaire, the respondent would be instructed to skip that section). When the filter questions involve objective information ("Are you over 65?"), their use is relatively straightforward. Caution must be exercised, however, in using behavioral or attitudinal questions as filter questions. Smith (1981) first asked respondents whether they approved of hitting another person in "any situations you can imagine." Logically, a negative response to this most general question should imply a negative response to any more specific questions. Nonetheless, over 80 percent of the people who responded "no" to the general question then reported that they approved of hitting another person in specific situations, such as in self-defense. Although findings such as this suggest that filter questions should be used cautiously, the need to demand as little of the respondent's time as possible makes filter questions an essential tool in the design of effective questionnaires.

SUMMARY

Survey research provides an accurate and efficient means of describing people's thoughts, opinions, and feelings. Surveys differ in purpose and scope, but they generally involve sampling, the procedure whereby results obtained with a carefully selected sample are used as a basis for describing the entire population of interest. Surveys also involve the use of a predetermined set of questions, generally in the form of a questionnaire. Survey research is typically not very effective for exploratory studies, but the greatest limitation of survey research is the problem of interpreting causal relationships.

Sampling is a procedure whereby a specified number of elements are drawn from a sampling frame that represents an actual list of the possible elements in the population. Our ability to generalize from the sample to the population depends critically on the representativeness of the sample, the extent to which the sample has the same characteristics as the population. Representativeness is best achieved by using probability sampling rather than nonprobability sampling. In simple random sampling, the most common type of probability sampling, every element is equally likely to be included in the sample. Stratified random sampling and cluster sampling provide alternatives when simple random sampling is not sufficient.

There are three general survey methods: mail surveys, personal interviews, and telephone interviews. Mail surveys avoid problems of interviewer bias and are especially well suited for examining personal or embarrassing topics. The problem of response bias is a serious limitation of mail surveys. Personal interviews and phone surveys usually have much higher response rates and provide greater flexibility. The phone survey is the method of choice for most brief surveys.

The survey is administered according to an overall plan called a research design. There are three survey research designs: the one-shot or cross-sectional study, the successive independent samples study, and the panel or longitudinal study. Cross-sectional surveys focus on describing the characteristics of a population or the differences between two or more populations. Describing changes in attitudes or opinions over time requires the use of successive independent samples or of a panel study. The panel study is generally preferred because it allows the assessment of changes for specific individuals and avoids the problem of noncomparable successive samples.

The analysis of survey results begins with coding open-ended questions and preparing frequency distributions for each item. Measures of relative frequency, such as percentages, are often used to allow comparisons between surveys. If the survey involves interval data, measures of central tendency (such as the mean) and measures of dispersion (such as the standard deviation) should be reported. One analyzes the correlational relationships between variables by using correlational coefficients and cross tabulations. The use of control variables in such analyses can greatly strengthen the evidence for a particular explanation. The validity of survey results, like that of other verbal reports, can be accepted at face value unless there is reason to do otherwise. One such reason is the pressure on respondents to give socially desirable responses. People's behavior does not always conform to what they say they would do, so survey research will never replace direct observation. However, survey research does provide an excellent way to determine people's attitudes and opinions.

Careful planning is required in preparing a questionnaire. Issues requiring attention include the wording of individual questions and the design of the format of the questionnaire itself. The editing and pretesting of questionnaires are essential steps in successful survey research. Individual questions should be simple, direct, clear, and specific. Double-barreled, leading, and loaded questions should be avoided. Open-ended questions are easier to write but more difficult to score; the reverse is true of closed questions. The order of asking questions varies for mail and phone surveys.

KEY CONCEPTS

population	cluster sampling
sampling frame	interviewer bias
sample	one-shot or cross-sectional study
element	successive independent samples
representativeness	panel or longitudinal study
biased sample	respondent mortality
nonprobability sampling	confidence interval
probability sampling	social desirability
accidental sampling	open-ended or free-response
purposive sampling	questions
simple random sampling	closed or multiple-choice
stratified random sampling	questions

REVIEW QUESTIONS

1 What two characteristics do surveys have in common even when they differ widely in scope and purpose?
2 State two advantages and two limitations of the consistent use of the same phrasing and ordering of questions in a survey.
3 Give an example of a sampling plan that would be likely to result in each of the two sources of a biased sample.
4 What is the greatest danger when an accidental sample is used in survey research?
5 Explain the relationship between the size of a sample needed to ensure representativeness and the homogeneity of the population.
6 Why would a researcher choose to use stratified random sampling instead of simple random sampling?
7 When is cluster sampling likely to be used?
8 What are the strengths and weaknesses of a mail survey?
9 What procedures can be followed to enhance response rate in a mail survey?
10 What are the strengths and weaknesses of personal interviews?
11 Why does the use of probes increase the possibility of interviewer bias? How can this problem be avoided?
12 What advantages do phone surveys have over personal interviews?
13 What are the two most common purposes of a cross-sectional study?
14 Why must researchers be cautious in using successive independent samples to interpret changes in attitudes over time?
15 What are the strengths and weaknesses of a panel (longitudinal) study?
16 What is the principal purpose of correlational studies?
17 What is the implication of each of the possible outcomes for interpreting the original relationship when a control variable is used to analyze the relationship?
18 What general guideline that we follow in everyday life can be used in assessing the validity of survey responses?
19 What are the six basic steps in preparing a questionnaire?
20 What are the relative advantages and disadvantages of open-ended questions compared to closed questions?
21 What six characteristics should a well-written questionnaire item exhibit?
22 Define and give an example of each of the following: (a) double-barreled question; (b) leading question; (c) loaded question.
23 How do the formats of self-administered questionnaires differ from those used in personal or telephone interviews?
24 What are two ways in which to handle effects due to order when several questions of the same level of specificity are included in a survey?

CHALLENGE QUESTIONS

1 **A** A survey researcher selected a random sample of households for a survey of consumer attitudes. In conducting the survey he often found that no one was home at the households he had selected. His solution to this problem was a simple one. He interviewed whichever next-door neighbor of the selected household happened to be home. Comment critically on the researcher's "solution" to his problem.

 B Two student researchers have been asked to do a survey to determine the attitudes of other students toward fraternities and sororities on campus. There are 2,000 students in the school. About 25 percent of the students belong to the Greek organizations and 75 percent do not. One researcher plans to draw a stratified random sample of 200 students: 100 from among those students who belong to Greek organizations and 100 from among the independent students. The second researcher plans to draw one simple random sample of 100 students from the campus as a whole. Comment critically on these two sampling plans. Finally, develop your own sampling plan if you decide that neither of the ones proposed so far is optimal.

2 A small national business manufactured and marketed a single product, Brand X. Members of the marketing department decided to do a mail survey of people who used Brand X to determine how satisfied they were with the product. They carefully selected a random sample of 100 people from the company's list of registered users of the product. Of the 30 people who returned the mail survey, 28 of them indicated that they were very pleased with the performance of Brand X. An advertising campaign was prepared in which the company boasted that 93 percent of those who use Brand X are very pleased with its performance. Explain what conditions would have to be met for this ad campaign to be defensible on the basis of the survey results, and explain why it is unlikely that these conditions would be met.

3 A recent observational study by the Swedish Road Safety Office showed that in running traffic 20 percent of drivers were found *not* to be wearing seatbelts. In a subsequent survey of Swedish drivers (75 percent of the sample returned the questionnaire), only 10 percent of the drivers admitted to being consistent nonusers of seatbelts.

 A Name two reasons to suspect that the survey results may overestimate the use of seatbelts.

 B Assume for the moment that the results of both the observation study and the survey are accurate. How might you account for the higher estimate of nonuse in the observation study?

4 A report in a 1986 issue of a major metropolitan newspaper indicated that an estimated 40 million Americans suffer from chronic pain and 9 million each year have

severe pain after surgery that is not adequately treated. Not surprisingly, then, pain is patients' number one complaint and the major reason for their seeking medical attention. A graphic entitled "The healers" reported the percentage of patients who had been treated by a professional and who then rated whether that professional had been very successful or unsuccessful in relieving pain. Physicians were rated by 73 percent of their patients as very successful; the corresponding value for dentists was 67 percent, for medical pain specialists 65 percent, for chiropractors 70 percent, for nutritionists 69 percent, for acupuncturists 35 percent, and for spiritual counselors and faith healers 83 percent.

A Explain what sampling problems would lead you to question whether these data validly reflect differences in professionals' abilities to relieve pain.

B Do the criticisms you raised in Part A of this problem assure that the reported findings do *not* validly reflect differences in professionals' abilities to relieve pain? Why or why not?

ANSWER TO CHALLENGE QUESTION 1

1 A The interviewer's solution is likely to introduce a selection bias, thereby threatening the representativeness of the sample and the subsequent generality of any findings. Factors such as employment or socioeconomic status might make those who happen to be home systematically different from those who were originally selected for the sample who happened not to be available to be interviewed.

  B The student who chose the equal-sized strata would have representative samples for each stratum, but the overall sample would overrepresent the views of students belonging to Greek organizations. The student who used the simple random sample of 100 would have a more representative sample as a whole, but the likely numbers of members of Greek organizations included in the sample (approximately 25) would make it unlikely that a reliable description would be possible of the different views of Greeks and non-Greeks. The preferred sampling plan would be a proportional stratified random sample including 150 non-Greeks and 50 Greeks.

CHAPTER

4

Alternatives to Direct Observation and Surveys: Physical Traces, Archival Data, and Case Studies

OUTLINE

The behavioral scientist generally learns about behavior through some form of direct observation (Chapter 2) or from data obtained through interviews and questionnaires (Chapter 3). In this chapter we consider some alternatives to these major approaches to the study of behavior. Although these alternative methods are often important in themselves, they also frequently provide a means of confirming the validity of conclusions reached on the basis of direct observation or surveys.

One major alternative is the examination of **physical traces** produced by persons engaged in some form of behavior. Consider, for example, the possibility that Latin Americans differ from North Americans in their concern for punctuality. Possible cultural differences in the importance of punctuality *could* be investigated by surveying people in both North American and Latin American countries as to how they feel about concerts or sporting events that begin later than the scheduled starting time. However, an alternative method would be to examine clocks in cities of North America and South America. It seems reasonable to assume that people's concern for time will be reflected in how accurately they set their clocks. In fact, researchers have found that public clocks (those located in banks) in a Brazilian city were less accurate than those in a similar-sized city in the United States (Levine et al., 1980). Although there may be alternative explanations for this finding, differences in this physical-trace measure support the notion that cultural differences in concern for being on time do exist.

Archives constitute another important source of information about behavior. **Archival data** are obtained by inspecting the records and documents produced by society, as well as by analyzing reports in the media. For example, researchers have claimed that analyses of mortality data reveal a lower than expected frequency of deaths before important events, such as birthdays and religious holidays, and a higher than expected frequency of deaths after these important events. One provocative interpretation of these findings is that timing of death is psychologically determined, perhaps by an individual's motivation to live in order to experience an important occasion. We will examine this interpretation of archival data in more detail later (see Box 4.2).

In this chapter we present the rationale for using physical traces and archival data. Particular kinds of physical traces are identified and examples of their use in psychological studies are offered. Types of archives and the kinds of data that can be drawn from archival sources are also reviewed. Several important advantages of the use of physical traces or archival data are highlighted. There are some limitations and problems with these measures, and they too are discussed. Finally, we examine the case study method in psychology. Case studies are frequently the source of valuable hypotheses about behavior and can be an important complement to more rigorously controlled approaches to understanding behavior. Both advantages and disadvantages of the case study method are reviewed.

PHYSICAL TRACES

RATIONALE

As everyone who has read a few detective stories knows, examining physical evidence of past behavior can provide important clues to the characteristics (or even identity) of individuals, as well as information about the conditions under which an event occurred. The size of footprints in the ground says something about the size and age of the person who stepped there. The distance between footprints can indicate whether the person was walking or running. And so on. As we have already seen, physical evidence (in the form of clock settings) can be of value to the behavioral scientist. Physical traces (like the archival data that are discussed later in this chapter) are especially valuable because they provide nonreactive measures of behavior (Webb et al., 1981).

You will recall from Chapter 2 that a behavioral measure is reactive when the subjects' awareness of an observer's presence affects the measurement process. This is often the case when direct observations are made, and it is nearly always the case when surveys are conducted. Reactivity introduces the problem of response bias. Aware that their responses are being recorded, subjects may behave in a way that does not correspond to their normal behavior. Survey data are particularly susceptible to reactive effects, because respondents may give answers that they feel the researcher wants to hear or may answer in a way that makes them (the respondents) look good.

We mentioned one example of response bias in the context of survey research in Chapter 3, when we discussed obesity charts used by physicians to assess the degree to which people are overweight. The charts were constructed on the basis of data obtained from a survey of prospective insurance clients. It was later found that those who were surveyed had not provided accurate estimates of their weight; rather, they had reported less than their actual weight in order to look better or perhaps to be charged a lower insurance premium. Physical trace measures are unobtrusive (because they are obtained in the absence of the subject), so they are valuable alternatives to the reactive measures obtained via direct observation or surveys.

Although a physical trace measure might be the only measure of behavior in some studies, physical traces are more commonly used in combination with other measures. A research study can be strengthened considerably by including several different measures of behavior. A **multimethod approach** to hypothesis testing is recommended because it reduces the likelihood that research findings are due to some artifact of the measurement process (Webb et al., 1981). There are few (if any) perfect measures in the social sciences. Therefore, the results of a study must be carefully scrutinized to determine whether some characteristic of the measurement instrument (such as its reactivity) has contributed to the results. Even then, it is possible that some artifact has been overlooked. The most persuasive argument supporting the validity of a particular research hypothesis is one based on evidence obtained by applying a combination of measures.

Researchers investigating cultural differences in time perception used such a multimethod approach. As we mentioned, they surveyed individuals living in Latin America and in the United States to find out how frequently their subjects were late for appointments and to discover their attitudes toward being late (Levine et al., 1980). Citizens of Brazil reported themselves more often late for appointments and expressed less regret at being late than did citizens of the United States. However, response bias could be present if people described themselves in a way that fit their cultural "image," rather than as they actually behaved. As already noted, however, the researchers also found that public clocks were less accurate in Brazil than in the United States. Further, the researchers observed that watches worn by people in the United States deviated less from the correct time (as reported by the telephone company) than watches worn by people in Brazil. The data obtained by examining public clocks and the watches worn by citizens of each country tended to confirm the validity of the survey responses and, in combination with the survey results, provided impressive evidence for the research hypothesis.

TYPES OF PHYSICAL TRACES

Physical traces are the remnants, fragments, and products of past behavior. Two broad categories of physical traces are use traces and products. *Use traces* are what the label implies—the physical evidence that results from use (or nonuse) of an item. Clock settings are an example of a physical use trace. So are the remains of cigarettes in ashtrays and the marks made on school desks. *Products* are the creations, constructions, or other artifacts of earlier behavior. Anthropologists are often interested in the surviving products of ancient cultures. By examining the types of vessels, paintings and other artifacts that remain, the anthropologist can often describe precisely the pattern of behavior exhibited in a setting that is thousands of years old. Psychologists may also examine physical products in order to describe behavior or to test hypotheses. Psychologists who study animal behavior, for instance, may learn about the behavior of different species by examining the types of nests that are constructed.

Use Traces   An examination of physical evidence provides measures of both accretion and erosion (Webb et al., 1981). *Accretion measures* are based on the accumulation of material. Measuring the amount of litter, for example, would be taking an accretion measure. *Erosion measures* are obtained when the physical evidence is the result of selective wear. The degree to which a young child's dolls show signs of wear is an erosion measure that might indicate which dolls the child likes best. The distinction between accretion measures and erosion measures is not always so obvious. Settings of clocks, for instance, resist ready classification. Nevertheless, classifying physical use traces in terms of accretion or erosion is often a meaningful description of physical traces, and the distinction calls our attention to two important dimensions of use traces.

Physical use traces are also classified as either natural or controlled (planned). *Natural* use traces are produced without any intervention by the investigator. Their appearance is the result of naturally occurring events. *Controlled* or planned measures result to some degree from the intervention or manipulation of an investigator.

Friedman and Wilson (1975) employed both controlled and natural accretion measures to investigate college students' use of textbooks. They affixed tiny glue seals between adjacent pages of textbooks before the students purchased the books for a course. At the end of the semester the investigators obtained the books from the students and recorded how many seals in the textbooks had been broken and where the broken seals were located. This constituted a controlled accretion measure. The investigators also analyzed the frequency and nature of underlining in the textbooks, a natural accretion measure. Analysis of these physical use measures indicated that students more often read (and presumably studied) the chapters that appeared early in the book than those appearing later in the book.

Table 4.1 contains examples of physical use traces and the variables being measured. These measures either actually were used as part of a scientific study or represent suggestions by researchers of possible novel and nonreactive measures of behavior (see Webb et al., 1981). The examples given in Table 4.1 have been organized according to whether they are accretion or

TABLE 4.1   EXAMPLES OF PHYSICAL USE TRACES AND VARIABLES BEING MEASURED*

Trace	Variable
Natural accretion	
Inscriptions (graffiti) on walls of public restrooms	Sexual preoccupation
Radio dial settings	Popularity of radio stations
Fingerprints or smudges on pages of books	Book usage
Liquor bottles in trash cans	Alcohol consumption of households
Odometer readings in cars	Conservation of gasoline
Litter	Effectiveness of antilitter posters
Dust on books	Frequency or recency of use
Garbage	Food use and life-style
Locked/unlocked cars	Concern for property
Lengths of cigarette butts	Cultural differences in death rate due to cancer
Controlled accretion	
Glue seals broken (seals inserted prior to distribution)	Index of specific pages read
Noseprints on windows of museum exhibit (windows wiped clean each night)	Popularity (frequency) and age (height of prints) of viewers
Natural erosion	
Wear on floor or steps	Amount of foot traffic
Wear on library books	Frequency of use
Food consumed	Eating behavior
Spots (produced by rubbing) on statues or religious objects	Level of religious belief
Controlled erosion	
Wear on children's shoes (measured at two points in time)	Activity level of children
Removal of "tear-away" tags on ads or notices	Interest in notice
Wear on mats or other floor coverings placed in specific areas	Amount of foot traffic
Change in statues or objects coated with substances sensitive to touching	Superstitious behavior

*From Webb et al. (1981).

erosion measures and whether their use is natural or controlled. As you examine the contents of Table 4.1, try to think of other possible physical traces that could serve as measures of the variables listed.

Products   Physical products have been examined less frequently in psychological studies than have physical use traces. Nevertheless, this category of physical traces has been used in interesting and meaningful ways to test hypotheses about behavior. A particularly good example of the use of physical products is found in a study by Coren and Porac (1977). They investigated the extent of human right-handedness in various cultures since ancient times. To determine manual preference they examined more than 12,000 works of art, including paintings, sculpture, and other products that spanned more than 50 centuries of human endeavor. The researchers recorded instances of unambiguous tool or weapon use depicted in the art works. They looked for any differential trend in the depiction of right- or left-handers in different cultures and at different times in human history. No trend was evident. Rather, across many cultures and in every epoch, 93 percent of the art works examined showed persons using their right hand. The results provide evidence for a physiological rather than a sociocultural theory of handedness.

Brandt (1972) points out that the products that people own harbor important clues to their life style and behavior patterns. What personality differences, for instance, are reflected in the purchase of different models of cars or in the extras and options that are ordered with a car? Besides serving as a measure of social status or personality, the products a person owns can be used to assess the validity of certain kinds of verbal reports. Are individuals' statements about their attitude toward energy conservation, for instance, related to the kinds of products they own and use?

Mooney and Brabant (1987) cite data indicating that various kinds of greeting cards, for example, those celebrating birthdays or holidays, as well as those conveying sympathy, represent over half of all the personal mail moved annually by the U.S. Postal Service. It is not surprising, therefore, that this particular product of society has proved to be a veritable treasure trove for researchers investigating attitudes toward such social phenomena as drinking, aging, and death. Mooney and Brabant (1987), for instance, randomly sampled birthday cards from fourteen retail outlets in a metropolitan area as part of a study of the use of deviant messages in interpersonal communications. The cards were classified according to various categories of deviant behavior, for example, making reference to obesity, violence, marital infidelity, or mental illness, as well as to a category of nondeviant behavior. Approximately 16 percent of the cards sampled contained some form of deviant message. Among the many differences noted between deviant and nondeviant cards was that deviant cards were more likely to present stereotypes, particularly of males, than were nondeviant cards. According to Mooney and Brabant, because cards containing deviant messages are the "moral opposite" of traditional birthday greetings, they likely signal a "unique moral order" between those involved, and, according to the authors, are perhaps appropriate when "you care enough to send the very worst" (Mooney and Brabant, 1987, p. 386).

PROBLEMS AND LIMITATIONS

Physical measures offer a researcher valuable and sometimes novel means to study behavior. And the measures available are limited only by the ingenuity of the investigator. However, the validity of physical traces must be carefully examined and verified through independent sources of evidence. Bias can be introduced in the way physical use traces are laid down and in the manner in which traces survive over time. Does a well-worn path to the right indicate people's interest in objects in that direction or simply a natural human tendency to turn right? Is the setting of clocks a good measure of people's regard for punctuality, or do inaccurate clock settings indicate poor artisanship, inadequate maintenance, or irregular electrical service?

Problems associated with the analysis of physical traces are illustrated in a classic study of honesty carried out using the "lost-letter technique" (see Merritt and Fowler, 1948). We can consider the method as planned accretion. The investigators dropped post cards and envelopes at various locations in cities of the East and Midwest. Two types of envelopes were discarded. One contained a written message, and the other contained a lead slug the size of a 50-cent piece. All the letters were addressed and bore proper postage, but no return address was shown. Although 85 percent of the "empty" envelopes were returned, only 54 percent of the envelopes with a slug found their way to a mailbox. Further, more than 10 percent of the envelopes with a slug were returned after having been opened.

Before the researchers could conclude that the return rates represented a valid measure of the public's honesty (or dishonesty), several possible biases associated with this physical trace had to be considered. Post cards, for instance, were less likely than sealed envelopes to be returned, but the fact that post cards are more easily disturbed by natural conditions no doubt contributed to this difference. On the other hand, envelopes with a slug are heavier and less likely to be blown away—and these were still less likely to be returned. Letters that were dropped in certain locations (for example, where many children are present) or at certain times of the day (for example, just before nightfall) are also likely to be "lost" for reasons other than the public's dishonesty or apathy.

Some of these possible biases associated with the lost-letter technique were avoided by the methods of dispersal used by the researchers, whereas others were checked via direct observation of a letter's fate. Observation of a sample of dropped letters revealed that a letter was picked up 90 percent of the time by the first person who saw it.

Whenever possible, supplementary evidence for the validity of physical traces should be obtained (see Webb et al., 1981). Alternative hypotheses for changes in physical traces must be considered, and data must be collected that allow different interpretations to be dismissed.

ARCHIVAL DATA

RATIONALE

When we were born a record was made of our birth. Information on the birth record probably included the city and state in which we were born, the date and time of our birth, our parents' names, and our name. When we die another record will be made. It will include such details as probable cause of death, date and time of death, and our age. In between these two events in-numerable records are made of our behavior. Physicians record visits. Hospitals keep a record of when we enter and when we leave. Schools record our grades and extracurricular activities. Businesses may record the number of times we are late or how often we fail to show up for work. Newspapers describe notable successes and failures. Local governments record when we get married and to whom, as well as when we buy a house and how much it costs. The federal government records, among other things, what we pay in income taxes.

Records are kept not only of individuals but also of countries, institutions, cities, and businesses. The gross national product of a country, its major exports and imports, the size of its navy, and the distribution of its population are but a few of the facts that are recorded. How much profit a company makes is part of its report to stockholders. Voting behaviors of state and federal legislators are recorded, as is the amount of money a city spends on social services. Analysis and interpretation of local and world events flood the media. The contents of the media and of documents and books (published and unpublished) are a source of information about current fads and prejudices, changing patterns of belief, and the ideas of important (and not so important) members of society.

Archives are records or documents recounting the activities of individuals or of institutions, governments, and other groups. As measures of behavior, archival data share some of the same advantages as physical traces. Archival measures are nonreactive and therefore provide an alternative to data collection via surveys or questionnaires. Like physical trace measures, archival data can be used to check the validity of other measures and as a part of multimethod approaches to hypothesis testing (see Box 4.1).

An examination of archival information may also provide a way to test the external validity of laboratory findings. Lau and Russell (1980) analyzed the contents of the sports pages in eight daily newspapers in order to test whether results obtained from laboratory-based experiments investigating causal attributions (the reasons people give for a certain outcome, or the cause they attribute the outcome to) were relevant to "real-world" settings. A major finding of attribution research is that people tend to make internal attributions (assuming that the outcome is due to some characteristic within themselves) for success and to make external attributions (assuming that the outcome is due to something beyond their control) for failure. Lau and Russell's analysis of explanations given by sportswriters or team members for the outcome of baseball and football games supported this conclusion that originally emerged from laboratory research. Specifically, they identified 594 explanations for success and failure involving 33 major sporting events. From the perspective of the winning team, 75 percent of the attributions were internal, whereas only 55 percent of the attributions of the losing team were internal.

Support for this laboratory-based attribution theory has also been obtained by analyzing letters and replies published in two widely syndicated newspaper advice columns: "Ann Landers" and "Dear Abby" (see Fischer et al.,

BOX 4.1

COMING OVER TO THE THE DARK SIDE

As Frank and Gilovich (1988) point out, in vintage American Western movies you could always tell the good guys from the bad guys. The good guys, of course, wore white hats and the bad guys wore black hats. There is a strong cultural association between black and badness. We speak of people being "blackballed," "blacklisted," "blackmailed," and a reputation being "blackened." When terrible things happen it is a "black day." Black is seen in many cultures as the color of death. The good and bad sides of human nature are also contrasted using black-and-white images, as was illustrated by the characters of the famous *Star Wars* movie. Viewers of this movie (first of a classic trilogy) likely will remember the confrontation between the villain, Darth Vader (dressed completely in black) and the young hero, Luke Skywalker (dressed in white or light colors). Vader, unfortunately, had "gone over" to the dark side.

Frank and Gilovich (1988) wanted to find out if this strong cultural association between black and evil would affect the way people behave. Specifically, they asked whether professional sports teams that wear black uniforms are more aggressive than those that wear nonblack uniforms. Using archival data obtained from the central offices of the National Football League (NFL) and the National Hockey League (NHL), Frank and Gilovich analyzed penalty records of each major professional team in these sports between 1970 and 1986. Yards penalized were analyzed in the NFL and minutes that a player was assigned to the penalty box were calculated in the NHL. These particular measures were deemed more appropriate given the study's hypothesis than was number of infractions. Penalties for overaggressiveness are generally more severe (in yards or minutes) than are those for simple rule violations. The operational definition of a "black uniform" was that the colored version of the team's uniform (the one used typically for away games in the NHL and for home games in the NFL) was more than 50 percent black. (An exception was made for the Chicago Bears of the NFL, who wear dark-blue uniforms but which many people mistakenly remember as

black.) According to the authors' hypothesis teams wearing black should be penalized more than would be expected simply by chance. And they were. Thus, teams with black uniforms, such as Oakland, Chicago, and Cincinnati in the NFL, and Philadelphia, Pittsburgh, and Vancouver in the NHL, were reliably more aggressive than many other teams.

As a further test of their hypothesis, the investigators examined the archives for penalty records of any teams that switched their uniform color from nonblack to black sometime during the period under observation. The notion that a team which switched from nonblack to black would become more aggressive after it switched was supported by data provided by two NHL teams. When these two teams donned black uniforms they were penalized more. One NHL team that switched from nonblack to nonblack did not show any increase in aggressiveness, which helps to some degree to rule out an effect of simply switching uniforms, as, for example, might occur if players compete more energetically after any change.

What are the possible psychological processes accounting for these effects? Frank and Gilovich suggest both social-perception and self-perception processes are at work. They argue that others (specifically, referees) "see" players in black as more aggressive than those players not wearing black (and award more penalties to players in black), and that the players themselves behave more aggressively when they put on a black uniform. In support of these explanations the authors provide data from laboratory experiments. In one experiment both college students and referees watched "staged" football games between teams wearing black or white uniforms and rated aggressiveness. In a second study students donned either black or white uniforms in anticipation of an athletic competition before choosing a game from a list of aggressive and nonaggressive games. In the first experiment both actual referees and college students were more likely to penalize a team when it was wearing black. The second experiment showed that subjects who donned black uniforms chose more aggressive games. In addition to providing an example of the ingenious use of archival data to test an hypothesis about human behavior, the Frank and Gilovich (1988) study is a good illustration of the multimethod approach to hypothesis testing.

1987; Schoeneman and Rubanowitz, 1985). The investigation was based on fifteen randomly selected columns of each advisor from 1980. The researchers, along with two-person teams of undergraduates trained for this task, first identified explanatory statements. The explanations were then coded according to whether the locus of the explanation was internal, that is, inherent to the subject, or external, implicating situations and circumstances. For one analysis, explanations were also coded in terms of temporal stability and controllability (see Fischer et al., 1987). A stable cause is one that is unchanging over time; an unstable cause is changeable. Attributions reflected controllable causes only when a subject was deemed capable of exercising control over them. One major finding of this archival study was that people view their own problems as the result of others' (external) invariable (stable) willful (controllable) tendencies. One letter-writer illustrated this attribution bias when she identified the source of her problematic vacations as follows: "Sydney is a drag on a trip (because) he has no interest in seeing new places or meeting new people" (Fischer et al., 1987, p. 461).

Other reasons for using archival data are to test hypotheses about previous behavior and to assess the effect of a natural treatment. It is possible, for instance, to obtain a measure of television viewing habits by studying the water pressure records of a city (see Webb et al., 1981)! When a television show is watched by many of a city's residents, water pressure levels are found to fluctuate in accordance with the show. For example, in one city a "30-million-gallon effect" was found for half-time and end-of-game breaks in a Super Bowl game, whereas only a "15-million-gallon effect" was found at the end of a Presidential debate. Changes in level of water pressure presumably reflect trips that viewers make to get a drink of water or to use the toilet when a convenient break appears in a television show that they are watching.

Natural treatments are naturally occurring events that have significant impact on society at large or on particular members. Because it is not always possible to anticipate these events, the investigator who wishes to assess their impact must be prepared to use a variety of behavioral measures, including archival data. School records of absenteeism have been used as an indirect measure of health in a study investigating the effect of aircraft noise on children (see Cohen et al., 1980). Assassinations of world leaders, drastic changes in the stock market, and the passage of new laws are examples of the kinds of events that may have important effects on behavior and that might be investigated using archival data.

Another reason for considering archival data as a behavioral measure is simply because archival data are so plentiful. We noted earlier the extensive records that society keeps on individuals, groups, and institutions. Through careful analysis of archival information, the industrious researcher can seek evidence to support numerous hypotheses. One goal of this chapter is to alert you to the possible rich rewards of analyzing archival data in the context of psychological studies of behavior.

TYPES OF ARCHIVAL DATA

The sheer diversity and extent of archival sources make their classification rather arbitrary. One scheme is to distinguish between records that are continuously kept and updated, such as tax records and records of various government agencies, and those that are discontinuous or episodic (see Webb et al., 1981). Included in the latter category are sales records of businesses, absentee and tardiness records, and personal documents. These two types of records are often also distinguished by the degree of their availability for public inspection. Many continuous records, frequently referred to as *running records,* are kept by government agencies and are easily obtainable. Most discontinuous records of private institutions and businesses, however, are not open to public scrutiny or can be obtained only after many requests and a display of considerable patience on the part of the researcher. Because of their continuous nature, running records are particularly useful in longitudinal studies or in the documentation of trends.

The media are yet another important source of archival information. Both continuous and discontinuous records are published in newspapers and reported on television. The content of media reports is also a form of archival record and is subject to analysis. Earlier we described how the contents of sports pages were used to test a theory of causal attribution. The placement of "Found" advertisements in the Lost and Found section of a newspaper can be used to measure public altruism (see Goldstein et al., 1978).

Phillips (1977) used running records of motor vehicle fatalities kept by the California Highway Patrol and a measure of suicide publicity derived from California newspapers to determine whether there is a significant suicidal component to motor vehicle fatalities. He hypothesized that a substantial number of deaths arising from motor vehicle accidents are actually the result of individuals using their cars to commit suicide. To test this hypothesis, Phillips investigated whether motor vehicle fatalities would, like suicides in general, increase after a well-publicized suicide story. Components of the publicity measure included the daily circulation of each newspaper and the number of days the newspaper carried the suicide story. This measure correlated significantly with changes in motor vehicle fatalities after each story. The number of motor vehicle fatalities increased significantly during the few days after a well-publicized suicide story, reaching a peak on Day 3. This result is shown in Figure 4.1. Changes in frequency were determined by comparing experimental periods (the week right after the story) with control periods that were free from suicide stories and were matched with the experimental periods in terms of day of the week, presence or absence of holidays, and time of the year. Phillips concluded that "suicide stories stimulate a wave of imitative suicides, some of which are disguised as motor vehicle accidents" (Phillips, 1977, p. 1464).

Table 4.2 contains a list of selected sources of archival information and the nature of the data that might be obtained from them. The types of archival data shown in Table 4.2 have been rather arbitrarily classified as running records, those pertaining to the media, and "other records," including records of businesses, schools, and other private institutions. An examination of the sources described in Table 4.2 will introduce you to the variety of possible measures that can be obtained from archival sources. Then, following a brief discussion of content analysis of archival sources, we will review several specific illustrations of the use of archival data in the context of hypothesis testing.

CONTENT ANALYSIS

Although many sources of archival data can be identified (see Table 4.2), the usefulness of these sources ultimately depends on how their content is analyzed. In the simplest case the analysis required may be quite minimal. Recording the votes of state legislators may be as simple as transcribing vote tallies found in legislative documents. Similarly, determining the average sales figure for divisions of a corporation may be only a matter of adding and dividing sets of numbers provided by the corporation's accountant. In many cases, however, extracting relevant data from an archival source requires careful procedures and relatively complex analysis of the source's content. Furthermore, problems of sampling, reliability, and validity of measures must

Figure 4.1   Daily fluctuations in motor vehicle accident fatalities for a 2-week period before, during (Day 0), and after publication of suicide stories. (*From Phillips, 1977.*)

TABLE 4.2   SELECTED SOURCES OF ARCHIVAL INFORMATION AND ILLUSTRATIVE DATA FOR THREE TYPES OF ARCHIVES*

Source	Illustrative data
Running records	
Congressional Record	Statements of position on particular issues
Telephone directories	Community ethnic group membership
Salaries of teachers or government employees	Community support
Government agency records (labor, commerce, agriculture departments)	Living trends
Judicial records	Uniformity in sentencing for antisocial behavior
Moody's Handbook	Corporate financial structure
Who's Who in America	Nature of cited accomplishments of successful people
Federal and state laws	Official societal restrictions
Tax records	Regional differences in patterns of living
Property transfer listings	Commercial activity of individuals
Legislative roll calls	Actions taken by individual legislators
City budgets	Perceived value or extent of support of various activities
Media	
Reader's Digest	Mathematics vocabulary in common usage
Society section of metropolitan newspaper	Upper-middle-class and lower-upper-class activities
Associated Press releases (available in complete form at the National Press Club, etc.)	Details of news events of various sorts
Children's books on sale	Qualities of models (heroes and heroines)
Movie announcements in newspapers	Changing taboos and enticements
Want ads	Employer inducements
Obituary columns	Charity preferences
Picture displays on front of movie houses	Changing taboos and enticements
Mail order catalogs	Apparel vogues, merchandise as reflection of living patterns
Published speeches	Political, social, economic attitudes
Newspaper headlines	Press bias
Other records†	
Absentee and tardiness records	Work habits or motivation
List of unsolicited complaints and commendations about various salespeople	Customer reaction
Military re-enlistment and longevity figures	Morale indicator
Pay increase and promotion lists	Perceived value of individuals to an organization
Number of people one supervises	Measure of management responsibility
Production and other output figures	Performance of individuals, departments, etc.
Sales contest records	Selling effectiveness, effectiveness of incentive plans
Sales slips at Delegates' Lounge bar in UN	Tension indicator
Peanut sales at ball games	Excitement indicator (greater after than before seventh inning)
Sales level of consumer goods	Effectiveness of display location, advertisement, or style of packaging
Air trip insurance figures	Public concern before and after air crashes
Sales of layettes by color (blue or pink)	Sex preference in different social classes
Sale price of autographs	Popularity indicator
Soap usage rate (amount of money spent on bars of soap)	Value of cleanliness to personnel
Admission rate in psychiatric hospitals	General overall anxiety in culture

TABLE 4.2 SELECTED SOURCES OF ARCHIVAL INFORMATION AND ILLUSTRATIVE DATA FOR THREE TYPES OF ARCHIVES* *(Continued)*

Source	Illustrative data
Club membership list	Indicator of segment of society involved
Committee reports	Institutional modification attempts
Board minutes	Official institutional policies
Actuarial records: birth, baptismal, death records, marriage licenses	Comparative demographic data (occupation, religion, time of day, cause of death, etc.)
Cemetery documents, burial lot records	Family membership

*Adapted from Brandt (1972).
†Institutions, businesses, hospitals, schools, etc.; may or may not be open to public inspection.

be addressed, just as these problems are addressed in situations where behavior is observed directly.

Content analysis is generally defined as any technique for making inferences by objectively identifying specific characteristics of messages (Holsti, 1969). Though it is associated primarily with written communications, content analysis may be used with any form of message, including television and radio programs, speeches, films, and interviews. Weigel et al. (1980) used content analysis to study race relations as they are depicted on prime-time television. They analyzed the frequency of appearances of blacks and whites on evening television shows carried by all three major networks. In addition, they rated the quality of black-white and white-white interactions. Appearances by blacks involved less than 9 percent of the human appearance time in programs and commercials, and compared to white-white interactions, black-white interactions were relatively infrequent and more formalized when they did appear.

There are several discernible steps in conducting research using content analysis. First is the identification of a relevant archival source. What is relevant, of course, depends on the goals of the study and the questions the researcher is asking. In some cases merely a statement of the purpose of the study is sufficient to pinpoint an appropriate archival source. A researcher who sets out to study humor in tombstone messages, the manifest content of suicide notes, or race relations on television has already identified the general source for content analysis. In other situations the identification of relevant sources depends on the ingenuity of the researcher. Lau and Russell's (1980) choice of the sports pages represented an appropriate and clever use of archival sources as a test of the external validity of laboratory findings related to attribution.

Having identified an archival source, the researcher must sample selections from this source appropriately. Sampling procedures similar to those described in previous chapters can be used. As is the case when behavior or events are sampled, the goal of sampling is to obtain a sample that is representative of all the data of interest. To investigate race relations on television, Weigel et al. (1980) videotaped a full week's broadcasts by the three major networks in the spring of 1978. Only programs with a story line and all product commercials were included in the sample. The decision not to use documentaries, news broadcasts, and sports shows further reduced the sample of viewing time by about 20 percent. As always, the extent to which the results of an archival study can be generalized depends on the nature of the sample that is taken.

The next step in performing a content analysis is coding. This step is similar to the scoring of narrative records (see Chapter 2) and requires that relevant descriptive categories and appropriate units of measure be defined (see Holsti, 1969). As with the choice of the archival source itself, what determines a relevant descriptive category is related to the goals of the study. This aspect of a content analysis task can be illustrated by examining the categories used by Weigel et al. (1980) in their study of race relations. Four major categories were defined: (1) human appearance time, (2) black appearance time, (3) cross-racial appearance time, and (4) cross-racial interaction time. Each category was operationally defined. For instance, cross-racial interaction was defined as "the time during which black and white characters were engaged in active, on-screen interactions (talking, touching, or clear nonverbal communication)" (p. 886). The use of precise operational definitions permitted coders viewing the sample broadcasts to make reliable judgments of events.

In many content analysis studies, the communication is written. The units of classification in this case generally include single words, characters, sentences or paragraphs, themes, or particular items (Holsti, 1969). Lau and Russell (1980), for instance, determined the frequency of attribution statements that were categorized as either internal or external and were made by members of the winning or losing team. Another unit of measure often used when newspaper content is analyzed is that of space—for instance, number of column inches devoted to a particular topic. When television or radio broadcasts are studied, the unit of measure may be time. Such was the case for the study by Weigel et al. (1980). Both black appearances and black-white appearances were expressed in terms of the percentage of total human appearance time.

Qualitative measures are also occasionally used as part of content analysis. These qualitative assessments may be in the form of ratings. In addition to measuring time of cross-racial interactions on prime time television, Weigel et al. (1980) sought to determine the "degree to which cross-racial interactions on television were characterized by the conditions that promote friendliness and mutual respect in face-to-face encounters" (pp. 886–887). To do this, they developed a series of rating scales that emphasized interpersonal dimensions found to be important in previous race-related research. Videotapes of broadcasts taken a year earlier were used to define levels of the scales, and coders were trained in the use of the scales before real data were collected. As has been mentioned, the quality of black-white interactions, relative to white-white interactions, differed on several dimensions.

ILLUSTRATIVE USES OF ARCHIVAL DATA

Analysis of Communications   Osgood and Walker (1959) compared the content of real suicide notes, simulated suicide notes (notes deliberately faked), and ordinary letters. Working under the assumption that language behavior changes as a function of heightened motivation, they suggested that suicide notes should differ from ordinary letters and faked notes in several ways. Specifically, the researchers hypothesized that, relative to other messages, suicide notes would show: (1) greater stereotypy (more repetitions, fewer modifiers, more familiar words and phrases); (2) greater disorganization of language (more grammatical errors, shorter units); (3) more frequent use of self-destructive motives (greater use of self-critical statements); and (4) more evidence of conflict (greater qualification of statements, more frequent use of constructions with "however," "but," and "if").

The investigators chose sixteen different measures to test their hypotheses regarding the content of these messages (for example, number of syllables per word and number of distress-expressing phrases). Many of these measures revealed significant differences between suicide notes and ordinary letters, lending support to three of the four major hypotheses. Interestingly, suicide notes did not show greater disorganization. When quantitative measures that were successful in distinguishing between suicide notes and ordinary letters were used to differentiate between faked and real suicide notes, the analysis correctly predicted the real suicide note in ten of thirteen matched pairs.

Analysis of Trends   Etaugh (1980) investigated attitudes toward nonmaternal child care as conveyed in the popular media and in child care books during the period 1957–1976. The possible effect of nonmaternal care on the adjustment of children has become an important issue because of the increased numbers of women who have children and also work full-time. Included in Etaugh's archival sample were all issues of seven leading women's magazines published during this period. As she points out, most women are likely to obtain their information about child care from such sources rather than from reading professional journals. Therefore, it is important to determine whether information presented in popular periodicals agrees with current research findings, which, according to Etaugh, show that "high-quality nonmaternal care does not appear to have harmful effects on the preschool child's maternal attachment, intellectual development, social-emotional behavior, or physical health" (Etaugh, 1980, p. 313). This determination is particularly important in light of the fact that there is a correlation between women's attitudes toward work and adjustment of their children (see Etaugh, 1980). Women with positive attitudes toward work have better-adjusted children than those with less favorable attitudes.

The results of this archival study revealed that there has been a major shift in the direction of more favorable views of working women and nonmaternal care in these sources, especially between the 1960s and 1970s. Views expressed in the popular magazines were generally found to be more favorable than those in child care books, a fact that may reflect the ability of magazines (which have shorter publication lags than books) to reflect the most recent research findings. Etaugh (1980) also points out that attacks on day care by the popular press have generally been directed toward existing day-care facilities, whereas research has largely emphasized high-quality day care.

Assessing the Effect of a Natural Treatment A study investigating the effect of a natural treatment (one that we have mentioned previously) is that of Phillips (1977). In this study the "treatment" was the publicity given by major newspapers to suicides and the effect of this variable on motor vehicle fatalities was assessed. In a subsequent study, Phillips (1978) used records of the U.S. National Transportation Safety Board (*Briefs of Accidents: U.S. Civil Aviation*) to show a relationship between well-publicized murder-suicides and changes in fatal aircraft accidents. This archival study revealed a sharp increase in multi-fatality crashes (implying both a murder and a suicide component) in the period following the widespread publicizing of a murder-suicide story. Interestingly, the peak increase in aircraft fatalities occurred on Day 3 following the story, just as was found when suicide stories were related to motor vehicle fatalities (see Figure 4.1).

Yet another finding by Phillips (1983) is that homicides increased significantly following heavyweight championship prize fights during the period 1973–1978. At the time this study was conducted, daily counts of homicides in the United States for this 6-year period were publicly available from the National Center for Health Statistics. Particularly intriguing is the fact that deaths due to homicides peaked 3 days following the prize fight, as had been found in previous analyses of motor vehicle and airplane fatalities following well-publicized suicide stories. According to Phillips (1983), the heavyweight prize fights provoke a brief, sharp increase in homicides. As evidence that this effect is due to some type of modeling of aggression, Phillips (1983) carried out additional analyses showing that homicides increased with an increase in the level of publicity surrounding the event. He operationally defined level of publicity in terms of whether or not the fight was discussed on television network news. He found that the increase in homicides was significantly greater when the fight was given more publicity by being on the network news.

This series of studies by Phillips and his colleagues provides an impressive demonstration of the use of archival data to provide external validity to the results of laboratory findings. Phillips (1983) noted that laboratory studies have shown that exposure to violent films and television produces brief increases in aggression by laboratory subjects. Often, however, neither the setting nor the nature of the violence studied (for example, hitting inflatable toys) is similar to that found in the real world. In contrast, studies using archival data, although lacking the rigorous control possible in the laboratory, provide evidence of what happens to real people who are exposed to real media violence.

PROBLEMS AND LIMITATIONS

When discussing the validity of physical traces, we mentioned that biases may result from the way physical traces are established and from the manner in which they survive over time. These biases are referred to as selective deposit and selective survival, respectively, and they are no less a problem for archival records (see Webb et al., 1981). Either of these biases can impose severe limitations on the generality of research findings.

Problems of **selective deposit** arise when biases exist in the production of archival sources. An interesting example of selective deposit is that associated with suicide notes. We mentioned earlier the research of Osgood and Walker (1959), who performed a content analysis of suicide notes and compared real suicide notes to ordinary letters and to faked suicide notes. We might ask whether the thoughts and feelings expressed in suicide notes are representative of all suicides. It happens that fewer than a fourth of all suicides leave notes, so it is possible that those who do leave notes are not representative of no-note suicides (Webb et al., 1981).

Problems of selective deposit may also arise when individuals associated with archival sources have the opportunity to edit and alter records before they are permanently recorded. This is illustrated by legislators' use of the *Congressional Record*. Though the *Congressional Record* is ostensibly a spontaneous record of speeches and remarks made before the Congress, legislators actually have the opportunity to edit their remarks before they are published (Webb et al., 1981) and even to enter into the record documents and accounts that were never really read aloud. No doubt remarks that are, in hindsight, viewed as less than politically expedient are changed prior to publication in the *Congressional Record*. Researchers who use archival data must be aware of the biases that may enter in when an archive is produced. Consider, for example, what types of biases might cause selective recording of crime statistics, income expense accounts, or sales figures.

Problems associated with **selective survival** arise when records are missing or incomplete (something an investigator may or may not even be aware of). It is important to consider whether there are reasons to suspect systematic biases in the survival of certain records. Are documents missing that are particularly damaging to certain individuals or groups? Following a change of Presidential administrations, are some types of archives destroyed or misplaced? Are "letters to the editor" representative of all letters that were received? Schoeneman and Rubanowitz (1985) cautioned that when analyzing the contents of advice columns they could not avoid a possible preselection bias given that advice columnists print only a fraction of the letters they receive. As one prominent group of researchers has commented, when one examines archival data, "the gnawing reality remains that archives have been produced for someone else and by someone else" (Webb et al., 1981, p. 140).

In addition to problems arising from selective deposit and survival, the researcher using archival sources must be aware of possible errors in record keeping and changes over time in the manner in which records are made. It is important to demonstrate that record keeping was relatively constant and stable over the period of the study. When running records are kept, there is always the possibility that the definitions of categories have been changed "midstream." For example, had the U.S. National Transportation Safety Board made important changes in the definition of "noncommercial" aircraft during the period of Phillips' (1978) study, it would have seriously affected the statistics he used to implicate murder-suicides in aircraft fatalities.

Although archives represent nonreactive measures of behavior, their classification as such applies only to archival analysis; it does not imply that reactivity was not a problem when the archive was produced. Statements that are made by public figures, printed in newspapers, and reported by other media must be evaluated for their reactive components. Politicians and others who are constantly exposed to media publicity no doubt learn how to "use" the media, and their public stance may not match their private views. Lau and Russell (1980) had to consider whether public statements made by players and coaches about a team's performance were really the same as those made in private. They concluded that differences between public and private statements of attribution no doubt existed but that these differences do not invalidate their generalization of laboratory findings to real-world settings. The only way to control for reactive effects in archival data is to be aware that they may exist and, when possible, to seek other forms of corroborative evidence.

Yet another problem in the analysis of archival data is identifying spurious relationships. A **spurious relationship** exists when evidence falsely indicates that two or more variables are associated. Such evidence may be the result of inadequate or improper statistical treatment. This problem may exist in studies showing a relationship between frequency of deaths and important occasions (see Box 4.2). Although many people appear to endorse the view that individuals can somehow prolong their life in order to experience certain important events, such as birthdays, Schulz and Bazerman (1980) reanalyzed data from several studies to show that supportive evidence may be the result of statistical artifacts—for example, the way in which the period of time before and after a death was measured.

Spurious relationships can also exist when variables are accidentally or coincidentally related. This is sometimes the case when changes in two variables are the result of another, usually unknown, third variable. For instance, Kidder and Judd (1986) point out that ice cream sales and crime rate are positively correlated. However, before concluding that eating ice cream prompts people to commit crimes, she suggests we consider the fact that both variables are affected by temperature; neither ice cream nor crime directly affects the other.

That Phillips' (1983) finding of a relationship between the occurrence of heavyweight prize fights and frequency of homicides in the United States is a spurious one has been the subject of several studies (e.g., Baron and Reiss,

BOX 4.2

DEATH AND IMPORTANT OCCASIONS: A SPURIOUS RELATIONSHIP?

Many people apparently believe that the timing of death is psychologically determined. One source of evidence for this view has come from studies showing a relationship between frequency of deaths and various positive events, such as birthdays and religious holidays. Two related hypotheses have received support in the psychological literature. One hypothesis is that there is a lower than expected frequency of deaths before important events (the so-called death-dip hypothesis). The other hypothesis claims that there is a greater than expected frequency of deaths after important dates (the death-rise hypothesis). Schulz and Bazerman (1980) took a closer look at the evidence supporting these hypotheses and found it equivocal.

The general procedure behind studies investigating the relationship between death and important occasions is to examine archival data revealing the death dates of individuals in relation to certain important events. Three major positive events have been examined by researchers: birthdays, national elections, and religious holidays. For instance, one of the early studies to offer data supporting a death-dip hypothesis used birth dates and death dates of persons listed in the book *Four Hundred Notable Americans*. The number of deaths in the month immediately prior to the month of an individual's birth was lower than what we would expect if chance alone was operating, thus giving credence to the death-dip hypothesis. A general explanation for this type of finding is that people are somehow able to prolong their lives or delay death until a certain event has been experienced. Exactly how one might do this is not particularly clear. One sug-

gestion is that looking forward to a positive event creates a state of positive anticipation that precipitates beneficial neurochemical changes. Another possible explanation is that elderly persons are more likely to follow their health and medical regimens closely as an important date nears, so as to reduce the chances of dying before the event arrives.

Schulz and Bazerman (1980) indicate that the relationship observed by previous investigators between death and important occasions may be spurious. For example, they applied a more sensitive measure to the archival data that had shown a death dip in the month prior to individuals' birthdays. They calculated the number of deaths in the 31-day period before and after individuals' birthdays. This measure should be more sensitive, because it classifies individuals who died in the same month of their birth but who died either before or after their birthday (except when they died exactly on their birthday). This reanalysis of the data eliminated any evidence for the death-dip hypothesis. These researchers also reanalyzed data from other studies supporting the death-dip and death-rise hypotheses and showed how statistical artifacts could account for the results. Although stating that "it has thus far been impossible to obtain the relevant data from archival records that would enable one to test the death-dip or death-rise hypothesis with respect to important positive events" (p. 260), Schulz and Bazerman suggest that supporting data "may well be within reach if we use the proper methodologies and carefully select important events" (p. 261).

1985). Some of the criticisms raised have to do with possible statistical artifacts in the complex analyses, while others suggest that important variables were not controlled. Baron and Reiss (1985) suggested that the third-day peak, which Phillips (1983) admitted he could not readily interpret, was quite possibly due to the occurrence of holidays or weekends near prize fight dates or even to fluctuations in the unemployment rate.

There is no easy way to deal with spurious relationships except to gather additional data from independent sources that will help confirm a relationship and to subject available archival data to more than one kind of analysis. Extensive reanalysis of Phillips' (1983) original data has tended to reaffirm a link between violence portrayed in the media and violence acted out in society (see Molcan et al., 1987; Phillips and Baron, 1985).

THE CASE STUDY METHOD

CHARACTERISTICS

A **case study** is an intensive description and analysis of a single individual. The "data" for a case study may be obtained from several different sources, including naturalistic observation (Chapter 2), interviews (Chapter 3), personal documents, and archival records (this chapter). A case study occasionally describes the application and results of a particular "treatment," as, for example, when a new therapeutic technique is used to treat an emotionally disturbed person. However, in the context of a case study, treatment variables are rarely varied systematically in an effort to control extraneous variables, and several different treatments are often applied simultaneously. The case study method can be contrasted with the "$N = 1$" approaches discussed in Chapter 8 which are based exclusively on experimental methods. Although it is most closely associated with the field of clinical psychology, the case study method has been used by child psychologists, memory researchers, and animal behaviorists, as well as by researchers in such fields as anthropology, criminology, and sociology.

In actual practice, the form and content of case studies are extremely varied. Published case studies may be only a few printed pages long or they may fill a book. Kirsch (1978) described an attempt to implement SMT with a woman experiencing low self-confidence and social inhibition (see Box 4.3). The case study described her treatment during nine therapy sessions and a 5-month follow-up. The complete case study was presented in four pages of the journal *Psychotherapy: Theory, Research and Practice.* In another case study, the personality psychologist Gordon W. Allport described the relationship between a mother and son as revealed in 301 letters that the mother wrote to friends. First reported in two consecutive issues of the *Journal of Abnormal and Social Psychology* (1946, Vol. 41, Nos. 3 and 4), this classic case study was eventually published as a 223-page book under the title *Letters from Jenny,* in 1965.

The cognitive psychologist Ulric Neisser (1981) presented a case study based on John Dean's memory for events and conversations surrounding the Watergate scandal. Dean was President Richard Nixon's legal counsel. In his testimony before the Senate Watergate Investigating Committee, Dean demonstrated an apparent ability to recall literally dozens of episodes that occurred during a several-year period prior to the Watergate investigation. Neisser compared Dean's memory for conversations with tape recordings of the actual con-

BOX 4.3

CAN CLIENTS BE THEIR OWN THERAPISTS?
A CASE STUDY ILLUSTRATION

This article reports on the use of Self-Management Training (SMT), a therapeutic strategy which capitalizes on the advantages of brief therapies, while at the same time reducing the danger of leaving too many tasks not fully accomplished....The essence of this approach involves teaching the client how to be his or her own behavior therapist. The client is taught how to assess problems along behavioral dimensions and to develop specific therapeutic tactics, based on existing treatment techniques, for overcoming problems. As this process occurs, the traditional client-therapist relationship is altered considerably. The client takes on the dual role of client and therapist, while the therapist takes on the role of supervisor.

The Case of Susan

Susan, a 28-year-old married woman, entered therapy complaining that she suffered from a deficient memory, low intelligence, and lack of self-confidence. The presumed deficiencies "caused" her to be inhibited in a number of social situations. She was unable to engage in discussions about films, plays, books, or magazine articles "because" she could not remember them well enough. She often felt that she could not understand what was being said in a conversation and that this was due to her low intelligence. She attempted to hide her lack of comprehension by adopting a passive role in these interactions and was fearful lest she be discovered by being asked for more of a response. She did not trust her own opinions and, indeed, sometimes doubted whether she had any. She felt dependent on others to provide opinions for her to adopt.

Administering a Wechsler Adult Intelligence Scale (WAIS), I found her to have a verbal IQ of about 120, hardly a subnormal score. Her digit span (scale score = 12, raw score = 13) indicated that at least her short-term memory was not deficient. The test confirmed what I had already surmised from talking with her: that there was nothing wrong with her level of intelligence or her memory.

After discussing this conclusion, I suggested that we investigate in greater detail what kinds of things she would be able to do if she felt that her memory, intelligence, and level of self-confidence were sufficiently high. In this way, we were able to agree upon a list of behavioral goals, which included such tasks as stating an opinion, asking for clarification, admitting ignorance of certain facts, etc. During therapy sessions, I guided Susan through overt and covert rehearsals of anxiety-arousing situations ...structured homework assignments which constituted successive approximations of her behavioral goals, and had her keep records of her progress. In addition, we discussed negative statements which she was making to herself and which were not warranted by the available data (e.g., "I'm stupid"). I suggested that whenever she noticed herself making a statement of this sort, she counter it by intentionally saying more appropriate, positive statements to herself (e.g., "I am not stupid—there is no logical reason to think that I am").

During the fifth session of therapy, Susan reported the successful completion of a presumably difficult homework assignment. Not only had she found it easy to accomplish, but, she reported, it had not aroused any anxiety, even on the first trial....It was at this point that the nature of the therapeutic relationship was altered. During future sessions, Susan rated her progress during the week, determined what the next step should be, and devised her own homework assignments. My role became that of a supervisor of a student therapist, reinforcing her successes and drawing attention to factors which she might be overlooking.

After the ninth therapy session, direct treatment was discontinued. During the following month, I contacted Susan twice by phone. She reported feeling confident in her ability to achieve her goals. In particular, she reported feeling a new sense of control over her life. My own impressions are that she had successfully adopted a behavioral problem-solving method of assessment and had become fairly adept at devising strategies for accomplishing her goals.

Follow-up

Five months after termination of treatment, I contacted Susan and requested information on her progress. She reported that she talked more than she used to in social situations, was feeling more comfortable doing things on her own (i.e., without her husband), and that, in general, she no longer felt that she was stupid. She summarized by saying: "I feel that I'm a whole step or level above where I was."

I also asked her which, if any, of the techniques we had used in therapy she was continuing to use on her own....Finally, she reported that on at least three separate occasions during the five-month period following termination of treatment, she had told another person: "I don't understand that—will you explain it to me?" This was a response which she had previously felt she was not capable of making, as it might expose her "stupidity" to the other person.

Three months after the follow-up interview, I received an unsolicited letter from Susan (I had moved out of state during that time), in which she reminded me that "one of [her] imaginary exercises was walking into a folk dancing class and feeling comfortable; well, it finally worked."

Kirsch, I. (1978). Teaching clients to be their own therapists: A case-study illustration. *Psychotherapy: Theory, Research, and Practice, 15*, pp. 302–305. Reprinted by permission.

versations that had been secretly recorded in Nixon's Oval Office (published as *The Presidential Transcripts*). Although Dean's testimony was basically accurate, Neisser was able to show that his memory underwent systematic distortion. This 21-page case study appeared in the journal *Cognition*.

Many aspects of the case study method make it a unique means of studying behavior. It can be viewed as differing from more experimental approaches in terms of its goals, the methods used, and the types of information that are obtained (see Kazdin, 1980b). For example, the case study method is often characterized as "exploratory" in nature and a source of hypotheses and ideas about behavior (Bolgar, 1965). Experimental approaches, on the other hand, are frequently viewed as opportunities to test specific hypotheses. The case study method has sometimes been viewed as antagonistic to these more controlled methods of investigation. A more appropriate perspective is suggested by Kazdin (1980b), who sees the case study method as interrelated with and complementary to other research methods in psychology.

The case study method offers both advantages and disadvantages to the research psychologist (see, for example, Bolgar, 1965; Hersen and Barlow, 1976; Kazdin, 1980b). Some of these are reviewed briefly in the following sections.

ADVANTAGES OF THE CASE STUDY METHOD

Source of Ideas and Hypotheses about Behavior The "power" of the case study method, according to Bolgar (1965), "lies in its ability to open the way for discoveries" (p. 30). It acts as a breeding ground for hypotheses that may subsequently be pursued with more rigorous methodologies. This aspect of the case study method was acknowledged by Kirsch (1978) in discussing the successful treatment of a woman in psychotherapy (see Box 4.3). He stated that the "conclusions [of this study] share the limitations of any inferences drawn from case study material. At this point they should be viewed as tentative. It is hoped that the utility of [this technique] will be established by more controlled research" (p. 305). The case study method is a natural starting point for a researcher who is entering an area of study about which relatively little is known. In psychology, the development of psychoanalytic theory stands as a classic example of hypothesis formation based on the case study method.

Opportunity for Clinical Innovation   The case study method provides an opportunity to "try out" new therapeutic techniques or to attempt unique applications of existing techniques. In this way it offers an opportunity for clinical innovation. The use of SMT in psychotherapy changes the typical client-therapist relationship. The approach is based on teaching clients to be their own therapists—in other words, to identify problems and to design behavioral techniques for dealing with them. The client is both client and therapist, while the therapist acts as supervisor (see Box 4.3). In a similar vein, Van Nuys (1975) used the case study method to call attention to the wording of hypnotic suggestions in helping a woman stop smoking. Information gained from this case study may provide guidance to other therapists who use hypnosis as a psychotherapeutic technique.

Method to Study Rare Phenomena   Certain events appear so infrequently in nature that it is possible to describe them only through the intensive study of single cases. An interesting example is a case study prepared by the Russian psychologist A. R. Luria, which describes a man with nearly a perfect memory. This case study was published as a book entitled *The Mind of a Mnemonist* (1968). In it Luria details at length the nature of this man's memory and the effect his prodigious ability to remember had on events in his life and on his personality. The case study material was based on more than 30 years of observation and informal experiments. Luria reported that the subject's use of visual imagery not only helped him to remember but also allowed him to exercise an amazing control over his body. He could increase his heart rate from a resting rate of 70–72 beats a minute to a rate approaching 100 beats per minute simply by imagining that he was running to catch a train!

Challenge to Theoretical Assumptions   A theory that all Martians have three heads would quickly collapse if a reliable observer spotted a Martian with only two heads. The case study method can often advance scientific thinking by providing a "counterinstance": a case that violates a general proposition or universally accepted principle (Kazdin, 1980b). Consider the idea that the mind is unitary, that human consciousness is inseparable. This view was challenged when surgeons who were trying to control a patient's epileptic seizures performed an operation that involved severing the corpus callosum, the brain pathway connecting the two cerebral hemispheres. The result was an individual who had, in fact, a "split brain." Normal conscious unity was disrupted, producing, in the words of one researcher, a "patient with two minds" (Gazzaniga, 1972, p. 311). Although he behaved normally, careful testing of the split-brain patient revealed peculiar aspects of this individual's cognitive functioning. It is possible for the right brain (mind?) to know something that the left brain (mind?) does not, and vice versa.

Tentative Support for a Psychological Theory Few researchers would accept the results of a case study as conclusive evidence for a particular hypothesis (see the treatment of disadvantages of the case study method that follows). The results of a case study generally must be viewed as tentative and must await investigation via more carefully controlled procedures before they are accepted by the scientific community. Nevertheless, the outcome of a case study can sometimes provide important evidence in support of a psychological theory. As an illustration, we can take another example from the memory literature.

In 1968 Atkinson and Shiffrin proposed a model of human memory that was to have considerable influence on research in this field. The model, which was based on principles of information processing, described both a short-term memory (STM) system and a long-term memory (LTM) system. Human memory, in other words, should be thought of as containing at least two memory structures, each with different characteristics and functions. STM was identified with "working memory" and represented the locus of conscious rehearsal and elaboration of information. It was the kind of memory we might use when looking up a telephone number and "holding" it until we had dialed it correctly. Information in LTM did not have to be actively processed in order to be remembered; rather, information in this memory system was stored on a relatively permanent basis, from whence it could be retrieved and brought into conscious memory (into STM).

Although results of numerous experiments provided evidence for this dual nature of our memory, Atkinson and Shiffrin (1968) considered the results of several case studies as "perhaps the most convincing demonstrations of a dichotomy in the memory system" (p. 97). These case studies involved patients who had been treated for epilepsy via surgical removal of parts of the brain within the temporal lobes, including a subcortical structure known as the hippocampus.

Of particular importance to Atkinson and Shiffrin's theory was the case study of a patient known as H. M. (see Scoville and Milner, 1957). Following the brain operation, H. M. was found to have a disturbing memory deficit. Although he could carry on a normal conversation and remember events for a short period of time, H. M. apparently could not put new information into long-term memory. He could not remember day-to-day events. He was able to read the same magazine over and over again without finding its contents familiar. It looked as though H. M. had an intact short-term memory system but could not get information into a long-term memory system. Subsequent testing of H. M. and patients with similar memory deficits has shown that the nature of this memory problem is more complex than originally suggested (see Zechmeister and Nyberg, 1982), but the case study of H. M. continues to be important whenever theories of human memory are discussed (for example, see Stern, 1981).

Complement to the Nomothetic Study of Behavior Psychology is a **nomothetic** discipline. This means that psychology (like science in general) seeks to establish broad generalizations, universal "laws" that apply to a wide population of organisms. As a consequence, psychological research is often characterized by studies that involve large numbers of subjects and seek to determine the "average" or typical performance of a group (see especially Chapters 5–7). This average may or may not represent the value of any one individual in the group. Rather, a researcher hopes to be able to predict, on the basis of this mean performance, what organisms will be like "in general."

Some psychologists, notably Allport (1961), argue that a nomothetic approach is inadequate—that the individual is more than what can be represented by the collection of average values on various dimensions. Allport argues that the individual is both unique and lawful (operates in accordance with internally consistent principles) and that the study of the individual (**idiographic** research) is an important goal. The need for an idiographic approach can be illustrated by the task confronting the clinical psychologist. As Allport (1961) points out, the clinician's goal "is not to predict the aggregate, but to foretell 'what any one man will do.' In reaching this ideal, actuarial predictions may sometimes help, universal and group norms are useful, but they do not go the whole distance" (p. 21). Allport suggests that our approach to understanding human nature should be neither exclusively nomothetic nor exclusively idiographic but should represent an "equilibrium" between the two. At the very least the idiographic approach, as represented by the case study method, permits the kind of detailed observation that has the power to reveal various nuances and subtleties of behavior that a "group" approach may miss.

DISADVANTAGES OF THE CASE STUDY METHOD

Difficulty of Drawing Cause-and-Effect Conclusions As we saw in Chapter 1, it is a goal of science to discover the causes of phenomena—to reveal in an unambiguous manner the specific factors that produce a particular event. The nature of the case study method is such that cause-and-effect conclusions can rarely be drawn on the basis of the results that are obtained. The major limitation of the case study method in this regard is the failure to control extraneous variables. Numerous plausible hypotheses are generally present to "explain" behavior change.

Consider, for instance, the treatment of Susan through SMT reported by Kirsch (1978; see Box 4.3). Although Susan apparently benefited from the SMT therapy, can we be sure that this particular factor accounted for her improvement? Many illnesses and certainly numerous emotional disorders are known to subside spontaneously. That is, over the course of time a certain number of people generally report a decrease in symptoms and an overall improvement. The case study method generally does not permit one to dismiss the hypothesis that improvement would have been observed even had the specified treatment never been administered. In addition, numerous aspects of the situation may be seen as responsible for Susan's improvement. Her care was in the hands of a "clinical psychologist" who assured her that she should not trust her own feelings and discussed with her the reasons for these feelings. The "insight" provided by a professional therapist may be sufficient to change Susan's attitudes toward herself. The therapist also asked Susan, as part of her therapy, to rehearse anxiety-arousing situations covertly and overtly. This technique is similar to rehearsal desensitization, which may be an effective therapeutic treatment in itself (see Rimm and Masters, 1979).

The fact that several "treatments" were used simultaneously makes it difficult to argue conclusively that the SMT therapy "caused" Susan's improvement. As we have seen, Kirsch (1978) himself was sensitive to the limitations of his results and suggested that the inferences drawn from his study should be considered tentative until they were investigated more rigorously.

Sources of Bias in Interpretation   The "outcome" of a case study often depends on inferences drawn by a researcher who is both participant and observer (see Bolgar, 1965). A therapist is an observer but is also certainly a participant in the therapeutic process. Problems of observer bias can arise in the context of the case study, as they do in other types of observation (see Chapter 2). In the absence of observable measures, the outcome of a case study may be based mainly on the "impressions" of the observer (see Hersen and Barlow, 1976). Kirsch (1978) described the patient Susan's "feelings" about her ability to achieve her goals and told how she reported a "sense of control" over her life. He stated that his "impressions are that she successfully adopted a behavioral problem-solving method of assessment and had become fairly adept at devising strategies for accomplishing her goals" (p. 304). Interpretation of an outcome solely on the basis of the subjective impressions of the observer can be seen as a serious weakness in the case study method.

Possible Biases in Data Collection   The material of a case study often includes several kinds of information, including that which is obtained from personal documents and psychological tests. Each of these sources of information must be carefully examined for possible biases. Archival records, as we have shown earlier in this chapter, are open to several sources of bias.

Further, when information is based on self-reports, there is always the possibility of distortion or falsification. Such was a possibility (although not necessarily a significant one) in the case of Susan's treatment. We have no way of knowing whether the patient's self-reports of improvement are exaggerated or even false.

Reports of even the most intelligent and well-intentioned individuals are susceptible to biases and reconstructions, especially when memory for remote events is concerned. Consider the following excerpt from a self-analysis by the well-known personality psychologist Alfred Adler (1973, pp. 179–180):

> Shortly after I went to a board[ing] school. I remember that the path to the school led over a cemetery. I was frightened every time and was exceedingly put out at beholding the other children pass the cemetery without paying the least attention to it, while every step I took was accompanied by a feeling of fear and horror. Apart from the extreme discomfort occasioned by this fear I was also annoyed at the idea of being less courageous than the others. One day I made up my mind to put an end to this fear of death. Again (as on my first resolve), *I decided upon a treatment of hardening* (Proximity of death!). I stayed at some distance behind the others, placed my school-bag on the ground near the wall of the cemetery and ran across it a dozen times, until I felt that I had mastered the fear. After that, I believe, I passed along this path without any fear.
>
> Thirty years after that I met an old schoolmate and we exchanged childhood reminiscences of our school days. It happened to occur to me that the cemetery was no longer in existence and I asked him what had happened to it remembering the great uneasiness it had at one time caused me. Astonished, my former schoolmate who had lived longer in that neighborhood than I had, insisted that *there never had been a cemetery* on the way to our school. Then I realized that the story of the cemetery had been but a poetic dress for my longing to overcome the fear of death.

Problem of Generalizing from a Single Individual   As Bolgar (1965) has stated, "Much of the criticism leveled against the case study method of research is based on the accepted canon that it is impossible to generalize from one case" (p. 30). As Kazdin (1980) notes, however, the ability to generalize from a single case depends on the degree of variability in the population from which the case was selected. Psychologists who study visual perception are often able to make wide generalizations based on the study of one individual. The assumption is that visual systems in humans are very similar and are related to the biological make-up of all humans. When significant variability exists among individuals, as would be the case when measures are made of learning and memory, emotionality, or personality, it becomes impossible to claim that what is observed in one individual will hold for all individuals. Even if we accept the validity of Kirsch's (1978) conclusion regarding the effectiveness of the SMT technique of psychotherapy, we do not know whether this particular treatment would be as successful for other individuals who might differ from the patient Susan in any of numerous ways, including intelligence, age, family background, and gender.

THE CASE STUDY METHOD: FINAL COMMENTS

Kazdin (1980) points out that case studies sometimes offer "dramatic" demonstrations of "new" or "unusual" findings or provide evidence for "success" of a particular treatment. These reports are often highly persuasive. Everyday examples are found in the media and in advertisements for various products. How many people with receding hairlines can resist the example of a formerly bald man who is shown to have grown an amazing amount of hair in the span of a few weeks! The persuasive value of case study examples are both an asset and a liability to the scientific community. Demonstrations of new or unusual findings based on a case study may lead scientists to rethink their original theoretical assumptions or may lead them into new and fruitful avenues of research. However, the results of case studies are often accepted by nonscientists with little regard for the limitations of such evidence. This is particularly likely when individuals are in a position to identify with the subject of the case study.

A person who suffers from a life-threatening illness may see more than a ray of hope in the results of a dramatic "new cure" based on treatment of an individual with the same illness. If this treatment worked for him, why wouldn't it work for me? For people who have (or think they have) few alternatives, this grasping at straws may not be totally unreasonable. Nevertheless, too often people do not consider (perhaps they do not want to consider) the reasons why a particular treatment would *not* work for them. They fail, in other words, to recognize the limitations of the case study method. This may have unfortunate consequences, as was illustrated in the recent controversy surrounding the supposed cancer-curing drug Laetrile (see Sun, 1981). Few respectable scientists or medical researchers considered this drug beneficial in the treatment of cancer. Positive results, however, based on individual "case studies," were presented as evidence by advocates of the drug. Largely because of public (not scientific) pressure, the government carried out systematic tests of the drug under controlled conditions. No beneficial effect of the drug was found. As others have commented, by using Laetrile instead of traditional therapies, many patients no doubt contributed to the spread of their cancer by postponing or interrupting valid courses of treatment.

SUMMARY

The use of physical traces and archival data are important alternatives to direct observation and surveys. Physical traces are the remnants, fragments, and products of past behavior. Physical use traces are based on the accumulation of evidence (accretion measures) or are the result of selective wear (erosion measures). Furthermore, use traces can either result naturally, without any intervention by the investigator, or be planned by the investigator. Physical traces may provide important nonreactive (unobtrusive) measures of behavior and can be used as the sole dependent variable or in combination with other measures of behavior. Multimethod approaches to the study of behavior are particularly recommended, because they reduce the chance that results are due to some artifact of the measurement process. In obtaining physical traces, an investigator must be aware of possible biases in the way in which traces accumulate or survive over time.

Archival data are found in records and documents that recount the activities of individuals, institutions, governments, and other groups. These sources of information are valuable because they provide a way of investigating the external validity of laboratory findings, assessing the effect of a natural "treatment" (such as a political assassination), analyzing the content of communications, and describing trends. Archival records are nonreactive measures of behavior and, like physical traces, can be used in multimethod approaches to hypothesis testing. The analysis of archival data typically requires some form of content analysis, a process that can involve problems of sampling and coding that are not unlike those that arise in the analysis of narrative records (see Chapter 2). Problems of selective deposit and selective survival must be investigated when archival data are used, and evidence should be presented showing that spurious relationships have not been obtained.

The case study method can be an important source of hypotheses about behavior, can provide an opportunity for clinical innovation (for example, trying out new approaches to therapy), can permit the intensive study of rare phenomena, can challenge theoretical assumptions, and can provide tentative support for a psychological theory. The intensive study of individuals that is the hallmark of the case study method is called idiographic research, and it can be viewed as complementary to the nomothetic inquiry (seeking general laws or principles) that is also characteristic of psychology. Problems arise when the case study method is used to draw cause-and-effect conclusions, or when biases of interpretation or in the collection of data are not identified. The case study method also suffers from a problem of generalizability: how to generalize on the basis of studying a single individual. Moreover, the "dramatic" results obtained from some case studies, though they may offer important insights to scientific investigators, are frequently accepted as valid by nonscientists who are not aware of the limitations of this method.

KEY CONCEPTS

physical traces	selective survival
archival data	spurious relationship
multimethod approach	case study
content analysis	nomothetic approach
selective deposit	idiographic approach

REVIEW QUESTIONS

1 What characteristic of physical traces and archival data makes them an especially attractive measurement alternative, compared to direct observation and surveys?

2 Why are multimethod approaches to hypothesis testing recommended?

3 What are the different kinds of physical trace measures used by psychologists, and in what ways do they differ?

4 What possible sources of bias exist when physical use traces are the dependent variable in a research study, and how can the validity of these measures be verified?

5 Give four reasons for using archival data as an alternative to, or in conjunction with, direct observation and surveys.

6 What dimensions distinguish the various types of archival sources used by psychologists?

7 What three basic steps must be taken in any research in which content analysis is done?

8 Explain the role of precise operational definitions in content analysis, and give one example of a quantitative unit and one example of a qualitative unit of measurement in content analysis.

9 Identify and give an example of the problems that researchers must be aware of when they make use of archival sources.

10 Explain the two ways in which evidence indicating spurious relationships most often arises.

11 Cite and give an example of the advantages of the case study method.

12 Distinguish between a nomothetic and an idiographic approach to research.

13 Cite and give an example of the disadvantages of the case study method.

14 What is the major limitation of the case study method in drawing cause-and-effect conclusions?

CHALLENGE QUESTIONS

1 A case study showing how "mud therapy" was successful in treating an individual exhibiting excessive anxiety was recently reported in a popular magazine. The patient's symptoms included having trouble sleeping, loss of appetite, extreme nervousness when in groups of people, and general feelings of arousal that led the individual always to feel "on edge" and fearful. The California therapist who administered the mud therapy was known for this treatment, having appeared on several TV talk shows. He first taught the patient a deep relaxation technique and a "secret word" to repeat over and over in order to block out all disturbing thoughts. Then the patient was asked to lie submerged for two hours each day in a special wooden "calm tub" filled with mud. During this time the patient was to practice the relaxation exercises and to concentrate on repeating the secret word whenever the least bit of anxiety was experienced. The therapy was very costly, but after six weeks the patient reported to the therapist that he no longer had the same feelings of anxiety that he had had before. The therapist pronounced him cured and attributed the success of the treatment to immersion in the calming mud. The conclusion drawn by the author of the magazine article describing this therapy was that "it is a treatment that many people could benefit from." On the basis of your

knowledge of the limitations of the case study method, answer the following questions:

A What possible sources of bias were there in the study?

B What alternative explanations can you suggest for the successful treatment?

C What problem arises from studying only one individual?

2 [A] Suggest *two* sources of archival data for *each* of the following variables. Be sure to specify an operational definition of each variable.

A Public's interest in cultural events

B Students' political attitudes

C Community concern about crime

D Amount of mobility in a corporation

E Citizens' attitudes toward their schools

F Ethnic grouping of neighborhoods

G Current fads in dress

[B] For *each* of the following archival sources, specify *two* kinds of data that might be useful in a psychological study. Once again, be sure to specify the operational definition that could be used for the variable you have identified.

A Weekly news magazine

B Television soap operas

C Classified section of newspaper

D Annual city budgets

E Student yearbooks

F List of donors to a university

G Television commercials

3 A bright female graduate student in psychology has been offered a job with both *Newsweek* and *Time.* The salary offers of the two companies are basically the same, and it appears that both the working conditions and the job responsibilities are similar. To help her decide which job to accept, she resolves to determine whether one magazine has a better attitude toward women than the other. She appeals to you to help her with a content analysis of these two news magazines. What specific advice would you give her regarding each of the following steps of her content analysis?

A Sampling

B Coding

C Reliability

D Quantitative and qualitative measures

4 An educational specialist was convinced that schoolyard fights among young boys were more violent than those among young girls. To gather evidence relevant to her hypothesis, she checked the records at the nurse's office of her school. She found that, of the 100 injuries resulting from fights which were reported to the school nurse, 75 percent involved boys and only 25 percent involved girls. The investigator was convinced on the basis of these findings that her hypothesis was correct. Criticize this conclusion by showing how these very same findings *could result if exactly the opposite* of the investigator's hypothesis were true—namely, that fights among young girls are more violent. (Be sure to confine your answer to the adequacy of the data that the investigator has presented to support her conclusion; *don't* get embroiled in problems of gender bias or in the various theories of violent behavior.)

5 A researcher wishes to test the hypothesis that children attending private grade schools are not as "dirty-minded" as students attending public grade schools. He chooses two schools (one a parochial school and one public) that are located in the same neighborhood, approximately one mile apart. Both schools include grades 1 through 8. To test the hypothesis, the investigator decides to use measures both of natural accretion and of controlled accretion. Specifically, he operationally defines "dirty-mindedness" as the number of obscene words (from a predetermined list) that are found in the restrooms of each school. The natural accretion measure is simply the number of new target words appearing on the walls of the restrooms at the end of each week. As a measure of planned accretion, the investigator obtains permission from the school authorities to place pads of paper and pencils in the toilet stalls of the restrooms at each school. On each pad of paper is written "Leave me a note." At the end of each week the investigator replaces the pad with a fresh one and examines the pages that have been written on for the appearance of obscene words.

  A Comment on possible problems of selective deposit and survival for the physical trace measures proposed in this study.

  B Frame questions that might be asked concerning the external validity of this study.

  C Suggest ways in which the investigator might use a multimethod approach to this problem.

ANSWER TO CHALLENGE QUESTION 1

1 A One source of bias in this case study was that the same individual served as therapist and as researcher with the commensurate problems of observer bias. A second source of bias is that the therapist based his conclusion solely on the self-reports of the patient.

  B The successful treatment may have resulted from the relaxation technique alone, the use of the "secret word" in the face of anxiety, attention the patient received from the therapist, or even the high cost of treatment.

  C The major problem that arises from studying one individual is a potential lack of generality.

Experimental Methods

CHAPTER

5

Independent Groups: Design and Analysis

OUTLINE

Psychologists use the experimental method to construct artificial situations (usually in the laboratory) to isolate the process they want to investigate. For instance, no matter how long or how carefully you observed adult readers, you would be unlikely to be able to tell whether they were saying the words to themselves as they read silently. The process you were interested in would literally be unobservable. Haber and Haber (1982) constructed a situation in which they were able to make the unobservable available to inspection. The term they used for the unobservable process of talking to oneself while reading was "subvocal articulation." They gave college students two types of sentences to read, tongue-twisters (Francis Forbes' father fries five flounders) and control sentences that were not tongue-twisters (Mary Wright's uncle cooks red lobsters). The logic of their experiment was that, if the students *did* say the words to themselves as they read silently, the tongue-twister sentences would be harder to read and thus take longer to read than the control sentences. This is exactly what they found, so they concluded that we do "talk to ourselves" as we read. Haber and Haber never did observe subvocal articulation directly. They constructed a situation in which a difference in behavior occurred as a result of a process that they presumed was occurring, and the situation they constructed allowed this process to "show itself."

Much of the experimental research in psychology is like that illustrated in the study we have just described. Theoretical explanatory processes are proposed, experiments are done in which outcomes are predicted on the basis of these explanatory processes, and the outcomes of the experiments either confirm or refute the existence of these unobservable theoretical processes. The role of theories in psychological research was discussed in Chapter 1. In the next few chapters we will explore the use of the experimental method to test psychological theories.

In this chapter we will discuss the most commonly used experimental design when different conditions are administered to different groups of subjects—namely, the random groups design. The topics we will address include the underlying logic of this design, the procedures for forming random groups, the ways in which the external validity of experiments using this design can be established, and the challenges to internal validity that apply specifically to the random groups design. We will then consider two alternative experimental designs involving independent groups: the matched groups design and the natural groups design. We will also describe special control and design problems that are applicable to the independent groups designs. Once we have covered the basics of the independent groups design, we will turn our attention to data analysis. Our discussion of data analysis will include the general logic of null hypothesis testing and specific procedures for performing the most commonly used statistical test in the analysis of experiments, the analysis of variance.

CHARACTERISTICS OF SOUND EXPERIMENTS

Up to this point we have been discussing research methods that serve primarily to meet the *descriptive* function of the science of psychology. Psychologists use observational methods to develop detailed descriptions of behavior, often in natural settings. Survey research methods allow psychologists to describe people's attitudes and opinions. The analysis of archival data provides a nonreactive means of obtaining converging evidence to enhance the validity of the descriptions of behavior that are based on observation and survey research. As essential as they are to the scientific study of behavior, descriptive methods are not sufficient. Psychologists seek to move beyond description to understanding—the *why* behind the *what* of behavior. As we mentioned in Chapter 1, scientific understanding is achieved when the causes of a phenomenon have been identified. This part focuses on the best available research method for specifying *causal* relationships: the experimental method.

The distinction between experimental methods and descriptive research methods should not be drawn too sharply. Observation, survey research, and archival data can certainly contribute to our understanding of the causes of behavior. Field experiments and longitudinal survey research designs clearly embody the principles of the experimental methods, although we have discussed them in the context of descriptive research methods. Similarly, experimental methods can be used effectively to develop accurate descriptions of behavior, especially when the methods are applied to practical research problems such as those involving the effectiveness of a behavior modification program (see Chapter 8). Perhaps the best approach to research is the multimethod approach (see Chapter 4). If researchers reach comparable conclusions about a research question after using different methods to study it, our confidence in their conclusions increases. The conclusions are said to have *convergent validity*. Each method has different shortcomings, but the methods have complementary strengths that overcome these shortcomings. The experimental method, however, is especially effective in establishing cause-and-effect relationships.

An experiment involves the *manipulation* of one or more factors and measurement of the effects of this manipulation on behavior. The factors that the researcher controls or manipulates are called the independent variables. The measures that are used to assess the effect (if any) of the independent variables are called **dependent variables.** For example, students might be asked to listen to a tape of segments of either familiar or unfamiliar rock songs. Song segments would be played varying numbers of times and the students' task would be to estimate how many times each segment had been played. In this experiment the familiarity of the songs would be the independent variable and the students' estimates of the songs' frequencies would be the dependent variable.

Four characteristics distinguish sound experiments from unsound experiments. Sound experiments are internally valid, reliable, sensitive, and externally valid. An *internally valid experiment* is one in which other plausible causes for the outcome that was obtained have been ruled out. The purpose of an experiment is to produce a difference in behavior; thus, a *reliable experiment* is one in which the obtained difference is likely to be found again if the experiment is repeated. Independent variables differ in terms of how large an effect they have on behavior. A *sensitive experiment* is one that is likely to detect the effect of an independent variable even when that effect is a small one. The findings of an *externally valid experiment* are generalizable to individuals, settings, and conditions beyond the scope of the specific experiment. Unfortunately, the four characteristics of a sound experiment cannot always be maximized simultaneously. For instance, the procedures that increase the sensitivity of an experiment can reduce its external validity. Nonetheless, the goal of the following chapters is to prepare you to conduct sound experiments, to interpret them appropriately, and to analyze them properly.

EXPERIMENTAL CONTROL

Three aspects of control are involved in implementing a particular research design: *manipulation, holding conditions constant,* and *balancing.* As we mentioned in Chapter 1, these three aspects of control share a common objective: to meet the three conditions necessary for a causal inference (covariation, time order, and elimination of plausible alternative causes) and thereby to ensure the internal validity of the experiment. The covariation condition is met when we observe systematic changes in the dependent variable as a function of the manipulated independent variable. That is, when the experimenter changes the level of the independent variable, the subjects' responses as measured by the dependent variable also change. Because we manipulate the independent variable *before* measuring the changes in the dependent variable, the time order condition is also met. Other factors that could influence subjects' performance must be controlled either by holding them constant or by balancing in order to meet the third and most critical condition of eliminating plausible alternative causes.

An experiment from the classic series of studies by Harlow on the development of affectional responses in rhesus monkeys illustrates these principles of control (Harlow, 1958; Harlow and Harlow, 1969). The purpose of the experiments was to assess the relative importance of two factors in the development of bonding between infant and mother: contact comfort (the softness of the mother's body) and nourishment (the opportunity to nurse at the mother's breast). Harlow constructed two types of surrogate mothers that differed in their ability to provide contact comfort (see Figure 5.1). The "cloth

FIGURE 5.1   Cloth and wire mother-surrogates were used to test the preferences of infant monkeys. The infants spent most of their time clinging to the soft cloth "mother" (*right*), even when nursing bottles were attached to the wire mother (*left*). (*From Harlow.*)

mother" was made of wood with a sponge rubber cover wrapped with terry cloth and with a light bulb behind the surrogate mother to radiate heat. The "wire mother" was made of wire mesh and warmed by radiant heat. By holding other factors constant, Harlow (1958) ensured that the wire mother "differs in no essential way from that of the cloth mother surrogate other than in the quality of the contact comfort which she can supply" (p. 676). The results of Harlow's research were clear-cut—the infant monkeys spent much more time in contact with the cloth mother regardless of which surrogate mother provided nourishment.

In order for a valid comparison of the effects of these two types of surrogate mothers to be made, it was essential that they differ only in degree of contact comfort. If, for example, Harlow had allowed the cloth surrogate mother to radiate heat while the wire mother was cold, then any differences in time spent in contact with the two surrogates could have been due to the warmth and not just to the softness of the cloth mother. The warmth and softness of the two mothers would have been "confounded." Holding warmth constant avoided this **confounding,** because a factor that does not change cannot possibly covary with the intended independent variable.

It is important to recognize, however, that we choose to control only those factors that we think might influence the behavior of interest. For example, look closely at the two surrogate mothers pictured in Figure 5.1. Notice that the heads, and especially the faces, of the two surrogates are not identical.[1] The round shape and pronounced eyes of the cloth mother may be more attractive to the infants than the rigid face and "beady" eyes of the wire mother. Harlow apparently assumed that these facial differences were irrelevant, because he described the two surrogates as differing in no essential way other than in quality of contact comfort. It is unlikely that the large difference in time spent on the two surrogates was solely attributable to these facial differences, but the facial differences are nonetheless confounded with the contact comfort differences. The point of this discussion is that we control only those factors we believe are potentially relevant. For instance, Haber and Haber (1982) equated their tongue-twister and control sentences in grammatical complexity, syllable count, and pattern of stressed syllables because previous research had shown that these three factors influenced the speed with which sentences could be read. Nevertheless, we should constantly remain alert to the possibility that there may be confounding factors in our experiments whose influence we had not anticipated.

The third type of experimental control in addition to manipulation and holding conditions constant is balancing. For example, consider that you were going to do an experiment and had two rooms available for testing. You could choose to control any potential effect of the testing room by using only one room thereby holding this factor constant. Balancing gives you another option. You could use both rooms but you would have to be sure that the

---

[1]We are grateful to our colleague Tom Ludwig for pointing out this difference to us.

same number of subjects is tested in each room in each of your experimental conditions. We will discuss a specific technique for carrying out this balancing later in this chapter. At this point it is important that you recognize that balancing provides a third control technique that is effective.

For factors such as testing rooms, the use of balancing or holding conditions constant is optional. For at least one set of factors, however, balancing is the only control option. This set of factors is the characteristics of the subjects tested. Researchers have two types of designs from which to choose in dealing with these factors: the independent groups designs and the within-subjects designs. Both types of designs control factors that are not manipulated and that cannot be held constant by balancing the influence of these factors across the levels of the independent variable. In the **independent groups designs,** each group represents a different condition as defined by the level of the independent variable. The most common type of independent groups design is the **random groups design.** In this design, the groups are formed in such a way that they are presumed to be equal at the start of the experiment. Then, if the groups perform differently, it is presumed that the independent variable is responsible. In Chapter 6 we will discuss the appropriate balancing techniques in within-subjects designs in which there is only one group of subjects, all of whom are given all the treatments in the experiment. In the present chapter, we will examine the most commonly used design involving independent groups of subjects, the random groups design.

RANDOM GROUPS DESIGN

RANDOM SELECTION VERSUS RANDOM ASSIGNMENT

The simplest experiments involve two *conditions*. That is, two levels of an independent variable are administered to subjects, and differences in the dependent variable between these two levels of the independent variable are used to measure the effect of the independent variable. In the independent groups design, each level represents a different group of subjects. In an experiment done by Loftus and Burns (1982), for example, one group of subjects was assigned to view a violent version of a film while a second group of subjects viewed a nonviolent version. Both groups were then tested for their memory of details included in the films. As we mentioned earlier, the logic of the design is straightforward. If the two groups are equivalent on all important characteristics at the start of the experiment *and* if, in the experiment itself, the two groups are treated the same *except* for the level of the independent variable, then, if the two groups perform differently, the difference must be due to the independent variable.

In a *random groups design*, equivalent groups are formed prior to the introduction of the independent variable. This is accomplished by sampling subjects in a way that ensures that each subject has an equal likelihood of being included in each group of the experiment. In practice, there are two ways to do this: random selection and random assignment. We discussed random selection procedures when we introduced survey research designs (see Chapter 3). Briefly, *random selection* involves drawing two or more random samples from the same population. Sampling theory assures us that, on the average, these randomly selected samples will not differ at the start of the experiment. In addition, we know that random samples, if sufficiently large, are representative of the population from which they were drawn. Thus random selection contributes to the internal validity of the experiment by balancing the differences among subjects across groups, and it enhances the external validity of the results by ensuring that the samples are representative.

Although random selection *could* be used to form equivalent groups, it is used only rarely in psychology experiments. When descriptive research methods such as surveys are used, it is essential that the samples be representative of a well-defined population. After all, the goal of descriptive research is to describe a population by observing only a sample of it. In experiments, however, the emphasis is on identifying the independent variable as the source of the difference between otherwise comparable groups. Usually, populations of potential participants in psychology experiments are defined by convenience. For instance, human subjects are often students from introductory psychology courses who volunteer for experiments for extra course credit. Animal subjects are those who happen to be shipped to the researcher by the supplier. Although you could form equivalent groups by randomly selecting subjects, the procedure would be time-consuming and impractical. And you would not enhance the external validity of your experiment by drawing random samples from such ill-defined populations. The most common solution to the problem of forming equivalent groups is to *assign* subjects randomly to the conditions of the experiment.

A closer look at the details of the Loftus and Burns (1982) experiment will illustrate both the procedures of **random assignment** and the power of the random groups design. Their experiment concerned the effect of viewing a violent scene on a person's memory for information that was processed seconds before the individual witnessed the mentally shocking event. The experiment was done at the University of Washington, and 226 students volunteered to participate in order to fulfill a course requirement. The students participated in small groups and each small group was randomly assigned to view one of two films. Approximately half of the subjects (115) were assigned to view a violent version of a film. Near the end of the film these subjects saw a robber, while running to a getaway car, turn and fire a shot toward two men who are pursuing him. The shot hits a boy in the face and the boy falls bleeding to the ground. The other half of the subjects viewed a nonviolent version of the film that was identical to the violent version until just before the shooting. At this point in the film the camera switches back to inside the bank, where subjects see the bank manager telling the customers and employees what has happened and asking them to remain calm. The two versions of the film (violent and nonviolent) represent the levels of the independent variable in the experiment.

After viewing the film, subjects in both groups were asked to answer twenty-five questions about events in the film. One question was critical; it asked for the number on the football jersey worn by a boy playing in the parking lot outside the bank. The boy wearing the jersey was visible for 2 seconds during the film—the 2 seconds before the shooting (violent version) or the 2 seconds before the scenes back in the bank (nonviolent version). The dependent variable was the percentage of subjects who correctly recalled the jersey number. The results were clear-cut: just over 4 percent of the subjects correctly recalled the number in the violent condition, whereas nearly 28 percent did so in the nonviolent condition.

The major benefit of randomly assigning subjects to groups is to balance the characteristics of the subjects in the two groups. These two random samples of over one hundred subjects are unlikely to differ, on the average, in memory ability, in attentiveness, or in any other way that might influence their performance on the memory test. Thus, if they had seen the same version of the film, their performance would not have been expected to differ. Moreover, it is important to remember that random assignment was not the only method of control used in the Loftus and Burns (1982) experiment. For instance, the equipment used to present the films, the quality of the films, the instructions given prior to showing the films, the tone of voice used by the experimenter in giving these instructions, and any other factors that could be controlled by being held constant were identical in the two conditions of the experiment. Because subjects' performances *did* differ, and because other potential causal factors were controlled, we conclude that the different versions of the film caused the difference in test performance.

The balancing accomplished through random assignment applies to factors other than the characteristics of the subjects. It is unlikely, for example, that Loftus and Burns were able to hold the temperature of the room constant during the various showings of the films. These variations in room temperature would threaten the internal validity of the experiment only if they systematically covaried with the levels of the independent variable, the two types of films. The random assignment of small groups of subjects to the two film conditions makes it unlikely that the room was consistently warmer or colder when the violent film was shown. Thus, although most of us associate the concept of control with holding conditions constant, the balancing accomplished through random assignment is an equally effective control technique. The most common procedure for carrying out random assignment, **block randomization,** is described in Box 5.1.

ESTABLISHING EXTERNAL VALIDITY

As we have already mentioned, random assignment, not random selection, is the most commonly used procedure for carrying out a random groups design. And random assignment alone is not sufficient to ensure that the results can be generalized beyond the particular subjects who happened to par-

BOX 5.1

BUILDING BLOCKS OF RANDOM ASSIGNMENT

Picture a researcher who is preparing to conduct a random groups design experiment. Now envision a long line of participants outside the door to the laboratory. As each participant gets to the door, he or she must be assigned to one of the conditions of the experiment. This long line never actually forms because human participants usually make an individual appointment to come to the laboratory at a prearranged time, and animal participants are brought from the animal room to the laboratory one at a time. Nonetheless, the image of the long line of participants gives you a good way to think about the process of assigning subjects to conditions over the course of the entire experiment. One way to assign participants to conditions would be to use simple random assignment, with each individual independently randomly assigned to a condition. When the experiment to be performed called for only two conditions, a simple coin toss or odd-even roll of a die would suffice for assigning subjects to a condition. Another alternative would be to use the Table of Random Numbers in Appendix A and assign odd-numbered entries to one group and even-numbered entries to the other group.

There is one minor problem with the use of simple random assignment. The different groups in the experiment are unlikely to come out with equal numbers of subjects. This problem of unequal numbers in each group becomes especially troublesome when you have five or six different conditions in the experiment. There are two advantages to having equal sample sizes in each group of a random groups design. The first advantage is that statistical computations with hand calculators are easier with equal sample sizes. The second, and perhaps more important, advantage concerns the reliability of the descriptive statistics that you use to summarize the results in each group of the experiment. Because the number of observations contributing to a descriptive statistic influences the reliability of that measure, and because you will be comparing such descriptive statistics across the groups in your experiment, the measures taken in each group should be based on the same number of observations. With small numbers of conditions and large samples within each condition, this concern with equal-sized groups is a very minor one. For example, in the study done by Loftus and Burns (1982) two groups of 115 and 111 subjects were tested. These two sample sizes clearly provide equally reliable estimates of performance. As the number of conditions increases and the sample size within each condition decreases, however, it becomes more critical that the groups contain equal numbers of subjects. Fortunately, a technique is available for randomly assigning subjects to groups in such a way that the groups will be of equal size. This technique is called *block randomization*.

A block in a block-randomized schedule is made up of a random order of the conditions of the experiment. If our experiment involved five conditions (A, B, C, D, and E), then the first five subjects in our fictitious line outside the laboratory would constitute the first block, and one of these five individuals would be assigned to each of the five conditions. The next five individuals would make up the second block, and each of them would similarly be randomly assigned to one of the five conditions. In block randomization, one subject is assigned to *each* group before a second subject is assigned to *any* group. There are as many blocks in the block-randomized schedule as there are subjects in each group of the experiment. For example, if we wanted to have twenty subjects in each of five groups, then there would be twenty blocks in our block-randomized schedule. Each block would be formed using the Random Number Table in Appendix A. We would assign each condition a number, such as A = 1, B = 2, C = 3, D = 4, and E = 5, and then enter the Random Number Table. If the sequence in the random number table were 1-4-1-9-4-6-2-5-9-0-3-6, then (ignoring repeated numbers and numbers higher than 5) the first block in our schedule would be A-D-B-E-C. Thus the first participant would be tested in Group A, the second in Group D, etc. We form each successive block in the same way. The result is a schedule by which we can ran-

Subject	Name	Condition	Dropped subject
1	J.Swim	A	
2	D.DeWolff	D	
3	D.Morier	B	
4	E. Greij/J. Gentile	E	E.Greij
5	R. Cutler	C	
6		D	
7		B	
8		E	
9		C	
10		A	
11		E	
12		C	
13		D	
14		A	
15		B	
16		E	
17		B	
18		D	
19		C	
20		A	

domly assign each subject in the long line outside our laboratory to a condition and end up with equal numbers of subjects in each group.

The table in this box shows a partially completed portion of a block-randomized schedule. Each subject is given a number, which also appears on any data sheets for that subject in the experiment. In this way, the subject can be identified while the confidentiality of the subject's data is maintained. The subject's name is recorded so that the experimenter can be sure not to test the same person more than once. If a subject begins the experiment but fails to complete it successfully, the subject's name appears on the block sheet under the column "dropped subject," and the reason why the subject did not complete the experiment should be recorded on the back of the block sheet. (See the section on challenges to internal validity, later in this chapter, for a discussion of the problem of subject loss.) The dropped subject is replaced by the next subject who comes to the laboratory. The block sheets contain a vital record of the sequence in which subjects were tested. It should be carefully prepared before beginning the experiment and followed closely throughout the experiment. It represents one of the basic building blocks of a good experiment.

ticipate in the experiment. How, then, do we establish the external validity of experiments?

One answer to this question is a bit unsettling, at least initially. For some experiments we do not establish external validity. Mook (1983) has argued that, when the purpose of an experiment is to test a specific hypothesis derived from a psychological theory, the question of the external validity of the findings is irrelevant. An experiment is often done to determine whether subjects *can* be induced to behave in a certain way. The question of whether subjects *do* behave that way in their natural environment is secondary to the question raised in the experiment. The issue of the external validity of experiments is not a new one, as reflected in the following statement by Riley (1962, p. 413):

> In general, laboratory experiments are not set up to imitate the most typical case found in nature. Instead, they are intended to answer some specific question of interest to the experimenter.

There are occasions, however, in which it *is* critical to obtain results that can be generalized beyond the boundaries of the experiment itself. It is important in these instances to obtain representative samples on all dimensions on which we wish to generalize. In experiments of this type, random selection of subjects is preferable to random assignment. Keep in mind, however, that random selection of subjects ensures only that we can generalize our results to the population from which we drew our subjects. If we also want to generalize our results to specific settings, for example, we must be equally careful to select a representative sample of settings in our experiment. The general rule is a simple one. The results of our experiment can be generalized on any dimension on which we have included a representative sample.

External validity is not likely to be established on the basis of the results of a single experiment. Instead, as Underwood and Shaughnessy (1975) have argued, the generality of a research finding is established through the continuity assumption and, more important, through replication. The **continuity assumption** asserts that we should assume that behavior is relatively continuous across time, subjects, and settings unless we have reason to assume otherwise. Researchers use the continuity assumption as an initial basis for generalization. For instance, most experiments are carried out in individual laboratory rooms, but we would not be likely to argue that the results of the experiment apply only to those particular rooms. Similarly, the particular subjects tested in an experiment are considered, according to the continuity assumption, to be generally representative of other similar individuals who might have been tested. The continuity assumption is not a call to blind faith. It is based on the fact that the history of research in psychology offers a wealth of examples of replicated findings.

Replication involves repeating the exact procedures used in an experiment to determine whether the same results are obtained. When the same experiment is done in a large metropolitan public university and in a small rural private college, the subjects and settings in the experiment are very different. When we obtain the same results in these two replications of the experiment, we can be confident that the findings are not peculiar to the particular types of subjects tested in each experiment or to the particular setting in which either experiment was performed. Notice that neither experiment alone has external validity; it is the findings that occur in both experiments that have external validity.

The boundaries of the continuity assumption are set by consensus of the research community. The research community may agree, for example, that introductory psychology students who volunteer for experiments are representative of college students in general but not of young children or of the elderly. There is always a technique available, however, to test the limits of the continuity assumption. The technique involves *including the dimension on which you want to generalize as an independent variable* in your experiment. Singer (1982) noted that most studies conducted on reading comprehension in the past decade had been based on reading in the laboratory. He was concerned that laboratory reading might involve goals or techniques different from those used in natural reading. In Singer's experiment, subjects who had not read a particular newspaper article were asked to read the article in the laboratory. These subjects were then given the same memory tests that had been given to subjects who had read the article outside the laboratory. The two groups performed similarly on the tests, leading to Singer's conclusion: "These effects, coupled with the similarity of the natural and laboratory readers, provide reassurance that it is reasonable to treat laboratory reading as an approximation of natural reading" (p. 331). Such direct tests of the continuity assumption represent perhaps the best way to establish the external validity of research findings.

CHALLENGES TO INTERNAL VALIDITY

Balancing Nuisance Factors A number of factors in an experiment may vary as a result of practical considerations in carrying out the study. For example, in order to complete an experiment more quickly, a researcher might decide to test small groups of participants having several different experimenters do the testing. The sizes of the groups and the experimenters themselves become potentially relevant variables that could confound the experiment if their effects are not somehow balanced across conditions. If all the subjects in the experimental group were tested by one experimenter and all those in the control group were tested by a second experimenter, differences between the experimenters would confound the intended independent variable.

Potential independent variables that are not directly of interest to the researcher but serve only as vexing sources of confounding can be called **nuisance factors.** But don't let the term fool you! An experiment confounded by such nuisance factors is no less confounded than if the confounding factor were of considerable inherent interest. For instance, if all the small groups in one condition of the experiment included two or three subjects, while all those in another condition included eight or nine subjects, any difference between these two conditions *could* result from the influence of the different group sizes on subjects' performance. Evans and Donnerstein (1974) studied a similar nuisance factor, specifically, differences among subjects who volunteer early in the term as compared to those who volunteer late in the term.

Their results indicated that those who volunteered early were more academically oriented and were more likely to have an internal locus of control (to emphasize their responsibility for their actions rather than to emphasize external factors). These findings suggest it would not be wise to test an additional control group at the end of the term if the subjects in the other conditions of the completed experiment had been tested in the first half of the term.

Fortunately, block randomization provides an easy and effective way to balance nuisance factors (see Box 5.1). All that is required is that entire blocks be tested at each level of the nuisance variable. Normally, the blocks of a block-randomized schedule are tested sequentially—the first block, then the second block, and so on. It is possible, however, to balance the possible effects of nuisance variables by assigning different blocks to each of the levels of the nuisance variable. For example, if there were four different experimenters, entire blocks of the block-randomized schedule would be assigned to each experimenter. Because each block contains all the critical conditions of the experiment, this strategy guarantees that each condition has been tested by each experimenter. We would probably assign the same number of blocks to each experimenter, but this is not essential. What is essential is that whole blocks be tested at each level of the nuisance factor. The balancing act can become a bit tricky when there are several nuisance factors, but careful advance planning can avoid confounding by such factors.

Even when their potential effects have been neutralized through balancing, nuisance factors affect the sensitivity and generality (external validity) of an experiment. For example, if five different experimenters test an equal number of subjects in each of two conditions, the experiment will be free of confounding due to the differences across experimenters. The performance of the subjects *within* each condition, however, is likely to vary more than if one experimenter had tested all the subjects. Subjects are likely, after all, to respond differently to the different experimenters, even when the experimenters try to treat all subjects within a condition the same way. This increased variation within each group makes it harder to detect differences between the groups, thus reducing the sensitivity of the experiment. If a difference is obtained between the two conditions, however, this finding has greater generality than it would have had if only one experimenter had done the testing.

The general principle that emerges is that controlling nuisance factors by holding them constant leads to more sensitive experiments with less generality, whereas controlling nuisance factors by balancing leads to lower sensitivity but increased generality. Both balancing and holding nuisance factors constant are equally effective, however, in meeting the primary objective of a sound experiment: ensuring that the experiment is internally valid.

Subject Loss Internally valid experiments involving the random groups design need not only to start with comparable groups but also to end with comparable groups. When subjects begin an experiment but fail to complete the experiment successfully, the internal validity of the experiment is threatened. There are two types of subject loss, mechanical and selective. Only selective subject loss poses a threat to internal validity (Underwood and Shaughnessy, 1975). **Mechanical subject loss** occurs when a subject fails to complete the experiment because of an equipment failure, and in this instance the experimenter is considered part of the equipment. If a light bulb burns out, or if someone inadvertently interrupts an experimental session, or if the experimenter reads the wrong set of instructions, the subject who was being tested represents a mechanical subject loss. Mechanical loss is unrelated to any characteristic of the subject, so it should not lead to systematic differences between the characteristics of the subjects who successfully complete the experiment in the various conditions of the experiment. When mechanical subject loss occurs, the name of the dropped subject and the reason for the loss are recorded on the block-randomized schedule. The lost subject is then simply replaced by the next subject who is tested.

Selective subject loss is a far more serious matter. **Selective subject loss** occurs when subjects are lost differentially across the conditions of the experiment and some characteristic of the subject that is related to the outcome of the study is responsible for the loss. Selective subject loss destroys the equivalence of groups that is essential to the random groups design and can render the experiment uninterpretable. This problem can arise in a variety of experimental situations—physiological studies involving surgical or drug treatments, memory experiments testing retention over days or weeks, and longitudinal survey research designs (see Chapter 3). For our purposes, the problems associated with selective subject loss can be illustrated by considering a fictitious but realistic example.

Assume that the directors of a local fitness center decide to do an experiment to test the effectiveness of a one-week fitness program they have developed. They identify eighty people who are willing to volunteer for the experiment, and they randomly assign forty to each of two groups. Members of the control group are simply asked to come to the center on Friday and they are given a fitness test. Those in the experimental group participate in the fitness program for one week prior to the Friday test. All forty control subjects are given the final fitness test, but only twenty-five of the experimental subjects stay with the rigorous fitness program and only these twenty-five people are given the final test. The average final fitness score is significantly higher for the experimental group, leading the directors of the fitness center to insert in the brochure describing their program the following claim: "A scientifically based research study has shown that our program leads to better fitness."

Is the fitness center's claim justified? Not on the basis of the study we have described. This example perfectly fits the criteria for selective subject loss. The loss occurred differentially across conditions in that subjects were lost only from the experimental group. The problem is *not* that the groups ended up different in size. If twenty-five people had been randomly assigned to the experimental group and forty to the control group, and all subjects had completed the experiment, the results would have been interpretable (although the results in each group would have had slightly different reliabilities). The problem is that the twenty-five experimental subjects who were tested are not likely to be comparable to the forty control subjects. In addition to occurring differentially, the loss is traceable to a characteristic of the subjects, and this characteristic is relevant to the outcome of the study: their original level of fitness. It is reasonable to expect that only the more fit experimental subjects could complete the rigorous program. Accordingly, their final fitness scores might have been higher even if they had not taken the fitness program!

If selective subject loss is not identified until after the experiment is completed, little can be done except to chalk up the experience of having conducted an uninterpretable experiment. Some preventive steps can be taken, however, if the researcher realizes in advance that selective loss may be a problem. One alternative is to administer a pretest and screen out subjects who are likely to be lost. In our example, an initial test of fitness could have been given and only those subjects who scored above some minimal level would have been allowed into the experimental and the control groups. The cost associated with this alternative is decreased generality because the results could be generalized only to people above the minimal fitness level. However, an interpretable study of limited generality seems preferable to an uninterpretable study.

The second way to minimize the risk of selective subject loss also involves a pretest. Here all subjects are given the pretest, but they are then simply randomly assigned to one of the conditions. Then, if a subject is lost from the experimental group, a subject with a comparable pretest score is dropped from the control group. In a sense, this approach tries to restore the comparability of the groups, but once again, the cost of this approach is decreased generality. The advantage of this approach is that generality is lost only if selective subject loss *does* occur. When a pretest is used in this situation, it is essential that it be a measure of the dimension responsible for the loss. For instance, a pretest of visual acuity could not be used to restore the comparability of groups in our fitness example.

ALTERNATIVE INDEPENDENT GROUPS DESIGNS

MATCHED GROUPS DESIGN

The random groups design is by far the most common variant of the independent groups design. To function effectively, however, the random groups design requires samples of sufficient size to guarantee that individual differences among subjects will average out across groups. The number of subjects required for a sufficient sample size cannot be specified exactly, because the required number increases as the heterogeneity of the population from which the subjects are drawn increases. However, we can be relatively confident that, when small numbers of subjects are tested from heterogeneous populations, random assignment will not suffice to balance the differences among subjects. This is exactly the situation researchers face in several areas of psychology. For example, some developmental psychologists study newborn infants and others study elderly people. These psychologists often have available only limited numbers of subjects, and both newborns and the elderly certainly represent diverse populations.

One alternative that researchers have in this situation is to administer all the treatments to all the subjects, using the within-subjects designs that we will discuss in the next chapter. Some independent variables require separate groups of subjects for each level, however, and for these variables the within-subjects designs are of no use. For instance, when the effects of participation in a special program for senior citizens are being assessed, a separate control group that does not participate in the program is essential. The matched groups design is a viable alternative when neither the random groups design nor the within-subjects designs can be used effectively.

The logic of the **matched groups design** is simple and compelling. Instead of trusting randomization in the formation of comparable groups, the researcher makes the groups equal by matching subjects. One approach to accomplishing the matching that is used in research with animals is the *split-litter technique*. The offspring from the same litter are randomly assigned to different conditions. The genetic similarity of the offspring constitutes the basis for the matching. The different experimental groups are expected to be comparable initially even if only relatively few subjects are in each group. A similar approach to the matched groups design is used when identical twins are the subjects. Since identical twins are homozygotic (develop from a single zygote) their genetic makeup is the same. Thus, if one in each set of pairs of twins is assigned to one of two experimental groups, the groups should be comparable. Studies involving identical twins have been critical in research examining whether intellectual abilities (i.e., IQ) are influenced more by hereditary or by environment (see discussion of IQ research in Appendix B).

Most uses of the matched groups design do not involve the split-litter technique or the testing of identical twins. Instead, a pretest task is used to match subjects. The challenge in this approach to the matched groups design is *to select a pretest task* (also called a *matching task*) *that equates the groups on a dimension that is relevant to the outcome of the experiment.* We discussed a similar problem earlier in this chapter when we described techniques to deal with the problem of subject loss. We noted then that it is of little help to match subjects on visual acuity if the experiment is designed to test subjects' physical fitness. Similarly, the matched groups design is useful only when a good matching task is available.

Researchers have three options in selecting a matching task. The most widely preferred option is to match subjects on the same task that will be used in the experiment itself. If the dependent variable in the experiment will be blood pressure, subjects should be matched on blood pressure. The matching is accomplished by measuring the blood pressure of all subjects and then forming pairs or triples or quadruples of subjects (depending on the number of conditions in the experiment) who have identical or similar blood pressures. After these matched sets are formed, the investigator must assign subjects randomly to the conditions of the experiment in order to balance individual differences other than those included in the matching task.

In some experiments, the experimental task cannot be used as the matching task. For example, if the experiment involved various approaches to solving a puzzle and a pretest were given to see how long it took subjects to solve the puzzle, their learning the solution to the puzzle during the pretest would make it impossible to observe differences in the speed with which the same problem could be solved in the experiment itself. After having experience with the puzzle in the pretest, all subjects might solve the puzzle very quickly. The next best alternative to using the experimental task as the matching task is to use a task from the same class as the experimental task. In our problem-solving experiment, subjects could be matched on their performance solving a different puzzle from the experimental puzzle, so long as it had been shown that performance on the experimental puzzle correlated with performance on the matching puzzle. The least preferred alternative is to use a task from a class different from the experimental task. For our problem-solving experiment, subjects could be matched on some test of general ability such as an intelligence test. Once again, to be useful, this general matching task must correlate with performance on the experimental task.

The matched groups design is not without problems. Several of these problems arise from practical considerations in carrying out the matching. Matching requires testing each subject twice (once on the matching task and once on the experimental task). It is often difficult to find appropriate matches for all subjects. Even when matched sets of subjects can be obtained, the matching process may so severely restrict the people included in the study that the groups may no longer be representative of the general population. For example, in an experiment involving a comparison of the emotional disorders of college students with those of elderly people who had been matched for general health and amount of education, the researcher would be studying a very unrepresentative group of the elderly population.

A more serious problem with matching, however, is that the matching task ensures comparable groups *only* on the dimension measured by the matching task. There are many potentially relevant characteristics of the subjects in addition to those assessed by the matching task. The groups must also be comparable on these other characteristics if any differences that emerge between groups are to be attributed solely to the effect of the independent variable. Random assignment bears the burden of balancing these additional factors, and, as we mentioned at the beginning of this section, we turn to the matched groups design when we fear that randomization may not be sufficient to accomplish this balancing. Nonetheless, when only a small number of subjects is available for an experiment that requires separate groups for each treatment, and when a good matching task is available, the matched groups design is a better alternative than the random groups design.[2]

NATURAL GROUPS DESIGN

So far we have been considering individual differences among subjects as a pesky source of potential confounding that must be neutralized in our experiments. In many areas of psychology, such as personality research, abnormal psychology, and social psychology, individual differences represent much more than a source of confounding and error variation. The characteristics that subjects bring with them to the laboratory (called *subject variables*), such as their gender, their degree of introversion-extroversion, or their aggressiveness, are important variables in many areas of psychology. Subject variables are different from manipulated independent variables because researchers *select* the levels of subject variables. They do so, however, to determine systematic relationships between the subject variables and other aspects of behavior. As such, subject variables are usually treated as if they were independent variables. To differentiate experiments involving subject variables and those involving manipulated independent variables we refer to those involving subject variables as **natural groups designs.**

The natural groups design can also be used in situations when ethical and practical constraints limit the scope of problems that can be studied by directly manipulating independent variables. No matter how interested we might be in the effects of traumatic events such as major surgery on subsequent depression, we could not ethically perform major surgery on a randomly selected group of introductory psychology students and compare them with another group of students on whom we did not perform surgery! Similarly, if we were interested in the relationship between divorce and emotional disorders, we could not randomly assign some people to get divorced. By using the natural groups design, however, we can compare people who have had surgery to those who have not. Similarly, people who have chosen to become divorced can be compared with those who have chosen to stay married. The intent of these studies is to determine whether these natural treatments result in other systematic differences between the groups. For example, studies have shown that people who are separated or divorced are much more likely to receive psychiatric care than are those who are married, who are widowed, or who have remained single (Bloom et al., 1978). The natural groups design essentially involves looking for correlations between subjects' characteristics and their performance. Because of this, these designs are also called *correlational research designs* (see also Chapter 3).

---

[2]The analysis procedures for the matched groups design are different from those for the random groups design. McGuigan (1983) provides a good introduction to the procedures for the matched groups design.

Natural groups designs are highly effective in meeting the first two objectives of the scientific method—description and prediction. Unfortunately, serious problems can arise when the results of these designs are used as a basis for causal inference. People have a tendency to conclude that all three conditions for a causal inference have been met when really only the first condition, covariation, has been met. For instance, the finding that divorced persons are more likely than married persons to receive psychiatric care shows that these two factors covary. This result could be taken to mean that divorce causes emotional disorders that lead to the need for psychiatric care. Before reaching this conclusion, however, we must assure ourselves that the time-order condition for a causal inference has been met—namely, that divorce *preceded* the emotional disorder. Demonstrating covariation does nothing to specify the *direction* of the causal relationship. Perhaps those who suffer from emotional disorders are more likely to get divorced because of the strain placed on the relationship by the disorder or because the emotional disorder contributed to their marrying unwisely in the first place.

The most critical problem in drawing causal inferences based on the natural groups design is in meeting the third condition for demonstrating causality: eliminating plausible alternative causes. As you might suspect, this problem arises because the experimenter has far less control in the natural groups design. The subject variables being studied in the natural groups design are usually confounded. For example, introverts and extroverts differ with respect to a number of characteristics other than their degree of introversion. For example, extroverts are apt to prefer excitement and practical jokes but not like quiet reading, while introverts generally show the opposite pattern. The manipulation done "by nature" is rarely the controlled type we have come to expect in establishing the internal validity of an experiment. The most effective approach to the problem of confounding in the natural groups design is *to study subject variables in combination with independent variables that can be manipulated.* We will be discussing the procedures for experiments involving more than one independent variable in Chapter 7. We will resume our discussion of the natural groups design in Chapter 7 after we have covered the basics of complex designs. For now, it is sufficient for you to recognize that drawing causal inferences based on the natural groups design is a treacherous enterprise.

SPECIAL CONTROL AND DESIGN PROBLEMS

PLACEBO CONTROL AND DOUBLE-BLIND EXPERIMENTS

Additional problems of control may arise in psychology experiments because of expectations held by both subjects and experimenters. In our discussion of the problem of reactivity in observational research (see Chapter 2), we introduced the concept of **demand characteristics** (Orne, 1962). As you may remember, Orne used the term to refer to the cues and other information used by subjects to guide their behavior in a psychological study. For example, if subjects knew that they had been given alcohol, they might expect certain effects such as feeling relaxed or giddy. In addition to the problems posed by subjects' expectations, there are also problems traceable to the expectations of the experimenters. These expectations may lead the experimenters to treat subjects differently in the different groups of the experiment in ways other than those required to implement the independent variable. The experimenters' observations may also be biased by their knowing which treatment the subject has received. Continuing with our alcohol experiment example, experimenters might read the instructions more slowly to subjects who had been given alcohol. The experimenters might also be more likely to notice any unusual motor movements or slurred speech among the "drinkers." The general term used to describe these biases is **experimenter effects** (Rosenthal, 1963).

The problems of demand characteristics and experimenter effects can never be eliminated, but their effects can be greatly diminished by following the principles of sound research methods. Every effort must be made to ensure that the only systematic difference in the way subjects are treated across the groups of the experiment is traceable to the independent variable of interest. The more mechanized the procedures for administering instructions and recording results, for example, the less likely it is that problems with experimenter effects will arise.

One approach to these problems is to do an experiment to see just how serious the problems are. Intons-Peterson (1983) directly manipulated experimenters' expectations to determine the effects of these expectations on subject responses in a number of different tests that the experimenters were administering to these subjects. In one experiment, imaginal and perceptual scanning of maps were compared. Subjects were asked to estimate the distances between two cities either while looking at a map or while imagining the map. One group of experimenters was led to believe that subjects' estimates would be more accurate when the subjects were imagining the map. Other experimenters were led to expect better estimates when subjects were looking at the map. Sure enough, subjects' estimates varied with the experimenters' beliefs; that is, whichever estimates the experimenter expected to be more accurate were more accurate!

In a separate study, observers were able to identify correctly the expectations held by the experimenters, but the observers were *not* able to detect differences in the ways in which the experimenters presented the instructions. An illustration of the potentially subtle influence of demand characteristics comes from research reported by Kallio and Cutler (1987). They were testing how the wording of questions influences the accuracy of eyewitness recall. Their experiments, unlike prior studies, did not show an effect of question wording. They argued that demand characteristics may have caused the wording effects found in previous studies. Specifically, they argued that when the critical questions appear in a short questionnaire the critical items stand out and lead subjects to respond to them differently. They argued that such demand characteristics are far less likely when the critical questions are embedded in a lengthy questionnaire like the one they used. Demand characteristics may not be the only factor responsible for the discrepancy between Kallio and Cutler's (1987) findings and those of previous studies. Nonetheless, once demand characteristics and experimenter effects are known to affect subjects' performance in a certain research paradigm, the only solution is to search for tasks that allow one to study the process of interest while minimizing the impact of the expectations held by subjects and experimenters.

Special research designs are available to control for both demand characteristics and experimenter effects in experiments testing the efficacy of drugs or of an approach to therapy. The first research design involves the use of *placebo control groups.* A **placebo** (from the Latin word meaning "I shall please") is a substance that looks like a drug or other active substance but that is actually an inert, or inactive, substance. Pishkin and Shurley (1983) used a placebo control group in demonstrating the effectiveness of two drugs, doxepin and hydroxyzine, in reducing the arousal levels of psychiatric patients in response to the stress of failure on a cognitive task. The placebo subjects were given capsules that were identical to those used to administer the two drugs, but the placebo capsules contained only lactose, a sugar found in milk. Because no subject in the placebo control group realized that the pill she or he was taking contained no medicine, all the groups had the same "awareness" of taking a drug, and any differences between the experimental groups and the placebo control group could legitimately be attributed to an effect of the drug the experimental subjects took.

Placebo control groups are often used in psychotherapy research to control for the nonspecific components of the therapy situation, such as time spent with the therapist and the client's expectations of improvement. Placebo control groups in psychotherapy research generally receive treatment that is considered "theoretically inert" in that no specific procedure related to the psychotherapy is included (O'Leary and Borkevec, 1978).

Placebo control groups are typically used in combination with a second research design that even more effectively controls for demand characteristics and experimenter effects. This second design is called a **double-blind experiment** because both the subject and the observer are kept unaware of (blind to) what treatment is being administered. In an experiment such as the Pishkin and Shurley (1983) study, two researchers would be needed to accomplish the double-blind control. The first researcher would prepare the drug capsules and code each capsule in some way, and a second researcher would distribute the drugs to subjects, recording the code for each drug as it was given to a subject. Hence there would be a record of which drug each subject received, but neither the subject nor the experimenter who actually administered the drugs would know which treatment the subject had received.

YOKED-CONTROL DESIGN

Yoked control designs provide an elegant solution to a somewhat rare but challenging control problem. As an example, consider an experiment done by Joffe et al. (1973) to test the influence of control over the environment on emotionality in rats. We discussed this research in Chapter 1 in the context of the theory that motivated the experiment. Here we are focusing on the role played by the yoked-control design in this research. Members of the experimental group of animals were given control over their environment. These animals were reared in a chamber in which pressing each of three different levers controlled the delivery of food, water, and lighting. Members of the control group of animals did not have control over their environment. They were reared in an environment identical to that of the experimental animals and they received the same amount of food, water, and lighting with the same distribution schedule as in the experimental group, but delivery of these substances was not contingent on the control animals' lever pressing. The yoked-control design provided a means to meet these conditions by making the experiences of the control subjects dependent on the performance of the experimental subjects.

Joffe and coworkers literally yoked an experimental chamber to a corresponding control chamber. Whenever an experimental animal pressed one of the levers, the consequence was the same in the experimental chamber and in the control chamber. After spending 2 months in these chambers, the rats were given an open field test for 2 minutes on each of four consecutive days. The animals reared in the contingent environment (those who had control) defecated less and were more active during the open field test than were the yoked-control animals who had been reared in the noncontingent environment (those who lacked control). These results indicate that control over the environment clearly affects emotionality in rats. The greater degree of control provided by the yoked-control design increases our confidence in the validity of this important conclusion.

TESTING INTACT GROUPS

Sometimes noncomparable groups are formed even when random assignment appears to have been used. This occurs when intact groups (and not individual subjects) are randomly assigned to the conditions of an experiment. *Intact groups* are those that were formed prior to the start of the experiment. For example, the different sections of an introductory psychology class are intact groups. If a researcher were to assign different sections randomly to the different conditions in the experiment, it would be highly likely that the experiment would be confounded by differences in the characteristics of the subjects in the different groups. The introductory psychology classes were not formed randomly. They probably meet at different times of the day, have different instructors, and exhibit any number of other factors influencing the choices students made to be in their section rather than in one of the others. Random assignment of such intact groups to experimental conditions is simply not sufficient to balance the differences among the intact groups that are almost guaranteed to confound the independent variable under investigation.

The solution to this problem is simple—do not use intact groups in an independent groups design. Sometimes practical constraints may force you to test intact groups in what is called the nonequivalent control group design (see Chapter 9). In such situations, however, it is essential that some effort be made to show that the groups are comparable on dimensions that might be critical to the outcome of the experiment. For example, if you were doing a problem-solving experiment, the least you would need to do is to administer a pretest of general problem-solving ability to both groups to show that the groups were comparable on this critical dimension. It is far better, however, to avoid whenever possible the use of intact groups.

REGRESSION TO THE MEAN

The final design problem we will describe is called *regression to* (or *toward*) *the mean.* It is a problem that corresponds somewhat to several everyday expressions. We often refer to the "law of averages," or we say that "things will even out," or that "we are due" for a good day after a string of bad ones. Each of these sayings expresses that extreme experiences tend to be balanced by less extreme experiences. Cook and Campbell (1979) provide a somewhat more formal analogy but one that still makes reference to students' common experience. They suggest that you consider your own experience in taking classroom tests. Sometimes you do more poorly than you expected because you lost some sleep, because you misread some questions, or because your instructor happened to ask several questions on a portion of the text you had not studied. If you took another version of the test the next day, your score would probably be higher, even without additional study, because it is unlikely that all the negative factors affecting the first test would "gang up on you" again during the second test.

In general, a test score or a subject's score on an experimental task is made up of two components: (1) the true score, reflecting what the test is validly measuring and likely to be stable from one measurement to the next, and (2) the error component, reflecting random error and unlikely to be stable from one time to another. The error component includes nonsystematic factors such as lack of sleep and question wording that affect the measurement. This error component is what "averages out" from one measurement to another. Those who have extremely high scores on the first test are likely to score lower on a second test simply because their error component is likely to be less extreme and closer to the average. The complement is true for those with extremely low scores on the first test. Hence, the name given to this phenomenon is **regression to the mean.** The less reliable the test the more regression to the mean will occur. Levin (1982) provides an excellent demonstration of statistical regression that can be carried out by anyone who needs to be convinced that the phenomenon exists by "seeing it happen" (see Box 5.2).

Regression to the mean plays a role in experiments when subjects are selected because of their extreme scores on a pretest. For example, students

---

BOX 5.2

REGRESSION TO THE MEAN: SEEING IS BELIEVING

Levin's (1982) procedure for demonstrating regression to the mean requires two standard decks of playing cards that are designated Decks A and B. Two partial decks from Deck A are formed by removing all 7s and putting all aces, 2s, 3s, 4s, 5s, and 6s in Deck A1 and all 8s, 9s, 10s, jacks, queens, and kings in Deck A2. Deck B is left intact. You then draw three cards from Deck A1 and three cards from Deck A2 and record the sum of each draw (using ace = 1 to king = 13). You replace the cards in the two decks and repeat this process five times or so. You then compute a mean for the A1 and A2 groups.

The next step in the procedure is to draw two cards from Deck A1 *or* Deck A2 and one card from Deck B. You again sum the three cards you draw each time. The card from Deck B represents the "drifting" *due to error variation alone* of some individuals from the extreme group back to their more usual position in the general population. When you repeat this process five times for each deck, you will be able to "see regression to the mean." That is, when you compute the means for Decks A1 and A2 after drawing only two cards from Decks A1 or A2 and one from Deck B, the mean difference should be smaller than it was when all three cards were drawn only from the decks representing the "extreme groups."

---

scoring the highest and lowest on a reading test might be selected. In the experiment a reading enhancement program would be given to those scoring lowest, and those scoring highest would serve as the control group. On the surface this seems to be a stringent test because you are using the best readers as the standard for determining the effectiveness of the program. In fact, this is not a good test at all; the poorest readers are likely to do better on a subsequent test even if they didn't have the program. Similarly, the best readers are likely to do worse. Both of these changes reflect the effects of regression to the mean.

The moral of this story about regression to the mean is a simple one. If you have a treatment that is intended only for subjects at one extreme (such as a program to help poor readers), form both an experimental group and a control group from these extreme subjects so that the control group can serve as a check on regression to the mean. If you want to show that the effect appears for one extreme and not for the other, you will need four groups with half of each extreme randomly assigned to receive the treatment. Designs of this type will be explained more fully in Chapter 7. In most instances, however, these special conditions do not apply and the best way to test the effectiveness of a treatment is to use the random groups design. This approach offers the greatest generality with the fewest threats to internal validity.

ANALYSIS OF INDEPENDENT GROUPS DESIGN EXPERIMENTS

As you now know, the purpose of an experiment is to determine whether an independent variable has had an effect on behavior. Evidence for an effect is found when the different levels of the independent variable are associated with differences in the dependent variable. Another way to say this is to say that there are differences in the dependent variable across the levels of the independent variable. If these differences are to be attributable to the independent variable, however, control techniques must be properly implemented to ensure the internal validity of the experiment. And even when this has been accomplished, a problem remains. Differences in the dependent variable across levels of an independent variable may or may not reasonably be attributed to the effect of the independent variable. We will illustrate this problem and its solution by focusing on the procedures and results of an experiment from a classic series of studies by Asch (1951, 1955) on conformity to group pressure.

The task in Asch's experiments was a simple one. Male subjects were shown two cards. The first card contained one line called "the standard." The second card contained three lines of different lengths, only one of which matched the standard. The subject's task was to select the line that matched the standard. Eighteen tests of this kind were given to each subject. During a test session there were varying numbers of other men present who were introduced to the subject as fellow participants in the experiment but who were actually working as confederates (see Chapter 2 for definition of confederates) of the experimenter. These confederates responded with the same incorrect responses on twelve of the eighteen trials. Thus the independent variable was the number of confederates present, and there were seven levels of this variable (0, 1, 2, 3, 4, 8, and 16). Subjects were randomly assigned to a group representing one of these seven levels. The dependent variable was the number of trials (out of the twelve possible on which the confederates gave incorrect responses) on which the subject conformed to group pressure by choosing the incorrect response instead of what was obviously the correct choice.

Two questions were addressed in Asch's experiment. First, would subjects conform? That is, would they choose the incorrect line more in the conditions when others were present than when they were alone? Second, would conformity increase with increasing size of the incorrect majority? Asch conducted a properly controlled experiment, so it is possible to use the results of the study to answer these two questions.

The first and most important step in analyzing an experiment is to summarize the results using an appropriate descriptive statistic. The most commonly used descriptive statistic in psychology experiments is the mean. The mean number and the range of errors for the ten subjects[3] who had been randomly assigned to each of the seven groups in the Asch experiment are presented in Table 5.1. The results seem clear. Fewer errors, on the average,

---

[3]In Asch's experiment there were actually varying numbers of subjects in each group, but all groups contained at least ten subjects. We have made the groups equal in size to make it easier to carry out certain analyses later in this chapter. The analysis plan of the original Asch experiment was also different from the one we describe here. We are describing how the experiment would be analyzed if it were done today.

TABLE 5.1   MEAN NUMBERS OF ERRORS AS A FUNCTION OF THE SIZE OF THE DISSENTING MAJORITY

	Size of dissenting majority						
	0	**1**	**2**	**3**	**4**	**8**	**16**
Mean number of errors	0.08	0.33	1.53	4.00	4.20	3.84	3.75
Range of errors	0–2	0–1	0–5	1–12	0–11	0–11	0–10

Adapted from Asch (1951).

were made when the subjects were alone than when they were confronted with the incorrect responses of other "subjects," and mean errors increased with increasing size of the dissenting majority, at least up to groups of four.

Descriptive statistics alone are not sufficient, however, to provide definitive answers to the two questions that Asch's experiment addressed. The problem rests with the nature of the control provided by balancing through random assignment. Random assignment (and random selection, for that matter) do not eliminate the differences among subjects. They simply distribute these differences equally across the groups in the experiment. That is, the differences among subjects are not allowed to vary systematically *across* groups.

The nonsystematic variation due to differences among subjects *within* each group is called **error variation.** The individual differences within each group are reflected in the range of errors presented in the second row of Table 5.1. Even with a dissenting majority of sixteen, at least one subject made no errors, while another subject made ten errors. The problem confronting the researcher is that, because individual differences among subjects are balanced and not eliminated, the means of the groups in the experiment may differ even if the independent variable has had no effect. Thus, by themselves, the results of the best-controlled random groups design experiment do not permit a definite judgment about whether the "treatment" was effective.

A good way to determine whether the differences obtained in an experiment are reliable would be to replicate the experiment and see if the same outcome is obtained. But replication is a cumbersome and inefficient solution to the problem for experiments that are as extensive as Asch's. Participants for experiments are a scarce resource, and each replication costs us a study that could be done to ask new and different questions about behavior. (Actually the problem is not quite so severe as the previous statement implies, because replication usually occurs in the natural course of research on a topic. For example, subsequent experiments that were done to locate the basis of conformity in the Asch experiment included at least some conditions from the original study.) In any case, some alternative to replication is needed to determine whether the differences obtained in a single experiment are larger than would be expected on the basis of error variation alone.

NULL HYPOTHESIS TESTING

Inferential statistics provide a means of testing whether the differences in a dependent variable that are associated with various conditions of an experiment should be attributed to an effect of the independent variable. The most commonly used inferential statistic in psychology experiments, the analysis of variance, is discussed in the next section. First, we will briefly describe the underlying logic of all inferential tests, a logic that unfortunately is not always intuitively clear.

Statistical inference is inductive and indirect. It is inductive because we draw *general* conclusions about populations on the basis of the *specific* samples that we test in our experiments. Statistical inference is indirect because it begins by assuming the null hypothesis. As the name implies, the **null hypothesis** is the assumption that the independent variable has had *no* effect. Once we make this assumption, we can use probability theory to determine the likelihood of our obtaining the difference that we did obtain in our experiment if the null hypothesis were true (if the independent variable had no effect). If this likelihood is small, we reject the null hypothesis and conclude that the independent variable *did* have an effect. Outcomes that lead us to reject the null hypothesis are called **statistically significant.** By this we mean only that the difference we have obtained in our experiment is larger than would be expected if error variation alone were responsible for the outcome.

Perhaps you can appreciate the process of statistical inference by considering the following dilemma. A friend offers to toss a coin with you to see who pays for the meal you just enjoyed at a restaurant. Your friend happens to have a coin ready to toss. Now it would be convenient if you could *directly* test whether your friend's coin were biased. The best you can do, however, is to test your friend's coin *indirectly* by assuming that it is not biased and seeing if you consistently get outcomes that differ from the expected 50–50 split of heads and tails. If the coin does not exhibit the ordinary 50–50 split, you might surmise that your friend is trying, by slightly underhanded means, to get you to pay for the meal. Similarly, researchers would like to test any obtained difference directly for significance, but the best they can do is to compare their outcome to the expected outcome of no difference. The key to understanding null hypothesis testing is to recognize that *we can use the laws of probability to estimate the likelihood of an outcome only when we assume that chance factors are the sole cause of that outcome.*

As we have said, a statistically significant outcome is one that has only a small likelihood of occurring if the null hypothesis is true. But just how small is small enough? Although there is no definitive answer to this important question, the consensus among members of the scientific community is that outcomes associated with probabilities of less than 5 times out of 100 (or .05) if the null hypothesis were true are judged to be statistically significant. The probability that we elect to use to indicate that an outcome is statistically significant is called the **level of significance.** The level of significance is indicated by the Greek letter α (alpha). Thus we speak of the .05 level of significance, the .10 level, or the .01 level, which we report as $\alpha = .05$, $\alpha = .10$, or $\alpha = .01$.

You must choose the level of significance *before* you begin your experiment, not after you have done the statistical analysis. This procedure allows you to avoid the temptation of using the probability of the obtained outcome as the level of significance you *would have chosen*. The level of significance is like a pregnancy test—just as you are either pregnant or not pregnant, an outcome either is statistically significant or it isn't. An outcome can't be a little bit statistically significant! Strictly speaking, there are only two conclusions possible when you do an inferential statistics test: reject the null hypothesis or fail to reject the null hypothesis. (See Box 5.3 for a less stringent approach to statistical inference.)

There is one final troublesome aspect to the process of statistical inference. No matter what decision you reach and no matter how carefully you reach it, there is always some chance that you are making an error. The two possible "states of the world" and the two possible decisions an experimenter can reach are listed in Table 5.2. The independent variable either does or does not have an effect on behavior. The two possible correct decisions the researcher could make are represented by the upper-left and lower-right cells of the table. If the independent variable does have an effect, the researcher should reject the null hypothesis; if it does not, the researcher should fail to reject the null hypothesis.

The two potential errors are represented by the other two cells of Table 5.2, and these two types of errors have the highly descriptive names of Type I error and Type II error. These errors arise because of the probabilistic nature of statistical inference. When we decide that an outcome is statistically significant because its probability of occurring under the null hypothesis is less than .05, we acknowledge that 5 times out of every 100 tests the outcome *could* occur even if the null hypothesis were true. The level of significance, therefore, represents the probability of making a *Type I error:* rejecting the null hypothesis when it is true. The probability of making a Type I error can be reduced simply by making the level of significance more stringent, perhaps .001. The problem with this approach is that it increases the likelihood of making a *Type II error:* failing to reject the null hypothesis when it is false.

TABLE 5.2   POSSIBLE OUTCOMES OF DECISION-MAKING WITH INFERENTIAL STATISTICS

	States of the world	
	Null hypothesis is false	Null hypothesis is true
Reject null hypothesis	Correct decision	Type I error
Fail to reject null hypothesis	Type II error	Correct decision

BOX 5.3

CAN THE NULL HYPOTHESIS EVER BE ACCEPTED AS TRUE?

When we take a strict approach to null hypothesis (H_0) testing—that the only acceptable decisions are to reject H_0 or to fail to reject H_0—we are essentially acknowledging the fact that it is impossible to prove that something does not exist. For example, if we were to propose that there was a monster in Lake Michigan, you would be unable to prove to us that this was not so. Putting ecological considerations aside for the moment, you might drain Lake Michigan and show that no monster is there. We could simply assert that the monster dug into the bed of the lake. You might then begin to dredge the lake and still come up with no monster; we could argue that our monster is digging faster than you are dredging. Becoming more desperate, you might fill the lake with explosives, and after detonating them, find no remains of the monster. We could calmly propose that our monster is impervious to explosives. So long as we were free to add characteristics to our monster, there is no test that you could perform that would convincingly show that the monster does not exist. (By the way, this problem of proving a negative contributes to the persistent belief of some people in ESP.) Practically speaking, however, if we continued to believe in our monster after reasonable efforts had failed to yield evidence of its existence, we would be judged unreasonable and would lose credibility with other members of the community.

A similar practical problem faces the community of researchers in psychology. Although we recognize the logical impossibility of proving that H_0 is true, we also must have some method of deciding which independent variables are not worth pursuing. Most often experiments are done to show that an independent variable causes a change in behavior. We should not get too discouraged, however, if the particular independent variable we are studying does not produce a statistically significant difference in our experiment. The discipline of psychology also progresses by identifying factors that do *not* influence behavior. Somewhat ironically, the standards for experiments that show that an independent variable is irrelevant are even higher than

for those that show that the independent variable is relevant. This is understandable when you recognize that experiments showing differences are likely to be subject to replication, whereas experiments finding no effects may discourage investigators from pursuing those avenues of investigation any further.

An experiment must meet three standards to serve as the basis for a conclusion that the null hypothesis is true (beyond, of course, avoiding confoundings to ensure internal validity). First, the experiment must represent a reasonable test of the hypothesis. If the hypothesis being tested is that a drug reduces tension, then the experiment must first induce tension in subjects to represent a fair test of the hypothesis. Second, the experiment must not contain any mitigating factors that would work against the expected differences. For example, if an experiment involved testing an hypothesis concerning reasons for alcohol consumption, the laboratory setting might influence how willing subjects might be to drink alcohol. The third and final standard is that the experiment must be sensitive enough to detect a difference if one were to exist. Every effort must be made to minimize error variation and to use sample sizes large enough to provide a reasonable opportunity to reject H_0. All too often after failing to reject H_0, researchers do a small (and insensitive) "replication" to confirm their original conclusion. If anything, the second experiment should be more sensitive than the first if it is to strengthen the conclusion that the independent variable has had no effect (Tversky and Kahneman, 1971).

Yeaton and Sechrest (1986, pp. 836–837) argue persuasively that no difference findings (those that would lead us to accept the null hypothesis) are especially critical in applied research. They cite several questions to illustrate their point: "Does Agent Orange increase the risk of health problems? Are the pollutants in Love Canal associated with an increased risk of genetic defects? Are children who are placed in daycare centers as intellectually, socially, and emotionally advanced as children who remain in the home? Is a new, cheaper drug with fewer side effects as effective as the existing standard in preventing heart attacks? Does saccharin increase one's risk of developing bladder cancer?" These important questions clearly illustrate situations in which accepting the null hypothesis involves more than a theoretical issue— life and death consequences rest on making the correct decision. Yeaton and Sechrest (1986) provide advice on how to approach this challenging aspect of applied research. For now, we are trying to make the point that issues like null hypothesis testing can be relevant to the "real world."

In summary, when a reasonable experiment with no mitigating factors is done to provide a sensitive test of an hypothesis, the absence of a difference between groups can lead us to accept H_0. We know that our decision will sometimes be in error; but as a community, we need some way to assure ourselves that some monsters are just not worth searching for.

The problem of Type I errors and Type II errors should not immobilize us. But it should help us understand why researchers rarely use the word "prove" when they describe the results of an experiment that involved inferential statistics. Instead they describe the results as "consistent with the hypothesis," or "confirming the hypothesis," or "supporting the hypothesis." These more tentative statements are a way of indirectly acknowledging that the possibility of making a Type I error or a Type II error always exists. The .05 level of significance represents a compromise position that allows us to strike a balance and avoid making too many of either type of error. The problem of Type I errors and Type II errors also reminds us that statistical inference can never replace replication as the ultimate test of the reliability of an experimental outcome. In spite of its limitations, however, statistical inference is an essential tool for the analysis of experiments. We now turn our attention to the most commonly used inferential test, the analysis of variance.

ANALYSIS OF VARIANCE

There are two sources of variation in a random groups experiment. First, variation *within each group* can be expected because of the individual differences among subjects who have been randomly assigned to that group. As we have already mentioned, however, in a properly conducted experiment these differences within each group should represent only error variation, because all the subjects in the group have been treated the same way. The second source of variation in the random groups design is variation *between the groups*.

If the null hypothesis is true, the nonsystematic variation among the means of the groups can also be attributed to error variation. Remember, when the null hypothesis is true, the performance in each group reflects the same underlying population, and thus the average performance in each group should be the same as the average performance in every other group. If several random samples are drawn from the same population, however, the means of these samples would not be expected to be identical. Fluctuations produced by chance make it likely that the means for the different random samples will vary somewhat. Thus the variation among the group means, under the condition that the null hypothesis is true, provides a second estimate of error variation. If the null hypothesis is true, this estimate of error variation between groups should be comparable to the earlier estimate we described of error variation within groups.

Now suppose that the null hypothesis is false. That is, suppose that the independent variable has had an effect. If the independent variable does have an effect, it will result in systematic differences across the groups of the experiment. This systematic variation will be *added to* the differences in the group means that always result from error variation.

We are now in a position to develop a statistic that will allow us to tell whether the variation due to our independent variable is larger than would be expected on the basis of error variation alone. The statistic is called an *F*-test; it is named after Ronald Fisher, the statistician who developed the test. The conceptual definition of the *F*-test is as follows:

$$F = \frac{\text{variation between groups}}{\text{variation within groups}}$$

$$= \frac{\text{error variation} + \text{systematic variation}}{\text{error variation}}$$

If the null hypothesis is true, there is no systematic variation and the resulting *F*-ratio has an expected value of 1. As the extent of the systematic variation increases, however, the expected size of the *F*-ratio becomes greater than 1.

The analysis of experiments would be easier if we could isolate the systematic variation produced by the independent variable. Unfortunately, the systematic variation between groups comes in a "package" along with error variation. Consequently, the *F*-ratio may sometimes be larger than 1 simply because our estimate of error variation between groups happens to be larger than our estimate of error variation within groups. This problem becomes less and less likely to arise with increasingly larger *F*-ratios, but we are still faced with a nagging question: How much greater than 1.00 does the *F*-ratio have to be before we can be relatively sure that it reflects systematic variation? Our discussion of null hypothesis testing in the previous section provides one answer to this question. The *F*-ratio needs to be large enough so that its probability of occurring if the null hypothesis were true is less than our chosen level of significance, usually .05.

The size of the *F*-ratio required to reject the null hypothesis, which is called the **critical value**, depends on three factors: the level of significance, the number of groups in the experiment, and the number of subjects within the groups in the experiment. Because of this, the *F*-test is not really one test but rather a family of tests. Fortunately, tables exist that list the critical values for the *F*-test depending on the three factors we have just listed. One such table appears in Appendix A.

To use this table you must be familiar with one additional concept we have not yet introduced, the concept of degrees of freedom. A particular member of the family of *F*-tests is identified by a pair of degrees of freedom—one associated with the numerator (variation between groups) and one associated with the denominator (variation within groups). In general, the statistical concept of **degrees of freedom (df)** is defined as the number of entries of interest minus 1. Thus, for the numerator the number of degrees of freedom is equal to the number of groups minus 1. If there are five groups, there are 4 degrees of freedom between groups (df_{BG}). Within each group, the number of degrees of freedom is equal to the number of subjects minus 1. For the experiment as a whole, the number of degrees of freedom within groups is equal to the sum of the degrees of freedom within each of the groups. When the groups are of equal size, the number of degrees of freedom within groups is equal to the number of groups times the number of degrees of freedom in one group. For example, if there are five groups of nine subjects each, there are 8 degrees of freedom in each group and 40 degrees of freedom within groups (df_{WG}).

To identify a critical value in the *F*-table, we locate the column associated with the number of degrees of freedom for the numerator (we will continue with our example of five groups or 4 df_{BG}) and the row associated with the number of degrees of freedom for the denominator (in our example, $df_{WG} = 40$). Finally, we identify the specific value associated with the level of significance we have chosen ($\alpha = .05$). The table yields a critical value of 2.61 for our example. If the *F*-ratio we obtain is larger than 2.61, we reject the null hypothesis and conclude that our independent variable had an effect. If the *F*-ratio we obtain is smaller than 2.61, we fail to reject the null hypothesis.

We are now ready to apply the principles of null hypothesis testing and the procedures of the analysis of variance to analyze the Asch experiment with which we began this section. The first step in the analysis of any experiment is to state the research question the analysis is intended to answer. Typically, this first step takes the general form of "Did the independent variable have any overall effect on performance?" In the Asch experiment this question would read as follows: "Did varying the size of the incorrect majority have any effect on the number of errors subjects made?" Once the research question is clear, the next step is to develop a null hypothesis for the analysis.

The initial overall analysis of the experiment is called an **omnibus *F*-test.** The null hypothesis for such omnibus tests is that all the group means are equal. The formal statement of a null hypothesis (symbolized H_0) is always done in terms of population characteristics. These population characteristics are indicated by Greek letters, and the population mean is symbolized as μ (mu). We can use a subscript for each mean in the Asch experiment to reflect the size of the incorrect majority for that group. Our null hypothesis then becomes

$$H_0: \mu_0 = \mu, \ldots = \mu_1 = \mu_2 = \mu_3 = \mu_4 = \mu_8 = \mu_{16}$$

The alternative to the null hypothesis, of course, is that the means for all the groups are not equal. If the size of the incorrect majority does produce systematic variation, we will be led to reject H_0.

The next step is to carry out the necessary computations to obtain the estimates of variation that make up the numerator and denominator of the F-ratio. These estimates are called mean squares (MS), and the procedures for computing them are presented in Appendix A. The results of the computations are presented in an Analysis of Variance Summary Table. The summary table for the omnibus analysis of the Asch experiment is given in Table 5.3. The obtained F-ratio in this analysis is $F(6,63) = 27.18$. The critical value for $\alpha = .05$ and for $F(6,60)$ [the denominator degrees of freedom in our example, 63, does not appear in the table—in such cases, we use the next *lower* degrees of freedom in the table, in this case, 60] is 2.25. Clearly our obtained F-ratio exceeds the critical value, so we reject the null hypothesis and conclude that the overall effect of the size of the incorrect majority is statistically significant.

Just what have we learned when we find a statistically significant outcome in an omnibus analysis of variance? In one sense, we have learned something very important. We are now in a position to state with confidence that manipulation of the independent variable produced a change in performance. In another sense, merely knowing that our outcome is statistically significant tells us nothing about the *nature* of the effect of the independent variable. The descriptive statistics (in our case, the means in Table 5.1) are the basis for our description of the nature of the effect. For example, if subjects had made the most errors when they were alone, the results could also have been statistically significant but in the opposite direction, leading to a very different conclusion from the one we draw from the means shown in Table 5.1. The point is that you should never try to interpret a statistically significant outcome without referring to the corresponding descriptive statistics.

Knowing that the omnibus test is statistically significant also does not tell us the *source* of the significant effect. All we know is that there is systematic variation somewhere in our experiment. On the basis of the omnibus test we could respond to a person who asked, "What happened in your experiment?" by saying, "Something." This response is not very satisfying and would almost surely prompt the exasperated query, "Yes, but

TABLE 5.3   ANALYSIS OF VARIANCE SUMMARY TABLE

Source of variation	df	SS	MS	F	p
Between groups	6	198.98	33.16	27.18	$< .05$
Within groups	63	77.13	1.22		
Total	69	276.11			

what?'' Fortunately, there are analysis techniques that allow us to locate more specifically the sources of systematic variation in our experiments. These techniques are called analytical comparisons, and they are linked directly to the hypotheses that led the researcher to do the experiment in the first place.

ANALYTICAL COMPARISONS

Asch did not do his experiment to find out whether something would happen when he manipulated the size of the incorrect majority. Instead, he had at least two specific questions to address in his experiment. Would subjects choose the incorrect line more in the conditions when others were present than when they were alone? And would conformity increase with increasing size of the incorrect majority? **Analytical comparisons** provide a way to translate these research questions into a form that allows us to locate a specific source of systematic variation in our experiment. We will illustrate this process with the first of Asch's research questions.

The first step in doing an analytical comparison, like the first step in doing an omnibus analysis, is to state the null hypothesis for the analysis. The verbal statement of the null hypothesis for the first of Asch's research questions is as follows: The mean for the group when subjects are alone is equal to the mean of all the groups in which other subjects were present. More formally, the null hypothesis is

$$H_0: \mu_0 = \frac{\mu_1 + \mu_2 + \mu_3 + \mu_4 + \mu_8 + \mu_{16}}{6}$$

Using computational procedures outlined in Appendix A, we can compute a mean square for this particular comparison. The mean square for the comparison reflects a combination of error variation and systematic variation due to this specific comparison. An F-ratio can then be formed with the comparison mean square in the numerator and the mean square within groups in the denominator as an estimate of error variation alone. Because this analytical comparison essentially involves the contrast between two means (subjects alone and subjects in groups), it has only 1 df. We then evaluate the resulting F-ratio by using the same procedures we described earlier for omnibus F-tests to determine whether the comparison has resulted in a statistically significant outcome.

The computations for the first analytical comparison in the Asch experiment result in $F(1,63) = 57.53$. Because the critical value given in the table for $\alpha = .05$ and for $F(1,60)$ is 4.00, the analytical comparison is statistically significant. This outcome allows us to state with confidence that one source of systematic variation in the Asch experiment was that subjects in groups performed differently from subjects who were alone. Because the mean number of errors for subjects in groups[4] (2.94) was higher than that for subjects alone (.08), we can conclude that Asch's first hypothesis was confirmed. That is, conformity did occur in Asch's experiment. This conclusion based on the analytical comparison is much more useful than the general conclusion (based on the omnibus test) that something happened in Asch's experiment.

LIMITS OF STATISTICAL SIGNIFICANCE

Like any tool, statistical inference can be and often is misused. At times researchers seem to forget that the statistical significance of a finding does nothing to enhance the internal validity of an experiment. Although we might be tempted to accept an interpretation if it is based on a "statistically significant" finding, we must remember that our ability to draw appropriate conclusions depends most of all on the internal validity of the study. And internal validity, as we have seen, depends mainly on whether the investigator has been able to exert enough control to eliminate alternative explanations. In other words, confounded experiments can easily produce statistically significant outcomes.

One illustration of a statistically significant finding in a confounded experiment is the famous "executive monkey" study (Brady, 1958). In this study four pairs of monkeys were tested. One monkey in each pair was the "executive," in that whenever it pressed a lever, it and its companion were spared strong unsignaled shocks. If the "executive" failed to press the lever within twenty seconds, however, shocks were delivered to both monkeys. The second monkey in each pair, called the "yoked monkey," had no control over the shocks; it simply received them whenever the executive monkey failed to press the lever in time. The results of this study were not only statistically significant, they were dramatic. All four executive monkeys developed ulcers and died, while the yoked monkeys showed no signs of ulcers. The conclusion seemed clear—"being in charge" is stressful and can be hazardous to health.

After several attempts to replicate this finding failed, however, researchers began to look more closely at the procedures employed in the original experiment. Rather than being randomly assigned, the four "executive" monkeys had been selected because they had shown higher rates of responding than their yoked partners on a pretest. Subsequent research has shown that higher response rates are associated with an increased likelihood of developing ulcers (Weiss, 1977). In fact, the more recent research findings lead to the conclusion that "being in charge" *reduces* the likelihood of developing ulcers. The original research represents a substantial contribution to psychology because it was at the forefront of research on an important problem. But it also

---

[4]The mean for subjects in groups can be obtained by simply averaging the six means for groups 1, 2, 3, 4, 8, and 16. However, this can be done only when all groups have the same number of subjects.

serves as a reminder that we must pay close attention to the procedures used in producing a statistically significant outcome.

Another problem with statistical inference is that it is always possible to produce statistically significant findings merely by reducing error variation. Our best estimate of error variation alone is the variation within groups in the random groups design, which serves as the denominator of the F-ratio. The size of the F-ratio can be shown to vary with changes in the size of error variation. For example, if there are three units of systematic variation in an experiment, then the expected value of the F-ratio is 2.0 when error variation is three units [$F = (3 + 3)/3 = 2$]. With the same amount of systematic variation, however, the F-ratio will grow to 4.0 when error variation is reduced to one unit and will shrink to 1.50 when error variation is increased to six units. The sensitivity of an experiment to detect an effect of a given size due to the independent variable is critically dependent on the amount of error variation in the experiment.

Sensitivity can be increased by drawing subjects from homogeneous populations rather than from heterogeneous populations, by holding as many factors constant as possible, and by testing large numbers of subjects within each group. For instance, error variation would be reduced in a vision experiment if subjects were selected from a homogeneous population of those students having 20-20 vision rather than from the more heterogeneous population represented by the general student body. When error variation is reduced by testing subjects from a homogeneous population or by holding many factors constant, the generality of the findings decreases while the sensitivity of the experiment increases. We briefly discussed this *sensitivity-generality trade-off* when we described procedures for balancing nuisance factors.

There is a way to increase sensitivity without involving the sensitivity-generality trade-off. Increasing the sample size within each group will provide a better estimate of the true (population) mean in each group (see confidence intervals in Appendix A). These better estimates can be accompanied by a decrease in error variation within groups and lead to a more sensitive experiment while also increasing generality. The best way to insure that your experiment is sensitive is to increase the sample size in each group.

The brief introduction we have given in this section to the use of inferential statistics is intended to show how closely the analysis of an experiment is tied to the questions and hypotheses that motivated the investigator to perform the experiment. Statistical analysis is not a necessary evil in experimentation; it is a critical step on the path from asking a research question to answering it.

SUMMARY

Experimental research allows us to observe the unobservable. Predictions based on proposed explanatory processes can be either confirmed or refuted by experimental outcomes. Sound experiments are internally valid, reliable, sensitive, and externally valid. The experimental method is ideally suited to identifying cause-and-effect relationships when the control techniques of manipulation, holding conditions constant, and balancing are properly implemented. In this chapter we have focused on the application of these control techniques in experiments in which different groups of subjects are given different treatments represented by the levels of the independent variable. In the most common design of this type, the random groups design, the groups are formed in such a way that they are equal at the start of the experiment. If they perform differently, it is presumed that the independent variable is responsible.

Random assignment, not random selection, is the most common means of forming comparable groups. By distributing subjects' characteristics equally across the conditions of the experiment, random assignment ensures that the differences among subjects are balanced. The most common technique for carrying out random assignment is block randomization.

Random assignment contributes to the internal validity of an experiment, but external validity must be established in some other way. One approach to enhancing external validity is to select representative samples of *all* dimensions on which you wish to generalize. A more common approach is to base judgments of external validity on the continuity assumption and replication. When we obtain the same outcomes in two replications of the same experiment done in two widely different settings, our confidence in the external validity of that finding increases. Direct tests of the boundaries of the continuity assumption provide perhaps the best way to establish the external validity of research findings.

Nuisance factors, such as different rooms or different experimenters, must not be allowed to confound the independent variable of interest. Even when such nuisance factors are controlled, however, they can contribute to the sensitivity and generality of an experiment. Holding nuisance factors constant increases sensitivity and decreases generality, whereas balancing nuisance factors decreases sensitivity and increases generality. A more serious threat to the internal validity of the random groups design is involved when subjects fail to complete the experiment successfully. Selective subject loss occurs when subjects are lost differentially across the conditions and some characteristic of the subject that is related to the outcome of the experiment is responsible for the loss. We can help prevent selective loss by restricting subjects to those likely to complete the experiment successfully or we can compensate for it by selectively dropping comparable subjects from the group that did not experience the loss.

The matched groups design is an alternative to the random groups design when only a small number of subjects is available along with a good matching task and when the experiment requires separate groups for each treatment. Practical problems in carrying out the matching can prove troublesome. The biggest problem with the matched groups design, however, is that the groups are equated *only* on the characteristic measured by the matching task. In the natural groups design, researchers select the levels of independent variables (usually subject variables) and look for systematic relationships between these independent variables and other aspects of behavior. Essentially, the natural groups design involves looking for correlations between subjects' characteristics and their performance. Such correlational research designs pose problems in drawing causal inferences.

Demand characteristics and experimenter effects can be minimized through the use of proper experimental procedures, but they can best be controlled by using placebo control and double-blind procedures. The yoked control design is a somewhat specialized but effective approach for investigating certain problems. Testing intact groups and regression to the mean are two easily avoidable threats to the internal validity of experiments involving the independent groups design.

The analysis of independent groups design experiments begins with a summary of descriptive statistics in a table or figure. The problem of chance variation, however, makes it necessary to use inferential statistics to determine whether the obtained differences are larger than would be expected on the basis of error variation alone. The inductive and indirect process of null hypothesis testing provides a set of guidelines for deciding on the statistical significance of a finding. By agreeing on a level of significance (usually $\alpha = .05$), we can determine whether an outcome occurs *less* frequently than we would judge to be the result of chance factors alone. The problems of Type I error and Type II error prevent null hypothesis testing from ever replacing replication; replication remains the ultimate test of the reliability of a research finding.

The most common inferential test used in the analysis of experiments is the analysis of variance. The numerator of an F-ratio (variation between groups) represents error variation and systematic variation; the denominator (variation within groups) represents only error variation. If the obtained F-ratio exceeds the critical value at the chosen level of significance, we conclude that the independent variable has had a statistically significant effect. Significant omnibus F-tests reveal only that something has happened, whereas analytical comparisons provide a means of locating the source of the systematic variation more precisely. The F-test is actually a family of tests with individual Fs defined by their numerator and denominator degrees of freedom. Tests of statistical significance are not without limits.

KEY CONCEPTS

independent variable	continuity assumption
dependent variable	replication
confounding	nuisance factors
independent groups design	mechanical subject loss
random groups design	selective subject loss
random assignment	matched groups design
block randomization	natural groups design

demand characteristics
experimenter effects
placebo
double-blind experiment
regression to the mean
error variation
inferential statistics

null hypothesis
statistically significant
level of significance (α)
critical value
degrees of freedom (df)
omnibus F-test
analytical comparison

REVIEW QUESTIONS

1 What role do manipulation, holding conditions constant, and balancing play in ensuring the internal validity of an experiment?
2 Briefly outline the logic of the independent groups design.
3 Distinguish between random selection and random assignment in terms of their use in carrying out the random groups design.
4 Briefly describe the procedures you would follow in order to use block randomization to assign subjects in an experiment involving four different groups.
5 What rule of thumb can be applied to the question of whether the results of an experiment can be generalized on any given dimension?
6 Describe the roles of the continuity assumption and replication in establishing the external validity of a research finding.
7 How are nuisance factors balanced in the random groups design? What impact do nuisance factors have on the sensitivity and generality of an experiment?
8 What preventive steps can a researcher take when he or she anticipates that selective subject loss may pose a problem in an experiment?
9 What is the logic of the matched groups design? When is it most likely to be used? What three options do researchers have in selecting a matching task?
10 How do subject variables differ from manipulated independent variables?
11 Why is drawing causal inferences on the basis of the natural groups design so difficult?
12 Briefly explain the logic and procedures involved in a yoked-control design.
13 Why should the use of intact groups be avoided in the independent groups design?
14 Briefly explain the problem of regression to the mean, and outline at least one approach to dealing with this problem when testing extreme groups.
15 Why is statistical inference said to be inductive and indirect?
16 Distinguish between Type I error and Type II error in statistical significance, and explain the role that level of significance (α) plays in influencing the likelihood of making each of these two types of error.
17 What three criteria must be met before we can accept the findings of an experiment in which the null hypothesis cannot be rejected as evidence against a theory predicting that the independent variable under investigation should have had an effect?
18 What are the two sources of variation in the analysis of a random groups experiment, and what does each of these sources estimate?
19 In what ways can researchers increase the sensitivity of their experiments by reducing error variation (that is, variation *within* groups)?

CHALLENGE QUESTIONS

1 Consider a random groups design experiment involving one independent variable. Specifically, the independent variable is Rate of Presentation and it is manipulated at four levels (Very Fast, Fast, Slow, and Very Slow).

A Use the following table of random numbers to prepare a block randomization schedule such that there will be four participants in each of the four conditions.

15-8-11-14-9-4-12-10-13-7-16-1-3-2-5-6
10-3-4-16-7-8-9-13-2-1-6-12-5-11-15-14
11-8-12-2-16-10-14-3-15-7-4-6-5-1-13-9
11-9-14-15-16-4-3-8-5-13-2-6-1-10-7-12

B The experimenter is considering restricting participants to those who pass a stringent reaction time test so as to be sure that they will be able to perform the task successfully with the Very Fast presentation rate. Explain what factors the experimenter should consider in making this decision, being sure to describe clearly what risks, if any, are taken if only this restricted set of participants is tested.

C The experimenter discovers that it will be necessary to test participants in two different rooms. How should the experimenter arrange the testing of the conditions in these two rooms so as to avoid possible confounding by this nuisance factor?

2 A chemical company wanted to test a new drug to be used for the treatment of nervousness. They obtained one hundred volunteers and gave all the volunteers a pretest to assess how nervous they were. The researchers then randomly assigned fifty people to the control group. These people were simply asked to return one month later for a second test. The fifty people in the experimental group agreed to take the drug each day for one month and then they too were to return for a second test.

Of course, the people in the experimental group had to be forewarned about the experimental nature of the drug and advised that there could be unknown side effects. There were forty-five people in the control group who returned for the second test, but only thirty-five people in the experimental group returned. On this second test, the experimental group showed a lower mean nervousness score than the control group.

A Explain why these results are likely to represent an overestimate of the effectiveness of the drug.

B Explain how you could use the pretest scores to verify that the difference had been overestimated.

3 A certain social worker was interested in reducing the amount of prejudice expressed by the members of the community in which she worked. She designed what she thought was an effective program for changing people's prejudicial attitudes. She decided to test her program in the most stringent way she knew. On the basis of a pretest measure of attitudes, she selected the ten most prejudiced people in her community (these people had a mean prejudice score of 9 on the 10-point paper-and-pencil test of prejudice that the investigator had quickly prepared for the purpose of selecting the most prejudiced people). She also selected the ten least prejudiced people (they had a mean prejudice score of 1.0 on her pretest). She administered her program to the ten most prejudiced people for a month and then tested all twenty people again. She found that the mean prejudice score for the ten most prejudiced was now 7.5 and that for the ten least prejudiced it was 1.5. Because she had reduced the difference between the least and most prejudiced groups by 25 percent, she decided that her program was highly successful.

A Explain why you would be hesitant to accept this conclusion. Be sure to explain the role of the reliability of the pretest in this problem.

B Describe how the investigator should have tested her program.

4 An experiment was done comparing the effectiveness of three methods of instruction for vocabulary acquisition to each other and to an uninstructed control condition. The independent groups design was used for the experiment. Thus there were four groups, one for each instructional condition. The three experimental methods were: studying a synonym of the to-be-learned word (Synonym Method), studying a dictionary definition of the to-be-learned word (Definition Method), and studying the to-be-learned word in the context of a literary passage (Passage Method). The researcher expected all three experimental methods to be better than

the uninstructed control group (Control Method), but the Passage Method was expected to be the best of all. The test given to all participants was a vocabulary usage test in which the participants had to select one sentence from a set of three for which the vocabulary word was appropriate. The values presented below are the eb mean numbers correct, out of a possible 20, on this test for each of the four groups. There were 25 participants randomly assigned to each group.

Control	Synonym	Definition	Passage
10.2	13.4	14.2	13.5

A Complete the Analysis of Variance Summary Table.

Source of variation	df	SS	MS	F	p
Method of instruction	—	240	—	—	.01
Within-groups error	—	1440	—		
Total	99	1680			

B Is the omnibus F-test in this analysis statistically significant? Be sure to provide the evidence on which you base your decision.

C Present the null hypothesis to be tested for an analytical comparison to determine whether the average of the three experimental conditions exceeds the performance in the control condition.

D Finally describe the analysis plan you would follow to determine whether the conceptual hypotheses described in this problem were supported by the results of the experiment.

5 Subject variables (individual differences) play a critical role in the random groups design. Comment critically on their role in each of the following areas:

A What method of control is used to deal with subject variables, and how is this control accomplished?

B What source of variation in the analysis of variance for the single-factor random groups design reflects differences due to subject variables?

C If you wanted to increase the sensitivity of your experiment, would you select from a homogeneous or a heterogeneous population of potential subjects? Why? What effect would this choice have on the generality of your findings?

D What one option do you have in the random groups design that allows you to increase both the sensitivity and the generality of your experiment simultaneously?

E Explain how the generality of an experiment done with the matched groups design would differ from an experiment done with the random groups design.

ANSWER TO CHALLENGE QUESTION 1

A Assigning the numbers 1 to 4 to the respective conditions Very Fast to Very Slow, and following the random number sequences (across the rows), the order of the four conditions in each of the four blocks would be

Block 1	Very Slow, Very Fast, Slow, Fast
Block 2	Slow, Very Slow, Fast, Very Fast
Block 3	Fast, Slow, Very Slow, Very Fast
Block 4	Very Slow, Slow, Fast, Very Fast

B The investigator is taking a reasonable step to avoid selective subject loss, but restricting participants to those who pass a stringent reaction time test entails the risk of decreased generality of the obtained findings.

C The rooms can be balanced by assigning entire blocks from the block-randomized schedule to be tested in each room. Usually, the number of blocks assigned to each room is equal, but this is not essential. For effective balancing, however, several blocks should be tested in each room.

6

Within-Subjects: Design and Analysis

OUTLINE

As we have repeatedly emphasized, the experimental method involves administering at least two treatments to subjects to determine their differential influence, if any, on behavior. Thus far we have considered experimental designs in which each treatment is administered to a separate group of subjects. These independent groups designs (random groups, matched groups, and natural groups) are powerful tools for studying the effects of a wide range of independent variables. There are times, however, when it is inefficient to give a different treatment to each of several separate groups of subjects. In such circumstances, it is still possible to do an interpretable experiment by administering all the treatments to each subject. In a sense, the experiment is done within each subject, so these designs are called **within-subjects designs.**

There are at least three reasons why a researcher might choose a within-subjects design. First, the within-subjects designs require fewer subjects, so they are ideal for situations in which only a small number of subjects is available. The within-subjects designs are especially useful when no acceptable matching task exists with which to equate small independent groups of subjects.

The second reason for choosing a within-subjects design applies even when sufficient numbers of subjects are available for an independent groups design. A researcher might choose to use a within-subjects design for the sake of convenience or efficiency. For example, Posner (1973) describes a series of experiments dealing with the cognitive processes required to identify individual letters while reading. In one of these experiments, Chase and Posner measured how long it took subjects to decide whether two briefly presented letters had the same name. There were two conditions in the experiment: either the two presented letters were physically identical (AA) or the two letters had the same name but were physically different (Aa). Even though the subjects' task was the same in the two conditions (to decide whether the two letters had the same name), Chase and Posner found that subjects could respond 80 milliseconds faster when the letters were physically identical than when the letters had only the same name in common. Each trial in this experiment required only a few seconds to complete. Chase and Posner could have tested separate groups of subjects for each of the two conditions, but this approach would have been horribly inefficient. It would have taken more time to instruct subjects regarding the nature of the task than it would to do the task itself. A within-subjects design in which each subject was tested on both types of pairs of letters provided Chase and Posner with a far more efficient way to answer their research question.

The third reason for choosing a within-subjects design is that some areas of psychological research require its use. When the research question involves studying changes in subjects' behavior over time, such as in a learning experiment or in a longitudinal design (see Chapter 3), a within-subjects design is needed. Further, whenever the experimental procedure requires that subjects compare two or more stimuli relative to one another, a within-subjects design must be used. For example, a within-subjects design would have to be used if a researcher wanted to measure the minimum amount of light that must be added before subjects could detect that a spot of light had become brighter. It would also be called for if a researcher wanted subjects to rate the relative attractiveness of a series of photographs. In general, the research areas of psychophysics (illustrated by the light-detection experiment) and scaling (illustrated by the ratings of attractiveness) rely heavily on within-subjects designs. We describe these two areas in greater detail in Appendix D.

We begin this chapter by examining the problem of practice effects in the within-subjects designs. Practice effects arise because subjects undergo changes as they are repeatedly tested; they may improve with practice or they may get worse because of fatigue. Unless these practice effects are balanced across the conditions of the experiment, the independent variable of interest will be confounded by the practice effects and the experiment will be uninterpretable. This chapter discusses various techniques for accomplishing this balancing. There are other limitations besides practice effects in the within-subjects designs, and you will need to become familiar with them in order to use these designs effectively.

One serious limitation of the within-subjects designs can be recognized from the outset. Within-subjects designs are not appropriate to study subject variables. Subject variables require separate groups of subjects as in the natural groups design. Finally, analysis procedures for within-subjects designs are similar to those we discussed in Chapter 5 for analysis of the independent groups design, but the within-subjects design procedures are sufficiently distinct to warrant separate consideration.

STAGE-OF-PRACTICE EFFECTS

At first glance the within-subjects designs might appear far superior to the independent groups design. The within-subjects designs require fewer subjects than the independent groups designs, and experiments can usually be completed more quickly when the within-subjects designs are used. In addition to their greater efficiency, the within-subjects designs offer another advantage—the problem of confounding the conditions of the experiment with the characteristics of the subjects within each condition is avoided. The same subjects are tested in all conditions of a within-subjects design, so it is impossible to end up with brighter, more aggressive, or more anxious subjects in one condition than in another condition. Stated formally, there can be no confounding by subject variables in the within-subjects designs.

The apparent elegance of the within-subjects designs vanishes, however, when we realize that these designs require that the same subject must be tested more than once. Subjects may change across repeated testings even if all tests are done under the same conditions. That is, subjects may get better and better at doing a task if a skill is being developed, or they may get worse and worse at the task because of such factors as fatigue and boredom. The repeated testing of each subject in the within-subjects designs gives the subjects practice with the experimental task. Thus, the changes subjects undergo with repeated testing are called **stage-of-practice effects** or just *practice effects*.

These changes with repeated testing are also sometimes called *progressive error* and they can be understood as temporary subject variables—temporary changes in the characteristics of the subject. In the random groups design the individual differences among subjects (subject variables) contribute to the error variation in the experiment. This error variation is controlled by randomly assigning subjects to groups. Similarly, the temporary changes subjects undergo in a within-subjects design contribute to progressive error. Progressive error (or stage-of-practice effects) must also be balanced if a within-subjects design experiment is to have internal validity. We describe techniques for doing this balancing in this chapter.

Wortman and Loftus (1981) describe a series of experiments that illustrate what happens when stage-of-practice effects are not balanced. Several hundred children from 3 to 10 years of age were tested to determine whether children perceive colors as adults do. The children were told to arrange fifteen colored caps in a specific order. The fifteen caps represented various shades of one color, such as red or blue, and there were several different colors tested. In early published reports, 50 percent of 3-year-olds made errors on the color blue, whereas only 11 percent of 10-year-olds did so. This suggested that the ability to detect differences in the color blue increased with age. But careful examination of the procedures revealed a serious problem: the early investigators had always tested the color blue last. These investigators failed to consider that children, especially young children, quickly become bored with a repetitive task and begin to make mistakes. When a second group of researchers repeated the experiment, they balanced for practice effects by administering the color tests in different orders. The younger children continued to make the most errors on colors tested last, but there were no consistent differences in errors made on the color blue (or on any other color) as a function of age. If the second group of researchers had not done experiments to balance practice effects, we might still be trying to explain why 3-year-olds have trouble seeing the color blue!

BALANCING STAGE-OF-PRACTICE EFFECTS

There are two types of within-subjects designs. In the **complete within-subjects design** practice effects are balanced by administering the conditions several times to each subject, using different orders each time, such that the results for each subject are interpretable. In the **incomplete within-subjects design** each condition is administered to each subject only once and the order of administering the conditions is varied across subjects, such that practice effects can be neutralized by combining the results for all subjects. The specific techniques for balancing practice effects in the two within-subjects designs are different, so we will discuss the two designs separately.

COMPLETE WITHIN-SUBJECTS DESIGN

Does one side of your face express emotion more intensely than the other side? Sackheim et al. (1978) used a within-subjects design to attempt to answer this question. Earlier research had shown that subjects given photographs depicting posed facial expressions of six basic human emotions (happiness, surprise, fear, sadness, anger, and disgust) could readily and accurately identify the expressed emotion. Sackheim and coworkers took advantage of a technique developed in earlier work on facial recognition whereby a full photograph of a face can be constructed using only one side of a person's face. The technique involves developing both a photograph of a full face and a photograph of its mirror image. These two photographs are then split down the middle and two composite photographs are made—one from the two versions of the left side of the face and one from the two versions of the right side. Illustrative photographs are presented in Figure 6.1. In the center is a photograph of a person showing disgust. The two composite photographs made from the center photograph are presented on either side of the original.

Subjects were shown slides of photographs like those in Figure 6.1 and were asked to rate each slide on a 7-point scale indicating the intensity of

FIGURE 6.1 (a) Left-side composite, (b) original, and (c) right-side composite of the same face. The face is expressing disgust. (*From Sackheim et al., 1978.*)

expressed emotion. The slides were presented individually for 10 seconds and subjects were then given 35 seconds to make their rating. To increase the external validity of their experiment, the investigators had photographs of fourteen different people depicting the six identifiable emotions and one neutral expression. The critical independent variable in the experiment, however, was the *version* of the photograph (left composite, original, or right composite). Each subject rated fifty-four slides: eighteen left composites, eighteen originals, and eighteen right composites.

Does one of the two composites in Figure 6.1 look more disgusted than the other? Subjects' ratings of emotional intensity were consistently higher for the left composite than for the right composite. Sackheim et al. (1978) interpreted these findings in terms of hemispheric specialization of the brain. In general, the left hemisphere controls the right side of the body and the right hemisphere controls the left side of the body. Thus, the left composite reflects control by the right hemisphere, and the right composite reflects control by the left hemisphere. The higher ratings of emotional intensity for the left composite photographs suggest that the right hemisphere may be more heavily involved than the left hemisphere in the production of emotional expression.

The interpretation of the differences in mean ratings assigned to the three versions of the photographs depends critically on the order in which the slides were presented to subjects. If all the original versions were presented first, followed by all the right composites, then by all the left composites, higher ratings for the slides shown at the end of this long sequence may reflect the intensity of the subjects' boredom and fatigue rather than the intensity of the emotions actually depicted in the photographs. The problem is the same as the one we described earlier in the experiments dealing with children's perception of color. If you imagine yourself in this experiment making a rating for each of the slides in this long sequence, you will get a sense of what we mean by practice effects. Surely your attention, motivation, and experience in rating the emotionality of photographs will change as you work through the sequence of slides. Sackheim et al. (1978) used balancing techniques specifically developed for use in the complete within-subjects design to ensure that each of the three versions of the photographs was equally likely to appear at any point in the long series of slides.

In the complete within-subjects design subjects are given each treatment enough times to balance stage-of-practice effects for each subject. Of course, this is possible only when each treatment can be administered more than once. When the task is simple enough and not too time-consuming (such as judging the emotional intensity of photographs), it is often possible to give one subject several experiences with each treatment. In fact, in some complete within-subjects designs, only one or two subjects are tested and each subject experiences literally hundreds of trials. More commonly, however, researchers use procedures like those used by Sackheim et al. (1978). That is, several subjects are tested and each subject is given each treatment only a relatively small number of times. Researchers have two choices in deciding how to arrange the order in which the treatments in a complete within-subjects design are administered: block randomization and ABBA counterbalancing.

Block Randomization   The first option for balancing practice effects in the complete within-subjects design represents a new use of a familiar technique. We introduced block randomization in Chapter 5 as an effective technique for assigning subjects to conditions in the random groups design. Block randomization can also be used to order the conditions for each subject in a complete within-subjects design. For instance, Sackheim et al. (1978) administered each of the three versions of their photographs (left composite, original, and right composite) eighteen times to each subject. The sequence of trials shown in Table 6.1 illustrates how block randomization could be used to arrange the order of the three conditions in their experiment. The sequence of fifty-four trials is broken up into eighteen blocks of three. Each block contains the three conditions of the experiment in random order. In general, the number of blocks in a block-randomized schedule is equal to the number of times each condition is administered, and the size of each block is equal to the number of conditions in the experiment.

If a subject rated the photographs following the sequence in the block-randomized schedule shown in Table 6.1, it is unlikely that changes in the subject's attention, motivation, or experience with rating photographs would affect any one of the conditions more than any other. The practice effects can reasonably be expected to "average out" over the three experimental conditions. Determining the average position of each of the three conditions in the block-randomized sequence gives a rough indication of the balancing of prac-

TABLE 6.1 BLOCK-RANDOMIZED SEQUENCE OF TRIALS IN AN EXPERIMENT WITH THREE CONDITIONS ADMINISTERED EIGHTEEN TIMES EACH

Trial	Cond.	Trial	Cond.	Trial	Cond.	Trial	Cond.	Trial	Cond.	Trial	Cond.
1	O	10	L	19	R	28	O	37	L	46	R
2	L	11	O	20	L	29	L	38	R	47	L
3	R	12	R	21	O	30	R	39	O	48	O
4	R	13	O	22	L	31	R	40	O	49	O
5	O	14	L	23	R	32	L	41	R	50	R
6	L	15	R	24	O	33	O	42	L	51	L
7	R	16	R	25	R	34	O	43	R	52	R
8	O	17	L	26	L	35	R	44	O	53	O
9	L	18	O	27	O	36	L	45	L	54	L

Note: The conditions are the three versions of the photographs used in Sackheim et al. (1978). L = left composite; O = original; R = right composite.

tice effects. This can be done by summing the trial numbers on which each condition appears and dividing by 18. For instance, the original photograph appeared on trials 1, 5, 8, 11, 13, 18, 21, 24, 27, 28, 33, 34, 39, 40, 44, 48, 49, and 53. The average position of the original photographs, therefore, was 27.6. The corresponding values for the left and right composite photographs are 27.7 and 27.2, respectively.

As you may have already recognized, block randomization requires several repetitions of each condition before practice effects can be expected to average out. We should not expect practice effects to be balanced after two or three blocks—any more than we would expect sample sizes of two or three in the random groups design to equate the characteristics of subjects across groups. Fortunately, a technique is available to balance practice effects when it is not possible to administer each condition often enough for the averaging process of block randomization to work effectively.

ABBA Counterbalancing In its simplest form, ABBA counterbalancing can be used to balance practice effects in the complete within-subjects design with as few as two administrations of each condition. **ABBA counterbalancing** involves presenting the conditions in one sequence followed by the opposite of that same sequence. Its name describes the sequences when there are only two conditions (A and B) in the experiment, but ABBA counterbalancing is not limited to experiments with just two conditions. Sackheim et al. (1978) could have presented the versions of their photographs according to the sequence outlined in Table 6.2.

Note that the order of the three conditions on the first three trials is simply reversed for trials 4 to 6. The values in the second row show the hypothetical amount of practice effects that would be added on each trial of the ABBA sequence when practice effects are linear. When practice effects are linear, the same amount is added to or subtracted from performance on each suc-

TABLE 6.2 ABBA COUNTERBALANCED SEQUENCE OF TRIALS IN AN EXPERIMENT WITH THREE CONDITIONS (LEFT COMPOSITE, ORIGINAL, AND RIGHT COMPOSITE)

Condition	Trial 1 Left	Trial 2 Original	Trial 3 Right	Trial 4 Right	Trial 5 Original	Trial 6 Left
Practice effect (linear)	+0	+1	+2	+3	+4	+5
Practice effect (nonlinear)	0	+6	+6	+6	+6	+6

cessive trial. In our example, practice effects add one unit to performance on each trial. If you add up the practice effects for each condition, you will see that all the totals are the same, namely, 5. The left composite condition gets the least and the greatest influence from practice effects, while the right composite condition gets two intermediate amounts. The ABBA cycle can be applied with any number of conditions and can be repeated any number of times. It balances practice effects even more effectively with larger numbers of repetitions of the cycle. Usually, however, ABBA counterbalancing is used when the number of conditions and the number of repetitions of each condition are relatively small.

Although ABBA counterbalancing provides a simple and elegant means to balance practice effects, it is not without limitations. ABBA counterbalancing is most effective when practice effects are linear. When practice effects for a task involve abrupt initial changes followed by relatively little change thereafter, ABBA counterbalancing would be ineffective, especially if only one ABBA cycle was used. This is illustrated in the bottom row of Table 6.2. The left composite receives only six hypothetical units of practice effects, and the other two conditions receive twelve units each. When practice effects of this type are anticipated, researchers often ignore performance on the early trials and wait until the practice effects reach a "steady state." Even in these situations, however, researchers still use either block randomization or ABBA counterbalancing after the steady state has been achieved—just in case the steady state does not stay steady. (See Box 6.1 for an example of this approach.)

A second limitation of ABBA counterbalancing is the problem of anticipation effects. **Anticipation effects** arise when a subject develops expectations about which condition should occur next in the sequence. The subject's response to that condition may then be influenced more by this expectation than by the actual experience of the condition itself. For example, consider a time perception experiment in which the subject's task is to estimate the length of time that has passed between when the experimenter says "Start" and when the experimenter says "Stop." (Of course, subjects would have to be prevented somehow from marking off time during the interval by counting or rhythmic tapping.) If the time intervals in such an experiment were 12, 24, and 36 seconds, then one possible ABBA sequence of conditions could be

BOX 6.1

HOW FAST DOES A NERVE IMPULSE TRAVEL?

Precise measurement of the speed of a nerve impulse obviously requires the use of reliable measurement devices such as millisecond timers. Rozin and Jonides (1977) describe a technique for making a rough estimate of nerve impulse speed with only a standard stop watch. Besides being educationally beneficial, the procedure can also be fun to do.

Rozin and Jonides (1977) describe their technique as follows:

The logic of this demonstration follows directly from Helmholtz's 1850 experiment. Simple reaction time to a pinch of the ankle is compared to simple reaction time to a pinch of the shoulder. The difference between these times should be an estimate of the time for the nerve impulse to traverse the equivalent of the distance between the ankle and the shoulder. Between ten and twenty students are needed for this

experiment. Each student grasps the ankle of his neighbor (this can be arranged with a minimum of acrobatics if the person at the end of a row of seats links with the person in front of him). Subjects are instructed to close their eyes and to simply squeeze their neighbor's ankle as soon as their own ankle is squeezed. The last person in the series is instructed to yell "Stop" when he feels squeezed. The experimenter starts the series by tapping the ankle of the first subject with the starting pin of a stop watch, thus starting the stop watch and the squeeze simultaneously. The experimenter stops the watch on the agreed signal from the last person (i.e., the "Stop" signal).

As you might suspect, there is considerable instability in the group's reaction times over the first few trials of this task. To combat this problem, Rozin and Jonides suggest that several ankle and shoul-

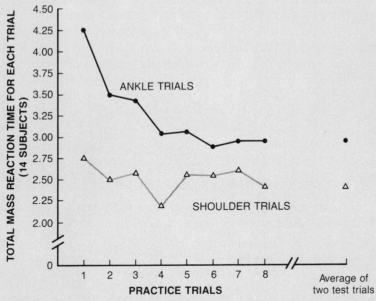

FIGURE 6.2 Waiting for a "steady-state" in order to minimize practice effects. (*From Rozin and Jonides, 1977.*)

der trials be done until the respective reaction times decrease and stabilize. As you can see in Figure 6.2, the reaction times are quite stable for both types of trials after about eight trials. Once the stable baselines are achieved, the complete within-subjects design experiment actually begins. ABBA counterbalancing can be used to order four test trials (Ankle, Shoulder, Shoulder, Ankle) to ensure that any possible continuing practice effects are balanced. The mean reaction times for one group of fourteen subjects are presented at the right in Figure 6.2. To obtain an estimate of the speed of a nerve impulse, one divides the mean difference between the ankle and shoulder reaction times into the difference between the mean ankle-to-shoulder distance for the tested subjects. Using this procedure, Rozin and Jonides obtained estimates of between 15 and 50 meters per second. By the way, it is possible to use this procedure with as few as six people (five subjects and an experimenter). The only difference is that you cycle four times around the group of five subjects.

Achieving a stable baseline prior to beginning the experiment offers an additional advantage beyond increasing the likelihood that balancing techniques will prove effective. Practice effects add variability to performance within each condition, thereby reducing the sensitivity of the experiment. Thus, when practice effects are minimized, the sensitivity of the experiment is increased. (The counterpart to this in the random groups design would be testing subjects from homogeneous rather than heterogeneous populations.) It is important to recognize, however, that the internal validity of an experiment takes precedence over its sensitivity and that, so long as appropriate balancing techniques have been used, the internal validity of a complete within-subjects design experiment is ensured.

12-24-36-36-24-12. If this cycle were repeated several times, subjects would be very likely to recognize the pattern and to expect a series of increasing and then decreasing intervals. Their time estimates might soon begin to reflect this pattern rather than their perception of each independent interval.

Anticipation effects usually do not pose a serious problem, because the ABBA cycle is not repeated enough times to allow subjects to recognize the pattern. The possibility that subjects might recognize the pattern can be reduced even further by using a random sequence of the conditions for the first half of the ABBA cycle. In the time perception experiment, the ABBA pattern of 24-36-12-12-36-24 would be less likely to be detected than the pattern of 12-24-36-36-24-12. In general, however, ABBA counterbalancing should not be used if anticipation effects are likely.

INCOMPLETE WITHIN-SUBJECTS DESIGN

To illustrate the techniques for balancing practice effects in the incomplete within-subjects design, we will focus on one of the oldest experimental tasks in psychology, the Stroop interference task. The Stroop task was first systematically investigated by the researcher after whom the task is named, J. Ridley Stroop. In the control condition, subjects are simply asked to name the color of each of a series of color patches. In the experimental condition, subjects are required to name as quickly as possible the colors in which a series of words are printed. The words are color names printed in an ink of a *different* color. Researchers have consistently found that subjects take longer to name the colors in which the color words are printed than to name the colors of the color patches. The Stroop interference phenomenon is presumed to occur because experienced readers cannot ignore the meanings of the color words—they read those words even when doing so makes the task harder.

Klein (1964) explored the basis of the Stroop effect by varying the nature of the words that were printed in the different colors. He argued that the interference effect should get stronger as the meaning of the printed word more closely approximated the meanings of the color names. There were six conditions in Klein's experiment. The printed items were nonsense syllables (strings of consonants that did not form an English word); rare English words (sol, helot, eft); common English words not closely associated with the color names (put, heart, friend); color-related words that were not color names but that implied color (lemon, grass, sky) and were printed in colors other than the one implied by the word; distant color words—that is, words that were color names but not the colors used to print the words (tan, purple, grey); and, finally, close color names, the incongruous color names used in the original Stroop task.

All subjects were also required to complete the color patch test, and the speed with which the subjects could name the color patches was used as a baseline against which to compare their performance in the experimental conditions. The mean difference between the baseline condition and each of the experimental conditions is plotted in Figure 6.3. The results are remark-

FIGURE 6.3 Increments of color-naming time with different word-color combinations, from baseline of subjects' reading time on colors alone. (*From Klein, 1964.*)

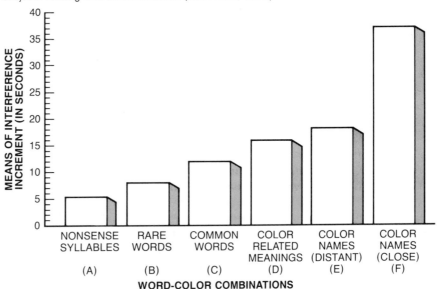

ably orderly and support Klein's hypothesis that interference increases systematically as similarity increases between the required response (the color name) and the competing response (the item printed in that color).

Klein (1964) actually used the independent groups design to carry out the analytical experiment we have just described; each subject was tested in only one experimental condition along with the baseline color patch test. The incomplete within-subjects design could have been used in this experiment, however, and we will describe the techniques for balancing practice effects using a variation of Klein's experiment as our example. We will consider an experiment involving four of the conditions from Klein's experiment: the Color Patch control condition, the Nonsense Syllable condition, the Color-Related Word condition, and the standard Incongruent Color Word condition.

In the incomplete within-subjects design, each subject is given each treatment only once. For any given subject, therefore, any differences produced by the independent variable are uninterpretable, because the levels of the independent variable of interest are perfectly confounded with the ordinal positions in which those levels appeared. For instance, the first two conditions given to the first subject in our Stroop experiment might be in the order Color Patch, then Nonsense Syllable. Any differences in the subject's performance in these two conditions could be due to the independent variable or to the order in which the conditions were administered. To break this confounding of ordinal position and the independent variable of interest, we administer different orders of the conditions to different subjects. The second subject in our Stroop experiment might be tested in the order Nonsense Syllable, then Color Patch. When several different subjects are tested in several different orders, it is possible to balance the ordinal position differences across conditions.

The general rule for accomplishing the balancing of practice effects in the incomplete within-subjects design is a simple one. Each condition of the experiment must appear in each ordinal position equally often. Several techniques are available to satisfy this general rule. These techniques differ in what additional balancing they accomplish; but so long as the techniques are properly used, the basic rule will be met and the experiment will be interpretable.

All Possible Orders The preferred technique for balancing practice effects in the incomplete within-subjects design is to use all possible orders of the treatments. Each subject is randomly assigned to one of the orders. With only two treatments there are only two possible orders (AB and BA); with three treatments there are six possible orders (ABC, ACB, BAC, BCA, CAB, CBA). In general, there are $N!$ (which is read "N factorial") possible orders with N treatments, where $N!$ equals $N(N - 1)(N - 2) \cdots (N - [N - 1])$. The number of required orders increases dramatically with increasing numbers of treatments. For instance, for only five treatments there are 120 possible orders. Because of this, the use of all possible orders is usually limited to experiments involving four or fewer conditions.

The twenty-four sequences that would be required to use all possible orders to carry out our four-condition Stroop experiment are presented in the left half of Table 6.3. Using all possible orders certainly meets the general rule of ensuring that all conditions appear in each ordinal position equally often. The first ordinal position shows this balancing most clearly; the first six sequences begin with the Color Patch condition, and each succeeding set of six sequences begins with one of the other three conditions. The same pattern applies at each of the four ordinal positions. The use of all possible orders also provides two other potentially useful types of balancing. First, careful examination of the twenty-four sequences reveals that each condition precedes and follows every other condition equally often. For instance, the Color-Related Word condition (R) precedes the Incongruent Color Word condition (I) six times, and the order IR also appears six times. Second, each condition precedes and follows every other condition equally often at each ordinal position. That is, the orders RI and IR appear exactly twice in ordinal positions 1 and 2, 2 and 3, and 3 and 4.

There is one other issue that must be addressed in deciding to use all possible orders. For this technique to be effective, it is essential that at least one subject be tested with each of the possible orders of the conditions. Therefore, the use of all possible orders requires at least as many subjects as there are possible orders. That is, if there are four conditions in the experiment, you must test twenty-four subjects (or forty-eight or seventy-two or some other multiple of twenty-four). This restriction makes it very important that you have a good idea of the number of potential subjects *before* you begin to test the first subject.

TABLE 6.3 ALTERNATIVE TECHNIQUES TO BALANCE PRACTICE EFFECTS IN AN INCOMPLETE WITHIN-SUBJECTS DESIGN EXPERIMENT WITH FOUR CONDITIONS

All possible orders								Selected orders							
									Latin Square			Random starting order with rotation			
Ordinal position				Ordinal position				Ordinal position				Ordinal position			
1st	2nd	3rd	4th	1st	2nd	3rd	4th	1st	2nd	3rd	4th	1st	2nd	3rd	4th
C	N	R	I	R	C	N	I	C	N	R	I	N	R	I	C
C	N	I	R	R	C	I	N	N	I	C	R	R	I	C	N
C	R	N	I	R	N	C	I	I	R	N	C	I	C	N	R
C	R	I	N	R	N	I	C	R	C	I	N	C	N	R	I
C	I	N	R	R	I	C	N								
C	I	R	N	R	I	N	C								
N	C	R	I	I	C	N	R								
N	C	I	R	I	C	R	N								
N	R	C	I	I	N	C	R								
N	R	I	C	I	N	R	C								
N	I	C	R	I	R	C	N								
N	I	R	C	I	R	N	C								

Note: The four conditions in this variation of Klein's (1964) Stroop experiment are the Color Patch control condition (C), the Nonsense Syllable condition (N), the Color-Related Word condition (R), and the standard Incongruent Color Word condition (I).

Selected Orders Klein's (1964) experiment on the Stroop effect involved six experimental conditions and a baseline control condition. If we were trying to replicate Klein's experiment using the incomplete within-subjects design with all possible orders, we would need to test 840 subjects, one for each of the possible orders of the seven conditions (7! orders). We obviously need some alternative to using all possible orders if we are to use the incomplete within-subjects design for experiments with five or more conditions.

Practice effects can be balanced by using just *some* of all the possible orders. The number of selected orders will always be equal to some multiple of the number of conditions in the experiment. For example, to replicate Klein's experiment we would need to select seven, fourteen, twenty-one, twenty-eight, or some other multiple of seven orders to balance practice effects. There are two basic variations of using selected orders and these are illustrated in the right half of Table 6.3. To allow you to compare the types of balancing more directly, we have illustrated the techniques for selected orders with the four-condition version of Klein's experiment we described in the previous section.

The first type of balancing using selected orders is the *Latin Square.* In a Latin Square each condition appears at each ordinal position once (the essential characteristic to meet the general rule for balancing practice effects), but each condition also precedes and follows each other condition exactly once. The only difference between using all possible orders and a Latin Square is that in the Latin Square, each condition does not precede and follow every other condition equally often at each ordinal position. For instance, in the Latin Square shown in Table 6.3, the orders RI and IR both appear, but RI appears only in ordinal positions 3 and 4 whereas IR appears only in positions 1 and 2. The procedures for constructing Latin Squares are illustrated in Box 6.2.

The second balancing technique using selected orders requires you to begin with a random order of the conditions and systematically to rotate this sequence with each condition moving one position to the left each time (see the example given in Table 6.3). When a random starting order with rotation is used, practice effects are balanced because each condition appears in each ordinal position. The systematic rotation of the sequences means that each condition always follows and always precedes the same other conditions. For example, in the illustration in Table 6.3, condition C always precedes condition N and follows condition I. Therefore, each condition does not precede and follow every other condition, as is true with the Latin Square technique.

The characteristics of the three balancing techniques in the incomplete within-subjects design are summarized in Table 6.4. The use of all possible orders, the Latin Square, and random starting orders with rotation are equally effective in balancing practice effects, because all three techniques ensure that each condition appears in each ordinal position equally often. Regardless of which technique one uses to balance practice effects, the sequences of conditions should be fully prepared prior to testing the first subject and subjects should be *randomly* assigned to these sequences. The ad-

BOX 6.2

SQUARING OFF AGAINST LATIN SQUARES

There is a simple procedure to follow when generating Latin Squares based on an even number of conditions. It is only slightly more complicated when there is an odd number of conditions.

First, let us outline the procedure when there is an even number of conditions in your experiment. Follow these steps:

1 Randomly order the conditions of your experiment. The number of conditions that you have is designated N. The size of the square will be $N \times N$. (At this time we are considering only situations where N is even.) Number your randomly ordered conditions 1 through N. For example, suppose there are six conditions in your experiment that when randomly ordered appear as White, Yellow, Blue, Green, Red, and Purple. Assign White the number 1, Yellow the number 2, and so on. We are looking to build a square that is 6×6.

2 To generate the first row of your square, use the following rule:

1, 2, N, 3, $N - 1$, 4, $N - 2$, 5, $N - 3$, 6, $N - 4$, 7, etc.

In our example, the first row is 1–2–6–3–5–4, or White–Yellow–Purple–Blue–Red–Green.

3 The second row is generated by adding 1 to each number in the first row with the understanding that 1 added to N equals 1. For our example, the second row is 2–3–1–4–6–5. Thus, condition 2 appears first, condition 3 appears second, etc.

4 The third row is generated by adding 1 to each number in the second row (and $N + 1 = 1$). The example third row is 3–4–2–5–1–6.

5 Similar steps are followed until N rows are completed. The Latin Square for our example is

1(W)	2(Y)	6(P)	3(B)	5(R)	4(G)
2(Y)	3(B)	1(W)	4(G)	6(P)	5(R)
3(B)	4(G)	2(Y)	5(R)	1(W)	6(P)
4(G)	5(R)	3(B)	6(P)	2(Y)	1(W)
5(R)	6(P)	4(G)	1(W)	3(B)	2(Y)
6(P)	1(W)	5(R)	2(Y)	4(G)	3(B)

6 Subjects are assigned randomly to rows of the Latin Square with the restriction that each row be used an equal number of times. Thus, the total number of subjects must be a multiple of N.

When there is an odd number of conditions, two squares must be constructed. The first square is generated according to the steps outlined above. The second square is generated by reversing the rows in the first square. The squares are then joined so that the original $N \times N$ square is now $N \times 2N$ in size. For example, if $N = 5$, then we are looking to build a 5×10 square. Suppose we have five conditions that when randomly arranged and numbered yield 1 = Red, 2 = Blue, 3 = Purple, 4 = White, 5 = Yellow. The Latin Square we would generate is

1(R)	2(B)	5(Y)	3(P)	4(W)	4(W)	3(P)	5(Y)	2(B)	1(R)
2(B)	3(P)	1(R)	4(W)	5(Y)	5(Y)	4(W)	1(R)	3(P)	2(B)
3(P)	4(W)	2(B)	5(Y)	1(R)	1(R)	5(Y)	2(B)	4(W)	3(P)
4(W)	5(Y)	3(P)	1(R)	2(B)	2(B)	1(R)	3(P)	5(Y)	4(W)
5(Y)	1(R)	4(W)	2(B)	3(P)	3(P)	2(B)	4(W)	1(R)	5(Y)

As when an even number of conditions is used, subjects are assigned randomly to the rows of the square with each row used the same number of times.

TABLE 6.4 CHARACTERISTICS OF ALTERNATIVE TECHNIQUES TO BALANCE PRACTICE EFFECTS IN THE INCOMPLETE WITHIN-SUBJECTS DESIGN

All possible orders
1. Each condition appears at every ordinal position equally often.
2. Each condition precedes and follows every other condition equally often.
3. Each condition precedes and follows every other condition equally often at every ordinal position.

Latin square
1. Each condition appears at every ordinal position equally often.
2. Each condition precedes and follows every other condition equally often.

Random starting order with rotation
1. Each condition appears at every ordinal position equally often.

ditional characteristics present with the use of all possible orders are especially helpful when it becomes necessary to track down possible interpretive problems in the incomplete within-subjects design. We will discuss these possible interpretive problems later in this chapter.

The Problem of Irreversible Tasks Sharma and Moskowitz (1972) asked subjects to come to their laboratory on four different days. Each day the subjects were given twenty minutes to smoke two cigarettes that contained one of four doses of marijuana—a placebo control and doses of 50, 100, and 200 units (1 unit = 1 µg/kg of body weight). The doses reflected the amount of tetrahydrocannabinol (THC) (the active agent in marijuana) in the two cigarettes combined. The experiment involved the incomplete within-subjects design, so each subject was given each dose once. The order of the doses across subjects was determined using a Latin Square. Immediately after the subjects smoked the two cigarettes, they were tested on an autokinetic illusion task. In this task the subject is placed in a darkened room and asked to focus on a pinpoint of light. The illusion that subjects often experience in this situation is that the pinpoint of light appears to move, even though it is really stationary. Sharma and Moskowitz (1972) found that the size of the autokinetic illusion—that is, the amount of apparent movement—increased with increasing doses of marijuana. Such an outcome indicates that there may be hazards associated with driving a car or flying an airplane at night under the influence of marijuana, especially at relatively high doses.

The task designed to measure the autokinetic illusion can be given repeatedly to subjects without their "mastering" it. Subjects continue to experience the illusion even after being tested several times. Therefore, Sharma and Moskowitz needed to balance practice effects only for the marijuana variable. Consider, however, how the situation would change if Sharma and Moskowitz had been interested in the effects of marijuana on people's ability to learn and remember new information.

One way to carry out such an experiment would be to give each subject a different list of words to learn under each dose of marijuana. A different list of words would be needed each time because a memory task of this type is an **irreversible task**—one that cannot be administered more than once without risking that the subject will master the task. Once subjects master the task, their performance under subsequent conditions is not likely to vary. In a sense, irreversible tasks result in a "ceiling effect" (see Chapter 7) for all conditions after the first one under which the task has been done.

The solution to the problem of irreversible tasks is outlined in Table 6.5. The solution requires two steps. The first step is to balance practice effects for (in our case) the marijuana variable. A random starting order with rotation has been used to accomplish the balancing of the four dose levels (0, 50, 100, 200). Only four subjects are needed to do this balancing, and the sequences for these four subjects appear in the upper-left quadrant of the table. Because each dose appears with each list exactly once, the marijuana variable is also balanced for the possible effects of the list variable.

A problem would arise, however, if the researcher were to try to assess differences among the four lists. The lists for the first four subjects are perfectly confounded by the ordinal position variable. The confounding of lists and ordinal position can be overcome by taking the second step in dealing with the problem of irreversible tasks. In general, this second step requires testing additional subjects so that the list variable and the ordinal position variable are also balanced. In our example, twelve additional subjects would need to be tested, with the order of the lists systematically rotated for each successive set of four subjects. This is illustrated in Table 6.5. Each quadrant

TABLE 6.5 BALANCING EXPERIMENTS WITH IRREVERSIBLE TASKS IN THE INCOMPLETE WITHIN-SUBJECTS DESIGN

	Ordinal position					Ordinal position			
	1st	2nd	3rd	4th		1st	2nd	3rd	4th
		List					List		
Subject	A	B	C	D	Subject	B	C	D	A
1	050	200	000	100	5	050	200	000	100
2	200	000	100	050	6	200	000	100	050
3	000	100	050	200	7	000	100	050	200
4	100	050	200	000	8	100	050	200	000

	Ordinal position					Ordinal position			
	1st	2nd	3rd	4th		1st	2nd	3rd	4th
		List					List		
Subject	C	D	A	B	Subject	D	A	B	C
9	050	200	000	100	13	050	200	000	100
10	200	000	100	050	14	200	000	100	050
11	000	100	050	200	15	000	100	050	200
12	100	050	200	000	16	100	050	200	000

Note: The numbers 000, 050, 100, and 200 refer to dose levels.

of the table includes the same order of the marijuana doses. The list order for each group of four subjects is different, however. The order of the lists has been determined using a random starting order with rotation. The two-step process of balancing in experiments involving irreversible tasks ensures that each of three variables (independent variable of interest, stage of practice, and task) are balanced for the other two. Thus, the effects of all three variables are interpretable.

LIMITATIONS OF THE WITHIN-SUBJECTS DESIGNS

An obvious limitation of the within-subjects designs is that they cannot be used to study subject variables such as age and gender. It is unlikely that any such subject characteristics could be successfully balanced. A 40-year-old person cannot be 20 years old, then 60 years old, and then back to 40 years old (though we've all known people who *act* that way!). Similarly, within-subjects designs are not appropriate when the levels of the independent variable represent an unfolding sequence of successive events. A study of brain lesions would require controls such as Anesthesia Only and a Sham-Operated condition, and the sequential nature of these treatments seems to demand separate groups. That is, an animal could not be tested in the Anesthesia Only group once the animal was lesioned. Third, experiments in which each condition takes a great deal of time to implement are not likely to be suitable for the within-subjects designs. If the treatment involved participation in a year-long program, one ABBA sequence in the complete within-subjects design would take four years! It is unlikely that the random groups design will be completely replaced by the within-subjects designs. In the next section we introduce a fourth and final limitation of the within-subjects designs, the problem of differential transfer.

DIFFERENTIAL TRANSFER

The most consistent and vocal critic of the within-subjects designs has been E. C. Poulton (1973, 1975, 1982; Poulton and Freeman, 1966). While conceding that balancing techniques control practice effects, Poulton has argued that they do not eliminate a more serious problem he calls *asymmetric transfer*. Asymmetric transfer arises when a strategy learned in one condition of a within-subjects design experiment is carried over and used in another condition of the experiment in which it is not appropriate. When performance in one condition differs depending on which of two other conditions precedes it, we say that the original condition has been influenced by **differential transfer.**

Consider a problem-solving experiment in which two types of instructions are being compared in an incomplete within-subjects design. One set of instructions (A) is expected to enhance problem solving, whereas the other set of instructions (B) serves as the neutral control condition. It is reasonable to expect that subjects tested in the order AB will be unable or unwilling to abandon the approach outlined in the A instructions when they are supposed to be following the B instructions. Giving up the "good thing" subjects had under instruction A would be the counterpart of successfully following the admonition "Don't think of pink elephants!" When subjects fail to give up the instruction from the first condition (A) when they are supposed to be following instruction B, any difference between the two conditions is reduced. For those subjects, after all, condition B was not really tried.

In general, the presence of differential transfer tends to underestimate differences between the conditions and thereby drastically reduces the generality of any findings. Psychologists are rarely interested in interpreting phenomena that are traceable to a problem in the design of the experiment. Thus the within-subjects design should not be used when differential transfer may arise. Differential transfer is sufficiently common with instructional variables to advise against the use of within-subjects designs for these variables (Underwood and Shaughnessy, 1975). Unfortunately, differential transfer can arise in any within-subjects design. For instance, the effect of 50 units of marijuana may be different if it is administered after the subject has received 200 units than after the subject has received the placebo. There are ways, however, to determine whether differential transfer is likely to have occurred.

DOCUMENTING DIFFERENTIAL TRANSFER

The first method for documenting differential transfer can be applied when all possible orders have been used to balance practice effects and when several subjects have been tested with each of the possible orders. Table 6.6 presents the sequences for twenty-four subjects who were each tested once with each of three doses of marijuana. Because all possible orders were used, each dose level precedes and follows each other dose level at each ordinal position. The orders have been repeated four times, so there are eight measurements when the 100-unit dose follows the 0-unit dose and eight measurements when the 100-unit dose follows the 50-unit dose. If differential transfer has occurred, the average performance for the 100-unit dose will differ in these two situations. That is, the 100-unit dose will have had a different effect when it followed the 50-unit dose than when it followed the 0-unit dose. Of course, similar tests would need to be done for the 0-unit and the 50-unit doses before the search for differential transfer would be complete.

There are alternative methods available to document differential transfer when all possible orders have not been used to balance practice effects. Poulton (1982) maintains that the best way to determine whether differential transfer is a problem is to do two separate experiments. The same independent variable would be studied in both experiments, but a within-subjects design would be used in one experiment and a random groups design in the other. The random groups design cannot possibly involve differential transfer because each subject is tested in only one condition. Thus, the logic of

TABLE 6.6 DOCUMENTING DIFFERENTIAL TRANSFER WHEN ALL POSSIBLE ORDERS HAVE BEEN USED TO BALANCE PRACTICE EFFECTS

	Ordinal position				Ordinal position		
Subject	1st	2nd	3rd	Subject	1st	2nd	3rd
*1	0	50	100	*13	0	50	100
**2	0	100	50	**14	0	100	50
**3	50	0	100	**15	50	0	100
*4	50	100	0	*16	50	100	0
5	100	0	50	17	100	0	50
6	100	50	0	18	100	50	0
*7	0	50	100	*19	0	50	100
**8	0	100	50	**20	0	100	50
**9	50	0	100	**21	50	0	100
*10	50	100	0	*22	50	100	0
11	100	0	50	23	100	0	50
12	100	50	0	24	100	50	0

Note: The text refers to eight measurements when the 100-unit dose follows the 50-unit dose. These sequences are marked with one asterisk (*). The eight measurements when the 100-unit dose follows the 0-unit dose are marked with two asterisks (**).

Poulton's recommended approach is that, if the within-subjects design shows the same effect as that shown in a random groups design, differential transfer is not a problem. If the two types of design show different effects for the same independent variable, however, differential transfer is likely to be guilty of producing the different outcome in the within-subjects design. When differential transfer does occur, the results of the random groups design experiment should be used to provide the best description of the effect of the independent variable.

Perhaps the most efficient way to follow Poulton's advice is to do experiments involving a relatively large incomplete within-subjects design. For example, if forty-eight subjects were tested in a four-condition experiment with all possible orders of the conditions, there would be twelve subjects tested in each of the four conditions at the first stage of practice. So long as subjects have been randomly assigned to sequences, the incomplete within-subjects design contains a random group design at the first stage of practice. The results for the first stage can then be compared to the overall results to achieve the comparison Poulton recommends between the random groups design and the within-subjects design for the same independent variable.

It may be discouraging at first to learn that the outcome of your experiment may depend critically on your choice of experimental design. One encouraging note, however, is that differential transfer itself may provide clues to the working of important psychological processes. For example, research in animal learning has consistently shown that the size of the reward given for correct responses influences the learning rate for those responses. As might be expected, larger rewards lead to better performance. A finding that may not be so intuitively obvious is that the effect of the size of the reward is larger when it is manipulated in a within-subjects design experiment than in a random groups design experiment (Flaherty et al., 1977). The differential transfer from one reward size to another influences the animals' performance beyond the effects of the reward size per se. Learning theorists currently are debating whether this occurs because of a perceptual contrast effect (the large reward looks even larger when compared to a small reward) or because of an emotional response such as frustration (the animal is "disappointed" by the small reward after having had experience with the large reward). Regardless of which of these (or other) explanations eventually proves true, the research on the effects of size of reward illustrates that differential transfer can be more than an interpretive problem in the within-subjects designs—it may also provide a window for the study of important psychological processes.

ANALYSIS OF WITHIN-SUBJECTS DESIGN EXPERIMENTS

The analysis of within-subjects design experiments involves the same general procedures that are used in the analysis of independent groups design experiments. The principles of null hypothesis testing are applied to determine whether the differences obtained in the experiment are larger than would be expected on the basis of error variation alone. The analysis begins with an omnibus analysis of variance to determine whether the independent variable has produced any systematic variation. Should this omnibus analysis prove statistically significant, analytical comparisons can be done to specify the source of the systematic variation. Because we have already described the logic and procedures for this general analysis plan in the context of the independent groups design (see Chapter 5), we will focus in this section on the analysis procedures that are specific to the within-subjects designs.

DETERMINING THE EFFECT OF THE INDEPENDENT VARIABLE

The first step in the analysis of any experiment is to prepare a matrix summarizing performance in each condition of the experiment. In the random groups design, this means simply listing the scores for those subjects tested in each of the conditions of the experiment and then summarizing these scores with some descriptive statistic such as the mean. Similarly, in the within-subjects designs, we prepare a matrix in which the scores for each subject in each condition of the experiment are listed.

An example of such a matrix appears in the upper half of Table 6.7. The data represent performance for five subjects tested in a time perception experiment that was done as a classroom demonstration of a within-subjects design. Each subject was tested on all four interval lengths (12, 24, 36, and 48 seconds). If the incomplete within-subjects design had been used, the matrix shown in Table 6.7 would have been prepared by "unraveling" the different sequences in which the subjects had been tested so that the results for each

TABLE 6.7 DATA MATRIX AND ANALYSIS OF VARIANCE SUMMARY TABLE FOR A WITHIN-SUBJECTS DESIGN EXPERIMENT

Data Matrix

Interval length

Subject	12	24	36	48
1	13	21	30	38
2	10	15	38	35
3	12	23	31	32
4	12	15	22	32
5	16	36	69	60
Mean	12.6	22.0	38.0	39.4

Summary table

Source of variation	df	SS	MS	F	p
Subjects	4	1553.5	—	—	
Interval length	3	2515.6	838.5	15.6	< .05
Residual (error variation)	12	646.9	53.9		
Total	19	4716.0			

subject were in the same order. For example, the first subject might have received the intervals in the order 12-24-36-48, whereas the second subject received the order 24-36-48-12. The time estimates for each interval for the first subject could just be placed directly in Table 6.7. The estimates for the second subject, however, would have to be rearranged so that they would be listed in Table 6.7 in the proper order. In fact, the complete within-subjects design was used for this experiment, so the preparation of the data matrix is a bit more involved.

Each of the four interval lengths was tested six times in the experiment, and block randomization was used to determine the order in which the intervals were presented. Thus, each subject provided twenty-four time estimates: six estimates for each of the four interval lengths. Any one of these six estimates for a given interval is contaminated by practice effects, so some measure that combines information across the six estimates is needed. Typically, the mean across the six estimates for each interval for each subject would be used to provide a single estimate of performance in each condition. As you may remember, however, the mean is influenced by extreme scores; it is quite possible that subjects gave extreme estimates of the time intervals for at least one of the six tests of each interval. Thus, the median of the six estimates probably provides the best measure to reflect subjects' estimates of the time intervals. It is these median estimates (rounded to the nearest whole number) that are listed in Table 6.7. For example, the median estimate by Subject 3 for the 24-second interval was 23 seconds.

Once the problem of obtaining an individual score to reflect performance by each subject in each condition has been solved, the next step is to summarize the results across subjects, using an appropriate descriptive statistic. (From this point on, by the way, the procedures for the analysis of the complete and the incomplete within-subjects designs are identical.) The mean estimates across subjects for each of the four intervals are listed near the center of Table 6.7. Even though the data for only five subjects are included in the table, these mean estimates are reasonably accurate reflections of the actual interval lengths, at least for intervals up to 36 seconds. The collective judgments of this small group of undergraduates provide a fair approximation to a stop watch. The focus on the analysis of this experiment was not on the accuracy of subjects' time estimates compared to the actual interval lengths. Instead, the purpose of the analysis was to determine whether subjects' estimates increased systematically with increasing interval lengths. In other words, could subjects discriminate between intervals of different lengths? As you probably have already realized, we cannot confirm subjects' ability to discriminate intervals of varying length until we know that the mean differences in Table 6.7 are greater than would be expected on the basis of error variation alone.

The null hypothesis for an omnibus analysis of variance for the data in Table 6.7 is that the mean estimates for each interval are the same. A formal statement of this hypothesis is H_0: $\mu_{12} = \mu_{24} = \mu_{36} = \mu_{48}$. To form an F-ratio to test this null hypothesis, we need an estimate of error variation plus systematic variation (the numerator of an F-ratio) and an estimate of error variation alone (the denominator). The variation among the mean estimates across subjects for the four intervals provides the information we need for the numerator. Even if these five subjects had been tested on only one interval length several times, we would not expect their mean estimates of this interval to be identical. Thus, we know that the mean estimates we have for each interval reflect error variation. We also know, however, that if the different interval lengths *did* systematically affect subjects' judgments, then the mean estimates for the intervals will reflect this systematic variation.

There is another source of systematic variation in a within-subjects design in addition to the independent variable. In a within-subjects design there is systematic variation among subjects. You can see in the data matrix in Table 6.7 that Subject 5 gave consistently higher estimates for each interval than did Subject 4. In the random groups design, subjects participate in only one condition. The systematic differences among subjects are balanced through random assignment, but these differences contribute to the amount of error variation in the experiment. Because each subject participates in each condition of a within-subjects design, differences among subjects contribute equally to the mean performance in each condition. Accordingly, any differences among the means for each condition *cannot* be the result of systematic differences among subjects. In the within-subjects design, then, differences among subjects are not balanced. They can be eliminated from the analysis using procedures we will describe in a moment.

But how do we get an estimate that involves only error variation in the within-subjects designs? As implied in the preceding paragraph, we get our estimate of error variation "by default." We first determine how much total variation there is in our data matrix. Then we subtract the potential sources of systematic variation (Subjects and Interval Length), and the remainder (called *Residual Variation*)[1] is our estimate of error variation alone. The analysis of variance summary table in the bottom half of Table 6.7 lists the four sources of variation in the analysis of a within-subjects design with one manipulated independent variable. Working from the bottom of the summary table up, these sources are: Total Variation, Residual Variation, Variation produced by the independent variable (in this case, the Interval Length), and Subject Variation. The procedures for computing the values in the summary table can be found in Appendix A. Our focus now, however, is on interpreting the information in the summary table.

As in any summary table, the most critical pieces of information are the F-ratio for the effect of the independent variable of interest and the probability associated with that F-ratio under the null hypothesis. The important F-ratio in Table 6.7 is the one for Interval Length. The numerator of this F-ratio is the mean square (MS) for Interval Length, and the denominator is the Residual MS. There are four interval lengths, so there are 3 degrees of freedom (df) for the numerator. There are 12 df for the denominator. We can obtain the df for the denominator by subtracting the df for Subjects and Interval Length from the Total df ($19 - 4 - 3 = 12$). The critical F-value of 3.49 for these degrees of freedom with $\alpha = .05$ can be found in Appendix A. The obtained F of 15.6 clearly exceeds this critical value, so we reject the null hypothesis and conclude that the interval length was a source of systematic variation.

This omnibus analysis of variance would almost certainly be followed by analytical comparisons (such as comparing each interval to its succeeding one) to determine the exact source of the variation in the mean estimates of the interval lengths. Once again, the logic of these analytical comparisons corresponds exactly to the logic we discussed in considering analytical comparisons in the random groups design (see Chapter 5). In most instances, the Residual MS can be used as an estimate of error variation alone in computing the F-ratios for the analytical comparisons. [See Keppel (1982), however, for a discussion of complications that can arise in doing analytical comparisons in the within-subjects designs.]

DETERMINING STAGE-OF-PRACTICE EFFECTS

So far we have discussed practice effects solely as a source of potential confounding in the within-subjects designs. It is also possible to analyze the results of a within-subjects design experiment to determine the nature of the stage-of-

---

[1]The Residual Variation can, of course, be computed directly. It reflects what is called the interaction effect of Interval Length and Subjects. The interaction of two or more independent variables is a critical concept that we will treat in our discussion of complex designs in Chapter 7. Because we have not yet introduced the idea of experiments involving more than one independent variable, we chose to describe the "subtraction method" for obtaining the Residual Variation. For a more complete discussion of Residual Variation and why it is an estimate of error variation alone, see Keppel (1982).

practice effects themselves. In some areas of psychology these stage-of-practice effects can reflect important psychological processes. For instance, changes in performance as a consequence of experience with different tasks or with repetitions of the same task provide one definition of the concept of learning.

In most cases, though, stage-of-practice effects are examined to help researchers design future experiments more effectively. For example, suppose you did an experiment that required subjects to perform some task with which they were not very familiar, such as solving anagrams. An anagram is a string of letters which, when unscrambled, forms a word (hicra = chair). What you might find is that performance on this task changes rather abruptly after subjects have had some initial practice. That is, subjects may "catch on quickly" and show a large practice effect at first. After this initial spurt, however, subjects' performance may stabilize and there may be little more evidence of substantial practice effects. Based on these results, in future experiments you might want to give subjects a brief practice period before beginning to collect the data you will actually analyze. By waiting for practice effects to become more stable, you would increase the sensitivity of your future experiments. Performance within each condition would not vary so much because the variation due to practice effects would be reduced.

Just as in the analysis of the effect of the independent variable, the first step in the analysis of stage-of-practice effects is to prepare a data matrix like that shown in Table 6.7. The procedures for preparing this data matrix differ slightly for the complete and the incomplete within-subjects designs, so we will describe these two designs separately.

In the time perception experiment summarized in Table 6.7, the complete within-subjects design was used. Each subject in this experiment made six estimates of each of four time intervals. In the complete within-subjects design, a stage of practice is defined as the administration of each condition in the experiment once. Therefore, there are as many stages of practice as there are repetitions of each condition. In our time perception experiment there were six repetitions of each condition, so there were six stages of practice. The data listed at the top of Table 6.8 represent the time estimates given by each of the five subjects for each of the twenty-four trials in the experiment. The actual interval lengths for each trial are also shown. The data matrix for the analysis of practice effects in this experiment appears in the lower half of Table 6.8. The data matrix was made by dividing the twenty-four trials for each subject into six blocks, one for each stage of practice. The mean estimates (rounded to the nearest whole second) for the four intervals in each block were then used to provide a value for each of the six stages of practice for each subject. For the first subject these mean estimates were 25, 13, 16, 11, 12, and 26; and, as you can see in Table 6.8, these six values make up the first row of the data matrix for the analysis of practice effects.

The bottom row of Table 6.8 presents the mean estimates across subjects for each of the six stages of practice. An omnibus analysis of variance of these means confirmed that there were statistically significant practice effects, $F(5, 20) = 7.0$, $p < .05$. The practice effects in this experiment turned out to be

TABLE 6.8 PROCEDURES FOR PREPARING DATA MATRIX FOR ANALYSIS OF STAGE-OF-PRACTICE EFFECTS IN THE COMPLETE WITHIN-SUBJECTS DESIGN

Trial	Block I				Block II				Block III				Block IV				Block V				Block VI			
Subject	1	2	3	4	5	6	7	8	9	10	11	12	13	14	15	16	17	18	19	20	21	22	23	24
1	33	35	13	20	10	15	8	20	8	23	15	17	12	17	6	8	10	7	15	17	13	22	23	24
2	45	35	10	15	10	25	5	15	5	15	10	15	10	15	5	15	10	10	15	20	10	15	25	40
3	25	32	10	23	24	34	10	30	13	38	26	30	22	31	10	19	18	16	27	34	15	23	40	30
4	35	25	15	15	15	25	10	20	10	25	15	20	15	25	10	15	15	10	25	25	10	15	30	20
5	69	60	15	41	30	40	10	47	10	35	15	30	20	35	10	15	25	10	35	53	17	32	78	51

Stage of practice

Subject	I	II	III	IV	V	VI
1	25	13	16	11	12	26
2	26	14	11	11	14	22
3	22	24	27	13	24	27
4	22	18	18	16	19	19
5	46	32	22	20	31	44
Mean	28.2	20.2	18.8	14.2	20.0	27.6

somewhat complex, as you can see in Figure 6.4. It would be possible to clarify the nature of these effects by performing analytical comparisons. There are even techniques available to analyze the effects of the independent variable and the stage-of-practice effects in the same analysis (see Keppel, 1982). But for now, we will have to rely on our descriptive statistics and simply indicate that subjects' time estimates in this experiment first decreased and then increased across stages of practice. One possible explanation for these rather unusual practice effects is that the decreasing estimates reflect improvement due to subjects' developing skill in making the judgments, whereas the increasing estimates at later stages reflect time beginning to "drag" as subjects become bored with this task.

The Sharma and Moskowitz (1972) marijuana experiment illustrates the incomplete within-subjects design. As you may remember, each subject in their experiment was tested once with each of four doses of marijuana, and the size of the autokinetic illusion was found to increase with increasing dose levels. In the incomplete within-subjects design, each ordinal position represents a stage of practice. Thus there are as many stages of practice as there are conditions in the experiment. Table 6.9 represents a possible order of the conditions for four hypothetical subjects in the Sharma and Moskowitz experiment. The values in parentheses are fictitious but reasonable estimates of apparent movement (in centimeters) for each subject in each condition.

The mean reported amount of apparent movement across subjects for each stage of practice is listed in the bottom row of the diagram. The amount of apparent movement appears to increase across the stages in this experiment. Of course, we would have to do an omnibus analysis of variance to ensure that the apparent practice effects are not the result of error variation alone. What is most important for you to recognize for now, however, is that stage-of-practice effects can be determined in any within-subjects design. Practice effects such as those in the Sharma and Moskowitz experiment are interpretable because, just as the marijuana variable is balanced for stage of practice, the stage-of-practice variable is balanced for the marijuana variable.

FIGURE 6.4   Example of stage of practice in a time perception experiment involving the complete within-subjects design.

TABLE 6.9 DATA MATRIX FOR DETERMINING STAGE-OF-PRACTICE EFFECTS IN THE INCOMPLETE WITHIN-SUBJECTS DESIGNS

Subject	Ordinal position			
	1st	2nd	3rd	4th
1	0(4)	50(6)	100(13)	200(18)
2	50(5)	200(16)	0(6)	100(14)
3	100(11)	0(5)	200(17)	50(8)
4	200(15)	100(12)	50(7)	0(7)
Mean	8.75	9.75	10.75	11.75

SUMMARY

The within-subjects designs provide an effective and efficient way to conduct an experiment by administering all the treatments in the experiment to each subject. For the within-subjects design experiment to be interpretable, however, stage-of-practice effects must be balanced. Practice effects are changes that subjects undergo because of repeated testing. In the complete within-subjects design, practice effects are balanced for each subject. In the incomplete within-subjects design, each subject receives each treatment only once and the balancing is accomplished across subjects.

Block randomization and ABBA counterbalancing can be used to balance practice effects in the complete within-subjects design. ABBA counterbalancing should not be used, however, if practice effects are expected to be nonlinear or if anticipation effects are likely. The alternative techniques for balancing practice effects in the incomplete within-subjects design involve either the use of all possible orders or selected orders (the Latin Square and rotation of a random starting order). When irreversible tasks are used, three independent variables must be balanced (the independent variable of interest, stage of practice, and the task variable). The most serious problem in any within-subjects design is differential transfer—when performance in one condition differs depending on which other condition it follows. Procedures for detecting the presence of differential transfer are available, but there is little that can be done to salvage a study in which it occurs. In an incomplete within-subjects design, however, it is possible to analyze the results of the random groups design included at the first stage of practice if differential transfer arises in the experiment as a whole.

The procedures for analyzing the results of experiments involving the within-subjects designs are basically the same as those used in the analysis of independent groups designs. Data reduction procedures are somewhat different, and it is possible to assess stage-of-practice effects in any within-subjects design. The greatest difference involves the role of differences across subjects. In the random groups design these subject differences are balanced, but they contribute to error variation. Systematic differences across subjects are eliminated in the analysis of within-subjects designs, making within-subjects designs generally more sensitive than random groups designs.

KEY CONCEPTS

within-subjects design
stage-of-practice effects
complete within-subjects design
incomplete within-subjects design

ABBA counterbalancing
anticipation effects
irreversible task
differential transfer

REVIEW QUESTIONS

1 For what three reasons might a researcher choose to use a within-subjects design?
2 Distinguish between the complete within-subjects design and the incomplete within-subjects design.
3 What options do researchers have in balancing practice effects in the complete within-subjects design?
4 Under what circumstances would you recommend against the use of ABBA counterbalancing to balance practice effects in the complete within-subjects design?
5 State the general rule for balancing practice effects in the incomplete within-subjects design.
6 What techniques can be used to balance practice effects in the incomplete within-subjects design? Which technique is preferred? Why?
7 Explain what is meant by an irreversible task. What additional balancing procedures must be used when an irreversible task is used in the incomplete within-subjects design along with another independent variable of interest?
8 For which types of independent variables is the within-subjects design unlikely to prove useful?
9 Describe how researchers can document differential transfer in a complete within-subjects design.
10 Outline the procedures that are used to determine whether an independent variable has had a statistically significant effect in a within-subjects design experiment.
11 What values are used for the numerator and denominator of the F-ratio for the omnibus analysis of a within-subjects design?
12 Explain the different roles played by systematic differences across subjects in the analysis of random groups designs and within-subjects designs. Include in your explanation the role of this factor in the likely differences in sensitivity of the two types of design.
13 How does the definition of a stage of practice differ in the complete and the incomplete within-subjects designs?

CHALLENGE QUESTIONS

1 The following problems represent different situations in the within-subjects design in which stage-of-practice effects need to be balanced.

A Consider a complete within-subjects design experiment involving one independent variable. The independent variable has three levels (Low, Medium and High). You are to prepare an order for administering the conditions of this experiment so that the independent variable is balanced for stage of practice. You are first to use block randomization to balance the variable and then to use ABBA counterbalancing to balance the variable. Each condition should appear twice in the order you prepare. Use the following table of random numbers in doing your block randomization.

15-8-11-14-9-4-12-10-13-7-16-1-3-2-5-6
10-3-4-16-7-8-9-13-2-1-6-12-5-11-15-14

B Consider an experiment to be done using the incomplete within-subjects design. One independent variable is to be manipulated at six levels (A, B, C, D, E, and F). Present a table showing how you would determine the order of administering the conditions to the first six subjects of the experiment. Be sure that practice effects are balanced for these subjects.

C Consider an experiment in which the incomplete within-subjects design is used to manipulate an environmental variable, room temperature. There are three levels of the variable (60, 65, and 70 degrees). The dependent variable of interest is the amount of time taken to solve a list of word problems. Thus three different word problem lists are required (designated as Lists A, B, and C). Present a table showing how you could administer the conditions of the experiment in order to determine the effect of each of the three independent variables: room temperature, stage of practice, and list. You have only *nine* people available for participants, but previous research indicates that you need not be concerned with problems of differential transfer.

2 The following table represents the order of administering the conditions to participants in an incomplete within-subjects design in which the independent variable was the difficulty of the task given to the participant (High, Medium, or Low Difficulty). The values in parentheses represent the number correct for each participant in each condition. Use this table, when necessary, to answer questions that follow.

Participant	Order of Conditions		
1	High (2)	Medium (9)	Low (9)
2	Medium (3)	Low (5)	High (7)
3	Low (4)	High (3)	Medium (5)
4	High (6)	Low (10)	Medium (8)
5	Medium (7)	High (8)	Low (6)
6	Low (8)	Medium (4)	High (4)

A What method was used to balance the stage-of-practice effects?

B Why is it unlikely that the experimenter would have considered the experiment completed when she had collected data from only six participants?

C Present the values you would use as a basis for your verbal description of the effect of the task difficulty variable.

D Present the values you would use as a basis for your verbal description of the stage-of-practice effects.

E Show which values you would compare in order to determine whether there had been differential transfer influencing performance in the High Difficulty conditions.

3 Subject	UNF	SYL	FREQ	FREQ	SYL	UNF
1	33	15	23	17	17	44
2	45	25	15	15	20	25
3	25	34	38	31	34	40
4	35	25	25	25	25	30
5	69	40	35	25	53	78
6	65	25	15	25	20	35
7	35	25	25	25	35	45
8	45	35	35	45	40	45
9	50	30	27	30	37	42
10	70	55	40	50	50	55

The foregoing table indicates the order in which the three conditions of a complete within-subjects design experiment were administered to each of the ten participants. The experiment was a time perception experiment, and the independent variable was the nature of the activity in which the participant engaged while the to-be-judged interval passed. Unbeknown to the participant, the interval was always the same length: 48 seconds. Six such intervals were presented, and the data shown represent the judged length of the intervals for each participant. During two of the intervals the participant did nothing [Unfilled (UNF) Intervals]; during two of the intervals the participant classified each word on a list as to the number of syllables in the word [Syllables (SYL) Intervals]; and during two of the intervals the participant classified each word as to its frequency of usage in printed English [Frequency (FREQ) Intervals]. You are to use these data to carry out the following analyses.

A Present the values you would use to describe the stage-of-practice effects in this experiment.

B Present the values you would use to describe the overall effect of the Interval Activity variable. You are to include a verbal description of the effect along with the descriptive statistics that are the basis for your description.

C Indicate any analytical comparisons you would do to locate the source of the overall effect of the Interval Activity variable. Be sure to explain why you would make each comparison.

D For how many individual participants does the overall pattern of the results hold? Of what value is this type of information?

4 The following table represents the order of administering the conditions to subjects in an incomplete within-subjects design in which room temperature was manipulated at three levels (50, 65, and 80 degrees). Three tasks were required—one for each of the stages of practice. Practice effects were balanced for the Task and Temperature variables through the use of random starting orders with rotation. The values in parentheses represent the number correct for each subject in each condition. Use this table to answer the questions that follow.

Subject	Stage 1 Task I	Stage 2 Task II	Stage 3 Task III
1	50(2)	65(4)	80(6)
2	65(3)	80(5)	50(4)
3	80(4)	50(3)	65(5)
	Task II	**Task III**	**Task I**
4	50(2)	65(4)	80(6)
5	65(3)	80(5)	50(4)
6	80(4)	50(3)	65(5)
	Task III	**Task I**	**Task II**
7	50(2)	65(4)	80(6)
8	65(3)	80(5)	50(4)
9	80(4)	50(3)	65(5)

A State the effect of the temperature variable verbally, being sure to include the values you use as a basis for your description.

B Did the three tasks differ in difficulty? Again, be sure to include the values you use to answer this question.

C Describe the nature of the stage-of-practice effects in this experiment. As always, be sure to include the values on which your description is based.

ANSWER TO CHALLENGE QUESTION 1

A Assigning the values 1, 2, and 3 to the Low, Medium, and High conditions, respectively, and using the accompanying random numbers, the block-randomized sequence is Low–High–Medium–High–Medium–Low. One possible ABBA counterbalanced sequence is Low–Medium–High–High–Medium–Low.

B Because there are six conditions, all possible orders is not feasible. Therefore, either a Latin Square or a random-starting order with rotation is needed to balance practice effects. A possible set of sequences using rotation is:

Subject	Position					
	1st	**2nd**	**3rd**	**4th**	**5th**	**6th**
1	B	D	E	C	A	F
2	D	E	C	A	F	B
3	E	C	A	F	B	D
4	C	A	F	B	D	E
5	A	F	B	D	E	C
6	F	B	D	E	C	A

C The required sequences to balance room temperature, stage of practice, and list, with only nine participants, are constructed by first balancing room temperature for the first three subjects and then repeating these three sequences while rotating the lists for successive sets of three subjects.

	Stage of practice		
Subject	1st List A	2nd List B	3rd List C
1	60	65	70
2	65	70	60
3	70	65	60
	List B	List C	List A
4	60	65	70
5	65	70	60
6	70	60	65
	List C	List A	List B
7	60	65	70
8	65	70	60
9	70	60	65

7

COMPLEX DESIGNS AND ANALYSIS

OUTLINE

In the last two chapters we described the basic designs that psychologists use to study the effect of an independent variable. We discussed how an independent variable could be implemented by administering each treatment to a separate group of subjects (Chapter 5) or by administering all the treatments to each subject (Chapter 6). We limited our discussion in these two chapters to experiments involving only one independent variable. We did this primarily because we wanted you to concentrate on the characteristics of each research design. Experiments involving only one independent variable are not, however, the most common type of experiment in current psychological research. Instead, researchers most often use **complex designs** in which two or more independent variables are studied simultaneously in one experiment.

Johnson et al. (1983) used a complex design to compare the memory performance of depressed and nondepressed people. Specifically, these investigators were testing the hypothesis that depressed individuals would be more likely to remember tasks they had not completed, whereas nondepressed individuals would be more likely to remember tasks they had completed. If depressed people do tend to dwell on the negative, this tendency may contribute to sustaining their depression. In the experiment, groups of depressed and nondepressed subjects were asked to do twenty tasks, ten of which were interrupted by the experimenter before they were completed. After the last task, the subjects were asked to recall the names or descriptions of as many tasks as they could.

As indicated in the following diagram, this experiment involved four conditions: Completed and Uncompleted tasks for Depressed and for Nondepressed subjects.

	Type of task	
Type of subject	**Completed**	**Uncompleted**
Depressed		
Nondepressed		

In a complex design such as this one, the levels of each of the two independent variables are combined factorially. *Factorial combination* involves pairing each level of one independent variable with each level of a second independent variable. Factorial combination makes it possible to assess the effect of each independent variable alone (main effect) *and* the effect of the two independent variables in combination (interaction). For example, Johnson et al. (1983) found, as they had predicted, that depressed subjects recalled more uncompleted than completed tasks and that nondepressed subjects recalled more completed than uncompleted tasks. The task variable, then, had opposite effects on depressed and nondepressed subjects. This type of effect, called an *interaction effect,* can be discovered only when two or more independent variables are included in the same experiment. In general, an **interaction** occurs when the effect of one independent variable differs depending on the level of a second independent variable. The procedures for producing, analyzing, and interpreting interactions are the subject of the present chapter.

We begin with a review of a set of guidelines for identifying or selecting an experimental design. The major advantages of using a complex design are then briefly introduced, along with the basic concepts of main effects and interactions. Next we examine the nature of interactions in the simplest of complex designs, the 2 × 2 design. We also discuss designs having more than two levels of each of two independent variables and designs having more than two independent variables. Special attention is given to the problems of interpretation that complex designs pose, and to the role of interactions in the natural groups design (see Chapter 5). This chapter concludes with the analysis procedures for complex designs.

INTRODUCTION TO COMPLEX DESIGNS

GUIDELINES FOR IDENTIFYING AN EXPERIMENTAL DESIGN

As we have already mentioned, an experiment involving a complex design is one in which more than one independent variable is being studied. Each independent variable in a complex design must be implemented using either a within-subjects or an independent groups design according to the procedures described in the previous two chapters. Before examining complex designs themselves, we need to review briefly the characteristics of the various experimental designs that can be used to study a single independent variable. You will be better able to understand descriptions of complex designs if you can quickly and accurately identify the independent variables, their levels, and the design used to implement each independent variable. Similarly, your ability to carry out your own experiments using complex designs will be enhanced if you can confidently select the most appropriate design for each independent variable in which you are interested.

The flow diagram presented in Figure 7.1 summarizes the distinctions among experimental designs by taking you through a series of questions. The diagram will probably prove most useful to you when you are reading about a particular experiment in either your text or a journal article. As you identify each independent variable in the experiment you are reading about, you can track the variable through Figure 7.1 to determine what design has been used to implement the independent variable. The first question at the top of the diagram is the most critical one. The answer to this question (number of levels of the independent variable administered to each subject) determines whether the independent groups or the within-subjects designs have been used. Answering the subsequent questions for the independent groups designs will allow you to identify the particular type of design by examining the procedures whereby the groups were formed. For the within-subjects designs, we have included questions to help you to identify which balancing technique has been used.

Complex designs require that you go through the diagram as many times as necessary to identify the design for each independent variable in the experiment. In a complex design, the two or more independent variables need not be implemented in the same way. In the Johnson et al. (1983) study, the type of subject (Depressed versus Nondepressed) represented a natural groups design, whereas the type of task (Completed versus Uncompleted) was manipulated using the within-subjects design. When the independent variables in a complex design are implemented using different designs for each independent variable, the experiment is sometimes described as a **mixed design.** Choosing a label to describe the design of the experiment as a whole is less critical than knowing that you must identify the type of design used for *each* independent variable in an experiment.

ADVANTAGES OF COMPLEX DESIGNS

Resolving Contradictions When only one independent variable is manipulated in an experiment, it is essential that all other potential independent variables be controlled by holding them constant or by balancing them across conditions. A problem can arise, however, if two researchers choose to hold the same potential independent variable constant at different levels in their respective experiments. For example, two memory researchers might be studying the relative effectiveness of two different learning strategies (A and

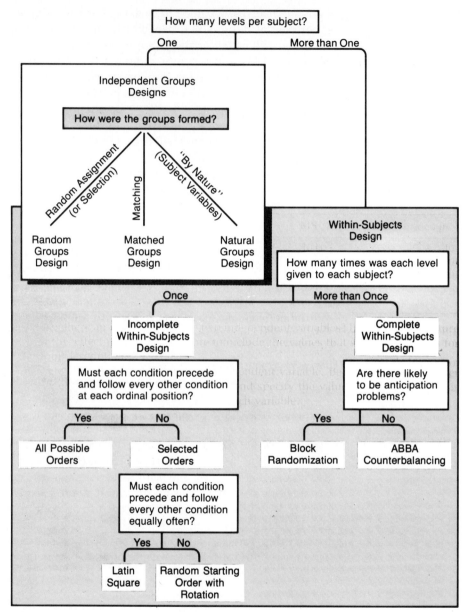

FIGURE 7.1   Flowchart for identifying experimental designs.

B). These two strategies would represent the levels of the manipulated independent variable in both experiments. One potential independent variable that would clearly need to be controlled in these experiments is the difficulty of the material to be learned. The first researcher might decide to control the level of difficulty of the material by giving subjects in both conditions relatively easy textbook passages to learn. The second researcher, who is equally concerned with the problem of controlling the difficulty of the material, might decide to give subjects in both conditions relatively hard textbook passages to learn. It would not be surprising if these two researchers were to obtain different results. One such possible outcome is illustrated in the following diagram.

Passage difficulty	Learning strategy	
	A	B
Easy (Researcher 1)	50	50
Hard (Researcher 2)	25	10

The first researcher has found that the two learning strategies are equally effective, while the second researcher has found that strategy A is more effective than strategy B! Why couldn't these two researchers replicate each other's findings?

At first, we might try to account for the different outcomes in the two experiments by focusing on the difficulty of the textbook passages. We could argue that the two strategies are equally effective for learning easy textbook passages but that strategy A is better for learning hard passages. This argument would not be convincing, however, unless the two types of passages represented the only independent variable that was held constant at two different levels in the two experiments. This seems highly unlikely. For example, the passages may very well have been studied for different lengths of time in the two experiments, the passages were probably on different topics, and the experimenters and subjects in the two experiments were undoubtedly different. Clearly, the difficulty of the passages is not the only factor that *could* be responsible for the different effects of the strategy variable in the two experiments.

The best way to identify which factor is responsible for the discrepant findings is to *use a complex design in which you manipulate the factor you think is responsible along with the strategy variable in the same experiment.* For instance, you might do an experiment in which both the strategy variable and the passage difficulty variable were manipulated. There would be four conditions in this complex design; both easy and hard passages would be tested under both strategies. Two possible outcomes of such an experiment are shown in the following diagram.

Passage difficulty	Outcome 1		Outcome 2	
	Strategy A	Strategy B	Strategy A	Strategy B
Easy	50	50	50	50
Hard	25	10	15	15

The pattern of results outlined in Outcome 1 has the same form as the original discrepancy between the outcomes in the two separate experiments involving *only* the strategy variable. That is, the strategies are equally effective for easy material and strategy A is better for hard material. If you obtain this outcome, you can be confident that the difficulty of the text was responsible for the different effects of the strategy variable in the two original experiments.

The situation would be very different, however, if you were to obtain results in your new experiment like those in Outcome 2. The pattern of results in Outcome 2 is *not* like the original pattern distinguishing the two experiments. The strategy variable has had no effect with either the easy or the hard text material. Because the strategy variable has the same effect with both types of material, differences in degree of difficulty between the materials in the two original experiments cannot be responsible for the different outcomes in those experiments. You must select another variable that you "suspect" and manipulate *it* along with the strategy variable. Both trial and error and the guidance of theory are involved in the selection of the variable. The process can be a painstaking one, but complex designs are extremely useful in tracking down the reasons for the seemingly contradictory finding that the same independent variable has had different effects in two different experiments.

Testing Theories Complex designs are useful for more than just clarifying contradictory research findings. Researchers often need to use complex designs to test predictions derived from psychological theories. For instance, the optimal arousal theory of motivation predicts that performance will be best when our arousal level is moderate—neither too low nor too high. If you have ever had to perform in either an athletic or an artistic event, you may have some sense of what is meant by optimal arousal. Your performance was not likely to be at its best if your arousal level was too low (you didn't care how well you did) or too high (you were scared out of your wits). Optimal arousal theory further predicts that the level of arousal that is best depends on the complexity of the task to be performed. Specifically, the theory predicts that higher arousal levels will lead to better performance on simple or well-learned tasks but that lower arousal levels will lead to better performance on complex tasks. You would probably be able to do simple arithmetic problems at a high arousal level, but the same arousal level would probably be disastrous if you were solving differential equations. Our focus for now is not on the details of optimal arousal theory but on the use of complex designs to test predictions derived from such a theory.

If we were to test the prediction that optimal arousal varied with task complexity, we would need to manipulate two independent variables: arousal level (High or Low) and task complexity (Simple or Complex). Our experiment would therefore have four conditions:

	Arousal level	
Task complexity	**High**	**Low**
Simple	50	35
Complex	10	25

The dependent variable entered in the body of our table is the mean number of tasks completed correctly in each of the four conditions. As you can see, the effect of arousal level depended on the level of task complexity—an interaction occurred. For the simple task, high arousal led to better performance, but for the complex task, low arousal led to better performance. This hypothetical but reasonable outcome supports the prediction derived from optimal arousal theory.

As in the example we just described, complex designs are often used to test a predicted interaction of two independent variables. In any complex design, however, it is also always possible to determine the overall effect of each independent variable in the experiment. The overall effect of an independent variable in a complex design is called a **main effect.** The following diagram contains the same information we used to examine the interaction of task complexity and arousal level.

	Arousal level*		**Main effect of task complexity**
Task complexity	**High**	**Low**	
Simple	50	35	42.5
Complex	10	25	17.5
Main effect of task complexity	30	30	

In addition, the means for the main effect of task complexity are presented in the far right-hand column, and the means for the main effect of arousal level are presented in the bottom row. These means were obtained by averaging the two entries in each respective row or column of the table.[1] For example, the mean for simple tasks (42.5) was obtained by averaging the two values for high and low arousal level: (50 + 35)/2. The means for the main effects represent the overall performance at each level of each individual variable *collapsed across* (averaged over) the levels of the other independent variable.

Analysis procedures for determining the statistical significance of the interaction and main effects will be described later in this chapter. For now, we need only note that the interpretation of main effects is critically dependent

---

[1]The simple averaging of the values within each row and column to obtain the means for the main effects is possible *only* when there are equal numbers of subjects contributing to each mean in the table. For procedures to use when the cells of the table involve different sample sizes, see Appendix A.

on whether an interaction is or is not present. For instance, the main effect of arousal level in the preceding table indicates no effect of this variable (the means for the high and low arousal levels are both 30). The absence of a main effect of arousal level, however, is totally determined by the equal and opposite effects of arousal level at the two levels of task complexity. The main effect of this variable was nonsignificant, but it would clearly be inappropriate to conclude that arousal level had no effect. Instead, the *interaction* of arousal level and task complexity indicates that the effect of arousal level *depends* on the complexity of the task. In general, main effects should be interpreted with caution whenever an interaction is present in the experiment. When no interaction occurs, the main effects of each independent variable can be interpreted as though they had been manipulated in two separate experiments, each of which involved only one independent variable.

THE NATURE OF INTERACTIONS

THE 2 × 2 DESIGN

The simplest possible experiment involves one independent variable manipulated at two levels. Similarly, the smallest possible complex design involves two independent variables, each of which is manipulated at two levels. Complex designs are identified by specifying the number of levels of each of the independent variables in the experiment. A 2 × 2 (which is read "2 by 2") design, then, identifies the most basic complex design. The number of conditions in a complex design can be determined by multiplying the number of levels of the independent variables. For instance, there are four conditions in a 2 × 2 design, eight conditions in a 4 × 2 design, and twelve conditions (and three independent variables) in a 3 × 2 × 2 design. As we mentioned earlier, a complex design can be used to identify interactions between independent variables. The nature of an interaction is essentially the same in all complex designs, but an interaction can be seen most easily in a 2 × 2 design. We will now consider one such experiment.

There are few events in a court of law that are as dramatic or as compelling as when an eyewitness identifies the accused as the perpetrator of the crime. Just how reliable is such eyewitness testimony? Several laboratory-based studies involving staged crimes indicate that the testimony of eyewitnesses is unreliable, with the number of false identifications being unacceptably high. Wells et al. (1979) realized that these laboratory-based studies could be discounted by members of the criminal justice system because the studies have not generally included procedures to challenge the testimony of eyewitnesses. For example, inaccurate eyewitnesses may be less able to stand up under the pressure of cross-examination. Wells et al. set out to do a laboratory-based study that included such procedures.

In the first phase of the experiment, subjects who had been designated as witnesses were escorted to individual cubicles where they were to await the arrival of the experimenter. A confederate of the experimenter came into each subject's cubicle and "discovered" a calculator that had apparently been left by a previous subject. The confederate then posed as a thief by placing the calculator in her purse and exiting quickly. After several minutes the experimenter came into the cubicle, explained that the theft had been staged, and asked the "witness" to identify the thief from a set of six photographs. Some witnesses were successful in identifying the thief; others were not. The question that Wells et al. were asking was whether another group of students who were designated as jurors would be able to distinguish between accurate and inaccurate eyewitnesses.

The subject jurors were tested in the second phase of the experiment. The jurors were told that other students had witnessed a staged theft of a calculator and that the witnesses had been asked to identify the thief from a set of six photographs. The jurors were next told that they would observe the cross-examination of one of these witnesses and that they must then decide whether the witness was right or wrong.

There were actually four groups of student jurors in the experiment. These four groups were formed by factorially combining two independent variables in the following 2 × 2 design:

Type of witness	Type of cross-examination	
	Pressured	Neutral
Inaccurate		
Accurate		

The subject jurors observed the cross-examination of either an accurate or an inaccurate witness who was given either a pressured or a neutral cross-examination. The person doing the cross-examining did not know whether the witness had previously made an accurate or an inaccurate identification. The pressured cross-examination involved many leading questions, whereas the neutral cross-examination involved nonleading questions. Two questions in the cross-examination were the same: one asked the witness to re-identify the photograph of the thief and the other asked how confident the witness was of that decision.

The critical question for the subject jurors was whether they believed the testimony of the witness. The dependent variable, therefore, was the proportion of jurors in each of the four groups who believed the witness. These values are presented in Table 7.1.[2]

[2]Complex designs are usually analyzed using the analysis of variance, the procedures for which we will describe later in this chapter. In this example, however, the proportions are based on frequency counts which require the use of the chi-square test (see Appendix A). The important point to be drawn from the table is that you understand the pattern of results that indicates an interaction.

TABLE 7.1   EXAMPLE OF A 2 × 2 DESIGN WITH AN INTERACTION

Proportion of Jurors Believing the Witnesses

| | Type of cross-examination | |
Type of witness	Pressured	Neutral
Inaccurate	.73	.86
Accurate	.84	.76

From Wells et al. (1979).

The first thing to note in the table is that subject jurors believed most witnesses; almost three-fourths of the witnesses were believed even in the conditions with the lowest values. For our purposes, though, the most important aspect of this table is that it reflects an interaction between the two independent variables, type of witness and type of cross-examination. If all the witnesses in the experiment had been given pressured cross-examination, we would have concluded that jurors are less likely to believe inaccurate witnesses than accurate witnesses (.73 versus .84). If all the witnesses had received neutral cross-examination, however, we would have concluded that jurors are more likely to believe inaccurate witnesses than accurate witnesses (.86 versus .76). Wells et al. (1979) were unable to determine why inaccurate witnesses were more believable in the neutral condition. Their results do clearly demonstrate, however, that the effect of the type of witness variable depends on the nature of the cross-examination. An interaction has apparently occurred.

As you may have suspected, however, statistical analysis is required before we can conclude with confidence that an interaction has occurred. For now, it is sufficient if you recognize that, when our conclusion about the effect of one independent variable changes as we move across the levels of the second independent variable, an interaction is likely.

When one independent variable interacts with a second independent variable, the second independent variable must interact with the first one. For example, we described the interaction in Table 7.1 by stating that the effect of the type of witness varies with the type of cross-examination. The reverse is equally true; the effect of the type of cross-examination varies with the type of witness. Neutral cross-examination leads to greater belief for inaccurate witnesses, but pressured cross-examination leads to greater belief for accurate witnesses. How you choose to describe the results of an interaction depends on which aspects of the interaction you want to emphasize.

Mastering the concept of an interaction requires practice in identifying various types of outcomes that can arise in a complex design. Therefore, we will conclude this section on the 2 × 2 design with an exercise that will give you an opportunity to identify main effects and interactions using only descriptive statistics. Inferential statistics would be required to confirm the statistical significance of any obtained effects, but the effects themselves can best be seen in a table or graph of the means for the conditions of the experiment.

There are three common ways to report a summary of the descriptive statistics in a complex design: tables, bar graphs, and line graphs. The procedures for preparing such tables and figures and the criteria for deciding to use each type of presentation are described in Appendix C. In general, tables can be used for any complex design and are most useful when the exact values for each condition in the experiment need to be known. Bar graphs and line graphs, on the other hand, are especially useful for showing patterns of results without dwelling on the exact values. Bar graphs are typically used when the independent variables represent nominal or ordinal scales (categories such as Easy-Hard, Slow-Fast, etc.). Line graphs are typically used when the independent variables represent interval or ratio scales (temperatures measured in degrees Centigrade or Fahrenheit or retention intervals measured in minutes or hours). Line graphs are particularly useful for depicting the results of complex designs, because an interaction can be seen so readily in a line graph. *Nonparallel lines in the graph suggest an interaction; parallel lines suggest no interaction.*

When the results of a 2 × 2 design are summarized in a table, it is easiest to assess the presence or absence of an interaction by using the subtraction method. One determines the differences between the means in each row (or column) of the table and then compares these differences. If the differences are different, an interaction is likely. The mechanics of the subtraction method can best be illustrated by examining an actual research example.

The following table presents the results of the Johnson et al. (1983) study we described earlier. The dependent variable entered in the table is the mean number of correctly recalled tasks out of a possible 10.

Type of subject	Type of task	
	Completed	Uncompleted
Depressed	6.75	7.85
Nondepressed	7.70	6.70

As we mentioned earlier, Johnson et al. did obtain an interaction when they analyzed their recall results. The subtraction method can be used to confirm the presence of this interaction. In the first row of the table (for depressed subjects) the difference between the mean recall of uncompleted tasks and that of completed tasks is 1.10 (7.85 − 6.75). For nondepressed subjects, on the other hand, computing the difference in the same direction results in a value of −1.00 (6.70 − 7.70). Applying the subtraction method reveals that the mean differences in the two rows of the table are different, thereby confirming that an interaction is likely. In applying the subtraction method, it is essential that the difference always be determined in the same direction (for example, Uncompleted Tasks − Completed Tasks) and that the sign of the obtained difference be carefully noted. You can practice applying the subtraction method by determining the mean differences in the two columns of the Johnson et al. table. For more practice, see Box 7.1.

BOX 7.1

HERE AN INTERACTION, THERE AN INTERACTION, EVERYWHERE AN INTERACTION

In the spirit of practice makes perfect, let us now turn our attention to the exercise we have prepared to help you learn to identify interactions. Your task is to identify main effects and interactions in each of six complex design experiments (A through F). That is, in each table or graph in this box you are to determine whether the effect of each independent variable differs depending on the level of the other independent variable. That is, is there an interaction? After checking for the interaction, you can also check to see whether each independent variable produced an effect when collapsed across the other independent variable. That is, is there a main effect of one or both independent variables? The exercise will be most useful if you also practice translating the data presented in a table (Figure 7.2) into a graph and those presented in graphs (Figures 7.3 and 7.4) into tables. The idea of the exercise is to become as comfortable as you can with the various ways of depicting the results of a complex design.[3]

FIGURE 7.2 Mean number of correct responses as a function of task difficulty and anxiety level.

FIGURE 7.3 Mean number of errors as a function of type of task and brain hemisphere tested.

[3]Answer key for exercises in this box: An interaction occurs in A, D, and E.

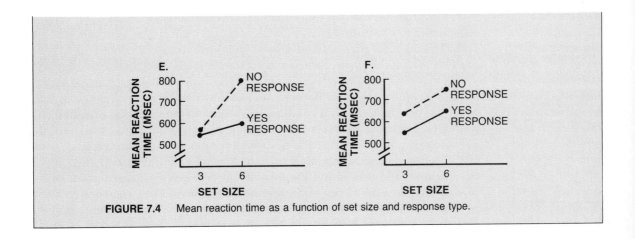

FIGURE 7.4   Mean reaction time as a function of set size and response type.

BEYOND THE 2 × 2: TWO ILLUSTRATIONS

The opportunity to identify an interaction makes the 2 × 2 design more useful analytically than designs involving only one independent variable. Nonetheless, the 2 × 2 design barely scratches the surface when it comes to tapping the potential of complex designs. The 2 × 2 design can be extended in one of two ways. Additional levels of one or both of the independent variables can be included in the design, yielding designs such as the 3 × 2, the 3 × 3, the 4 × 2, the 4 × 3, and so on. Or additional independent variables can be studied in the same experiment with the number of levels of each variable ranging from 2 to some unspecified upper limit. The addition of a third or fourth independent variable yields designs such as the 2 × 2 × 2, the 3 × 3 × 3, the 2 × 2 × 4, the 2 × 3 × 3 × 2, and so on. It is obviously not feasible to illustrate each possible complex design. It is also not necessary. One illustration of each type of extension of the 2 × 2 should suffice.

   What Was That Number?   Hinrichs and Novick (1982) used a 2 × 4 design to investigate the way people remember the order of a string of unrelated digits. Memory researchers have consistently found that serial recall of unrelated strings of digits, letters, or words follows a familiar pattern called the *bowed serial position curve* (Zechmeister and Nyberg, 1982). Recall of the first few items in a string is best and recall of the last few items in the string is almost as good, but recall of items from the middle of the string is much poorer. The bowed appearance of the serial position curve arises because the point of poorest recall is often just beyond the middle of the string. Although the bowed serial position curve is one of the most reliable phenomena of human memory, Hinrichs and Novick wondered whether our memory for a sequence of numbers would *always* conform to this pattern.

Hinrichs and Novick (1982) distinguished between two different ways in which people use numbers. We sometimes use numbers as arbitrary strings, as is the case with telephone numbers. In this instance, Hinrichs and Novick argued, it would be reasonable to expect a person's memory for the number string to follow the bowed serial position effect. Most of the time, however, we use numbers to reflect amounts or magnitudes, as when a number indicates the cost of a new car. In this case Hinrichs and Novick expected the number to be remembered not as a string of unrelated digits but as an approximate amount. That is, the first digit should be remembered best, with each successive digit being less critical and thus less likely to be remembered. For example, the digit string 8362 would need to be remembered exactly if it were a phone number, but remembering $8,300 would be close enough if the original number was intended to reflect the price of a car. When numbers reflected amounts, Hinrichs and Novick saw no reason why the serial recall of the digits should show a bowed serial position curve.

The experiment Hinrichs and Novick did closely followed the logic described in the preceding paragraph. They manipulated two independent variables, using the within-subjects design for both. The first independent variable in their experiment was the type of list subjects were asked to learn. Half of the lists that subjects were asked to learn included thirty 4-digit numbers, each of which was paired with a person's name. Subjects were told to consider the numbers the 4-digit extensions of campus phone numbers for a group of thirty students. For the other half of the lists, the 4-digit numbers were paired with the names of cars, and subjects were told to remember the numbers as the prices of new and used cars they might be interested in purchasing. In both lists, the pairs were shown for study for 5 seconds and a given pair was tested after either zero, one, two, four, or eight other pairs had been presented. The test for both lists required subjects to respond with the appropriate number when the name of the person or of the car was presented.

The second independent variable in the experiment was the serial position variable. The accuracy of subjects' recall was determined for the digits at each of the four positions within the 4-digit numbers. Thus Hinrichs and Novick used a 2×4 design (two types of lists and four serial positions). They expected to find an interaction. That is, they expected the pattern of recall across serial positions to differ depending on the type of list the subject was trying to remember.

The proportion of digits recalled correctly at each serial position for the two different lists is presented in Figure 7.5. As predicted by Hinrichs and Novick, recall was best for serial positions 1 and 4 when the list was "phone numbers"—the bowed serial position curve appeared. For the "prices" list, however, recall systematically decreased across serial positions, at least across the first three positions. As we previously mentioned, the appearance of nonparallel lines in a line graph like that shown in Figure 7.5 suggests that an interaction has occurred. The interaction can also be verified by applying

FIGURE 7.5 Illustration of an interaction in a complex design (2 × 4). (*From Hinrichs and Novick, 1982.*)

the subtraction method to determine the differences between the points plotted above each serial position. The prices list led to higher recall for serial positions 1 and 2 but to lower recall for serial positions 3 and 4. The different patterns of recall across serial positions for the two types of lists confirm that our memories for numbers differ depending on what those numbers represent.

The experiment by Hinrichs and Novick illustrates an intriguing fact about human memory. For our purposes, however, their experiment also illustrates that the concept of an interaction can be extended to complex designs beyond the 2 × 2. You should now be beginning to see how complex designs allow psychologists to test predictions that specify how two independent variables can work together to produce an interaction.

The power and complexity of complex designs increase substantially when the number of independent variables in the experiment increases from two to three. In the two-factor design there can be only one interaction, but in the three-factor design each independent variable can interact with each of the other two variables and all three independent variables can interact together. Thus the change from a two-factor to a three-factor design introduces the possibility of obtaining four different interactions. If the three independent variables are symbolized as A, B, and C, the three-factor design allows a test of the main effects of A, B, and C; the two-way interactions of A × B, A × C, B × C; and the three-way interaction of A × B × C. The efficiency of an experiment involving three independent variables is remarkable. We would have to perform three experiments involving two variables at a time (A and B, A and C, and B and C) in order to assess the three main effects and the three two-way interactions that we can examine in a single three-factor design. Furthermore, we can assess the simultaneous interaction of all three independent variables *only* by including all three variables in the same experiment.

We Don't All Think Alike   When a college student reads the words "cat" and "robin," there is good reason to believe that the student automatically also registers the concepts "animal" and "bird" in memory. The student may not be consciously aware of her or his spontaneous production of these concept labels, but memory research suggests that they do occur. For example, suppose a college student in a free-recall experiment was asked to memorize a list of conceptually related words (such as cow, green, sparrow, blue, horse, robin). In free-recall experiments words are presented one at a time for a brief period of study. After the last word is presented the subject recalls as many words as possible in any order. The student's subsequent recall of related words would be greater than it would be if he or she were asked to memorize a comparable list of words that were not conceptually related. Presumably, what makes the former task easier is that implicit category labels serve to organize the conceptually related list.

However, conceptually related items do not always facilitate memory performance. In a paired-associate task, the subject must learn to give a specific response whenever a cue word is given. For instance, for the pair *mother-picnic*, the subject would have to learn to respond with the word *picnic* whenever the word *mother* was shown. When a paired-associate list contains several conceptually related items with different instances of two categories forming the pairs (ocean-tea, lake-milk, river-coffee), learning is often slower than when no conceptual relationships exist among pair members. This interfering effect of conceptual relationships in the paired-associate task, like the facilitating effect of such relationships in the free-recall task, is traceable to the automatic and implicit occurrence of category labels to category instances.

The preceding brief summary of research on conceptual relatedness aptly characterizes one important aspect of the thinking of typical college students—at least their thinking in memory researchers' laboratories. But what about adults who are mentally retarded? Do the mentally retarded think in the same way as college students but not as efficiently? Or do mentally retarded adults think in ways different from typical college students? Wallace and Underwood (1964) used a complex design involving three independent variables to address one question about the thinking of mentally retarded adults: whether they spontaneously produce category labels when they come across category instances.

The overall design of Wallace and Underwood's (1964) experiment was $2 \times 2 \times 2$. There were two different types of subjects (college students and mentally retarded young adults), two different types of memory tasks (free-recall and paired-associate), and two different types of lists for each task (conceptually related or conceptually unrelated). There were thus eight conditions in the experiment, and a separate group of twenty subjects participated in each of the eight groups. On the basis of the research we have already summarized, Wallace and Underwood expected that the college students would do better with the conceptually related list in the free-recall task but worse with the conceptually related list in the paired-associate task. Wallace and Underwood went on to argue, however, that the mentally retarded adults would *not* spontaneously think of the category labels. Thus, the mentally retarded adults were expected to perform equally well on the conceptually related and the conceptually unrelated lists in both the free-recall and the paired-associate tasks.

The outcome of an experiment involving three independent variables can be summarized by using a two-panel graph like that shown in Figure 7.6. The performance of the college students is presented in the left panel and that of the mentally retarded adults in the right panel. As expected, the college students did better with conceptually related lists in the free-recall task but worse with conceptually related lists in the paired-associate task. The pattern shown for the mentally retarded adults in the right panel is very different; conceptual relatedness has little or no effect in either the free-recall or the paired-associate task. You may have recognized that the graph in the left panel reflects an interaction of conceptual relatedness and task. The right panel reflects no such interaction. The findings depicted in Figure 7.6 represent a specific example of a triple interaction involving three independent variables. In general, when the interaction of two independent variables dif-

FIGURE 7.6 The results of a complex design involving three independent variables in which there was a triple interaction. (*From Wallace and Underwood. 1964.*)

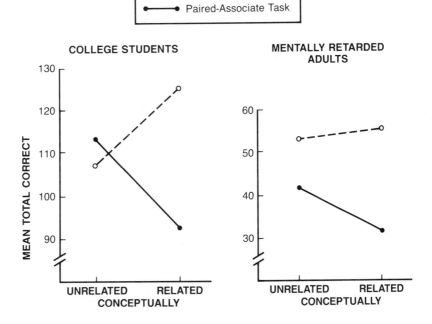

fers depending on the level of a third independent variable, there is evidence of a triple interaction. The description of this one experiment only hints at the power and complexity of experiments involving three independent variables. For now, however, we will turn to a discussion of the interpretation of interactions.

INTERPRETING INTERACTIONS

GENERALITY OF FINDINGS

In Chapter 5 we discussed at some length the procedures for establishing the generality, or external validity, of a research finding when an experiment involved only one independent variable. We noted at that time that replication and inferences drawn on the basis of the continuity assumption were the primary means by which external validity, could be established. Complex designs provide a means of establishing the generality of a finding that is more manageable than replication and more satisfying than the consensual agreement required when the continuity assumption is applied. As you might have suspected, the presence or absence of an interaction is critical in determining the external validity of the findings in a complex design.

When a complex design is used and when no interaction occurs, we know that the effects of each independent variable can be generalized across the levels of the other independent variable. For instance, Dittmar et al. (1982) tested hearing and deaf subjects in a vigilance task that required subjects to detect intermittent blips on a radar screen. They found that performance did decline across three 15-minute vigilance periods, but the decline occurred at approximately the same rate for hearing and deaf subjects. That is, there was no interaction of the subject variable (hearing or deaf) and the period variable. Thus, declining performance in a vigilance task can be generalized to both hearing and deaf people. This same generalization across types of subjects could have been made on the basis of the continuity assumption if only deaf subjects or only hearing subjects had been tested. That is, we could have argued that there would be no reason to expect that deaf subjects' performance would decline but that of hearing subjects would not. The inference is far less risky, however, when it is based on the empirical finding of the absence of an interaction.

Of course, the continuity assumption would still be needed to establish the external validity of a finding beyond the boundaries that were included in the complex design. For example, the absence of an interaction of the subject variable and periods in the vigilance task does not allow us to conclude that detection performance would decline at the same rate if young children or trained observers were tested. Similarly, we do not know whether the same decline across periods would occur if there were short breaks after each observation period. We must also exercise caution in making generalizations based on the *absence* of an interaction. This situation involves problems associated with the failure to reject the null hypothesis, such as the sensitivity of the experiment to detect any interaction that might be present (see Chapter 5, Box 5.3).

As we have seen, the absence of an interaction increases the generality of the effects of each independent variable in the experiment. Perhaps more important, the presence of an interaction specifies *limits* on the generality of a finding. When they tested college students, Wallace and Underwood (1964) found that there was an interaction between conceptual relatedness of the material to be remembered and the type of memory test. This interaction clearly sets limits on the generality of the nature of the effects of conceptual relatedness on memory. Given this finding, the best way to respond to someone's query regarding the general effect of conceptual relatedness on memory is to say "it depends." The presence of the interaction limits generality but also specifies what those limits are. In the case of conceptual relatedness the nature of the effects differs depending on the type of test. For instance, Dittmar et al. (1982) would have obtained an *ordinal interaction* if vigilance performance had declined across periods for both hearing and deaf subjects but the decline was less steep for the deaf subjects. With an ordinal interaction we can generalize that vigilance performance declines over time, but we would need to add the slight modification that the *size* of the effect depends on the type of subject tested.

The second type of interaction, called a *disordinal interaction*, places far greater limits on the generality of a finding. In a disordinal interaction the effects at different levels of the second independent variable are opposite in direction. In general, an interaction in a complex design places limits on the generality of the effects of each independent variable in the experiment, and these limits are greater with disordinal than with ordinal interactions. When Wallace and Underwood (1964) found that conceptual relatedness enhanced performance on a free-recall test and interfered with performance on a paired-associate test, they obtained a disordinal interaction. They could reach no general conclusion regarding the effect of conceptual relatedness; their conclusions had to be specific to the particular type of memory test that had been used.

To help you recognize ordinal and disordinal interactions, we have illustrated idealized versions of each type in Figure 7.7. In the left panel, the ordinal interaction is reflected in the convergence of the two curves. The disordinal interaction in the right panel is also called a *crossover interaction* because of the distinctive shape of the two crossing lines.

IDENTIFYING RELEVANT INDEPENDENT VARIABLES

One of the primary tasks facing researchers who use the experimental method is identifying relevant and irrelevant independent variables. A **relevant independent variable** is one that has been shown to influence behavior, and an *irrelevant independent variable* is one that has been shown not to influence behavior. Identifying factors that do affect behavior and those that do not is essential both for developing adequate theories to explain behavior and

FIGURE 7.7   Illustrations of ordinal and disordinal interactions.

for designing effective interventions to deal with problems in applied settings such as schools, hospitals, and factories (see Chapter 8 and 9).

If independent variables did not interact with one another, the task of identifying relevant independent variables would be a long one, but not a particularly challenging one. Each independent variable would simply be manipulated across a wide range of levels in separate single-factor experiments. The variables would be classified as either relevant or irrelevant, depending on whether or not they produced a significant difference in the dependent variable. Independent variables do interact, however, and we must adjust our definition of relevant and irrelevant independent variables accordingly.

Sprague and Sleater (1977) have reported that as many as 600,000 children in the United States receive drug treatment for hyperactivity in any one year. A reasonable question is whether dosage of the drugs is a relevant independent variable in determining the effectiveness of treatment. A hypothetical but typical experiment that could be done to address this question might include two dose levels (Low and High) and three types of tasks (Easy, Moderate, and Difficult). One possible outcome of such an experiment is summarized in the following table, with the dependent variable being the percent correct performance in each condition.

Task	Dose level* Low	Dose level* High	Overall mean
Easy	75	90	82.5
Moderate	70	70	70.0
Difficult	65	50	57.5
Overall mean	70.0	70.0	

The overall means for the main effect of dose level are identical, and this information could mistakenly be used to argue that dose level was an irrelevant independent variable. By now you recognize, however, that the dose level produced different effects depending on the difficulty of the task to be performed. For difficult tasks a low dose is better, for moderate tasks there is no effect of dose level, and for easy tasks a high dose is better. Dose level is a relevant independent variable, because it enters into a significant interaction with the difficulty variable. In general, a relevant independent variable is one that influences behavior directly (results in a main effect) or that produces an interaction when studied in combination with a second independent variable.

The knowledge that interactions of independent variables can occur in complex designs should make us cautious about identifying any independent variable as irrelevant solely on the basis of having found that the independent variable failed to produce an effect in a single-factor experiment. It is always possible that some factor that was held constant in the experiment would have resulted in an interaction if it had been manipulated along with the original independent variable. (Imagine what would have happened if our hypothetical experiment testing the effects of drug doses had been done using only problems of moderate difficulty.) Theories about the processes underlying behavior help us to deal effectively with interactions (Underwood and Shaughnessy, 1975). For now, it is best if you avoid being dogmatic about identifying any independent variable as irrelevant.

CEILING AND BASEMENT EFFECTS

Consider the results of an experiment investigating the effects of increasing amounts of practice on performance on a physical-fitness test. There were six groups of subjects in this fictitious experiment. Subjects were given either 10, 30, or 60 minutes to practice doing either easy or hard exercises just prior to their being given a fitness test using one of these types of exercise. The dependent variable was the percentage of the assigned number of exercises that each subject was able to complete in a 15-minute test period. Hypothetical results of the experiment are presented in Figure 7.8.

The pattern of results in Figure 7.8 looks like a classic interaction; the effect of practice time was different for the easy and the hard exercises. Test performance increased with increasing amounts of practice for the hard exercises, but performance leveled off after 30 minutes of practice with the easy exercises. If a standard analysis of variance were applied to these data, the interaction effect would be very likely to be statistically significant. Unfortunately, this interaction would be essentially uninterpretable. For those groups given practice with the easy exercises, performance reached a maximum after 30 minutes of practice, so no improvement beyond this point could be shown in the 60-minute group. Even if the subjects given 60 minutes of practice had further benefited from the extra practice, the experimenter could not measure this improvement on the chosen dependent variable.

FIGURE 7.8 Illustration of a ceiling effect.

The preceding experiment illustrates the general measurement problem referred to as a **ceiling effect.** Whenever performance reaches a maximum in any condition of an experiment, there is danger of a ceiling effect. The corresponding name given to this problem when errors are used to measure performance is **basement effect** (or floor effect). In general, one can avoid ceiling and basement effects by selecting dependent variables that allow ample "room" for performance differences to be measured across conditions. For example, in the fitness experiment it would have been better to test subjects with a greater number of exercises than anyone could be expected to complete in the time allotted for the test. The mean number of exercises completed in each condition could then be used to assess the effects of the two independent variables without the danger of a ceiling effect.

INTERACTIONS AND THE NATURAL GROUPS DESIGN

The natural groups design, which we described briefly in Chapter 5, is one of the most popular research designs in psychology. Groups of subjects are formed by selecting individuals who differ on some characteristic such as the subjects' gender, introversion-extroversion, or aggressiveness. Researchers then look for systematic relationships between these subject variables and other aspects of behavior. The natural groups design is an effective one for establishing correlations between subjects' characteristics and their performance. As we also noted in Chapter 5, however, the natural groups design is perhaps the most challenging design when it comes to drawing conclusions about cause and effect.

The difficulty in interpreting the natural groups design arises when we try to conclude that differences in performance are *caused* by the characteristics of the subjects we used to define the groups. For instance, consider an experiment in which subjects are selected because of their musical training. One group of subjects includes people with ten or more years of formal musical training, and one group includes people with no formal training. Both groups are tested on their ability to remember the musical notation for simple ten-note melodies. The results of these tests show that those with musical training perform far better than those without such training.

We can conclude on the basis of these results that memory for simple melodies varies with (is correlated with) amount of musical training. But we cannot conclude that the superior memory performance was *caused* by the musical training. Why not? There are probably many ways in which people with ten years of musical training differ from those without such training other than the characteristic of amount of training. The groups may differ in amount and type of general education, family background, socioeconomic status, and amount and type of experience they have had listening to music. Those with musical training may have generally better memories than those without such training, and their superior memory for musical notation of simple melodies may reflect this general memory ability. Finally, those who sought out musical training may have done so because they have a special aptitude for music. Accordingly, they might have done better on the memory-for-melodies task even if they had not had any musical training. In short, there are many possible causes other than musical training for the difference in memory performance that was observed.

There is a potential solution to the problem of drawing causal inferences based on the natural groups design (Underwood and Shaughnessy, 1975). The reasoning on which the solution is based can best be illustrated by examining a specific example. Halpern and Bower (1982) were interested in the question of how memory for musical notation differs between musicians and nonmusicians. They expected that musicians would do better on a test of memory for the notation of simple melodies, but they recognized that it would not be sufficient to attribute this difference to the fact that one group had had ten years of formal musical training and the other group had not. Instead, they developed a theory of how musical training would influence the cognitive processing of musical notation by those who had such training.

Halpern and Bower's theory was based on a memory concept called "chunking." Earlier research by de Groot (1965) had shown that chess experts were better able than novices to remember the position of chess pieces on a chessboard that they were allowed to observe for 5 seconds. The superior performance of the experts, however, was limited to those arrangements that could reasonably be expected to occur during a chess game. If the pieces were randomly arranged on the board, the experts and novices did equally well on the memory test. Chase and Simon (1973) subsequently argued that the chess experts were grouping or "chunking" segments of the chessboard into familiar patterns or "chunks." You can get some sense of the memory advantage provided by chunking if you imagine trying to memorize the following strings of letters: IBMTWASOSUSAUSSR versus IBM-TWA-SOS-USA-USSR.

Halpern and Bower argued that musical training led musicians to "chunk" musical notation into meaningful musical units, thereby reducing the amount of information they needed to remember in order to reproduce the notation for a simple melody. If this process were responsible for the difference between the memory performance of musicians and nonmusicians, then the difference should be greater for melodies with good musical structure than for those with poor musical structure. Halpern and Bower chose to manipulate the independent variable of musical structure to test their theory.

Halpern and Bower used three different types of melodies to test their groups of musicians and nonmusicians. They prepared sets of simple melodies whose notations had similar visual structures but that were either Good, Bad, or Random in musical structure. The design of their experiment was a 2 (Musician versus Nonmusician) × 3 (Type of Musical Structure) factorial, and the critical test was whether they would obtain an interaction of the two independent variables. Specifically, they expected that the difference in memory performance between musicians and nonmusicians would be largest for the melodies exhibiting good structure, next largest for the melodies exhibiting bad structure, and smallest for the random melodies. The results of Halpern and Bower's experiment conformed exactly to these expectations.

The obtained interaction allowed Halpern and Bower to rule out many alternative hypotheses for the difference in memory performance between musicians and nonmusicians. Such characteristics as amount and type of general education, socioeconomic status, and family background are not likely to explain why there is a systematic relationship between the structure of the melodies and the size of the difference in memory performance between musicians and nonmusicians. The interaction makes such simple correlational explanations much less plausible. In addition, the interaction provides support for Halpern and Bower's theory about the way musicians process information differently from nonmusicians. Their experiment does not, however, eliminate all alternative hypotheses. It is still possible that people classified as musicians have experience listening to more music and to more different types of music. Such differences in listening experience could result in the obtained interaction. A more stringent test of Halpern and Bower's hypothesis would involve selecting a group of nonmusicians who have listening experiences comparable to those of the musicians. If musical training is essential for developing the "chunking" of good musical structures, then the same type of interaction should occur when these two groups are tested on the three types of melodies.

There are several steps that the investigator must take in carrying out the general procedure for drawing causal inferences based on the natural groups design. The first step is to develop a theory explaining why a difference should occur in the performance of the groups that have been differentiated on the basis of a subject variable. The second step is to select an independent variable that can be manipulated and that is presumed to influence the like-lihood that this theoretical process will occur. This independent variable is then applied to both natural groups. The most critical aspect of the recom-mended approach is to continue to strive to produce an interaction between the manipulated variable and the subject variable. The approach can be strengthened even further by testing predictions of interactions of three in-dependent variables: two manipulated independent variables and the subject variable (see, for example, Anderson and Revelle, 1982).

ANALYSIS OF COMPLEX DESIGNS

LOGIC OF ANALYSIS PROCEDURES

The analysis of complex designs builds on the logic used in the analysis of experiments with only one independent variable. The first step in the anal-ysis of such single-factor experiments is to perform an omnibus F-test to de-termine whether the independent variable has produced any systematic vari-ation. If the omnibus test is statistically significant, analytical comparisons are used to pinpoint more precisely the source of the systematic variation.

The tracking of sources of systematic variation applies equally to the anal-ysis of complex designs, and the same basic tool, the analysis of variance, is used. However, in complex designs with two independent variables there are three potential sources of systematic variation. Each independent variable can produce a significant main effect, and the two independent variables can combine to produce a significant interaction.

An example of an analysis of variance summary table for a complex design is presented in Table 7.2. A table of means is included for completeness, but

TABLE 7.2 ANALYSIS OF VARIANCE SUMMARY TABLE FOR A 3 × 3 DESIGN

Source of variation	df	MS	F	p
Age (A)	2	100	10.0	< .05
Condition (B)	2	200	20.0	< .05
Age × Condition (A × B)	4	150	15.0	< .05
Error Variation Within Groups	81	10		
Total	89	——		

TABLE OF MEAN TIMES (IN MINUTES) SPENT PLAYING WITH NOVEL TOYS

	Age		
Condition	4	5	6
Alone	5	5	10
With a Parent	15	25	35
With Another Child	10	15	15

we will focus on the summary table. The hypothetical experiment being analyzed was a 3 × 3 design with nine groups of subjects. Children of three different ages (4, 5, and 6) were tested under one of three conditions (Alone, With a Parent, and With Another Child). The dependent variable in the experiment was the amount of time the child spent playing with novel (compared to familiar) toys. There were ten children of each age tested under each of the three conditions, so there were ninety subjects in the experiment, ten in each of the nine conditions.

As indicated in the first three rows of the first column of Table 7.2, there are three potential sources of systematic variation in this complex design: the main effect of age, the main effect of condition, and the interaction between age and condition. Using appropriate computational procedures (see Appendix A), we can determine a mean square for each main effect and for the interaction. These mean squares reflect error variation plus any systematic variation produced by each type of effect. As was true in the analysis of single-factor experiments, we need some estimate of error variation alone to use as the denominator for an F-ratio for each of the three effects. In this experiment, the variation within the groups serves as the estimate of error variation alone. We then use this MS within groups to form three different F-ratios, one for each main effect and one for the interaction:

$$\frac{MS_A}{MS_{WG}} \quad \frac{MS_B}{MS_{WG}} \quad \text{and} \quad \frac{MS_{A \times B}}{MS_{WG}}$$

We need the degrees of freedom for each of the F-ratios in order to test for statistical significance. We determine the number of degrees of freedom for a main effect by subtracting 1 from the number of levels of the independent variable. For instance, there were three levels of the age variable, so there are 2 df for the variable of age. We determine the df for an interaction by multiplying the degrees of freedom for the two independent variables entering into the interaction. Thus, there are 4 df for the Age × Condition interaction (2 × 2 = 4). The df for the MS_{WG} is obtained by multiplying the df within each group times the number of groups. In our example, there are ten subjects in each group and therefore 9 df within each group. Because there were nine groups in the study, there were 81 df within groups. The closest critical value in the table is an $F(2,60)$ at $\alpha = .05$ of 3.15, and the obtained F-ratios for the main effects exceed this critical value. Thus, both main effects are statistically significant. Similarly, the critical F-ratio for the interaction $F(4,60)$ at $\alpha = .05$ is 2.53, and the obtained F-ratio for the A × B interaction exceeds this value and is hence statistically significant.

Knowing that all three major effects in a complex design are statistically significant tells us little about what actually happened in our experiment. Each of the three effects represents an omnibus analysis that tells us only that three different "somethings" happened. Just as analytical comparisons can be used to locate the source of an omnibus effect in a single-factor experiment, so there are analysis procedures that can be used to locate more precisely the sources of systematic variation in a complex design. The guidelines for applying these procedures in the analysis of a complex design are outlined in Table 7.3.

Not all the terms in Table 7.3 are familiar to you at this point, but the table will serve as a guide for the analysis procedures we will be describing. As we mentioned previously in this chapter, the interpretation of a complex design differs depending on whether an interaction is or is not obtained in the initial overall analysis. Therefore we will track through Table 7.3 twice, once describing an experiment in which there is no interaction and once describing a study in which there is an interaction. In the next two sections, we will concentrate on the logic and interpretation of the analysis of complex designs. Computational procedures for these analyses are described in Appendix A.

ANALYSIS OF A COMPLEX DESIGN WITH NO INTERACTION

Earlier we described a study by Dittmar et al. (1982), who used a 3 × 3 design to test whether people who are deaf perform better on a visual vigilance task than people who can hear. As you may remember, a visual vigilance task requires a person to detect intermittent visual signals such as blips on a radar screen for a long period of time. Dittmar et al. expected that deaf people would have an advantage on such a task because their deafness would keep them from being distracted. The deaf subjects who participated were offered a prize if their vigilance performance was the best in their group. To assess the possible effect of the prize as an incentive, two additional groups of hearing subjects were tested, one offered a prize and one not. These three groups represent the levels of the first independent variable in the experiment. The subjects were all tested in a 45-minute session divided into three continuous 15-minute periods, and these three periods were the levels of the second independent variable.

TABLE 7.3   GUIDELINES FOR THE ANALYSIS OF A TWO-FACTOR EXPERIMENT

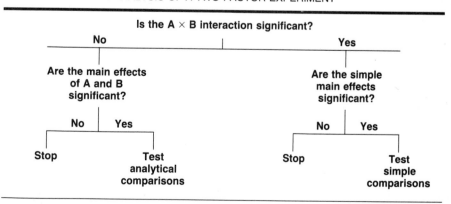

The mean percentage of correct detections across the three periods for the three different groups of subjects is presented in Table 7.4. The same data are depicted graphically in Figure 7.9. The interaction, or more accurately the lack of an interaction, can best be seen in Figure 7.9. Although the three lines in the figure are not perfectly parallel, the mean percentage of correct detections appears to decrease in all three groups at approximately the same rate. An analysis of variance confirmed that the performance decline across periods was comparable for the three groups of subjects; the interaction of Period × Group was not statistically significant, $F(4,134) < 1$.

The guidelines for the analysis of a complex design listed in Table 7.3 suggest that, when the interaction effect is not significant, the next step is to examine the main effects of each independent variable. This can be done most easily by referring to the data in Table 7.4. By collapsing across the three vigilance periods, we can obtain the means for the main effect of the Group variable. These means are 86.0, 81.7, and 78.3 for the Deaf, Hearing—Prize, and Hearing—No Prize groups, respectively. The overall analysis of the Group main effect was statistically significant, $F(2,67) = 4.16$, $p < .025$, suggesting that there was systematic variation produced by the Group variable. As indicated in Table 7.3, the source of a significant main effect can be specified more precisely by performing analytical comparisons. For example, a comparison of performance in the Hearing—Prize and Hearing—No Prize groups (81.7 and 78.3) was not statistically significant, but the average performance of the two groups of hearing subjects (80.0) was significantly lower than the performance of the deaf subjects (86.0). These two analytical comparisons allow us to confirm that deaf subjects were better at the vigilance task than hearing subjects and that the offer of a prize did not affect the vigilance performance.

A similar approach would be followed in assessing the main effect of the Period variable. By collapsing across the three groups of subjects, we obtain the means 93.7, 80.3, and 72 for the main effect of the Period variable. The main effect of this variable was statistically significant, $F(2,134) = 19.1$, $p < .001$. Analytical comparisons could then be used to determine whether the decreases over each successive period (93.7 to 80.3 and 80.3 to 72) were significant. The analysis of Dittmar et al.'s vigilance experiment illustrates

TABLE 7.4   MEAN PERCENTAGE OF CORRECT DETECTIONS ACROSS THREE PERIODS OF A VIGILANCE TASK FOR DEAF AND HEARING SUBJECTS

	Period		
Group	**1**	**2**	**3**
Deaf	95	85	78
Hearing—Prize	93	82	70
Hearing—No Prize	93	74	68

Adapted from Dittmar et al. (1982).

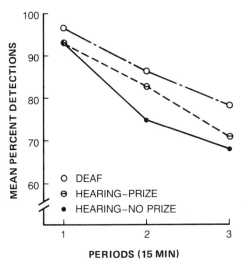

FIGURE 7.9   Results of a 3 × 3 complex design in which there was no interaction effect but there were two main effects. (*Adapted from Dittmar et al., 1982.*)

that much can be learned from a complex design even when there is no interaction. We turn now to the analysis of an experiment that *does* contain an interaction.

ANALYSIS OF A COMPLEX DESIGN WITH AN INTERACTION

One of the many approaches psychologists have tried to use to understand depression is based on investigating the differences between the thought patterns of depressed and nondepressed people. One aspect of this cognitive approach to depression deals with attributions, the causal explanations we use to try to account for our own behavior and the behavior of others. For example, nondepressed people tend to overestimate how much control they have over their lives while depressed people more realistically estimate that they have less control (Bootzin and Acocella, 1988, p. 244). According to the cognitive approach, this tendency toward less optimistic thinking on the part of depressed people may be critically involved in causing the onset of depression, maintaining depression once it occurs, and alleviating depression by changing this way of thinking. The Johnson et al. (1983) study with which we began this chapter fits well in the cognitive perspective—depressed subjects were more likely to remember unfinished than finished tasks. The study we will be using to illustrate the analysis of a complex design with an interaction represents another of the many experiments investigating the cognitive bases of depression.

Rodman and Burger (1985) investigated a particular phenomenon called the *defensive attribution effect*. In previous experiments nondepressed subjects read a description of an accident in which a person suffers mild or severe consequences. These nondepressed subjects attributed more responsibility to the perpetrator in the severe than in the mild accident condition. One interpretation of this phenomenon is that people do not want to attribute the cause of a severe accident to chance. If they did attribute chance as the cause, then they would be increasing the perceived possibility that they would be involved in a severe accident. Their attribution of greater responsibility to the perpetrator in the severe accident represents a defensive attribution, protecting themselves against a greater likelihood of future severe accidents. Rodman and Burger reasoned that depressed people might be less likely to show this type of defensive attribution effect because their negative thinking would lead them to be less self-protective. Stated more formally, they tested the hypothesis that the defensive attribution effect would decrease as a person's level of depression increased.

Rodman and Burger (1985) tested fifty-six college students in a 2 × 3 design. The first independent variable was the severity of the described accident (Severe and Nonsevere), and this was manipulated using the random groups design. The natural groups design was used for the second independent variable; students were selected on the basis of their scores on a paper-and-pencil test of depression to represent Nondepressed, Slightly Depressed, and Mildly Depressed subjects. The dependent variable was a single item on a longer questionnaire that asked subjects to divide 100 percent among four potential sources of responsibility: each of the three drivers in the accident and "uncontrollable circumstances." The defensive attribution effect would be reflected in a larger value assigned to uncontrollable circumstances for the Nonsevere than for the Severe accident. The mean percentage values for this uncontrollable factor for each of the six conditions are presented in Table 7.5.

As Rodman and Burger had predicted, there is an apparent interaction; as degree of depression increases, the differences between the percentage values for Severe and Nonsevere accidents change. Nondepressed subjects show the defensive attribution effect and Mildly Depressed subjects do not. As usual, however, inferential statistics tests must be done to confirm the presence of the interaction. Rodman and Burger performed the necessary test and obtained $F(2, 50) = 7.02$. The closest tabled critical value for $\alpha = .05$ with 2 and 40 df is equal to 3.23, so we know that the obtained F-ratio for the interaction is statistically significant.

TABLE 7.5 MEAN PERCENTAGE OF RESPONSIBILITY ATTRIBUTED TO UNCONTROLLABLE CIRCUMSTANCES

Type of accident	Degree of depression		
	Nondepressed	**Slightly depressed**	**Mildly depressed**
Severe	7.00(9.2)	14.00(16.1)	16.90(16.0)
Nonsevere	30.50(22.2)	16.50(12.7)	3.75(3.5)

Note: Standard deviations appear in parentheses. Adapted from Rodman and Burger (1985).

Once we have confirmed that there is an interaction of two independent variables, we must locate more precisely the source of that interaction. As outlined in Table 7.3, there are statistical tests specifically designed for tracing the source of a significant interaction. These tests are called *simple main effects* and *simple comparisons.*

A **simple main effect** represents the effect of one independent variable at *one* level of a second independent variable. In fact, one definition of an interaction is that the simple main effects in an experiment are different. We can illustrate the use of simple main effects by returning to the analysis of the Rodman and Burger experiment. There are *five* simple main effects in Table 7.5: the effect of the type of accident at each of the three levels of degree of depression and the effect of degree of depression at each of the two levels of type of accident. Rodman and Burger predicted that the defensive attribution effect (the difference between the means for severe and nonsevere accidents) would decrease as severity of depression increased. Therefore, they chose to test the simple main effects of type of accident at each of the three levels of depression. They found, as predicted, that the simple main effect of type of accident was statistically significant for Nondepressed subjects, but the simple main effects of type of accident for the Slightly Depressed and for the Mildly Depressed subjects were not statistically significant.

Simple comparisons are analytical comparisons done on simple main effects rather than on the overall main effect. Simple comparisons are not necessary when the simple main effect has only two levels as was the case for the simple main effects of type of accident at each level of degree of depression. If Rodman and Burger had tested the simple main effects of degree of depression at the two levels of type of accident, these simple main effects likely would have been statistically significant. Once again, finding significant simple main effects does not tell us the source of these omnibus effects. Simple comparisons must be done. For example, one way to break down the simple main effect of degree of depression for the nonsevere accident would be to use a simple comparison that contrasts the average of the two Depressed groups to the mean for the Nondepressed group. This comparison would be testing the effect of depression versus nondepression. A second simple comparison could then be made between the means of the Slightly Depressed group (16.50) and the Mildly Depressed group (3.75). Remember, these analyses are called simple comparisons because they break down a simple main effect which is the effect of one independent variable at only one level of a second independent variable.

When students are introduced to the analysis of simple main effects and simple comparisons, they sometimes tend to overuse them. That is, the students analyze all possible simple main effects and every conceivable simple comparison. More often than not, this "barrage" approach to the analysis of a complex design that involves an interaction leads to utter confusion. Usually a researcher selects one set of simple main effects to break down a significant interaction. This choice is based on the rationale behind the predicted interaction and is not a "search and destroy" mission. With experience, students also can learn to use these powerful analytical tools effectively and judiciously.

Once an interaction has been thoroughly analyzed, researchers can also examine the main effects of each independent variable. As we mentioned earlier in this chapter, however, the main effects are of much less interest when we know that an interaction is significant. For instance, once we know that the effect of the type of accident varies depending on the degree of depression, we have not added much when we learn that, overall, the nonsevere accident led to a higher mean percentage than did the severe accident. Nonetheless, there are experiments in which the interaction and the main effects are all of interest. In such cases, the guidelines in Table 7.3 can be followed to track down all sources of systematic variation in a complex design.

SUMMARY

A complex design is one in which two or more independent variables are studied in the same experiment. A complex design involving two independent variables allows one to determine the overall effect of each independent variable (the main effect of each variable). More important, complex designs can be used to reveal the interaction of two independent variables that exists when the effect of each independent variable depends on the level of the other independent variable. Complex designs are essential to resolve contradictions that arise when two experiments involving the same independent variable result in different findings. Investigators can trace the source of the contradictory findings by using a complex design in which both the original independent variable and the independent variable that is presumed to be responsible for the discrepant findings are manipulated in the same experiment. Complex designs also play a critical role in the testing of predictions derived from psychological theories.

The smallest possible complex design is the 2×2 design, in which two independent variables are both studied at two levels. The analytical power of complex designs increases when additional levels of one or both of the independent variables are included in the design, yielding designs such as the 3×2, the 3×3, the 4×2, the 4×3, and so on. Additional independent variables can also be included to yield designs such as the $2 \times 2 \times 2$, the $3 \times 3 \times 3$, and so on. Experiments involving three independent variables are remarkably efficient. They allow determination of the main effects of each of the three variables, the three two-way interactions of the three independent variables, and the simultaneous interaction of all three variables.

When a complex design is used and no interaction occurs, we know that the effects of each independent variable can be generalized across the levels of the other independent variable(s). When an interaction does occur, however, limits on the generality of a finding can be clearly specified. If an ordinal interaction is obtained, these limits pertain to the size of the effect of an independent variable but not to its direction. Disordinal interactions, on the other hand, place far greater limits on the generality of a finding in that the effects of one independent variable at different levels of a second independent variable are opposite in direction. The possibility of interactions requires that we expand the definition of a relevant independent variable to include those that influence behavior directly (produce main effects) and those that produce an interaction when studied in combination with another independent variable.

Interactions that may arise because of measurement problems such as ceiling or basement effects must not be confused with interactions that reflect the true combined effect of two independent variables. Interactions can also be most helpful in solving the problem of drawing causal inferences based on the natural groups design.

The analysis of complex designs with two independent variables involves three potential sources of systematic variation. Each independent variable can produce a significant main effect, and the two independent variables can combine to produce a significant interaction. Interactions can be initially identified by using the subtraction method when the descriptive statistics are reported in a table or by the presence of nonparallel lines when the results appear in a line graph. Inferential statistics tests, however, are required to confirm the presence of the interaction. If the interaction does prove to be statistically significant, we can locate its source by analyzing simple main effects and by using simple comparisons. When no interaction arises, we analyze the main effects of each independent variable, using analytical comparisons when necessary.

KEY CONCEPTS

complex design	relevant independent variable
interaction	ceiling (basement) effect
mixed design	simple main effect
main effect	simple comparison

REVIEW QUESTIONS

1 Explain how a complex design can be used to resolve contradictions that arise when two researchers obtain different results after manipulating the same independent variable in their respective single-factor experiments.

2 Use an example to illustrate how a complex design can be used to test predictions derived from a psychological theory.

3 How is the interpretation of a main effect influenced by the presence or absence of an interaction in a complex design?

4 Use the Wells et al. eyewitness experiment to illustrate that there is one possible interaction in a 2 × 2 design but that there are *two* possible ways to describe the interaction.

5 Describe the guidelines you would follow in deciding which of the three most common formats (table, bar graph, line graph) you would use to report a summary of the descriptive statistics in a complex design.

6 In what two ways can the basic 2 × 2 design be expanded to create more extensive complex designs?

7 How is the generality (external validity) of the findings in a complex design influenced by the presence or absence of an interaction?

8 What is the role of the continuity assumption in establishing the generality of findings in a complex design?

9 Why must we be cautious in making generalizations based on the absence of an interaction in a complex design?

10 What different effects on the generality of a finding do ordinal and disordinal interactions have?

11 What expansion in the definition of a relevant independent variable is required by the use of complex designs?

12 What potential solution is there for the problem of drawing causal inferences on the basis of the natural groups design?

13 List the *seven* possible effects in a three-factor complex design involving independent variables A, B, and C.

14 Describe the steps in the analysis of a complex design involving two independent variables when there is an interaction and when there is not an interaction.

CHALLENGE QUESTIONS

1 Consider an experiment in which two independent variables have been manipulated. Variable A has been manipulated at three levels, and Variable B has been manipulated at two levels.

A Draw a graph showing an effect of Variable B, no effect of Variable A, and no interaction between the two variables.

B Draw a graph showing no effect of Variable A, no effect of Variable B, but an interaction between the two variables.

C Draw a graph showing an effect of Variable A, an effect of Variable B, *and* no interaction between the A and B variables.

2 A psychologist is interested in whether older people suffer a deficit with respect to their reaction time in processing complex visual patterns. He selects a random sample of 65-year-old people and another random sample of young adults (such as college students). He tests both groups of fifty people in the same reaction time task. He presents a simple figure to each subject, then a complex pattern, and asks the subject to indicate as quickly as possible whether the simple figure is present in the complex pattern. Subjects are timed only for their reaction to the complex patterns. This test is called an embedded figures test. As he had expected, the mean reaction time for the older adults was markedly longer than that for the young adults. By any standard the results were statistically significant.

A Explain what minimal set of conditions the psychologist would have to include in his experiment before he could conclude that older adults suffered a deficit in their processing of *complex* visual patterns. That is, state what additional reaction time test must be given to both groups. Finally, describe an outcome of the test you propose which would support his position and one which would lead you to question his conclusion.

B Recognizing that his original study is flawed, the psychologist tries to use post hoc matching to try to equate his two groups. He decides to match on general health (i.e., the better your general health, the faster your reaction time). Although he cannot get an exact matching across groups he does find that when he looks only at the fifteen healthiest older adults, their reaction times are only slightly longer than the mean for the college students. Explain how this outcome would change the psychologist's conclusion concerning the effect of age on reaction time. Could the psychologist reach the general conclusion that older adults do not suffer a deficit in reaction time in this task? Why or why not?

3 The data presented in the following table represent the mean number of analogy problems correctly solved in a random groups design experiment involving two independent variables. The first independent variable was the difficulty of the analogies and there were two levels: Hard and Very Hard. The second independent variable was the stress under which the participant was working, and there were three levels: High, Medium, and Low. There were 10 participants in each of the six groups and the mean in each group is reported in the table. Use these means to answer the questions that follow.

Difficulty	Stress		
	Low	**Medium**	**High**
Hard	7.0	6.5	6.0
Very hard	3.0	2.5	2.0

A Explain why you think there is or is not an interaction present in this experiment.

B What values would you use to describe the overall main effect of the Difficulty variable?

C Fill in the blanks in the following analysis of variance summary table.

Source of variation	df
Difficulty (A)	—
Stress (B)	—
A × B	—
Within-Group Error	—
Total	59

D Briefly describe the analysis plan you would follow after having completed the overall analysis outlined in the preceding part of this problem. For purposes of this question, you may assume that the interaction is *not* statistically significant but that both main effects are statistically significant.

4 The following data represent the number of words correctly recalled by the participants in each of the four conditions of an experiment. Each of the forty people was randomly assigned to one of the four conditions, which were differentiated on the basis of the type of rehearsal the people used to try to learn the words (Maintenance or Elaborative) and the time at which the recall test was given (Immediately or After a Delay). Use these data and the accompanying analysis of variance summary table to answer the questions that follow.

Maintenance, immediate		Maintenance, delayed		Elaborative, immediate		Elaborative, delayed	
Subject	No. Recalled	Subject	No. Recalled	Subject	No. recalled	Subject	No. recalled
1	38	11	8	21	28	31	16
2	40	12	10	22	30	32	20
3	36	13	6	23	26	33	12
4	42	14	12	24	32	34	24
5	44	15	14	25	34	35	28
6	34	16	4	26	24	36	8
7	32	17	2	27	22	37	4
8	46	18	6	28	36	38	12
9	48	19	8	29	38	39	16
10	40	20	10	30	30	40	20

Source of Variation	df	SS	MS	F	p
Type of Rehearsal (A)	1	10.00	10.00	.33	$> .10$
Time of Test (B)	1	5290.00	5290.00	176.33	$< .001$
Type × Time (A × B)	1	810.00	810.00	27.00	$< .001$
Within-Groups Error	36	1080.00	30.00		
Total	39	7190.00			

A Was there an interaction of the two independent variables? If so, state the nature of this effect verbally, being sure to include the values that serve as the basis for your description.

B State verbally the effect of each independent variable. Be sure to state whether the effect was statistically significant and specify the values you used as a basis for your description of the effect of each variable.

ANSWER TO CHALLENGE QUESTION 1

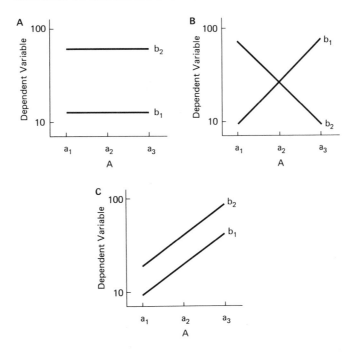

THREE

APPLIED RESEARCH

N = 1 DESIGNS

OUTLINE

For the most part, thus far in this book, we have emphasized group methodology—research designed to examine the average performance of one or more groups of subjects. This was particularly evident in the last few chapters, in which experimental methods were examined. This emphasis on group methodology is warranted given the nomothetic nature of the science of psychology, and it reflects well the activities of researchers in this field. The most common research design in psychological research is one involving many subjects, whose behavior is observed following one or more experimental treatments. A decision about the effectiveness of an independent variable is made when other potential independent variables have been controlled either within or between groups of subjects.

In this chapter you are introduced to an alternative research methodology. The distinctive characteristic of this alternative approach is its emphasis on the single subject. In fact, in many textbooks this area of research is called "N = 1." This approach is derived from an **experimental analysis of behavior** that has been promoted by the well-known psychologist B. F. Skinner. Respondent and operant conditioning are major experimental methods used by researchers in this field. In this chapter we first briefly review Skinner's brand of behaviorism and the experimental procedures associated with it. Understanding the experimental analysis of behavior is not necessary to learn about single-subject designs, so that depending on your background and interest in this field of psychology, or given the emphasis of a classroom instructor, you may want to omit this first section of Chapter 8. However, included in this section of Chapter 8 is information intended to help you to see the relationship between various experimental procedures and their applied counterparts—for instance, that between establishing conditioned reinforcers and the use of tokens as part of token economies. We also describe some practical suggestions of B. F. Skinner for training animals and reveal some of his informal observations on the scientific enterprise.

Our major focus, however, is on **applied behavior analysis,** and, more specifically, *N* **= 1 designs.** Techniques derived from laboratory studies of animal and human behavior have been found to be effective in managing behavior in numerous situations, including schools, the home, hospitals, and businesses. Use of the single-case or $N = 1$ experimental design is characteristic of this approach. The rationale behind this type of research design will be discussed. Specific illustrations of the more common types of $N = 1$ designs will be given. Although there are many advantages to the use of $N = 1$ experimental designs, particularly in applied settings, there are important limitations to their use, and these also will be discussed. The $N = 1$ design is a special case of a within-subjects design that was introduced in Chapter 6.

INTRODUCTION

BEHAVIORISM

Behaviorism, or behavior theory, was officially launched in 1913 with the publication of John B. Watson's article "Psychology as the Behaviorist Views It." Watson argued that psychology would be able to take its place among the natural sciences, such as chemistry and biology, only when it abandoned subjective methods of inquiry, such as introspection, and emphasized observable behavior instead. As the behaviorist viewed it, psychology's goal was the prediction and control of behavior.

Watson (1913) further argued that the behaviorist saw "no dividing line between man and brute" (p. 158). This meant, of course, that the experimental psychologist could learn about human behavior through the study of animals. The behaviorist assumes that human behavior, although it appears complex, is the product of certain fundamental behavioral principles. These are the same principles that operate to control the behavior of relatively simple organisms, such as the rat and the pigeon. Consequently, the behavioristic approach tends to prefer animal subjects and laboratory procedures (Hintzman, 1978). The laboratory setting permits a high degree of experimental control and has traditionally been assumed to be "unbiased" in that it does not call forth various genetically determined or specially adapted patterns of behavior, as might be true of "natural" environments (however, see Schwartz and Lacey, 1982).

A particularly important form of behaviorism that emerged in the 1930s, and now dominates this field, is that associated with B. F. Skinner. Skinner's approach is synonymous with what is called an *experimental analysis of behavior.* It presents a unique behavioral view of human nature that not only contains prescriptions for the way psychologists should do research but also has implications for the way society should be organized. Several of Skinner's books, including *Walden Two* and *Beyond Freedom and Dignity,* describe how the principles of behavior control that have been and will be derived from an experimental analysis of behavior can be put to work improving society. In addition, techniques of behavior control based on this approach have been applied successfully in educational settings, in institutions where therapists work with the emotionally disturbed or mentally retarded, in businesses, in the home, and in many other areas where behavior change is often desired. Although you have probably been introduced to the major laboratory methods associated with behavior theory as part of an introductory course in psychology, a brief review of them is provided in the next section. These methods are the basis for an applied behavior analysis, which is the major focus of this chapter.

EXPERIMENTAL METHODS

In the experimental analysis of behavior all behaviors can be classified as one of two types: respondents and operants (Reynolds, 1968). A response that is *elicited* naturally by an environmental event is a **respondent.** It is usually an innate reflex. Examples of respondents are the withdrawal of a hand from a hot stove, salivation in response to dry food placed in the mouth, the startle response made to a loud noise, and constriction of a pupil in response to a bright light. Respondents are clearly adaptive and help to ensure the safety and survival of an organism. That your eyelid closes "automatically" when a puff of air hits the eye serves to protect the eye from damage due to objects carried in the air.

Although it is clearly important, respondent behavior represents only a small part of all human behavior. Most human behaviors are classified as **operants.** These are responses that operate directly on the environment (Skinner, 1937). Operants have no identifiable eliciting stimulus; their "cause" is within the organism (Reynolds, 1968). Consequently, operants are said to be *emitted* by an organism rather than elicited by an environmental stimulus. Behaviors that we normally view as "voluntary" are operants. Walking, talking, sitting, jumping, standing, and hitting are good examples.

Research methods employed in the experimental analysis of behavior are those associated with respondent and operant conditioning.

Respondent (Classical) Conditioning   The Russian physiologist I. P. Pavlov carried out the first systematic experiments using respondent conditioning. Hence the procedure is also called Pavlovian or (most frequently) classical conditioning. Pavlov's experimental subjects were dogs. The eliciting stimulus was food or mild acid placed on the dog's tongue. The respondent was salivation. Pavlov demonstrated that an environmental event that reliably preceded the eliciting stimulus also acquired the power to elicit salivation. This was true even for events that were originally "neutral" in that they did not have any pre-experimental capability of producing salivation. A common neutral stimulus used by Pavlov was the sound of a metronome. For example, he found that the sound of a metronome, after being repeatedly presented prior to the dog's receiving food, would cause the animal to salivate.

In the terminology of the behavioral scientist, an eliciting stimulus is an **unconditioned stimulus (US),** whereas the respondent that is elicited is an **unconditioned response (UR).** The environmental event that is initially neutral is the **conditioned stimulus (CS),** whereas the response that it comes to elicit is the **conditioned response (CR).** Note that CS refers both to a neutral stimulus that is selected for a conditioning experiment and to the stimulus that is shown, after repeated pairings with the US, to elicit a CR.

Many everyday behaviors are the product of classical conditioning. Salivation at the thought of biting into a juicy lemon or at the sight of a steak frying on the grill, crying at a sad movie, feeling anxious in front of a group of people—all are likely to have their basis in respondent conditioning. Classical or respondent conditioning has adaptive value to an organism (Schwartz and Lacey, 1982). A conditioned response may help the organism prepare for an unconditioned stimulus. Salivation in response to the sight and sound of a steak frying readies the organism for digestion of the steak.

Operant Conditioning   Operant conditioning is the process by which behavior is modified by its consequences.[1] Changes in behavior are usually measured in terms of frequency of responding, although other measures (such as duration or latency) may be used. When frequency is measured, it is typically reported as a function of some unit of time, such as a day, a minute, or a 10-second interval. Thus, rate of responding is a major dependent variable (perhaps *the* major dependent variable) in operant conditioning. The task of the operant researcher is to relate changes in rate of responding to changes in the environment.

An increase in rate of responding is brought about by a procedure known as **reinforcement.** The giving of "rewards" (such as praise, candy, flowers, ribbons, or high grades) following a response is one way to increase the subject's rate of responding. This particular procedure is called *positive reinforcement*. A stimulus that an organism normally seeks to obtain and that brings about an increase in rate of responding when presented after a response is called a *positive reinforcer*. Candy and praise, for example, are potent positive reinforcers, especially for children. As we get older we appreciate different

---

[1]The term *operant conditioning* is virtually synonymous with *instrumental conditioning*, and no important theoretical distinction is made between them. However, *operant conditioning* is often used when referring to situations wherein a response can be made at any time (such as in a classroom), whereas *instrumental conditioning* is more likely to be used when referring to trial-by-trial kinds of learning (such as trials to learn a maze) (see Hintzman, 1978). Moreover, *operant conditioning* is the preferred term in the experimental analysis of behavior. Skinner (1966) objects to the use of the term *instrumental* because it implies the use of tools and therefore has undesirable "purposive overtones" (p. 15).

kinds of positive reinforcers—money or a dinner at a fancy restaurant, for instance.

Presenting a stimulus contingent on a particular response is not the only way to produce an increase in response rate. Frequency of responding can also be increased by removing certain stimuli following a response. When car manufacturers first experimented with attempting to control drivers' use of seat belts, they put irritating buzzers in cars that sounded when the key was inserted in the ignition and did not stop sounding until the seat belt was coupled. The car maker's intent was to increase rate of seat belt use by making removal of an aversive stimulus contingent on use of the seat belt. Analogously, the researcher may control the rate of responding of a laboratory rat by turning off an electric current delivering shock to the animal's feet after it makes a response. Rats, like humans, generally show an increase in rate of responding due to removal of an aversive stimulus. However, people (and no doubt rats as well) do not like to be controlled by aversive events. Although many people apparently increased their rate of seat belt use in order to escape the car makers' noxious buzzer, others reacted by going under their cars and disconnecting the wires on the buzzer system. More recent models of cars have buzzers that shut off automatically after a brief interval whether or not the seat belt is coupled.

An event that an organism normally seeks to avoid and that produces an increase in rate of responding when it is removed following a response is a *negative reinforcer*. Buzzers that go off when you couple your seat belt, headaches that are relieved by aspirin, smoke-filled air that can be escaped by leaving the room, and a parent's nagging that is stopped by a child doing her chores are examples of negative reinforcers. These aversive events lead to an increase in responding by their cessation or removal following a response. This procedure is *negative reinforcement.* It is important to note and to remember that *both* positive and negative reinforcement are procedures that lead to an *increase* in response rate.

Decreases in rate of responding can be brought about by a procedure known as **punishment.** And, just as there are two ways to apply reinforcement (positive and negative) and increase rate of responding, there are two ways to inflict punishment and decrease rate of responding. One method is to present an aversive (repugnant) event following a response. The laboratory rat that is shocked when it presses a bar will soon stop bar pressing. The child who is spanked after telling a lie will probably stop lying (at least in the presence of the person delivering the aversive stimulus). Following a response with the removal of a positive stimulus—something that an organism would normally want—is also a form of punishment. The parent who takes away the keys to the family car after a teenager gets a traffic ticket and the teacher who denies recess privileges to students who misbehave are using this form of punishment. The use of punishment in behavior therapy, especially when it involves aversive stimuli, raises serious ethical questions. A conflict can arise between the patient's right to be kept free from physical harm and the possible beneficial effects of aversive therapy. (See the Lovaas study in Appendix B for a specific example of this conflict.)

In conducting the experimental analysis of behavior, experimenters frequently make observations on single subjects. As we said earlier, it is often the case in the experimental analysis of behavior (unlike the group methodologies discussed in previous chapters) that $N = 1$. Experimental control is demonstrated by arranging experimental conditions such that the individual's behavior changes systematically with the manipulation of an independent variable. As Skinner (1966, p. 21) has commented,

> instead of studying a thousand rats for one hour each, or a hundred rats for ten hours each, the investigator is likely to study one rat for a thousand hours. The procedure is not only appropriate to an enterprise which recognizes individuality, it is at least equally efficient in its use of equipment and of the investigator's time and energy. The ultimate test of uniformity or reproducibility is not to be found in the methods used but in the degree of control achieved, a test which the experimental analysis of behavior usually passes easily.

There is a minimum of statistical analysis. Conclusions regarding the effect of an experimental variable are made by visually inspecting the behavioral record in order to observe whether behavior changes systematically with the introduction and withdrawal of the experimental treatment.

The typical experimental apparatus used in the experimental analysis of behavior consists of an *operant chamber*, or what is often referred to as a "Skinner box" (see Figure 8.1 and Box 8.1). Although its furnishings are relatively modest, the operant chamber contains several important features that provide a basis for research. The chamber contains some type of device for the subject to operate. For the pigeon it is a disc that, when pecked, causes grains of food to be delivered automatically to a food dish. For the rat it is a bar that, when pressed, delivers food pellets. Frequency of responding is automatically recorded by means of a *cumulative recorder* (see Figure 8.1). The cumulative recorder is designed to record responses through the movement of a pen on moving paper. Each time a rat presses the bar, the pen moves up a notch. Thus rate of responding is reflected by the slope of the curve that is obtained. A fast rate of responding causes the pen to jump quickly on the moving paper, and a steep line is produced. Slow rates of responding are indicated by gradual slopes on the cumulative record. When no responses are being made, the record shows a straight line. The cumulative record is the most common means of reporting the results of an operant conditioning experiment.

Two additional and important concepts related to the control of operant behavior are shaping and stimulus control. These concepts can be easily defined in terms of the laboratory procedures with which each is associated. After defining these concepts in this way, however, we will illustrate their significance in an important area of behavior control—specifically, that of animal training. **Shaping** is a process of reinforcing "successive approximations" to a desired response. As a laboratory example, consider the behavior

FIGURE 8.1   Illustrations of major kinds of apparatus typically used in laboratory operant conditioning. Responses of the organism are registered electronically, and automatically cause a movement of the pen on the cumulative recorder. (*From Ferster and Skinner, 1957.*)

of a rat when it is first introduced to the Skinner box. Rats do not naturally know that pressing a lever will gain them reinforcers. Rather, the behavior of bar pressing has to be shaped. One method is to deliver food reinforcement when the rat first approaches the area of the bar. The rat will soon repeat this behavior. The experimenter then withholds reinforcement until a response occurs that more closely approximates bar pressing. It might be the response of touching the bar. This behavior is reinforced until the rat begins to repeat it. Then reinforcement is withheld once again until a closer approximation to bar pressing is observed, such as raising a paw and putting it on the bar. This

BOX 8.1

SKINNER ON SCIENTIFIC PRACTICES AND THE "SKINNER BOX"

From reading several autobiographical accounts, we find how Skinner first began to do research in psychology (Skinner, 1956; 1967). He did not have any formal psychology courses while an undergraduate at Hamilton College (although he did have "a lot of biology"); rather, he majored in English with the possible goal of becoming a writer. In fact, it was Skinner's literary interests that carried him toward a career in psychology. Reading articles by the philosopher Bertrand Russell in a literary magazine led him to Russell's book *Philosophy,* which described John B. Watson's book *Behaviorism.* Skinner read some of Watson's publications as well as Pavlov's book *Conditioned Reflexes,* which had been recommended by a biology professor. As Skinner commented, "Pavlov had shown the way," and upon entering Harvard graduate school, he was ready to begin the study of what he described simply as "looking for lawful processes in the behavior of the intact organism" (Skinner, 1956, p. 223). Skinner's early investigations led him to make some important, although somewhat unconventional, observations regarding the practice of science and, if we can believe him, led directly to the development of the operant chamber, or what psychologists know as the "Skinner Box."

Skinner's initial research led him to the following conclusions about the scientific process (see also Epstein, 1982): (1) "When you run into something interesting, drop everything else and study it." (2) "Some ways of doing research are easier than others." (3) "Some people are lucky." (4) "Apparatuses sometimes break down." According to Skinner these informal principles were the basis for his developing the operant chamber (Skinner, 1956). The first principle (being ready to pursue an interesting finding even if you have to drop what you are doing) was occasioned by the fact that his early work with rats, which was aimed at studying these animals' reactions to a novel stimulus, produced little of consequence. Nevertheless, in observing the infant rats' behavior, Skinner found their reflexive behavior interesting and designed an apparatus to study it. The piece of equipment would allow Skinner to measure precisely the movement of a baby rat in response to a stimulus. Infant rats, however, did not hold any special fascination for Skinner and he figured that his apparatus would work just as well in the study of adult rats. He redesigned the apparatus to allow him to measure automatically adult rats' reactions to a noise stimulus. But the equipment involved a long runway that required

shaping procedure continues until the rat is successfully pressing the bar and receiving reinforcement.

Shaping is likely to be used whenever a response is absent from a subject's repertoire but is a response that the subject is capable of making. (Rats cannot be shaped to fly, nor can very young infants be shaped to use the toilet.) Once the behavior has been shaped, it can be brought under control of a schedule of reinforcement.

Another way to control frequency of responding once a behavior is emitted regularly is to establish a discriminative stimulus. A **discriminative stimulus** signals the organism that reinforcement is available and, once established, can be used to control operant responding. Consider the bar pressing behavior of the rat once again. Assume that the rat has been shaped to press the bar and does so regularly, receiving reinforcement each time the bar is pressed. This would be a *continuous schedule of reinforcement* because behavior is reinforced continuously (that is, each time the bar is pressed). Now assume that a light is switched on in

Skinner to remove the rat from one end and take it back to the other end in order to begin a new trial. Skinner rapidly got tired of this. Hence the next informal scientific principle: some ways of doing things are easier than others. He added a back alley so the rat could get back itself. Because behavior was measured using a kymograph (a pen scratching the surface of a moving drum), the experimenter had little to do but put the rats in the apparatus and make sure they got some food as reinforcement. Unfortunately, the rats sometimes would spend a lot of time waiting before they went back to the beginning, so Skinner invoked the second principle again and shortened the runway while working out a way for the rat to deliver its own food. A new apparatus was built. It used a wooden disc that, when turned by the movement of the rat in the apparatus, dropped a piece of food. Then Skinner got lucky (third principle). The wooden disc originally had attached to it a spindle that Skinner had removed. However, this later led him to think that if he attached the spindle and wound string around it, he could improve considerably on his invention. A string being unwound whenever the spindle moved would produce not just little marks following each response but a cumulative curve. That is, having been lucky enough to use a piece of wood that gave him the idea of using a spindle, Skinner was now in the position of automatically measuring the rate of responding of an animal. The moving spindle with its unwinding string leading to a mark on a polygraph showed Skinner that high frequency of responding produced fast movement of the spindle and a steep curve, whereas a slow rate of responding produced a less steep cumulative record.

Finally, the fourth principle came into play: laboratory apparatuses (particularly complicated ones) sometimes break down. The one Skinner had devised did break down, but this led him to another discovery. What Skinner observed when the feeding mechanism stopped delivering food was an extinction curve. Having been used to getting its food reward automatically, the rat would slowly stop making responses whenever the machine broke down. A reduction in frequency of responding due to the removal of positive reinforcement is called experimental extinction. Skinner saw that, by controlling the food delivery, he could systematically observe the animal's reactions to different schedules of reinforcement. As Skinner stated, "I then built four soundproofed ventilated boxes, each containing a lever and food magazine and supplied with a cumulative recorder, and was on my way to an intensive study of conditioned reflexes in skeletal behavior." (Skinner, 1956, p. 226)

the operant chamber. The rat is continuously reinforced in the presence of the light. Now the light is switched off. When the rat presses the bar with the light off, no reinforcement is delivered. Soon the rat slows down its rate of bar pressing. Now the light is switched on again and, when the rat presses the bar, it receives reinforcement. Rate of bar pressing will pick up. If this procedure of pairing light with the opportunity for reinforcement and absence of light with nonreinforcement continues, the rat soon exhibits a predictable pattern of behavior. It will press the bar only when the light is on. The light has become a discriminative stimulus signaling the rat when reinforcement is available. Bar pressing is said to be under *stimulus control*. Turn the light on and the animal bar-presses; turn the light off and it stops bar-pressing. Most of our behaviors are under some form of stimulus control. We walk at an intersection only when the light is green. We throw baseballs outside but not indoors. We hug friends and relatives but not strangers.

Shaping and stimulus control are very important in the field of animal training. This can be illustrated by examining the procedures used to train dolphins at Chicago's Brookfield Zoo (and in similar situations, such as SeaWorld, around the world). Spectators at the dolphin shows held daily at the Brookfield Zoo see an amazing display of animal behavior. The dolphins jump hurdles, retrieve objects thrown into the water, shake hands with the trainer, do flips, "walk" on their tails, "beach" themselves, and even play basketball (see Figure 8.2). The animal trainers use positive reinforcers exclusively. However, for reasons that will soon be apparent, the reinforcer is not always a **primary reinforcer** (one that has reinforcing properties that do not depend on the prior experience of the animal, such as food). It may be what is called a **secondary** or **conditioned reinforcer** instead. For the dolphins at Brookfield Zoo the secondary reinforcer is the sound of a high-frequency whistle (one that the spectators cannot hear).

The procedure for establishing a secondary reinforcer is to pair it consistently with a primary reinforcer. When the dolphins are first brought to the zoo, one of the first stages in their training is to establish the sound of the whistle as a secondary reinforcer. The trainers take the new dolphin aside and feed fish to the animal after blowing the whistle. This is done many

FIGURE 8.2 Dolphins at the indoor Seven Seas Panorama facility of Chicago's Brookfield Zoo entertain and educate audiences the year round.

(a) Basketball

(b) Tailwalking

(c) Beached with Liz and John

(d) Beached with trainer

times over the course of days. Whistle then food, whistle then food, over and over again. You should recognize this procedure as respondent or classical conditioning. A secondary reinforcer acquires its reinforcing properties through classical conditioning. Once the sound of the whistle is firmly established as a secondary reinforcer, the trainers begin to shape the behavior of the dolphin. Indeed, a critical test of whether a conditioned reinforcer has been successfully established is whether it can be used, just as a primary reinforcer can, to modify behavior. Even after the conditioned reinforcer is established, "refresher courses" are periodically used in training to maintain the connection between the conditioned and the primary reinforcer.

The major reason why a conditioned reinforcer (rather than a primary reinforcer such as food) is used to train animals is that food would take too long to deliver following a response. An important principle in using reinforcement to control behavior is that reinforcement must be delivered as quickly as possible following the target response. Successful shaping of a response requires that the reinforcement be delivered immediately after the desired response has been made. Throwing a piece of fish across the pool to a dolphin takes too much time (and also interrupts the behavior). Skinner (1951), in one of his more famous articles, "How to Teach Animals," suggests that even a whistle is too slow to be most effective because it takes time to draw a breath before blowing the whistle. He suggests a "cricket" be used in animal training, the kind that makes a click when you squeeze a piece of metal. Nevertheless, the dolphin trainers at Brookfield Zoo use a whistle. One reason is that it allows their hands to be free to throw objects or to move equipment while working with the dolphins.

Training the dolphins to perform their various tricks generally follows the shaping procedure we described for training the laboratory rat to press the bar. The whistle is blown whenever the dolphin makes an approximation to the desired response. Consider, for example, the "beaching" behavior of the dolphins. On signal, the dolphins will swim out of the water in order to meet visitors (see Figure 8.2). While delighting children of all ages, this particular behavior has proved to be important in protecting the health of the dolphins.

Specifically, it is necessary periodically to take the dolphins from the water for a physical examination by a zoo veterinarian. This physical checkup usually includes drawing blood to be tested in the laboratory in the same manner as human blood would be tested as part of a complete physical examination by one's family doctor. Getting the dolphins to cooperate with this procedure has not always been easy. For example, in order to prepare the dolphins for this exam, trainers at Chicago's Brookfield Zoo once had to lower the water level in the pool to permit the trainers to walk into the pool and put the dolphins on stretchers prior to their being lifted out for the exam. The dolphins found this procedure uncomfortable (as did the trainers), and, as a consequence, it was done only twice a year. At some dolphinariums around the country trainers now rely on the beaching response as well as other reinforced behaviors to carry out these physical examinations.

To train the beaching response, the trainers first reinforce, via the blown whistle, the dolphin for approaching an object, such as a ball. Once the dolphin learns to approach the object in the water, the object is fixed to the end of a pole so that it can be gradually pulled to the edge of the water by the trainer. The dolphin is then reinforced for approaching the object in the water and for following the object to the edge of the pool. Finally, the animal is reinforced for following the object out of the pool, that is, for beaching itself. To permit the veterinarian to draw blood, again a shaping procedure is used. For example, the dolphin is first reinforced for lying still while being poked slightly by the trainer's finger. Once the animal is comfortable with this, the trainer pokes the animal with a dull metal object, such as a door key. Then, a toothpick is used to poke the dolphin. Finally, a sterilized needle is used. These shaping procedures are based entirely on the use of positive reinforcement and take several months to complete.

After being trained to permit the drawing of blood, the dolphins can be examined either in the water, where they also have been taught to lie still, belly-up, or at the edge of the pool, by making use of the beaching procedure. When the beaching response is used, observers witness a rather amazing demonstration of trainer and dolphin interaction. When a hand signal is given, the dolphin swims toward the trainer at the side of the pool, beaches at the feet of the trainer, lies still while being examined and while blood is drawn, and then, on signal, returns to the water. A dolphin's "physical," which previously could take several hours to complete and thus could be performed only infrequently, can now be done in minutes at more frequent intervals with no discomfort to the dolphin (or the trainer). This successful use of behavior modification procedures has helped to ensure better care and treatment of these marvelous animals.

The dolphins are signaled to begin their tricks either by hand signals (which have been consistently paired with the availability of reinforcement) or by the appearance of a particular object. A basketball, for example, becomes a discriminative stimulus. When it is thrown into the pool, the dolphin "knows" that it will be reinforced if it puts the ball through the hoop. You may have noticed a similarity between the procedures for establishing a CS as a conditioned reinforcer and those for establishing a discriminative stimulus. These two concepts are related; a discriminative stimulus often can be used as a conditioned reinforcer, and vice versa. These stimuli differ, however, in the kinds of information provided to the organism. A CS tells an organism what is about to happen to it, whereas a discriminative stimulus tells an organism what it has to do (Schwartz and Lacey, 1982). As you will see when we discuss principles of applied behavior analysis, conditioned reinforcers in the form of "tokens" have been used to manage human behavior in a wide variety of settings. The presence of tokens often serves as a signal that certain behaviors will be reinforced.

APPLIED BEHAVIOR ANALYSIS

HISTORICAL BACKGROUND

Kazdin (1978a), in his *History of Behavior Modification*, points out that it was during the 1950s and early 1960s, about two decades after Skinner's seminal work, that researchers began to extend operant conditioning research to humans. The principles of behavior control based on the experimental analysis of behavior, which had been so successfully explored with nonhuman subjects such as rats and pigeons, began to be applied to human behavior. Initially, the goal of this research was to demonstrate that the techniques that had been worked out using animal subjects would control the behavior of human subjects in a similar fashion. Normal human subjects were tested by being placed in settings not so very different from that of the operant chamber. As Kazdin (1978a, pp. 240–241) has commented,

> the bulk of early human laboratory investigations focused on lever-pressing behavior in very much the same way as had the work with animals. Indeed, the experimental situation for human operant research was modeled after the laboratory.

The focus of this work gradually shifted from basic to applied research, however, as investigators observed how effective operant methods were in changing behaviors in a wide variety of human populations. Numerous studies showed how operant techniques could be successfully employed to shape the behavior of psychotic individuals, normal and retarded children, retarded adults, autistic children, individuals diagnosed as schizophrenic, stutterers, psychiatric patients, children with learning problems, and many others (Kazdin, 1978a). At this same time, extensions of operant research were being promoted in education. Skinner (1958) advocated the use of teaching machines. Based on operant principles of immediate and positive reinforcement, these machines permitted students to work at their own pace and to master complex material by progressing in small steps that reduced, if not eliminated, the probability of errors. In 1967, The Society for the Experimental Analysis of Behavior voted to sponsor a journal which would publish studies on applications of behavior modification (see Bailey, 1987). In 1987, the *Journal of Applied Behavior Analysis* marked its twentieth anniversary.

One of the most influential developments during this period was the successful design and implementation of **token economies** (Kazdin, 1978a). Tokens are conditioned reinforcers. They achieve their "value" by being paired with a variety of positive reinforcers, such as food, candy, activities, and privileges. The tokens themselves may be plastic discs, paper stars, or even tally marks on a chart. In a token economy the tokens act like money does in our economic system. Behaviors are reinforced by the paying out of tokens, which can then be used to "purchase" desired reinforcers. A token economy can be (and has been) implemented on entire psychiatric wards in hospitals, in classrooms, and in numerous other settings (see Kazdin, 1982b; Kazdin and Bootzin, 1972, for evaluative reviews).

The application of learning-conditioning principles to clinical populations is called **behavior therapy,** a term that was first used synonymously with the term **behavior modification** (Wilson, 1978). Behavior therapy approaches grew rapidly in the 1960s. To many, they offered an important alternative to traditional psychodynamic approaches to understanding and treating psychopathology. The psychodynamic perspective is a collection of theories and therapies that have in common a "concern with the dynamics, or interaction, of forces lying deep within the mind" (Bootzin and Acocella, 1988, p. 25). Behavior, in this view, is often determined unconsciously by inner forces that have been affected by early-childhood experiences. Freud's psychoanalytic theory is particularly representative of this approach. Behavior therapy, with its emphasis on observable behavior rather than hypothesized inner forces, was seen by many as a more effective approach to clinical treatment than that based on the psychodynamic model. For example, by conceptualizing self-stimulatory behaviors, such as prolonged body-rocking, gazing at lights, or spinning, that often characterize so-called autistic children, as operant behaviors, clinicians and teachers may be able to control their frequency of occurrence (see Lovaas et al. 1987). Applied behavior analysis can be viewed as a subarea of the more general field of behavior modification or behavior therapy (Kazdin, 1978a). In it, the methods that are developed within an experimental analysis of behavior are applied to socially relevant problems.

SINGLE-CASE (*N* = 1) EXPERIMENTAL DESIGNS

The use of single subjects, which we have seen is often characteristic of the experimental analysis of behavior, is also a hallmark of an applied behavior analysis. Like its classic cousin, the case study (see Chapter 4), the **single-case experiment** typically focuses on an examination of behavior change in one individual. This methodology can be extended, however, to treatments applied to single groups of individuals as well (Kazdin, 1980b). Single-case experiments differ from the traditional case study method in that they systematically contrast conditions within an individual whose behavior is being continuously monitored. Consequently, single-case designs are an important alternative to the relatively uncontrolled case study method (Kazdin, 1982a).

For certain kinds of applied research, $N = 1$ experimental designs may be more appropriate than designs based on multiple-group methodology (see Hersen and Barlow, 1976). This is likely to be true when research is directed toward changing the behavior of specific individuals. For example, the average response of a group of subjects will not necessarily be the same as the response of any one individual in the group. Therefore, the outcome of a group experiment may lead to recommendations about what treatments "in general" should be applied to modify behavior, but it is not possible to say what the effect of that treatment will be on any particular individual. As

Kazdin (1982a) has commented, "Perhaps the most obvious advantage [of single-case experimental designs] is that the methodology allows investigation of the individual client and experimental evaluation of treatment for the client" (p. 482).

Another disadvantage of multiple-group methodology, particularly in the context of clinical research, is that ethical problems arise when a potentially beneficial treatment is withheld from subjects in order to provide a control group that satisfies the requirements of internal validity. Because single-case experimental designs contrast conditions of No Treatment and Treatment within the same individual, this problem can be avoided. Moreover, investigators doing clinical research often find it difficult to gain access to enough clients to do a group experiment. For instance, a clinician may be able to identify from a list of clients only a few individuals experiencing claustrophobia (excessive fear of enclosed spaces). The single-case experiment provides a practical solution to the problem of investigating cause-and-effect conclusions when only a few subjects are available.

The first stage of a single-case experiment is usually an observation stage or **baseline stage.** During this stage a record is made of the individual's behavior prior to any intervention. A typical measure is frequency of behavior per some unit of time, such as a day, hour, or other recording interval (see Box 8.2). An applied researcher might record the number of times during a 10-minute interview that an excessively shy child makes eye contact, the number of headaches reported each week by a depressed migraine sufferer, or the number of verbal pauses per minute made by a chronic stutterer. The baseline record provides information about what behavior would be like if treatment were not provided (Kazdin, 1978b).

Once behavior is shown to be relatively stable—that is, it exhibits little fluctuation between recording intervals—an intervention is introduced. Behavior immediately following an intervention is contrasted with that seen during baseline performance. The effect of a behavioral intervention is typically evaluated by visual inspection of the behavioral record. How did behavior change, in other words, following the experimental treatment? Traditionally, tests of statistical significance have not been used, although there is some controversy surrounding this aspect of single-case methodology (Kratochwill and Brody, 1978). Later in this chapter we will discuss some of the problems that arise when visual inspection is used to determine whether a treatment was effective.

Another approach to treatment evaluation is to assess the **clinical significance** of an experimental result. Information, for instance, about the strength of a treatment—how likely it is to improve the life of a client in a real-world setting—is often more important for the applied researcher than a treatment's statistical significance or even its "obvious" effect on behavior as contrasted with baseline performance (Yeaton and Sechrest, 1981). Two methods for determining clinical significance of a treatment are social comparison and subjective evaluation (Kazdin, 1977; 1982a). In a **social compari-**

BOX 8.2

FIRST STEPS IN APPLIED BEHAVIOR ANALYSIS: DEFINING, OBSERVING, AND RECORDING

The first stage of applied behavior analysis is to state in general terms the goals of a behavior modification program. What, in other words, should be accomplished by behavioral intervention? Often this statement of goals will be in terms of increasing or decreasing the frequency of some behavior. A parent might want to decrease the frequency with which a child bites her nails, or hits a sibling, or uses obscene language. A teacher may wish to reduce the frequency with which a child leaves his seat in the classroom without permission. An employer may wish to reduce absenteeism or increase productivity. A dentist may want to increase patients' compliance with a dental hygiene program. A behavior therapist may seek to reduce a client's stuttering.

A general statement of purpose, however, is insufficient when carrying out applied behavior analysis. One reason why is that many different behaviors are likely to be related to a general goal. Consider what behaviors might be related to a goal of "losing weight." Particular relevant behaviors might include eating less food, exercising regularly, avoiding between-meal snacks, and eating less junk food. In most cases only one behavior will be selected as a "target" for change. A more important reason why general goals are inappropriate for behavior analysis is that they are simply that—too general. A critical step in applied behavior analysis is to define a target behavior explicitly and objectively so that behavior can be easily measured. "Behaviors" such as aggression, anxiety, rudeness, sloppiness, laziness, and studying cannot be measured. Rather, *specific* target behaviors must be defined that are related to these more general behaviors. The number of minutes spent reading a textbook, for instance, is a behavior that defines "studying" in an objective way.

If a behavior has been defined objectively, it should be possible to observe it reliably and record some measure of its occurrence. In fact, a good way to determine whether you have defined a behavior clearly enough is to see whether two observers can agree on its description and its rate of occurrence. As with other methodologies based on observation, it is important to provide measures of observer agreement as evidence of the reliability of observations.

In the context of applied behavior analysis, the most common measure of behavior is frequency of occurrence, although measures of duration (for example, time on task) are also used. Often the frequency of a target behavior is recorded during some convenient unit of time, such as a day or week. There are alternatives to simply counting occurrences during an observation period. One of the more widely used recording strategies is *interval recording* (Kazdin, 1980a). In this procedure a block of time is identified, such as a 30-minute period during the day. This block of time is divided into a series of smaller equal intervals, such as intervals of 15 seconds. The observer records whether or not the behavior occurs during each interval. Only the first occurrence of a behavior during an interval is counted. That is, the observer notes whether or not the behavior occurred, not how many times during the interval it occurred.

As observations are made, a graph or "chart" is constructed showing the rate of occurrence of behavior across observation periods. The goal of this observation is to provide a measure of baseline behavior prior to implementing a treatment. Many possibilities of behavioral intervention exist and are described in many different textbooks on behavior modification. Reese (1978), for example, describes in detail the general procedures for applied behavior analysis and illustrates many of the more popular techniques for behavior change.

son approach to clinical significance, the researcher compares the behavior of a client after treatment with the behavior of a "normal" group of subjects. For example, following treatment aimed at reducing aggressive behavior of a child in the classroom, a researcher may compare the treated child's behavior with that of children who are not normally aggressive. A **subjective evaluation** approach uses the judgments of people who have contact with the client to help decide whether a treatment has been effective. Family members, teachers, friends, and staff members in a hospital are examples of the types of people who might be asked to judge whether the behavior of the individual is perceptibly different after treatment from what it was before treatment.

Although there are numerous design possibilities for the researcher who uses the single-case approach (Hersen and Barlow, 1978; Kazdin, 1980a), the most commonly employed are the ABAB and multiple-baseline designs (Kazdin, 1978b).

SPECIFIC EXPERIMENTAL DESIGNS

The ABAB Design The **ABAB design** seeks to confirm a treatment effect by demonstrating that behavior changes systematically with alternating conditions of No Treatment and Treatment. An initial baseline stage (A) is followed by a treatment stage (B), next by a return to baseline (A), and then by another treatment stage (B). Because treatment is removed during the second A stage, and any improvement in behavior is likely to be reversed at this point, this design is also called a *reversal design*. The researcher using the ABAB design observes whether behavior changes immediately upon introduction of a treatment variable (first B), whether behavior reverses when treatment is withdrawn (second A), and whether behavior improves again when treatment is reintroduced (second B). When variations in behavior follow the introduction and withdrawal of treatment in this way, there is considerable evidence supporting the conclusion that the treatment caused behavior change.

Horton (1987) used an ABAB design to assess the effects of facial screening on the maladaptive behavior of a severely mentally retarded 8-year-old girl. Facial screening is a mildly aversive technique involving the application of a face cover (for example, a soft cloth) contingent on the appearance of the undesirable behavior. Previous research had shown this technique to be effective in reducing the frequency of self-injurious behaviors, such as face slapping. Horton sought to determine whether it would reduce the frequency of spoon banging by his young subject at mealtime. The spoon banging prevented the girl from dining with her classmates at the school for exceptional children which she attended. Banging was disruptive because of the noise, and because it often led her to fling food on the floor, or resulted in her dropping the spoon on the floor.

A clear definition of spoon banging was made to distinguish it from normal scooping motions. Then, a paraprofessional was trained to make observations and to administer the treatment. A frequency count was used to assess the magnitude of spoon banging within each 15-minute eating session. During the initial or baseline period the paraprofessional recorded frequency and, with each occurrence of the response, said "no bang," gently grasped the subject's wrist, and returned her hand to her dish. The procedure was videotaped, and an independent observer viewed the films and recorded frequency as a reliability check. Interobserver reliability was approximately 96 percent. The baseline was conducted for 16 days.

The first treatment period began on Day 17 and lasted for 16 days. Each time spoon banging was observed, the paraprofessional continued to give the corrective feedback of "no bang" and returned the girl's hand to her dish. However, the paraprofessional also pulled a terrycloth bib over the subject's entire face for 5 seconds. Release from facial screening was contingent on the subject not banging for 5 seconds. The first treatment phase was followed by a second baseline period and another treatment phase. Post-treatment observations were also made at 6, 10, 15, and 19 months.

Figure 8.3 shows changes in the frequency of the retarded girl's spoon banging behavior as a function of alternating baseline and treatment phases. Facial screening was not only effective in reducing this behavior during treatment phases; follow-up observations revealed that the target behavior was still absent months later. Following the final treatment phase, the girl no longer required direct supervision during mealtime at either school or home and was permitted to eat with her peers. The facial screening technique was a successful procedure for controlling the maladaptive behavior of the young

FIGURE 8.3 Frequency of spoon-banging responses across baseline, treatment, and follow-up phases of study. (*Adapted from Horton, 1987.*)

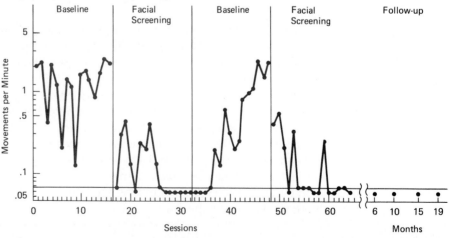

child when other, less intrusive procedures had failed. Because only one treatment was administered, and because visual inspection revealed that behavior changed systematically with the introduction and withdrawal of treatment, it can be concluded that application of an aversive stimulus was responsible for eliminating spoon banging.

A major methodological problem that sometimes arises in the context of an ABAB procedure can be illustrated by looking again at the results of the Horton (1987) study shown in Figure 8.3. In the second baseline stage, when application of the facial screening was withdrawn, spoon banging increased in frequency. That is, the improvement observed under the preceding treatment stage was reversed. What if behavior was not found to change when the treatment was withdrawn? What can be concluded? Behavior in a second baseline stage may not revert to what it was during the initial baseline period, and when that occurs it raises serious problems of interpretation.

One reason why improvement in behavior may not reverse is that the behavior that is the focus of treatment would not logically be expected to become worse once improvement was observed. This might be the case if treatment involved training an individual in a new skill. Once the skill is acquired, it cannot reasonably be expected to be unlearned. The solution to this problem is one of foresight. That is, the ABAB design should not be used when the target behavior could not logically be expected to show reversal when treatment is withdrawn.

Given that the experienced researcher is likely to avoid using an ABAB design in situations wherein behavior would not be expected to reverse, the failure to observe a reversal of performance is probably due to one of two factors. One possibility is that a variable other than the treatment variable was responsible for the improvement in behavior in the first shift from baseline to treatment stages. For example, the subject may receive increased attention from staff or friends during treatment. This increased attention—rather than the treatment—may produce an improvement in behavior. If the attention persists even though the specific treatment is withdrawn, the behavior change is likely to persist as well. It is also possible that, although the treatment caused behavior to improve, other variables "took over" to control the new behavior. Again, we might consider attention as a variable having an effect on behavior. When family and friends witness a change in behavior, they may pay increased attention to the subject. Positive reinforcement in the form of attention may maintain the behavior change that was initiated by the treatment.

In either case, when improvement in behavior does not reverse, it is not clear whether the experimental treatment or some other factor led to the initial behavior change (Kazdin, 1980a). The solution to this set of circumstances is to examine the situation carefully in hopes of finding variables that might be confounding the treatment variable or to replicate the procedure with the same subject or with different subjects (Hersen and Barlow, 1976).

From an applied researcher's point of view, in some situations there is also an ethical problem in using the ABAB design. As you might imagine, the withdrawal of a beneficial treatment may not be justified in all cases. For example, although spoon-banging behavior would not be considered life-threatening or exceptionally debilitating, other kinds of behavior might be, and it would not be ethical in these cases to remove or even suspend treatment once a positive effect was observed. Some autistic children exhibit self-injurious behaviors such as head banging or face slapping. If a clinical researcher succeeded in reducing the frequency of such behavior, it might be considered unethical to withdraw treatment to meet the requirements of an experimental design. Fortunately, there are other single-case experimental designs that do not involve withdrawal of treatment and that may be appropriate in such situations.

The Multiple-Baseline Design   The **multiple-baseline design** demonstrates the effect of a treatment by showing that behaviors in more than one baseline change as a consequence of the introduction of a treatment. There are several variations on the multiple-baseline design, depending on whether multiple baselines are established for different individuals, for different behaviors in the same individual, or for the same individual in different situations. In each case, the conclusion that an experimental variable produced a reliable effect rests on the demonstration that behavior changed only when the experimental variable was introduced. Although they sound complex, multiple-baseline designs are frequently used and easily understood. Let us refer to a specific example of each type from the applied research literature.

A *multiple-baseline across subjects design* refers to a procedure wherein more than one individual is observed simultaneously. Specifically, baselines are first established for different individuals. When the behavior of each individual has stabilized, an intervention is introduced for one individual, then for another individual, later for another; and so on. That is, the experimental treatment is introduced at a different time for each subject. If the treatment is responsible for changing behavior, then an effect in the behavioral record will be seen immediately following the application of the treatment in each individual.

An interesting example of the use of a multiple-baseline design across subjects is from a study by Allison and Ayllon (1980). Their study also illustrates how an applied behavior analysis can be employed in the area of sports psychology. This blossoming field involves the application of psychological principles to the improvement of recreation and sports (see, for example, Browne and Mahoney, 1984). Specifically, Allison and Ayllon investigated the effect that a coaching method based on several behavioral techniques had on the acquisition of specific football, tennis, and gymnastic skills. To evaluate this new coaching method they used a multiple-baseline design. Although their investigation was successful in each sport, we will examine the effects of behavioral coaching only as it was applied to the acquisition of a football skill.

The subjects in this experiment were second-string members of a citywide football program [chosen because they "completely lacked fundamental football skills" (Allison and Ayllon, 1980, p. 299)]. The skill to be acquired was blocking, which was defined operationally in terms of eight elements, ranging from the body first being behind the line of scrimmage to maintaining body contact until the whistle was blown. Behavioral coaching involved specific procedures implemented by the team coach. The procedures included systematic verbal feedback, positive and negative reinforcement, and several other behavioral techniques. The experimenter first established baselines for several different members of the football team under "standard coaching" conditions. In this procedure the coach used verbal instructions, provided occasional modeling or verbal approval, and, when execution was incorrect, "loudly informed the player and, at times, commented on the player's stupidity, lack of courage, awareness, or even worse" (p. 300). In short, an all-too-typical example of coaching behavior.

The experimenter and a second, reliability observer made observations of the frequency of correct blocks made in sets of ten trials. Behavioral coaching was begun, in accordance with the multiple-baseline design, at different times for various football players. Results of this intervention are shown in Figure 8.4.

FIGURE 8.4   Multiple baselines showing percentage of football blocks executed correctly by four players as a function of standard coaching and of behavioral coaching. (*From Allison and Ayllon, 1980.*)

Across four individuals, behavioral coaching was shown to be effective in increasing the frequency of correctly executed blocks. Observer agreement on blocking performance ranged from 84 to 94 percent, indicating that the observation of behavior change was reliable. The skill execution changed for each player at the point where behavioral coaching was introduced. Thus, it can be argued that this method caused the change in each player's performance.

When two or more baselines are established by observing different behaviors in the same individual, the design is called a *multiple-baseline across behaviors design*. A treatment is directed first at one behavior, then at another, and so on. A causal relationship between treatment and behavior is assumed if each behavior responds directly to treatment. For example, Bornstein et al. (1977) successfully treated an 8-year-old elementary schoolgirl who was judged to be excessively shy, unassertive, and passive. Multiple baselines were established for behaviors of eye contact, number of requests, and loudness of speech. Intervention consisted of prompting, feedback, and modeling of behaviors and was instituted at different times across behaviors. An inspection of the behavioral record showed that the different behaviors changed immediately after introduction of the new intervention.

The third major variation on the multiple-baseline design is that across situations. In a *multiple-baseline across situations design,* baselines are established for a behavior in different situations. For example, a researcher might establish baselines showing frequency of a target behavior in the clinic and frequency of this same behavior in the home. As with other variations of this design, the treatment is applied at different times and the behavioral records are examined to determine whether behavior changes systematically with the introduction of treatment.

VanBiervliet et al. (1981) used a multiple-baseline across situations design to demonstrate how changes in the way meals are served can influence the frequency of mealtime language of institutionalized retarded persons. The investigators suggested that the typical institutional method of serving meals does not encourage peer interaction and that an alternative procedure, serving "family style," would increase verbal interactions. Baselines for frequency of verbalizations of five residents were made for three different situations (actually, three meals)—dinner, lunch, and breakfast. An analysis of behavior change both in terms of the average number of vocalizations made by the five residents and in terms of an examination of individual behavioral records showed that frequency of verbal behavior increased at each meal following this change in the way meals were served.

Often the first question to arise when one is doing a multiple-baseline experiment is "How many baselines do I need?" As with many other aspects of single-case methodology, there are no hard-and-fast rules. The bare minimum is clearly two baselines, but this is generally considered inadequate. Three to four baselines are recommended (Hersen and Barlow, 1976).

Because a convincing demonstration of a treatment rests on the observation that behavior changes immediately when the experimental variable is introduced, problems arise when changes are seen in a baseline *before* an experimental intervention. This may occur in any of the types of multiple-baseline designs we have considered, and the reasons are not always clear. When changes in baseline performance occur prior to an experimental intervention, it is often difficult to draw a conclusion about the efficacy of the experimental treatment. However, the multiple-baseline design can still be interpreted with some confidence when preintervention changes appear in only one of several baselines that are being recorded—so long as plausible explanations for the baseline change that are based on procedural or situational variables are available. For instance, Kazdin and Erickson (1975) used a multiple-baseline across subjects design to develop responsiveness to instructions in severely retarded individuals. Subjects who followed instructions were reinforced with candy-coated cereal and praise, and this intervention was introduced in each of four small groups at different points in time. Performance changed directly with the application of the positive reinforcement procedure in three groups, but not in the fourth. In this group, which had the longest baseline, behavior gradually improved prior to the intervention. The researchers reasonably suggested that this occurred because subjects in this group saw other patients comply with instructions and then imitated the treated subjects' behavior.

Another problem sometimes seen in the context of a multiple-baseline design occurs when changes in one behavior generalize to other behaviors or situations. For example, when VanBiervliet et al. (1981) successfully increased the degree of verbal interaction of retarded persons at a dinner meal, we might not have been totally surprised if the residents increased their amount of talking at other meals. Once behavior at dinner was changed, at other meals the sight of food being served or the act of sitting down beside an acquaintance might prompt an increased level of verbal interaction. Such generalization effects were not seen, however, so the effect of the mealtime variable was clearly demonstrated.

To circumvent possible problems, we must again bring foresight to bear. If altering the behavior of one individual is likely to affect the behaviors of others, if behavior in one situation is likely to influence behavior in another situation, or if changing one type of behavior is likely to affect other behaviors, then multiple-baseline designs should not be used (Kazdin, 1980a). As we have noted, unless behavior improves directly following an experimental intervention, concluding that the treatment variable was effective is problematic. Unfortunately, anticipating when changes will occur simultaneously in more than one baseline is not always easy, but these problems appear to be relatively infrequent exceptions to the effects usually seen in a multiple-baseline design (Kazdin, 1980a).

PROBLEMS AND LIMITATIONS COMMON TO ALL SINGLE-CASE DESIGNS

Increasing or decreasing baseline trends, or excessive variability, in behavioral records can make it difficult to evaluate the effects of an intervention. An ideal baseline record and response to an intervention are shown in panel

A of Figure 8.5. Behavior during baseline is very stable, and behavior changes immediately following the introduction of treatment. If this were the outcome of the first stages of either an ABAB or a multiple-baseline design, we would be headed in the direction of showing that our treatment is effective in modifying behavior. However, consider the baseline and treatment stages shown in panel B of Figure 8.5. The baseline shows extreme variability, and, although behavior appears to increase in frequency following an intervention, it is difficult to know whether the treatment produced the change or behavior just happened to be on the upswing. In this case it would be hard to decide whether our intervention successfully changed behavior.

There are several approaches to the problem of excessive baseline variability. One is to look for variables in the situation that might be producing variability and that we might be able to remove. The presence of a particular staff member, for instance, might be causing changes in the behavior of a psychiatric patient. Another approach is to "wait it out"—to continue taking baseline measures until behavior stabilizes. It is, of course, not possible to predict *when* and *if* this might occur, but introducing an intervention before behavior has stabilized would jeopardize a clear interpretation of the experimental outcome. Another approach is to average data points. By charting a behavioral record using averages of several points, we can sometimes reduce the "appearance" of variability (Kazdin, 1978b).

Another problem arises when the baseline record shows an increasing or a decreasing trend. In panel C of Figure 8.5, we see how behavior might change following an intervention when the initial baseline stage was charac-

FIGURE 8.5 Examples of behavioral records showing possible relationships between baseline and intervention phases of a behavior modification program.

terized by a decreasing trend in frequency of behavior. If the goal of the intervention was to increase frequency of behavior, the change described in panel C offers little problem of interpretation. An intervention that reversed the decreasing trend can be taken as evidence that the treatment was effective. However, should the goal of intervention be to *reduce* frequency of behavior, it would be difficult to know whether the decrease in frequency of behavior following the intervention is due to the intervention or to continuation of a trend. This situation is illustrated in panel D. Here we see a decreasing trend in the baseline stage and continued reduction of frequency in the treatment stage. It is difficult in this case to know whether the experimental treatment had an effect. Generally speaking, when an intervention is expected to have an effect in the same direction as a baseline trend, the effect must be very marked in order to conclude that behavior was modified by the application of a treatment (Kazdin, 1978b). Moreover, because a treatment effect in a single-case design is usually judged by visually inspecting the behavioral record, in cases where baseline trends are evident it is often difficult to say what a "marked" change in the behavioral record is. In such cases other means of evaluation should be employed, such as social comparison or subjective evaluation.

When an effect is demonstrated using an *N* = 1 design, a frequent criticism is that external validity is limited. In other words, the *N* = 1 experiment appears to have the same limitation as the traditional case study method. Because each person is unique, it can be argued that there is no way of knowing whether the effect of a particular intervention will generalize to other individuals. There are several reasons why this problem may not be as serious as it seems. First, the types of intervention used in single-case studies are often ones that produce dramatic and sizable changes in behavior (Kazdin, 1978b). Consequently, these types of treatments are often found to generalize to other individuals. Other evidence for the generality of effects based on single-case studies comes from the use of multiple-baseline designs. A multiple-baseline across-subjects design, for example, is often able to show that a particular intervention was successful in modifying the behavior of *several* individuals. Similarly, multiple baselines across situations and behaviors attest to the external validity of a treatment effect.

A treatment effect can also be shown to generalize to other individuals when a "single group" of subjects is used in a single-case experiment. As was mentioned before, the procedures associated with single-case designs are sometimes used with small groups of individuals as well. We have already seen two examples of this. VanBiervliet et al. (1981) showed that changes in a mealtime procedure were effective in increasing the average frequency of verbalizations of five retarded individuals who were treated simultaneously. Similarly, Kazdin and Erickson (1975) found that positive reinforcement improved responsiveness to instructions in small groups of retarded individuals. In both these experiments, the researchers were able to demonstrate that an experimental treatment was effective for a small group of subjects as well as for individuals in the group. In other words, an effect was replicated several times across members of a group each time an experimental manipulation was introduced. Such studies offer impressive evidence for both internal and external validity.

One limitation of the $N = 1$ methodology is not easily dismissed, and it illustrates again the lesson that no one research methodology is able to provide all the answers to questions that psychologists ask. The $N = 1$ experiment is often not appropriate for examining the effect of interactions among variables. Although a single-case design can provide evidence of the effect of one variable (a main effect) by showing, for example, that behavior changes between conditions of No Treatment and Treatment, it is difficult if not impossible to examine adequately the differential effect of *combinations* of various levels of experimental variables. It was pointed out in Chapter 7 that, when a subject variable is investigated, any "effect" of that variable must be considered essentially the same as correlational evidence. Therefore, when subject variables are of concern, it is best to do a factorial design that combines levels of the subject variable and levels of a manipulated variable. The subject variable and the manipulated variable may work together to produce an interaction. This interaction effect may offer crucial information about what characteristics of the subject are important in producing an effect of the treatment variable on the dependent variable. Or it may demonstrate under what conditions a difference between levels of the subject variable will be found. Questions about interactions between treatment variables and subject variables are not easily answered using single-group methodology (Kazdin, 1982a). In this situation, a between-groups design is most appropriate. The experienced research psychologist realizes that there are problems and limitations associated with most methodologies. The methodology best suited to answering a particular question should be used. And, when possible, multi-method approaches to data collection are recommended (see Chapter 4).

SUMMARY

Behaviorism is an approach to the study of psychology that emphasizes the study of observable behavior under strictly controlled conditions. The behaviorist often uses animal subjects, working under the assumption that human behavior and animal behavior differ only quantitatively and not qualitatively. The behaviorism of B. F. Skinner is called an experimental analysis of behavior. Research methods associated with this approach are those of respondent and operant conditioning. Skinner developed an operant chamber in which he could observe and record automatically how animal subjects respond as a function of various types of reinforcement and punishment. In order to control behavior in an operant chamber, principles of shaping and stimulus control are frequently used. We saw in this chapter how these experimental techniques are also important in the field of animal training.

The application of principles derived from an experimental analysis of behavior to socially relevant problems is called applied behavior analysis. The major methodology of this approach is the single-case or $N = 1$ experimental design. Although there are many kinds of $N = 1$ designs, the most common are the ABAB design and the multiple-baseline design. An important consideration in applied behavior analysis is obtaining evidence for clinical significance of a treatment—that is, how likely a treatment is to modify the behavior of a client in a real-world setting.

An ABAB design, or reversal design, allows a researcher to confirm a treatment effect by showing that behavior changes systematically with conditions of No Treatment (baseline) and Treatment. Methodological problems arise in this design when behavior that changed during the first treatment (B) stage does not reverse when treatment is withdrawn during the second baseline (A) stage. When this occurs, it is difficult to establish that the treatment variable, rather than some other variable, was responsible for the initial change. One may encounter ethical problems when using the ABAB design if a treatment that has been shown to be beneficial is withdrawn during the second baseline stage.

A multiple-baseline design demonstrates the effectiveness of a treatment by showing that behaviors across more than one baseline change as a consequence of the introduction of a treatment. Baselines are first established across different subjects, across behaviors in the same subject, or across situations. Methodological problems arise when behavior does not change immediately with the introduction of a treatment or when a treatment effect generalizes to other subjects, other behaviors, or other situations.

Problems of increasing or decreasing baselines, as well as excessive baseline variability, sometimes make it difficult to interpret the outcome of single-case designs. The problem of excessive baseline variability can be approached by seeking out and removing sources of variability, by extending the time during which baseline observations are made, or by averaging data points to remove the "appearance" of variability. Increasing or decreasing baselines may require the researcher to obtain other kinds of evidence for the effectiveness of a treatment—for example, measures of social comparison or subjective evaluation. Finally, the $N = 1$ design is often criticized for its lack of external validity. However, because treatments typically produce substantial changes in behavior, these changes can often be easily replicated in different individuals. The use of "single groups" of subjects can also provide immediate evidence of generality across subjects. The fact that the $N = 1$ design usually is not appropriate for testing the possible interactions of variables emphasizes the importance of selecting the research methodology that is most relevant to answering the particular question under investigation.

KEY CONCEPTS

experimental analysis of behavior
applied behavior analysis
$N = 1$ designs
behaviorism
token economy
behavior therapy
behavior modification
single-case experiment

baseline stage
clinical significance
social comparison
subjective evaluation
ABAB design (reversal design)
multiple-baseline design (across
    subjects, across behaviors, across
    situations)

REVIEW QUESTIONS

PRINCIPLES OF CONDITIONING

1 Briefly describe the procedures associated with respondent or classical conditioning and with operant or instrumental conditioning.
2 Distinguish between the members of the following pairs: reinforcement and punishment, positive reinforcer and negative reinforcer, positive reinforcement and negative reinforcement.
3 Explain how our everyday behaviors are often under stimulus control.
4 Outline the procedures for establishing (a) a discriminative stimulus and (b) a conditioned reinforcer.
5 Describe how dolphin trainers might shape, in a dolphin, the behavior of "beaching."

APPLIED BEHAVIOR ANALYSIS

6 Under what conditions might an $N = 1$ design be more appropriate than a multiple-group design?

7 Distinguish between baseline and intervention stages of an $N = 1$ experimental design.

8 How does clinical significance differ from statistical significance? Explain how clinical significance can be evaluated.

9 Why is an ABAB design also called a reversal design?

10 What major methodological problems are specifically associated with an ABAB design?

11 Outline the general rationale behind all the major forms of multiple-baseline designs.

12 What major methodological problems are specifically associated with multiple-baseline designs?

13 What major methodological problems are inherent in all $N = 1$ experimental designs?

14 What answers are given to the frequent criticism that $N = 1$ experimental designs lack external validity?

15 What types of research questions are not easily answered using single-case ($N = 1$) experimental designs?

CHALLENGE QUESTIONS

1 A 5-year-old child frequently gets skin rashes, and the mother has been told by her family doctor that the problem is due to "something" that the child eats. The doctor suggests that she "watch carefully" what the child eats. The mother decides to approach this problem by recording each day whether the child has a rash and what the child has eaten the day before. She hopes to find some relationship between eating a particular food and the presence or absence of the rash. Although this approach might help discover a relationship between eating certain foods and the appearance of the rash, a better approach might be one based on the logic and procedures associated with $N = 1$ designs. Explain how the mother might use such an alternative approach. Be specific and point to possible problems that may arise in this application of behavioral methodology.

2 During the summer months you find employment in a camp for mildly retarded children. As a counselor you are asked to supervise a small group of children, as well as to look for ways to improve their attention to various camp activities that take place indoors (for example, craft making and sewing). You decide to explore the possibility of using a system of rewards (M & M candies) for "time on task." You realize that this behavior must be shaped before it can be maintained through some schedule of reinforcement. Furthermore, you realize that the camp director will want evidence of the effectiveness of your intervention strategy as well as some assurance that it will work with other children in the camp. Therefore you are to:

  A Plan an intervention strategy based on operant principles that has as its goal an increase in the time children spend on a camp activity.

  B Explain what behavioral records you will need to keep and how you will determine whether your intervention has produced a change in the children's behavior. You will need, for example, to specify exactly when and how you will measure behavior, as well as to justify your use of a particular design to carry out your "experiment."

  C Describe the argument you will use to convince the director that your intervention strategy (assuming that it works) will work with other, similar children.

3 A schoolteacher asks your help in planning a behavioral intervention that will help manage the behavior of children in the classroom. Many of the children do not stay at their desks when asked to do so, do not remain quiet during "quiet times," and exhibit other behaviors that disrupt the teaching environment. Explain how a token economy might be established to help control the children's behavior. Identify what the tokens are and what specific things might be "purchased" with the tokens. Also explain under what conditions the tokens will be awarded (the contingencies of reinforcement). Finally, explain how an ABAB $N = 1$ experimental design could be used with this group of children in order to demonstrate the effectiveness of the intervention.

4 You have been asked to address a research methodology class on the topic $N = 1$ versus $N = $ Many. The idea behind the presentation is to show the advantages and disadvantages of single-case experimental designs relative to multiple-group designs. What would you say regarding the role of $N = 1$ research in psychology compared to research using multiple groups of subjects?

ANSWER TO CHALLENGE QUESTION 1

1 The mother would probably be better served by identifying likely candidates for the allergic reactions and then applying an ABAB design to each candidate one at a time. That is, she should include milk in her child's diet and measure the rash over a baseline period and then eliminate milk from the diet and note whether the rash subsides or even disappears, followed by a return to the baseline with milk in the diet again, and concluding with a final "treatment" period without milk. The major problems with this approach are the likelihood of identifying the correct offending foods, but, more important, if the rash is the result of an interactive reaction to particular food combinations, these will be most difficult to detect by eliminating foods one at a time.

9

QUASI-EXPERIMENTAL DESIGNS AND PROGRAM EVALUATION

OUTLINE

In the most general sense, an experiment is a test; it is a procedure used to find out something not presently known. In this sense we experiment when we add new ingredients to the chili in order to see whether they improve its taste. We experiment with new ways to catch fish by changing the lures we use. We experiment by driving a different route in order to find a quicker way to commute to work. As you have seen, however, in the conduct of psychological research, experiments are usually carried out in order to discover the causes of a phenomenon. Experimental methods, unlike other research techniques such as observation and surveys, are viewed as the most efficient way to determine causation. Indeed, in one way or another, all discussions found in Chapters 5 through 8 have emphasized experimental methods in psychological research.

By now you probably appreciate the complexity of the task facing the researcher who seeks to understand a phenomenon by discovering what caused it. In this chapter we continue our discussion of experimental methods, but we focus on experiments as they are often conducted in natural settings. You will see that the task of drawing cause-and-effect conclusions often becomes even more difficult, and that new problems arise, when an investigator leaves the confines of the laboratory to experiment in natural settings.

There are numerous reasons why experiments are carried out in natural settings. One important reason (mentioned in Chapter 5) is to test the external validity of a laboratory finding. Other reasons for doing field experiments are likely to be associated with attempts to improve conditions under which people live and work. The government may experiment with a new tax system or a new method of training military enlistees. Schools may experiment by changing lunch programs, after-school care, or curricula. A business may experiment with new product designs, methods of delivering employee benefits, or flexible work hours. In these cases, as is true in the laboratory, it is important to determine whether the "treatment" caused a change. Did a change in the way patients are admitted to a hospital emergency room cause patients to be treated more quickly and efficiently? Did a college energy conservation program cause a decrease in energy consumption?

Knowing whether a treatment was effective permits us to make important decisions about continuing the treatment, about spending additional money, about investing more time and effort, or about changing the present situation on the basis of our knowledge of the results. Research that seeks to determine the effectiveness of changes made by institutions, government agencies, and other units of society is called **program evaluation.**

In this chapter we discuss the problems of conducting experiments in natural settings. We describe obstacles to doing true experiments in such settings, and we discuss ways of overcoming these obstacles so that true experiments are done whenever possible. Nevertheless, true experiments are sometimes not feasible outside the laboratory. In these cases, experimental procedures that only approximate the conditions of laboratory experiments must be considered. We discuss several of these "quasi-experimental" techniques. The problems attendant on quasi-experimentation make us realize the value of true experiments, so we briefly consider alternatives to quasi-experiments in natural settings. One such alternative is the extension of single-case experimental designs (which we discussed in Chapter 8) to research in natural settings. We conclude the chapter by providing a brief introduction to the logic, procedures, and limitations of program evaluation.

DIFFERENCES BETWEEN LABORATORY EXPERIMENTS AND EXPERIMENTS IN NATURAL SETTINGS

There are some important considerations to keep in mind as we discuss experimentation in natural settings. Experimentation outside the confines of the psychology laboratory is likely to differ from laboratory research in a number of significant ways. Not every experiment in a natural setting differs from laboratory experiments in all of these ways, of course. But, when considering research in a natural setting, it is important to weigh the following points.

CONTROL

More than anything else, the scientist is concerned with control. Only by controlling those factors that are assumed to influence a phenomenon can one make a decision about causation. As you have seen in previous chapters, control takes several forms. The assignment of subjects to conditions of an experiment is a method of control used to balance subject characteristics in Treatment and No Treatment conditions. Other factors that are likely to influence a phenomenon may be controlled by holding them constant.

In a natural setting, a researcher may not always have the same degree of control over conditions of an experiment or over assignment of subjects as in a laboratory. A field experiment may have to be conducted according to the availability of subjects or at the discretion of an administrator or government official. Natural settings place various restrictions on an experiment that limit the researcher's control. It is even possible that an investigator may not directly participate in the planning and conduct of the "experiment," but may be asked afterward whether a treatment "worked." This kind of situation is clearly the most difficult, because vital factors may not have been considered in planning or executing the intervention.

EXTERNAL VALIDITY

Field experiments are often conducted with the goal of establishing the external validity of a laboratory finding. The "artificial" environment of the psychology laboratory, which increases the internal validity of research, often decreases the external validity of the findings. Experiments in natural settings may therefore need to be conducted in order to generalize results beyond the laboratory situation.

The external validity of research done in natural settings may be emphasized more if social experimentation is the basis for large-scale social changes. That is, if the results of an experiment are to be used to plan further interventions or to implement similar programs outside the domain in which the experiment was conducted, then it is vital to know to what extent the treatment and results can be generalized. For example, legislators may wish to generalize to a different state certain procedures that have been shown to produce an increase in voter registration in one state. A method to increase employee morale that succeeded in one branch of a company may be considered by company officials for all branches of the company. Will the results of a reading program that is judged to be beneficial at one grade level in one school generalize to other grade levels, other schools, or conditions where it is implemented by different personnel? These are, of course, all questions of external validity.

GOALS

Experimentation in natural settings often has different goals from laboratory research. One major difference in goals is that which exists between basic and applied research. *Basic research* is often carried out with the single goal of understanding a phenomenon, of determining how "nature" works. **Basic research** may be done to gain knowledge merely for knowledge's sake. **Ap-**

plied research is also directed toward discovering the reasons for a phenomenon, but it is likely to be done only when knowing the reasons for an event will lead to a change in the status quo. That is, applied research is carried out with the goal of gaining knowledge that will modify or improve the present situation. Experimentation in natural settings, therefore, is more likely to have practical goals.

CONSEQUENCES

During the 1970s the U.S. government experimented with the "new town" concept. Thirteen new towns were created under government sponsorship. Beginning from scratch, designers tried to avoid all the problems of older unplanned urban communities. Towns such as Columbia, Maryland and Reston, Virginia are examples. Also in the decade of the 1970s, the government experimented with a program designed to aid prisoners following release from incarceration (see Berk et al., 1987). Individuals released from prison often have little in the way of resources to help them begin a new life and they frequently have difficulty finding jobs. This economic hardship can contribute to new crime. The program involved random assignment of ex-prisoners to groups that either received financial assistance on leaving prison or did not receive financial assistance. The program targeted as subjects about 2,000 ex-prisoners in Texas and Georgia. In 1988 the National Cancer Institute debated whether to fund a $130 million study to investigate a possible link between breast cancer and fat consumption. The proposed study would require rigorous control over the diets of 10,000 women and monitoring them over 10 years (Sun, 1988).

Clearly, these examples of society's "experiments," as well as those we might imagine being carried out on a smaller scale in natural settings (such as those conducted in schools or businesses), are likely to have consequences of greater immediate impact than laboratory research. Although a few planned communities worked, others did not, and planners and builders went bankrupt (see *Time*, October 16, 1978, p. 84). While the prison release program produced some identifiable positive results, it was also found to be responsible for an increase in crime, apparently due to the ex-prisoners' freedom from having to work (see Berk et al., 1987). The breast cancer study was voted down when administrators decided that monitoring 22,000 women needed for a control group could not reasonably be accomplished. A decision was not made at that time as to whether a different study would be undertaken to investigate the cancer link.

The Head Start program for disadvantaged children and the "Sesame Street" television show were experiments designed to improve the education of literally hundreds of thousands of children across the nation. Experiments in businesses may be carried out with the eventual goal of reducing the number of employees or in other ways affecting the quality of employees' lives. Unfortunately, drawing a meaningful conclusion about the effects of many of these experiments may be impossible without giving more consideration to the design and implementation of these "treatments" (see Box 9.1). This is particularly disturbing, because the consequences of such experiments are often so great in terms of money spent and the number of people whose lives are affected. By contrast, the consequences of a laboratory experiment are often likely to be minimal. They may directly affect only the lives of a few researchers and of those relatively few subjects recruited to participate.

TRUE EXPERIMENTS AND QUASI-EXPERIMENTS

CHARACTERISTICS OF TRUE EXPERIMENTS

Although many everyday activities (such as altering the ingredients of a recipe) might be called "experiments," we would not consider them "true" experiments in the sense in which experimentation has been discussed in this textbook. Analogously, many of the various "social experiments" that are carried out by the government (such as the "new town" concept) and those that are conducted by company officials or educational administrators are also not true experiments. A true experiment is one that leads to an unambiguous outcome regarding what caused an event.

True experiments exhibit three important characteristics. First, in a true experiment some type of intervention or treatment is implemented. Using the language of the laboratory researcher, we say that an independent variable is manipulated. Second, true experiments are marked by the high degree of control that an experimenter has over the arrangement of experimental conditions, assignment of subjects, choice of dependent variables, and systematic manipulation of independent variables. The ability to assign subjects randomly to experimental conditions is often seen as the most critical defining characteristic of the true experiment (Kidder and Judd, 1986). Finally, true experiments are characterized by an appropriate comparison. Indeed, the experimenter exerts control over a situation principally in order to establish a proper comparison to evaluate the effectiveness of an independent variable. In the simplest of experimental situations, this comparison is one between two groups that are treated exactly alike except for the variable of interest. Any differences in a dependent variable that arise in such a situation can logically be assigned to the differences between levels of the independent variable.

OBSTACLES TO CONDUCTING TRUE EXPERIMENTS IN NATURAL SETTINGS

Although we have tried to convince you in this and preceding chapters that experimental research is an effective tool for solving problems and answering questions, not everyone agrees with this approach. Those who disagree would hasten to point out the two obstacles that arise when we try to carry out experiments in natural settings. The first problem is obtaining permission to do the research from individuals in positions of authority. Unless they be-

BOX 9.1

SOCIAL REFORMS AS EXPERIMENTS

Each year, governments at both local and national levels propose, plan, and execute various types of social reforms. Tax relief programs, work incentive programs, educational reforms, police reforms, and medical care for senior citizens are just a few of the types of social reform programs that a government might initiate. Unfortunately, as Donald Campbell (1969), past president of the American Psychological Association, points out, the outcome of these social reforms often cannot be meaningfully evaluated. Did a change in police techniques lead to greater crime stoppage? Are more elderly people gaining access to public transportation after a reduction in fares? Does a work incentive program take more people off the unemployment rolls? The answers to such questions often cannot be found, says Campbell, because most social reforms are instituted in a political climate that is not ready for hard-headed evaluation. What public official, for instance, wants to be associated with a program that failed? As Campbell suggests, there is "safety under the cloak of ignorance" (pp. 409–410). Furthermore, many social reforms are begun under the assumption that they are certain to be successful. Otherwise why spend all that tax money? For many public administrators it is advantageous to leave that assumption in people's minds rather than face the true facts.

Campbell (p. 409) argues that:

> The United States and other modern nations should be ready for an experimental approach to social reform, an approach in which we try out new programs, in which we learn whether or not these programs are effective, and in which we retain, imitate, modify, or discard them on the basis of apparent effectiveness on the multiple imperfect criteria available.

Social scientists must convince administrators to use "true" experiments if at all possible, or quasi-experiments at the very least, when executing social reform. For example, a randomization procedure, perhaps based on public lottery, could be used to decide which group receives a pilot program or gains access to scarce resources. Groups not receiving the program or the available resources would become control groups. The effect of a social "treatment" could then be meaningfully evaluated. At present, decisions regarding who gets what are often influenced by particular interest groups—as the result of intense lobbying, for example—or made on the basis of political favoritism.

When true experiments are not possible, quasi-experimental procedures should be used. Campbell, for instance, demonstrated how an interrupted time-series design (see text) could be used to determine whether a 1955 crackdown on speeding by then Connecticut governor Abraham Ribicoff was successful in reducing traffic fatalities. This experimental analysis showed that the crackdown had beneficial effects but that they were not so great as statements by public officials suggested.

According to Campbell, the most significant change needed in the thinking of public officials is that they must begin to emphasize the importance of the problem rather than the importance of the solution. Rather than pushing for one certain cure-all (which, in most cases, has little opportunity for success), officials must be ready to execute reform in a manner that permits the clearest evaluation and must be prepared to try different solutions if the first one fails. Public officials must, in other words, be ready to use the experimental method to identify society's problems and to determine effective solutions.

Perhaps every elected official should be required to take a course in research methods. What do you think?

lieve that the research will be useful, school board presidents and government and business leaders are unlikely to support research financially or otherwise. We will discuss the problem of the credibility of research later in this chapter when we introduce program evaluation.

The second, and often more pressing, obstacle to doing experiments in natural settings is the problem of access to participants. This problem can prove especially troublesome if participants must agree to be randomly assigned to either a treatment group or a control group before they are allowed to participate in the experiment.

Random assignment to conditions appears unfair at first—after all, random assignment requires that a potentially beneficial treatment be withheld from at least some participants. Suppose that a new approach to the teaching of foreign languages was to be tested at your college or university. Suppose further that, when you went to register for your next semester's classes, you were told that you would be randomly assigned to one of two sections taught at the time you selected—one section involving the old method and one involving the new method. How would you react? Your knowledge of research methods tells you that the two methods must be administered to comparable groups of students and that random assignment is the best way to ensure such comparability. Nonetheless, you might be tempted to feel that random assignment is not fair, especially if you are assigned to the section using the old (old-fashioned?) method. Let's take a closer look at the fairness of random assignment.

If those responsible for selecting the method of foreign language instruction already knew that the new method was more effective than the old method, there would be little justification for testing the method again (unless, of course, the effectiveness of the new method had been demonstrated at schools very different from yours). Under such circumstances we would agree that withholding the new method from students in the control group would be unjust. If we do not know whether the new method is better, however, any approach other than conducting a true experiment will leave us in doubt about the new method's effectiveness. Random assignment to treatments—call it a "lottery" if you prefer—may be the most fair procedure for assigning students to sections. The old method of instruction, after all, was considered effective before the development of the new method. If the new method proves *less* effective, random assignment will have actually "protected" the control participants from receiving an ineffective treatment.

There are ways to offer a potentially effective treatment to all participants while still maintaining comparable groups. Atkinson (1968) randomly assigned students to receive computer-assisted instruction in either English *or* math and then tested both groups in English *and* math. Each group served as a control for the other on the test for which its members had not received instruction. After completing the experiment, both groups could then be given computer-assisted instruction in the subject matter to which they had not been previously exposed.

Establishing a proper control group is possible if there is more demand for a service than an agency can meet. People who are waiting to receive the service can act as what is called a "waiting list" control group. It is essential, however, that people be assigned to the waiting list randomly. As Campbell (1969) points out (see Box 9.1), when scarce social treatments are to be applied, randomization may be preferred to a process that depends on political lobbying or favoritism toward selected groups.

There are also circumstances in which random assignment simply cannot be used. For example, in clinical trials involving tests of new medical treatments, it may be extremely difficult to get patients to agree to be randomly assigned to either the treatment group or the control group. Quasi-experimental designs such as the nonequivalent control group design can be used in these situations. The logic and procedures for these quasi-experimental designs will be described later in this chapter.

THREATS TO INTERNAL VALIDITY CONTROLLED BY TRUE EXPERIMENTS

One way to evaluate an experiment is to determine what kinds of alternative explanations for a phenomenon have been controlled. Prior to doing an experiment, we might look to see what major classes of possible explanations are ruled out by our experimental procedure. Only by eliminating all possible alternative explanations are we able to arrive at a definite conclusion about cause and effect. In previous chapters we have referred to various uncontrolled factors that threaten the internal validity of an experiment as confounding factors (they are also called *confounds*). Several types of confounds have been identified in earlier chapters (see especially Chapter 5). We will now list eight classes of confounds, using the terminology of Campbell and Stanley (1966; see also Cook and Campbell, 1979). You have already been introduced to some of these **threats to internal validity;** others will be new. After reviewing the major classes of confounds, we will be able to judge the extent to which various experimental procedures control for these kinds of alternative explanations of a treatment effect.

History   The occurrence of an event other than the treatment can threaten internal validity if it produces changes in subjects' behavior. A true experiment requires that subjects in the experimental group and the control group be treated the same (have the same history of experiences) except for the treatment. In the laboratory, this is usually accomplished by balancing or holding conditions constant. For example, the same experimenter might be asked to test subjects in all conditions of an experiment. If different experimenters were to test experimental and control subjects we would confound the possible effect due to the experimenter and that of the treatment. When doing experiments in natural settings, the researcher may not always be able to exercise these forms of control, so confounding due to history can be a threat to internal validity.

Maturation   Subjects in an experiment necessarily change as a function of time. They grow older, become more experienced, and so forth. Change associated with the passage of time per se is called *maturation*. For example, without a proper comparison a researcher might attribute the changes in performance between a pretest and a posttest of a group of schoolchildren to the effect of an intervention when, in reality, the changes were simply due to normal processes of maturation.

Testing   Taking a test generally has an effect on subsequent testing. Consider, for example, the fact that many students often improve from the initial test in a course to the second test. The familiarity with the testing procedure and with the instructor's expectations that they gain during the first test affects their performance on the second test. In the context of a psychology experiment, testing is a threat to internal validity if the effect of a treatment cannot be separated from an effect of testing.

Instrumentation   It is possible that changes over time take place not only in the subjects of an experiment but also in the instruments used to measure subjects' performance. This is most clearly a possibility when human observers are used to assess behavior. As you learned in previous chapters (see especially Chapter 2), effects of observer bias are possible due to fatigue, expectations, and other characteristics of observers. For example, as a researcher becomes more experienced in conducting observations, there is likely to be a change in the quality of the observations that she or he makes. Unless controlled for, these changes in instrumentation can threaten internal validity by providing alternative explanations for differences in behavior between one observation period and another. Mechanical instruments also may change with repeated use. A researcher known to the authors once found that a machine used to present material in a learning experiment was not working the same at the end of the experiment as it was at the beginning.

Regression   Statistical regression is always a problem when subjects have been selected for an experiment because of "extreme" scores. This source of confounding was discussed in some detail in Chapter 5. As summarized by Cook and Campbell (1979, pp. 52–53), statistical regression

> (1) operates to increase obtained pretest–posttest gain scores among low pretest scores, since this group's pretest scores are more likely to have been depressed by error; (2) operates to decrease obtained change scores among persons with high pretest scores since their pretest scores are likely to have been inflated by error; and (3) does not affect obtained change scores among scorers at the center of the pretest distribution since the group is likely to contain as many units whose pretest scores are inflated by error as units whose pretest scores are deflated by it. Regression is always to the population mean of a group.

Selection When, from the outset of a study, differences exist between the kinds of subjects in one group of an experiment and those in another, there is a confounding due to selection. In the laboratory, this threat to internal validity is generally handled by balancing subject characteristics through random assignment. When one is doing experiments in natural settings, there are often many obstacles to randomization of subjects to Treatment and No Treatment conditions. These obstacles prevent doing a true experiment and hence present a possible confound due to selection.

Subject Mortality When subjects are lost from an experiment there is a threat to internal validity. Possible reasons for subject loss were discussed in Chapter 5. The threat to internal validity rests on the assumption that subject loss (attrition) changes the nature of a group from that established prior to the introduction of the treatment—for example, by destroying the equivalence of groups that had been established through randomization.

Interactions with Selection Several of the foregoing threats to internal validity can be a source of additional concern to the extent that they interact with characteristics of groups of subjects selected for an experiment. Specifically, there are possible problems due to interactions between (a) selection and history, (b) selection and maturation, and (c) selection and instrumentation. Basically, what this means is that one or more groups of subjects respond differentially to effects associated with history, maturation, or instrumentation. For example, if groups of subjects in an experiment mature at different rates, then differences between groups in the form of changes from pretest to posttest may be due to an interaction of selection and maturation rather than to any treatment. Such might be the case if freshmen in college who served as an experimental group were compared with sophomores who served as a control group. Changes in subjects that occur during the freshman year (as students gain their first acquaintance with the college environment) might be presumed to be greater than those that occur during the sophomore year, and thus they might explain any observed effects.

An interaction of selection and history results when events occurring in time had a different effect on one group of subjects than on another. This is particularly a problem when intact groups are compared. Perhaps due to events that are peculiar to one group's situation, an event may have more of an impact on that group than on another. Consider, for example, research involving a comparison between two classrooms of students at the same school. If the principal of the school were changed during the experiment, it might be expected to have an equal effect on children in both classrooms. However, this would not be the case if children in one classroom had more familiarity with the principal (perhaps because the principal was a previous teacher of these students). Similarly, an interaction of selection and history might be a problem if classrooms at different schools are compared and an event other than the treatment occurs at one school (the principal is changed) and not at the other.

Finally, an interaction of selection and instrumentation might occur should the test instrument be relatively more sensitive to changes in one group's performance than to changes in another's. This occurs, for instance, when "ceiling" or "floor" effects are present. Such is the case when a group scores initially so low on an instrument (*floor effect*) that any further drop in scores cannot be reliably measured, or so high (*ceiling effect*) that any more gain cannot be assessed. As you can imagine, a confound would be present if an experimental group showed relatively no change (due to floor or ceiling effects) while a control group changed reliably because its mean performance was near neither the low end nor the high end of the measurement scale.

A true experiment controls all of these eight major classes of threats to internal validity. Quasi-experiments can be viewed as compromises between the general aim of gaining valid knowledge regarding the effectiveness of a treatment and the realization that true experiments (and hence control of the major factors threatening internal validity) are not always possible. As Campbell (1969) emphasizes, so-called true experiments should be conducted when possible, but if they are not feasible, quasi-experiments should be conducted. "We must do the best we can with what is available to us" (p. 411). Again, see Box 9.1.

PROBLEMS THAT EVEN TRUE EXPERIMENTS MAY NOT ELIMINATE

Before considering specific quasi-experimental procedures, we should point out that even true experiments may not control for all possible factors that might cloud the interpretation of an experimental result. Although major threats to internal validity are typically eliminated by the true experiment, there are some additional threats that the investigator must guard against, particularly when working in natural settings. We will use the term "contamination" to describe one general class of threats to internal validity. **Contamination** occurs when there is communication of information about the experiment between groups of subjects. The result of this communication can be resentment on the part of subjects receiving less desirable treatments, rivalry among subjects receiving different treatments, or a general diffusion of treatments across the groups (see Cook and Campbell, 1979).

Consider a situation in which a group of subjects has been randomly assigned to a control group. Further, assume that information is obtained by subjects in this group indicating that "other" subjects are receiving a treatment which appears to be obviously beneficial. What do you think might be the reaction of the control subjects? One possibility is resentment and demoralization. As Cook and Campbell explain, in an industrial setting the person receiving the less desirable treatment may retaliate by lowering productivity. In an educational setting teachers or students might "lose heart" or become angry. This unwanted effect of information about the treatment may make a treatment look better than it ordinarily would because of the lowered performance of the control group that is demoralized.

Another possible effect of a No Treatment group's learning about another group's good fortune is to generate a spirit of competition. That is, a control group might become motivated to reduce the expected difference between itself and the treatment group. As Cook and Campbell point out, this may be likely when intact groups (such as departments, work crews, branch offices, and the like) are assigned to various conditions. Realizing that another group will look better depending on how much it distinguishes itself from the control group, subjects comprising the control group may be motivated to "try harder" so as not to look bad by comparison. Cook and Campbell (1979) call this problem compensatory rivalry. Like other contamination effects, it cannot always be assumed to be absent in an experiment.

Yet another possible effect of contamination is diffusion of treatments. According to Cook and Campbell, this occurs when subjects in a No Treatment group use information given to others to help them change their own behavior. For example, control subjects may use the information given to subjects in the treatment group to imitate the behavior of the treated subjects. Of course, this reduces the differences between the treated and untreated groups and affects the internal validity of the experiment.

In addition to problems resulting from contamination, true experiments can also be weakened by threats to external validity. As you have learned in previous chapters, the extent to which one can generalize across persons, settings, and times depends mainly on how representative one's sample is of the persons, settings, and times to which one wishes to generalize. Representativeness is normally achieved through random sampling. However, because random sampling is used so infrequently, we can rarely say that our sample of subjects, or the situation in which we are making observations, or the times during which we test subjects, are representative samples of all persons, settings, or times. Therefore, the investigator must be aware of possible interactions between the independent variable of an experiment and the type of subject, setting, or time of the experiment. Is a difference between an experimental group and a control group that is found when only volunteers are used, when the setting is an inner-city school, or when the experiment is conducted in the winter also likely to be found when nonvolunteers are tested, when a suburban school is the setting, or when the experiment is performed in the spring of the year?

Cook and Campbell (1979) describe several approaches to evaluating threats to external validity, the foremost being determination of the representativeness of the sample. However, they point out that in the last analysis the best test of external validity is replication. External validity is an empirical question that is best answered through repetition of the experiment with different types of subjects, in different settings, and at different times. Occasionally these replications can be "built into" an experiment—for example, by selecting more than one group to participate.

Finally, true experiments do not always protect the experimenter from confounding due to experimenter expectancy effects or to a "Hawthorne effect." Effects due to experimenter expectancies were discussed in earlier chapters. They occur when the experimenter unintentionally influences the results. Systematic errors in interpretation or mistakes in recording data can be the result of experimenter expectancy effects. Various ways to control experimenter or observer effects were outlined in Chapter 2. The **Hawthorne effect** refers to changes in persons' behavior brought about by the interest that "significant others" show in them (see Box 9.2). Consider, for example, prisoners who are sampled to participate in research examining the relationship between changes in prison cell conditions and attitudes toward prison life. If positive changes in prisoners' attitudes are obtained, the result could be due to the actual changes in cell conditions that were made, or it could be due to an increase in morale because prisoners saw the prison administration as expressing concern for them.

Hawthorne effects may be inextricably linked to the action of an independent variable intended to alter the subjects' environment (Sommer, 1968). As Sommer (1968) points out, people naturally interpret changes in their environment according to various expectations that they have, according to their needs, and so forth. Just as prisoners may view changes in prison conditions as reflecting concern on the part of the prison staff, so factory workers, schoolchildren, college faculty members, and other groups may interpret changes made in their environment as reflecting interest in them on the part of significant others. Although there is as yet no evidence for widespread Hawthorne effects in field research (see Cook and Campbell, 1979), the psychology investigator must be conscious of the fact that changes in subjects' behavior may be at least partially due to their awareness of the fact that others are interested in them.

QUASI-EXPERIMENTS

A dictionary will tell you that one definition of the prefix *quasi-* is "resembling." A quasi-government, for example, is one resembling, but not actually the same as, a true government. **Quasi-experiments** involve procedures that resemble those that are characteristic of true experiments. Generally speaking, quasi-experiments include some type of intervention or treatment and provide a comparison, but they lack the degree of control that is found in true experiments. Just as randomization is the hallmark of true experiments, so *lack of randomization* is the hallmark of quasi-experiments. As Campbell and Stanley (1963, p. 34) explain,

> There are many natural social settings in which the research person can introduce something like experimental design into his scheduling of data collection procedures (e.g., the *when* and to *whom* of measurement), even though he lacks the full control over the scheduling of experimental stimuli (the *when* and to *whom* of exposure and the ability to randomize exposures) which makes a true experiment possible. Collectively, such situations can be regarded as quasi-experimental designs.

BOX 9.2

WHAT REALLY HAPPENED AT HAWTHORNE?

From 1924 to 1932 officials at the Hawthorne plant of the Western Electric Company in Cicero, Illinois, near Chicago, conducted a series of studies examining the relationship among productivity, satisfaction, and motivation of workers (Roethlisberger, 1977). The initial studies were conducted in association with the National Academy of Sciences and were intended to examine the relationship between illumination level in the plant and productivity in simple, repetitive tasks, such as inspecting small parts and assembling relays and winding coils (Huse and Bowditch, 1977). Results of these early studies were difficult to interpret. Therefore, the staff of the Western Electric Company, on its own, continued experiments over the following years to investigate further the "mysterious" factors that were responsible for the results originally obtained (Hicks and Gullett, 1975).

What really happened at the Hawthorne plant? The answer to that question is surrounded by much controversy and the issue may never be entirely resolved. Nevertheless, several facts emerge. First, the results of the initial studies, which examined the relationship between level of illumination and productivity, produced results that were "not only inconclusive but also rather curious" (Roethlisberger, 1977, p. 46). Specifically, in one experiment workers were divided into two groups, one working under increasing levels of illumination and the other working under constant illumination. The result was increased productivity in *both* groups, with the rise in output being approximately the same magnitude. A well-known and respected industrial researcher associated with the project was F. J. Roethlisberger of the Harvard Business School. He commented that, "Several further experiments of this character exhibited similar curious outcomes. It looked as if the workers were reacting more to the positive concern of the experimenters about their working conditions than to the actual physical changes in illumination. This response later came to be called the 'Hawthorne effect'" (Roethlisberger, 1977, p. 46).

In the field of business management, the Hawthorne studies mark the beginning of a separate human relations school of management (wherein was recognized the "importance of the worker's needs,

---

Quasi-experiments are recommended when true experiments are not feasible. Some knowledge about the effectiveness of a treatment is more desirable than none. The list of possible confounds provided by Campbell and Stanley (1963; Cook and Campbell, 1979), which we reviewed earlier, can be used as a check list in deciding just how good that knowledge is. Moreover, although a particular experimental procedure may not control for one or more possible types of confounds, the investigator must be prepared to look for additional kinds of evidence that might rule out a confound that is not specifically controlled by an experimental procedure. For example, suppose that a quasi-experiment explicitly controls for only six of the eight major classes of confounds that are eliminated by a true experiment. It may be possible, on the basis of supplementary data or through evidence offered by a logical analysis of the situation, to rule out the remaining two classes of explanations as implausible. In this case a strong argument can be made for the internal validity of the research design, even though a true experiment was not performed. What is important is that the researcher always recognize the specific shortcomings of quasi-experimental procedures and be prepared to address these shortcomings through whatever evidence or logic is available.

desires, and feelings") (Huse and Bowditch, 1977, p. 22). In the field of experimental psychology, results of the studies at the Western Electric Company have been interpreted as evidence of behavior change as a consequence of unwanted effects of the experimental operations themselves (Parsons, 1974). The "Hawthorne effect" refers to behavior change resulting from subjects' awareness that someone is interested in them.

Nevertheless, Parsons (1974), writing in the journal *Science,* suggests that the actual source of the Hawthorne effect was a series of studies conducted after the illumination experiments. This research was called the "Relay Assembly Test Room Experiment," and it included two independent variables: timing of rest pauses and hours worked (Parsons, 1974). The experiment lasted from 1927 until 1932 and involved a small group of women employees singled out for participation. Following observation of productivity in their "regular department," the women were introduced to a special testing room and observations of productivity were made during the next few years as a function of changes in rest pauses and number of hours worked. A general finding was that productivity showed a gradual increase over the course of the experiment and appeared to be relatively independent of changes in working conditions. According to Par-

sons (1974) this "discovery" was unexpected. "The observed overall increase in production rates yielded the Hawthorne effect. Some uncontrolled, extraneous variable was at work" (p. 926). Moreover, Parsons suggests that this other variable was not increased "morale," as traditionally thought. Rather, it was a combination of feedback and financial reward. Based on existing records of the Hawthorne experiments and interviews with persons directly involved in the research, Parsons has built a case for operant conditioning (see Chapter 8) as a critical factor contributing to the increase in productivity. Specifically, he presents evidence that one of the changes made in the workers' situation was a new method of recording output, which was available for inspection by the workers, as well as a new method of payment. These factors, according to Parsons, resulted in the "shaping" of the workers' rate of productivity. The lesson for research design, based on this interpretation, is "Don't let subjects see the data or reward them according to their performance" (p. 930).

Operant conditioning or increased morale? Whatever the source of the "Hawthorne effect," the psychology investigator must always be on the lookout for unintended effects of the introduction of an experimental treatment.

With full knowledge of their limitations, then, we present the following information about specific quasi-experimental designs so that you will understand the routes remaining open to an investigator when the path to a true experiment is hopelessly blocked. At the same time, this presentation should help you appreciate the clarity of inference provided by the true experiment. Following a discussion of specific quasi-experimental designs, we look at an alternative to quasi-experimentation—the extension of single-case experimentation to research in natural settings. You may also want to refer to the previous discussion of obstacles to true experiments in natural settings. The difference between the power of the true experiment and that of the quasi-experiment is such that, before facing the problems of interpretation that result from quasi-experimental procedures, the researcher should make every effort possible to approximate the conditions of a true experiment.

SPECIFIC QUASI-EXPERIMENTAL DESIGNS

THE NONEQUIVALENT CONTROL GROUP DESIGN

Perhaps the most serious limitation on experimentation in natural settings is that the experimenter is frequently unable to assign subjects randomly to conditions. This occurs, for instance, when an intact group is singled out for treatment and when administrative decisions or practical considerations prevent randomly assigning subjects. Children in one classroom or school and workers at a particular plant are examples of groups that might be treated in the absence of any random assignment of individuals to conditions. If we assume that behavior is measured both before and after treatment, such an "experiment" can be described as follows:

$$O_1 \quad X \quad O_2$$

where O_1 refers to the first observation, or pretest, X indicates a treatment, and O_2 refers to the second observation, or posttest.

Campbell and Stanley (1963) call this particular design the "one-group pretest-posttest design." Although it is often used in psychological research, the design has very little internal validity. You should be able to see, for instance, that this design does not control for many factors that can threaten the internal validity of a study. For example, should a difference between pretest and posttest measures be found, how do we know that this difference was not due to some event other than the treatment (history threat), that it was not due to the fact that subjects benefited from initial testing (testing threat), or that it didn't occur simply because the group of subjects changed over time (maturation threat)? This particular design has so little going for it, in terms of allowing cause-and-effect inferences, that it is sometimes referred to as a "preexperimental design," or one that serves as a "bad experiment" to illustrate possible confounds (see Campbell and Stanley, 1966).

The one-group pretest-posttest design can be modified to create a quasi-experimental design with greatly superior internal validity if two conditions are met: (1) there exists a group "like" the treatment group that can serve as a comparison group and (2) there is an opportunity to obtain pretest and posttest measures from individuals in *both* the Treatment and the No Treatment groups. Because a comparison group is selected on bases other than random assignment, it cannot be assumed that individuals in the treatment and control groups are equivalent on all important characteristics (a selection threat arises). Therefore it is essential that a pretest be given to both groups to assess their similarity on the dependent measure. Campbell and Stanley (1966) call this quasi-experimental procedure a **nonequivalent control group design.** It can be outlined as follows:

$$\begin{array}{ccc} O_1 & X & O_2 \\ \hline O_1 & & O_2 \end{array}$$

The dashed line indicates that the treatment and comparison groups were not formed by assigning subjects randomly to conditions. Before considering the strengths and weaknesses of this experimental procedure, let us examine an actual study using this particular quasi-experimental design.

ILLUSTRATION OF THE NONEQUIVALENT CONTROL GROUP DESIGN: THE LANGER AND RODIN STUDY

Langer and Rodin (1976) hypothesized that environmental changes associated with old age contribute, in part, to feelings of loss, inadequacy, and low self-esteem among the elderly. Of particular importance is the change that occurs when elderly persons move into a nursing home. Although they usually care for the elderly quite adequately in physical terms, nursing homes often provide what Langer and Rodin call a "virtually decision-free" environment. The elderly are no longer called on to make even the simplest decisions, such as what time to get up, whom to visit, what movie to watch, and the like. In a nursing home, many or most of these everyday decisions are made for the elderly, leaving them with little personal responsibility and choice.

To test the hypothesis that the lack of opportunity to make personal decisions contributes to the psychological and even the physical debilitation sometimes seen in the elderly, Langer and Rodin carried out an experiment in a Connecticut nursing home. The independent variable was the type of communication given to two groups of nursing home residents. One group was given a communication stressing the many decisions that the patients needed to make regarding how their rooms were arranged, visiting, care of plants, movie selection, and so forth. These residents were also given a small plant as a gift (if they decided to accept it) and told to take care of it as they wished. This was the Responsibility Induced condition. The second group of residents, the comparison group, was also called together for a meeting, but the communication given to this group stressed the staff's responsibility for them. These residents also received a plant as a gift (whether they chose to have one or not) and were told that the nurses would water and care for the plants for them.

Residents of the nursing home had been assigned to a particular floor and room on the basis of availability, and some residents had been there for a long time. As a consequence, randomly assigning residents to the two communication groups was impractical—and probably undesirable from the administration's point of view. Therefore the two communications were given to residents on two different floors of the nursing home. These floors were chosen, in the words of the authors, "because of similarity in the residents' physical and psychological health and prior socioeconomic status, as determined from evaluations made by the home's director, head nurses, and social worker" (Langer and Rodin, 1976, p. 193). A different floor was randomly selected for each treatment. In addition, questionnaires containing items that related to "how much control they felt over general events in their lives and how happy and active they felt" (p. 194) were given to residents 1 week before and 3 weeks after the communications. Furthermore, staff members on each floor were asked to rate the residents, before and after the experimental communications, on such traits as alertness, sociability, and activity. The investigators also included a clever posttest measure of social interest by holding a competition that asked participants to guess the number of jelly beans in a large jar. Residents entered the contest if they wished by simply filling out a piece of paper giving their estimate and name.

The Langer and Rodin (1976) study nicely illustrates a nonequivalent control group procedure. Moreover, differences between pretest and posttest measures showed that the residents in the Responsibility Induced group were generally happier, more active, and more alert than residents in the comparison group. Behavioral measures such as frequency of movie attendance also favored the Responsibility Induced group, and, although ten residents from this group entered the jellybean contest, only one resident from the comparison group participated! The investigators point to possible practical implications of these findings. Specifically, they suggest that some of the negative consequences of aging can be reduced or reversed by giving the aged the opportunity to make personal decisions and to feel competent.

SOURCES OF INVALIDITY IN THE NONEQUIVALENT CONTROL GROUP DESIGN

According to Cook and Campbell (1979), the nonequivalent control group design generally controls for all major classes of potential confounds except those due to interactions of (a) selection and maturation, (b) selection and history, (c) selection and instrumentation, and (d) those due to differential statistical regression. We will explore how each of these potential sources of invalidity might pose problems in an effort to interpret the results of the Langer and Rodin study. Then we will explain what evidence or argument the authors offered in defense of their interpretation, which was that the differential communication *caused* the differences in posttest behavior between the two groups of residents. We will also examine how experimenter bias and problems of contamination were controlled, and we will comment briefly on problems of external validity inherent in the nonequivalent control group design.

First, it should be mentioned that Langer and Rodin found that the residents in the two experimental groups did not differ significantly on the pretest measures. Because the residents were not randomly assigned to conditions, it might not have been surprising to find a difference between the two groups before the treatment was introduced. Moreover, it is important to recognize that, even when pretest scores show no difference between groups, as Langer and Rodin reported, one cannot assume that the groups are "equivalent" (Campbell and Stanley, 1966). Why this is so will become apparent in the discussion that follows.

Interaction between Selection and Maturation   An interaction between selection and maturation occurs when individuals in one group are growing more experienced, more tired, or more bored at a faster rate than individuals in another group (Cook and Campbell, 1979). Campbell and Stanley (1966) illustrate this problem by describing a nonequivalent control group design using psychotherapy patients in a treatment group and normals in a comparison group. The psychotherapy patients would normally be expected to show some spontaneous remission without the treatment, a change that could be falsely interpreted (given no change in the comparison group) as a treatment effect. Whenever the treatment group consists of individuals who are brighter or more competent than those in the comparison group, differences in rate of maturation may be a confounding factor.

In examining the Langer and Rodin study, we have to ask whether there is any reason to suspect an interaction of selection and maturation. For instance, would residents on the Treatment floor be expected to change naturally at a faster rate than patients on the No Treatment floor? Several kinds of evidence suggest that this would not be the case. First, the procedure of assigning residents to floors was basically random, and floors were selected randomly for Treatment and No Treatment. The authors also point out that various measures showed that the residents of the two floors were, on the average, equivalent in socioeconomic status and length of time at the nursing home. Finally, although it is not sufficient evidence in itself, residents on the two floors did not differ on the pretest measures. There is little in the Langer and Rodin study to suggest a confound due to an interaction of selection and maturation.

An interaction of selection and maturation is more likely to be an actual source of invalidity (as are other sources) when the treatment group is self-selected (the members deliberately sought out exposure to the treatment) and when the comparison group is from a different population than the treatment group (Campbell and Stanley, 1966). This occurs when a particular group is singled out for treatment in order to determine whether behavior will improve as a function of treatment. The example of psychotherapy patients who are compared to normals, which was mentioned earlier, is an example.

An investigator must be aware that, even when pretest scores are the same on the average for the treatment and control groups, it cannot be concluded that the groups are equivalent. This is true for two reasons. First, the pretest is likely to measure respondents on only one measure, or at best on a few measures. The mere fact that individuals do not differ on one measure does not mean that they don't differ on other measures that are relevant to their behavior in this situation. Second, the natural growth rate of two groups from different populations might be different, but the pretest may have been taken at a time when both groups were approximately the same. This problem is illustrated in Figure 9.1. The normal rate of change is greater in Group A than in Group B, but the pretest is likely to show that the groups do not differ. On the other hand, and again because of the differential growth rate, the groups would probably show a difference at the posttest that could be mistaken for a treatment effect. Langer and Rodin selected their groups (but not individuals) randomly from the same population of individuals. Consequently, their design more closely approaches a true experiment than it would if individuals in the two groups came from different popula-

FIGURE 9.1   Possible differential growth rates for two groups (A and B) in the absence of a treatment.

tions (Campbell and Stanley, 1966), as would be the case if residents in a nursing home were compared to those attending a sheltered workshop program for the elderly.

Interaction between Selection and History   Another type of confound that is not controlled in the nonequivalent control group design is the interaction between selection and history. Cook and Campbell (1979) refer to this problem as *local history* effects. This problem arises when an event other than the treatment affects one group and not the other. Local history, for example, could be a problem in the Langer and Rodin study if an event affecting the residents' happiness and alertness occurred on one floor of the nursing home and not on the other. You can probably imagine a number of possibilities. A change in nursing staff, for instance, might bring about either an increase or a decrease in residents' morale, depending on the nature of the change and the relationship between the behavior of a new nurse and that of an old one. Problems of local history become more problematic the more the locations or settings of the individuals in the treatment and comparison groups differ. Langer and Rodin do not specifically address the problem of local history.

Interaction between Selection and Instrumentation   An interaction of selection and instrumentation occurs when changes in a measuring instrument are more likely to be detected in one group than they are in another. Floor or ceiling effects, for instance, could make it difficult to detect behavior change from pretest to posttest. If this is more of a problem in one group than in another, an interaction of selection and instrumentation is present. Cook and Campbell (1979) point out that this confound is likely to be more of a problem the greater the nonequivalence of the groups. Because Langer and Rodin's groups did not differ on the pretest, and because performance of the groups did not suggest floor or ceiling effects on the measurement scales that were used, this confound seems implausible in their study.

Differential Statistical Regression Finally, the nonequivalent control group design does not control for differential statistical regression (Cook and Campbell, 1979). This is especially a problem when one group has been singled out for treatment because of its poor performance on some measure. As you probably are aware by now, *whenever* subjects have been selected on the basis of extreme scores (the poorest readers, workers showing the lowest productivity, patients reporting the most severe problems), regression toward the mean is to be expected. Changes in behavior from pretest to posttest that are due to regression may be mistakenly interpreted as a treatment effect if regression is more likely in the treatment group than in the control group. Because the groups in the Langer and Rodin study came from the same population and there is no evidence that one group's scores were more extreme than another's, a problem of differential statistical regression is not plausible in their study.

Observer Bias and Contamination It is worthwhile to consider how Langer and Rodin handled problems of observer bias and possible effects of contamination, and to inquire whether a Hawthorne effect was present. If observers in their study had been aware of the experimental hypothesis, it is possible that they might inadvertently have rated residents as being better after the experimental communication than before. However, all the observers were kept unaware of the experimental hypothesis. Thus, observer bias appears to have been controlled. Langer and Rodin were aware of possible contamination effects. Residents in the control group might have become demoralized if they learned that residents on another floor were given more opportunity to make decisions. In this case, the use of different floors of the nursing home was advantageous; Langer and Rodin indicate that "there was not a great deal of communication between floors" (p. 193). Thus, if one accepts Langer and Rodin's argument, contamination effects do not seem to be present, at least on a scale that would destroy the internal validity of the study.

Hawthorne Effect A Hawthorne effect would be present in the Langer and Rodin study if residents on the treatment floor interpreted the responsibility-inducing communication as a form of special attention. Such an interpretation might lead residents on the treated floor to feel better about themselves. The changes in behavior that Langer and Rodin observed could then be attributed to a change in morale due to a Hawthorne effect as easily as to the opportunity to make decisions and assume personal responsibility that was available to residents in the treatment group. It is difficult to rule out completely a Hawthorne effect in this study. According to the authors, however, "there was no difference in the amount of attention paid to the two groups" (p. 194). In fact, communications to both groups stressed that the staff cared for them and wanted them "to be happy."

Thus, without additional evidence to the contrary, we can conclude that the changes in behavior that Langer and Rodin observed were due to the effect of the independent variable and not to the effect of an extraneous variable that the investigators failed to control.

What should be apparent at this point is that, for an investigator to decide, in the context of a particular experiment, whether an independent variable "worked," it is necessary that he or she be something of a detective. Evidence for and against the interpretation that the treatment actually caused behavior change must be systematically (and sometimes ingeniously) collected and carefully weighed. As Cook and Campbell (1979, pp. 55–56) explain,

> Estimating the internal validity of a relationship is a deductive process in which the investigator has to systematically think through how each of the internal validity threats may have influenced the data. Then, the investigator has to examine the data to test which relevant threats can be ruled out. In all of this process, the researcher has to be his or her own best critic, trenchantly examining all of the threats he or she can imagine. When all of the threats can plausibly be eliminated, it is possible to make confident conclusions about whether a relationship is probably causal. When all of them cannot, perhaps because the appropriate data are not available or because the data indicate that a particular threat may indeed have operated, then the investigator has to conclude that a demonstrated relationship between two variables may or may not be causal.

The Issue of External Validity The investigator must make the same systematic inquiry into the external validity of an experiment. What evidence is there that the particular pattern of results is restricted to a particular group of subjects, setting, or time? For example, although Langer and Rodin suggest that certain changes be made in the way the elderly are cared for, we might question whether the effectiveness of the responsibility-inducing communication would hold for all elderly residents, for all types of nursing homes, and at different times. That the particular nursing home selected by Langer and Rodin was described as "rated by the state of Connecticut as being among the finest care units" (p. 193) suggests that the residents, facilities, and staff there would be different from those found in other homes. For instance, if residents at this particular home were relatively more independent before coming to the home than residents at other homes (perhaps because of differences in socioeconomic status) then the changes experienced upon moving into a home might have had greater impact on them. Consequently, the opportunity to be more independent of staff might be more important to those residents relative to residents in other homes. Similarly, if staff members at this home were more competent than those at other homes, they might be more effective in communicating the experimental communications than the staff at other homes.

As we indicated earlier, in the last analysis, the investigator must be ready to replicate an experimental finding under different conditions in order to establish external validity. The deductive process applied to questions of internal validity must also be used to examine a study's external validity. Moreover, an investigator must be ready to live with the fact that one experiment is very unlikely to answer all questions about an experimental hypothesis.

INTERRUPTED TIME-SERIES DESIGNS

In situations where one can observe changes in a dependent variable for some time before and after a treatment is introduced, another quasi-experiment is possible. It is called a **simple interrupted time-series design** (Cook and Campbell, 1979). The essence of this design is the availability of periodic measures before and after a treatment has been introduced. It can be outlined in the following way:

$$O_1 \quad O_2 \quad O_3 \quad O_4 \quad O_5 \quad X \quad O_6 \quad O_7 \quad O_8 \quad O_9 \quad O_{10}$$

Situations such as this may arise when a new product has been introduced, a new social reform instituted, or a special advertising campaign begun. Campbell's (1969) analysis of the effect on traffic fatalities of a crackdown on speeding ordered by the Connecticut governor made use of an interrupted time-series design (see Box 9.1). Because statistics related to traffic accidents are regularly kept by state agencies, a wealth of archival data was available to yield pretreatment and posttreatment measures. Besides number of fatalities, Campbell looked at number of speeding violations, number of drivers having their licenses suspended, and other measures related to driving behavior. Figure 9.2 shows the percentage of suspensions of licenses for speeding (as a percentage of all license suspensions) before and after the crackdown. There is a clear discontinuity in the time graph that provides evidence for an effect of the treatment. Indeed, the discontinuity in the time series is the major evidence for an effect.

As Campbell (1969) points out, only abrupt changes in the time graph can be evaluated, because gradual changes are indistinguishable from normal fluctuations over time. Unfortunately, changes often are not nearly so dramatic as seen in Figure 9.2. In fact, Campbell's analysis of traffic fatalities over the same time period, while revealing evidence of an effect of the crackdown, did not show as abrupt a change as that associated with suspension of drivers' licenses (see Campbell, 1984, Figure 2). A typical outcome of an interrupted time-series design is illustrated by the findings of Ross and White (1987), who examined the effect of newspaper publicity on subsequent crime rates. In June 1984, a metropolitan newspaper instituted a policy of publishing the court results of people convicted of shoplifting, impaired driving, or failure to take a breathalyzer test. The published information identified the individual by name and also furnished details of the incident. For instance, in the case of shoplifting, the item that the individual attempted to shoplift and its value also were noted. Ross and White (1987) sought to assess the impact of this publication policy on the frequency of similar offenses. They obtained data from several police and government agencies detailing the in-

FIGURE 9.2 Suspensions of licenses for speeding, as a percentage of all suspensions. (*From Campbell, 1969.*)

cidence of these crimes over a time period beginning several years before the new policy was instituted and continuing for approximately 18 months after the new policy was implemented. The number of shoplifting offenses during this period is shown in Figure 9.3. Visual inspection, confirmed by the results of statistical analyses, revealed an effect of the publication policy on incidence of shoplifting. Interestingly, the policy showed no effect on the incidence of drinking and driving or refusing the breathalyzer test. The investigators suggested that being associated with shoplifting carries a greater social stigma than is the case for driving under the influence of alcohol.

Campbell and Stanley (1966) summarize the problem facing researchers using the simple interrupted time-series type of quasi-experiment: "The problem of internal validity boils down to the question of plausible competing hypotheses that offer likely alternate explanations of the shift in the time series other than the effect of X" (p. 39). An effect of history is the main threat to internal validity in this type of design (Cook and Campbell, 1979). For instance, considering the results in Figure 9.3, is it possible that some factor other than newspaper publicity was responsible for the reduction in frequency of shoplifting offenses?

Particularly threatening to the internal validity of the time-series design are influences of a cyclical nature, including seasonal variation (Cook and Campbell, 1979). Thus, when Maki et al. (1978) assessed the effect of a water conservation program on water use in a California water district, they had to

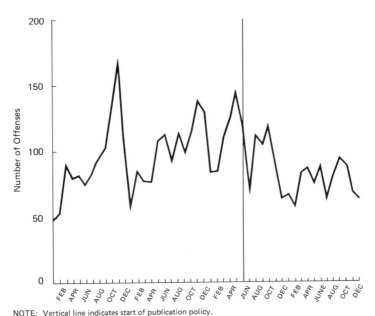

NOTE: Vertical line indicates start of publication policy.

FIGURE 9.3   Shoplifting offenses between January 1980 and December 1985. (*From Ross and White, 1987.*)

be sensitive to possible influences of weather changes, such as increased rainfall. Water use also would be expected to drop if population decreased because residents fearful of water shortages left the area when the conservation program was announced. The time series graph depicting water use revealed a slight dip in water use after the water conservation program was initiated, and only through a detailed and sophisticated analysis, taking into account other facts related to water use, could these researchers conclude that the reduction in water use could reasonably be attributed to the conservation program. When analyzing the effect of the Connecticut governor's crackdown on speeding, Campbell (1969) gathered data from neighboring states in order to rule out possible regional trends due to weather or the introduction of automotive safety features in order to strengthen his case for the effect of this particular social policy change.

Instrumentation must also be considered a threat to internal validity in the simple interrupted time-series design (Cook and Campbell, 1979). When new programs or new social policies are instituted, for example, there are often accompanying changes in the way that records are kept or in the procedures used to collect information. A program intended to reduce crime may lead authorities to modify their definitions of particular crimes or to become more careful when observing and reporting criminal activities. Nevertheless, for an instrumentation threat to be plausible, it must be shown how changes in instrumentation could occur at exactly the time of the intervention (Campbell and Stanley, 1966). Ross and White (1987) showed that they were aware of possible influences due to instrumentation effects. They noted in their Method section that data more than 18 months after the newspaper's new policy were not comparable to prior data due to changes in the laws defining a shoplifting offense. Hence, data were collected only during the 18-month period immediately after the policy change.

Most other threats to internal validity are controlled in the simple interrupted time-series design. Problems of maturation, testing, and regression are pretty much eliminated by the presence of multiple observations both before and after treatment. None of these threats can be ruled out when only a single pretest and posttest measure is available, as in the single-group pretest-posttest design mentioned earlier. For example, an effect of maturation would not normally be expected to show a sharp discontinuity in the time series, although this might be possible in some situations (Campbell and Stanley, 1966). When only one pretest and one posttest observation are available, it is not possible to decide whether performance changes from pretest to posttest reflect a treatment effect or are simply due to maturational processes. The simple time-series design generally permits this decision to be made.

Threats to external validity in the simple interrupted time-series design must be examined carefully. It should be obvious that, if pretreatment observations of behavior are based on multiple tests, then an effect of the treatment on behavior may be restricted to those subjects who have had multiple test experiences. Moreover, because only a single group is generally tested, one that was not randomly selected, it is always possible that the results are limited to subjects with characteristics similar to those who took part in the experiment.

TIME SERIES WITH NONEQUIVALENT CONTROL GROUP

The interrupted time-series design can be enhanced greatly by including a control group. This procedure is identical to that followed in constructing a nonequivalent control group design, which we discussed previously. In this case the researcher must find a group that is comparable to the treatment group and that allows a similar opportunity for multiple observations before and after the time that the treatment is administered to the experimental group. This **time series with nonequivalent control group** design is outlined as follows:

$$O_1 \quad O_2 \quad O_3 \quad O_4 \quad O_5 \quad X \quad O_6 \quad O_7 \quad O_8 \quad O_9 \quad O_{10}$$
$$\overline{O_1 \quad O_2 \quad O_3 \quad O_4 \quad O_5 \quad\quad O_6 \quad O_7 \quad O_8 \quad O_9 \quad O_{10}}$$

As before, a dashed line is used to indicate that the control group and the experimental group were not randomly assigned. This interrupted time series with nonequivalent control group permits one to control many threats due to history. As was mentioned earlier, Campbell (1969) used traffic fatality data obtained from neighboring states to provide a comparison with traffic fatality data following the crackdown on speeding in Connecticut. Although traffic fatalities in Connecticut showed a decline immediately following the crackdown, data from comparable states did not exhibit any such decline. This fact tends to rule out changes that might have been due to favorable weather conditions, improved automobile design, or other potentially positive factors.

Archival data, rather than direct observation, frequently provide the basis for time-series designs. For example, the extensive archival data in various fields of sport have furnished social psychologists with an opportunity to test the real-life implications of laboratory-based theories. In particular, Lord and Hohenfeld (1979) used an interrupted time-series design with nonequivalent control group to assess the effects on baseball players' performance of failure to reach a negotiated contract with their club. On the basis of an equity theory, they predicted that players who were playing without a contract would perform more poorly during the year they played out their option because they would feel undercompensated for their services. Their results tended to bear out this prediction, although Duchon and Jago (1981) obtained results suggesting that the external validity of the effect may be limited due to characteristics of the original sample of baseball players. As part of another study in the same vein (see Jackson et al., 1988), researchers compiled statistics on baseball players who were traded in midseason to a new team. A quasi-experimental analysis revealed that the batting average of these players was higher when playing for the new club than for the old club, confirming a prediction made from a drive theory of social facilitation. The possibility that baseball players, regardless of whether they are traded, increase their batting average over the full-year season was ruled out as an alternative explanation for these findings by demonstrating that averages of a random sample of nontraded players did not show a similar rise.

A particularly good illustration of the interrupted time-series design is provided by McSweeney (1978), who analyzed the frequency of telephone calls asking for directory assistance following initiation of a charge for such calls. Directory assistance calls requesting information about phone numbers listed in standard directories cost the telephone company money, and they pay these expenses by charging more for other services. As McSweeney (1978) pointed out, an intervention that would effectively reduce the frequency of these unnecessary calls would benefit both the telephone company and the consumer.

In 1974, officials at Cincinnati Bell Telephone company initiated charges for local directory assistance calls in excess of three per month. Subscribers were charged 20 cents for each additional call. Because the telephone company keeps extensive archival records, the effect of this intervention could be assessed using a time-series analysis. Furthermore, a simple time series could be expanded by seeking a comparison group. McSweeney chose to use as a control measure the long-distance directory assistance calls that were made from outside the Cincinnati area, for which no charge was made. Although the exact number of "participants" could not be known, it was estimated that the service charge for local directory assistance calls affected more than a million users. From data provided by Cincinnati Bell administrative records, McSweeney created the time-series graph shown in Figure 9.4. The frequency of local calls decreased dramatically after the charge was initiated, while directory assistance calls from outside the area continued to increase gradually.

The time-series analysis revealed a small dip in frequency of local calls before the actual charges were levied. This was apparently in response to the announcement by telephone company officials of the upcoming cost to the user. McSweeney reasonably argued that this change was due to the fact that

FIGURE 9.4 Number of local and long-distance directory assistance calls placed per average business day before and after charges were introduced. (*From McSweeney, 1978.*)

some individuals misunderstood the announcement in news reports and thought the charges were already being made. Others may simply have begun to change their calling habits in anticipation of the charges. The clear discontinuity in the time series associated with the treatment group, in conjunction with the absence of any decrease in calls by the comparison group, provides nearly incontrovertible evidence that the effect was due to the intervention made by the telephone company. A subsequent analysis showed that the decrease in local directory assistance calls resulted in an average savings of 65 cents on the telephone bill of each individual residential consumer.

AN EXTENSION OF SINGLE-CASE EXPERIMENTAL DESIGNS TO RESEARCH IN NATURAL SETTINGS

RATIONALE

You may have noticed a similarity between the simple time-series design and the single-case experimental designs discussed in Chapter 8. In both situations, observations made prior to a treatment represent a "baseline" that is compared with observations obtained after the treatment. If there is a clear discontinuity in the behavioral record following the application of an independent variable, this is evidence for the effect of the treatment. Furthermore, for both types of design the major threat to internal validity is history. It is possible that some factor affecting the subjects' behavior, other than the independent variable, is responsible for the observed behavior change. However, the two types of design handle this threat differently.

When a simple time series is used, the investigator must search for historical factors (for example, seasonal variation) that might explain a change in the behavioral record. The addition of a nonequivalent control group greatly enhances the internal validity of the time-series design but does not completely rule out history or other threats, such as instrumentation. Moreover, unless the discontinuity in the time-series record is abrupt and obvious, the investigator must consider the possibility that one of numerous subtle factors produced a change and must rely on sophisticated mathematical models to determine whether an effect is present (see, for example, McCain and McCleary, in Cook and Campbell, 1979). A single-case experimental design controls for effects due to history when changes in the behavioral record correspond systematically to the repeated introduction and withdrawal of an independent variable (as in an ABAB design) or to the staggered introduction of a treatment (as in a multiple-baseline design). Unless observed changes are very small, it may be possible to avoid using complex statistical procedures and to rely instead on visual inspection of the pattern of change associated with the sequential manipulation of a treatment.

Single-case experimental designs offer an alternative to quasi-experimental procedures when one is conducting research in natural settings (for example, Horn and Heerboth, 1982). Although it is typically used to evaluate changes in a single subject, the single-case experimental design strategy can be used for a group of individuals, such as a classroom singled out for treatment. Examples of single-case experimental designs using groups of subjects are found in Chapter 8 (see, for instance, VanBiervliet et al., 1981). To use an **ABAB design,** the investigator must have control over the application and withdrawal of a treatment and an opportunity must be present for periodic observation both during No Treatment (baseline) stages and during Treatment stages. Clearly this is not always possible in natural settings.

Treatments are often initiated under the assumption that they will "work," and, unfortunately, their effects are often not evaluated (see Box 9.1). A water conservation program, for example, is not likely to be applied, withdrawn, and then applied again in an attempt to measure its effectiveness on water consumption. However, when control over the application and withdrawal of a treatment is feasible, a single-case experimental design may be used to determine whether a treatment effect exists. The advantage to the researcher is a design whose internal validity is close to, if not the same as, that of a true experiment (see Horn and Heerboth, 1982). The following actual experiment illustrates the possibilities of using this experimental approach in natural settings. This example makes use of a variation of an ABAB design; the multiple-baseline design can also be employed in natural settings (see Horn and Heerboth, 1982).

THE ABAB DESIGN

Schnelle and his associates have used a single-case methodology to evaluate the effect of police procedures on reducing crime rate (see, for example, Schnelle et al., 1978). In one study they sought evidence for the effect of a combined police car and helicopter patrol in reducing the frequency of home burglaries in a neighborhood of Nashville, Tennessee. The area was selected because police records showed that it had a chronically high number of burglaries. (Do you see how the *chronic* nature of this extreme measure neutralizes the problem of statistical regression?) The plan was to increase surveillance of the area by adding a helicopter patrol to the usual police car patrol. When the helicopter was used, the pilots were told to fly low enough to observe suspicious activity. Pilots were in radio contact with the police in the patrol car. The helicopter was flown between 9 A.M. and 5 P.M. (weather permitting), a time that coincides with most home burglaries.

An ABAB procedure was used. Following a baseline observation of frequency of home burglaries in the experimental area, the helicopter was introduced for a period of time, then withdrawn, and then introduced again. The addition of the helicopter was an experimental program by the Nashville police, so the helicopter was again removed following the second treatment stage, providing an additional (and final) baseline period.

Figure 9.5 shows daily frequency of home burglaries during baseline and treatment periods. Visual inspection of the behavioral record clearly shows that the frequency of burglaries decreased when the helicopter was added to the police surveillance and increased when no helicopter was present. Inter-

FIGURE 9.5 Daily frequency of home burglaries. Arrows indicate the days the helicopter was prevented from flying. (*From Schnelle et al., 1978.*)

estingly, a check of police records showed no displacement of burglary activity to surrounding neighborhoods. That is, when frequency of burglaries dropped in the experimental area, there was no corresponding rise in these types of crime in nearby neighborhoods. Note that the dependent variable in this example is frequency based on a *group* of individuals—in this case, residents in an approximately 6-square-mile area. Except for this change in the way behavior is assessed, the design strategy is exactly the same as might be used with a single individual.

PROGRAM EVALUATION

Organizations that produce goods have a ready-made index of success. If a company is set up to make hammers, its success is ultimately determined by its profits from the sale of hammers. At least theoretically, the efficiency and effectiveness of the organization can be easily assessed by examining the company's ledgers. Increasingly, however, organizations of a different sort play a critical role in our society. Because these organizations typically provide services rather than goods, Posavac and Carey (1989) refer to them as *human service organizations*. For example, hospitals, schools, police departments, and government agencies provide a variety of services ranging from emergency room care to fire prevention inspections. Because profit making is not their goal, some other method must be found to distinguish between effective and ineffective agencies. One useful approach to assessing the effectiveness of human service organizations is the newly emerging discipline of program evaluation.

Posavac and Carey (1989, p. 3) define *program evaluation* as "a collection of methods, skills, and sensitivities necessary to determine whether a human service is needed and likely to be used, whether it is sufficiently intense to meet the need identified, whether the service is offered as planned, and whether the human service actually does help people in need without undesirable side effects."

Program evaluation represents a hybrid discipline that draws on political science, sociology, economics, education, and psychology. We discuss program evaluation at the end of this chapter on research in natural settings because it represents perhaps the most large-scale application of the principles and methods we have been describing throughout this book. In fact, the brief introduction we provide to the methods used in program evaluation will serve primarily as a review of the objectives of the different research methods in psychology.

Program evaluations are done to provide feedback to administrators of human service organizations to help them decide what services to provide to whom and how to provide them most effectively and efficiently. There are four general types of evaluation studies, and each type is most closely associated with particular research methods. The first type of evaluation involves an *assessment of the needs* of the people for whom an agency plans to provide a service. If a city government were considering instituting a program of recreational activities for senior citizens in the community, it would first want to determine whether the senior citizens actually needed or wanted such a program. The methods of survey research are used extensively in studies designed to assess needs.

A second type of evaluation study involves gathering information to assist in *program planning*. Questions regarding the makeup of a recreational program for senior citizens need to be addressed before one can begin to ask about the effectiveness of the program. Where should the program be conducted? What time of day is best? What activities should be included in the program? Once again, surveys and archival data can provide useful information for setting up a program. Participant observation might also be an effective means of gathering information about the interests and activities of senior citizens.

Once the program has been set up, a third type of evaluation, called *formative evaluation*, may be necessary. Programs are not always implemented the way they were planned, and it is essential to know what actually *is* being done when a program is implemented. If the planned activities were not being used by the activity directors in the program for senior citizens, it would make little sense to test the effectiveness of the "program." Formative evaluation can be used in such a case to try to adjust the specifics of a program in response to problems that may arise when the program is first implemented. Observational methods, especially unobtrusive methods, are best suited to successful formative evaluation.

The fourth and final type of evaluation study is called *summative evaluation*. A summative evaluation is done to answer questions such as whether the senior citizen program is effective, whether it should be continued or expanded, and whether it is preferable to an alternative program. Summative evaluation draws most directly on the experimental and quasi-experimental methods for research in natural settings. It is also possible to use archival data like those described in Chapter 4 to carry out a summative evaluation. For example, one could use the number of visits to local physicians before and after implementation of the recreation program among senior citizens as a measure of the program's effectiveness. A difference in number of doctor visits might be expected between those senior citizens who participate in the program and those who do not.

Earlier in this chapter we described differences between basic and applied research. Program evaluation is perhaps the extreme case of applied research. The purpose of program evaluation is practical, not theoretical. Nevertheless, even in the context of blatantly practical goals, there is an intimate relationship between applied and basic research (see also Box 9.3). Consider, for example, a recent definition by a group of social scientists involved in program evaluation of social policy experiments, the kind advocated by Campbell (1969) more than 20 years ago (see Box 9.1). They defined this type of experiment as "A theoretically based effort to introduce social change in a way that permits discerning the net effect of the change on social outcomes" (Berk et al., 1987, p. 650). In this view, social policy experiments, such as those associated with rehabilitating prisoners, removing people from welfare, and Sesame Street have two goals: informing policy decisions and advancing scientific theory and knowledge. Basic and applied research, in this view, have often been artificially separated. As these social scientists commented further:

> It is, in fact, difficult to imagine good social policy not capitalizing on the accumulated wisdom of the social sciences, and equally difficult to imagine changes in social policy from which social scientists could not learn (Berk et al., 1987, p. 650).

Perhaps the greatest difference between basic research and program evaluation lies in the political and social realities surrounding program evaluation. Campbell's (1969) idea that social reforms and experimental methods be routinely brought together has had some impact on social policy makers, but it is still underutilized (see Berk et al., 1987). The reasons are some of the same ones initially identified by Campbell (see Box 9.1). Nevertheless, without social experimentation, especially that which makes use whenever possible of randomized field experiments, policy makers and the community at large may believe a treatment works, when it doesn't or vice versa. Such incorrect decisions lead us to allocate money and resources to ineffective programs.

Not too many years ago, a show called "Scared Straight" aired on national television which described a juvenile education program implemented at Rahway State Prison in New Jersey. The program involved taking youthful offenders into a prison to meet with selected convicts from the inmate population. The goal was to inform juveniles about the reality of prison life and,

BOX 9.3

BASIC AND APLIED RESEARCH: A CIRCULAR STREET

Basic and *applied research* can be differentiated in terms of goals and products and in terms of constraints placed on the problem-solving aspects of these kinds of research (see Voss, 1987). While basic research seeks a better understanding of human nature through the development of conceptual tools, applied research looks for an improvement of human life through the scientific discovery of practical solutions (see Salomon, 1987). However, a case can be made for a reciprocal relationship between basic and applied research. Writing in the *International Journal of Psychology,* Salomon (1987) argues that each domain of research serves the other in an ongoing circular way. Specifically, basic research provides us with certain abstractions (for example, scientifically based principles) that express certain regularities in nature. When these principles are examined in the complex and "dirty" world where they supposedly apply, new complexities are recognized and new hypotheses are called for. These new complexities are then tested and evaluated before being tried out again in the real world. Salomon's model looks like this (from Salomon, 1987, p. 444):

Salomon points to the work of Ellen Langer as a concrete example of this circular relationship. She identified a decline in elderly people's health, once they entered nursing homes (see Langer, 1987; and Langer and Rodin, 1976, described in this chapter). This led her to develop a theory of mindlessness which she has tested under controlled experimental conditions, and which has implications for more general theories of cognitive development (for example, see Langer and Piper, 1987). The theory provides a guide for her applied work—designing new models of nursing homes. Tests of the practical effects of changes in the care given by nursing homes on the residents' health and well-being undoubtedly will lead to modifications of her theory of mindlessness.

thereby, the program leaders hoped, dissuade them from further illegal activity. Unsubstantiated claims were made for the effectiveness of the program, including some suggesting a success rate as high as 80 to 90 percent (see Locke et al., 1986). The Rahway program is just one of several similar programs around the country. But do these programs really work?

Several evaluation studies of the exposure-to-prison programs have produced mixed results, including positive findings, findings of no difference between control and experimental subjects, as well as results suggesting that the program may actually increase juvenile crime rate among some types of delinquents. There is a possibility that less frequent juvenile offenders may increase their criminal activity after meeting the prisoners. It has been suggested that because these less hardened offenders have recently begun a lifestyle wherein they are being recognized and reinforced by their peers for their toughness, this image is also reinforced by the tough image often projected by the prisoners. On the other hand, more frequent juvenile offenders, who have achieved a level of status among their peers for some period of time, may be more threatened by the prospects of prison life because it would mean loss of that status (see Locke et al., 1986). Attempts to evaluate the effectiveness of this significant social program provide good examples of the difficulties inherent in evaluation research: difficulty of randomly assigning subjects, getting administrators to cooperate with experimental procedures, and dealing with loss of subjects during the evaluation. Nevertheless, program evaluation based on sound experimental methodology offers policy makers at all levels (institution, community, city, state, federal) the information that can be helpful in making rational choices among possible treatments for social problems. Since resources inevitably are in short supply, it is critical that those that are available to help society be put to the best possible use.

Our hope is that your knowledge of research methods will allow *you* to participate knowledgeably and perhaps contribute constructively to the ongoing debate concerning the role of experimentation in society.

SUMMARY

Experimentation in natural settings differs in many ways from that done in psychology laboratories. There are likely to be more problems in exerting experimental control in a natural setting, and establishing external validity or generality of results is more often a key objective. The stated goals of the research and its possible consequences also differ when research is conducted in natural settings. Reasons for doing experiments in natural settings include testing the external validity of laboratory findings and assessing the effects of "treatments" aimed at improving conditions under which people work and live.

Campbell and others have argued that society must be willing to take an experimental approach to social reform—one that will allow the clearest evaluation of the effectiveness of new programs. In many situations (for instance, when available resources are scarce), true experiments involving randomization of individuals to Treatment and No Treatment conditions are recommended. However, if a true experiment is not feasible, quasi-experimental procedures are the next best approach. Quasi-experiments differ from true experiments in that fewer plausible rival hypotheses for an experimental outcome are controlled. When specific threats to the internal validity of an experiment are not controlled, then the experimenter, by logically examining the situation and by collecting additional evidence, must seek to rule out these threats to internal validity.

A particularly strong quasi-experimental procedure is the nonequivalent control group design. This procedure generally controls for all major threats to internal validity except those associated with interactions of (a) selection and history, (b) selection and maturation, (c) selection and instrumentation, and (d) threats due to differential statistical regression. In addition to the major threats to internal validity, an experimenter must be sensitive to possible contamination effects that result when there is communication between groups of subjects. Problems of observer or experimenter bias, questions of external validity, and Hawthorne effects are potential problems in all experiments, whether conducted in the laboratory or in the field.

When it is possible to observe changes in a dependent measure before and after a treatment is administered, one can carry out a simple interrupted time-series design. The researcher using this design looks for an abrupt change in the time series that coincides with the introduction of treatment. The major threat to internal validity in this design is that of history—some event other than the treatment may have been responsible for the change in the time series. Instrumentation also can be a problem, especially when the treatment represents a type of social reform that may lead to changes in the way records are kept or data collected. By including a control group that is as similar as possible to the experimental group, one can strengthen the internal validity of a simple time-series design. A time series with nonequivalent control group, for example, controls for many possible history threats.

In this chapter we also discussed how the logic and methodology associated with single-case experimental designs (see Chapter 8) can be applied to experimentation in natural settings. For instance, an ABAB design may be used when a researcher can control the application and withdrawal of a treatment. In such cases the internal validity of the experiment can approach that of a true experiment.

A particularly important goal of research in natural settings is program evaluation. Persons other than psychologists (such as educators, political scientists, and sociologists) are often involved in this process. Types of program evaluation include assessment of needs, program planning, formative evaluation, and summative evaluation. Perhaps the most serious constraints on program evaluation are the political and social realities that surround it. The reluctance of public officials to seek an evaluation of social reforms is often an obstacle to be overcome. Nevertheless, social scientists have called on individuals who are knowledgeable about the procedures of program evaluation to make themselves available to those who are responsible for the delivery of social services. By answering this call, perhaps we can help change society in a way that brings the most effective services to those most in need.

KEY CONCEPTS

program evaluation
basic research
applied research
threats to internal validity
contamination
Hawthorne effect
quasi-experiment

nonequivalent control group
  design
simple interrupted time-series
  design
time series with nonequivalent
  control group
ABAB design

REVIEW QUESTIONS

1 What special reasons are there for carrying out experiments in natural settings?
2 Explain how laboratory experiments and those in natural settings differ in control, external validity, goals, and consequences.
3 Distinguish between basic research and applied research.
4 Briefly explain what Donald Campbell meant when he called for an experimental approach to social reform.
5 What are the three distinguishing characteristics of true experiments?
6 What obstacles arise in trying to carry out experiments in natural settings?
7 Comment critically on the "fairness" of random assignment.
8 How can participants be randomly assigned to treatments while still giving all participants access to the experimental treatment?
9 Define by means of an example the eight major threats to internal validity as summarized by Campbell and Stanley (1966).
10 Explain how contamination, threats to external validity, experimenter expectancy effects, and Hawthorne effects threaten the clear interpretation of an experimental result.
11 How are subjects in the control group likely to respond when contamination occurs?
12 What do Cook and Campbell (1979) consider the best test of external validity?
13 Why is the use of a pretest critical in the nonequivalent control group design?
14 Cite one example of a threat to internal validity that is controlled in the nonequivalent control group design and two examples of threats that are not controlled.
15 Explain why we cannot conclude that the treatment and control groups in a nonequivalent control group design are equivalent even when the pretest scores are the same for both groups.
16 What is meant by a local history effect in the nonequivalent control group design?
17 How did Langer and Rodin handle problems of observer bias and possible effects of contamination in their study of elderly residents of a nursing home?
18 What is the major evidence for an effect of the treatment in a simple interrupted time-series design?

19 Explain how the addition of a nonequivalent control group to a simple interrupted time-series design reduces the threat to the internal validity of the design.

20 How can single-case experimental designs be used to determine whether an effect is due to a treatment or to the threat to internal validity called history?

21 What is the purpose of each of the four types of study used in program evaluation?

22 In what sense can it be said that basic and applied research have a reciprocal relationship to one another?

CHALLENGE QUESTIONS

1 Because of your extensive background in research design, you have been appointed by a local school board committee to design a definitive study of the effect of a newly developed nutritious breakfast on the school performance of young children. The school board is trying to decide whether to establish a "breakfast program" at the school, and, because of the expense of this proposed program (and because of your persuasive arguments), they have decided to test the effectiveness of the breakfast before implementing the program. For this problem, pretend that you are meeting with the principal of the school to work out the details of the study. You are to respond to each of the following suggestions made by the principal.

A The principal first suggests that students be selected for the treatment during the test phase on the basis of their need. That is, the students who have the lowest nutrition level now will be given the treatment. Explain to the principal why this is not an advisable procedure.

B Having given up his suggestion in Part A, the principal next suggests that the only fair procedure for the test is to give the treatment to all the students to see if there is any improvement in their performance. Explain to the principal what you would have to do under these circumstances to verify the effectiveness of the program, and explain why this could be a "risky" way to test the program.

C Finally, the principal gives up and asks you to outline the design you would propose for the study. Outline the essentials of the design you would propose. In your design be sure to use double-blind procedures and explain to the principal the how and why of these procedures.

2 A certain assistant professor moved into a new (old) house on November 1 of this year. On or around December 1 of the same year, he was to have some aluminum siding installed on his house, and he decided to determine whether the investment in the siding would prove to be worthwhile in terms of savings on his heating bills. He recognized that this situation corresponded to that quasi-experimental procedure known as time-series analysis. He is seeking your advice on the following questions.

A In order for this time-series analysis to prove at all effective, what measures must the investigator be sure to collect before beginning to examine the effect of the aluminum siding "treatment"?

B What problem is likely to arise if the investigator tries to use his total monthly heating bill as a response measure for his analysis? What alternative measure would you suggest?

C What potentially confounding factor is present, given the time of year when the "treatment" must be administered?

3 The police force of a large city had to decide between two different approaches to keeping the officers on the force informed about the changes in laws. An enlightened administrator of this force decided to put the two approaches to test in a research study. She decided to use the random groups design and she assigned thirty officers randomly to each of the two programs for a period of 6 months. At the end of this time all the officers who successfully completed the training required under the two approaches were given a final test on their knowledge of the law. The twenty officers who completed Program A showed a reliably higher mean score on this test than did the twenty-eight officers who completed Program B. The administrator wisely chose not to accept these results as decisive evidence of the effectiveness of the two programs. Using only the data reported in this problem, explain why she made this decision. Next, explain how her decision would have been different if twenty officers completed both programs (from the original thirty assigned to each) and there was still a sizable difference favoring Program A. Be sure to mention any limitations on the conclusions she could reach concerning the overall effectiveness of these programs.

4 A small undergraduate college with a new physical fitness center decided to introduce a health enhancement program for faculty and staff. The program is designed to take one semester to complete with three 1-hour sessions per week. Comment critically on each of the following questions regarding the evaluation of this program.

A What role would formative and summative evaluation play in the evaluation of the program?

B What obstacles generally exist in real-world settings, and probably apply in this situation, to prevent the conduct of a true experiment to evaluate the program? (Be sure to define the three characteristics of a true experiment.)

C As an alternative to a true experiment, a nonequivalent control group design is proposed in which a group of faculty who did not participate in the program agree to take the performance tests before the program begins and after the program has ended. Explain why this nonequivalent control group design is superior to a pretest-posttest design in which only the program participants would be tested. State one threat to internal validity that is controlled in the nonequivalent control group design.

ANSWER TO CHALLENGE QUESTION 1

1 A Selecting students on the basis of need may result in problems with regression to the mean, especially if the students are identified on the basis of an unreliable measure of need. If regression were to be a problem, the nutrition program could falsely appear to be effective.

B Administering the program to all students would necessitate projecting what students' performance would have been without the program on the basis of their prior school performance, as is the case in a time-series design. Their prior performance would serve as a baseline, and the risks associated with variable baselines would apply to this situation. The test of the effectiveness of the program would also be potentially challenged by the threats to internal validity that apply to the time-series designs, such as history.

C The most appropriate design for this problem would be a two-group experiment using the random groups design. Both groups should receive comparably packaged breakfast foods that had been previously coded by the manufacturer as containing the newly developed nutritious breakfast or the previously used (and presumably less nutritious) diet. Neither the students nor those responsible for assessing their school performance should know which diet a given student has received. This double-blind procedure avoids potential problems of demand characteristics (students working harder in school because they know they have received the "super" breakfast) and experimenter effects (teachers showing observer bias by varying their assessments of students in light of which treatment the student has received or influencing students' performance differentially by giving more individual attention and instruction to students whom the teachers know are receiving the new diet).

P A R T

FOUR

Appendixes

APPENDIX

A

Statistical Methods

OUTLINE

NOTES ON NOTATION

To learn the computational procedures for specific statistical tests, you need first to learn some general characteristics of statistical notation. A subject's score on a dependent variable is typically called "X." The scores of individual subjects are indicated by subscripts (X_1 X_2, X_3); thus, we refer to the score for the first subject as X_1, that for the second subject as X_2, and so on. If we have two scores for each subject on two different dependent variables, we typically refer to the first score as X and the second score as Y. For example, if we measured the first subject's height as 60 inches and weight as 120 pounds, then $X_1 = 60$ and $Y_1 = 120$.

The number of subjects in each group within a study is indicated using the symbol n. Once again, we use subscripts to differentiate the different groups. If there are thirty subjects in Group 1 and twenty-five subjects in Group 2, we indicate this in symbols as $n_1=30$; $n_2=25$. The subscripts need not be numbers; if there are ten subjects in the control group and twelve subjects in the experimental group, we could write $n_c=10$; $n_e=12$. The total number of subjects across all the groups in the study is indicated by the symbol N. If there are three groups in an experiment and if $n_1=10$, $n_2=15$, and $n_3=5$, then $N=30$.

The summation sign, Σ, indicates that you are to add all the values represented by the symbol(s) that appear to the right of the summation sign. If you had the three scores $X_1=4$, $X_2=5$, and $X_3=6$, the expression ΣX would indicate that you should do the following computation:

$$\Sigma X = X_1 + X_2 + X_3 = 4 + 5 + 6 = 15$$

There are two other common expressions involving the summation sign that appear in many statistical computations, ΣX^2 and $(\Sigma X)^2$. These two expressions look very similar, but they require very different computations. The expression ΣX^2 indicates that each individual score should first be squared and then the sum of these squared scores should be determined. The expression $(\Sigma X)^2$ requires the determination of the sum of the individual scores first and then the squaring of this sum. Using our sample of three scores ($X_1=4$, $X_2=5$, and $X_3=6$), the differences between the two calculations can be made clear.

$$\Sigma X^2 = X_1^2 + X_2^2 + X_3^2 = 4^2 + 5^2 + 6^2 = 16 + 25 + 36 = 77$$
$$(\Sigma X)^2 = (X_1 + X_2 + X_3)^2 = (4 + 5 + 6)^2 = (15)^2 = 225$$

DESCRIPTIVE STATISTICS

The scores representing performance of subjects in a particular group can be summarized most completely by constructing a frequency distribution. In a frequency distribution, the possible values of the dependent variable are listed from lowest to highest and the number of subjects obtaining each score is tabulated. While a frequency distribution provides the most complete summary of the results, reporting the frequency distributions for each of the six conditions in an experiment is too cumbersome. Most frequency distributions can be well summarized by reporting one measure of central tendency and one measure of dispersion. We will now describe each type of measure in turn.

MEASURES OF CENTRAL TENDENCY: MODE, MEDIAN, AND MEAN

Measures of central tendency indicate the score that identifies the center of the frequency distribution. The *mode* is the crudest measure of central tendency in that it simply indicates the score in the frequency distribution that occurs most often. If two scores in the distribution occur with much higher frequency than do other scores in the distribution, and if these two scores occur at two different locations in the frequency distribution, this two-humped distribution is said to be *bimodal* (to have two modes).

The *median* is defined as the middle score in the frequency distribution. The median is calculated by ranking all the scores from lowest to highest. If there is an odd number of scores, then the middle score is equal to the median. If there is an even number of scores, then the median is the average of the two scores in the middle. For example, if a distribution of scores included the values 4, 7, 2, 1, 9, we would compute the median by first ranking the scores—1, 2, 4, 7, 9—and then selecting the third of the five scores (4) as the median. If a sixth score were included in the distribution (4, 7, 2, 1, 9, 5), we would again rank the scores (1, 2, 4, 5, 7, 9), but this time we would average the third and fourth scores to obtain the median

$$\left(\frac{4 + 5}{2}\right) = 4.5$$

The median is the best measure of central tendency when the distribution includes extreme scores because it is less influenced than is the mean by the extreme scores. For example, the median of the distribution of scores 1, 2, 3, 4, 5 is 3. The median would remain the same even if the distribution were changed to 1, 2, 3, 4, 50.

The *mean* is the most commonly reported measure of central tendency and it is determined by dividing the sum of the scores (ΣX) by the number of scores contributing to that sum (n). The mean of the five scores 4, 7, 2, 1, 9 would be calculated as follows:

$$\text{Mean} = \frac{\Sigma X}{n} = \frac{4 + 7 + 2 + 1 + 9}{5} = 4.6$$

The mean of a population is symbolized as μ (Greek letter mu); the mean of a sample of scores is usually indicated as $\overline{X}$ (read "X bar"), but it is sometimes symbolized as M. The mean should always be reported as a measure of central tendency unless there are extreme scores in the distribution.

The mean of several samples of the same size can be determined by averaging the means of the individual samples. For example, if each of the five groups included ten subjects and the means for these five groups were as follows, $\overline{X}_1=4.6$, $\overline{X}_2=4.3$, $\overline{X}_3=6.2$, $\overline{X}_4=4.7$, and $\overline{X}_5=5.2$, then the mean across all five groups can be computed using the following equation in which K is the number of groups:

$$\text{Overall mean} = \frac{(\Sigma\overline{X})}{K} = \frac{4.6 + 4.3 + 6.2 + 4.7 + 5.2}{5}$$

$$= \frac{25}{5} = 5.00$$

When the overall mean for a group of samples of different sizes needs to be computed, the simple averaging of the sample means is not appropriate. Simple averaging would give undue weight to the scores for subjects in the smaller groups and would give too little weight to subjects' scores in the larger groups. The overall mean can be computed in a way that gives equal weight to the score for each individual subject. For example, if in Group 1 there are twenty subjects and $\overline{X}_1= 4.45$, and in Group 2 there are 10 subjects and $\overline{X}_2=6.20$, and in Group 3 there are twenty subjects and $\overline{X}_3=4.95$, then the overall mean can be computed as follows:

$$\text{Overall mean} = \frac{\Sigma(n)(\overline{X})}{N} = \frac{(20)(4.45) + (10)(6.2) + (20)(4.95)}{50}$$

$$= \frac{89 + 62 + 99}{50}$$

$$= \frac{250}{50} = 5.00$$

MEASURES OF DISPERSION: RANGE, SEMI-INTERQUARTILE RANGE, AND STANDARD DEVIATION

Whenever you report a measure of central tendency, it should always be accompanied by an appropriate measure of dispersion. Measures of central tendency indicate the center of a frequency distribution, measures of dispersion indicate the breadth or variability of the distribution. The two distributions shown below have the same mean (13), but they clearly differ in how the scores are distributed about that mean. In Distribution A, the scores are tightly packed about the mean, indicating low dispersion. The scores in Distribution B, on the other hand, are more widely distributed about the mean, indicating greater dispersion.

Distribution A	Distribution B
13	9
13	11
13	13
13	15
13	17

The crudest measure of dispersion (the counterpart of the mode) is the range. The *range* is determined by subtracting the lowest score in the distribution from the highest score. In the small distribution made up of the scores 1, 3, 5, 7, the range would be equal to 7−1, or 6.

The semi-interquartile range is a useful measure of dispersion, particularly when the median is used as a measure of central tendency because of the presence of extreme scores in a distribution. The *semi-interquartile range* is equal to one-half of the difference between the score in the distribution at the seventy-fifth percentile and the score at the twenty-fifth percentile. A percentile defines the percentage of scores below a given score. The computation of the semi-interquartile range begins by ranking the scores from lowest to highest. For example, if a distribution of ten scores included 13, 14, 18, 50, 11, 15, 12, 16, 15, and 20, the ranked scores would be 11, 12, 13, 14, 15, 15, 16, 18, 20, 50. The score at the seventy-fifth percentile in this distribution of ten scores would be the average of the seventh and eighth scores in the ranked distribution

$$\left(\frac{16 + 18}{2}\right) = 17$$

The score at the twenty-fifth percentile is the average of the second and third scores

$$\left(\frac{12 + 13}{2}\right) = 12.5$$

The semi-interquartile range for this distribution would then be equal to (17−12.5)/2 or 2.25. This value is a better indication of the dispersion in this relatively tightly packed distribution than the range (50− 11=39) would be. The semi-interquartile range is most commonly used to compare dispersions in two or more distributions, at least one of which contains extreme scores.

The most commonly used measure of dispersion (the counterpart of the mean) is the standard deviation. The *standard deviation* tells you approximately how far on the average a score is from the mean. It is equal to the square root of the average squared deviations of the scores in the distribution about the mean. The definitional formula for the standard deviation is

$$\sqrt{\frac{\Sigma(X - \overline{X})^2}{n - 1}}$$

For reasons that need not concern us here the average of the squared deviations about the mean must involve division by $n-1$ rather than n so as to provide an unbiased estimate of the population standard deviation based on the sample. The standard deviation of a population is symbolized as σ (Greek letter sigma); the standard deviation of a sample of scores is usually indicated as s, but it is sometimes symbolized as SD. The computational formula for the standard deviation is

$$s = \sqrt{\frac{\Sigma X^2 - \frac{(\Sigma X)^2}{n}}{n - 1}}$$

The use of this computational formula can be best illustrated by working through an example for a small distribution of scores: 2, 6, 10, 14, 18.

1 Compute $\Sigma X^2 = 2^2 + 6^2 + 10^2 + 14^2 + 18^2$

$$= 4 + 36 + 100 + 196 + 324$$

$$= 660$$

2 Compute $\Sigma X = 2 + 6 + 10 + 14 + 18$

$$= 50$$

3 Compute $\dfrac{(\Sigma X)^2}{n} = \dfrac{(50)^2}{5} = \dfrac{2,500}{5} = 500$

4 Compute $\Sigma X^2 - \dfrac{(\Sigma X)^2}{n} = 660 - 500 = 160$

5 Compute $\dfrac{\Sigma X^2 - \dfrac{(\Sigma X)^2}{n}}{n - 1} = \dfrac{160}{4} = 40$

6 Compute $\sqrt{\dfrac{\Sigma X^2 - \dfrac{(\Sigma X)^2}{n}}{n - 1}} = \sqrt{40} = 6.32$

STANDARD ERROR OF THE MEAN

In doing inferential statistics, we use the sample mean as a point estimate of the population mean. That is, we use a single value $(\overline{X})$ to estimate (infer) the population mean (μ). It is often helpful to be able to determine how much error there is in estimating μ on the basis of $\overline{X}$. The Central Limit Theorem in mathematics tells us that if we draw an infinite number of samples of the same size and we compute $\overline{X}$ for each of these samples, the mean of these samples means ($\mu_{\overline{x}}$) will be equal to the population mean (μ), and the standard deviation of the sample means ($\sigma_{\overline{x}}$) will be equal to the population standard deviation (σ) divided by the square root of the sample size ($\sqrt{n}$). The standard deviation of this theoretical sampling distribution of the mean is called the *standard error of the mean*.

Typically, we do not know the standard deviation of the population so we estimate it on the basis of a sample. Thus, the standard error of the mean ($s_{\overline{x}}$) is computed using the formula $s_{\overline{x}} = s/\sqrt{n}$. Small values of $s_{\overline{x}}$ suggest that we have a good estimate of the population mean, and large values of $s_{\overline{x}}$ suggest that we have only a rough estimate of the population mean. The formula for the standard error of the mean indicates that our ability to estimate the population mean on the basis of a sample is dependent on the size of the sample (large samples lead to better estimates) and on the variability in the population from which the sample was drawn, as estimated by the sample standard deviation (the less variable the scores in a population, the better our estimate of the population mean will be).

If the standard deviation of a sample of twenty-five scores (which can be computed from a set of scores following the procedures described in the previous section) is 5, then the standard error of the mean ($s_{\overline{x}}$) is equal to $s/\sqrt{n}$, which in this case is $5/\sqrt{25} = 5/5 = 1.00$.

CONFIDENCE INTERVALS

Imagine that you are having a physical examination at the campus health clinic. The technician reports that your pulse is 75 beats per minute. You are unlikely to be concerned that your heart is racing if you are also told that the average pulse rate at rest for a person your age is 72 beats per minute. Your knowledge of the variability of pulse rates keeps you from being alarmed. In both physiological and psychological measurement we are often more interested in knowing a range of values that define a "normal" range than we are in specifying a single estimate of a population value. These normal ranges are based on the standard error of the mean and are called *confidence intervals*. In computing a confidence interval we specify a range of values within which we can have a certain degree of confidence that the population mean is included within the interval. As you may suspect, the larger the interval we specify, the greater our confidence that the mean will be included; but larger intervals give us less specific information about the exact value of the population mean. As a compromise, researchers have agreed that the 95 percent confidence interval and the 99 percent confidence interval will be used when an interval estimate of the population mean is desired. The confidence interval is centered about our point estimate of the mean ($\overline{X}$), and the boundaries of the 95 percent confidence interval can be calculated using the following formulas:

Upper limit of 95 percent confidence interval $= \overline{X} + [t(n-1)]_{\alpha = .05}[S_{\overline{X}}]$

Lower limit of 95 percent confidence interval $= \overline{X} - [t(n-1)]_{\alpha = .05}[S_{\overline{X}}]$

We have already described procedures for computing the sample mean $(\overline{X})$ and the standard error of the mean $(s_{\overline{X}})$. The unfamiliar symbols in the two equations for the limits of the 95 percent confidence interval are $[t(n-1)]$ and $\alpha = .05$. The level of significance $(\alpha = .05)$ may be familiar to you if you have studied the procedures for inferential statistics tests described in Chapter 5. In the case of confidence intervals, $\alpha = (1 -$ level of confidence), expressed as a proportion. So, for the 95 percent confidence interval, $\alpha = 1 - .95 = .05$ and for the 99 percent confidence interval, $\alpha = 1 - .99 = .01$. The t statistic included in the equation is defined by the number of degrees of freedom $(n-1)$, and the t is determined by looking it up in Table A.5.

We are now ready to compute the 95 percent confidence interval for the mean of a sample in which $\overline{X} = 12$, $s = 4$, and $n = 25$.

1 Compute $s_{\overline{X}} = \dfrac{s}{\sqrt{n}} = \dfrac{4}{\sqrt{25}} = \dfrac{4}{5} = .8$

2 Determine degrees of freedom for t: $n - 1 = 25 - 1 = 24$

3 Determine $\alpha = 1 - .95 = .05$

4 Look up in Table A.5 the value for $t(24)_{\alpha = .05} = 2.06$

5 Compute upper limit of 95 percent confidence interval

$$
\begin{aligned}
&= \overline{X} + [t(n-1)]_{\alpha = .05}[s_{\overline{X}}] \\
&= 12 + [2.06][.8] \\
&= 12 + 1.65 = 13.65
\end{aligned}
$$

6 Compute lower limit of 95 percent confidence interval

$$
\begin{aligned}
&= \overline{X} - [t(n-1)]_{\alpha = .05}[s_{\overline{X}}] \\
&= 12 - [2.06][.8] \\
&= 12 - 1.65 = 10.35
\end{aligned}
$$

7 The 95 percent confidence interval for a sample mean of 12 from a sample size of 25 with a standard deviation of 4 is bounded by 10.35 and 13.65. We can thus be 95 percent confident that the specified interval captures the mean of the population from which the sample was drawn.

CORRELATION COEFFICIENTS

The degree of relationship between two dependent measures for the same sample of subjects is determined by calculating a correlation coefficient. If the two dependent measures both represent at least an interval scale of measurement (see Chapter 1), then the Pearson Product-Moment Correlation Coefficient r is used. If one or both dependent measures represent only an ordinal scale of measurement, however, then the appropriate correlation coefficient is Spearman's Rank-Order Correlation Coefficient r_s. We will illustrate the computational procedures for both correlation coefficients.

PEARSON PRODUCT-MOMENT CORRELATION COEFFICIENT *r*

Each of ten subjects agreed to keep track of how many hours were spent practicing the week before a ping-pong tournament. During the week of the tournament the number of games won by each of these ten subjects was also determined. We will refer to the number of hours of practice as X and to the number of games won as "Y." The data for each of the ten subjects on each of these two measures are listed in the following table, and these data were used to carry out the necessary computations for determining *r*.

Subject	Hours of practice (X)	Games won (Y)
1	40	10
2	20	3
3	10	1
4	15	2
5	18	4
6	35	6
7	27	9
8	16	8
9	4	5
10	33	7

1 Compute $\Sigma X = 40 + 20 + 10 + \ldots + 33 = 218$

2 Compute $\Sigma Y = 10 + 3 + 1 + \ldots + 7 = 55$

3 Compute $\Sigma X^2 = 40^2 + 20^2 + 10^2 + \ldots + 33^2 = 5{,}964$

4 Compute $\Sigma Y^2 = 10^2 + 3^2 + 1^2 + \ldots + 7^2 = 385$

5 Compute $\Sigma XY = (40)(10) + (20)(3) + \ldots (33)(7) = 1{,}404$

6 Compute $\Sigma XY - \dfrac{(\Sigma X)(\Sigma Y)}{n} = 1{,}404 - \dfrac{(218)(55)}{10} = 205$

7 Compute $\Sigma X^2 - \dfrac{(\Sigma X)^2}{n} = 5{,}964 - \dfrac{(218)^2}{10} = 1{,}211.60$

8 Compute $\Sigma Y^2 - \dfrac{(\Sigma Y)^2}{n} = 385 - \dfrac{(55)^2}{10} = 82.50$

9 Multiply step 7 by step 8 $= (1{,}211.60)(82.50) = 99{,}957$

10 Take the square root of step 9 $= \sqrt{99{,}957} = 316.16$

11 Divide step 6 by step 10 to obtain $r = \dfrac{205}{316.16} = .65$

The eleven steps we have just outlined have led you successfully through the computational formula for r. The computational formula in its complete form is as follows:

$$r = \frac{\Sigma XY - \dfrac{(\Sigma X)(\Sigma Y)}{n}}{\sqrt{\left(\Sigma X^2 - \dfrac{(\Sigma X)^2}{n}\right)\left(\Sigma Y^2 - \dfrac{(\Sigma Y)^2}{n}\right)}}$$

To determine whether your obtained r is greater than zero, you can use Table A.2. The degrees of freedom (df) are $n - 2$, and Table A.2 lists the critical values of r for the .05 and .01 levels of significance. If your obtained r is *greater* than the tabled value, then the correlation you have obtained is statistically significant. In our example, the degrees of freedom for r would be 8 since n is 10. The obtained r of .65 is larger than the tabled r for a .05 level of significance (.632), so it would be considered statistically significantly larger than zero. Notice, however, if we had used a .01 level of significance, our obtained r of .65 would be *less* than the tabled value (.765) and thus judged to be *not* statistically significant. If we concluded the correlation was significant, then we would also conclude that the more hours a player practices Ping Pong, the more games he or she is likely to win.

SPEARMAN'S RANK-ORDER CORRELATION COEFFICIENT r_s

The director of the admissions office at a very small college selected a random sample of ten students from this year's incoming class to determine whether there was a correlation between the students' high school class ranks and their scores on a national college board test. The scores on the college board test represent an interval scale, with higher scores indicating better performance. The high school ranks, however, represent only an ordinal scale and so Spearman's rank-order correlation must be used.

Student	Class rank	Test score	Test rank	D	D²
1	2	675	1	1	1
2	4	525	6	−2	4
3	7	500	7.5	−.5	.25
4	9	450	9	0	0
5	6	650	2	4	16
6	1	600	3	−2	4
7	3	550	5	−2	4
8	8	500	7.5	.5	.25
9	10	425	10	0	0
10	5	575	4	1	1

Note: The students' actual high school class ranks would have ranged over ranks larger than 1 to 10. These are their converted class ranks within this sample of 10.

1 Rank the students from highest to lowest on their test scores. For students with the same test score, take the ranks these students would have received and average them. Then, assign the next rank to the next lowest student. For example, students 3 and 8 both have a score of 500. They are in ranks 7 and 8, so both receive a rank of

$$7.5 \left(\frac{7 + 8}{2} \right)$$

and the next lowest student (student 4 with a score of 450) receives a rank of 9.

2 Compute D—the difference in the two ranks for each student. See column D in the table.

3 Compute D^2—square each difference score. See column D^2 in the table.

4 Compute $\Sigma D^2 = 1 + 4 + .25 + 0 + 16 + 4 + 4 + .25 + 0 + 1 = 30.5$

5 Multiply ΣD^2 by $6 = (6)(30.5) = 183$

6 Compute $n(n^2 - 1) = 10(10^2 - 1) = 10(100 - 1) = 10(99) = 990$

7 Divide step 5 by step 6: $\dfrac{183}{990} = .18$

8 Subtract step 7 from step 1 to obtain $r_s = 1 - .18 = .82$

Once again, the eight steps we have just outlined have led you successfully through the computational formula for r_s. The computational formula in its complete form is

$$r_s = 1 - \frac{6(\Sigma D^2)}{n(n^2 - 1)}$$

To determine whether your obtained r_s is greater than zero, you can use Table A.3. The critical information you need in Table A.3 is n (in our example n = 10), and the level of significance you want to use. If the obtained r_s is *greater* than the tabled value, then the correlation you have obtained is statistically significant. In our example, the obtained r_s of .82 is larger than the tabled value for the .05 level of significance (.648), so it would be considered statistically significantly larger than zero. Thus, as you might expect, students' high school class ranks and college board test scores are correlated, although the actual correlation is usually less than .82.

INFERENTIAL STATISTICS TESTS

CHI-SQUARE (χ^2) TEST: GOODNESS OF FIT

The chi-square (χ^2) goodness-of-fit test is used to determine whether the obtained frequencies in each of several nominal scale categories correspond to the expected frequencies in each category. The expected frequencies are often based on the laws of chance, but they can also represent expectations based on a formal psychological theory. It is essential that each individual observation be independent and that each observation be classified into one—and only one—category.

The example we will use to illustrate the computation of this test will involve testing the "fairness" of a six-sided die rolled sixty times. You could also consider these data to represent the responses of sixty students to a six-alternative multiple-choice test item on material the students have *not* studied. A fair die and a good test item should lead to equal frequencies across categories. The observed and expected frequencies on which the computations will be based are as follows:

	Outcome categories					
	1	2	3	4	5	6
Observed frequency	7	12	10	12	8	11
Expected frequency	10	10	10	10	10	10
(O−E)	−3	2	0	2	−2	1

1 Compute Observed (O)−Expected (E) frequencies in each category. (See last row of table.)

2 Compute $\chi^2 = \Sigma \dfrac{(O - E)^2}{E}$

$$= \frac{(-3)^2}{10} + \frac{(2)^2}{10} + \frac{(0)^2}{10} + \frac{(2)^2}{10} + \frac{(-2)^2}{10} + \frac{(1)^2}{10}$$

$$= \frac{9}{10} + \frac{4}{10} + 0 + \frac{4}{10} + \frac{4}{10} + \frac{1}{10}$$

$$= .9 + .4 + 0 + .4 + .4 + .1 = 2.20$$

3 Determine degrees of freedom for χ^2: (number of categories − 1) = 6 − 1 = 5

4 Use Table A.4 to determine critical χ^2 values for 5 degrees of freedom and $\alpha = .05$

$$\chi^2(5)_{\alpha = .05} = 11.07$$

5 Compare obtained χ^2 to tabled χ^2 value.
  a If obtained $\chi^2 <$ tabled χ^2, then the expected frequencies provide a "good fit" for the obtained frequencies.
  b If obtained $\chi^2 >$ tabled χ^2, then the expected frequencies do *not* provide a good fit for the obtained frequencies.

6 Our result conforms to step 5a, and so we know we have a fair die or a good test item.

CHI-SQUARE (χ^2) TEST: CONTINGENCY TABLE

The chi-square (χ^2) contingency test is used to determine whether there is a relationship between two nominal scale variables. As described in Chapter 3, this version of the chi-square test is used in the analysis of cross tabulations in survey research. The observations entering into this analysis must be independent, and each observation must be classified into one and only one cell of the contingency table. These assumptions are generally met by making only one observation of each subject, thereby ensuring that the total number of observations entering into the table equals the total number of subjects. In contingency tables having only one degree of freedom (2 × 2 tables), the computations we describe here should not be used if any expected values are less than 10. For chi-square contingency tests with two or more degrees of freedom, it is best if there are no expected frequencies less than 5.

The data presented in the following table are the same as those presented in Table 3.5 in Chapter 3. The category listed along the rows of the table is the number of hours that subjects reported they habitually slept each night. The category listed across the columns of the table is the frequency with which these same subjects experienced headaches. The observed frequencies in the body of the table represent the numbers of subjects who experienced the particular combination of sleep and headache frequency.

Hours of sleep	Frequency of headaches			Row totals
	Never	Sometimes	Often	
≥ 8	38	17	3	58
	30.98	22.74	4.28	
7	37	21	5	63
	33.65	24.70	4.65	
≤ 6	19	31	5	55
	29.37	21.56	4.06	
Column totals	94	69	13	176

1 Compute row and column totals of observed frequencies. See table.

2 Compute overall total. Check to be sure both row and column totals sum to the same overall total. See boxed entry in lower right corner of the table.

3 Compute expected frequencies in each cell of the table by multiplying the row total by the column total for that cell and dividing by the overall total. For example, for the cell in the table for subjects getting more than 8 hours of sleep and never reporting headaches, the expected value is equal to

$$\frac{(58)(94)}{176} = \frac{5{,}452}{176} = 30.98$$

The expected values for each cell of the table are entered in the brackets below and to the right of each observed frequency.

4 Compute $\chi^2 = \Sigma \dfrac{(O - E)^2}{E} =$

$$\dfrac{(38 - 30.98)^2}{30.98} + \dfrac{(17 - 22.74)^2}{22.74} + \dfrac{(3 - 4.28)^2}{4.28} + \dfrac{(37 - 33.65)^2}{33.65}$$

$$+ \dfrac{(21 - 24.70)^2}{24.70} + \dfrac{(5 - 4.65)^2}{4.65} + \dfrac{(19 - 29.37)^2}{29.37}$$

$$+ \dfrac{(31 - 21.56)^2}{21.56} + \dfrac{(5 - 4.06)^2}{4.06}$$

$= 1.59 + 1.45 + .38 + .33 + .55 + .03 + 3.66 + 4.13 + .22$

$= 12.34$

5 Determine degrees of freedom for χ^2: (number of rows $-$ 1) $\times$ (number of columns $-$ 1)

$$= (3 - 1)(3 - 1)$$
$$= (2)(2)$$
$$= 4$$

6 Use Table A.4 to determine critical χ^2 value for 4 degrees of freedom and $\alpha = .05$

$$\chi^2(4)_{\alpha = .05} = 9.49$$

7 Compare obtained χ^2 to tabled χ^2 value.
  a If obtained χ^2 is greater than the tabled χ^2, then the two variables in the contingency table are significantly related.
  b If obtained χ^2 is less than the tabled χ^2, then the two variables in the contingency table are *not* significantly related.

8 Our result conforms to step 7a, so we conclude that habitual sleep duration and headache frequency are related.

INDEPENDENT SAMPLES *t*-TEST

The independent samples *t*-test is used to determine whether two sample means are sufficiently different so as to be unlikely to have been drawn from the same population. This test is applicable for the analysis of two-group designs involving either the random groups design or the natural groups design, although the assumptions underlying the test strictly apply only to the random groups design. If the independent variable has had no effect, then the two samples represent random samples drawn from the same population and they would therefore be expected to provide comparable estimates (within the bounds of sampling error) of the population mean. The independent samples t-test is based on the difference between the two sample means, so the expected value of t when the independent variable has had no effect is zero. If the independent variable has had an effect, however, the t will differ from zero. If the larger mean is subtracted from the smaller mean, the t will become increasingly smaller than zero as the mean difference increases. If the smaller mean is subtracted from the larger mean, the t will become increasingly larger than zero. The difference may be taken in either direction, but you must be careful to note whether it is a positive or negative t value. Because sampling error can never be eliminated, the obtained t must be compared to a critical value from the appropriate t-distribution to determine if it is statistically significant.

The data presented in the following table represent the number of correct responses on a test given after subjects studied the material in one of two groups in a random groups design. Subjects were randomly assigned to either the experimental ($n_e = 4$) or to the control group ($n_c = 6$), and the hypothesis tested in the experiment was that the experimental group would do better on the test.[1]

Subject	Experimental group	Subject	Control group
2	20	1	16
5	14	3	15
8	17	4	12
9	21	6	12
		7	14
		10	15

1 Compute $\bar{X}_e = \dfrac{\Sigma X_e}{n_e} = \dfrac{20 + 14 + 17 + 21}{4} = \dfrac{72}{4} = 18$

2 Compute $\bar{X}_c = \dfrac{\Sigma X_c}{n_c} = \dfrac{16 + 15 + 12 + 12 + 14 + 15}{6}$

$\qquad = \dfrac{84}{6} = 14$

3 Compute $\Sigma X_e^2 = 20^2 + 14^2 + 17^2 + 21^2 = 400 + 196 + 289 + 441$

$\qquad = 1{,}326$

[1]Some investigators distinguish between directional statistical tests (also called "one-tailed" tests) and nondirectional tests (also called "two-tailed" tests). In a nondirectional test you are testing simply to see if the groups differ from each other; in a directional test you are testing to see if one group has done better (or worse). In this appendix we have tested all hypotheses as if they were nondirectional because we believe it is rare in psychology that an investigator knows a priori that a difference can *only* occur in one direction. Any introductory statistics textbook can be consulted if you need further information concerning the rationale and procedures for one-tailed tests. Table A-5 in this appendix is for nondirectional tests.

4 Compute $\Sigma X_c^2 = 16^2 + 15^2 + 12^2 + 12^2 + 14^2 + 15^2 = 256 + 225$

$+ 144 + 144 + 196 + 225 = 1,190$

5 Compute $SS_e = \Sigma X_e^2 - \dfrac{(\Sigma X_e)^2}{n_e} = 1,326 - \dfrac{(72)^2}{4} = 1,326 - \dfrac{5,184}{4}$

$= 1,326 - 1,296 = 30$

6 Compute $SS_c = \Sigma X_c^2 - \dfrac{(\Sigma X_c)^2}{n_c} = 1,190 - \dfrac{(84)^2}{6} = 1,190 - \dfrac{7,056}{6}$

$= 1,190 - 1,176 = 14$

7 Compute pooled $s^2 = \dfrac{SS_e + SS_c}{n_e + n_c - 2} = \dfrac{30 + 14}{4 + 6 - 2} = \dfrac{44}{8} = 5.50$

8 Compute $s_{\bar{X}_e - \bar{X}_c} = \sqrt{\dfrac{s^2}{n_e} + \dfrac{s^2}{n_c}}$

$= \sqrt{\dfrac{5.50}{4} + \dfrac{5.50}{6}} = \sqrt{1.38 + .92} = \sqrt{2.30} = 1.52$

9 Compute $t = \dfrac{\bar{X}_e - \bar{X}_c}{s_{\bar{X}_e - \bar{X}_c}} = \dfrac{18 - 14}{1.52} = \dfrac{4}{1.52} = 2.63$

10 Determine degrees of freedom for $t = n_e + n_c - 2 = 4 + 6 - 2 = 8$

11 Use Table A.5 to determine critical value for t with 8 degrees of freedom and $\alpha = .5$

$$t(8)_{\alpha = .05} = 2.31$$

12 Compare the *absolute value* of your obtained t value to the tabled value.
  a If the absolute value of your obtained t is larger than the tabled value, then the two sampled means represent two different populations. That is, the mean difference is statistically significantly larger than zero.
  b If the absolute value of your obtained t is smaller than the tabled value, then the two sample means represent the same population. That is, the mean difference is *not* statistically significantly larger than zero.

13 Our outcome conforms to step 12a, so we would conclude that the experimental group did better.

DIRECT DIFFERENCE *t*-TEST

The direct difference *t*-test is used to determine the statistical significance of a mean difference in two-condition experiments in which each subject has participated in both conditions. The direct difference *t*-test is applicable, therefore, to the analysis of complete and incomplete within-subjects design experiments involving two conditions. The procedures for data reduction in these two designs are described in Chapter 6; in this appendix we will assume that these procedures have been completed successfully, and we will present the data for our computational example in its final tabular form.

The following data represent the scores for six subjects, each of whom was tested under the experimental and control conditions in a within-subjects design. The higher the score, the better the subject's performance.

| Subject | Condition | | D |
	Experimental	Control	
1	80	60	20
2	90	75	15
3	65	75	−10
4	95	75	20
5	85	60	25
6	75	55	20

1 Compute a difference score (D) for each subject (see table). Be sure to compute the difference in the same direction for each subject and retain the sign of the difference score.

2 Compute $\Sigma D = 20 + 15 + (-10) + 20 + 25 + 20 = 90$

3 Compute $\overline{D} = \dfrac{\Sigma D}{n} = \dfrac{90}{6} = 15.0$

4 Compute $\Sigma D^2 = 20^2 + 15^2 + (-10)^2 + 20^2 + 25^2 + 20^2$
$$= 400 + 225 + 100 + 400 + 625 + 400$$
$$= 2{,}150$$

5 Compute $s_D = \sqrt{\dfrac{\Sigma D^2 - \dfrac{(\Sigma D)^2}{n}}{n-1}}$

$$= \sqrt{\dfrac{2{,}150 - \dfrac{(90)^2}{6}}{6-1}} = \sqrt{\dfrac{2{,}150 - \dfrac{8{,}100}{6}}{5}} = \sqrt{\dfrac{2{,}150 - 1{,}350}{5}}$$

$$= \sqrt{\dfrac{800}{5}} = \sqrt{160} = 12.65$$

6 Compute $s_{\overline{D}} = \dfrac{s_D}{\sqrt{n}} = \dfrac{12.65}{\sqrt{6}} = \dfrac{12.65}{2.45} = 5.16$

7 Compute $t = \dfrac{\overline{D}}{s_{\overline{D}}} = \dfrac{15.0}{5.16} = 2.91$

8 Determine degrees of freedom for t: $(n-1) = 6 - 1 = 5$

9 Use Table A.5 to determine critical value for t with 5 degrees of freedom and $\alpha = .05$

$$t\,(5)_{\alpha\,=\,.05} = 2.57$$

10 Compare the *absolute value* of your obtained t value to the tabled value.

    a If the absolute value of your obtained t is larger than the tabled value, then the mean difference (D) is statistically significantly larger than zero.

    b If the absolute value of your obtained t is smaller than the tabled value, then the mean difference (D) is *not* statistically significantly larger than zero.

11 Our result conforms to step 10a, and so we conclude that the experimental group did better.

SINGLE-FACTOR ANALYSIS OF VARIANCE FOR INDEPENDENT GROUPS DESIGNS

The single-factor analysis of variance for independent groups designs is used to analyze the results of random groups and natural groups designs involving one independent variable with two or more levels. The logic of this statistical test is described in detail in Chapter 5. In this appendix we will focus entirely on the computational procedures necessary to carry out the analysis. We will first describe the procedures for computing an omnibus F-test, and we will then describe the procedures for developing the coefficients for analytical comparisons and for computing the F-ratio necessary to test the statistical significance of the comparison. We will consider only the case when all groups in the experiment are the same size.

The data in the following table represent the number of words correctly identified (out of a possible twenty) on a vocabulary test. Five subjects were randomly assigned to each of four groups (defined by the method of study that subjects were instructed to use to learn the words in preparation for the vocabulary test). The control method involved no specific instructions, but in the three experimental methods subjects were instructed either to study a synonym of the to-be-learned word (synonym method), or a dictionary definition of the to-be-learned word (dictionary method), or a literary passage in which the to-be-learned word was used in context (passage method). The independent variable being manipulated is instruction, and it can be symbolized by the letter A. The levels of this independent variable can be differentiated by using the symbols a_1, a_2, a_3, and a_4 for the four respective groups. The number of subjects within each group is referred to as n; in this case, n = 5. The total number of subjects in the experiment is symbolized as N; in this case, N = 20. Finally, the number of groups is referred to as a; in this case, a = 4.

Instruction (A)							
Subject	Control (a_1)	Subject	Synonym (a_2)	Subject	Definition (a_3)	Subject	Passage (a_4)
1	12	6	15	11	16	16	14
2	10	7	14	12	16	17	14
3	9	8	13	13	13	18	15
4	11	9	12	14	12	19	12
5	8	10	12	15	15	20	12

1 Complete the following table by computing ΣX, ΣX^2, $\overline{X}$, and $SS = \Sigma X^2 - \dfrac{(\Sigma X)^2}{n}$ in each group.

Subject	Control (a_1)	Synonym (a_2)	Definition (a_3)	Passage (a_4)
ΣX	50	66	72	67
ΣX^2	510	878	1,050	905
$\overline{X}$	10.0	13.2	14.4	13.4
SS	10.0	6.8	13.2	7.2

2 Compute $SS_{total} = \Sigma X^2 - \dfrac{(\Sigma X)^2}{N}$, where N = total number of subjects. (For the SS_{total}, you accumulate the ΣX^2 and ΣX across all four groups.)

$$= (510 + 878 + 1,050 + 905)$$
$$- \frac{(50 + 66 + 72 + 67)^2}{20}$$
$$= 3343 - \frac{(255)^2}{20}$$
$$= 3,343 - 3,251.25 = 91.75$$

3 Compute $SS_{WG} = SS_{a_1} + SS_{a_2} + SS_{a_3} + SS_{a_4}$
$$= 10.0 + 6.8 + 13.2 + 7.2$$
$$= 37.20$$

4 Compute $SS_{BG} = \dfrac{(\Sigma X_{a_1})^2 + (\Sigma X_{a_2})^2 + (\Sigma X_{a_3})^2 + (\Sigma X_{a_4})^2}{n} - \dfrac{(\Sigma X)^2}{N}$
$$= \frac{50^2 + 66^2 + 72^2 + 67^2}{5} - \frac{(255)^2}{20}$$
$$= \frac{16,529}{5} - 3,251.25$$
$$= 3,305.8 - 3,251.25 = 54.55$$

5 Carry out computational check: $SS_{total} = SS_{BG} + SS_{WG}$
$$91.75 = 54.55 + 37.20$$

6 Compute degrees of freedom $BG = a - 1$
$$= 4 - 1 = 3$$

7 Compute $MS_{BG} = \dfrac{SS_{BG}}{df_{BG}} = \dfrac{54.55}{3} = 18.18$

8 Compute degrees of freedom $WG = a(n - 1)$
$$= 4(5 - 1)$$
$$= (4)(4)$$
$$= 16$$

9 Compute $MS_{WG} = \dfrac{SS_{WG}}{df_{WG}} = \dfrac{37.20}{16} = 2.33$

10 Compute omnibus $F(3, 16) = \dfrac{MS_{BG}}{MS_{WG}} = \dfrac{18.18}{2.33} = 7.80$

11 Use Table A.6 to determine critical value of $F(df_{BG}, df_{WG})$ for $\alpha = .05$

$$F(3, 16)_{\alpha = .05} = 3.24$$

12 Compare your obtained F with the tabled F.
   a If the obtained F is greater than the tabled F, then the overall effect of the independent variable is statistically significant.
   b If the obtained F is less than the tabled F, then the overall effect of the independent variable is *not* statistically significant.

13 Our outcome conforms to step 12a, so we conclude that the methods had an effect on the number of recalled words.

Having completed the omnibus F-test we now know that something happened in the experiment—the overall effect of the independent variable was statistically significant. We are now in a position to carry out analytical comparisons to determine the source of the overall effect. We will illustrate the procedure for doing analytical comparisons by carrying out only one comparison; typically a small set of comparisons would be required to locate the sources of systematic variation in a single-factor experiment (see Chapter 5). The analytical comparison we will use as an example will involve a comparison of the control method to the average of the three experimental methods.

STEPS IN DEVELOPING COEFFICIENTS FOR ANALYTICAL COMPARISON

1 State hypothesis in words: Compare control method to average of three experimental methods.

2 State null hypothesis for comparison: $\mu_{a_1} = \dfrac{\mu_{a_2} + \mu_{a_3} + \mu_{a_4}}{3}$

3 Set null hypothesis statement equal to zero:

$$\mu_{a_1} - \left[\frac{\mu_{a_2} + \mu_{a_3} + \mu_{a_4}}{3}\right] = 0$$

4 Expand expression by taking minus sign inside brackets and isolating terms over common denominator:

$$\mu_{a_1} - \frac{\mu_{a_2}}{3} - \frac{\mu_{a_3}}{3} - \frac{\mu_{a_4}}{3} = 0$$

5 Eliminate fractions by multiplying expression by common denominator:

$$3\mu_{a_1} - \mu_{a_2} - \mu_{a_3} - \mu_{a_4} = 0$$

6 The coefficients for each group are the multipliers for each mean in this equation.

$$C_1 = +3$$
$$C_2 = -1$$
$$C_3 = -1$$
$$C_4 = -1$$

7 Computation check: The coefficients for an analytical comparison must sum to zero.

8 If a group is not included in a comparison, its coefficient is 0.

STEPS IN COMPUTING *F*-TEST FOR ANALYTICAL COMPARISON ONCE COEFFICIENTS HAVE BEEN DETERMINED

1 Compute $\Sigma c\overline{X}$ by multiplying coefficient for each group times the mean for that group and summing these products.

$$\begin{aligned}
\Sigma c\overline{X} &= (3)(10) + (-1)(13.2) + (-1)(14.4) + (-1)(13.4) \\
&= 30 - 13.2 - 14.4 - 13.4 \\
&= -11
\end{aligned}$$

2 Compute $(\Sigma c\overline{X})^2 = (-11)^2 = 121$

3 Compute $n(\Sigma c\overline{X})^2 = 5(121) = 605$

4 Compute $\Sigma c^2 = 3^2 + (-1)^2 + (-1)^2 + (-1)^2$
$$\begin{aligned}
&= 9 + 1 + 1 + 1 \\
&= 12
\end{aligned}$$

5 Compute $SS_{comparison} = \dfrac{n(\Sigma c\bar{X})^2}{\Sigma c^2} = \dfrac{\text{step 3}}{\text{step 4}} = \dfrac{605}{12} = 50.42$

6 Compute $MS_{comparison} = \dfrac{SS_{comparison}}{df_{comparison}} = \dfrac{50.42}{1} = 50.42$

> *Note:* The df for all analytical comparisons is 1, but it is important to remember that you must convert the $SS_{comparison}$ to an $MS_{comparison}$ before computing an *F*-ratio.

7 Compute $F_{comparison} = \dfrac{MS_{comparison}}{MS_{WG}} = \dfrac{50.42}{2.33} = 21.64$

> *Note:* The MS_{WG} is calculated in the omnibus *F*-test and is simply used again here. The degrees of freedom for the MS_{WG} are also the same as those determined for the omnibus *F*-test. Therefore, the degrees of freedom for the comparison *F*-test are 1 and 16.

8 Use Table A.6 to determine the critical value for $F(1, df_{WG})$ for $\alpha = .05$.

$$F(1, 16)_{\alpha = .05} = 4.49$$

9 Compare the *F* for your comparison with the tabled *F* value.
  a If the comparison *F* is larger than the tabled *F* value, then the analytical comparison resulted in statistically significant systematic variation.
  b If the comparison *F* is smaller than the tabled *F* value, then the analytical comparison did *not* result in statistically significant systematic variation.

10 Our outcome conforms to Step 9a, so we conclude that the control group recalled fewer words than the average of the three experimental groups.

SINGLE-FACTOR ANALYSIS OF VARIANCE FOR WITHIN-SUBJECTS DESIGNS

The single-factor analysis of variance for within-subjects designs is used to analyze the results of experiments involving one independent variable with two or more levels. The logic of this statistical test is described in detail in Chapter 6. In fact, the data we will use to illustrate the computations are those included in Table 6.5 in the text. The computations for the omnibus *F*-test for the analysis of within-subjects designs are sufficiently different from those necessary for the analysis of independent groups designs to warrant a full description here. The procedures for analytical comparisons in the within-subjects designs and the independent groups designs are so similar, however, that only the few differences between them will be highlighted in this section of the appendix.

The data presented in the following table represent the median time judgments by each of five subjects in a complete within-subjects design. The independent variable was the actual length of a time interval, and it was manipulated at four levels (12, 24, 36, and 48 seconds). The subjects' judgments are their median estimates of the length of the interval, based upon six presentations of each interval length. The independent variable, interval length, will be referred to as A, with the four levels referred to as a_1, a_2, a_3, and a_4, respectively. The far-right column of the table represents the total estimates for each subject across the four intervals, and these values will be referred to as the *subject totals* (S_1, S_2, etc.).

	Interval length (A)				
Subject	12 (a_1)	24 (a_2)	36 (a_3)	48 (a_4)	Subject totals (S)
1	13	21	30	38	102
2	10	15	38	35	98
3	12	23	31	32	98
4	12	15	22	32	81
5	16	36	69	60	181
ΣX	63	110	190	197	n = 5
ΣX^2	813	2,716	8,550	8,317	
$\overline{X}$	12.6	22.0	38.0	39.4	N = 20

1 Compute ΣX, ΣX^2, and $\overline{X}$ for each level of A. (See table above.)

2 Compute $SS_{total} = \Sigma X^2 - \dfrac{(\Sigma X)^2}{N}$, where N = total number of *scores*

$$= (813 + 2{,}716 + 8{,}550 + 8{,}317) - \frac{(63 + 110 + 190 + 197)^2}{20}$$

$$= 20{,}396 - \frac{(560)^2}{20}$$

$$= 20{,}396 - 15{,}680 = 4{,}716$$

3 Compute $SS_A = \dfrac{(\Sigma X_{a_1})^2 + (\Sigma X_{a_2})^2 + (\Sigma X_{a_3})^2 + (\Sigma X_{a_4})^2}{n} - \dfrac{(\Sigma X)^2}{N}$

$$= \frac{(63)^2 + (110)^2 + (190)^2 + (197)^2}{5} - \frac{(560)^2}{20}$$

$$= \frac{3{,}969 + 12{,}100 + 36{,}100 + 38{,}809}{5} - \frac{(560)^2}{20}$$

$$= \frac{90{,}978}{5} - 15{,}680$$

$$= 18{,}195.60 - 15{,}680 = 2{,}515.60$$

4 Compute

$$SS_s = \frac{(S_1^2 + S_2^2 + S_3^2 + S_4^2 + S_5^2)}{a} - \frac{(\Sigma X)^2}{N}$$

$$= \frac{102^2 + 98^2 + 98^2 + 81^2 + 181^2}{4} - \frac{(560)^2}{20}$$

$$= \frac{10{,}404 + 9{,}604 + 9{,}604 + 6{,}561 + 32{,}761}{4} - 15{,}680$$

$$= \frac{68{,}934}{4} - 15{,}680$$

$$= 17{,}233.50 - 15{,}680 = 1{,}553.50$$

5 Compute $SS_{Residual} = SS_{total} - SS_A - SS_s$
$$= \text{step } 1 - \text{step } 3 - \text{step } 4$$
$$= 4{,}716 - 2{,}515.60 - 1{,}553.50$$
$$= 646.90$$

6 Compute degrees of freedom for $A = a - 1$
$$= 4 - 1 = 3$$

7 Compute degrees of freedom total $= N - 1$
$$= 20 - 1 = 19$$

8 Compute degrees of freedom for subjects $= n - 1$
$$= 5 - 1 = 4$$

9 Compute degrees of freedom for Residual $= df_{total} - df_A - df_s$
$$= 19 - 3 - 4$$
$$= 12$$

10 Compute $MS_A = \dfrac{SS_A}{df_A} = \dfrac{2{,}515.6}{3} = 838.53$

11 Compute $MS_{Residual} = \dfrac{SS_{Residual}}{df_{Residual}} = \dfrac{646.90}{12} = 53.91$

12 Compute omnibus F-test for effect of A:

$$F(3, 12) - \frac{MS_A}{MS_{Residual}} = \frac{838.53}{53.91} = 15.6$$

13 Use Table A.6 to determine the critical value of $F(df_A, df_{Residual})$ for $\alpha = .05$. $F(3, 12)_{\alpha = .05} = 3.49$

14 Compare the obtained F with the tabled F.
 a If the obtained F is greater than the tabled F, then the overall effect of variable A is statistically significant.
 b If the obtained F is less than the tabled F, then the overall effect of variable A is not statistically significant.

15 Our outcome conforms to step 13a, so we conclude that the subjects' estimates were influenced by the length of the actual interval.

The procedures for developing coefficients for analytical comparisons following the omnibus F-test in within-subjects designs are identical to those used for independent groups designs. These procedures are described in this appendix under the single-factor analysis of variance for independent groups. The computation of the $SS_{comparison}$ is also identical for the within-subjects and independent groups designs. The F-test for an analytical comparison in the within-subjects design differs from that in the independent groups design. The MS Residual is used as the denominator of the F-ratio for the analytical comparison in the within-subject designs.

TWO-FACTOR ANALYSIS OF VARIANCE FOR INDEPENDENT GROUPS DESIGNS

The two-factor analysis of variance for independent groups designs is used for the analysis of experiments in which each of two independent variables has been manipulated at at least two levels. The logic of complex designs with two independent variables and the conceptual basis for the analysis of these experiments are described in Chapter 7. We will focus in this appendix on the computational procedures for the omnibus analysis of a complex design which involves an F-test for the main effect of A, the main effect of B, and the interaction effect, A × B. Our example will involve a significant A × B interaction, and so we will also describe the computations for simple main effects to track down the source of the interaction effect. The two-factor analysis for independent groups is applicable to experiments in which both independent variables are manipulated using a random groups design, in which both independent variables represent the natural groups design, and in which one independent variable represents the natural groups design and the other represents the random groups design. This last case is technically a "mixed design," but for purposes of analysis both independent variables represent the independent groups design. In the last section of this appendix we will describe the computations for a mixed design in which one independent variable represents an independent groups design and the second independent variable represents a within-subjects design.

The data in the following table represent the number of correct responses on a simple motor learning task as a function of two independent variables. The first independent variable was the hand the subject used to perform the task, and the two levels of this variable were the dominant and the nondominant hand. The second independent variable was the delay (in seconds) between successive trials on the task, and it was manipulated at three levels (0, 30, and 60 seconds). The hand variable will be referred to as A, with the dominant hand being a_1, and the nondominant hand being a_2. The delay variable will be referred to as B with the 0-second delay as b_1, the 30-second delay as b_2, and the 60-second delay as b_3. Five subjects were randomly assigned to each of the six groups resulting from the factorial combination of the two independent variables.

Hand Dominance (Variable A) × Delay Interval (Variable B)

Group 1		Group 2		Group 3	
Subject	a_1b_1	Subject	a_1b_2	Subject	a_1b_3
1	18	6	17	11	18
2	17	7	19	12	20
3	19	8	22	13	21
4	21	9	20	14	22
5	20	10	17	15	19

Group 4		Group 5		Group 6	
Subject	a_2b_1	Subject	a_2b_2	Subject	a_2b_3
16	9	21	15	26	16
17	11	22	17	27	19
18	10	23	16	28	18
19	11	24	17	29	20
20	12	25	14	30	18

1 Complete the following table for the AB matrix.

		Delay Interval		
		b_1	b_2	b_3
Dominant hand (a_1)	ΣX	95	95	100
	ΣX^2	1815	1823	2010
	$\overline{X}$	19.0	19.0	20.0
	SS	10.0	18.0	10.0
Nondominant hand (a_2)	ΣX	53	79	91
	ΣX^2	567	1255	1665
	$\overline{X}$	10.6	15.8	18.2
	SS	5.2	6.8	8.8

Just to be sure the procedures for completing the table for the AB matrix are clear, we will illustrate them more fully for the a_1b_1 cell (0-seconds, dominant hand). Note that n = number of subjects in each ab cell.

$$\Sigma X_{a_1b_1} = 18 + 17 + 19 + 21 + 20 = 95$$

$$\Sigma X^2_{a_1b_1} = 18^2 + 17^2 + 19^2 + 21^2 + 20^2 = 1{,}815$$

$$\overline{X}_{a_1b_1} = \frac{\Sigma X}{n} = \frac{95}{5} = 19.0$$

$$SS_{a_1b_1} = \Sigma X^2_{a_1b_1} - \frac{(\Sigma X_{a_1b_1})^2}{n}$$

$$= 1{,}815 - \frac{(95)^2}{5}$$

$$= 1{,}815 - \frac{9{,}025}{5} = 1{,}815 - 1{,}805 = 10.0$$

2 Compute SS_{total} by accumulating ΣX^2 and ΣX across all cells of the AB matrix and applying the formula (where N = total number of subjects)

$$SS_{total} = \Sigma X^2 - \frac{(\Sigma X)^2}{N}$$

$$= (1{,}815 + 1{,}823 + 2{,}010 + 567 + 1{,}255 + 1{,}665)$$

$$- \frac{[95 + 95 + 100 + 53 + 79 + 91]^2}{30}$$

$$= 9{,}135 - \frac{(513)^2}{30}$$

$$= 9{,}135 - 8{,}772.3 = 362.70$$

3 Compute $SS_{WG} = SS_{a_1b_1} + SS_{a_1b_2} + SS_{a_1b_3} + SS_{a_2b_1} + SS_{a_2b_2} + SS_{a_2b_3}$

$$= 10.0 + 18.0 + 10.0 + 5.2 + 6.8 + 8.8$$

$$= 58.80$$

4 Compute $SS_{BG} =$

$$\frac{(\Sigma X_{a_1b_1})^2 + (\Sigma X_{a_1b_2})^2 + (\Sigma X_{a_1b_3})^2 + (\Sigma X_{a_2b_1})^2 + (\Sigma X_{a_2b_2})^2 + (\Sigma X_{a_2b_3})^2}{n}$$

$$- \frac{(\Sigma X)^2}{N}$$

$$= \frac{95^2 + 95^2 + 100^2 + 53^2 + 79^2 + 91^2}{5} - \frac{(513)^2}{30}$$

$$= \frac{9{,}025 + 9{,}025 + 10{,}000 + 2{,}809 + 6{,}241 + 8{,}281}{5} - \frac{(513)^2}{30}$$

$$= \frac{45{,}381}{5} - 8{,}772.3$$

$$= 9{,}076.20 - 8{,}772.3 = 303.90$$

5 Compute $SS_A =$

$$\frac{(\Sigma X_{a_1b_1} + \Sigma X_{a_1b_2} + \Sigma X_{a_1b_3})^2 + (\Sigma X_{a_2b_1} + \Sigma X_{a_2b_2} + \Sigma X_{a_2b_3})^2}{(b)(n)}$$

$$- \frac{(\Sigma X)^2}{N}$$

$$= \frac{(95 + 95 + 100)^2 + (53 + 79 + 91)^2}{(3)(5)} - \frac{(513)^2}{30}$$

$$= \frac{(290)^2 + (223)^2}{15} - \frac{(513)^2}{30}$$

$$= \frac{84,100 + 49,729}{15} - 8,772.3$$

$$= \frac{133,829}{15} - 8,772.3$$

$$= 8,921.93 - 8,772.3 = 149.63$$

6 Compute $SS_B =$

$$\frac{(\Sigma X_{a_1 b_1} + \Sigma X_{a_2 b_1})^2 + (\Sigma X_{a_1 b_2} + \Sigma X_{a_2 b_2})^2 + (\Sigma X_{a_1 b_3} + \Sigma X_{a_2 b_3})^2}{(a)(n)}$$

$$- \frac{(\Sigma X)^2}{N}$$

$$= \frac{(95 + 53)^2 + (95 + 79)^2 + (100 + 91)^2}{(2)(5)} - \frac{(513)^2}{30}$$

$$= \frac{(148)^2 + (174)^2 + (191)^2}{10} - 8,772.3$$

$$= \frac{21,904 + 30,276 + 36,481}{10} - 8,772.3$$

$$= 8,866.1 - 8,772.3 = 93.80$$

7 Compute $SS_{A \times B} = SS_{BG} - SS_A - SS_B$

$$= 303.90 - 149.63 - 93.80$$

$$= 60.47$$

8 Compute $df_A = a - 1 = 2 - 1 = 1$

9 Compute $df_B = b - 1 = 3 - 1 = 2$

10 Compute $df_{A \times B} = (a - 1)(b - 1) = (2 - 1)(3 - 1) = (1)(2) = 2$

11 Compute $df_{WG} = (a)(b)(n - 1) = (2)(3)(5 - 1) = (2)(3)(4) = 24$

12 Compute $MS_{WG} = \dfrac{SS_{WG}}{df_{WG}} = \dfrac{58.80}{24} = 2.45$

13 Compute $MS_A = \dfrac{SS_A}{df_A} = \dfrac{149.63}{1} = 149.63$

14 Compute $F(df_A, df_{WG})$ for main effect of A:

$$F(1, 24) = \frac{MS_A}{MS_{WG}} = \frac{149.63}{2.45} = 61.07$$

15 Compute $MS_B = \dfrac{SS_B}{df_B} = \dfrac{93.80}{2} = 46.90$

16 Compute $F\,(df_B, df_{WG})$ for main effect of B:

$$F\,(2,\ 24) = \frac{MS_B}{MS_{WG}} = \frac{46.90}{2.45} = 19.14$$

17 Compute $MS_{A \times B} = \dfrac{SS_{A \times B}}{df_{A \times B}} = \dfrac{60.47}{2} = 30.24$

18 Compute $F\,(df_{A \times B}, df_{WG})$ for the interaction effect A $\times$ B:

$$F(2,\ 24) = \frac{MS_{A \times B}}{MS_{WG}} = \frac{30.24}{2.45} = 12.34$$

19 Use Table A.6 to determine critical values for F(1, 24) for $\alpha = .05$ and $F\,(2, 24)$ for $\alpha = .05$

$$F\,(1,\ 24)_{\alpha\,=\,.05} = 4.26 \qquad F\,(2,\ 24)_{\alpha\,=\,.05} = 3.40$$

20 Compare obtained F for main effect of A to tabled value for $F\,(1,\ 24)_{\alpha\,=\,.05}$ and compare obtained F for main effect of B and for interaction effect, A $\times$ B to tabled value for $F\,(2,\ 24)_{\alpha\,=\,.05}$. As usual, if obtained F is greater than tabled F, then the effect for that obtained F is statistically significant. If the obtained F is less than the corresponding tabled value, then the effect for that obtained F is not statistically significant. Because in our example the F for the A $\times$ B interaction was statistically significant, it is necessary to carry out an analysis of simple main effects. Because we expected in this experiment to find no effect of the delay with the dominant hand and an effect of delay for the nondominant hand, we will compute the effects of delay interval (B) at each level of the hand variable (a_1 and a_2).

COMPUTATION OF SIMPLE MAIN EFFECTS OF VARIABLE B AT EACH LEVEL OF VARIABLE A

1 The data for the computations that follow are included in the AB matrix for the two-factor analysis of variance for independent groups. The MS_{WG} used as the denominator of the F-ratio for the simple main effects comes from the omnibus analysis.

2 Simple main effect of B at a_1 (B/a_1).

   a Compute $SS_{B/a_1} =$

$$\frac{[(\Sigma X_{a_1 b_1})^2 + (\Sigma X_{a_1 b_2})^2 + (\Sigma X_{a_1 b_3})^2]}{n} - \frac{(\Sigma X_{a_1 b_1} + \Sigma X_{a_1 b_2} + \Sigma X_{a_1 b_3})^2}{(b)(n)}$$

$$= \frac{95^2 + 95^2 + 100^2}{5} - \frac{(95 + 95 + 100)^2}{(3)(5)}$$

$$= \frac{9{,}025 + 9{,}025 + 10{,}000}{5} - \frac{(290)^2}{15}$$

$$= \frac{28{,}050}{5} - \frac{84{,}100}{15}$$

$$= 5{,}610.00 - 5{,}606.67 = 3.33$$

b Compute $df_{B/a_1} = b - 1 = 3 - 1 = 2$

c Compute $MS_{B/a_1} = \dfrac{SS_{B/a_1}}{df_{B/a_1}} = \dfrac{3.33}{2} = 1.67$

d Compute $F\,(df_{B/a_1},\ df_{WG}) = \dfrac{MS_{B/a_1}}{MS_{WG}} = \dfrac{1.67}{2.45} = .68$

e Use Table A.6 to determine critical value for $F\,(df_{B/a_1},\ df_{WG})$ for $\alpha = .05$.

$$F\,(2,\ 24)_{\alpha = .05} = 3.40$$

f Compare obtained F for simple main effect of B/a_1 to tabled value. The obtained F is less than the tabled F, so the simple main effect of B/a_1 was not statistically significant. The delay had no effect when subjects used their dominant hand.

3 Simple main effect of B at a_2 (B/a_2).

a Compute $SS_{B/a_2} = \dfrac{(\Sigma X_{a_2b_1})^2 + (\Sigma X_{a_2b_2})^2 + (\Sigma X_{a_2b_3})^2}{n}$

$$- \frac{(\Sigma X_{a_2b_1} + \Sigma X_{a_2b_2} + \Sigma X_{a_2b_3})^2}{(b)(n)}$$

$$= \frac{(53)^2 + (79)^2 + (91)^2}{5} - \frac{(53 + 79 + 91)^2}{(3)(5)}$$

$$= \frac{2{,}809 + 6{,}241 + 8{,}281}{5} - \frac{(223)^2}{15}$$

$$= \frac{17{,}331}{5} - \frac{49{,}729}{15}$$

$$= 3{,}466.20 - 3{,}315.27 = 150.93$$

b Compute $df_{B/a_2} = b - 1 = 3 - 1 = 2$

c Compute $MS_{B/a_2} = \dfrac{SS_{B/a_2}}{df_{B/a_2}} = \dfrac{150.93}{2} = 75.47$

d Compute $F\,(df_{B/a_2},\ df_{WG}) = \dfrac{MS_{B/a_2}}{MS_{WG}} = \dfrac{75.47}{2.45} = 30.80$

e Use previously determined critical value for $F\,(2, 24)_{\alpha = .05} = 3.40$ to compare to obtained F.

f The obtained F for the simple main effect of B/a_2 is larger than the tabled value, so the simple main effect of B/a_2 was statistically significant. The delay had an effect when subjects used the nondominant hand.

g The significant simple main effect of B/a_2 could be followed up with simple comparisons. The computation is the same as that for analytical comparisons in the one-factor analysis of variance (ANOVA) for independent groups but coefficients are developed only for the b_1, b_2, and b_3 means at level a_2. See Chapter 7 for a discussion of the logic of these comparisons.

TWO-FACTOR ANALYSIS OF VARIANCE FOR MIXED DESIGN

The two-factor analysis of variance for mixed design is appropriate when one independent variable represents either the random groups or natural groups design and the second independent variable represents the within-subjects design. The first independent variable is called the *between-subjects factor* and is symbolized as A. The second independent variable is called the within-subjects factor and is symbolized as B. The two-factor analysis for mixed design is somewhat of a hybrid of the single-factor analysis for independent groups and the single-factor analysis for the within-subjects designs. Thus, it might prove useful to review the computations for those two analyses before beginning this one.

The data presented in the following table represent the mean frequency judgments subjects gave to four brief segments of popular songs. The subjects listened to a tape including several songs; half the subjects did not expect the frequency judgment test (incidental group), and half did expect the test (intentional group). In addition, all subjects judged songs that had been presented either one, two, or three times. Thus, the experiment was a 2×3 design in which instructions were manipulated in a random groups design with five subjects assigned to each of two groups and in which the presented frequency variable was manipulated in a complete within-subjects design. The data matrix, showing mean frequency judgments at three levels of presentation frequency for each subject, and a few preliminary computations are as follows.

	Subject	Presentation Frequency (B)			Subject total
		$1(b_1)$	$2(b_2)$	$3(b_3)$	
	1	1.2	2.2	3.0	6.4
	2	.8	2.0	3.2	6.0
	3	1.2	1.8	2.8	5.8
Incidental	4	1.5	2.0	2.5	6.0
group (a_1)	5	1.2	2.5	3.2	6.9
	ΣX	5.9	10.5	14.7	
	ΣX^2	7.2	22.3	43.6	
	$\overline{X}$	1.2	2.1	2.9	
	6	1.2	1.5	2.0	4.7
	7	1.0	2.0	2.5	5.5
	8	1.0	1.2	3.2	5.4
Intentional	9	1.2	2.2	2.8	6.2
group (a_2)	10	1.0	2.2	3.5	6.7
	ΣX	5.4	9.1	14.0	
	ΣX^2	5.9	17.4	40.6	
	$\overline{X}$	1.1	1.8	2.8	

Note that n = 5, or the number of subjects in each level of the between-subjects factor.

1 Compute $SS_{total} = \Sigma X^2 - \dfrac{(\Sigma X)^2}{N}$ where N = total number of *scores*

$$= (7.2 + 22.3 + 43.6 + 5.9 + 17.4 + 40.6)$$

$$- \frac{(5.9 + 10.5 + 14.7 + 5.4 + 9.1 + 14.0)^2}{30}$$

$$= 137 - \frac{(59.6)^2}{30}$$

$$= 137 - \frac{(3,552.16)}{30}$$

$$= 137 - 118.40 = 18.60$$

2 Compute $SS_{subjects} =$

$$\frac{S_1{}^2 + S_2{}^2 + S_3{}^2 + S_4{}^2 + S_5{}^2 + S_6{}^2 + S_7{}^2 + S_8{}^2 + S_9{}^2 + S_{10}{}^2}{b} - \frac{(\Sigma X)^2}{N}$$

$$= \frac{6.4^2 + 6.0^2 + 5.8^2 + 6.0^2 + 6.9^2 + 4.7^2 + 5.5^2 + 5.4^2 + 6.2^2 + 6.7^2}{3}$$

$$- \frac{(59.6)^2}{30}$$

$$= \frac{40.96 + 36 + 33.64 + 36 + 47.61 + 22.09 + 30.25 + 29.16 + 38.44 + 44.89}{3}$$

$$- \frac{(59.6)^2}{30}$$

$$= \frac{359.04}{3} - 118.40$$

$$= 119.68 - 118.40 = 1.28$$

3 Compute SS_B =

$$\frac{(\Sigma X_{a_1b_1} + \Sigma X_{a_2b_1})^2 + (\Sigma X_{a_1b_2} + \Sigma X_{a_2b_2})^2 + (\Sigma X_{a_1b_3} + \Sigma X_{a_2b_2})^2}{(a)(n)} - \frac{(\Sigma X)^2}{N}$$

$$= \frac{(5.9 + 5.4)^2 + (10.5 + 9.1)^2 + (14.7 + 14.0)^2}{(2)(5)} - \frac{(59.6)^2}{30}$$

$$= \frac{11.3^2 + 19.6^2 + 28.7^2}{10} - 118.40$$

$$= \frac{127.69 + 384.16 + 823.69}{10} - 118.40$$

$$= \frac{1{,}335.54}{10} - 118.40$$

$$= 133.55 - 118.40 = 15.15$$

4 Compute $SS_{S \times B} = SS_{total} - SS_S - SS_B$
$$= 18.60 - 1.28 - 15.15$$
$$= 2.17$$

5 Compute SS_A =

$$\frac{(\Sigma X_{a_1b_1} + \Sigma X_{a_1b_2} + \Sigma X_{a_1b_3})^2 + (\Sigma X_{a_2b_1} + \Sigma X_{a_2b_2} + \Sigma X_{a_2b_3})^2}{(b)(n)}$$

$$- \frac{(\Sigma X)^2}{N}$$

$$= \frac{(5.9 + 10.5 + 14.7)^2 + (5.4 + 9.1 + 14.0)^2}{(3)(5)} - \frac{(59.6)^2}{30}$$

$$= \frac{31.1^2 + 28.5^2}{15} - 118.40$$

$$= \frac{967.21 + 812.25}{15} - 118.40$$

$$= \frac{1{,}779.46}{15} - 118.40$$

$$= 118.63 - 118.40 = .23$$

6 Compute $SS_{S/A} = SS_{subjects} - SS_A = 1.28 - .23 = 1.05$

7 Compute $SS_{AB} =$

$$\frac{[(\Sigma X_{a_1b_1})^2 + (\Sigma X_{a_1b_2})^2 + (\Sigma X_{a_1b_3})^2 + (\Sigma X_{a_2b_1})^2 + (\Sigma X_{a_2b_2})^2 + (\Sigma X_{a_2b_3})^2]}{n} - \frac{(\Sigma X)^2}{N}$$

$$= \frac{5.9^2 + 10.5^2 + 14.7^2 + 5.4^2 + 9.1^2 + 14.0^2}{5} - \frac{(59.6)^2}{30}$$

$$= \frac{(34.81 + 110.25 + 216.09 + 29.16 + 82.81 + 196)}{5} - 118.40$$

$$= \frac{669.12}{5} - 118.40$$

$$= 133.82 - 118.40 = 15.42$$

8 Compute $SS_{A \times B} = SS_{AB} - SS_A - SS_B$
$$= 15.42 - .23 - 15.15$$
$$= .04$$

9 Compute $SS_{B \times S/A} = SS_{S \times B} - SS_{A \times B}$
$$= 2.17 - .04$$
$$= 2.13$$

10 Compute $df_A = a - 1 = 2 - 1 = 1$

11 Compute $df_{S/A} = a(n - 1) = 2(5 - 1) = 2(4) = 8$

12 Compute $df_B = b - 1 = 3 - 1 = 2$

13 Compute $df_{A \times B} = (a - 1)(b - 1) = (2 - 1)(3 - 1) = (1)(2) = 2$

14 Compute $df_{B \times S/A} = (b - 1)(a)(n - 1) = (3 - 1)(2)(5 - 1)$
$= (2)(2)(4) = 16$

15 Compute $MS_A = \frac{SS_A}{df_A} = \frac{.23}{1} = .23$

16 Compute $MS_{S/A} = \frac{SS_{S/A}}{df_{S/A}} = \frac{1.05}{8} = .13$

17 Compute $F(df_A, df_{S/A})$ for main effect of A:

$$F(1, 8) = \frac{MS_A}{MS_{S/A}} = \frac{.23}{.13} = 1.77$$

18 Compute $MS_B = \frac{SS_B}{df_B} = \frac{15.15}{2} = 7.58$

19 Compute $MS_{A \times B} = \frac{SS_{A \times B}}{df_{A \times B}} = \frac{.04}{2} = .02$

20 Compute $MS_{B \times S/A} = \dfrac{SS_{B \times S/A}}{df_{B \times S/A}} = \dfrac{2.13}{16} = .13$

21 Compute $F(df_B, df_{B \times S/A})$ for main effect of B:

$$F(2, 16) = \frac{MS_B}{MS_{B \times S/A}} = \frac{7.58}{.13} = 58.31$$

22 Compute $F(df_{A \times B}, df_{B \times S/A})$ for interaction effect A $\times$ B:

$$F(2, 16) = \frac{MS_{A \times B}}{MS_{B \times S/A}} = \frac{.02}{.13} = .15$$

23 Use Table A.6 to determine critical values of $F(1, 8)$ and $F(2, 16)$ at $\alpha = .05$ to compare to obtained F values with corresponding degrees of freedom.

$$F(1, 8)_{\alpha = .05} = 5.32 \qquad F(2, 16)_{\alpha = .05} = 3.63$$

24 Given the tabled critical values, only the main effect of B is statistically significant in this analysis because it is the only obtained F that is larger than the corresponding tabled F.

25 The significant main effect of presentation frequency (B) indicates that subjects' judged frequencies for the songs were influenced by the actual frequencies of their presentation.

26 The form of the Summary Table for the analysis of the two-factor mixed design is different from that of the two-factor design for independent groups. It is as follows:

Source of variation	df	SS	MS	F	p
Group (A)	1	0.23	0.23	1.77	> .05
S/A	8	1.05	0.13	—	—
Presentation frequency (B)	2	15.15	7.58	58.31	< .05
A $\times$ B	2	0.04	0.02	0.15	> .05
B $\times$ S/A	16	2.13	0.13	—	
Total	29	18.60			

27 The error term (denominator) for computing the F for the effect of Group is the MS S/A. For computing the F for both the main effect of B and the A $\times$ B interaction, the MS B $\times$ S/A is used. In fact, the MS B $\times$ S/A is used any time the effect being tested involves the within-subjects variable. For example, any simple main effects analysis of the A $\times$ B effect or analytical comparison of the effect of the B variable would be tested using the MS B $\times$ S/A. If the independent groups design variable has three or more levels, any analytical comparison would be tested using the error term involving only this variable, MS S/A.

STATISTICAL TABLES

TABLE A.1 TABLE OF RANDOM NUMBERS*

Col. Line	(1)	(2)	(3)	(4)	(5)	(6)	(7)	(8)	(9)	(10)	(11)	(12)	(13)	(14)
1	10480	15011	01536	02011	81647	91646	69179	14194	62590	36207	20969	99570	91291	90700
2	22368	46573	25595	85393	30995	89198	27982	53402	93965	34095	52666	19174	39615	99505
3	24130	48360	22527	97265	76393	64809	15179	24830	49340	32081	30680	19655	63348	58629
4	42167	93093	06243	61680	07856	16376	39440	53537	71341	57004	00849	74917	97758	16379
5	37570	39975	81837	16656	06121	91782	60468	81305	49684	60672	14110	06927	01263	54613
6	77921	06907	11008	42751	27756	53498	18602	70659	90655	15053	21916	81825	44394	42880
7	99562	72905	56420	69994	98872	31016	71194	18738	44013	48840	63213	21069	10634	12952
8	96301	91977	65463	07972	18876	20922	94595	56869	69014	60045	18425	84903	42508	32307
9	89579	14342	63661	10281	17453	18103	57740	84378	25331	12566	58678	44947	05585	56941
10	85475	36857	53342	53988	53060	59533	38867	62300	08158	17983	16439	11458	18593	64952
11	28918	69578	88231	33276	70997	79936	56865	05859	90106	31595	01547	85590	91610	78188
12	63553	40961	48235	03427	49626	69445	18663	72695	52180	20847	12234	90511	33703	90322
13	09429	93969	52636	92737	88974	33488	36320	17617	30015	08272	84115	27156	30613	74952
14	10365	61129	87529	85689	48237	52267	67689	93394	01511	26358	85104	20285	29975	89868
15	07119	97336	71048	08178	77233	13916	47564	81506	97735	85977	29372	74461	28551	90707
16	51085	12765	51821	51259	77452	16308	60756	92144	49442	53900	70960	63990	75601	40719
17	02368	21382	52404	60268	89368	19885	55322	44819	01188	65255	64835	44919	05944	55157
18	01011	54092	33362	94904	31273	04146	18594	29852	71585	85030	51132	01915	92747	64951
19	52162	53916	46369	58586	23216	14513	83149	98736	23495	64350	94738	17752	35156	35749
20	07056	97628	33787	09998	42698	06691	76988	13602	51851	46104	88916	19509	25625	58104
21	48663	91245	85828	14346	09172	30168	90229	04734	59193	22178	30421	61666	99904	32812
22	54164	58492	22421	74103	47070	25306	76468	26384	58151	06646	21524	15227	96909	44592
23	32639	32363	05597	24200	13363	38005	94342	28728	35806	06912	17012	64161	18296	22851
24	29334	27001	87637	87308	58731	00256	45834	15398	46557	41135	10367	07684	36188	18510
25	02488	33062	28834	07351	19731	92420	60952	61280	50001	67658	32586	86679	50720	94953
26	81525	72295	04839	96423	24878	82651	66566	14778	76797	14780	13300	87074	79666	95725
27	29676	20591	68086	26432	46901	20849	89768	81536	86645	12659	92259	57102	80428	25280
28	00742	57392	39064	66432	84673	40027	32832	61362	98947	96067	64760	64584	96096	98253
29	05366	04213	25669	26422	44407	44048	37937	63904	45766	66134	75470	66520	34693	90449
30	91921	26418	64117	94305	26766	25940	39972	22209	71500	64568	91402	42416	07844	69618
31	00582	04711	87917	77341	42206	35126	74087	99547	81817	42607	43808	76655	62028	76630
32	00725	69884	62797	56170	86324	88072	76222	36086	84637	93161	76038	65855	77919	88006
33	69011	65795	95876	55293	18988	27354	26575	08625	40801	59920	29841	80150	12777	48501
34	25976	57948	29888	88604	67917	48708	18912	82271	65424	69774	33611	54262	85963	03547
35	09763	83473	73577	12908	30883	18317	28290	35797	05998	41688	34952	37888	38917	88050
36	91567	42595	27958	30134	04024	86385	29880	99730	55536	84855	29080	09250	79656	73211
37	17955	56349	90999	49127	20044	59931	06115	20542	18059	02008	73708	83517	36103	42791

TABLE A.1 TABLE OF RANDOM NUMBERS* (*continued*)

Col. Line	(1)	(2)	(3)	(4)	(5)	(6)	(7)	(8)	(9)	(10)	(11)	(12)	(13)	(14)
38	46503	18584	18845	49618	02304	51038	20655	58727	28168	15475	56942	53389	20562	87338
39	92157	89634	94824	78171	84610	82834	09922	25417	44137	48413	25555	21246	35509	20468
40	14577	62765	35605	81263	39667	47358	56873	56307	61607	49518	89696	20103	77490	18062
41	98427	07523	33362	64270	01638	92477	66969	98420	04880	45585	46565	04102	46880	45709
42	34914	63976	88720	82765	34476	17032	87589	40836	32427	70002	70663	88863	77775	69348
43	70060	28277	39475	46473	23219	53416	94970	25832	69975	94884	19661	72828	00102	66794
44	53976	54914	06990	67245	68350	82948	11398	42878	80287	88267	47363	46634	06541	97809
45	76072	29515	40980	07391	58745	25774	22987	80059	39911	96189	41151	14222	60697	59583
46	90725	52210	83974	29992	65831	38857	50490	83765	55657	14361	31720	57375	56228	41546
47	64364	67412	33339	31926	14883	24413	59744	92351	97473	89286	35931	04110	23726	51900
48	08962	00358	31662	25388	61642	34072	81249	35648	56891	69352	48373	45578	78547	81788
49	95012	68379	93526	70765	10592	04542	76463	54328	02349	17247	28865	14777	62730	92277
50	15664	10493	20492	38391	91132	21999	59516	81652	27195	48223	46751	22923	32261	85653

Source: Table of 105,000 Random Decimal Digits, Statement no. 4914, File no.261-A-1, Interstate Commerce Commission, Washington, D.C., May 1949.

TABLE A.2 VALUES OF *r* AT THE .05 AND .01 LEVELS OF SIGNIFICANCE*

df	.05	.01	df	.05	.01	df	.05	.01
1	.997	1.000	16	.468	.590	35	.325	.418
2	.950	.990	17	.456	.575	40	.304	.393
3	.878	.959	18	.444	.561	45	.288	.372
4	.811	.917	19	.433	.549	50	.273	.354
5	.754	.874	20	.423	.537	60	.250	.325
6	.707	.834	21	.413	.526	70	.232	.302
7	.666	.798	22	.404	.515	80	.217	.283
8	.632	.765	23	.396	.505	90	.205	.267
9	.602	.735	24	.388	.496	100	.195	.254
10	.576	.708	25	.381	.487			
11	.553	.684	26	.374	.478			
12	.532	.661	27	.367	.470			
13	.514	.641	28	.361	.463			
14	.497	.623	29	.355	.456			
15	.482	.606	30	.349	.449			

*Adapted from Table VII of Fisher and Yates, *Statistical Tables for Biological, Agricultural, and Medical Research,* 6th ed., 1974. Published by Oliver and Boyd, Limited, Publishers, Edinburgh, by permission of the authors and publishers. Published by Longman Group Ltd., London.

TABLE A.3 VALUES OF RANK-ORDER CORRELATION COEFFICIENT (r_s) AT THE .05 AND .01 LEVELS OF SIGNIFICANCE*

N	.05	.01
5	1.000	—
6	.886	1.000
7	.786	.929
8	.715	.881
9	.700	.834
10	.649	.794
12	.588	.735
14	.539	.680
16	.503	.636
18	.474	.600
20	.447	.570
22	.426	.544
24	.407	.521
26	.391	.501
28	.376	.484
30	.363	.467

*Adapted from Table 1 (p. 385) of McCall, R. B. (1980). *Fundamental Statistics for Psychology,* 3d ed., Harcourt, Brace, Jovanovich. Reproduced by permission of publisher.

TABLE A.4 CRITICAL VALUES OF THE CHI SQUARE (χ^2) DISTRIBUTION*

Instructions for use: To find the critical value of χ^2, locate the row in the left-hand column of the table corresponding to the number of degrees of freedom (df) associated with χ^2, and select the value of χ^2 listed for the desired level of significance (α).

df	$\alpha = .05$	$\alpha = .01$	df	$\alpha = .05$	$\alpha = .01$
1	3.84	6.63	16	26.30	32.00
2	5.99	9.21	17	27.59	33.41
3	7.81	11.34	18	28.87	34.81
4	9.49	13.28	19	30.14	36.19
5	11.07	15.09	20	31.41	37.57
6	12.59	16.81	21	32.67	38.93
7	14.07	18.48	22	33.92	40.29
8	15.51	20.09	23	35.17	41.64
9	16.92	21.67	24	36.42	42.98
10	18.31	23.21	25	37.65	44.31
11	19.68	24.72	26	38.89	45.64
12	21.03	26.22	27	40.11	46.96
13	22.36	27.69	28	41.34	48.28
14	23.68	29.14	29	42.56	49.59
15	25.00	30.58	30	43.77	50.89

*This table is abridged from Table 8 in *Biometrika tables for statisticians,* vol. 1 (3d ed.), New York: Cambridge University Press, 1970, edited by E. S. Pearson and H. O. Hartley, by permission of the *Biometrika* Trustees.

TABLE A.5   SELECTED VALUES FROM THE *t* DISTRIBUTION*

Instructions for use: **To find a value of *t*, locate the row in the left-hand column of the table corresponding to the number of degrees of freedom (df) associated with the standard error of the mean, and select the value of *t* listed for your choice of α. The value given in the column labeled $\alpha = .05$ is used in the calculation of the 95 percent confidence interval, and the value given in the column labeled $\alpha = .01$ is used to calculate the 99 percent confidence interval.**

df	$\alpha = .05$	$\alpha = .01$	df	$\alpha = .05$	$\alpha = .01$
1	12.71	63.66	18	2.10	2.88
2	4.30	9.92	19	2.09	2.86
3	3.18	5.84	20	2.09	2.84
4	2.78	4.60	21	2.08	2.83
5	2.57	4.03	22	2.07	2.82
6	2.45	3.71	23	2.07	2.81
7	2.36	3.50	24	2.06	2.80
8	2.31	3.36	25	2.06	2.79
9	2.26	3.25	26	2.06	2.78
10	2.23	3.17	27	2.05	2.77
11	2.20	3.11	28	2.05	2.76
12	2.18	3.06	29	2.04	2.76
13	2.16	3.01	30	2.04	2.75
14	2.14	2.98	40	2.02	2.70
15	2.13	2.95	60	2.00	2.66
16	2.12	2.92	120	1.98	2.62
17	2.11	2.90	Infinity	1.96	2.58

*This table is adapted from Table 12 in *Biometrika tables for statisticians*, vol. 1 (3d ed.), New York: Cambridge University Press, 1970, edited by E. S. Pearson and H. O. Hartley, by permission of the *Biometrika* Trustees.

TABLE A.6 CRITICAL VALUES OF THE F-DISTRIBUTION*

Instructions for use: To find the critical value of F, locate the cell in the table formed by the intersection of the row containing the degrees of freedom associated with the denominator of the F-ratio and the column containing the degrees of freedom associated with the numerator of the F-ratio. The numbers listed in boldface type are the critical values of F at $\alpha = .05$; the numbers listed in Roman type are the critical values of F at $\alpha = .01$. As an example, suppose we have adopted the 5 percent level of significance and wish to evaluate the significance of an F with $df_{num} = 2$ and $df_{denom} = 12$. From the table we find that the critical value of $F(2,12) = 3.89$ at $\alpha = .05$. If the obtained value of F equals or exceeds this critical value, we will reject the null hypothesis; if the obtained value of F is smaller than this critical value, we will not reject the null hypothesis.

Degrees of freedom for numerator

df denom	1	2	3	4	5	6	7	8	9	10	12	15	20	24	30	40	60	Infinity
1	**161** 4052	**200** 4999	**216** 5403	**225** 5625	**230** 5764	**234** 5859	**237** 5928	**239** 5981	**241** 6022	**242** 6056	**244** 6106	**246** 6157	**248** 6209	**249** 6235	**250** 6261	**251** 6287	**252** 6313	**254** 6366
2	**18.5** 98.5	**19.0** 99.0	**19.2** 99.2	**19.2** 99.2	**19.3** 99.3	**19.3** 99.3	**19.4** 99.4	**19.4** 99.4	**19.4** 99.4	**19.4** 99.4	**19.4** 99.4	**19.4** 99.4	**19.4** 99.4	**19.4** 99.5	**19.5** 99.5	**19.5** 99.5	**19.5** 99.5	**19.5** 99.5
3	**10.1** 34.1	**9.55** 30.8	**9.28** 29.5	**9.12** 28.7	**9.01** 28.2	**8.94** 27.9	**8.89** 27.7	**8.85** 27.5	**8.81** 27.4	**8.79** 27.2	**8.74** 27.0	**8.70** 26.9	**8.66** 26.7	**8.64** 26.6	**8.62** 26.5	**8.59** 26.4	**8.57** 26.3	**8.53** 26.1
4	**7.71** 21.2	**6.94** 18.0	**6.59** 16.7	**6.39** 16.0	**6.26** 15.5	**6.16** 15.2	**6.09** 15.0	**6.04** 14.8	**6.00** 14.7	**5.96** 14.6	**5.91** 14.4	**5.86** 14.2	**5.80** 14.0	**5.77** 13.9	**5.75** 13.8	**5.72** 13.8	**5.69** 13.6	**5.63** 13.5
5	**6.61** 16.3	**5.79** 13.3	**5.41** 12.1	**5.19** 11.4	**5.05** 11.0	**4.95** 10.7	**4.88** 10.5	**4.82** 10.3	**4.77** 10.2	**4.74** 10.0	**4.68** 9.89	**4.62** 9.72	**4.56** 9.55	**4.53** 9.47	**4.50** 9.38	**4.46** 9.29	**4.43** 9.20	**4.36** 9.02
6	**5.99** 13.8	**5.14** 10.9	**4.76** 9.78	**4.53** 9.15	**4.39** 8.75	**4.28** 8.47	**4.21** 8.26	**4.15** 8.10	**4.10** 7.98	**4.06** 7.87	**4.00** 7.72	**3.94** 7.56	**3.87** 7.40	**3.84** 7.31	**3.81** 7.23	**3.77** 7.14	**3.74** 7.06	**3.67** 6.88
7	**5.59** 12.2	**4.74** 9.55	**4.35** 8.45	**4.12** 7.85	**3.97** 7.46	**3.87** 7.19	**3.79** 6.99	**3.73** 6.84	**3.68** 6.72	**3.64** 6.62	**3.57** 6.47	**3.51** 6.31	**3.44** 6.16	**3.41** 6.07	**3.38** 5.99	**3.34** 5.91	**3.30** 5.82	**3.23** 5.65
8	**5.32** 11.3	**4.46** 8.65	**4.07** 7.59	**3.84** 7.01	**3.69** 6.63	**3.58** 6.37	**3.50** 6.18	**3.44** 6.03	**3.39** 5.91	**3.35** 5.81	**3.28** 5.67	**3.22** 5.52	**3.15** 5.36	**3.12** 5.28	**3.08** 5.20	**3.04** 5.12	**3.01** 5.03	**2.93** 4.86
9	**5.12** 10.6	**4.26** 8.02	**3.86** 6.99	**3.63** 6.42	**3.48** 6.06	**3.37** 5.80	**3.29** 5.61	**3.23** 5.47	**3.18** 5.35	**3.14** 5.26	**3.07** 5.11	**3.01** 4.96	**2.94** 4.81	**2.90** 4.73	**2.86** 4.65	**2.83** 4.57	**2.79** 4.48	**2.71** 4.31
10	**4.96** 10.0	**4.10** 7.56	**3.71** 6.55	**3.48** 5.99	**3.33** 5.64	**3.22** 5.39	**3.14** 5.20	**3.07** 5.06	**3.02** 4.94	**2.98** 4.85	**2.91** 4.71	**2.85** 4.56	**2.77** 4.41	**2.74** 4.33	**2.70** 4.25	**2.66** 4.17	**2.62** 4.08	**2.54** 3.91
11	**4.84** 9.65	**3.98** 7.21	**3.59** 6.22	**3.36** 5.67	**3.20** 5.32	**3.09** 5.07	**3.01** 4.89	**2.95** 4.74	**2.90** 4.63	**2.85** 4.54	**2.79** 4.40	**2.72** 4.25	**2.65** 4.10	**2.61** 4.02	**2.57** 3.94	**2.53** 3.86	**2.49** 3.78	**2.40** 3.60
12	**4.75** 9.33	**3.89** 6.93	**3.49** 5.95	**3.26** 5.41	**3.11** 5.06	**3.00** 4.82	**2.91** 4.64	**2.85** 4.50	**2.80** 4.39	**2.75** 4.30	**2.69** 4.16	**2.62** 4.01	**2.54** 3.86	**2.51** 3.78	**2.47** 3.70	**2.43** 3.62	**2.38** 3.54	**2.30** 3.36
13	**4.67** 9.07	**3.81** 6.70	**3.41** 5.74	**3.18** 5.21	**3.03** 4.86	**2.92** 4.62	**2.83** 4.44	**2.77** 4.30	**2.71** 4.19	**2.67** 4.10	**2.60** 3.96	**2.53** 3.82	**2.46** 3.66	**2.42** 3.59	**2.38** 3.51	**2.34** 3.43	**2.30** 3.34	**2.21** 3.17
14	**4.60** 8.86	**3.74** 6.51	**3.34** 5.56	**3.11** 5.04	**2.96** 4.69	**2.85** 4.46	**2.76** 4.28	**2.70** 4.14	**2.65** 4.03	**2.60** 3.94	**2.53** 3.80	**2.46** 3.66	**2.39** 3.51	**2.35** 3.43	**2.31** 3.35	**2.27** 3.27	**2.22** 3.18	**2.13** 3.00

Degrees of freedom for denominator

TABLE A.6 CRITICAL VALUES OF THE *F*-DISTRIBUTION* *(CONTINUED)*

									DEGREES OF FREEDOM FOR NUMERATOR									
Degrees of freedom for denominator	1	2	3	4	5	6	7	8	9	10	12	15	20	24	30	40	60	INFINITY
15	4.54 / 8.68	3.68 / 6.36	3.29 / 5.42	3.06 / 4.89	2.90 / 4.56	2.79 / 4.32	2.71 / 4.14	2.64 / 4.00	2.59 / 3.89	2.54 / 3.80	2.48 / 3.67	2.40 / 3.52	2.33 / 3.37	2.29 / 3.29	2.25 / 3.21	2.20 / 3.13	2.16 / 3.05	2.07 / 2.87
16	4.49 / 8.53	3.63 / 6.23	3.24 / 5.29	3.01 / 4.77	2.85 / 4.44	2.74 / 4.20	2.66 / 4.03	2.59 / 3.89	2.54 / 3.78	2.49 / 3.69	2.42 / 3.55	2.35 / 3.41	2.28 / 3.26	2.24 / 3.18	2.19 / 3.10	2.15 / 3.02	2.11 / 2.93	2.01 / 2.75
17	4.45 / 8.40	3.59 / 6.11	3.20 / 5.18	2.96 / 4.67	2.81 / 4.34	2.70 / 4.10	2.61 / 3.93	2.55 / 3.79	2.49 / 3.68	2.45 / 3.59	2.38 / 3.46	2.31 / 3.31	2.23 / 3.16	2.19 / 3.08	2.15 / 3.00	2.10 / 2.92	2.06 / 2.83	1.96 / 2.65
18	4.41 / 8.29	3.55 / 6.01	3.16 / 5.09	2.93 / 4.58	2.77 / 4.25	2.66 / 4.01	2.58 / 3.84	2.51 / 3.71	2.46 / 3.60	2.41 / 3.51	2.34 / 3.37	2.27 / 3.23	2.19 / 3.08	2.15 / 3.00	2.11 / 2.92	2.06 / 2.84	2.02 / 2.75	1.92 / 2.57
19	4.38 / 8.18	3.52 / 5.93	3.13 / 5.01	2.90 / 4.50	2.74 / 4.17	2.63 / 3.94	2.54 / 3.77	2.48 / 3.63	2.42 / 3.52	2.38 / 3.43	2.31 / 3.30	2.23 / 3.15	2.16 / 3.00	2.11 / 2.92	2.07 / 2.84	2.03 / 2.76	1.98 / 2.67	1.88 / 2.49
20	4.35 / 8.10	3.49 / 5.85	3.10 / 4.94	2.87 / 4.43	2.71 / 4.10	2.60 / 3.87	2.51 / 3.70	2.45 / 3.56	2.39 / 3.46	2.35 / 3.37	2.28 / 3.23	2.20 / 3.09	2.12 / 2.94	2.08 / 2.86	2.04 / 2.78	1.99 / 2.69	1.95 / 2.61	1.84 / 2.42
22	4.30 / 7.95	3.44 / 5.72	3.05 / 4.82	2.82 / 4.31	2.66 / 3.99	2.55 / 3.76	2.46 / 3.59	2.40 / 3.45	2.34 / 3.35	2.30 / 3.26	2.23 / 3.12	2.15 / 2.98	2.07 / 2.83	2.03 / 2.75	1.98 / 2.67	1.94 / 2.58	1.89 / 2.50	1.78 / 2.31
24	4.26 / 7.82	3.40 / 5.61	3.01 / 4.72	2.78 / 4.22	2.62 / 3.90	2.51 / 3.67	2.42 / 3.50	2.36 / 3.36	2.30 / 3.26	2.25 / 3.17	2.18 / 3.03	2.11 / 2.89	2.03 / 2.74	1.98 / 2.66	1.94 / 2.58	1.89 / 2.49	1.84 / 2.40	1.73 / 2.21
26	4.23 / 7.72	3.37 / 5.53	2.98 / 4.64	2.74 / 4.14	2.59 / 3.82	2.47 / 3.59	2.39 / 3.42	2.32 / 3.29	2.27 / 3.18	2.22 / 3.09	2.15 / 2.96	2.07 / 2.81	1.99 / 2.66	1.95 / 2.58	1.90 / 2.50	1.85 / 2.42	1.80 / 2.33	1.69 / 2.13
28	4.20 / 7.64	3.34 / 5.45	2.95 / 4.57	2.71 / 4.07	2.56 / 3.75	2.45 / 3.53	2.36 / 3.36	2.29 / 3.23	2.24 / 3.12	2.19 / 3.03	2.12 / 2.90	2.04 / 2.75	1.96 / 2.60	1.91 / 2.52	1.87 / 2.44	1.82 / 2.35	1.77 / 2.26	1.65 / 2.06
30	4.17 / 7.56	3.32 / 5.39	2.92 / 4.51	2.69 / 4.02	2.53 / 3.70	2.42 / 3.47	2.33 / 3.30	2.27 / 3.17	2.21 / 3.07	2.16 / 2.98	2.09 / 2.84	2.01 / 2.70	1.93 / 2.55	1.89 / 2.47	1.84 / 2.39	1.79 / 2.30	1.74 / 2.21	1.62 / 2.01
40	4.08 / 7.31	3.23 / 5.18	2.84 / 4.31	2.61 / 3.83	2.45 / 3.51	2.34 / 3.29	2.25 / 3.12	2.18 / 2.99	2.12 / 2.89	2.08 / 2.80	2.00 / 2.66	1.92 / 2.52	1.84 / 2.37	1.79 / 2.29	1.74 / 2.20	1.69 / 2.11	1.64 / 2.02	1.51 / 1.80
60	4.00 / 7.08	3.15 / 4.98	2.76 / 4.13	2.53 / 3.65	2.37 / 3.34	2.25 / 3.12	2.17 / 2.95	2.10 / 2.82	2.04 / 2.72	1.99 / 2.63	1.92 / 2.50	1.84 / 2.35	1.75 / 2.20	1.70 / 2.12	1.65 / 2.03	1.59 / 1.94	1.53 / 1.84	1.39 / 1.60
120	3.92 / 6.85	3.07 / 4.79	2.68 / 3.95	2.45 / 3.48	2.29 / 3.17	2.17 / 2.96	2.09 / 2.79	2.02 / 2.66	1.96 / 2.56	1.91 / 2.47	1.83 / 2.34	1.75 / 2.19	1.66 / 2.03	1.61 / 1.95	1.55 / 1.86	1.50 / 1.76	1.43 / 1.66	1.25 / 1.38
INFINITY	3.84 / 6.63	3.00 / 4.61	2.60 / 3.78	2.37 / 3.32	2.21 / 3.02	2.10 / 2.80	2.01 / 2.64	1.94 / 2.51	1.88 / 2.41	1.83 / 2.32	1.75 / 2.18	1.67 / 2.04	1.57 / 1.88	1.52 / 1.79	1.46 / 1.70	1.39 / 1.59	1.32 / 1.47	1.00 / 1.00

*This table is abridged from Table 18 in *Biometrika tables for statisticians*, vol. 1 (3d ed.), New York: Cambridge University Press, 1970, edited by E. S. Pearson and H. O. Hartley, by permission of the *Biometrika* Trustees.

B

Ethical Issues in the Conduct of Psychological Research

OUTLINE

INTRODUCTION

ETHICAL ISSUES RELEVANT TO ALL THE SCIENCES

Numerous ethical issues are relevant to the conduct of psychological research, and ethical problems may arise at any stage of a research activity. Many of these issues concern all the sciences. They include the responsibility of the scientist to seek knowledge, to carry out research in a competent manner, to report results accurately, to manage available resources honestly, to acknowledge fairly in scientific communications those individuals who contributed ideas or their time and effort, to consider the consequences to society of a research endeavor, and to speak out publicly on societal concerns that are related to a scientist's specific knowledge and expertise (see especially Diener and Crandall, 1978). Consider, for example, ethical issues related to assigning credit to those who make contributions to a research project. Research is often a collaborative effort, involving, for instance, colleagues who offer suggestions about a study's design, graduate or undergraduate students who assist a principal investigator by testing subjects and organizing data, technicians who construct specialized equipment, and expert consultants who give advice about computer programs needed for statistical analyses. Because "authorship" of a published scientific study frequently is used to measure an individual's motivation and competence in a scientific field, it is important to acknowledge fairly those who have contributed to a project. However, deciding whether an individual should be credited by being an "author" of a scientific paper or whether that individual's contribution should be acknowledged in a less visible way, such as in a footnote, is not always easy. When research psychologists are surveyed about this issue, most believe that a contribution should be evaluated mainly in terms of its scholarly importance (e.g., aiding the conceptual aspects of a study) and not by the time and energy invested in the study (see Bridgwater et al., 1981).

Ethical problems arise, in other words, from both the *processes* and the *products* of research (Kelman, 1972). For example, the public sometimes views the products of psychological research as providing methods of controlling and manipulating human behavior. A nagging fear is that these methods will be used by some members of society at the expense of others. A report issued by an APA committee examining ethics aptly summarizes the dilemma psychologists face (American Psychological Association, 1982, p. 16).

> Just as the results of research in atomic physics can be used for the treatment of cancer as well as for destructive weapons so methods discovered to reduce prejudice toward minority groups, to eliminate troublesome behavior problems, or to facilitate learning in school may also be used to manipulate political allegiance, to create artificial wants, or to reconcile the victims of social injustice to their fate. The double-edged potentiality of scientific knowledge poses ethical problems for all scientists.

At one time or another, all the sciences have been tarnished by both major and minor scandals resulting from the unethical behavior of member scientists. In 1912, for instance, anthropologists were formally introduced to startling new evidence bearing on the origin of humans. An amateur archaeologist had uncovered a human-like skull and jawbone near Piltdown Common, England. "Piltdown man," as the fossil remains were called, was so different from anything previously discovered that anthropologists were forced to rethink all their ideas about human evolution. It was not until the 1950s, some 40 years later, that Piltdown man was shown to be fake. By that time enough other genuine remains had been collected to make Piltdown man stand out as unbelievably different. Modern tests indicated that the skull and jaw were of different ages. Close inspection also revealed that the teeth had been filed so as to give the appearance of having been worn by chewing. Piltdown man was a sophisticated hoax perpetrated by someone who had constructed the "evidence" from a human skull and the jaw of an ape (Campbell, 1976).

Psychologists were confronted in 1976 with evidence of fraud. According to *Science* magazine, this fraud, if proven, could rival the fraud of Piltdown man. The eminent English psychologist Cyril Burt was accused of misrepresenting data obtained in his studies on the basis of intelligence. Burt had been the first psychologist to be knighted in England, in 1971, and the first foreigner to receive the prestigious Thorndike Award from the American Psychological Association (APA). Burt died the same year that he received the APA award, and his acceptance speech, containing his most recent views on intelligence, was published posthumously (Burt, 1972). He had long maintained that intelligence was largely inherited rather than due to environmental factors, and both his data and his views were highly influential. As a government adviser, Burt was involved in setting up a tripartite system of British secondary education. Schoolchildren were assigned, on the basis of tests given at age 11, to whichever of three educational levels was judged suitable to each child's "aptitudes" (Hearnshaw, 1979). Such a system was in line with the view that intelligence is largely innate and that tests given at a relatively early age can predict the ultimate level of an individual's intelligence.

Particularly crucial to Burt's arguments were IQ data obtained from identical twins who had been raised apart. Over the years Burt claimed to have collected data from more than fifty sets of such twins. The correlation between the IQs of the separated twins was quite high, supporting his position on the innateness of intelligence. Burt also had data showing that the environments of separated twins (as measured by occupational status of biological and foster parents) were uncorrelated, indicating that the highly related IQ of the twins could not be explained by similarities in the different twins' environments (Wade, 1976b).

After Burt's death, evidence was found to indicate that he had falsified much of his data on identical twins (Kamin, 1974) and that he had even made up the names of fictitious co-workers. It is still not entirely clear whether Burt faked these data in order to perpetrate fraud or to bolster the defense of his views in the face of personal and professional criticism (Hearnshaw, 1979). Some of Burt's findings were later replicated by other psychologists, and the three-tier educational system in England has since been abandoned. Therefore, it is difficult to say how much of an impact the disclosures had on the intelligence issue or on education (however, see Wade, 1976).

The revelations surrounding Burt's work clouded the already controversial study of the basis of intelligence and undoubtedly lowered the prestige of psychology in the eyes of the public. As *Time* magazine so aptly put it in describing the Burt case to its readers, "When a leader in the field is shown to be either a fraud or spectacularly inept, it is psychology's loss" (*Time*, 1976, Dec. 8, p. 66). Although such cases of fraud and misrepresentation are said to be rare among well-established scientists, and apparently occur more frequently among less experienced scientists—and particularly among students and hired assistants (Diener and Crandall, 1978)—they do still occasionally occur (see Hostetler, 1987b). Moreover, fraudulent behavior by established scientists apparently is suspected by a substantial number of researchers (see Hostetler, 1987a). These suspicions, as well as the revelations yielded by well-publicized cases of actual fraud, have raised questions as to whether the scientific community is doing enough to police the ethical activities of its members.

ISSUES ESPECIALLY RELEVANT TO PSYCHOLOGY

In addition to those ethical concerns shared by all the sciences, certain issues are especially relevant to psychology. Foremost among these is the treatment of subjects in psychological research. The APA has adopted principles governing research with both human and animal subjects. (These sets of principles are reprinted later in this appendix.) Human participants in psychological research are also protected under provisions of the National Research Act, which was signed into law in 1974. This Act called for the creation of a National Commission for the Protection of Human Subjects of Biomedical and Behavioral Research. The National Research Act of 1974 also required that institutions, such as colleges and universities that seek research funds from specific federal agencies, establish committees to review research sponsored by the institution. These committees, referred to as Institution Review Boards (IRBs), are frequently called on to review psychological research in order to safeguard the rights and welfare of human participants. Similarly, in 1985, the Department of Agriculture, as well as the Public Health Service, formulated new guidelines for care of laboratory animals (Holden, 1987). As a result, every institution doing research with animal subjects is required to have an Institutional Animal Care and Use Committee (IACUC), whose members minimally must include a scientist, veterinarian, and at least one person not affiliated with the institution. Violation of federal regulations regarding the review of research involving human or animal subjects can bring a halt to research at an institution, spell the loss of federal funds, and result in substantial fines (see Holden, 1987; Smith, 1977).

It has become increasingly important that students of psychology be introduced at an early stage to the ethical principles related to the treatment of research subjects, as well as to the rules and regulations for institutional review. Failure to conduct research in an ethical manner can undermine the entire scientific process, retard the advancement of knowledge, erode the public's respect for the scientific and academic communities, and bring significant legal and financial penalties down on individuals and institutions.

INSTITUTIONAL REVIEW

Prior to enactment of the National Research Act of 1974, many institutions had already established committees to review research with human participants (see Gray, et al., 1978). However, federal regulations imposed very specific requirements on the makeup and duties of these committees (see *Federal Register*, March 13, 1975). For example, an IRB was to be comprised of at least five members with varying backgrounds and fields of expertise. Hence an IRB could not consist entirely of psychologists. Furthermore, the guidelines specified that at least one of the members of each IRB must not be affiliated with the institution. Responsible persons from the community, such as members of the clergy, lawyers, and nurses, are asked to serve on these committees. The regulations also prohibit an IRB from consisting either of all men or of all women (*Federal Register*, January 26, 1981).

The federal regulations were originally interpreted to mean that IRBs were required to review *all* research with human participants conducted at an institution, regardless of whether the research was supported by a specific federal agency. Accordingly, at many colleges and universities, research projects carried out by undergraduate students as part of a laboratory class in psychology, as well as research performed by faculty members, were reviewed by an IRB. Research conducted in an undergraduate psychology class might be reviewed by having the instructor file with the IRB a form describing the nature of the student research and the risks, if any, to participants. Recent federal regulations have relaxed somewhat the original provisions regarding IRBs, and certain categories of research are now exempt from review by an IRB (*Federal Register*, Jan. 16, 1981).

Nearly every college and university requires that all research conducted at the institution be reviewed at some stage by an independent committee. In the case of human subjects, this committee may be an IRB, or, when animal subjects are involved, the IACUC. A psychology student seeking to do research with human participants is apt to be asked first to satisfy the regulations of a departmental committee charged with reviewing research conducted in the psychology department. Depending on the association of this departmental committee with an IRB, research falling into various well-defined categories is either reviewed at the departmental level or referred to the IRB. For example, research that is sponsored by an agency of the Department of Health and Human Services must be reviewed by an IRB unless such a review is specifically exempted by federal regulations. Review of animal research by IUCACs extends to more than simply overseeing the research procedures. Federal regulations governing the conduct of animal research extend to specifications of animal living quarters and the proper training of personnel who work directly with the animals (see Holden, 1987).

Given the complex nature of federal regulations, and the policies of most institutions requiring review of research with human and animal subjects, any individual who wants to do research is obliged to inquire of the proper authorities, prior to starting research, about the appropriate procedure for institutional review.

APA PRINCIPLES GOVERNING THE TREATMENT OF HUMAN PARTICIPANTS

The decision to undertake research rests upon a considered judgment by the individual psychologist about how best to contribute to psychological science and human welfare. Having made the decision to conduct research, the psychologist considers alternative directions in which research energies and resources might be invested. On the basis of this consideration, the psychologist carries out the investigation with respect and concern for the dignity and welfare of the people who participate and with cognizance of federal and state regulations and professional standards governing the conduct of research with human participants.

a In planning a study, the investigator has the responsibility to make a careful evaluation of its ethical acceptability. To the extent that the weighing of scientific and human values suggests a compromise of any principle, the investigator incurs a correspondingly serious obligation to seek ethical advice and to observe stringent safeguards to protect the rights of human participants.

b Considering whether a participant in a planned study will be a "subject at risk" or a "subject at minimal risk," according to recognized standards, is of primary ethical concern to the investigator.

c The investigator always retains the responsibility for ensuring ethical practice in research. The investigator is also responsible for the ethical treatment of research participants by collaborators, assistants, students, and employees, all of whom, however, incur similar obligations.

d Except in minimal-risk research, the investigator establishes a clear and fair agreement with research participants, prior to their participation, that clarifies the obligations to honor all promises and commitments included in that agreement. The investigator informs the participants of all aspects of the research that might reasonably be expected to influence willingness to participate and explains all other aspects of the research about which the participants inquire. Failure to make full disclosure prior to obtaining informed consent requires additional safeguards to protect the welfare and dignity of the research participants who have impairments that would limit understanding and/or communication.

e Methodological requirements of a study may make the use of concealment or deception necessary. Before conducting such a study, the investigator has a special responsibility to (i) determine whether the use of such techniques is justified by the study's prospective scientific, educational, or applied value; (ii) determine whether alternative procedures are available that do not use concealment or deception; and (iii) ensure that the participants are provided with sufficient explanation as soon as possible.

f The investigator respects the individual's freedom to decline to participate in or to withdraw from the research at any time. The obligation to protect this freedom requires careful thought and consideration when the investigator is in a position of authority or influence over the participant. Such positions of authority include, but are not limited to, situations in which research participation is required as part of employment or in which the participant is a student, client, or employee of the investigator.

g The investigator protects the participant from physical and mental discomfort, harm, and danger that may arise from research procedures. If risks of such consequences exist, the investigator informs the participant of that fact. Research procedures likely to cause serious or lasting harm to a participant are not used unless the failure to use these procedures might expose the participant to risk of greater harm, or unless the research has great potential benefit and fully informed and voluntary consent is obtained from each participant. The participant should be informed of procedures for contacting the investigator within a reasonable time period following participation should stress, potential harm, or related questions or concerns arise.

h After the data are collected, the investigator provides the participant with information about the nature of the study and attempts to remove any misconceptions that may have arisen. Where scientific or humane values justify delaying or withholding this information, the investigator incurs a special responsibility to monitor the research and to ensure that there are no damaging consequences for the participant.

i Where research procedures result in undesirable consequences for the individual participant, the investigator has the responsibility to detect and remove or correct these consequences, including long-term effects.

j Information obtained about a research participant during the course of an investigation is confidential unless otherwise agreed upon in advance. When the possibility exists that others may obtain access to such information, this possibility, together with the plans for protecting confidentiality, is explained to the participant as part of the procedure for obtaining informed consent.

(*Source:* American Psychological Association (1982). *Ethical Principles in the Conduct of Research with Human Participants.* Washington: D.C.)

MAJOR ISSUES IN THE CONDUCT OF RESEARCH WITH HUMAN PARTICIPANTS

Reading the APA principles governing research with human participants suggests that there are few "absolutes." The principles attempt to strike a balance between the right—and indeed the ethical responsibility—of the psychologist to seek an understanding of human behavior, and the rights and welfare of the individuals who participate in psychological research. The decision to do psychological research rests on a subjective evaluation of the costs both to the individual and to society. Failure to do research may cost society the benefits of research findings and ultimately the opportunity to improve the human condition. To do research may at times exact a cost from individual participants—for example, by exposing them to potentially harmful circumstances or by inducing emotional stress.

Ethical dilemmas often arise. For instance, the principle of informed consent (APA Principle d) requires that subjects be informed about experimental procedures before they participate. However, an investigator may find that telling subjects the details of an experiment will affect the way they respond to a psychological treatment. A researcher who has reason to believe that a particular psychotherapeutic technique is beneficial in the treatment of psychoses may wish to use this technique only for some individuals and not for others. The object is to establish a comparison group by which to assess the effect of the treatment. Yet, ethical principles would seem to argue against depriving individuals of a possible beneficial treatment (for example, APA Principles g and i). In those cases where ethical dilemmas arise, a researcher is always obligated to seek advice from others who are more experienced or more knowledgeable about a particular research practice (APA Principal a).

Major ethical issues in the conduct of research with human subjects can be arbitrarily grouped into five general categories: the nature of risk, informed consent, deception, privacy, and the risk/benefit ratio. A brief discussion of these issues will serve to introduce the problems inherent in applying ethical principles and in deciding whether a particular research project should be undertaken.

NATURE OF RISK

Determination of Risk Serious ethical obligations exist whenever subjects risk injury by participating in psychological research (APA Principle b). However, determining whether subjects are "at risk" illustrates the difficulties involved in ethical decision making. Life itself is a risky affair. Commuting to work or school, crossing streets, and riding on elevators are all activities that have an element of risk. Simply showing up for an appointment to serve in a psychology experiment must be judged to entail some degree of risk. To say that human participants in psychological research can never risk injury would bring all research to a halt. Decisions about what constitutes risk must take into consideration those risks that are part of everyday life.

Any determination of risk must also consider the nature of the participants. Certain activities can reasonably be judged to pose a serious risk for some individuals but not for others. Running up a flight of stairs may substantially increase an elderly person's chance of suffering a heart attack; the same task would not be a serious risk for most young adults. Individuals who are exceptionally depressed or anxious might be expected to show more severe reactions to certain psychological treatments than would other people. Statements about what constitutes risk cannot be easily generalized to all individuals or populations.

Risk is often associated with the possibility of physical injury, as when bodily harm is threatened. More often, however, participants in social science research risk social or psychological injury. The potential for social risk exists when information gained about an individual through her or his participation in psychological research is revealed to others. Simply knowing that someone completed a questionnaire inquiring about deviant sexual practices could cause social injury if those who knew reacted differently to that individual as a consequence of their knowledge. Information collected during the conduct of research may include important personal facts about intelligence, personality traits, and political, social, or religious beliefs. A research participant is not likely to want this information divulged to teachers, employers, or peers. Failure to protect the confidentiality of a subject's responses may significantly increase the possibility of social injury.

Consider, for example, the dilemma recently faced by a graduate student seeking to interview adolescents receiving service from a family planning clinic (Landers, 1988). Parental permission was not required for the teens to attend the clinic; thus, if the investigator asked the parents for permission for their children to participate in the study, she would be revealing to the parents the teens' use of the clinic's services. Yet, obtaining permission of parents before conducting research with minors is standard ethical practice (see APA Principle d) and also is mandated by federal laws. To help make a decision regarding proper ethical procedures in this difficult case, the graduate student correctly sought advice from experts (see APA Principle a), specifically, from members of APA's Committee for the Protection of Human Participants in Research. The student used the information obtained from the experts to formulate the procedures that she proposed to use as part of her dissertation research. Although advice should be sought from knowledgeable others whenever ethical dilemmas arise, final responsibility for conducting research in an ethical manner always rests with the investigator (see APA Principle c).

The potential for psychological injury exists whenever the procedures associated with a research activity are likely to induce serious mental or emotional stress in the participants. A subject who participates in a social psychology experiment involving a simulated emergency, as when smoke enters a room where she is waiting, may experience a substantial amount of emotional stress until the true, simulated character of the event is revealed. Merely participating in a psychology experiment is anxiety-provoking for some individuals. After learning a list of nonsense syllables, a subject once volunteered that he was sure the researcher now knew a great deal about him! The subject assumed that the psychologist was interested in his mental state as revealed by the associations he used when learning the list. In reality, this subject was participating in a simple memory experiment designed to measure forgetting. Even here, the researcher is responsible for putting the subject's mind at ease. A researcher is under an obligation to protect subjects from emotional or mental stress, including, when possible, that which might arise due to a participant's misconceptions about the nature of a psychological task (APA Principle g).

Definition of Risk   As illustrated by the APA principles governing research with human participants, a distinction can be made between a subject "at risk" and a subject "at minimal risk" (see APA Principle b). One definition of "minimal risk" is that which is followed by IRBs in their review of biomedical and behavioral research (*Federal Register*, January 26, 1981).

> "Minimal risk" means that the risks of harm anticipated in the proposed research are not greater, considering probability and magnitude, than those ordinarily encountered in daily life or during the performance of routine physical or psychological examinations or tests.

An IRB may waive certain requirements if it is judged that the risks that research participants are exposed to are minimal. However, when the possibility of injury is judged to be more than minimal, each subject is considered to be "at risk." Correspondingly, more serious obligations fall on the researcher to obtain informed consent and to protect the welfare of such participants.

As an example of how this definition might be applied, consider the fact that many psychology laboratory experiments involve lengthy paper-and-pencil tests intended to assess various mental abilities. Participants are frequently under time pressure to complete the tests and may receive specific feedback regarding their performance. No doubt some degree of mental or even emotional stress is associated with participation in these kinds of activities. Within limits, however, the risk of psychological injury in this situation would generally be assumed to be no greater than that of being a student. Therefore, subjects who are college students would be judged to incur only "minimal risk" in such experiments.

Dealing with Risk   Even when only a slight potential for injury exists, the researcher should try to minimize the risk and provide safeguards for the participants. For instance, stating at the beginning of a memory experiment that the tasks are not intended to measure intelligence or personality reduces the level of stress that some participants experience. When substances are to be taken internally, subjects should be screened prior to participation in order to identify and excuse any individuals who might show unusual physical reactions. In situations where the possibility of harm is judged to be significantly greater than that occurring in daily life, the researcher's obligation to protect participants increases correspondingly. It is not unheard of for an IRB to require that a clinical psychologist be available to counsel subjects when, by participating in a psychology experiment, they are exposed to the possibility of serious emotional stress.

No research activity involving serious risk to subjects should be carried out unless alternative, low-risk methods of data collection have been explored. In some cases, descriptive approaches involving observation or questionnaires should be substituted for experimental treatments. It is also possible to take advantage of naturally occurring "treatments." For example, Anderson (1976) interviewed owner-managers of small businesses that had been damaged by hurricane floods. He found that the likelihood of problem-solving coping behaviors by the subjects showed an inverted-U-shaped function when related on a graph to perceived stress, indicating that there is an optimal level of stress and that, when stress is higher or lower than this optimal level, performance decreases. A similar relationship has been demonstrated in a number of experimental laboratory tasks using experimenter-induced stress.

Another alternative to placing subjects at risk is role playing. Rather than experiencing an experimental manipulation directly, subjects are asked to "act as if" they found themselves in a particular situation. Diener and Crandall (1978) suggest that role playing also can be usefully employed when it is unclear how a treatment will affect subjects. By first having subjects role-play in an imagined situation, experimenters can gather important information that they can use to assess the possible risks the subjects would run if they actually received the treatment.

In order to protect subjects from social injury, a method of data collection should be used that preserves the anonymity of participants or, when this is not possible, to ensure the confidentiality of responses (APA Principle j). If at all possible, a researcher should obtain information about participants in a manner that does not require individuals to be identified. Simply not having subjects sign their names to the test instruments is obviously one way to keep participation anonymous. When the researcher must test subjects on more than one occasion or otherwise track specific individuals, numbers can be randomly assigned to participants at the beginning of a study. Only these numbers need appear on subjects' response sheets.

When anonymity cannot be preserved, confidentiality should be protected through some type of code system. If the information supplied by participants is particularly sensitive, such a scheme is necessary to adequately minimize the risk of social injury. One procedure is to assign code numbers to participants. Names are linked with the code numbers on a master list. Access to this list is restricted by keeping it under lock and key. Even this system may not adequately protect participants if information about them is related to criminal activity. The master list could be legally subpoenaed. In at least one case, in order to safeguard the rights of his subjects, a researcher went so far as to place the master list with the information that linked coded data to specific individuals in the vault of a foreign bank (Diener and Crandall, 1978).

INFORMED CONSENT

Nature of Consent Ethical research practice requires that subjects be informed of all features of the research that reasonably might be expected to influence their willingness to participate (APA Principle d). The researcher is obligated to respond to any inquiries that subjects might have about the research and to inform subjects that they are free to withdraw their consent at any time without penalty or prejudice (APA Principles d, f). Consent must be given freely, without undue inducement or pressure. Informed consent should always be obtained and is absolutely essential when subjects are exposed to the possibility of serious injury (APA Principle g).

True informed consent cannot be obtained from certain individuals, such as the mentally handicapped, emotionally disturbed, young children, and others who are recognized as having limited ability to understand the nature of research and the possible risks. In these cases, consent must be obtained from the subjects' parents or legal guardians. Developmental psychologists who want to test school children are often faced with the task of contacting dozens (if not hundreds) of parents in order to secure permission for children to participate in psychological research. Moreover, ethical restrictions, such as those involving informed consent, raise methodological issues as well (see Adair et al., 1985.) Results of one study revealed that children of parents who did not provide parental consent for a research project were academically less successful and were less popular with their peers than were children of parents who did provide consent (Frame and Strauss, 1987).

It is not always easy to decide what constitutes undue inducement or pressure to participate. Paying college students $2 an hour to take part in a psychology experiment would not generally be considered improper coercion. Recruiting very poor or disadvantaged persons from the streets with a $2 offer may be more coercive and less acceptable (see Kelman, 1972). Prisoners may believe that any refusal on their part to participate in a psychology experiment will be viewed by the authorities as evidence of uncooperativeness and will therefore make it more difficult for them to be paroled. Parents of school children may fear that their children will be less well treated by teachers if they refuse to give permission for their children to participate in research. When college students are asked to fulfill a class requirement by serving as subjects in psychology experiments (an experience that presumably has some educational value), it is recommended that an alternative method of earning class credit be available to those who do not wish to participate in psychological research (American Psychological Association, 1982). Such options should be equivalent, in terms of time and effort, with the requirements of research participation.

Witholding Information from Subjects Serious ethical problems can arise when a researcher withholds certain information about a psychological treatment from a subject (APA Principle d). This is particularly true when substantial risk to the subject is present. The reason for withholding information may be a legitimate concern on the part of the researcher that informing subjects of all details of the experiment will negate the effect of a particular treatment. For example, research on conformity behavior often requires that subjects believe that responses of other persons in the situation represent those individuals' own opinions. Telling subjects before the experiment that responses made by other people will be purposely misleading would appear to make this type of research impossible. Certain types of field experiments and the use of unobtrusive measures would also be prohibited if informed consent were always required.

Failure to obtain informed consent from subjects was at the center of a recent controversy surrounding a researcher who submitted copies of a fake article to a number of academic journals in the field of social work (Coughlin, 1988). It is standard practice for editors of journals to ask individuals with expertise in the area to critique articles that are submitted for possible publication. On the basis of these expert evaluations, the editor makes a decision regarding the suitability of the article for the journal. The researcher in question wanted to investigate the possibility that social work journals exhibit a confirmational bias, namely, that editors tend to accept articles for publication that confirm the value of social work interventions and reject articles that do not. Using fictitious names, he submitted two different versions of a bogus research study to various journals. One version showed a positive outcome of a social work intervention; the other version revealed no positive outcome. Only when the journal editors accepted or rejected his article did he notify them that they had been subjects in an experiment.

When the researcher submitted his findings as part of a legitimate article to a scholarly journal, the article was rejected by the editors and a complaint lodged against the researcher with the National Association of Social Workers. The complaint said that the researcher practiced deception and failed to obtain informed consent from the subjects (the journal editors and expert reviewers). Critics of the research pointed out that the evaluation and processing of the manuscript cost time and money, which, in the view of at least some editors, was not justified by the potential benefits of the findings. The researcher argued that editorial policies of journals have a significant influence on the practice of science and thus warrant investigation. Many journal editors undoubtedly would agree. However, the question raised is whether the methods used by the researcher in this investigation were ethical.

Even when no deliberate attempt is made by the researcher to withhold information, strict adherence to the principle of informed consent is perhaps impossible. As Kelman (1972) has noted, the researcher could not possibly give a precise reason for every procedure that is used, and there is really no way to identify individuals who are participating out of some sense of obligation. As in other areas of ethical decision making, implementing the principle of informed consent requires that the investigator seek to balance the need to investigate human behavior on the one hand with the rights of human participants on the other. Leaving subjects utterly in the dark is always unethical. So is providing misinformation for the purpose of getting people to participate in an activity they would not normally engage in.

DECEPTION

The Controversy Surrounding Deception   No ethical issue related to research is more controversial than that of deception. There are those who would argue that subjects should *never* be deceived in the context of psychological research. Deception runs counter to the principle of openness and honesty that ethical practice says should characterize the relationship between experimenter and subject. Deception can occur either through omission, the withholding of information, or through commission, the presentation of misinformation to subjects about an aspect of the research. Either kind of deception contradicts the principle of informed consent. To some, deception is morally repugnant; it is no different from lying. Nevertheless, despite the increased attention over the last couple decades given to deceptive methodological practices, the use of deception in psychological research has not declined (Adair et al., 1985).

As we have seen, it would be impossible to carry out certain kinds of research unless subjects were not informed about some aspects of the research. In other situations, it may be necessary to misinform subjects in order to have them adopt certain attitudes or behaviors. A participant observer, for instance, may find it necessary to misrepresent herself in order to gain access to a particular group or setting. Rosenthal's (1966) research investigating experimenter bias was based on the assumption that the subjects believed that they were experimenters working for a principal investigator. The "experimenters" were actually the subjects. The data collected by these subject-experimenters sometimes differed as a function of the expectations they had about the research outcome. Although deception is sometimes said to be justified on methodological grounds (APA Principle e), deceiving subjects for the purpose of getting them to participate in research in which they would not normally take part, or research that involves serious risk, is difficult to justify.

Milgram (1977) has questioned whether the term "deception" is a fair description of the procedures used by psychologists. He suggests that more neutral terms, such as "masking" or "technical illusions," are more appropriate. After all, illusions are sometimes created in real-life situations in order to make people believe something. When listening to a radio program, people are not generally bothered by the fact that the thunder they hear or the sound of a horse galloping are merely technical illusions created by a sound-effects specialist. Milgram argues that technical illusions should be permitted in the cause of scientific inquiry. We deceive children into believing in Santa Claus. Why cannot scientists create illusions in order to better understand human behavior?

Just as illusions are often created in real-life situations, in other situations, Milgram (1977) points out, there can be a suspension of a general moral principle. If we learn of a crime, we are ethically bound to report it to the authorities. On the other hand, a lawyer who is given information by a client must consider this information privileged even if it reveals that the client is guilty. Physicians perform very personal examinations of our bodies. Although it is morally permissible in a physician's office, the same type of behavior would not be condoned outside the office. Milgram (1977) argues that, in the interest of science, psychologists should occasionally be allowed to suspend the moral principle of truthfulness and honesty.

Problems Arising from Casual Use of Deception A basic assumption underlying the use of deception is that it is necessary to conceal the true nature of an experiment so that subjects will behave as they normally would, or so that they will act in accordance with the stated instructions and cues provided by the experimenter. If people come to realize (and perhaps many already have) that psychologists often present misinformation and that serving in a psychology experiment means they are likely to be deceived, then the very assumption on which the use of deception is based will be lost. Subjects will no longer act in accordance with the instructions of the experimenter, because they will no longer believe that the experimenter is telling the truth. Frequent and casual use of deception undermines the usefulness of deception as a methodological tool (Kelman, 1967).

The fact that psychologists are often identified with deceptive practices, and the fact that deception may be the basis for experimental manipulations in natural settings, also may affect the way people react to emergencies or other events that they witness. On one college campus a student was attacked and shot by another student. Witnesses did not try to help and the assailant was not pursued. When bystanders were asked why they did not intervene, some said they thought it was just a psychology experiment (Diener and Crandall, 1978).

Role Playing as an Alternative In addition to its use in situations involving serious risk of injury to participants, role playing is sometimes suggested as an alternative to the use of deception (Kelman, 1968, 1972). Even when people know it is only a "game," they sometimes get quite involved and behave in a manner that is similar, if not identical, to the behavior of subjects in a "real" situation.

One problem with role playing as an alternative method of observing behavior is that participants can act only in the way they believe they would act if the situation were real. People sometimes see themselves as acting in one way but would actually behave in another way. Latané and Darley (1970) tested subjects' reactions to emergency situations when they were either in the presence of others or alone. One type of emergency involved subjects encountering another person in distress. Subjects were deceived as to the true nature of the experiment. Consistently, subjects were more likely to intervene (for example, by going to someone's aid) when they were alone than when they were with others. Then the researchers presented written descriptions of the emergency situations to another group of subjects. A person was described as being either alone or with others when an emergency occurred. The paper-and-pencil subjects were asked (a) what they would do in this situation and (b) whether the presence of others would affect their behavior.

Subjects rated themselves as equally likely to help whether they were alone or with others and said that their behavior would not be affected by the presence or absence of others in that situation.

Clearly, subjects' beliefs about their behavior in emergency situations do not necessarily correspond to their actual behavior in these circumstances. At some point, a real experiment would have to be done to determine whether all behavior observed in a role-playing situation is the same as that which is observed in a real situation (Milgram, 1977). Nevertheless, while acknowledging that role playing may not substitute for the use of deception in every experimental situation, Kelman (1972) suggests that its potential value for research warrants its use much more for this purpose than it presently is.

The Decision to Use Deception   Kelman (1972) suggests that, before using deception, a researcher give very serious consideration to (a) the importance of the study to our scientific knowledge; (b) the availability of alternative, deception-free methods; and (c) the "noxiousness" of the deception. This last consideration refers to the degree of deception involved and to the possibility of injury to the participants. In Kelman's (1972, p. 997) view, "Only if a study is very important and no alternative methods are available can anything more than the mildest form of deception be justified." (See also APA Principle e.)

When deception is used, the researcher must inform subjects after the experiment of the reasons for the deception, discuss any misconceptions that they may have, and remove any harmful effects of the deception (APA Principles e, h, and i). One goal of this "debriefing" is educating the subject about the need for deception. In addition, researchers should try to help subjects understand how they have made a contribution to science and, in general, help them come away with a positive feeling about having participated in psychological research.

PRIVACY

Threats to Privacy   Information about individuals, organizations, and institutions obtained in the course of psychological research should be kept confidential (APA Principle j). *Privacy* refers to the rights of individuals to decide how information about them is to be communicated to others. The manner in which information about subjects will be kept confidential should be explained to participants in psychological research so that they may judge for themselves whether the safeguards taken to ensure confidentiality are reasonable. Diener and Crandall (1978) identify three major dimensions to consider when deciding what information is private and what safeguards should be employed: sensitivity of the information, setting, and degree of dissemination of the information.

Clearly, some kinds of information are more sensitive than others. Subjects interviewed about sexual practices, religious beliefs, or criminal activities are likely to be more concerned about the dissemination of this information than subjects interviewed about who they believe will win the World Series. Similarly, organizations and businesses are likely to perceive some types of information about them as more sensitive than other types.

The setting in which behavior is observed is also a factor in defining what constitutes private activity. Individuals engaged in what reasonably might be considered public behaviors, such as attending a baseball game or other outdoor event, give up a certain degree of privacy. What is public behavior is not always easy to decide. Such behaviors as riding inside one's own car, using public bathrooms, or picnicking in a park are not easily classified. Decisions about ethical practice in these situations sometimes depend on the sensitivity of the data and the manner in which information is disseminated.

Dissemination of information in terms of group averages or proportions is unlikely to reflect on specific individuals. In other situations, code systems can be used to protect subjects' confidentiality. Dissemination of sensitive information about individuals or groups without their permission is a serious breach of ethics. When information about individuals has been collected unobtrusively (for example, by a concealed observer), one approach that has been suggested is to contact subjects after the observations have been made and ask whether this information can be used by the researcher. (People can be surprisingly generous with revelations about themselves, even when they think they may have been made to look silly. It would be fascinating to know what proportion of unwitting "performers" on the old TV show "Candid Camera" withheld permission to air segments involving them. It would also be interesting to know what—if any—monetary inducements were offered.)

Decision to Invade Privacy As Diener and Crandall (1978) indicate, the most difficult decisions regarding privacy involve situations in which there is an obvious ethical problem on one dimension but not on others and situations in which there is a slight problem on all dimensions. For instance, the behavior of individuals in the darkened setting of a movie theatre would appear to have the potential of yielding sensitive information about an individual, but the setting could be reasonably classified as public.

During the 1980s, the APA Committee for the Protection of Human Participants in Research became involved in a number of major ethical issues related to psychosocial research on acquired immune deficiency syndrome (AIDS) (Melton et al., 1988). Particularly salient among the ethical dilemmas posed by this research is that related to privacy. Control over knowledge about oneself and one's body is basic to respect for persons and is even constitutionally protected; on the other hand, the courts have supported the government's police power to curb threats to public health (see Melton and Gray, 1988). The transmission of AIDS is known to take place via the sharing of body fluids, such as sexual contact or sharing of needles for intravenous injections. Thus, to understand fully the spread of AIDS requires gathering data regarding individuals' sexual practices, drug use, medical history, travel, and acquaintances. Unfortunately, confidentiality cannot always be guaranteed to participants in AIDS research because of laws requiring the reporting of AIDS cases and the fact that records are sometimes able to be legally supoenaed (Gray and Melton, 1985). New federal and state laws may be needed in order to protect adequately the privacy of participants in research involving diseases of this nature (Melton and Gray, 1988).

As in other areas when ethical dilemmas arise, the investigator is obligated to seek advice from knowledgeable others regarding the appropriateness of a research procedure. For example, consultation with members of IRBs, experienced researchers, members of ethics committees, and even representatives of the population at risk (see Melton et al., 1988) will help to ensure that the rights of the participants are protected when psychosocial aspects of communicable diseases are investigated.

RISK/BENEFIT RATIO

Is It Worth It? The final decision concerning risks and benefits of a research project is most appropriately made by knowledgeable individuals who do not have a personal interest in the research. Nonetheless, it is the principal investigator who must first give some consideration to the risk/benefit ratio. The possible costs to the individual must be weighed against the benefits both to the individual and to society in general. In its simplest form, the question of risk/benefit is "Is it worth it?" When the inconvenience and possible risks to subjects are considered, is there sufficient potential benefit to the individual and to society to carry out this research?

Factors in the Ratio Many factors affect a decision regarding the proper balance of risks and benefits of a particular research activity. The most basic are the nature of the risk and the magnitude of the probable benefit to the participant and to society. When the benefits to an individual or society are clear and immediate, a greater risk can be tolerated than when the benefits are less clear or their application is less immediate. For instance, in the context of research investigating the antecedents of psychotic behavior, the possible benefits to both the participants and society may be substantial if a proposed treatment has a good possibility of having a beneficial effect. Society will also benefit as psychologists come to understand more completely such behaviors as aggression, bystander intervention, deviance, and suicide. The benefits to be gained by investigating these behaviors, however, must be continually weighed against the risks to the participants.

In determining the risk/benefit ratio, a researcher also must take into account the probability that valid and interpretable results will be produced. An established scientist with a history of successful research in her field would reasonably be judged to have a greater chance of obtaining important results than an undergraduate psychology major. When risk is present, a researcher must make sure that there are not alternative, low-risk procedures that might be substituted and that the research has been planned in a competent manner. Without a careful review of the psychological literature, for instance, a researcher just might carry out research that has already been done. In this case subjects would be exposed to risk needlessly.

APA PRINCIPLES FOR THE CARE AND USE OF ANIMALS

An investigator of animal behavior strives to advance understanding of basic behavioral principles and/or to contribute to the improvement of human health and welfare. In seeking these ends, the investigator ensures the welfare of animals and treats them humanely. Laws and regulations notwithstanding, an animal's immediate protection depends upon the scientist's own conscience.

a The acquisition, care, use, and disposal of all animals are in compliance with current federal, state or provincial, and local laws and regulations.

b A psychologist trained in research methods and experienced in the care of laboratory animals closely supervises all procedures involving animals and is responsible for ensuring appropriate consideration of their comfort, health, and humane treatment.

c Psychologists ensure that all individuals using animals under their supervision have received explicit instruction in experimental methods and in the care, maintenance, and handling of the species being used. Responsibilities and activities of individuals participating in a research project are consistent with their respective competencies.

d Psychologists make every effort to minimize discomfort, illness, and pain of animals. A procedure subjecting animals to pain, stress, or privation is used only when an alternative procedure is unavailable and the goal is justified by its prospective scientific, educational, or applied value. Surgical procedures are performed under appropriate anesthesia; techniques to avoid infection and minimize pain are followed during and after surgery.

e When it is appropriate that the animal's life be terminated, it is done rapidly and painlessly.

(*Source:* American Psychological Association. 1981. Ethical principles of psychologists. *American Psychologist 36:* 638.)

MAJOR ISSUES IN THE CONDUCT OF RESEARCH WITH ANIMAL SUBJECTS

Each year millions of animals become subjects in laboratory investigations aimed at answering a wide range of important questions. New drugs are tested on animals before they are used with humans. Substances introduced into the environment must first be given to animals to test their effects. Animals are exposed to diseases in order that investigators may observe symptoms and test various cures. New surgical procedures—especially those involving the brain—are often first tried out on animals. Many animals are also used for behavioral research, for example by ethologists and experimental psychologists. These investigations yield much information that contributes to human welfare (see Miller, 1985). In the process, however, many animals are subjected to pain and discomfort, stress and sickness, and death. Although rodents, particularly rats and mice, are the largest group of laboratory animals, researchers use a wide variety of species in their investigations, including monkeys, fish, dogs, and cats. Specific animals are frequently chosen because they are good models of human responses. For example, psychologists interested in audition sometimes use chinchillas as subjects because their auditory processes are very similar to those of humans. Apparently, chimpanzees are the only nonhuman primates that can harbor the virus linked to AIDS, which experts say will be contracted by more than a quarter of a million people by the early 1990s (Landers, 1988). Because of the dwindling numbers of these animals, concern has been expressed by both animal conservationists, who worry about the extinction of this species, and biomedical researchers, who may depend on the availability of these animals for laboratory research aimed at finding a vaccine for AIDS (Booth, 1988; Goodall, 1987).

The use of animals as laboratory subjects has often been taken for granted. In fact, the Biblical reference to man's "dominion" over all lesser creatures is sometimes invoked to justify the use of animals as laboratory subjects (see, for example, Rollin, 1985). More often, however, the research with animal subjects is justified by the need to gain knowledge *without putting humans in jeopardy* about aspects of nature that directly affect the human condition. Few cures, drugs, vaccines, or therapies have come about without experimentation on animals (see Rosenfeld, 1981). It would be difficult to contemplate the consequences of doing research on such diseases as cancer or muscular dystrophy without the opportunity first to examine the course of the disease or try out a new cure on animal subjects. Feeney (1987), for example, has called attention to the contributions that basic research with animal subjects has made to the treatment of patients recovering from brain and spinal cord injury. He also points out that our understanding of the relationship between brain and behavior was advanced significantly by the now classic work of Roger Sperry in the 1960s, who won a Nobel Prize for his work on the "split brain" (the functioning of the brain after the corpus callosum has been cut). Early investigations by Sperry and others, using cats and monkeys as subjects, demonstrated that the two hemispheres of the brain can function independently in learning and memory.

Recently, however, many questions have been raised about the role of animal subjects in laboratory studies. These questions include the most basic one, whether animals should be used at all in scientific investigations, as well as equally important questions about the care and protection of animal subjects. Many of the questions raised regarding research with animal subjects have been directed toward psychologists (see Larsen, 1982). In 1976, for instance, the research activities of an experimental psychologist working at the American Museum of Natural History attracted considerable media attention (see Wade, 1976a). For almost 20 years the investigator had been studying the sexual behavior of domestic cats. The research sometimes involved observing behavioral changes in cats when the cats had been deprived of various kinds of sensation or brain function. For instance, parts of the brains of the cats or the cats' testicles were removed. Animal-rights groups vigorously challenged the researcher's activities, which had been funded by the National Institute of Child Health and Human Development. Opponents of the research picketed the museum and tried to get people to stop making contributions to it. Threats to kill or maim the persons responsible for the research were also received. The major complaints by the animal-rights groups were that the cats were inhumanely treated, that the experimental manipulations were cruel and unethical, and that the research was unlikely to lead to significant new knowledge. The project was defended by the principal investigator; by the museum director, and by individuals who granted research funds for the project. Nevertheless, the case raised questions about similar research activities carried out by other behavioral scientists.

Clearly, according to the APA principles, the researcher who uses animal subjects in an investigation has an ethical obligation to look out for their welfare and to treat them humanely (see APA Principle b). Only individuals who are qualified to do research and to manage and care for the particular species that is used should be allowed to participate (APA Principle c). When research is to be done that exposes the animals to pain or discomfort, it must be justified by the potential scientific, educational, or applied goals (APA Principle d). However, it is also clear that the APA principles deal almost exclusively with the care and treatment of animal subjects and do little to restrict their use. Although researchers are morally obligated not to subject animals to needless harm or pain (APA Principles d and e), critics have suggested that the APA principles seem to imply researchers' absolute freedom to use the subjects in whatever way they deem necessary (see Wade, 1976). Nevertheless, as was noted earlier when institutional review was discussed, animal review boards (IACUCs) are now in place at research facilities receiving funds from the Public Health Service. These committees are charged with determining the adequacy of the procedures for controlling pain, carrying out euthanasia, housing animals, and training personnel, as well as determining whether the experimental design is sufficient to gain important new information and whether the animal model is appropriate or whether nonanimal models exist (Holden, 1987).

Partly in response to calls from members of animal-rights groups during the 1980s, investigators now must meet a host of federal and state requirements, including inspection of animal facilities by veterinarians from the U.S. Department of Agriculture (see, for example, Landers, 1987a; 1987b). These regulations often are welcomed by members of the scientific community, and many animal researchers belong to groups such as the APA Committee on Animal Research and Experimentation (CARE), which seek to protect laboratory animals. As with any ethically sensitive issue, however, it is clear that compromises must be reached. For example, until alternatives to animal research can be found, the need to conduct research using animal subjects in order to battle human disease and suffering must be balanced against the need for adequate control over the way animals are treated in laboratory research (see, for example, Goodall, 1987). Hovering above this discussion is the need for a balanced treatment of the issues (see, for example, Kelly, 1986). While few scientists would disagree that restrictions are necessary to prevent needless suffering in animals, most want to avoid a quagmire of bureaucratic restrictions and high costs that will undermine research. Feeney (1987) suggests that severe restrictions and high costs, as well as the negative publicity (and occasional terrorist acts) directed toward individuals and institutions by extremists within the animal-activists groups, may deter young scientists from entering the field of animal research. If such is the case, the result possibly could be to deprive the (presently) incurably ill or permanently paralyzed of the hope that comes through scientific research (see Feeney, 1987).

CASE STUDIES FOR DISCUSSION

The following descriptions of published studies are presented for analysis and discussion. Ethical issues are present in any psychological investigation. Some situations and procedures, however, pose more serious problems than others. These studies have been selected deliberately to identify various ethical dilemmas faced by investigators in the context of doing psychological research. Therefore the studies should not be considered representative of all psychological research, nor should their selection be interpreted to mean that they have been judged unethical.

The sensitivity of psychologists to ethical issues is evidenced by the fact that a number of these published studies contain lengthy discussions by the investigators about the ethical problems raised by their research. Some of the more recent studies were no doubt reviewed by an ethics committee or institutional review board prior to their being carried out. As you read these abstracts of published studies, consider what ethical issues are raised and how the rights and welfare of the subjects are protected. Try to think of similar situations or methodologies that pose ethical dilemmas for an investigator. Decide how you would resolve these issues. Remember, however, that you have an advantage over the researchers and the members of the institutional review boards. You know what results were obtained and can determine a risk/benefit ratio "after the fact." As you make your decisions, try to put yourself in the position of those who must try to *anticipate* what benefits the research might have.

(1) Newman, J., and Krzystofiak, F. Self-report versus unobtrusive measures: Balancing method variance and ethical concerns in employment discrimination research. 1979. *Journal of Applied Psychology* 64:82–85.

The impact of affirmative action pressures on employment practices of companies was assessed using two different data collection procedures. In one study 240 employment managers were sent fake résumés describing work and educational experiences of two racially different applicants. In a second study, another 240 managers from the same population were asked to provide self-reports on what employment action they would take *if* they had actually received the two different résumés.

In the self-report condition 86 percent of the companies said they would treat the applicants identically. When companies were not aware that they were subjects of a field experiment, less than one-half of the companies were found to treat the applicants equally. The authors concluded that self-report data on affirmative action practices are not likely to reveal the actual employment actions taken in the case of racially different applicants.

(2) Middlemist, R. D.; Knowles, E. S.; and Matter, C. F. Personal space invasions in the lavatory: Suggestive evidence for arousal. 1976. *Journal of Personality and Social Psychology 33:* 541–546.

Personal space is defined as an area with invisible boundaries surrounding an individual and into which others may not come. People seek comfortable interpersonal distances and will move away when others invade their space. A field experiment was conducted to test the hypothesis that personal space invasions produce arousal as measured by delay of onset and duration of men's urination. Men using a three-urinal lavatory at a Midwestern university were subjects. According to a previously determined schedule of random assignment a confederate either stood at the urinal directly adjacent to the subject, stood one urinal away, or was absent from the lavatory. An observer with a periscope was concealed in a toilet stall and recorded measures of urination. He did not see the faces of the subjects. Data were gathered on sixty users of the lavatory, all of whom did not know that they were subjects in an experiment. Delay of onset and persistence of urination were inversely related to closeness of another individual at the urinal. For example, urination delay (measured as the time between when a subject unzipped his fly and when urination began) was 4.8 seconds in the Confederate Absent condition, 6.2 seconds when the confederate was one urinal away, and 8.4 seconds when the confederate was at the adjacent urinal. Results were interpreted as supporting the hypothesis that increased arousal is a result of personal space invasions and this is a probable cause of certain behavioral responses (for example, moving away).

(3) Farrar, C. H.; Powell, B. J.; and Martin, L. K. Punishment of alcohol consumption by apneic paralysis. 1968. *Behavior Research and Therapy 6:* 13–16.

One approach to the treatment of alcoholics is aversion therapy. A noxious unconditioned stimulus is paired with alcohol consumption. At the time of the investigation, previous studies had shown mixed results using an aversion treatment based on a curare-like drug that produces rapid and complete paralysis of the skeletal muscles. Although patients remain conscious, there is a temporary suspension of respiration (apnea). Patients' response to this sudden inability to breathe is generally extreme fear. The subjects were twelve male alcoholics who had been admitted to a state psychiatric center and who had expressed a desire to stop drinking. All were on some form of drug therapy. In each case the patient exhibited evidence of a psychoneurotic or personality disorder or was classified as exhibiting "chronic brain syndrome." Patients were informed that they would receive a treatment that would help them stop drinking. They were told that "although frightening, the treatment involved minimal risk and actually was no more dangerous than extraction of a tooth" (p. 14). A physician and nurse assisted on the day of the treatment. Subjects lay down and an intravenous (IV) needle was inserted in their arm. The IV apparatus was hidden behind a screen, and patients were told that the IV contained only harmless salt solution. The paralyzing drug was injected via the IV and coincided with the subject's drinking a glass of alcohol. After 30 seconds of apnea, a manual resuscitator was used so that the total time during which breathing was interrupted did not last longer than 90 seconds. The subjects believed that the sudden cessation of respiration was related to alcohol consumption, and all spontaneously vowed during a postexperimental interview never to drink again. Twelve months later nine of the original twelve subjects were contacted. Only two had stopped drinking. One of these subjects reported that he was extremely anxious concerning anything to do with alcohol and had violent reactions to such substances as mouthwash and hair-spray. Although he believed that the aversion treatment had stopped his excessive drinking permanently, the subject felt that the cure had left him in worse than his original condition. Possible reasons for the failure of the treatment were discussed and suggestions given for future research.

(4) Humphreys, L. *Tearoom trade: Impersonal sex in public places.* 1975. Chicago: Aldine. (Enlarged edition with a retrospect on ethical issues. First edition published in 1970.)

Within the homosexual subculture, a tearoom is a public restroom where homosexual encounters occur. During a period between 1965 and 1968, the researcher investigated the nature of homosexual activity in restrooms located in public parks of a large city. In the initial stages of the project the researcher was a participant observer. He assumed the role of a "lookout-voyeur," someone who watches for the approach of intruders while simultaneously being permitted to observe the homosexual acts. In his role of "watchqueen," the researcher was able to observe homosexual activity directly without physically participating. The researcher made field research notes by using a portable tape recorder concealed in his car and by making written observation records when he got back to his office. The researcher also recorded the license numbers of cars of individuals he had observed engaging in homosexual activities. Using vehicle registration information, he obtained the home addresses of 100 subjects. Observations were then made of their residences. This provided information as to geographic distribution, socioeconomic status (size of house, location) as well as other characteristics (swing sets or bicycles indicated subjects had children). Fifty subjects were personally interviewed in their homes in the guise of conducting a health survey. Responses of these individuals were compared to responses made by a group of fifty control subjects. Interviews were made more than a year after the subjects had been observed in homosexual activity. The researcher had changed his appearance and was not recognized. The list of names identifying these particular individuals was kept in a safety deposit box, and other identifying information was destroyed immediately after an interview was completed. Twelve additional subjects gave their permission for an in-depth interview of their homosexual activities. Identities of all subjects in the study were scrupulously safeguarded. The study provided a comprehensive description of the settings, types of individuals, strategies and tactics governing encounters, signaling systems, contracting, and other behaviors associated with homosexual activities. Also included was evidence of blackmailing by local law enforcement personnel. In the Foreword to the published study, the director of the research project emphasizes the important knowledge gained and suggests that the results will provide a base for those trying to formulate rational social policies toward homosexual behavior.

(5) Hetherington, E. M., and Feldman, S. E. College cheating as a function of subject and situational variables. 1964. *Journal of Educational Psychology 55*:212–218.

The study seeks to identify factors associated with cheating behavior of college students. Subjects were students enrolled in two child psychology classes at a state university. All subjects had taken a large battery of tests, including the California Personality Inventory (CPI), the Minnesota Multiphasic Personality Inventory (MMPI), and the Taylor Manifest Anxiety Scale, and had answered a questionnaire asking about such personal characteristics as sex, birth order, religion, and grade-point average. Three situations were provided for students to cheat. Situation 1 was the first examination in the course, an hour-long multiple-choice test. Five observers in the class watched for cheating while the instructor pretended to be inattentive. Students were also allowed to grade their own test in the following class period, unaware that the examination had been graded in the interim. Situation 2 was the second examination in the course, an essay test. A week in advance, students had been given a list of five questions and told that two of the questions would be on the exam. Examination booklets were easily available at the university, and, at the time of the test, the booklets distributed by the instructor were unobtrusively marked so that any student substituting a booklet completed outside of class could be detected. In Situation 3 students were given an oral examination administered individually in the instructor's office. Part way through the exam, the instructor was called out of the room. The text from which the questions were being taken was left in a conspicuous position near the student. Its position was carefully marked so that the instructor could tell whether the book had been opened while she was absent from the room. After the data had been collected on cheating behaviors in the three situations, the class was told the nature of the experiment and those students who cheated were permitted to take a makeup examination. More than half (59 percent) of the students exhibited some form of cheating. Approximately 64 percent of those cheating did so in two situations, and 24 percent cheated in all three situations. The tendency to cheat was associated with certain demographic, intellectual, and personality characteristics of the subjects. Cheaters, relative to noncheaters, tended to be males and first-borns, to exhibit a set of behaviors that suggest maternal overprotection, and to be lower in intelligence. Cheaters also reported significantly *higher* frequency of church attendance than noncheaters. Characteristics of cheaters also differed according to the type of situation in which they were found cheating.

(6) Darley, J. M. Fear and social comparison as determinants of conformity behavior. 1979. *Journal of Personality and Social Psychology 4:73–78.*

Psychological conformity is generally defined as accepting the opinions or judgments of others in the absence of significant reasons to do so or in the face of evidence to the contrary. A laboratory experiment was conducted to test the hypothesis that increasing a person's fear level will lead to increases in conformity. A total of sixty-four female subjects volunteered for a psychology experiment and were paid $1.50 per hour for their participation. Subjects were told that the experiment concerned hearing mechanisms, that subjects in an experimental condition would receive electric shocks, and that subjects assigned to a control condition would not. An experimenter dressed in a white coat met each subject and took her to a room littered with electrical apparatus. The experimenter informed the subject of the particular condition (experimental or control) that she had been assigned to and informed her of the assignment of three other women whom the subject believed were also present in the situation. The "other" women were either in the same condition as the subject or in the other condition. The subject put on headphones through which she heard instructions by the experimenter and through which she believed responses of other subjects in the experiment could be heard. Subjects in the experimental group heard instructions intended to induce fear of electrical shock. They were told that physiological modification procedures involving electric shock were necessary to evaluate hearing mechanisms. The instructions went on to indicate that the shock would be painful but that the results of the experiment had great potential for alleviating suffering caused by hearing defects. Subjects were then given an opportunity to rate their feelings of nervousness about the experiment and to indicate whether they would prefer to wait with other women in the experiment or to wait alone during a period following the pretest and before the experimental subjects would be given their electroshocks. The conformity test was then administered in the guise of a pretest

of auditory acuity. Subjects were asked to count the number of tape-recorded metronome clicks that they heard. The subject gave her responses after three other subjects, working as confederates of the experimenter, had given their responses. The confederates gave wrong but unanimous judgments on twelve of the eighteen trials. The measure of conformity was the number of trials on which the subject gave the same wrong response. No subject actually received electric shock. After the experiment the subjects were told the true purpose of the experiment, and the experimenter discussed their reactions with them. The fear manipulation worked, as evidenced by the ratings subjects gave about their nervousness and by the fact that women threatened by shock wanted to wait with other subjects whom they thought would also be receiving shock. Subjects thinking they were to receive shock were more likely to conform to the confederates' responses than those believing they would not be shocked. Conformity was highest when subjects were in the shock condition and also believed that the other women were in the same condition. Results supported the hypothesis that increases in the level of fear increase subjects' degree of conformity and that conformity is highest when the pressure to conform comes from people toward whom the subject feels affiliative. The author points to possible relationships between his findings and mob behavior in a panicked crowd. People sometimes are led to imitate senseless and maladaptive acts of a panicked member of the crowd.

(7) Milgram, S. *Obedience to authority.* 1974. New York: Harper & Row.

During the early 1960s the researcher conducted a number of experiments designed to investigate the psychological mechanisms underlying obedience to authority. Although there were many variations, the basic methodology was as follows. Two people came to a psychology laboratory supposedly to participate in a verbal learning study. They were told that the study was concerned with the effects of punishment on learning. The individuals drew slips of paper to determine who would be the "teacher" and who would be the "learner." One person was actually an accomplice of the principal investigators, and the drawing was rigged so that the real subject was always given the role of teacher. The subject watched as the learner was taken to an adjacent room and strapped into a chair and an electrode attached to the wrist. The subject then heard the experimenter say that the learner would receive an electric shock for every error made while learning a list of word pairs. The teacher was then taken to the laboratory room, which housed an impressive-looking shock generator with thirty lever switches. Each switch was labeled with a voltage designation (ranging from 15 to 450 volts), and next to the switches were verbal labels describing the amount of shock, for example, "Slight Shock," "Strong Shock," and "Danger: Severe Shock." Two switches after the last verbal description are simply marked XXX. The teacher was given a sample shock and told to administer the electric shock to the learner whenever the learner made a mistake. The learner's responses were communicated via a set of four switches that lit up a number on the top of the shock generator. The teacher was also told to move one lever higher on the shock generator after each wrong response. As the experiment progressed, the learner offered various protests to the shock. These complaints could be heard through the walls of the room and included shouts to the effect that the shocks were becoming painful and, later, that the learner wanted the experimenter to end the procedure. When the teacher moved the switch at 180 volts, the learner yelled, "I can't stand it any more" and at 270 volts gave an agonizing scream. At 300 volts the learner yelled "I will not give any more answers" but continued to scream. After the switch corresponding to 330 volts was pressed, the learner was not heard from any more. The learner was not actually shocked, and the major dependent variable was the maximum shock that the subject would give in response to the "orders" of the experimenter.

Subjects usually exhibited intense conflict during the task and frequently turned to the experimenter to ask whether they should continue in the face of the learner's protests. A number of subjects expressed fear that they were seriously harming the learner. The experimenter always answered the subject's inquiries with predetermined responses that varied from "please continue" to "you have no choice, you must go on." Even when the learner fell silent, the experimenter told the teacher he had to continue giving shocks. Despite the obvious anguish experienced by the subjects, many followed the directions of the experimenter and administered the most extreme shocks possible. When subjects could hear the screams of the learner but not actually see the learner, approximately 60 percent of the subjects gave the maximum shock. In another variation of the experiment, when the learner was present in the room and the teacher was ordered to force the learner's hand onto a shock plate, 30 percent of the subjects complied despite the very convincing protests of the learner. All subjects were debriefed and at times talked to individually for some length of time. All received a follow-up questionnaire and were sent a summary of the major findings. The number of ordinary people (many subjects were recruited from the local community through advertisements in the newspaper) who would knuckle under to authority and commit blatantly immoral acts was not predicted either by a group of psychiatrists or by people from the same population as the subjects. When thirty-nine psychiatrists were given a description of the experiment and polled as to what they believed would be the maximum shock subjects would administer, none predicted that subjects would give the most extreme shock. The mean maximum shock predicted was 8.20, whereas in the actual experiment the mean maximum shock was 24.53 when the subject could be heard but not seen. The report contains a lengthy description of the possible mechanisms underlying these responses to authority and an extensive discussion of the ethics of the experiments. The major justification for continuing the experiment when the initial (and unexpected) responses of subjects were obtained was that no subjects were apparently seriously injured by the experiment and that an overwhelming majority of the subjects (84 percent) said they were glad to have been in the experiment. Many subjects (74 percent) said in a follow-up questionnaire that they had gained something of personal value from the experience. The investigator cooperated with a follow-up study in which an impartial medical examiner interviewed forty of the subjects. No evidence of traumatic reactions to the experiment was found.

(8) Aggleton, J. P., and Passingham, R. E. Syndrome produced by lesions of the amygdala in monkeys (*Macaca mulatta*). 1981. *Journal of Comparative and Physiological Psychology* 95: 961–977.

The amygdala is a subcortical structure of the brain associated with the expression of emotion and aggression. Total destruction of the amygdala in monkeys generally leaves them unnaturally tame, exhibiting a lack of emotional responsiveness, showing excessive exploratory behavior, deficient in certain learning tasks, and (occasionally) hypersexual. In the present study sixteen male rhesus monkeys were operated on, and either a portion of the amygdala or the total amygdala was destroyed. The operations were carried out with the monkeys under anesthesia and in sterile conditions. Lesions were produced by lowering an electrode through a hole cut in the skull and then briefly raising the temperature of the electrode tip in the target area. Some of the monkeys were operated on twice. One group of four monkeys was initially operated on but did not receive amygdala lesions. These animals served as a control group in stage one of the testing procedure. Three of the control monkeys were operated on again and the entire amygdala was removed. Four other monkeys also received a second operation in order to provide a control for the monkeys experiencing total destruction of the amygdala.

The goal of the study was to compare the effects of selective subtotal lesions of the amygdala with the effects of total lesions. In this way the researchers hoped to be able to discover whether certain areas of the amygdala mediated specific behavioral responses seen when the entire amygdala was destroyed. Various experiments were carried out to test the monkeys' food preferences, exploratory tendencies, emotional responsiveness, and willingness to approach a natural fear stimulus (an experimenter unknown to the animals or a plastic mask of a human face) as well as to examine learning of visual discriminations. Testing of emotional responsiveness involved observing the animals' reactions to various frightening stimuli presented to them in the testing apparatus. These stimuli were toys (for example, a snake or a bear) or the experimenter staring at them while wearing a surgical cap and gown as well as a face mask. After testing, all the animals were sacrificed by intracardial profusion using formolsaline. Brains of the monkeys were prepared for histological examination so as to reveal the exact position of the lesions.

Results of behavioral testing showed that only monkeys with total or near-total destruction

of the amygdala showed the typical amygdalectomy syndrome. Lesions in specific areas of the amygdala failed to fractionate the syndrome. Only mild behavioral changes were observed in these animals, compared to the dramatic change in emotional responsiveness and deficits in learning observed in the animals with total lesions. The results are seen as having particular relevance to psychosurgery with humans, because the procedure in the present experiment was similar to that used with human patients who are operated on in an attempt to control hyperaggressive and assaultive behavior. Psychosurgery is said to "normalize" the individuals, to have effects that are restricted to the patient's aggressive behavior, and not to involve global changes in the patient's emotional responsiveness. Results of the present experiment apparently showed that not only aggression may be affected but also other aspects of emotional, motivational, and cognitive functioning. In fact, one monkey appeared to show an *increase* in aggression following the lesioning of the amygdala. In addition to the serious implications raised for psychosurgery with humans, the results contributed further to knowledge of the function of the amygdala in mediating behavior.

(9) Seligman, M. E. P.; Maier, S. F.; and Geer, J. H. Alleviation of learned helplessness in the dog. 1968. *Journal of Abnormal Psychology 73:* 256–262.

Previous experiments had revealed a striking behavioral abnormality referred to as "learned helplessness." Specifically, dogs who have been given inescapable electric shock while strapped in a harness failed to behave normally when later given escape/avoidance training. In this type of training an animal is first placed on one side of a shuttlebox apparatus, where it is shocked. The naive dog generally runs frantically about, defecating, urinating, and howling until it manages to cross a barrier to the other side where it is not shocked. On successive trials, normal animals generally move more quickly to the other side when placed in the shock side. However, animals that have experienced inescapable shock prior to escape/avoidance training often stop running and fail to escape the shock. Rather, they passively "accept" the shock and hence experience as much as 50 seconds of severe pulsating electric shock. This reaction was termed learned helplessness, because it was hypothesized to result from the animal learning in the first stage of the procedure (during inescapable shock) that its behavior was independent of the presentation of the electric shock. This maladaptive response is seen as being similar to behavior disorders in humans in which individuals passively accept aversive consequences without attempting to escape. Such behavior was observed in the Nazi concentration camps wherein some prisoners were described as "walking corpses" who had apparently given up all hope and who felt that there was nothing whatsoever that they could do to change their environment.

In the present experiment the researchers investigated possible methods of alleviating learned helplessness in dogs. Animals that had previously failed to escape shock as a result of receiving prior inescapable shock served as subjects. Four mongrel dogs had been placed in a rubberized cloth hammock, constructed to allow their legs to hang beneath them. Shock was delivered through electrodes taped to the dogs' hind feet. Animals had received sixty-four trials of inescapable shock. Twenty-four hours later they had been tested for escape/avoidance learning and all four dogs had failed to escape after ten trials, having experienced 500 seconds of shock during these trials. This failure to escape was also observed 7 days later. Subsequently a procedure of behavior modification was used to attempt to remove the learned helplessness reaction. Treatment consisted of first calling to the dogs, with no barrier present in the escape/avoidance procedure and, for those dogs not responding to this treatment, physically pulling the animals to the safe side in the shuttle apparatus. One dog responded to the first stage of treatment; the remaining dogs began to show escape/avoidance after the "directive therapy." All animals were then given further testing with the barrier gradually being raised to shoulder height. The procedures were viewed as being entirely successful in breaking up the maladaptive failure of the dogs to escape and to avoid shock. Results were considered to be in line with a theoretical analysis provided for this phenomenon as well as to shed light on possible therapy procedures for humans who have experienced traumatic events and who then show passive responding to future aversive events. It is suggested that pathological behavior resulting from inescap-

able trauma may be alleviated by exposing individuals to situations wherein their behavior can be seen as instrumental in obtaining successful avoidance of aversive events.

(10) Lovaas, O. I.; Schaeffer, B.; and Simmons, J. Q. Building social behavior in autistic children by use of electric shock. 1965. *Journal of Experimental Research in Personality 1:* 99–109.

The usefulness of pain in modifying the behavior of two 5-year-old identical twins diagnosed as childhood schizophrenics was explored in this study. The twins had shown no improvement with conventional psychiatric therapy and were largely unresponsive to daily interpersonal events. They showed no social responsiveness, nor did they speak or play appropriately with objects. They showed considerable self-stimulatory behavior (rocking, repeated moving of hands and arms) and a fair amount of tantrum behaviors (screaming, throwing objects, and hitting themselves). Several studies were conducted using electric shock to modify the social responsiveness of the twins' behavior. It was noted that, at the time the studies began, the future of the children was certain to include institutionalization. They had already been under observation and treatment in a residential setting. In one study the children were placed in a room the floor of which had been covered with metal tape and from which shock could be delivered. The shock level was such that the three experimenters standing barefooted on the floor considered it painful and frightening. When the children were placed in the room, they were shocked immediately whenever pathological behaviors were observed. Shock was turned off when the children approached an adult who was present. In this way the adult represented a "safe" object in an otherwise painful environment. In a second study, the children were shocked by means of a portable apparatus strapped to their backs that could be signaled electronically to deliver shock via electrodes strapped to their buttocks. In this study the behavior to be modified was refusal to hug and kiss the experimenter. Children were shocked when they failed to respond to the experimenter's request to "hug me" or "kiss me." In a third study the children were trained to press a lever to obtain M & M candy and simultaneously to see the experimenter's face. The children were then trained to come to the experimenter to avoid shock. Finally, the reinforcing power of the experimenter was tested by phasing out the candy reward and letting the children see the experimenter's face only as a consequence of lever pressing. The studies compared behavior following shock with control or baseline periods of no shock and also tested for generalization of effects to other situations. Results showed that shock was effective in increasing the children's approach to adults and eliminating certain pathological behaviors. It also affected other social behaviors exhibited toward adults. Generalization of the shock procedures was observed, although not in all instances, and some effects were shortlived. The children actually appeared happier during successful shock therapy and did not show fearful behaviors, except at the onset of training. The researchers suggest that the successfulness of shock in modifying behavior will not come in the suppression of specific responses but in the establishment of social reinforcers through shock reduction. The question of the necessity of using electric shock was raised. However, it was pointed out that previous attempts to modify social behaviors through the use of food delivery had been unsuccessful and were both time-consuming and laborious compared to the use of electric shock.

APPENDIX C

Scientific Research Reports

OUTLINE

INTRODUCTION

Scientific research is a public activity. A clever hypothesis, an elegant research design, meticulous data collection procedures, reliable results, and an insightful theoretical interpretation of the findings are all useless to the scientific community unless they are made public. As one writer suggests most emphatically, "Until its results have gone through the painful process of publication, preferably in a refereed journal of high standards, scientific research is just play. Publication is an indispensable part of science" (Bartholemew, 1982, p. 233). A "refereed" journal is one in which submitted manuscripts are reviewed by other researchers who are experts in the field addressed in the paper under review. These so-called peer reviewers evaluate whether the research is methodologically sound and whether it makes a substantive contribution to the field of psychology. These reviews are then submitted to a senior researcher who serves as editor of the journal. It is the editor's job to decide which papers warrant publication.

As we have already noted, the most common vehicle for making a research study available to the scientific community is the journal article. *Memory & Cognition, Child Development, Journal of Personality and Social Psychology,* and *Journal of Clinical and Consulting Psychology* are but a few of the journals that publish research studies of interest to investigators in a variety of fields in psychology. Editors of these journals decide which manuscripts will be published. Their decisions are based on (a) *the quality of the research* and (b) *the effectiveness of its presentation in the written manuscript.* Thus both content and style are important. Editors seek the best research, clearly described. Journal editors set rigorous standards; only about one of every four manuscripts submitted to the leading psychology journals is accepted for publication (American Psychological Association, 1988).

Editorial review and the publication process itself are time-consuming. More than a year can elapse between when a paper is submitted and when it finally appears in the journal. To provide a more timely means of reporting research findings, professional societies such as the American Psychological Association, the American Psychological Society, the Psychonomic Society, and the Society for Research in Child Development sponsor conferences at which researchers give brief oral presentations describing their recent work. Such conferences also provide an opportunity for discussion and debate among investigators interested in the same research questions.

In order to do research, whether it will eventually be reported at a conference or published in a journal, investigators must often obtain financial support in the form of a grant from a government or private agency. These grants are typically awarded on the basis of a competitive review of research proposals. Because these proposals are written before the research is actually done, they require a slightly different style and format from a journal article.

What do journal articles, oral presentations, and research proposals have to do with you? If you attend graduate school in psychology, you will probably have to describe your research using all three types of scientific communication. Even if you do not pursue a professional career in psychology, the principles of good written and oral presentations are applicable to a wide variety of employment situations. For example, a memo to your department manager describing the outcome of a recent sale may have much the same content and format as a short journal article. Of more immediate concern, however, your course in research methods may require you to write or deliver a research report. This appendix will help you do it well. First we will review some guidelines for effective writing. Then we will discuss the preparation of research reports, both written and oral, as well as the writing of research proposals.

Throughout this appendix we have drawn heavily on the *Publication Manual* (3d ed., 1983) of the American Psychological Association. Editors and authors use this manual in order to ensure a consistent style across the many different journals in psychology. The manual answers questions ranging from appropriate content for each section of the article to rules for typing the final manuscript. If graduate study in psychology is in your future, we recommend that you add the *Publication Manual* to your personal library. (Order from the American Psychological Association, 1200 17th St. N.W., Washington, D.C. 20036.)

GUIDELINES FOR EFFECTIVE WRITING

Learning to write well is like learning to swim, drive a car, or play the piano. Improvement is unlikely to result solely from reading about how the activity is to be done. A person learns to write well by writing and by getting critical feedback from writing "coaches" (teachers, friends, editors). Nonetheless, reading over the "Rules of the Road" in preparation for a periodic driving test often proves beneficial even for experienced drivers. So, too, a brief look at the "Rules of Good Writing" should prove helpful. Even though the format of a research report may be new to you, the basic and familiar rules of effective writing still apply. Professional writer Jack Ridl provides a maxim for effective writing: "Write, not assuming that you will be understood, but trying to avoid being misunderstood." Good writing, like good driving, is best done defensively. Assume that whatever *can* be misunderstood will be!

The first way to avoid being misunderstood is to *know your audience*. If you assume your readers know more than they actually do, you will leave them confused. If you underestimate your readers, you risk boring them with unnecessary details. Either risk seriously increases the likelihood that what you have written will not be read. But if you must err, it is better to underestimate your readers. For example, in preparing research reports you might reasonably assume that your intended audience is your instructor. Writing for this audience might lead you to "leave a lot out of your paper" because, after all, your instructor knows all that anyway. It would probably be better to consider your fellow students your audience. This might result in your including more detail than necessary, but it will be easier for your instructor to help you learn to "edit out" the nonessential material than to "edit in" essential material that you have omitted. Whatever intended audience you choose, make the selection *before* you begin to write, and keep your audience in mind every step of the way.

A second task that you must complete before you begin to write is to *identify your purpose*. The principal purposes of a journal article are to describe and to convince. You want first to describe what you have done and what you have found, and second to convince the reader that your interpretation of these results is a sound one. A research proposal, on the other hand, is principally written to persuade someone that the proposed research is worth doing. Because they are typically brief, oral presentations can be expected to do little more than get the listener interested enough to read more about the topic. Knowing the purpose for which you are writing should help you choose what information to present and decide how that information should be presented.

Although the specific purposes of research reports and proposals vary, all reports and proposals represent the general category of expository writing. Webster's defines exposition as "discourse designed to convey information or explain what is difficult to understand." The foundation of good expository writing is clarity of thought and expression. The *Publication Manual* (1983) clearly outlines the road to clarity. "Clear communication, which is the prime objective of scientific reporting, may be achieved by presenting ideas in an orderly manner and by expressing oneself smoothly and precisely" (p. 31).

One avenue to clarity is adherence to grammatical rules, the mechanics of good writing. Table C.1 presents a helpful checklist of common mechanical errors (Trigg, 1979). If the problem in each of these examples is not apparent to you, a review of basic grammar may be in order. The "corrected" version of each item is found in Table C.2. The *Publication Manual* (pp. 34–35) also contains sage advice regarding diction: the choice of the right word at the right time.

> Make certain that every word means exactly what you intend it to mean. Sooner or later most authors discover a discrepancy between their accepted meaning of a term and its dictionary definition. In informal style, for example, *feel* broadly substitutes for *think* or *believe*, but such latitude is not acceptable in scientific style.
>
> Likewise, avoid colloquial expressions (e.g., *write up* for *report*), which diffuse meaning. Approximations of quantity (e.g., *quite a large part, practically all*, or *very few*) are interpreted differently by different readers or in different contexts. They weaken statements, especially those describing empirical observations.

Other mechanical problems are common in students' papers. For example, the words *affect* and *effect* are not interchangeable. As a verb, *affect* means *to influence*, and as a noun it means *emotion or feeling*. As a verb, *effect* means *to cause to come into being*, and as a noun it means *outcome or result*. The following incorrect statement could have been added to Table C.1: "You will have an adverse affect on your instructor's effect when you misuse affect and effect." Another problem that often arises involves words of Latin and Greek origin with unusual plural forms. Words such as "data," "phenomena," and "criteria" are plural. They require a plural verb form and plural adjective modifiers: "These data show that...."

TABLE C.1 CHECKLIST FOR AUTHORS: IN YOUR OWN WRITE

1. Make sure each pronoun agrees with their antecedent.
2. Just between you and I, the case of pronouns is important.
3. Watch out for irregular verbs that have crope into English.
4. Verbs has to agree in number with their subjects.
5. Don't use no double negatives.
6. Being bad grammar, a writer should not use dangling modifiers.
7. Join clauses good like a conjunction should.
8. A writer must not shift your point of view.
9. About sentence fragments.
10. Don't use run-on sentences you got to punctuate them.
11. In letters essays and reports use commas to separate items in series.
12. Don't use commas, that are not necessary.
13. Parenthetical words however should be enclosed in commas.
14. Its important to use apostrophes right in everybodys writing.
15. Don't abbrev.
16. Check to see if you any words out.
17. In the case of a report, check to see that jargonwise, it's A-OK.
18. As far as incomplete constructions, they are wrong.
19. About repetition, the repetition of a word might be real effective repetition—take, for instance the repetition of Abraham Lincoln.
20. In my opinion, I think that an author should definitely not get into the habit of making use of too many unnecessary words that are not needed in order to put the message across.
21. Use parallel construction not only to be concise but also clarify.
22. It behooves us all to avoid archaic expressions.
23. Mixed metaphors are a pain in the neck and ought to be weeded out.
24. Consult the dictionery to avoid mispelings.
25. To ignorantly split an infinitive is a practice to religiously avoid.
26. Remember to hyphenate two or more word modifiers that precede the words they modify.
27. Last but not least, lay off clichés.

Merely avoiding flagrant violations of grammatical rules does not guarantee effective writing. Grammatical rules do not address questions of organization and style. As you will see in the next section, a generally agreed-upon structure has evolved for research reports, and this structure dictates the basic organization of research papers. Although certain stylistic conventions are often suggested, these are less consistently adhered to than the structural conventions. For instance, at one time scientific writing was assumed to require the use of the third person passive: "It has been shown that behavior is affected by the drug." Such constructions were intended to connote increased objectivity, but all too often they resulted only in deadly dull prose. The sentence construction to use is the one that is the most direct and concise: "The drug affected behavior." Increasingly, the use of third person constructions ("The authors believe...") are being replaced by the use of the first person ("We believe...") (see Polyson and Levinson, 1982).

The American Psychological Association has issued a policy statement (APA Publication Manual, p. 43, regarding one aspect of the style of research papers:

TABLE C.2   "CORRECTED" VERSION OF TABLE C.1: CHECKLIST FOR AUTHORS

1. Make sure each pronoun agrees with its antecedent.
2. Just between you and me, the case of pronouns is important.
3. Watch out for irregular verbs that have crept into English.
4. Verbs have to agree in number with their subjects.
5. Don't use double negatives.
6. A writer should not use dangling modifiers.
7. Join clauses well as a conjunction should.
8. A writer must express a consistent point of view.
9. Avoid sentence fragments.
10. Don't use run-on sentences. You have to punctuate them.
11. In letters, essays, and reports use commas to separate items in series.
12. Don't use commas that are not necessary.
13. Parenthetical words, however, should be enclosed in commas.
14. It's important to use apostrophes right in everybody's writing.
15. Don't abbreviate.
16. Check to see if you left any words out.
17. In the case of a report, check to see that you have avoided jargon whenever possible.
18. As far as incomplete constructions go, they are wrong.
19. The repetition of a word might be effective.
20. An author should definitely not use unnecessary words.
21. Use parallel construction not only to be concise but also to clarify.
22. We should avoid archaic expressions.
23. Mixed metaphors ought to be weeded out.
24. Consult the dictionary to avoid misspellings.
25. To split an infinitive is a practice to avoid.
26. Remember to hyphenate two-or-more-word modifiers that precede the words they modify.
27. Avoid clichés.

> APA as a publisher accepts journal authors' word choices unless those choices are inaccurate, unclear, or ungrammatical. Because APA as an organization is committed both to science and to the fair treatment of individuals and groups, however, authors of journal articles are required to avoid writing in a manner that reinforces questionable attitudes and assumptions about people.

Although APA is concerned with the general problem of fair treatment of individuals and groups, one aspect of language use has received special attention. APA has developed guidelines for the use of nonsexist language "to help authors recognize and change instances in which word choices may be inaccurate, misleading, or discriminatory" (p. 43). These guidelines and a few examples of their use are presented in Tables C.3 and C.3A. Most psychology journals now require all published manuscripts to conform to the guidelines, so it would be wise (and considerate) to get into the habit of using nonsexist language.

As we noted at the outset, our review of the essentials of effective writing is neither exhaustive nor thorough enough to make you a good writer. Developing your writing skill requires several trips through the cycle of writing, reading, and rewriting, preferably with critical feedback from others in the reading stage. The *Publication Manual* again provides a clear statement of the

TABLE C.3   GUIDELINES FOR NONSEXIST LANGUAGE

Sexism in journal writing may be classified into two categories: problems of *designation* and problems of *evaluation.*

Problems of designation

When you refer to a person or persons, choose words that are accurate, clear, and free from bias. Long-established cultural practice can exert a powerful, insidious influence on even the most conscientious author. For example, the use of *"man"* as a generic noun can be ambiguous and may convey an implicit message that women are of secondary importance. You can choose nouns, pronouns, and adjectives to eliminate, or at least to minimize, the possibility of ambiguity in sex identity or sex role. In the examples given in the following table, problems of designation are divided into two subcategories: *ambiguity of referent,* where it is unclear whether the author means one or both sexes, and *stereotyping,* where the writing conveys unsupported or biased connotations about sex roles and identity.

Problems of evaluation

Scientific writing, as an extension of science, should be free of implied or irrelevant evaluation of the sexes. Difficulties may derive from the habitual use of clichés, or familiar expressions, such as "man and wife." The use of *"man and wife"* implies differences in the freedom and activities of each and may inappropriately prompt the reader to evaluate the roles. "Husband and wife" are parallel; "man and wife" are not. In the examples given in the following table, problems of evaluation, like problems of designation, are classified in terms of ambiguity of referent and stereotyping.

Avoiding sexist language

The task of changing language may seem awkward at first. Nevertheless, careful attention to meaning and practice in rephrasing will overcome any initial difficulty (Bass, 1979). The result of such effort, and the purpose of the guidelines in this table, is accurate, unbiased communication.

goal: "By developing ideas clearly and logically you invite readers to read, encourage them to continue, and make their task agreeable by leading them smoothly from thought to thought" (p. 31). With this goal in mind, we now turn our attention to the "nuts and bolts" of a research report by considering the structure of a typical journal article.

STRUCTURE OF A RESEARCH REPORT

The structure of a research report serves two major purposes. First, the structure offers an organizational framework with which the author can provide a clear description of the research and a convincing interpretation of the findings. In this sense, the structure is like that provided by the various acts of a Shakespearean play. Both the playwright and the audience share certain expectations about what should occur in each act as the play unfolds. For example, "the stage will be set" in the first act and the climax is expected in the third act. Similarly, in a research report both author and reader share expectations about the content of each section of the report. The structure is not intended to shackle the playwright or the author. It simply provides a vehicle to make it easier for the audience to focus on the particular point being made in the play or the research report.

A research report is like a play but it is also like a telephone directory. The structure of a telephone directory is intended to facilitate access to specific information. The structure of a research report also serves this "ready reference"

TABLE C.3A GUIDELINES FOR NONSEXIST LANGUAGE IN APA JOURNALS

Examples of common usage	Alternatives
Problems of designation: ambiguity of referent	
The *client* is usually the best judge of the value of *his* counseling.	The *client* is usually the best judge of the value of counseling. [Comment: *His* deleted] The client is usually the best judge of the value of his or her counseling. [Comment: *Or her* added (Use sparingly to avoid monotonous repetition.)] *Clients* are usually the best judges of the value of the counseling *they* receive. [Comment: Changed to plural] The best judge of the value of counseling is usually *the client.* [Comment: Rephrased]
The use of experiments in psychology presupposes the mechanistic nature of *man.*	The use of experiments in *psychology* presupposes the mechanistic nature of the *human being.* [Comment: Noun substituted]
Problems of designation: stereotyping	
Research scientists often neglect their *wives* and *children.*	Research scientists often neglect their *spouses* and *children.* [Comment: Alternative wording acknowledges that women as well as men are research scientists.]
Problems of evaluation: ambiguity of referent	
The authors acknowledge the assistance of *Mrs. John Smith.*	The authors acknowledge the assistance of *Jane Smith.* [Comment: Use given names.]
Problems of evaluation: stereotyping	
men and girls	men and women, women and men, boys and girls [Comment: Use parallel terms. Of course, use *men* and *girls* if that is literally what is meant.]
The boys chose typically male toys. The client's behavior was typically female.	The boys chose (specify). The client's behavior was (specify).
Subjects were 16 men and 4 women. *The women were housewives.*	The men were (specify), and the women were (specify). [Comment: Women and men described in parallel terms or description of both omitted. Do not use *housewife* to identify occupation, a term that indicates sex and marital status and excludes men. Use *homemaker*, which includes men.]

function. If you wanted to know how an experiment was done, you would look in the Method section; if you were seeking specific information about some particular research finding, you would look in the Results section.

Even though research reports can be used like telephone directories, they should not read like telephone directories. As the *Publication Manual* puts it, "Although scientific writing differs in form from literary writing, it need not and should not lack style or be dull" (p. 22). When writing a research report you should keep the analogy of the play in mind; when mining the research literature to set up your next experiment, you may find the telephone directory analogy more helpful.

The research report consists of the following sections:

	Title Page
	Abstract
	Introduction
Body of Report {	Method
	Results
	Discussion
	References
	Footnotes
	Appendixes

The four sections from the Introduction to the Discussion make up the body of the report (the four acts of the "play"). The Title Page and the Abstract are like the playbill you would see before the play itself begins, and the remaining sections are the counterpart of the credits. In this appendix we will provide descriptions of the content and format of each of these sections, but these descriptions will not suffice for teaching you how to write a report. The best preparation for that is to read journal articles in some area of psychology that interests you. Even so, you will perfect your skill at writing research reports only by actually writing them.

TITLE PAGE

The first page of a research report is the title page. It includes the title of the research report, the name(s) of the author(s), and the institutional affiliation(s) of the author(s). An illustration of a correctly typed title page and succeeding pages of a research report is presented in the sample paper at the end of this appendix. The title page indicates what the research is about, who did the research, and where the research was done. The title is perhaps the most critical aspect of your paper, because it is the part that is most likely to be read! The title should clearly indicate what the central topic of your paper is. In the words of the *Publication Manual* (pp. 22–23):

> A title should summarize the main idea of the paper simply and, if possible, with style. It should be a concise statement of the main topic and should identify the actual variables or theoretical issues under investigation and the relation between them.
>
> Titles are commonly indexed and compiled in numerous reference works. Therefore, avoid words that serve no useful purpose; they increase length and can mislead indexers. For example, the words *method* and *results* do not normally appear in a title, nor should such redundancies as "A Study of" or "An Experimental Investigation of" begin a title.

A common format for the title of students' research reports is "[The Dependent Variable(s)] as a Function of [the Independent Variable(s)]." For example, "Anagram Solution Time as a Function of Problem Difficulty" and "Accuracy of Mirror Tracing as a Function of Gender and Background

Luminence" would be good titles. The title must not only be informative, but it should also be brief; the recommended maximum length is fifteen words. At all costs avoid uninformative or ambiguous titles such as "Operant Conditioning Results," "Laboratory Report #1," or "Personality Differences in Subjects." Be sure your title describes as specifically as possible the content of your research.

ABSTRACT

The second page of the report, the Abstract, appears under that single word, which is typed as a centered heading (see sample paper). The abstract is a one-paragraph summary of the content and purpose of the research report. The abstract should be 100 to 175 words long (about ten to fifteen double-spaced typewritten lines), and it should highlight the critical points made in each of the four sections of the body of the report (Introduction, Method, Results, Discussion). The abstract should also specify the population from which subjects were drawn, the nature of the test instruments or research apparatus employed, and the data-gathering procedures—all in sufficient detail to reflect their importance in the research study. Next to the title, the abstract is the part of the paper that is most likely to be read. And, like the title, it will help determine whether readers will go on to the rest of the paper. Because so much information must be presented in a single paragraph, you may find the abstract difficult to write. The best approach is to write it last! If you write the abstract after you have written the rest of the report, you will be able to "abstract" or paraphrase your own words more easily. The *Publication Manual* (pp. 23–24) summarizes these points well.

> An abstract is a brief, comprehensive summary of the contents of the article; it allows readers to survey the contents of an article quickly and, like the title, is used by abstracting and information services to index and retrieve articles.
>
> A well-prepared abstract can be the single most important paragraph in the article....Do not include in an abstract information that does not appear in the body of the paper....Make each sentence maximally informative, especially the lead sentence. Be as brief as possible....An abstract that is accurate, succinct, quickly comprehensible, and informative will increase the audience and the future retrievability of your article.

INTRODUCTION

Objectives The title of your report appears at the top of the third page as a centered heading, and then the first paragraph of the introduction section begins immediately. This is the only section of the report that does *not* begin with a centered section heading (see sample paper). The introduction serves three purposes. The order in which these objectives are met in any given report may vary, but the order in which we will describe them here is the most common one.

First, the introduction should provide a general statement of the problem being addressed. This places the paper in perspective. The second objective is to summarize briefly the relevant background literature that led you to the present research problem and approach. Finally, the introduction includes an outline of the present study and a logical development of the predictions or hypotheses (if any) guiding the research. All three of these objectives share a common purpose: to give the reader a firm sense of what you are doing and why you are doing it.

The *Publication Manual* suggests four questions to keep in mind while writing the introduction: "What is the point of the study? How do the hypothesis and the experimental design relate to the problem? What are the theoretical implications of the study, and how does the study relate to previous work in the area? and What are the theoretical propositions tested, and how were they derived?" (p. 24).

The purpose of summarizing related research studies is *not* to provide an exhaustive literature review. Instead, care should be taken to select the most pertinent studies to develop the rationale of your experiment. In summarizing these selected studies, you should emphasize whatever details of the earlier work will best help the reader understand what *you* have done and why. You must acknowledge the contributions of other researchers to your understanding of the problem. Of course, if you quote directly from another person's work, you must use quotation marks.

More commonly, however, reference is made to the work of other researchers in one of two ways. Either you refer to the authors of the article you are citing by their last names, with the year in which the paper was published appearing in parentheses immediately after the names, or you make a general reference to their work and follow it with *both* the names and the year of publication in parentheses. For example, if you were citing a study by David G. Myers and Jane R. Dickie that was published in 1989, you would write either "Myers and Dickie (1989) have found...." or "Recent research (Myers & Dickie, 1989) has shown that...." Complete bibliographical information on Myers and Dickie's paper, including the journal title, volume number, and specific pages, would appear in the References section. Footnotes are *not* used to cite references in a research report in psychology.

You should include in your paper only those references that you have actually read. If you read a paper by Motiff (1990) in which the research of Ludwig (1988) is described, you should not cite the Ludwig paper unless you have actually read that paper. Instead, you should use some form such as "Ludwig (1988), as reported by Motiff (1990), found that..." You should use this approach for two reasons. The first and most obvious one is that you should accurately report what you have read. If this appeal to scholarly integrity does not suffice, you should recognize the risk you are taking. If Motiff (1990) has misreported the work of Ludwig (1988) and you repeat this misrepresentation, you are equally subject to criticism. You won't subsequently be able to say, "Motiff (1990) made me do it." The general rule is simple: *Cite only what you have read.*

Searching the Psychological Literature   In the long run, the best way to develop ideas for research and to become familiar with the relevant literature is to read regularly the journals in your area of interest. Reading journal articles requires an approach different from reading newspaper articles or textbooks. In the spirit of "well begun is half done," we present ten commandments for reading journal articles in Table C.4. The comments below the commandments provide a brief interpretation of each one. Following these dictums will help you to read more critically and successfully.

At the time you are taking your research methods course you may not have had a chance to read the research literature widely or to have settled on a principal area of interest in psychology. So, when you are faced with the task of writing a research report, you may need help in searching the psychological literature. For example, you may have an idea for an experiment and you may wonder whether this experiment has already been done. Or you may have read an article describing an experiment on which you would like to base your experiment, and you may be interested in finding other studies related to this topic. Fortunately, resources are available to help you answer such questions without plodding through every issue of every psychology journal in the campus library.

Perhaps the most useful reference tool for psychology students is *Psychological Abstracts,* in which the abstracts from over 1,000 national and international periodicals are published monthly. These abstracts are organized under sixteen general categories, such as "Experimental Psychology (Human)" and "Physical and Psychological Disorders." Under each category, abstracts are arranged alphabetically by the first author's name, and the abstracts are numbered consecutively in two volumes each year. One volume covers January–June issues and one covers July–December. In 1987 over 36,000 abstracts appeared in *Psychological Abstracts* (that's over 3,000 abstracts in each monthly issue). Obviously, browsing aimlessly through issues of the *Abstracts* would be only slightly less time-consuming than browsing through the journals themselves.

The most efficient way to search through *Psychological Abstracts* is to use one of the two indices that are published with each volume. An author index contains an alphabetical listing of authors of articles in that volume, along with the number of the abstract of each author's article. If you were interested in doing research in perception, you could use an undergraduate textbook to identify well-known researchers in this area and then use the author index to locate the abstracts of their most recent work. The second type of index, the subject index, is a bit more cumbersome to use, but it is obviously essential if you have not identified specific researchers whose work you want to locate. The subject index is psychology's version of the Yellow Pages. However, your fingers can do a lot of walking before you finally find what

TABLE C.4   TEN COMMANDMENTS FOR READING RESEARCH ARTICLES CRITICALLY

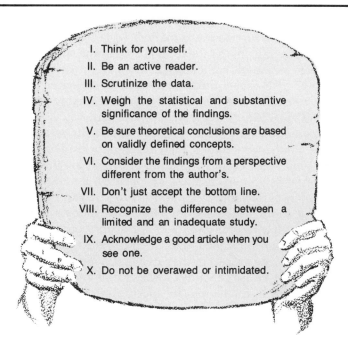

I. Think for yourself.

II. Be an active reader.

III. Scrutinize the data.

IV. Weigh the statistical and substantive significance of the findings.

V. Be sure theoretical conclusions are based on validly defined concepts.

VI. Consider the findings from a perspective different from the author's.

VII. Don't just accept the bottom line.

VIII. Recognize the difference between a limited and an inadequate study.

IX. Acknowledge a good article when you see one.

X. Do not be overawed or intimidated.

Comments on the Commandments

(1) Read the paper with the goal of gaining your own understanding of the research. The best source for an independent view of what was done and what was found is the Method and Results section, respectively.

(2) Read the paper actively from start to finish. Whenever possible, outline, paraphrase, or write down questions about the details of the study.

(3) Examine the data very carefully, especially those in tables and figures. Are the findings internally consistent; do they support the author's expectations?

(4) Examine not only whether a given effect is statistically significant, but also what its magnitude is. Are the conclusions based on strong or marginal results?

(5) Often conclusions found in the Discussion are stated in terms of theoretical concepts and make no mention of their defining operations. This is appropriate but only when the operations validly define the concepts.

(6) An independent view of the findings is one that is free of bias. Viewing the findings from a different perspective involves purposely adopting a bias different from the author's.

(7) Any "bottom line" conclusion is the result of several transformations of the original data. Be sure you get to the bottom of these transformations before accepting the bottom line.

(8) A study that confounds the age of the subjects in each of two treatment groups is inadequate. One that tests only fifth graders in both groups is of limited generality, but it is interpretable.

(9) A good study asks and answers a good question. If the method is sound and the conclusions are supported by the results, then the study passes the critical test for good research.

(10) Remember the tremendous assets you have in reading research articles. The article includes technical language, including statistics, and the author is likely an authority about the research itself, but you have the advantage of objectivity and a fresh perspective.

Adapted from Table 1 in Anisfeld, 1987. Used by permission of the author.

you are looking for. To make matters worse, the language of psychology is an ever-changing one, so the topics listed in the subject index vary somewhat from year to year. Nonetheless, careful and industrious use of the subject index can be an excellent route to invaluable references. If you want to use the subject index to locate abstracts of articles related to your research in perception, you must focus your topic. Perhaps terms such as "motion perception" or "apparent movement" would lead you to the references you want.

Once you have identified a few recent articles (within the last three to five years), your best bet for continuing to search the literature would be to use the References sections of these key articles. If an article keeps appearing in the References sections of other articles, you can be fairly sure that it is an important paper. There is even a reference index called the *Social Science Citation Index* that records the reference history of an article. That is, once an article has been published, the citation index searches the References sections of all future articles in that area and notes whenever the original article is cited. You can use the index to determine how many times a given article has been cited or to identify the specific articles in which the given article is cited. In a sense, *Psychological Abstracts* allows you to search backward from the present, and the *Social Science Citation Index* allows you to search forward from the past. Like *Psychological Abstracts*, the *Citation Index* permits you to trace the work of a specific author. Detailed instructions regarding the use of the *Citation Index* are best left to a reference librarian.

We will conclude this section on searching the psychological literature with a brief look at one search technique of the future that is already here: computerized literature search. A useful overview of online information retrieval is provided by Lewis (1986). Our discussion of this topic will be limited to the description of a computer-assisted search done by one of our undergraduate students, Janet Swim. Janet was interested in conducting a survey to determine the incidence of rapes and other sexual assaults on dates. She had come across a few references to this topic in her general reading in the area of women's studies, and now she wanted to make a more systematic search of the psychological literature. A reference librarian helped Janet make a search of the computer-based counterparts of both *Psychological Abstracts* and the *Social Science Citation Index*.

Janet used a keyword technique to search *Psychological Abstracts*, and she had a chapter on rape by Klemmack and Klemmack (1976) to serve as the basis of her search of the *Citation Index*. A keyword search is possible because of the computer's ability to access large amounts of information quickly. The computer is able to scan the titles and abstracts of articles in its memory and to identify all those that contain particular keywords. The most effective approach to this type of search is to have intersecting keywords *both of which* need to be present before the computer will "tag" an article. For example, Janet used the keyword RAPE and the letter string DAT to guide her search. She chose the letter string DAT in order to catch such variants as DATE, DATES, and DATING. This intersection led to the identification of seventy-five references, seventy-three of which were written in English. Janet also obtained eleven additional references that had cited the Klemmack and Klemmack (1976) paper when she had the computer search the *Social Science Citation Index.*

The major advantage of the computer-assisted search is speed; Janet completed both searches in less than half an hour. There are a few disadvantages of this approach. Computer searches are not yet as sophisticated as those done by a person, so many of the references the computer locates do not prove useful. For example, Janet obtained one reference on rape among mallard ducks on specific chronological dates. Keywords can also prove tricky. The string DAT identified all studies using the word DATA, so a number of Janet's references provided data about rape—but not solely in the context of dating. One final potential disadvantage of doing a computer search is that there is usually a fee associated with using this service. Nonetheless, when used properly, a computer-assisted literature search is a useful tool. Parr (1979) concludes that "Online information retrieval adds a new dimension to bibliographic inquiry while at the same time reinforcing use of traditional bibliographic sources" (p. 62).

METHOD

The second major section of the body of a research report is the Method section. The Method section is usually identified by a centered heading ("Method") with a double space separating it from the preceding and following text (see sample paper). The Method section follows right after the Introduction. The Introduction has provided a broad outline of the research you have done; the Method fills in the nitty-gritty details. The *Publication Manual* presents a straightforward description of the goals of the Method section: "The method section describes in detail how the study was conducted. Such a description enables the reader to evaluate the appropriateness of your methods and the reliability and the validity of your results. It also permits experienced investigators to replicate the study if they so desire" (p. 25). Writing a good Method section can be frustrating. It sounds easy because all you have to do is describe exactly what you have done. But if you want to get a sense of how challenging this can be, just try to write a clear and interesting paragraph describing how to tie your shoelaces.

The key to a good Method section is organization. Fortunately, the structure of this section is so consistent that a few basic subsections provide the pattern of organization you need for most research reports. Before describing the content of these subsections, however, we must address the question that students writing their first research report ask most frequently: "How much detail should I include?" The quality of your paper will be adversely affected if you include either too much or too little detail. The rule stated in the *Publication Manual* seems simple enough: "Include in these subsections only the information essential to comprehend and replicate the study" (p. 26). As we have said before, the best way to learn how to follow this rule is to read the Method sections of journal articles and to write your own research reports. Be sure to get feedback from your instructor concerning appropriate level of detail.

The four most common subsections of the Method section are Subjects (Participants), Design, Apparatus (Materials), and Procedure. Each of these subsections is introduced by an underlined subheading that usually begins at the left margin (see sample paper). The *Publication Manual* (p. 26) aptly summarizes the content of the Subjects subsection.

> The subsection on subjects answers three questions: Who participated in the study? How many participants were there? How were they selected? Give the total number of participants and the number assigned to each experimental condition. If any participants did not complete the experiment, give the number of participants and the reasons they did not continue. When humans are the participants, report the procedures for selecting and assigning subjects and the agreements and payments made. Give major demographic characteristics such as general geographic location, type of institutional affiliation, sex, and age. When animals are the participants, report the genus, species, and strain number or other specific identification, such as the name of the supplier. Give the number of animals and the animal's sex, age, weight, and physiological condition. In addition, specify all essential details of their treatment and handling so that the investigation can be successfully replicated.

The Design subsection contains such information as the operational definitions of independent and dependent variables, along with the specific design used for each independent variable. The procedures used to form groups of subjects (such as random assignment or matching) should be described. Counterbalancing or randomization techniques for arranging the levels of within-subjects variables could also be included in this subsection. Often the information in this subsection and that in the Subjects subsection are presented together in a combined subsection called Design and Subjects. Another common practice is to include the material that would be presented in the Design subsection in the Procedure subsection. Where the design information appears in the Method section is optional; that it appear *somewhere* in the Method section is required.

The Apparatus subsection is also optional. If the only equipment you used is paper, pencils, and a stopwatch, it is better to include this information in the Procedure subsection than in a separate Apparatus section. On the other hand, if the apparatus or materials played a central role in the study, a separate subsection is useful. In an operant conditioning experiment, it would be essential to describe the conditioning chamber in which the animal was trained. If complex or custom-made equipment has been used, a diagram or drawing is helpful for both the reader and the writer of an Apparatus subsection. In general, the label "Apparatus" is used when mechanical equipment is described. The label "Materials" is used when less mechanical instruments, such as a paper-and-pencil personality test, have been constructed or used. If you use equipment or materials developed by another investigator, you should cite the work of that investigator, but you should also include the general characteristics of the materials in your own report.

The Procedure subsection is the most critical component of the Method section. It is here that you describe what happened from the beginning to the end of the sessions in which you tested your participants. As the previous sentence implies, the organization of the Procedure subsection is usually chronological. You should begin writing this subsection by outlining the important steps in testing participants in each group of your study. Next you can either describe the procedure for each group in turn or describe the procedures common to all groups and then point out the distinguishing features of each group. Whichever organization you choose (you may not learn which works best until you have tried to write both), it is best to begin writing only after you have prepared a checklist of the important features of your procedure. The instructions given to subjects should be presented in paraphrase form unless they define an experimental manipulation, in which case they should be reported verbatim. The *Publication Manual* recommends that the Method section, and especially the Procedure subsection, "should tell the reader *what* you did and *how* you did it" (p. 26).

RESULTS

The centered heading "Results" introduces this third major section of the body of a research report (see sample paper). Like the third act of a dramatic play, the Results section contains the climax of the research report—the actual findings of the study. For many students, though, the excitement of describing the climax is blunted by anxiety. The source of their anxiety is the necessity of reporting statistical information in the Results section. The best way to alleviate this anxiety, of course, is to develop the same command of statistical concepts that you have of other concepts. While you are acquiring this mastery of statistics, however, you need a way to deal effectively with the problem of presenting statistical information. The solution to this problem is to adopt a simple organizational structure to guide your writing of the Results section.

You should use your Results section to answer the questions you raised in your Introduction. In a sense, the Results section is like the evidence presented during the testimony of witnesses in a criminal trial. The Introduction serves as the counterpart of the attorney's opening statement, and the Discussion (to be described in the next section of this appendix) parallels the attorney's closing statement to the jury. The guiding principle in the Results section is to "stick to the facts, just the facts."

Reporting Statistics   The *Publication Manual* provides a clear statement of the objectives of a Results section: "The Results section summarizes the data collected and the statistical treatment of them. First, briefly state the main results or findings. Then report the data in sufficient detail to justify the conclusions" (p. 27). As we mentioned, there is a structure for the paragraphs of the Results section that will help you meet these objectives. This structure is outlined in Table C.5, and an illustration of a paragraph from the Results section of a published article appears after the table. The paragraph should begin by identifying the descriptive statistic that will be used to summarize the results for a given dependent variable. For example, you might use the mean number of correct responses, the median reaction time, or the cumulative number of bar presses per minute to summarize the results in each condition of your study. Next, a summary of this descriptive statistic across conditions should be provided. Whenever possible, measures of central tendency should be accompanied by corresponding measures of variability. If there are only two or three conditions in your experiment, this summary can be presented in the text itself. For instance, you could summarize the results of a two-group study by saying, "The mean number of correct responses for the experimental group was 10.5 ($s = 2.1$) , whereas that for the control group was 5.2 ($s = 1.8$)."

More commonly, however, you will have more data to summarize and you will need to present your findings in either a table or a figure (graph). We will describe the procedures for constructing tables and figures later in this section. For now, it will be sufficient if you simply look at the examples of tables and figures in the sample paper at the end of the appendix.

TABLE C.5   STRUCTURE OF A TYPICAL PARAGRAPH IN THE RESULTS SECTION

1. Identify the descriptive statistic to be used to summarize results.
2. Present a summary of this descriptive statistic across conditions in the text itself, in a table, or in a figure.
3. If a table or figure is used, point out the major findings on which the reader should focus.
4. Present the reasons for, and the results of, inferential statistics tests.
5. State the conclusion that follows from each test, but do not discuss implications. These belong in the Discussion section.

SAMPLE PARAGRAPH

To examine retention as a function of instructions given at the time of study, the number of words recalled by each subject in each instruction condition was determined. Words were scored as correct only if they matched a word that had appeared on the target list. Thus, synonyms were not counted as correct; misspelled words were accepted if the spelling was sufficiently similar to a target item that it could be reasonably concluded that the intended word had actually appeared on the list. Mean numbers of words recalled were 15.6, 15.2, and 10.1 in the bizarre imagery condition, the standard imagery condition, and the control condition, respectively. Overall, mean recall differed significantly among the conditions, $F(2, 72) = 64.84$, $MS = 0.44$, $p < .05$. Two analytical comparisons were performed to determine the source of this effect. These tests revealed that the two groups given imagery instructions when averaged together differed significantly from the control condition, $F(1, 72) = 44.62$, $p < .05$; however, the two imagery conditions did not differ significantly from each other, $F(1, 72) = 1.66$, $p > .05$. In conclusion, retention by subjects instructed to use imagery was higher than that by subjects given no specific study instructions, but retention did not differ for the two types of imagery instructions.

A table or figure should not be expected to be self-sufficient. Instead, it should be used more like a map that you are given as you enter a large and unfamiliar museum. For most of us, the map is not sufficient to guarantee a satisfying visit to the exhibits without some commentary from a tour guide. Similarly, your reader needs some help to gain as much information as possible from a table or figure. You are in the best position to offer this assistance, because you are the person who is most familiar with your results. You should direct your reader's attention to the highlights of the data in the table or figure, focusing especially on those aspects of the results that are consistent (or discrepant) with the hypotheses you proposed in the Introduction. Usually the same data are not reported in both a table and a figure. Tables provide a more precise description of the results, but figures make it easier to see trends or patterns in the data. Whichever you choose, be sure to highlight in the text itself the critical results that the table or figure reveals.

The fourth step in writing a paragraph of the Results section is to present the reasons for, and the results of, inferential statistical tests. The reason(s) for doing an analysis should be stated succinctly; often, no more than a phrase is necessary. You might introduce an inferential test by saying, "An analysis of variance was done to determine the main effect of the drug variable" or "In order to determine the overall effect of the drug variable...." There are two reasons for making the rationale for each analysis explicit. It helps your reader follow the logic of your analysis plan. And it ensures that you will never try to report an analysis whose purpose you do not understand.

Three pieces of information should always be reported with any inferential statistics test: the name of the test (usually indicated by a symbol such as t, r, χ^2, or F); the degrees of freedom for the test; and the value of the test statistic that you obtained. Until quite recently, the convention had been to report the probability level along with each test relative to the chosen level of significance, such as $p < .05$ or $p < .01$. An example of the conventional format would be, "The mean in the experimental group (5.20) was significantly higher than the mean in the control group (3.00), $t(24) = 2.75$, $p < .05$." More recently, editors have suggested that the significance level for all inferential tests be specified early in the Results section and that each reported test be accompanied by the estimate of error variation for that test. For instance, you might see "The overall effect of the drug variable was statistically significant, $F(3, 64) = 7.15$, $MS_{error} = 2.4$." When you write the Results section, you should assume that your reader has a basic knowledge of inferential statistics. Therefore, you do not need to refer to concepts such as the null hypothesis or mention whether your outcome falls in or out of the critical region. All that is required is that you use the term "statistically significant" correctly.

The final step in writing a good paragraph in the Results section is to state a brief conclusion that follows from each test you report. This is accomplished by referring to the descriptive statistics on which the inferential test is based. For example, if the mean number correct in the experimental group is 10, that in the control group is 5, and this difference is statistically significant, an appropriate concluding statement would be "The control group did more poorly than the experimental group." In this simple example the conclusion may seem obvious, but appropriate concluding statements are essential in more complex analyses. It is discouraging when a student strings together a series of inferential statistical tests with appropriate commentary on the statistical significance of each test—and then never reports the descriptive statistics or any conclusion. It is almost useless for your readers to know that an independent variable has had a statistically significant effect if you have failed to describe the nature of that effect. *Descriptive* statistics are essential in providing such a description.

As we mentioned earlier, each paragraph of the Results section follows the structure outlined in Table C.5. The idea is not to overload your reader with statistics. The challenge is to select those findings that are most critical, being sure to report all the data pertinent to the questions raised in your Introduction. Before concluding our discussion of the Results section, we will briefly describe the basic procedures for constructing tables and figures, two key tools in reporting results effectively.

Presenting Data in Tables Tables provide an effective and efficient means of presenting large amounts of data in concise form. The table should supplement and not duplicate information in the text of the paper, but it should be well integrated into the text. The tables in your paper should be numbered consecutively (arabic numerals are used to number tables) so that they can be referred to easily in the text by their number. Each table should also have a brief explanatory title, and the columns and rows of the table should be labeled clearly. The data entries in the table should all be reported to the same degree of precision (that is, all values should have the same number of decimal places), and the values should be consistently aligned with the corresponding row and column headings. An appropriately constructed table appears in the sample manuscript at the end of this appendix.

When manuscripts are submitted for publication, each table is typed on a separate page and the tables appear at the end of the paper after the References and Footnotes sections. This is done principally for the convenience of the typesetter, who will be positioning the tables in the printed journal article. When this format is used, the position of the table in the paper is indicated by typing "Insert Table 1 about here" as a centered heading either immediately before or immediately after the paragraph in which the first reference to the table appears. You separate this heading from the preceding and the following paragraphs by double-spacing before and after typing the heading (see sample paper). Some instructors prefer to have their students type the table in the text itself at the point where reference to the table is made. A table number and title are required even when the table is placed directly in the text.

Presenting Data in Figures   Figures, like tables, provide a concise way to present large amounts of information. Of course, the format of a figure differs from that of a table. A figure has two principal axes: the horizontal axis or X-axis and the vertical axis or Y-axis. Typically, the levels of the independent variable are plotted on the X-axis, and those of the dependent variable are plotted on the Y-axis. When there are two or more independent variables, the levels of the second and succeeding independent variables serve as labels for the curves within the figure or are indicated in a figure legend. Two illustrations of the format for figures are presented in Figures C.1 and C.2. In Figure C.1 the values of the dependent variable are plotted on the Y-axis, the levels of one independent variable (serial position) are indicated on the X-axis, the levels of the second independent variable (C versus NC) label the curves, and the levels of the third independent variable (instructions) serve as the headings for each of the two panels of the figure. There are also three independent variables represented in Figure C.2: one on the X-axis and two differentiated by symbols that can be interpreted by using the legend at the top of the figure. For example, the reversal groups are represented by circles and the control groups are represented by squares. Here again, the Y-axis indicates values of the dependent variable.

The two sample figures illustrate that there are alternative ways to construct useful graphical presentations. All figures must include certain features, however. The X- and Y-axes must be clearly labeled, with each label printed parallel to the corresponding axis. Selected points (called grid points) on each axis must be identified with labeled grid marks, and the grid labels are always printed horizontally. Each figure is accompanied by a figure caption that corresponds to the title of a table.

Figures are numbered consecutively in the paper with arabic numerals, and they are referred to by number. The numbering of figures is done separately from the numbering of tables. It is common in psychology to enclose figures in a boxed outline, as had been done in Figures C.1 and C.2. The grid

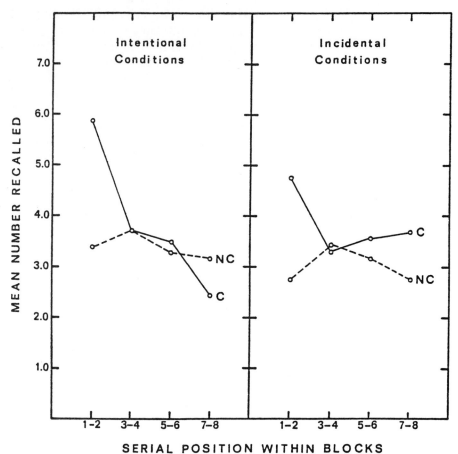

FIGURE C.1 Mean number of words recalled (of a possible ten) as a function of serial position within blocks and instructional condition (C = Cued; NC = Noncued).

points of the X-axis are repeated on the top and those of the Y-axis are repeated on the right for ease of reading the figure, but these additional grid points are usually not labeled. Finally, the grid scale for the X- and Y-axes should be chosen such that the plotted curves are legible and span the entire illustration. Although the word *caption* actually means *at the head,* the captions of Figure C.1 and Figure C.2 appear at the bottom of the corresponding figure because this is a common format that instructors use for students' research reports. The figure then appears as the page following the page of text on which reference to the figure is first made. When a manuscript is submitted for publication, each figure appears on a separate page but the figure captions do not appear on the figures themselves. They are presented on a separate page under the centered heading "Figure Captions." This page follows the tables at the end of the manuscript but precedes the figures, which are presented in order.

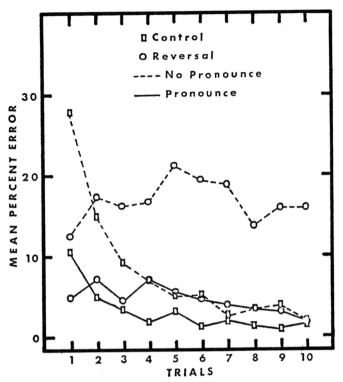

FIGURE C.2   Mean percent error across trials for TCC transfer as a function of type of transfer task and pronunciation instructions

Two general types of figures are commonly used in psychology: bar graphs and line graphs. A *bar graph* should be used when the independent variable plotted on the X-axis is a nominal-scale variable (see Chapter 1). For example, if you were plotting the mean GPA (dependent variable) of students enrolled in different academic majors (independent variable), you would use a bar graph. An illustration of a bar graph is presented in Figure C.3. By far the most common type of figure is the *line graph*. Figures C.1 and C.2 represent this type of figure, and we have already discussed the procedures for constructing it.

DISCUSSION

The fourth section of the body of your report, the Discussion, opens with a centered head (see sample paper). After presenting the evidence in the Results section, you are ready for your "closing statement to the jury." In the words of the *Publication Manual* (p. 27):

> After presenting the results, you are in a position to evaluate and interpret their implications, especially with respect to your original hypothesis. In the Discussion

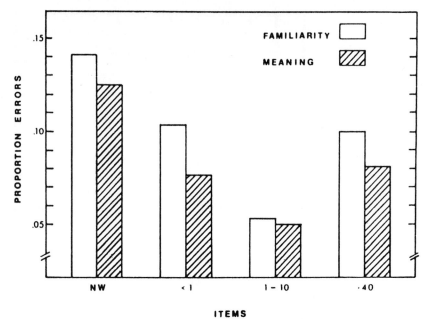

FIGURE C.3 Proportion recognition errors made by two groups of college students after rating verbal items for either familiarity or meaning. The items were nonwords (NW) and words appearing less than one time, one through ten times, and more than 40 times per million in the Thorndike-Lorge count.

section, you are free to examine, interpret, and qualify the results, as well as to draw inferences from them.

The Discussion should begin with a succinct statement of the essential findings, and you should give particular attention to how your findings support or refute your original hypotheses. You do not repeat the descriptive statistics in this summary, nor do you necessarily refer to the statistical significance of the findings. The Discussion is written in a tone and style consistent with the Introduction. Be careful, however, to keep the statements you make in the Discussion consistent with the data reported in the Results. For instance, you should not report that one group did better than another if the comparison between these groups was not statistically significant—at least not without some qualification on what you mean by "better."

The second step in the Discussion is to tie your findings in with the relevant literature, most of which you will have cited in the Introduction. "Similarities and differences between your results and the work of others should clarify and confirm your conclusions" (*Publication Manual,* p. 27). If your results are not consistent with your original hypotheses, you should suggest an explanation for these discrepancies. Such *post hoc* (after-the-fact) explanations should be considered tentative at best. If the reasons for your results are unclear, you should not hesitate to say so. In students' research reports, it is often necessary and helpful to include a paragraph describing limitations or problems in your research. As noted in the *Publication Manual,* however, "...do not dwell compulsively on every flaw" (p. 28). On the other hand, you should try to anticipate possible criticisms of your study that others might make.

If appropriate, you should conclude the Discussion by proposing additional research that should be done on the problem you are investigating. Avoid clichés such as "Additional research on this problem is needed before definitive conclusions can be reached." Instead, be specific about what research should be done and *why* it needs to be done. That is, be sure to explain what the new research should reveal that we do not already know. Do not just say, "It would be interesting to do this experiment with younger subjects." Explain how you would expect the results to differ with younger subjects and what you would conclude if the results of the proposed experiment were to turn out as expected. Remember, the watchword in proposing new research is to *be specific.* Your emphasis should definitely be on quality, not quantity.

Some students (as well as some professional researchers) find it hard to separate their description of their findings from their interpretation of the results. A potential solution for such students is to write a combined Results and Discussion section. If you choose this option, however, you must still meet the objectives of both sections. The objectives for the Discussion are clearly summarized in the *Publication Manual* (p. 28).

> In general, be guided by these questions: What have I contributed here? How has my study helped to resolve the original problem? What conclusions and theoretical implications can I draw from my study? The responses to these questions are the core of your contribution, and readers have a right to clear, unambiguous, and direct answers.

REFERENCES

We have already described the procedure for citing references within the body of a research report by using the name(s) of the author(s) and the date of publication. The References section, which appears with a centered heading on a separate page after the Discussion (see sample paper), includes the complete citation for each reference. "Just as data in the paper support interpretations and conclusions, so reference citations document statements made about the literature" (*Publication Manual,* p. 28).

There are three types of references that will cover almost all those needed for students' research reports: journal articles, books, and chapters in edited books. The reference format for each of these types is illustrated in Table C.6. As this table shows, the second and succeeding lines of each reference are slightly indented. The journal article reference includes the authors, the year of publication, the title of the article, the name of the journal, the volume number, and the page numbers. The book citation includes the authors, the copyright date, the title, the city in which the book was published, and the publisher. The reference for a chapter in an edited volume includes the author of the chapter, the date, the chapter title, the editors of the book, the title of the book, the city of publication, and the publisher. You can save your readers much aggravation if you

TABLE C.6   ILLUSTRATION OF FORMAT OF REFERENCE CITATIONS

Journal article

Loftus, E. F., & Burns, T. E. (1982). Mental shock can produce retrograde amnesia. *Memory & Cognition, 10,* 318–323.

Book

Posavac, E. J., & Carey, R. G. (1989). *Program evaluation* (3rd ed.). Englewood Cliffs, NJ: Prentice-Hall.

Chapter in an edited book

Weiss, J. M. (1977). Psychological and behavioral influences on gastrointestinal lesions in animal models. In J. D. Maser & M. E. P. Seligman (Eds.), *Psychopathology: Experimental models* (pp. 232–269). San Francisco: W. H. Freeman.

follow the reference format closely and proofread your reference list *carefully*. The references are listed in alphabetical order by the last name of the first author of each article. If there are two articles by the same author(s), they are arranged in ascending order by year of publication.

FOOTNOTES

Because they are not used for citing references, footnotes are rare in journal articles and even more rare in students' research reports. Should you find that you do need to use footnotes, number them consecutively in the text. They appear on a separate page following the References section under the centered heading, "Footnotes."

APPENDIXES

Appendixes are slightly less common than footnotes, and they, too, appear at the end of the paper following the References (or Footnotes, if there are any). Appendixes are a bit more common in students' research reports than in published articles. Instructors may require you to submit an appendix including your raw data, the worksheets for a statistical analysis, or the computer printout of the analyses. The appendix can also be used to provide a verbatim copy of the instructions to subjects or a list of the specific materials used in an experiment. Each appendix is identified by letter (A, B, C, etc.), and any reference to the appendix in the body of the text is made using this letter. For instance, you might write, "The complete instructions can be found in Appendix A."

ORAL PRESENTATIONS

Research psychologists regularly attend professional conventions at which they present brief oral descriptions of their research. Similarly, students in a research methods class may be required to give an oral presentation of their research either in class or at a research symposium involving students from a number of different classes or at Undergraduate Research Conferences (Palladino et al., 1982). All of these settings share one characteristic—the time allowed for the presentation will be no longer than 10 to 15 minutes. In this length of time it is impossible to provide the detailed description that is included in a journal article. In general, as noted in the *Publication Manual*, "Material delivered verbally should differ from written material in its level of detail, organization, and presentation" (p. 192). Schlosberg (1965) summarizes the task one faces in giving an oral presentation and offers a word of sage advice: "Your primary purpose is to communicate clearly to an audience [under less-than-ideal conditions]. The important thing is to concentrate your efforts on getting across only one or two main points" (p. 606). In getting the main points across, the person giving the oral presentation must remember that a listener, unlike a reader, has no opportunity to review what has been said before.

One consequence of the constraints we have just described is that a brief oral presentation may require more preparation than that required for writing a research report. In giving your presentation, you will draw on the same questions that you use to organize the body of a written research report: Why was the research done? What was done? What was found? What are the implications of the findings? You probably recognize these as the guiding questions for organizing the Introduction, Method, Results, and Discussion sections. All four questions are relevant to an oral presentation, but the time constraints (and the attention span of your listeners) require that you choose *one* of these questions as your focus. For example, if you were describing a completed research project, you would probably focus on the question "What was found?" But if the research had been done principally to develop a new technique to study a problem, you would probably focus on the question "What was done?" Choose one focus and stick to it.

A colleague[1] of ours in the biology department has developed five principles that he distributes to his cell physiology students to help them prepare the oral presentation required in his class. These five principles are listed in Table C.7. Like all good maxims these five sound simple enough, but they are all too frequently ignored even by experienced researchers. The temptation described in the first principle can best be avoided by following the advice we gave earlier about limiting your presentation to one or two main points. The brief time available for an oral presentation is barely sufficient to allow you to present the evidence supporting these main points. There simply will not be time to discuss any side issues.

The second principle, cultivation of a good platform presence, can best be achieved by developing public speaking skills. Most people need a written copy of their presentation in front of them while they are presenting, but your presentation will be more effective if you can *appear* not to be reading.

[1]We are grateful to Professor Donald Cronkite for allowing us to use the materials he has prepared for teaching students how to deliver oral presentations.

TABLE C.7   PRINCIPLES TO FOLLOW FOR AN EFFECTIVE ORAL PRESENTATION

1. Avoid the temptation to tell everything you know in 10 minutes.
2. Cultivate a good platform presence.
3. Accompany your talk with useful visual aids.
4. Leave at least two minutes of your allotted time for questions.
5. Practice your talk before a critical audience before you give it.

Many people speak too quickly in front of an audience, particularly if they are reading; it is best to use simple, direct sentences presented at a moderate rate. Most important, speak loudly and clearly.

The third principle, the use of effective visual aids, can help your listeners follow your presentation. To be effective, slides or material written on a blackboard must be distinct enough to be seen clearly at a distance (see Figure C.4). If you are not an audio-visual whiz, consider developing your skills in this area. In the meantime, use printed handouts for visual aids. Be sure that whatever visual aids you use are as close to self-explanatory as you can make them.

You need to keep in mind the fourth principle, leaving time for questions, because most professional conferences and classroom presentations will require that you reserve time for questions. Though it is somewhat intimidating, this opportunity for questions gives your listeners a chance to become actively involved in your presentation.

The final principle is perhaps the most important one. The presence of an audience is more critical than the practice you can get by simply rehearsing the talk over and over by yourself. Such private rehearsal is a good way to prepare for your "dress rehearsal," but it is no substitute for practicing before others.

The five principles listed in Table C.7 provide a good coaching manual for oral presentations. The best way to develop this skill, however, is to deliver as many oral presentations as possible under "game conditions." Practice may not make perfect, but it is the best route we know to improvement.

RESEARCH PROPOSALS

In the last section of this appendix, we discuss writing again—but this time the writing of research proposals. As we mentioned at the beginning of the appendix, researchers must often seek financial support for their research by submitting grant proposals to private or government agencies. Students in research methods classes are also sometimes required to submit proposals describing research they might do. Even if a written proposal is not required, only a foolhardy researcher would tackle a research project without careful *prior* consideration of related literature, possible practical problems, workable statistical analyses of the data, and eventual interpretation of the expected results. Without a carefully constructed plan for the research, the unprepared investigator is likely to produce an unworkable, unanalyzable, or uninterpretable piece of research.

For maximum legibility use a typeface that is simple in design. Some slightly more complex type styles are easily read because of their wide use. Type fonts especially designed for esthetic reasons are usually poor choices. AVOID THE USE OF ALL CAPITAL LETTERS, LEGIBILITY IS REDUCED. MANY EXTREMES EXIST IN TYPE STYLES AND SHOULD NEVER BE USED. Keep it simple.

Kodak

M3-193 Lettering Styles

FIGURE C.4   A visual aid that speaks for itself.

The purpose of a research proposal is to ensure a workable experimental design that, when implemented, will result in an interpretable empirical finding of significant scientific merit. No research proposal, no matter how carefully it is prepared, can guarantee important results. Researchers learn early in their careers about "Murphy's Law." In essence, Murphy's Law states that "anything that can go wrong will go wrong." Nonetheless, it is worthwhile to develop a research proposal, if only to avoid the research problems that *are* avoidable.

A written research proposal follows the general format of a journal article, but the headings of the various sections are slightly different. The proposal should include the following main sections:

Introduction
Method
Statistical Treatment

Expected Results
References
Appendix

An Abstract is not included in a research proposal. The Introduction of a research proposal should include a more extensive review of the relevant literature than is required for a journal article. The statement of the research problem and the logical development of hypotheses in a research proposal are the same as required in a journal article. Similarly, the Method section in the proposal should be as close as possible to the one that will accompany the finished research. Thus our remarks about the format and content of the Method section of a research report apply equally to the writing of a proposal.

The separate section on statistical treatment of the data does, of course, not appear in the final research report. The purpose of this section is to make sure that the obtained results can be analyzed appropriately. If you don't know what descriptive and inferential statistics to use before you collect the data, there is a good chance that *no* appropriate analysis will be possible once the data are collected. For example, if you don't know that the chi-square test is the most appropriate one for testing your research hypothesis, you may also not know how to ensure the independence of observations required by the chi-square test. This section also helps the researcher to organize the data records during the collection phase so that the most efficient system can be used to analyze the data.

The section of the proposal entitled "Expected Results" should include a brief discussion of the anticipated results of the research. In most cases the exact nature of the results will not be known. Nevertheless, you will always have some idea (in the form of an hypothesis or prediction) of the outcome of the research. The Expected Results section should outline what results might be expected and highlight those that are most important to the project. This section may include tables or figures of the results as you expect (hope) that they will come out. Reasonable alternatives to the expected results should also be mentioned, as well as possible problems of interpretation that will arise if the results deviate from the research hypothesis.

The References section should be exactly like that same section as it would be submitted with the final report. It is always possible that literature may have to be included in the Discussion section of the final manuscript that was not anticipated in the proposal. But this should be an exception. An Appendix should complete the research proposal and should include a list of *all* materials that will be used in doing the experiment. In most cases this will mean that a copy of the instructions to subjects will be included, as well as the type of apparatus used, a list of stimulus materials or a description of the stimuli, and so on. To repeat, *all materials* should be listed. For example, if you are doing a study involving subjects' memory for lists of words, the following must be included in the Appendix: actual lists with randomizations made, type of apparatus used for presentation, instructions to subjects for all conditions, and randomizations of conditions.

A SAMPLE RESEARCH REPORT

The first two or three words of the title are typed above each page number in order to identify the manuscript. Note that the title page is the first numbered page.

The title of the article, the author's name, and the institutional affiliation of the author are each typed on separate lines. Use uppercase and lowercase letters, with double spacing between lines; center these lines slightly above the middle of the page. A good title will identify for the reader the topic and the major variables under investigation.

A *running head* is an abbreviated title. It should be a meaningful phrase and appear, centered, in all-uppercase letters, near the bottom margin of the title page. The running head appears in the manuscript only here; however, it appears at the top of every other page in a journal article.

```
                                        Memory for Frequency

                                                1




                        Memory for Frequency of Hearing Popular Songs

                                   Nancy A. Norton

                            Loyola University of Chicago












                     Running head:  MEMORY FOR SONGS
```

The abstract is found on page 2 of the manuscript. The word *Abstract* appears centered on a line double-spaced above the first line of the abstract. The abstract is typed as a single paragraph, but without indenting the first line.

The abstract should be a concise summary of the problem, methodology, major findings, and conclusion of the study. It should not exceed approximately 150 words.

Double-space between *all* lines in a manuscript, including between lines in footnotes, tables, and figure captions. Page margins should be about 1 to 1½ inches on all sides of each page.

Abstract

Memory for frequency of occurrence of popular songs was investigated. College students ($\underline{N}$ = 26) listened to a lengthy series of 10-s excerpts from popular songs, judged the number of times each song was heard, and tried to identify the titles and artists of the songs. Each excerpt was presented 0, 1, 2, 3, or 4 times. All students were informed that their memory for the names of various popular songs would be tested, and that some songs would be repeated, but only half the students were also informed that a frequency test would be given. Mean frequency estimates corresponded closely to actual frequencies and did not differ as a function of instructions regarding a frequency judgment test. However, accuracy of frequency judgments was significantly correlated with degree of knowledge of the popular songs, suggesting that memory for frequency of songs may not be a strictly automatic process.

Memory for Frequency of Hearing Popular Songs

Memory for the number of times that an event has been experienced is often remarkably good. This is true whether the event to be remembered has been experienced in a particular situation, for example, as part of a laboratory experiment, or whether the event is one that an individual has experienced in many different situations as part of a lifetime of experiences (see Zechmeister & Nyberg, 1982, for a brief review of frequency judgment studies). This sensitivity to event frequency is assumed to play a role in many kinds of cognitive decisions. For example, frequency information is relevant when discriminating between old and new events as part of a recognition memory task (Underwood, 1971) or when assessing our degree of certainty about the truth or validity of statements (Hasher, Goldstein, & Toppino, 1977).

Hasher and Zacks (1979) have suggested that frequency information is encoded automatically. Automatic processes, in their view, are those that are completed without effort, are not affected by intention to learn, are not improved with practice, and are developmentally quite stable. Automatic encoding may, in fact, be something that humans are genetically "prepared" to do.

Hasher and Chromiak (1977) have provided empirical support for this theory of automatic encoding of frequency information. In one experiment, these investigators presented a list of 48 words to students in the second, fourth, and sixth grades, and to

The title of the article (without the author's name or affiliation) is typed in lowercase and uppercase letters and centered above the first line of the introduction to the study. Note that the word *Introduction* does not appear in the manuscript.

An ampersand (&) is used for "and" when referring to a study with more than one author when that reference is enclosed within parentheses.

The word *and* is used to join names of multiple authors when a reference is not enclosed within parentheses. First names or initials of authors are typically not used when identifying a reference.

college students. The critical words were presented zero to four times. Half the students at each grade level were warned that a frequency judgment test would be forthcoming; the other half were not told that memory for frequency would be tested. Results revealed that students at all levels judged frequency relatively accurately, that this ability did not differ across grade levels, and that students forewarned about a frequency test did not do better than those not forewarned. In a second experiment, Hasher and Chromiak investigated whether memory for frequency improved with practice. It did not.

Studies investigating memory for event frequency have generally examined retention of verbal stimuli, such as words or parts of words (e.g., letters, bigrams), or pictorial stimuli. Nevertheless, automatic encoding of frequency information is assumed to extend potentially to all stimuli, whether meaningful or not (Hasher & Chromiak, 1977). In the present experiment, the generality of automatic encoding of frequency was tested by examining memory for frequency of hearing popular songs. College students listened to a lengthy series of brief excerpts from popular songs that were presented zero to four times. After listening to the presentation series all students were asked to judge the number of times that different songs had been heard. Half of the students were informed that a frequency test would be administered; half were not informed. If frequency of hearing popular songs is encoded automatically then students' estimates

A useful analogy for writing an introduction is a funnel. A good introduction often begins with rather broad or general statements about the topic under consideration. Then, the author narrows somewhat the focus by referring to relevant examples of previous research on this topic. Finally, the author identifies the specific goals (hypotheses) of the present research.

After reading the introduction, does the reader know exactly why you are doing this study and what you expect to find?

The word *Method* is centered prior to the first line of the second major part of the body of the manuscript. Do not begin a new page when starting the Method, Results or Discussion sections.

It is advisable to use headings, such as Subjects, Materials, and Procedure, to sequence the writing of the Method section. Although there is no "right" order of appearance of headings, a Subjects heading most often appears first in a research manuscript. Sometimes a Design heading is used, particularly when the design is complex; moreover, headings can be combined, for example, Subjects and Design.

of situational frequency should correspond closely to actual frequency of occurrence and should not differ between students told that a frequency test would be given and those not told.

Method

Subjects

Twenty-six students from a college psychology class participated in the study. These students were randomly assigned to either the informed or uninformed groups. Thus, each group consisted of 13 students.

Materials

An audio cassette tape was prepared containing 52, 10-s segments of popular songs. All of the song segments were taken from rock songs that had been in the "top 20" at some point in the past 3 years. The same song segment was never repeated in successive positions on the tape; there were always 4 to 10 intervening presentations between the repetitions of any one song. Segments contained no lyrics and were taken from the beginning of the song. Each segment was separated from the next by silent intervals of 5 to 7 s.

The 16 critical songs were presented either 1, 2, 3, or 4 times on the tape. The tape was divided into two halves. In each half different critical songs were represented twice at each of the four levels of frequency. Therefore, there were four songs presented at each of the frequency levels. To increase the apparent range of frequencies on the tape, one song was recorded six times and presented through both halves of the tape. In addition, to avoid possible primacy or recency effects, one filler song segment was presented twice and two different segments were each played once at the beginning of the tape (primacy), and two songs were each played once at the end of the tape (recency).

The test tape was prepared in similar fashion. The 16 critical song segments, each of 10-s duration, were randomly ordered and recorded. In addition, four additional song segments that had not been on the presentation tape were included on the test. Thus, 20 song segments were on the test tape, four at each of five frequency levels: 0, 1, 2, 3, or 4. Each segment was separated by a 5-s silent interval to allow subjects time to record their frequency judgment for each song.

Test booklets were prepared for all students. The first page of these booklets contained instructions that were to be read prior to listening to the tape. The second page of the booklet was a questionnaire that was not to be inspected until the presentation tape had ended. The items on the questionnaire asked (a) how many hours per day the student spent listening to music, (b) which type of music the student preferred, and (c) whether the student had ever played a musical instrument. Additional items on the questionnaire asked students to use a 7-point rating scale to indicate (a) how much they liked rock music, (b) how knowledgeable they felt they were about

---

Numbers 10 or greater appear as numerals (e.g., 13), unless they begin a sentence, in which case they are expressed in words (e.g., Twenty-six. . .).

Words are used to express numbers less than 10 (e.g., five), unless they precede a unit of measure (3 years), occur in a series (4, 6, 8, 10, and 12), or represent specific numerical forms, such as dates, time, sums of money, points on a scale, and so forth (e.g., January 1; 7-point scale; $N = 9$).

contemporary music, and (c) how good they felt their memory was for music heard previously. The last page in the booklet was the answer sheet for the frequency judgment test. Space was provided for frequency judgments for each of the 20 songs. Space was also provided for identification of each song title and of the artist or group.

Procedure

All students were assembled in a classroom and a tape player was positioned at the front of the room so that each student could hear the song segments. The previously prepared booklets were distributed to the students in a random order. Students were then told to read the instructions on the first page of the booklet, but to keep the booklet closed until after the tape had been played. Booklets for students in the informed group contained general memory instructions indicating that the experiment involved a test of "your memory for the names of various popular songs." Students in the informed group were also asked to attend to the frequency of each song segment so that they could later make accurate frequency judgments. Students in the uninformed group received similar instructions but they were not told that their memory for the frequency of occurrence of song segments would be tested. The instructions also informed students in both groups about the general nature of what would be played on the tape, and the fact that some songs would be repeated.

Avoid including trivial details in the Method section (e.g., A Number 2 pencil was used.)

When writing the Procedure subsection of the Method section, try to tell a story from beginning to end of what happened.

Units of measure are abbreviated without trailing periods (e.g., seconds = s; minutes = min).

After the presentation tape was played, students were asked to fill out the brief questionnaire on the second page of the booklet. This took approximately 2 min. This questionnaire was used primarily as a filler activity to introduce a delay between hearing the tape and the frequency judgment test. The test tape, containing the 20 song segments, was then played and students were asked to estimate how many times each song was heard on the previous tape. Students were told to guess if they were not sure.

Finally, the test tape was played again, and students were asked to try to identify the title and the name of the artist for each song segment. The tape was stopped after each segment and approximately 30 s were allowed for the two identifications.

Results

After reading the Method section, can the reader carry out your study exactly as you did it?

The Results section begins immediately following the Method section. The word *Results* is centered above the first line of the Results section.

The Results section should begin with a description of the major dependent variables, the summary statistics used (e.g., means and standard deviations), and the results obtained across conditions of the study.

Before carrying out the analysis of the frequency judgment test, the characteristics of the students tested in the experiment were examined using their responses to the questionnaire. The mean responses of the students in the informed and uninformed groups to four critical items on the questionnaire are summarized in Table 1. Although there were slight differences across groups, the mean responses indicated that the two groups of students were comparable in terms of the number of hours each day they spent listening to music, their liking of rock music, and their self-assessed memory ability for previously heard music.

Tables or figures appear on separate pages toward the end of the manuscript. When a table or figure is included in the Results section, lines are used to separate a phrase telling the printer where to insert the relevant table or figure in the final printed version of the article. In the text do not refer to a table or figure by position (e.g., ''See Figure 1 below.) because the actual position will be determined when the article is typeset. Always refer to tables or figures by their number.

When writing the Results section, you may assume that your reader has a basic knowledge of statistical procedures and thus you may omit reference to such concepts as the null hypothesis or whether an outcome falls within the critical region for your test.

Insert Table 1 about here

Two dependent variables were considered in assessing the accuracy of students' frequency judgment performance. First, as a measure of what could be called absolute accuracy, the number of times each student correctly judged the actual frequency of presentation was recorded. The mean number of these "hits" was 9.46 ($\underline{SD}$ = 3.04) for students in the informed group, and 9.00 ($\underline{SD}$ = 2.89) for students in the uninformed group. The difference between these means was not statistically significant, $\underline{t}(24)$ = .40, $\underline{p}$ > .05.

An alternative method for measuring the accuracy of frequency judgment performance is to assess the ability to discriminate among items of different presentation frequencies. This relative measure of frequency judgment accuracy was used as a second dependent variable in this study. The mean estimated frequency as a function of actual frequency was determined on the basis of the four frequency judgments made at each of five levels of frequency. Thus, for each student the mean estimated frequency for the four zero-presented songs, the four once-presented songs, and so forth, was calculated. The means of these means for each frequency level and for both informed and uninformed students are shown in Figure 1. As can be seen in the figure, frequency estimates in both groups increased as actual

Note that a figure is a graph or other pictorial representation of results; a table is used to summarize numbers or verbal expressions (e.g., descriptions of scale labels).

An analysis of variance for a complex design is indicated by using numerals to represent the independent variables and the number of levels associated with each variable. Numerals are separated by an ×, which is read "by." For example, a 2 × 5 ("two by five") analysis of variance indicates that the statistical test involved two independent variables; one variable had 2 levels and the other variable had 5 levels. Degrees of freedom associated with results of an analysis of variance (F-test) are presented in parentheses with the obtained F values.

Be careful to use signs for inequality correctly when referring to the probability of a statistical outcome.

frequency of occurrence increased. Moreover, an inspection of the data in Figure 1 reveals that there were only slight differences in mean frequency judgments as a function of being informed or not being informed about an upcoming frequency judgment test.

Insert Figure 1 about here

A 2 x 5 analysis of variance including the two independent variables of instructions and frequency level was carried out on the data summarized in Figure 1. Although there was some suggestion of an interaction in the nonparallel lines in the figure, there was no statistically significant interaction between instructions and frequency level, $\underline{F}(4, 96) = 1.82$, $\underline{p} > .05$. There was also no significant difference in the mean judgments for students in the informed group (2.20) as compared to those in the uninformed group (2.34), $\underline{F}(1, 24) < 1$. However, actual frequency was a statistically significant variable, $\underline{F}(4, 96) = 129.40$, $\underline{p} < .01$. The mean estimates for frequencies 0, 1, 2, 3, and 4, were 0.39, 1.38, 2.52, 3.31, and 3.76, respectively. Therefore, there was evidence that accurate relative frequency judgments for excerpts from popular songs can be made. But there was no evidence that students differed in their memory for frequency of hearing songs as a function of the instructions given to them regarding a frequency judgment test.

The number of titles and artists correctly identified by each student was also determined. Among all 26 students the range of song titles (of 20 possible) identified correctly was 0 to 18, (M = 8.81). The range of correct identification of artists was the same (M = 8.27). The numbers of titles and artists correctly identified were highly correlated, r(24) = .90. Because of this close relationship, the number of titles correctly identified was chosen to indicate the degree of knowledge that a student had about the songs heard. The correlation was determined between students' knowledge of the songs and the accuracy of their frequency judgments as reflected by the number of "hits" on the frequency judgment test.[1] The obtained correlation was r(24) = .70, which is reliably larger than zero, t(24) = 4.79, p < .01. The significant correlation suggests that frequency judgment accuracy varies with a person's knowledge of the to-be-judged stimuli.

Discussion

The present experiment investigated people's abilities to judge the frequency with which they heard a number of popular songs. Prior to listening to the songs, college students were either informed or not informed about the later frequency judgment task. In agreement with results of other published studies in this area (e.g., Hasher & Chromiak, 1977), no significant difference in frequency judgment performance was observed as function of instructions to remember frequency.

All statistical terms are abbreviated and should be underlined to indicate italics printing (e.g., t, M, SD).

Footnotes should be used sparingly in a manuscript. A footnote is indicated with the proper numerical superscript at the end of a line, and the footnote itself is typed on a separate page following the reference section.

After reading the Results section, does your reader know all the important findings in your study?

The word *Discussion* is centered on a line immediately following the Results section and before the first line of the Discussion section.

The Discussion section should begin with a brief review of the rationale and procedure of the study, and then provide a succinct statement of the essential findings, emphasizing those findings that relate to the hypotheses or goals of the study that were stated in the Introduction.

The year of publication appears in parentheses after the authors' surnames even when that particular reference has appeared previously in the text.

A good Discussion section will mention possible alternative explanations for the results of the study.

Moreover, in both the informed and uninformed conditions of the experiment, frequency estimates increased as frequency of actual occurrence increased. These findings support the notion that frequency information for musical stimuli, like that for verbal or pictorial stimuli, is encoded "automatically."

The finding, however, that accuracy of frequency judgments correlated with students' knowledge of the musical stimuli, poses a challenge for the strictly automatic encoding process proposed by Hasher and Zacks (1979). There are apparently individual differences in frequency judgment performance that are linked to knowledge of the stimuli to be judged. One possibility is that memory for frequency is likely to be encoded more easily when stimuli are meaningful than when they are not meaningful. Although Hasher and Chromiak (1977) have indicated that meaningfulness is not a critical factor in determining automatic encoding of frequency information, the present results suggest otherwise.

Although meaningful elaboration of the stimuli to be judged may influence memory for frequency, this suggestion must be made tentatively. The relationship between knowledge (defined by number of song titles identified) and memory for frequency (defined by number of "hits") is only correlational. There are several other possible factors that may be responsible for this relationship. For example, students who know more song titles are likely to be more familiar with music in general than are

The conclusion of a good Discussion section often contains information that can direct future research; vacuous statements such as, "More research needs to be done" should be avoided.

students who do not know many titles. The correlation between knowledge of the songs and accuracy of frequency judgments may be attributable to this general expertise in music rather than to meaningful elaboration. An "expert" might be able to make finer discriminations among stimuli than can a nonexpert. This alternative explanation could be tested by administering a frequency judgment test for musical stimuli to groups of people selected on the basis of their musical expertise. If general musical expertise is a critical factor, then frequency judgment accuracy should be greater for groups with greater expertise. Of course, in testing this possible explanation it would be essential to demonstrate that frequency judgment accuracy for nonmusical stimuli does not vary with changes in musical expertise.

Because all students were advised that their memory for song titles would be tested, it is possible that students who knew many titles were less frustrated or less anxious than those who knew only a few titles. Such affective differences could account for the original correlation if it were argued that frequency judgment accuracy decreased with increasing anxiety or frustration. An account based on differences in frequency judgment performance as a function of mild emotional changes would also provide evidence against automatic encoding (see Hasher & Zacks, 1979).

In summary, the present results confirm that accurate frequency judgments can be made for musical stimuli, thereby extending the generality of frequency encoding beyond verbal and pictorial stimuli. The absence of a difference in frequency judgment accuracy for informed and uninformed groups supports the notion that frequency information is encoded automatically. The automatic encoding of frequency appears inconsistent, however, with the obtained correlation between knowledge of the musical stimuli and frequency judgment accuracy. The basis of this correlation and the extent of the challenge it poses to the automatic encoding theory are unclear at this time.

After reading the Discussion section, does your reader know what your findings mean?

The References
section begins on
a new page, with
the word
References cen-
tered on a line that
is two lines below
the page number.

The authors'
names are typed
flush with the
margin with the se-
cond and subse-
quent lines in-
dented three
spaces; initials, but
not first names of
authors, are pro-
vided. Names of
two authors, and
the last two names
in a series, are
separated by an
ampersand (&).
The year of
publication of a
book or article ap-
pears in paren-
theses followed by
a period im-
mediately after the
authors' names
and before a title.

Only the first letter
of the first word of
titles of articles
and books is
capitalized, where-
as the first letters
of all major words
in the name of a
journal are
capitalized.

Page numbers of a
specific article or
chapter are shown
in parentheses
following the title
of the book in
which the material
appears.

The volume num-
ber of a journal, as
well as the name
of a journal or book,
are underlined.

References

Hasher, L., & Chromiak, W. (1977). The processing of frequency

   information: An automatic mechanism? Journal of Verbal

   Learning and Verbal Behavior, 16, 173-184.

Hasher, L., Goldstein, D., & Toppino, T. (1977). Frequency and

   the conference of referential validity. Journal of Verbal

   Learning and Verbal Behavior, 16, 107-112.

Hasher, L., & Zacks, R. T. (1979). Automatic and effortful

   processes in memory. Journal of Experimental Psychology:

   General, 108, 356-388.

Underwood, B. J. (1971). Recognition memory. In H. H. Kendler &

   J. T. Spence (Eds.), Essays in neobehaviorism (pp. 313-335).

   New York: Appleton-Century-Crofts.

Zechmeister, E. B., & Nyberg, S. E. (1982). Human memory: An

   introduction to research and theory. Monterey, CA:

   Brooks/Cole.

Author notes are used to acknowledge technical, financial, editorial, or other forms of assistance with the study, and to identify the address of the author or authors from whom additional information about the study, as well as reprints (copies), may be obtained.

Author Notes

The data reported in this study are "real" and are based on an experiment performed as a classroom demonstration in an undergraduate course taught by E. B. Zechmeister. The author was asked, along with other members of the class, to be a subject in this experiment. Then, in order to pass the course the author was required to prepare a written manuscript, using strict American Psychological Association (APA) editorial style, which reported the results of this experiment. Subsequently, the instructor had the nerve to ask whether he might use the manuscript (after some "editing") in his book!

Both the author and the instructor wish to acknowledge the help of Jim Fidler in preparing the audio tapes used in this experiment.

Requests for reprints should be addressed to Nancy A. Norton, Psychology Department, Loyola University of Chicago, 6525 N. Sheridan Road, Chicago, IL 60626.

Footnotes, if they are present, are indicated in the text by typing numerals slightly above the last letter of the last word in a sentence or phrase that is noted (. . .end.[1]). The notes themselves are numbered consecutively and are typed on a separate page under the heading Footnote(s). The footnote page follows immediately after the page titled Author Notes.

Footnote

[1]Typically a single correlation should not be computed across two or more groups of subjects who have been treated differently. Instead, the correlation of interest should be computed within each group of subjects and an average correlation across groups would then be used to describe the overall correlation. In the present study there were no significant differences between groups in either knowledge of the songs or accuracy of frequency judgments. Therefore, for the sake of simplicity, only one correlation was computed.

Tables and figures appear on separate pages at the end of the manuscript following the References, Author Notes, and Footnotes. Tables are numbered consecutively (using arabic numerals) in the order that the tables appear in the manuscript.

Table titles are typed flush with the margin in uppercase and lower letters. The title is also underlined.

A note that clarifies or explains the table as a whole is put below the table with the word *Note,* underlined, followed by a period, typed flush to the left margin, introducing the note. If a specific footnote is needed to explain a particular item in the table, then a superscript letter is used following the item in the table (45[a]) and also before the first letter of the note which appears on the line after any general notes ([a]This number. . .).

Table 1

Mean Responses of Students in Informed and Uninformed Groups to Questionnaire Items

	Condition	
Item	Informed	Uninformed
Hours listening to		
music	2.44	2.29
Liking of rock		
music	4.92	5.71
Knowledge of contemporary		
music	4.54	4.85
Memory for music		
previously heard	5.38	5.15

Note. Means for "hours listening" item are based on students' judgments of number of hours; means for remaining items are based on students' responses using a 7-point scale, with 7 being the high end of the scale.

Figure captions are numbered consecutively (using arabic numerals) on one page in the order that they appear in the text.

Figure Caption

<u>Figure 1</u>. Estimated frequency of occurrence as a function of actual frequency of occurrence.

The actual figures are presented, each on a separate page, following the list of figure captions. When graphs are figures, they should be drawn carefully on white paper of good quality. Be sure to label correctly and clearly the axes and curves of any line graph.

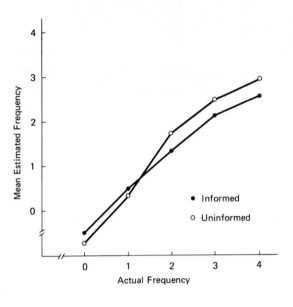

APPENDIX
D

Psychophysics and Scaling

OUTLINE

PSYCHOPHYSICS

In 1860, nearly twenty years before Wilhelm Wundt established the first psychological laboratory, Gustav Fechner published *Elemente der Psychophysik.* Because of his background as a physicist, Fechner wanted to obtain empirical evidence in support of a philosophical position he was developing. Specifically, Fechner wanted to quantify precisely the relationship between stimulation measured in physical units and the psychological sensation experienced in response to that stimulation. For instance, if you are in a dimly lit room, how much light needs to be added before you notice that the room has gotten brighter? Or how much weight needs to be added to a tin can you are lifting before you notice that the can is heavier? Questions such as these became the focus of an area of research called **psychophysics.**

Fechner had intended his book to serve as an introduction to what he hoped would be an influential theory of philosophy. The book has proved influential, but not for the reasons—or in the discipline—that Fechner had hoped. Philosophers rejected his theory, but the emerging discipline of psychology eagerly adopted the psychophysical methods Fechner introduced.

CLASSICAL METHODS

Three basic questions concerned the early experimental psychologists who used psychophysical methods. First, what are the minimum and maximum points on a physical dimension to which our sensory apparatus will respond? For example, what are the shortest and the longest wavelengths of light to which the human eye will respond? Second, how can we determine what point on a stimulus dimension is equal *psychologically* to a specified point defined physically? That is, how many grams would you have to lift to judge that the weight you just lifted was 50 grams? Third, how much of a change in physical stimulation will it take before an observer reports that the stimulus has changed? For instance, how much would you need to turn up your stereo before your roommate noticed that it was louder? We will now consider each of these general questions in more detail, at the same time providing a brief introduction to three different classical psychophysical methods.

The first general question led investigators to seek methods that would allow them to measure the limits of our ability to detect a stimulus. These limits or boundaries are called **absolute thresholds.** In the simplest terms, a lower absolute threshold is a point below which we do not detect the presented stimulus and above which we do. For some stimuli we also have an upper absolute threshold, that is, a point above which we do not detect the stimulus and below which we do. The situation is a bit more complex, however, than these statements imply. For example, the absolute threshold for a person with normal vision to detect a spot of light depends both on the wavelength of that light and on where the spot of light is presented in the person's visual field. The human eye is more sensitive to wavelengths near the center of the visible spectrum, and lights in the periphery are more likely to be detected than are those in the center of our visual field. Practically speaking, these findings suggest that you are more likely to see a dim stimulus if you do not look directly at it. For instance, you are more likely to see dimly lit stars in the nighttime sky if you look for them "out of the corner of your eye." For now, though, we need to shift our focus back to the classical psychophysical methods that were used to measure absolute thresholds.

One such classical method is called the **method of limits.** To use this method, the researcher begins with a stimulus that is known to be below the lower absolute threshold on some dimension (size, brightness, loudness) and slowly increases the stimulus along that dimension until the observer reports detecting the stimulus. The method of limits begins, therefore, with the presentation of an ascending series of stimuli, each one louder, brighter, or bigger than the preceding ones. This ascending series is followed by a descending series in which the experimenter begins with a stimulus above the lower absolute threshold and decreases it in steps until the subject reports being unable to detect the stimulus. The point at which the subject reports detecting the appearance or disappearance of the stimulus typically varies from trial to trial. The ascending and descending series are also likely to yield different points at which the change in stimulation is detected by the subject. That is, the subject may report detecting the stimulus during the ascending series at a point that is higher (louder, brighter, bigger) than the point at which the same subject reports no longer detecting the stimulus during the descending series.

Because of the variability in subjects' detection accuracy, the absolute threshold is actually a statistical concept defined as the point at which the subject is able to detect the stimulus 50 percent of the time. When the method of limits is used, the absolute threshold also represents an average of the two estimates based on the ascending series and the descending series. It can literally take hours to use the method of limits to establish a person's absolute threshold for detecting a spot of light at one point in that person's visual field. This may give you some idea of what a painstaking effort psychophysicists made to map out the limits of the visual system. You also should be developing a sense that the psychophysical methods (and science in general) are not intended for use by the impatient.

The second general question addressed by early experimental psychologists concerns the calibration of sensory dimensions. The objective of this calibration is to determine what point on a psychological scale is equal to a specified standard point on a physical scale. For example, what weight would appear to you to be equal to a standard weight of 100 grams? The general term used to describe such a value is the **point of subjective equality.** The measurement of points of subjective equality has been especially critical in the study of visual illusions like the one depicted in Figure D.1. In this Müller-Lyer illusion, the line on the right appears longer even though it is in fact the same length as the line on the left. What is critical to producing the illusion is the position of the inward and outward arrows at the end of each

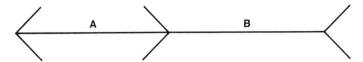

FIGURE D.1 The Müller-Lyer illusion. Line A appears to be shorter than line B, although both are the same length.

line. The Müller-Lyer illusion has been important in studies of the influence of cultural experiences on perception. People from Western cultures readily see the illusion, presumably because they have many opportunities to view right angles, both in everyday living and on the printed page. People from other cultures, such as members of the Zulu tribe in Africa, live in an environment that includes mostly rounded structures and few right angles. Individuals from such cultures tend not to see the illusion in the Müller-Lyer illusion—they see the two lines as the same length.

The relative effects of the Müller-Lyer illusion on different individuals can be measured by using the **method of adjustment,** which is also called the *method of average error.* With this method, one of the lines—say, the one with the arrows pointing in—is set as the standard. The subject is asked to adjust a variable line with arrows pointing out until the line appears equal psychologically to the standard line. To take into account the variability that is likely in subjects' responses, several such tests are given, with half of the trials beginning with the variable line set noticeably longer than the standard and half with the variable line set noticeably shorter. The average error a subject makes in setting the variable line equal to the standard provides a measure of the size of the Müller-Lyer illusion for that subject.

The third and final question addressed in psychophysics concerns our ability to detect changes in stimuli that are above our absolute threshold. How much the stimulus must change before we can detect that it has changed is called a **difference threshold** or a **just noticeable difference** (*JND*). The classic psychophysical method most frequently used to measure difference thresholds is the **method of constant stimuli.** In this method an observer is asked to compare a series of comparison stimuli to a standard, making a separate judgment for each comparison stimulus. In a weight-discrimination experiment, a standard weight of 100 grams could be used with comparison stimuli ranging from 75 to 125 grams in 5-gram increments. The observer is presented the standard stimulus, followed by a randomly chosen comparison stimulus, and is then asked to judge whether the comparison stimulus is lighter or heavier than the standard. This sequence is repeated until all comparison stimuli have been tested, and then the entire process is repeated several times.

The responses of a student in a classroom exercise involving the method of constant stimuli can be summarized in a graph like the one shown in Figure D.2. The percentage of times the student responded "heavier" is plotted as a function of the weights of the comparison stimuli. The difference thresh-

FIGURE D.2   Graphic illustration of the computation of a difference threshold based on a subject's responses in a weight-discrimination experiment using the method of constant stimuli.

old, or just noticeable difference, is defined as that increment or decrement in weight that the student could detect 50 percent of the time. (Just as was true for absolute thresholds, difference thresholds are defined statistically because subjects are not perfectly consistent in judging a given comparison stimulus as lighter or heavier than the standard.) The first step in computing a JND is to determine the interval of uncertainty (IU). This interval is equal to the difference between the weights corresponding to the points at which the subject responded "heavier" 75 percent and 25 percent of the time, respectively. The difference threshold is then computed by taking one-half of the interval of uncertainty. For the results plotted in Figure D.2, we obtained a difference threshold of 5 grams.

Psychology has very few laws, but one of them pertains to the measurement of difference thresholds. Stevens (1951) summarizes this law as follows: "The relation of the just noticeable difference to the size of the initial stimulus stands as a law of relativity in psychology: what must be added to produce a detectable difference is relative to what is already there" (pp. 34–35). We regularly experience instances of this law; a small amount of light in a darkened room is more noticeable than that same amount of light would be on a sunlit day.

Ernst Weber (1795–1878) was responsible for gathering the first sets of data demonstrating the relativity of difference thresholds. Weber was a professor of anatomy and later of physiology at the University of Leipzig (Boring, 1950). He did extensive work on the sense of touch, especially dealing with subjects' difference thresholds for detecting two simultaneously stimulated points on the skin. Using a "compass test" that he developed, Weber would vary the distance between two needle points that he simultaneously pressed against the subject's skin at various locations on the body. Subjects were then required to indicate whether they felt one or two needlepoints. Weber found that the threshold for detecting two different points varied widely for different parts of the body. For example, the upper arm yielded a threshold thirty times the size of the threshold on the little finger.

Weber's research on the sense of touch was influential, but not nearly so influential as his work on the relativity of difference thresholds. Weber did a series of experiments measuring difference thresholds for weights, line lengths, and the pitches of tones in which he systematically varied the standard stimulus. He summarized his observations by stating that the ratio between the increase in a stimulus needed to produce a JND and the original level of the stimulus was a constant.

This relationship can be illustrated in the context of Weber's weight discrimination experiments. Suppose that the subject needs an increase of 5 grams to detect a change when the standard weight is 100 grams. If Weber's idea is right, when the standard weight is 200 grams, the stimulus will have to be increased by 10 grams for the subject to detect a difference. That is, the relative change in both instances is the same: a ratio of 1 to 20. Gustav Fechner, whose role in introducing the discipline of psychophysics we described at the beginning of this section, called the relationship Weber's Law. Within limits, Weber's Law has proved effective in yielding precise predictions of the size of difference thresholds depending on the magnitude of the standard stimulus.

SIGNAL DETECTION THEORY

In recent years a new approach to the study of sensory processes has been developed. This new approach is called *signal detection theory* (Green and Swets, 1966), and it can best be understood by considering the standard testing situation used in signal detection experiments.

On each trial in a signal detection experiment, one of two events can occur: a stimulus (usually called a *signal*) is or is not presented. The subject is allowed one of two responses: yes or no. The possible outcomes of a trial in a signal detection experiment can thus be summarized by the fourfold table presented in Table D.1. This table may look somewhat familiar to you; it has the same general form as the table we used to outline the possible outcomes of making decisions regarding tests of the null hypothesis (see Chapter 5). As we indicated in that earlier discussion of null hypothesis testing, the decision

TABLE D.1   POSSIBLE OUTCOMES OF A TRIAL IN A SIGNAL DETECTION EXPERIMENT

	Signal presented	
Subject's response	Yes	No
Yes	Hit	False Alarm
No	Miss	Correct Rejection

maker always faces the possibility of making an error in situations involving uncertain decisions. Signal detection theory provides an explicit model of how the observer resolves this dilemma.

The basic features of a signal detection experiment are illustrated in a typical hearing test. On each of a series of test trials, an examiner might either present or not present a tone during a specified interval. The beginning and end of the interval could be indicated by a light on a panel in front of the person being tested. The person's task would be to decide whether a tone had been presented in the interval.

According to signal detection theory, a tone or any other sensory signal is always detected against the background of internal noise in the sensory system. Even if the hearing test were to be given in a soundproof room from which external sources of noise were excluded, one would still be faced with internal noise from sources such as one's own heartbeat. The noise would vary in magnitude around some average M_n, as indicated by the distribution shown on the left at the top of Figure D.3. Signal detection theory assumes that, when a tone actually *is* presented, it adds to this level of internal noise to form a second distribution, centered around a larger value on the X-axis (M_s) as pictured on the right in Figure D.3. If the tone were very loud, the two distributions would be far apart and the detection task would be easy. Such strong signals would be unlikely to be included in a hearing test or in a detection experiment. Instead, as shown in Figure D.3, the two distributions (called the *noise distribution* and the *signal-plus-noise distribution*) are likely to overlap. This overlap means that sometimes the noise distribution can result in a stronger stimulus than the signal-plus-noise distribution. Of course, the signal-plus-noise distribution can also sometimes produce a weaker stimulus than one from the noise distribution alone. The observer's task is to *decide* which distribution is the source of the sensory input on any given trial.

Signal detection theory makes a sharp distinction between a person's ability to detect the occurrence of a signal, called **sensitivity** d', and that person's willingness to report this decision, called **response bias** β. The hearing test is obviously intended to assess the person's sensitivity to various sounds. People differ, however, not only in how well they can hear but also in how willing they are to say they have heard something. One person might say that a tone occurred in the interval if there were the slightest chance that she heard something. Another person might say "Yes, a tone occurred" only if it is

FIGURE D.3   Illustration of signal-plus-noise and noise distributions with indication of d' and criterion. In bottom graph, hypothetical distributions of the psychological magnitudes of two confusable stimuli, A and B. The distance between their means d can be inferred from the observer's judgments and is a measure of discriminability. The dashed line C represents a symmetrical decision criterion, in anticipation of the ROC analyis, which emphasizes a variable criterion.

very likely that he heard something. According to signal detection theory, each person makes a decision by establishing a criterion or cutoff value on the two distributions shown in Figure D.3. If the stimulus exceeds this criterion, the person responds that a signal occurred; if the stimulus falls short of this criterion, the person responds that no signal occurred.

The placement of the decision criterion is influenced by the person's response bias. A person who was trying to identify a murder suspect in a police lineup would probably adopt a strict criterion for saying "Yes" because of the grave consequences of such a decision for the witness and the identified suspect. When a person wants to minimize the chance of being wrong in saying there is a signal when there is not (a false alarm), the criterion is set farther to the right on the noise distribution. As you can see, however, reducing the number of false alarms also reduces the number of hits (see Figure D.3). Varying the consequences of various decisions can induce a person to shift the criterion. For example, a subject could be paid for successful performance and the cost of making a false alarm could be varied systematically. Subjects also can be asked to give a confidence judgment with each decision. For example, the subject could use a 6-point scale ranging from 1 = Very Sure Signal Did Not Occur to 6 = Very Sure Signal Did Occur. The confidence judgment procedure presumably encourages subjects to adopt response criteria that vary in terms of how strict they are, a judgment of 1 representing a more strict criterion than a judgment of 3. By using either of these procedures it is possible to develop a receiver operator characteristic (ROC) curve. The ROC curve can then be used to compute direct measures of the observer's sensitivity in detecting the signal, called d', and of the subject's response bias, called *beta* (β). (See Swets, 1973, for a description of these procedures.)

In many experiments the investigator is not interested in measuring response bias but may want to control for its effects. In such situations a forced-choice procedure can be used. In a **forced-choice procedure,** each detection trial involves two intervals with a signal presented in one of them and not in the other. The two intervals could be indicated by different-colored lights. The subject's task is to identify which interval contained the signal. Because each subject is forced to choose one of the two intervals, there can be no problem with differences across subjects in their willingness to report that they detected a signal. The proportion correct on a forced-choice test can be translated directly into a d' measure of the subject's sensitivity (Green and Swets, 1966).

Signal detection procedures are not limited to the study of basic sensory processes. Swets et al. (1979) described the use of these procedures to decide which of two diagnostic tests is better for detecting, localizing, and diagnosing brain lesions in patients suspected of having a tumor. The two diagnostic tests compared in the study were computed tomography (CT) and radionuclide scanning (RN), two different types of x-ray techniques. The CT technique uses computer graphics to prepare a detailed picture of the target organ—in this case the brain. The RN technique involves the injection of a radioactive substance that is picked up by the body's metabolic processes and then detected by an isotope counter from which the x-ray picture is prepared. Twelve radiologists were asked to examine either CT scans or RN films for 136 cases. Autopsy and histological evidence were used to confirm that 84 cases were positive for a tumor and 52 were negative. A signal detection measure d' was used to assess the accuracy of each technique. Computed tomography was found to be substantially more accurate than radionuclide scanning. Similar applications of signal detection theory have been made to other aspects of the complex problem of medical diagnosis (Metz, 1978). Clearly, psychophysical techniques are proving beneficial to areas well outside the confines of experimental psychology.

SCALING TECHNIQUES

The psychophysical methods described in the previous section are all intended to assess a person's response to a clearly defined physical stimulus. As we mentioned in Chapter 1, however, psychologists are often faced with the challenge of measuring stimuli on dimensions for which there is no underlying physical scale. Aggressiveness, beauty, and pleasantness are but a few examples of such psychological dimensions. The procedures used to measure stimuli on psychological dimensions are generally described as **scaling techniques.** Scaling is an extensive and complex subdiscipline in psychology that often involves the use of sophisticated statistical techniques. In this brief section we intend only to provide an introduction to several basic scaling techniques. By discovering the strengths and weaknesses of these simple procedures, you will see that measurement of psychological dimensions is possible.

PAIRED COMPARISONS

The method of **paired comparisons** is perhaps the simplest scaling technique. In this method each stimulus to be measured is first paired with each other stimulus. Then the subject is asked to compare the members of each pair and to select the member that has the greater amount (or the lesser amount) of the characteristic of interest. For example, if four photographs were to be scaled for beauty, there would be six possible pairings of the photographs [$n(n-1)/2$]. Subjects would be presented with these six pairs and would have to select the more beautiful photograph in each pair. The logic of paired comparisons is the same as that of a round-robin tournament. If each of four teams plays each other, the team with the most wins after the required six games could be described as the best team. Of course, to take into account such factors as "hot nights" and "off nights" for each team, the results might be more reliable if each team played every other team several times. Similarly, the reliability of the paired comparison technique is enhanced when each observer judges each pair several times.

The data that result from the paired comparison method are the numbers of times each stimulus has been selected across all its possible pairings. If observers agree on the member of each pair that they found more beautiful, certain photographs will have been selected frequently and others will have been selected infrequently. In a sense, we can use subjects' responses just as we would use the records of the teams in our round-robin tournament. That is, we could rank the photographs from most to least beautiful on the basis of the number of "wins" for each photograph. Thus the paired comparison technique results in an ordinal scale (see Chapter 1) of measurement. Before discussing the relative advantages and disadvantages of such a rank-order scale, we need to examine another method that also results in an ordinal scale. This alternative method is needed because the paired comparison method is limited to situations in which only a small number of stimuli need to be measured. (This is because the number of possible pairings becomes prohibitively large when the number of stimuli is increased.)

RANK-ORDER SCALING

The method of **rank-order scaling** involves presentation of all the stimuli to be scaled in one list. The subject is then asked to rank the stimuli in terms of the amount of the characteristic of interest. If there were fifteen photographs to be scaled for beauty, the subject would assign a 1 to the most beautiful photograph, a 2 to the next most beautiful, and so on. Theoretically, to accomplish this task the subject must compare each photograph to every other photograph, just as in the paired comparison method. Practically speaking, however, the subject can reliably complete the required rankings without making all possible comparisons. Perhaps after ranking the five most beautiful photographs, the subject may rank the remaining photographs by making comparisons only among the last ten.

Several subjects are asked to scale the stimuli when rank-order scaling is used. The mean rank across subjects for each stimulus can then be used to obtain a final rank-ordering of the stimuli. If the subjects cannot discriminate among the stimuli, the mean rankings will all be approximately the same. If the subjects agree on their rankings of the stimuli, however, the mean ranks will vary accordingly.

The major advantage of rank-order scaling and the paired comparison method is that they force the subject to make discriminations among the stimuli. Hence these two methods are more sensitive to any differences subjects *can* detect. But from the source of this advantage springs the major disadvantage of these two methods. The ordinal nature of the scale that results tells us nothing about the size of the differences between the stimuli or about the absolute judgment of subjects for any one stimulus. For instance, the subjects might judge that all fifteen photographs were ugly but that, if forced to choose, they could reliably identify the "most beautiful" (least ugly) of the set. Some technique is obviously needed to allow subjects to indicate their overall reaction to each stimulus.

CATEGORY SCALING

The traditional method for having subjects indicate their absolute judgments of a set of stimuli is **category scaling.** In this method, subjects are asked to rate each stimulus on a scale with a fixed number of categories. For instance, subjects could be asked to rate the fifteen photographs on a 7-point scale ranging from very beautiful to very ugly. Often each point on the scale is given a verbal label (for example, 1 = very beautiful, 2 = moderately beautiful, and so on), but this is not essential. In using category scaling, however, it is essential to establish *anchors* for the scale. An anchor provides a point of reference for subjects in making their ratings. If you were told to rate how beautiful a photograph is, you might be inclined to ask, "Relative to what?" Anchors provide an answer to this question. Subjects can be asked to use anchors within the set of stimuli or from outside the set of stimuli. If anchors from within the set are used, the subject has to rate one of the fifteen presented photographs with the highest rating and one of them with the lowest. If external anchors are used, the subjects might be asked to think of the ugliest photograph and the most beautiful photograph they have ever seen and to consider these to be the stimuli corresponding to scale values of 1 and 7.

The mean ratings for each stimulus across subjects reflect an interval scale (see Chapter 1). Thus, the absolute level of rated beauty of each photograph is interpretable, as are the relative distances between mean ratings for different photographs. This represents the major advantage of category scaling. The major disadvantage is that subjects may fail to make discriminations that they are capable of making among stimuli. Subjects might even give all the photographs the same rating. If the investigator only wants to know how subjects feel about each photograph, the assignment of the same rating to all photographs poses no problem. If the scaling study was done to select one photograph to put on display, however, the subjects' failure to discriminate among the photographs does pose a problem. In order to choose between rank-order scaling and category scaling, the investigator should generally have a clear notion of whether absolute or relative ratings are more critical.

MAGNITUDE ESTIMATION

The last scaling technique we will describe was developed relatively recently (Stevens, 1956). Stevens originally introduced the technique as a psychophysical method to be applied to physical stimuli, but it has been most extensively used in scaling psychological stimulus dimensions. **Magnitude estimation** requires the subject to assign to each presented stimulus a number that reflects the apparent magnitude of that stimulus relative to a standard. A tone of a certain loudness could be presented, and the experimenter could instruct the subject to call the loudness of that tone 100. For all succeeding tones, the subject would then assign a number relative to that standard. If the next tone was judged half as loud, it would be assigned 50; if it was judged twice as loud, it would be assigned 200.

A variation of the magnitude estimation technique has been developed that does not even require the subject to assign numbers to each stimulus. This technique, called *cross-modality matching*, requires the subject to judge stimuli on one dimension by producing responses on a second dimension. For instance, subjects can judge the beauty of each photograph by varying the loudness of a tone. The louder the tone, the more beautiful they judge the photograph to be. Initially, the questions asked in cross-modality matching sound silly (How loud is a beautiful photograph?) but application of the technique has led to remarkably stable results. In most cases, magnitude estimation is the simplest and best technique for the psychological scaling of stimuli.

SUMMARY

We began with a discussion of psychophysics, one of the oldest areas of investigation in experimental psychology. Psychophysical methods such as the method of limits, the method of average error, and the method of constant stimuli are used to determine absolute thresholds, difference thresholds, and points of subjective equality. Increasingly, the classical psychophysical methods are being supplanted by signal detection methods that provide measures of detectability and response bias.

Four methods of scaling (paired comparisons, rank-ordering, category scaling, and magnitude estimation) are essential in carrying out psychological measurement. Paired comparisons and rank ordering ensure that all possible discriminations are made but yield no information about the absolute rating of any stimulus. Category scaling provides the absolute rating of each stimulus but may suffer because all stimuli can be given the same rating. In most circumstances, magnitude estimation is the simplest and best scaling technique for psychological measurement.

KEY CONCEPTS

psychophysics

absolute threshold

method of limits

point of subjective equality

method of adjustment (method of average error)

difference threshold (just noticeable difference)

method of constant stimuli

sensitivity d'

response bias β

forced-choice procedure

scaling techniques

paired comparisons

rank-order scaling

category scaling

magnitude estimation

Glossary

ABAB design (reversal design)   A single-case experimental design in which an initial baseline stage (A) is followed by a treatment stage (B), a return to baseline (A), and then another treatment stage (B); the researcher observes whether behavior changes on introduction of the treatment, reverses when the treatment is withdrawn, and improves again when the treatment is reintroduced.

ABBA counterbalancing   A technique for balancing stage of practice effects in the complete within-subjects design that involves presenting the conditions in one sequence followed by the opposite of the same sequence.

absolute threshold   The point at which the observer is able to detect a physical stimulus 50 percent of the time.

accidental sample   A type of nonprobability sample that results when availability and willingness to respond are the overriding factors used in selecting respondents; generally low in representativeness.

analytical comparisons   A statistical technique that can be applied (usually after obtaining a significant omnibus F-test) to locate the specific source of systematic variation in an experiment.

anticipation effects   A problem in the within-subjects design, especially when ABBA counterbalancing is used; whenever the subject's expectations about which condition should occur next influence how the subject responds.

applied behavior analysis   The use of techniques derived from laboratory studies of animal and human behavior to manage behavior in diverse settings, such as schools, the home, hospitals, and businesses; characterized by the use of single-case experimental designs.

applied research   See **basic versus applied research.**

archival data   A source of evidence that is based upon records or documents relating the activities of individuals, institutions, governments, and other groups; used as an alternative to or in conjunction with other research methods.

baseline stage   The first stage of a single-case experiment in which a record is made of the individual's behavior prior to any intervention.

basement effect   See **ceiling effect.**

basic versus applied research   Whereas basic research mainly seeks knowledge about nature simply for the sake of understanding it better, applied research seeks knowledge that will modify or improve the present situation; however, basic and applied research are considered to have a reciprocal relationship, for example, when basic research is used to identify abstract principles that can be applied in real-world settings, and applied research is used to reveal possible limitations or extensions of these principles.

487

behaviorism An approach to the study of psychology that emphasizes observable behavior as the only legitimate source of scientific evidence and that defines psychology's goal as the prediction and control of behavior.

behavior modification The application of learning-conditioning principles in order to change behavior; first used synonymously with behavior therapy.

behavior therapy The application of learning-conditioning principles to clinical populations; first used synonymously with behavior modification.

beta See **response bias.**

biased sample A sample in which the distribution of characteristics is systematically different from that of the parent population.

block randomization The most common technique for carrying out random assignment in the random groups design; each block includes a random order of the conditions and there are as many blocks as there are subjects in each condition of the experiment.

case study An intensive description and analysis of a single individual.

category scaling A scaling technique in which the subject provides a rating for each stimulus on a scale with a fixed number of categories to indicate the absolute amount of whatever quality is being measured.

causal inference The identification of the cause or causes of a phenomenon, by establishing covariation of cause and effect, a time-order relationship with cause preceding effect, and the elimination of plausible alternative causes.

ceiling (basement) effect A measurement problem whereby the researcher cannot measure the effects of an independent variable or a possible interaction because performance has reached a maximum (minimum) in any condition of the experiment.

checklist An instrument used to record the presence or absence of something in the situation under observation.

closed or multiple-choice questions Questionnaire items in which specific response alternatives are provided.

clinical significance A measure of the strength of a treatment as indicated by the extent to which it has improved the life of a client in a real-world setting; usually assessed using either subjective evaluation or social comparison.

cluster sample A type of probability sample in which the sampling unit is an aggregate or cluster of elements for which an appropriate sampling frame is available.

coding The initial step in data reduction, especially with narrative records, in which units of behavior or particular events are identified and classified according to specific criteria.

complete within-subjects design A type of within-subjects design in which practice effects are balanced by administering the conditions several times to each subject such that results for each subject are interpretable.

complex design An experiment in which two or more independent variables are studied simultaneously.

confederate Someone in the service of a researcher who is instructed to behave in a certain way in order to help produce an experimental treatment.

confidence interval An interval around the sample mean in which there can be a specified degree of confidence that the population mean is included in the interval; most common interval is the 95 percent confidence interval that spans approximately two standard error of the mean units on either side of the sample mean.

confounding When the independent variable of interest systematically covaries with a second, unintended independent variable.

contamination   When there is communication of information about the experiment between groups of subjects.

content analysis   Any of a variety of techniques for making inferences by objectively identifying specific characteristics of messages, usually written communications but may be any form of message; used extensively in the analysis of archival data.

continuity assumption   Assumption used in establishing generality of experimental findings that asserts that behavior is relatively continuous across time, subjects, and settings unless there is reason to assume otherwise.

control   A key component of the scientific method whereby the effect of various factors possibly responsible for a phenomenon are isolated; three basic types of control are manipulation, holding conditions constant, and balancing.

correlation   A correlation exists when two different measures of the same people, events, or things, vary together; the presence of a correlation makes it possible to predict values on one variable by knowing the values on the second variable.

correlation coefficient   A statistic that indicates how well two measures vary together; absolute size ranges from 0.0 (no correlation) to 1.00 (perfect correlation); direction of covariation is indicated by the sign of the coefficient, a plus (+) indicating that both measures covary in the same direction and a minus (−) indicating that the variables vary in opposite directions.

critical value   The size of a test statistic required to reject the null hypothesis; for F-ratio, it depends on the level of significance, the number of groups in the experiment, and the number of subjects within the groups.

d'   See **sensitivity.**

data reduction   The process in the analysis of behavioral data whereby results are meaningfully organized and statements summarizing important findings are prepared.

degrees of freedom   A statistical concept that can generally be defined as the number of entries of interest minus one.

demand characteristics   The cues and other information used by participants to guide their behavior in a psychological study, often leading participants to do what they believe the observer (experimenter) expects them to do.

dependent variable   Measures of behavior used by the researcher to assess the effect (if any) of the independent variables.

difference threshold   (or **just noticeable difference**)   That increment or decrement in a stimulus that an observer can detect 50 percent of the time.

differential transfer   Potential problem in within-subjects designs when performance in one condition differs depending on which of two other conditions precedes it.

double-blind experiment   Both the subject and the observer are kept unaware (blind) of what treatment is being administered.

element   Each member of the population of interest.

ecological psychology   Has as its goal the comprehensive description of individuals in everyday contexts.

empirical approach   An approach to acquiring knowledge that emphasizes direct observation and experimentation as a way of answering questions.

error variation   The nonsystematic variation in an experiment; in the random groups design, error variation is estimated on the basis of differences among subjects within each group.

ethogram   A complete catalog of all the behavior patterns of an organism, including information as to frequency, duration, and context of occurrence.

ethology   The study of the behavior of organisms in relation to their natural environment; generally considered a branch of biology.

event sampling   A procedure whereby the observer records each event that meets a predetermined definition; more efficient method than time sampling when event of interest occurs infrequently.

experimental analysis of behavior   A form of behaviorism (developed and promoted by B. F. Skinner) that presents a unique behavioral view of human nature with implications both for how psychologists should do research and how society should be organized.

experimenter effects   The experimenters' expectations that may lead them to treat subjects differently in different groups or to record data in a biased manner.

external validity   Is the extent to which the results of a research study can be generalized to different populations, settings, and conditions.

field experiment   A procedure in which one or more independent variables is manipulated by an observer in a natural setting to determine the effect on behavior.

field notes   Verbal records of a trained observer that provide running descriptions of participants, events, settings, and behaviors.

filter questions   General questions on a survey to determine whether the respondents need to be asked more specific questions.

funnel questions   When the questions dealing with a particular topic on a questionnaire are ordered from the most general to the most specific.

Hawthorne effect   Refers to changes in a person's behavior brought about by the interest shown in that person by significant others.

hypothesis   A tentative explanation for a phenomenon.

idiographic approach   The intensive study of an individual, with an emphasis on both individual uniqueness and lawfulness.

incomplete within-subjects design   A type of within-subjects design in which each condition is administered to each subject only once and the order of administering the conditions is varied across subjects such that practice effects are neutralized by combining the results for all subjects.

independent groups design   Each separate group in the experiment represents a different condition as defined by the level of the independent variable.

independent variable   A factor for which the researcher either selects or manipulates at least two levels in order to determine its effect on behavior.

inferential statistics   A means to test whether the differences in a dependent variable that are associated with various conditions of an experiment are reliable, that is, larger than would be expected on the basis of error variation alone.

interaction   Occurs when the effect of one independent variable differs depending on the level of a second independent variable.

internal validity   The degree to which differences in performance can be attributed unambiguously to an effect of an independent variable, as opposed to an effect of some other (uncontrolled) variable; an internally valid study is free of confounds.

interobserver reliability   The degree to which two independent observers are in agreement.

interrupted time-series design   See **simple interrupted time-series design** and **time series with nonequivalent control group**.

interval recording   An observational procedure in which a block of time is identified, divided into a series of smaller equal intervals, and records kept as to whether a target behavior occurs during each interval; only the first occurrence of a behavior during an interval is counted.

interviewer bias   Occurs when the interviewer tries to adjust the wording of a question to "fit" the respondent or records only selected portions of the respondent's answers.

introspection   A method of doing research wherein observers are asked to describe their feelings and sensations when presented with various stimuli.

irreversible task   A problem that arises in the incomplete within-subjects design when a specific task cannot be administered more than once to the same subjects; necessitates special balancing procedures to ensure that practice effects, task, and independent variable are appropriately controlled.

just noticeable difference   See **difference threshold.**

level of significance (alpha α)   When the probability of an outcome under the null hypothesis is less than this value, then the outcome is statistically significant.

magnitude estimation   The scaling technique, developed by S. S. Stevens, whereby the subject is required to assign a number to each presented stimulus that reflects the apparent magnitude of that stimulus relative to a standard.

main effect   The overall effect of an independent variable in a complex design.

matched groups design   A type of independent groups design in which the researcher forms comparable groups by matching subjects on a pretest task and then randomly assigning the members of these matched sets of subjects to the conditions of the experiment.

measurement scale   One of four levels of physical and psychological measurement: nominal (categorizing), ordinal (ranking), interval (specifying distance between stimuli), and ratio (having an absolute zero point).

mechanical subject loss   Occurs when a subject fails to complete the experiment because of equipment failure or because of experimenter error.

mixed design   When different designs (independent groups, within-subjects) are used for the different independent variables in a complex design the overall experiment is described as a mixed design.

multimethod approach   An approach to hypothesis testing that seeks evidence by collecting data using several different measures of behavior; a recognition of the fact that any single measure of behavior can result from some artifact of the measuring process.

multiple-baseline design (across subjects, across behaviors, across situations)   A single-case experimental design in which the effect of a treatment is demonstrated by showing that behaviors in more than one baseline change as a consequence of the introduction of a treatment; multiple baselines are established for different individuals, for different behaviors in the same individual, or for the same individual in different situations.

natural groups design   A type of independent groups design in which the conditions represent the selected levels of a naturally occurring independent variable, for example, the subject variable age.

$N = 1$ Research designs characteristic of the experimental analysis of behavior that provide an alternative to group methodology and in which the emphasis is on research involving a single subject.

narrative record   Intended to provide a more or less faithful reproduction of behavior as it originally occurred.

naturalistic observation   An observation of behavior in a more or less natural setting without any attempt by the observer to intervene.

nomothetic approach   An approach to research that seeks to establish broad generalizations or laws that apply to large groups (populations) of individuals; the average or typical performance of a group is emphasized.

nonequivalent control group design A quasi-experimental procedure in which a comparison is made between control and treatment groups that have been established on some basis other than through random assignment of subjects to groups.

nonprobability sampling A sampling procedure in which there is no way to estimate the probability of each element being included in the sample; two common types are accidental sampling and purposive sampling.

nuisance factors Potential independent variables that are not directly of interest to the researcher but serve as vexing sources of confounding.

null hypothesis The assumption used as the first step in statistical inference whereby the independent variable is said to have had no effect.

observer bias Systematic errors in observation often resulting from the observer's expectancies regarding the outcome of a study (i.e., *expectancy effects*).

omnibus *F*-test An initial overall analysis of the experiment for which the null hypothesis is that all the group means are equal.

one-shot or cross-sectional study A survey research design in which one or more samples of the population is selected and information is collected from the samples at one time.

open or free-response questions Questionnaire items that specify the area to be addressed in a response but no specific alternatives as possible answers are provided.

operational definition A procedure whereby a concept is defined solely in terms of the operations used to produce and measure it.

paired comparisons A scaling method in which each stimulus to be measured is paired with each other stimulus and the subject is asked to select the member in each pair that has the greater (or lesser) amount of the characteristic of interest.

panel or longitudinal study A survey research design in which the same sample of respondents is interviewed more than once.

participant observation An observation of behavior by someone who also has an active and significant role in the situation or context in which behavior is recorded.

physical traces A source of evidence that is based on the remnants, fragments, and products of past behavior; used as an alternative to or in conjunction with other research methods.

placebo A substance that resembles a drug or other active substance but that is actually an inert, or inactive, substance.

point of subjective equality That point that is equal psychologically to a specified standard on a physical scale.

population The set of all the cases of interest.

probability sampling A sampling procedure in which the probability that each element of the population will be included in the sample can be specified.

program evaluation Research that seeks to determine whether a change proposed by an institution, government agency, or other unit of society is needed and likely to have an effect as planned, or, when implemented, to actually have an effect.

purposive sample A type of nonprobability sample in which the elements to be included in the sample are selected by the investigator on the basis of special characteristics of the respondents.

psychophysics The experimental study of the relationship between stimulation measured in physical units and the psychological sensation experienced in response to that stimulation.

quasi-experiments   Procedures that resemble those characteristics of true experiments, for example, that some type of intervention or treatment is used and a comparison is provided, but are lacking in the degree of control that is found in true experiments.

random assignment   The most common technique for forming groups as part of an independent groups design; the goal is to establish equivalent groups by balancing subject characteristics.

random groups design   The most common type of independent groups design in which individuals are randomly selected or randomly assigned to each group such that groups are considered comparable at the start of the experiment.

random sampling   See **simple random sample.**

rank-order scaling   A method of scaling in which all stimuli are presented simultaneously and the subject is asked to rank them from highest to lowest, or vice versa.

reactivity   The influence that an observer has on the behavior under observation; behavior influenced by an observer may not be representative of behavior when an observer is not present.

regression to the mean   Because some component of a test score is due to error (as opposed to true score), extreme scores on one test are likely to be closer to the mean on a second test, thus posing a threat to the validity of an experiment in which extreme groups are selected; the amount of this regression will be greater for less reliable tests.

relevant independent variable   An independent variable that has been shown to influence behavior, either directly by producing a main effect, or indirectly by resulting in an interaction in combination with a second independent variable.

reliability   A measurement is reliable when it is consistent.

replication   Repeating the exact procedures used in an experiment to determine whether the same results are obtained.

respondent mortality   When a respondent fails to complete all phases of a panel or longitudinal survey research design.

representativeness   A sample is representative to the extent that it has the same distribution of characteristics as the population from which it was selected; our ability to generalize from sample to population is critically dependent on representativeness.

response bias (beta β)   A concept in signal detection theory referring to the observer's overall willingness to report that a signal has occurred.

sample   Something less than all the cases of interest; typically, a subset of the population actually drawn from the sampling frame.

sampling frame   A specific listing of all the members of the population of interest; an operational definition of the population.

scaling techniques   Procedures used to measure stimuli on psychological dimensions, such as aggressiveness or pleasantness.

scientific method   An approach to knowledge that emphasizes empirical rather than intuitive processes, testable hypotheses, systematic and controlled observation of operationally defined phenomena, data collection using accurate and precise instrumentation, valid and reliable measures, and objective reporting of results; scientists tend to be critical and, most importantly, skeptical.

selective deposit   The bias that results from the way physical traces are laid down and the way archival sources are produced, edited, or altered, as they are established; when present, the bias severely limits generality of research findings.

selective subject loss Occurs when subjects are lost differentially across the conditions of the experiment as the result of some characteristic of the subject that is related to the outcome of the study.

selective survival The bias that results from the way physical traces and archives survive over time; when present, the bias severely limits generality of research findings.

sensitivity *d'* Concept in signal detection theory referring to the observer's ability to detect the occurrence of a signal.

simple comparison A special type of analytical comparison that is used to determine the specific source of variation within a simple main effect in a complex design.

simple interrupted time-series design A quasi-experimental procedure in which changes in a dependent variable are observed for some period of time both before and after a treatment is introduced.

simple main effect The effect of one independent variable at one level of a second independent variable in a complex design.

simple random sample and random selection A type of probability sample in which each possible sample of a specified size in the population has an equal chance of being selected.

single-case experimental design A procedure that focuses on behavior change in one individual by systematically contrasting conditions within that individual while continuously monitoring behavior.

situation sampling The random or systematic selection of situations in which observations are to be made with the goal of representativeness across circumstances, locations, and conditions.

social comparison A measure of clinical significance of a treatment in which the researcher compares the behavior of a client after treatment with the behavior of a "normal" group of subjects.

social desirability The pressures on survey respondents to answer as they think they should respond in accordance with what is most socially acceptable, and not in accordance with what they actually believe.

split-ballot technique A procedure used in questionnaire construction in which different wordings of the same questions are used for equivalent samples of respondents to examine the effect of the wording directly.

spurious relationship Exists when evidence falsely indicates that two or more variables are associated.

stage-of-practice effects The changes subjects undergo across repeated testing in within-subjects designs; subjects may get better if a skill is being developed or worse because of factors such as fatigue or boredom.

statistically significant When the probability of an obtained difference in an experiment is smaller than would be expected if error variation alone were assumed to be responsible for the difference.

stratified random sample A type of probability sample in which the population is divided into subpopulations called *strata* and random samples are drawn from each of these strata.

structured observation A variety of observational methods using intervention in which the degree of control is often less than in field experiments; frequently used by clinical and developmental psychologists when making behavioral assessments.

subject variables The characteristics subjects bring with them to the laboratory, such as their gender; subject variables are often studied as independent variables in the natural groups design.

subjective evaluation A measure of clinical significance of a treatment in which the judgments of people who have contact with the client are used to assess whether the behavior of the client is perceptibly different after treatment from what it was before treatment.

successive independent samples A survey research design in which a series of cross-sectional surveys is done and the same questions are asked of each succeeding sample of respondents.

theory A logically organized set of propositions which serves to define events, describe relationships among events, and explain the occurrence of these events; scientific theories guide research and organize empirical knowledge.

threats to internal validity Possible causes of a phenomenon which must be controlled so that a clear cause-and-effect inference can be made.

time sampling The selection of observation intervals either systematically or randomly with the goal of obtaining a representative sample of behavior.

time series with nonequivalent control group (See also **simple interrupted time-series design.**) A quasi-experimental procedure that improves on the validity of a simple time-series design by including a nonequivalent control group; both treatment and comparison groups are observed for a period of time both before and after the treatment.

token economy A procedure in behavior modification in which behavior is reinforced with tokens which can then be used to "purchase" desired reinforcers.

unobtrusive (nonreactive) measures Measures of behavior that eliminate the problem of reactivity, because observations are made in such a way that the presence of the observer is not detected by those being observed.

validity The "truthfulness" of a measure; a valid measure is one that measures what it claims to measure.

within-subjects design A design in which the independent variable is implemented by administering all the levels of the independent variable to each subject.

References

Abramson, L. Y., and Seligman, M. E. P. 1977. Modeling psychopathology in the laboratory: History and rationale. In *Psychopathology: Experimental models*, ed. J. D. Maser and M. E. P. Seligman, pp. 1–26. San Francisco: Freeman.

Adair, J. G.; Dushenko, T. W.; and Lindsay, R. C. L. 1985. Ethical regulations and their impact on research practice. *American Psychologist* 40: 59–72.

Addison, W. E. 1986. Agonistic behavior in preschool children: A comparison of same-sex versus opposite-sex interactions. *Bulletin of the Psychonomic Society* 24: 44–46.

Adjang, O. M. J. 1986. Exploring the social environment: A developmental study of teasing in chimpanzees. *Ethology* 73: 136–160.

Adler, A. 1973. *Practice and theory of individual psychology*, trans. P. Radin. Totowa, N.J.: Littlefield, Adams.

Alevizos, P.; De Risi, W.; Liberman, R.; Eckman, T.; and Callahan, E. 1978. The behavior observation instrument: A method of direct observation for program evaluation. *Journal of Applied Behavior Analysis* 11: 243–257.

Allison, M. G., and Ayllon, T. 1980. Behavioral coaching in the development of skills in football, gymnastics, and tennis. *Journal of Applied Behavior Analysis* 13: 297–314.

Allport, G. W. 1946. Letters from Jenny. *Journal of Abnormal and Social Psychology* 41, nos. 3 and 4.

———. 1961. *Pattern in growth and personality*. New York: Holt, Rinehart, and Winston.

———. 1965. *Letters from Jenny*. New York: Harcourt, Brace & World.

Altmann, J. 1974. Observational study of behavior: Sampling methods. *Behavior,* 48: 1–41.

American Psychological Association. 1981. Ethical principles of psychologists. *American Psychologist* 36: 633–638.

———. 1982. *Ethical principles in the conduct of research with human participants*. Washington.

———. 1983. *Publication Manual*. 3d ed. Washington.

———. 1988. Summary report of journal operations: 1987. *American Psychologist* 43: 588.

Anderson, C. R. 1976. Coping behaviors as intervening mechanisms in the inverted-U stress-performance relationship. *Journal of Applied Psychology* 61: 30-34.

Anderson, K. J., and Revelle, W. 1982. Impulsivity, caffeine, and proofreading: A test of the Easterbrook hypothesis. *Journal of Experimental Psychology: Human Perception and Performance* 8: 614–624.

Anisfeld, M. 1987. A course to develop competence in critical reading of empirical research in psychology. *Teaching of Psychology* 14: 224–227.

Asch, S. E. 1951. Effects of group pressure upon the modification and distortion of judgments. In *Groups, leadership, and men*, ed. H. Guetzkow, pp. 177–190. Pittsburgh: Carnegie.

————. 1955. Opinions and social pressure. *Scientific American* 193: 31–35.

Atkinson, R. C. 1968. Computerized instruction and the learning process. *American Psychologist* 23: 225–239.

Atkinson, R. C., and Shiffrin, R. M. 1968. Human memory: A proposed system and its control processes. In *The psychology of learning and motivation*, ed. K. W. Spence and J. T. Spence, vol. 2, pp. 89–195. New York: Academic Press.

Babbie, E. R. 1979. *The practice of social research*. 2d ed. Belmont, Calif.: Wadsworth.

Bailey, J. 1987. The editor's page. *Journal of Applied Behavior Analysis* 20: 305–307.

Barash, D. P. 1977. Human ethology: Exchanging cheetahs for Chevrolets? *Environment and Behavior* 9: 487–490.

Barker, R. G.; Wright, H. F.; Schoggen, M. F.; and Barker, L. S. 1978. Day in the life of Mary Ennis. In *Habitats, environments, and human behavior*, ed. R. G. Barker et al., pp. 51–98. San Francisco: Jossey-Bass.

Baron, J. N., and Reiss, P. C. 1985. Same time, next year: Aggregate analyses of the mass media and violent behavior. *American Sociological Review* 50: 347–363.

Barron, D. D., and Yankelovich, D. 1980. *Today's American woman: How the public sees her.* Report prepared for the President's Advisory Committee for Women by the Public Agenda Foundation.

Bartholomew, G. A. 1982. Scientific innovation and creativity: A zoologist's point of view. *American Zoologist* 22: 227–335.

Bartlett, F. C. 1932. *Remembering: A study in experimental and social psychology.* Cambridge: Cambridge University Press.

Bass, B. M. 1979. Confessions of a former male chauvinist. *American Psychologist* 34: 194–195.

Becker, J. V.; Turner, S. M.; and Sajwaj, T. E. 1978. Multiple behavioral effects of the use of lemon juice with a ruminating toddler-age child. *Behavior Modification* 2: 267–278.

Benassi, V. A.; Singer, B.; and Reynolds, C. B. 1980. Occult belief: Seeing is believing. *Journal for the Scientific Study of Religion* 19: 337–349.

Benjamin, L. T., Jr. 1979. A century of science. *APA Monitor* (February): 1, 3.

Berk, R. A.; Boruch, R. F.; Chambers, D. L.; Rossi, P. H.; and Witte, A. D. 1987. Social policy experimentation: A position paper. In *Evaluation Studies Review Annual*, Vol. 11, ed. D. S. Cordray and M. W. Lipsey, pp. 630–672. Newbury Park, Calif. Sage.

Bernstein, C., and Woodward, B. 1976. *All the president's men.* New York: Simon and Schuster.

Bickman, L. 1976. Observational methods. In *Research methods in social relations*, ed. C. Selltiz, L. S. Wrightsman, and S. W. Cook, pp. 251–290. New York: Holt, Rinehart and Winston.

Bloom, B. L.; Asher, S. J.; and White, S. W. 1978. Marital disruption as a stressor: A review and analysis. *Psychological Bulletin* 85: 867–894.

Bolgar, H. 1965. The case study method. In *Handbook of clinical psychology*, ed. B. B. Wolman, pp. 28–39. New York: McGraw-Hill.

Bond, C. F., Jr., and Titus, L. J. 1983. Social facilitation: A meta-analysis of 241 studies. *Psychological Bulletin* 94: 265–292.

Booth, W. 1988. Chimps and research: Endangered? *Science* 241: 777–778.

Bootzin, R. R., and Acocella, J. R. 1988. *Abnormal psychology: Current perspectives.* 5th ed. New York: Random House.

Boring, E. G. 1950. *A history of experimental psychology.* New York: Appleton-Century-Crofts.

————. 1954. The nature and history of experimental control. *American Journal of Psychology* 67: 573–589.

Bornstein, M. T.; Bellack, A. S.; and Hersen, M. 1977. Social-skills training for unassertive children: A multiple-baseline analysis. *Journal of Applied Behavior Analysis* 10: 183–195.

Brady, J. V. 1958. Ulcers in "executive" monkeys. *Scientific American* 199: 95–100.

Brainerd, C. J. 1978. *Piaget's theory of intelligence.* Englewood Cliffs, N.J.: Prentice-Hall.

Brandt, R. M. 1972. *Studying behavior in natural settings.* New York: Holt, Rinehart and Winston; University Press of America, 1981.

Bridgwater, C. A.; Bornstein, P. H.; and Walkenbach, J. 1981. Ethical issues and the assignment of publication credit. *American Psychologist* 36: 524–525.

Bringmann, W. 1979. Wundt's lab: "humble...but functioning" [letter to the editor]. *APA Monitor* (September/October): 13.

Browne, M. A., and Mahoney, M. J. 1984. Sport psychology. *Annual Review of Psychology* 35: 605–625.

Burns, M. S.; Haywood, H. C.; and Delclos, V. R. 1987. Young children's problem-solving strategies: An observational study. *Journal of Applied Developmental Psychology* 8: 113–121.

Burt, C. 1972. Inheritance of general intelligence. *American Psychologist* 27: 175–190.

Campbell, A. 1981. *The sense of well-being in America.* New York: McGraw-Hill.

Campbell, A.; Converse, P. E.; and Rodgers, W. L. 1975. *The quality of American life: July–August, 1971.* Ann Arbor: ISR Social Science Archive.

Campbell, B. G. 1976. *Humankind emerging.* Boston: Little, Brown.

Campbell, D. T. 1969. Reforms as experiments. *American Psychologist* 24: 409–429.

Campbell, D. T., and Stanley, J. C. 1966. *Experimental and quasi-experimental designs for research.* Chicago: Rand McNally.

Chambers, J. H., and Ascione, F. R. 1987. The effects of prosocial and aggressive videogames on children's donating and helping. *Journal of Genetic Psychology* 148: 499–505.

Chase, W. G., and Simon, H. A. 1973. Perception in chess. *Cognitive Psychology* 4: 55–81.

Cohen, D. 1979. *J. B. Watson: The founder of behaviorism.* London: Routledge & Kegan Paul.

Cohen, S.; Evans, G. W.; Krantz, D. S.; and Stokols, D. 1980. Physiological, motivational, and cognitive effects of aircraft noise on children: Moving from the laboratory to the field. *American Psychologist* 35: 231–243.

Converse, P. E., and Traugott, M. W. 1986. Assessing the accuracy of polls and surveys. *Science* 234: 1094–1098.

Cook, T. D., and Campbell, D. T. 1979. *Quasi-experimentation: Design and analysis issues for field settings.* Chicago: Rand McNally.

Cordaro, L., and Ison, J. R. 1963. Psychology of the scientist: X. Observer bias in classical conditioning of the planarian. *Psychological Reports* 13: 787–789.

Coren, S., and Porac, C. 1977. Fifty centuries of right-handedness: The historical record. *Science* 198: 631–632.

Coughlin, E. K. 1988. Scholar who submitted bogus article to journals may be disciplined. *The Chronicle of Higher Education* 35: 1, A7.

Crusco, A. H., and Wetzel, C. G. 1984. The Midas touch: The effects of interpersonal touch on restaurant tipping. *Personality and Social Psychology Bulletin* 10: 512–517.

Curtiss, S. R. 1977. *Genie: A psycholinguistic study of a modern-day "wild child."* New York: Academic Press.

deGroot, A. D. 1965. *Thought and choice in chess.* The Hague: Mouton.

Department of Health, Education and Welfare. *Protection of human subjects: Technical amendments.* 40 Federal Register (p. 50, pt. 2, March 13, 1975).

Department of Health and Human Services. *Final regulations amending basic HHS policy for the protection of human subjects.* 46 Federal Register (p. 16, January 26, 1981).

Detterman, D. K., and Sternberg, R. J., eds. 1982. *How and how much can intelligence be increased.* Norwood, N.J.: Ablex.

Dickie, J. R. 1987. Interrelationships within the mother-father-infant triad. In *Men's transitions to parenthood: Longitudinal studies of early family experience,* ed. P. W. Berman and F. A. Pedersen, pp. 113–143. Hillsdale, N.J.: Erlbaum.

Diener, E., and Crandall, R. 1978. *Ethics in social and behavioral research.* Chicago: The University of Chicago Press.

Dittmar, M. L.; Berch, D. B.; and Warm, J. S. 1982. Sustained visual attention in deaf and hearing adults. *Bulletin of the Psychonomic Society* 19: 339–342.

Divorce of the year. Newsweek, March 12, 1973, pp. 48–49.

Duchon, D., and Jago, A. G. 1981. Equity and the performance of major league baseball players: An extension of Lord and Hohenfeld. *Journal of Applied Psychology* 66: 728–732.

Eibl-Eibesfeldt, I. 1975. *Ethology: The biology of behavior.* New York: Holt, Rinehart and Winston.

Epstein, R., ed. 1982. *Skinner for the classroom: Selected papers.* Champaign, Ill.: Research Press.

Etaugh, C. 1980. Effects of nonmaternal care on children: Research evidence and popular views. *American Psychologist* 35: 309–319.

Evans, R., and Donnerstein, E. 1974. Some implications for psychological research of early versus late term participation by college subjects. *Journal of Research in Personality* 8: 102–109.

Feeney, D. M. 1987. Human rights and animal welfare. *American Psychologist* 42: 593–599.

Ferster, C. B., and Skinner, B. F. 1957. *Schedules of reinforcement.* New York: Appleton-Century-Crofts.

Festinger, L.; Riecken, H.; and Schachter, S. 1956. *When prophecy fails.* Minneapolis: University of Minnesota Press.

Fischer, K.; Schoeneman, T. J.; and Rubanowitz, D. E. 1987. Attributions in the advice columns: II. The dimensionality of actors' and observers' explanations for interpersonal problems. *Personality and Social Psychology Bulletin* 13: 458–466.

Flaherty, C. F.; Hamilton, L.W.; Gandelman, R. J.; and Spear, N. E. 1977. *Learning and memory.* Chicago: Rand McNally.

Fossey, D. 1981. Imperiled giants of the forest. *National Geographic* 159: 501–523.

———. 1983. *Gorillas in the mist.* Boston: Houghton-Mifflin.

Frame, C. L., and Strauss, C. C. 1987. Parental informed consent and sample bias in grade-school children. *Journal of Social and Clinical Psychology* 5: 227–236.

Frank, M. G., and Gilovich, T. 1988. The dark side of self- and social perception: Black uniforms and aggression in professional sports. *Journal of Personality and Social Psychology* 54: 74–85.

Friedman, M. P., and Wilson, R. W. 1975. Application of unobtrusive measures to the study of textbook usage by college students. *Journal of Applied Psychology* 60: 659–662.

Gallup, G. H. 1976. Human needs and satisfaction: A global survey. *Public Opinion Quarterly* 40: 459–467.

Gazzaniga, M. S. 1972. One brain—Two minds? *American Scientist* 60: 311–317.

Geller, E. S.; Russ, N. W.; and Altomari, M. G. 1986. Naturalistic observations of beer drinking among college students. *Journal of Applied Behavior Analysis* 19: 391–396.

Goldstein, R. S.; Minkin, B. L.; Minkin, N.; and Baer, D. M. 1978. Finders, keepers?: An analysis and validation of a free-found-ad policy. *Journal of Applied Behavior Analysis* 11: 465–473.

Goleman, D. 1981. The new competency tests: Matching the right people to the right jobs. *Psychology Today*, January, pp. 35–46.

Goodall, J. 1987. A plea for the chimpanzees. *American Scientist* 75: 574–577.

Grammer, K.; Schiefenhovel, W.; Schleidt, M.; Lorenz, B.; and Eibl-Eibesfeldt, I. 1988. Patterns on the face: The eyebrow flash in crosscultural comparison. *Ethology* 77: 279–299.

Gray, B. H.; Cooke, R. A.; and Tannenbaum, A. S. 1978. Research involving human subjects: The performance of institutional review boards is assessed in this empirical study. *Science* 201: 1094–1101.

Gray, J. N., and Melton, G. B. 1985. The law and ethics of psychosocial research on AIDS. *Nebraska Law Review* 64: 637–688.

Green, D. M., and Swets, J. A. 1966. *Signal detection theory and psychophysics.* New York: Wiley.

Griffin, J. H. 1960. *Black like me.* New York: New American Library.

Guerin, B. 1986. Mere presence effects in humans: A review. *Journal of Experimental Social Psychology* 22: 38–77.

Haber, L. R., and Haber, R. N. 1982. Does silent reading involve articulation? Evidence from tongue twisters. *American Journal of Psychology* 95: 409–419.

Halpern, A. R., and Bower, G. H. 1982. Musical expertise and melodic structure in memory for musical notation. *American Journal of Psychology* 95: 31–50.

Harlow, H. F. 1958. The nature of love. *American Psychologist* 13: 673–685.

———. 1959. Love in infant monkeys. *Scientific American* 200: 68–74.

Harlow, H. F., and Harlow, M. K. 1966. Learning to love. *American Scientist* 54: 244–272.

———. 1969. Effects of various mother-infant relationships on rhesus monkey behaviors. In *Determinants of infant behavior IV,* ed. B. M. Foss, pp. 15–36. London: Methuen.

Hartup, W. W. 1974. Aggression in childhood: Developmental perspectives. *American Psychologist* 29: 336–341.

Hays, R. 1980. Honesty requiring a self-initiated response. *Psychological Reports* 46: 87–90.

Hearnshaw, L. S. 1979. *Cyril Burt, Psychologist.* London: Hodder & Stoughton.

Henderson, B. B., and Dias, L. 1987. An exploratory study of infant problem solving in natural environments. *Ethology and Sociobiology* 8: 205–213.

Hersen, M., and Barlow, D. H. 1976. *Single-case experimental designs: Strategies for studying behavior change.* New York: Pergamon Press.

Hicks, H. G., and Gullett, C. R. 1975. *Organizations: Theory and behavior.* New York: McGraw-Hill.

Hicks, R. A., and Kilcourse, J. 1983. Habitual sleep duration and the incidence of headaches in college students. *Bulletin of the Psychonomic Society* 21: 119.

Hinrichs, J. V., and Novick, L. R. 1982. Memory for numbers: Nominal vs. magnitude information. *Memory & Cognition* 10: 479–486.

Hintzman, D. L. 1978. *The psychology of learning and memory.* San Francisco: Freeman.

Hirschberg, N., and Itkin, S. 1978. Graduate student success in psychology. *American Psychologist* 33: 1083–1093.

Hite, S. 1987. *Women and love: A cultural revolution in progress.* New York: Knopf.

Holden, C. 1987. Animal regulations: So far, so good. *Science* 238: 880–882.

Holsti, O. R. 1969. *Content analysis for the social sciences.* Reading, Mass.: Addison-Wesley.

Hops, J.; Biglan, A.; Sherman, L.; Arthur, J.; Friedman, L.; and Osteen, V. 1987. Home observations of family interactions of depressed women. *Journal of Consulting and Clinical Psychology* 55: 341–346.

Horn, W. F., and Heerboth, J. 1982. Single-case experimental designs and program evaluation. *Evaluation Review* 6: 403–424.

Horton, S. V. 1987. Reduction of disruptive mealtime behavior by facial screening. *Behavior Modification* 11: 53–64.

Hostetler, A. J. 1987a. Many researchers see, speak no evil. *APA Monitor* (November): 16.

———. 1987b. The case of science ethics v. libel. *APA Monitor* (November): 16–17.

Hughes, H. M., and Haynes, S. N. 1978. Structured laboratory observation in the behavioral assessment of parent-child interactions: A methodological critique. *Behavior Therapy* 9: 428–447.

Huse, E. F., and Bowditch, J. L. 1977. *Behavior in organizations: A systems approach to managing,* 2d ed. Reading, Mass.: Addison-Wesley.

Intons-Peterson, M. J. 1983. Imagery paradigms: How vulnerable are they to experimenters' expectations? *Journal of Experimental Psychology: Human Perception and Performance* 9: 394–412.

Jackson, J. M.; Buglione, S. A.; and Glenwick, D. S. 1988. Major league baseball performance as a function of being traded: A drive theory analysis. *Personality and Social Psychology Bulletin* 14: 46–56.

Jacobson, E. 1979. I was there [letter to the editor]. *APA Monitor* (September/October): 13.

Jenni, D. A., and Jenni, M. A. 1976. Carrying behavior in humans: Analysis of sex differences. *Science* 194: 859–860.

Jenni, M. A. 1976. Sex differences in carrying behavior. *Perceptual and Motor Skills* 43: 323–330.

Jessor, R.; Chase, J. A.; and Donovan, J. E. 1980. Psychosocial correlates of marijuana use and problem drinking in a national sample of adolescents. *American Journal of Public Health* 70: 604–613.

Joffe, J. M.; Rawson, R. A.; and Mulick, J. A. 1973. Control of their environment reduces emotionality in rats. *Science* 180: 1383–1384.

Johnson, J. E.; Petzel, T. P.; Hartney, L. M.; and Morgan, R. A. 1983. Recall and importance ratings of completed and uncompleted tasks as a function of depression. *Cognitive Therapy and Research* 7: 51–56.

Kagan, J., Reznick, J. S.; and Snidman, N. 1988. Biological bases of childhood shyness. *Science* 240: 167–171.

Kahneman, D., and Tversky, A. 1973. On the psychology of prediction. *Psychological Review* 80: 237–251.

Kallio, K. D., and Cutler, B. L. 1987. Does lexical marking affect eyewitness recall? *The Journal of Psychology* 121: 249–258.

Kamin, L. J. 1974. *The science and politics of I.Q.* Hillsdale, N.J.: Erlbaum.

Kazdin, A. E. 1977. Assessing the clinical or applied significance of behavior change through social validation. *Behavior Modification* 1: 427–452.

———. 1978a. *History of behavior modification: Experimental foundations of contemporary research.* Baltimore: University Park Press.

———. 1978b. Methodological and interpretive problems of single-case experimental designs. *Journal of Consulting and Clinical Psychology* 46: 629–642.

———. 1980a. *Behavior modification in applied settings,* rev. ed. Homewood, Ill.: Dorsey Press.

———. 1980b. *Research design in clinical psychology.* New York: Harper & Row.

———. 1982a. Single-case experimental designs. In *Handbook of research methods in clinical psychology,* ed. P. C. Kendall and J. N. Butcher, pp. 461–490. New York: Wiley.

———. 1982b. The token economy: A decade later. *Journal of Applied Behavior Analysis* 15: 431–446.

Kazdin, A. E., and Bootzin, R. R. 1972. The token economy: An evaluative review. *Journal of Applied Behavior Analysis* 5: 343–372.

Kazdin, A. E., and Erickson, L. M. 1975. Developing responsiveness to instructions in severely and profoundly retarded residents. *Journal of Behavior Therapy and Experimental Psychiatry* 6: 17–21.

Keith, T. Z.; Reimers, T. M.; Fehrmann, P. G.; Pottebaum, S. M.; and Aubrey, L. W. 1986. Parental involvement, homework, and TV time: Direct and indirect effects on high school achievement. *Journal of Educational Psychology* 78: 373–380.

Keller, F. S. 1937. *The definition of psychology.* New York: Appleton-Century-Crofts.

Kelly, J. A. 1986. Psychological research and the rights of animals: Disagreement with Miller. *American Psychologist* 41: 839–841.

Kelman, H. C. 1967. Human use of human subjects: The problem of deception in social psychological experiments. *Psychological Bulletin* 67: 1–11.

———. 1972. The rights of the subject in social research: An analysis in terms of relative power and legitimacy. *American Psychologist* 27: 989–1016.

Kenny, D. A. 1979. *Correlation and causality.* New York: Wiley.

Keppel, G. 1982. *Design and analysis: A researcher's handbook,* 2d ed. Englewood Cliffs, N.J.: Prentice-Hall.

Kidder, L. H., and Judd, C. M. 1986. *Research methods in social relations.* 5th ed. New York: Holt, Rinehart and Winston.

Kirkham, G. L. 1975. *Doc cop. Human Behavior* 4: 16–23.

Kirmeyer, S. L., and Biggers, K. 1988. Environmental demand and demand engendering behavior: An observational analysis of the Type A pattern. *Journal of Personality and Social Psychology* 54: 997–1005.

Kirsch, I. 1978. Teaching clients to be their own therapists: A case-study illustration. *Psychotherapy: Theory, Research and Practice* 15: 302–305.

Klein, G. S. 1964. Semantic power measured through the interference of words with color-naming. *American Journal of Psychology* 77: 576–588.

Klemmack, S. H., and Klemmack, D. L. 1976. The social definition of rape. In *Sexual assault,* ed. M. J. Walker and S. L. Brodsky. Lexington, Mass.: Lexington Books.

Krantz, D. S. 1979. A naturalistic study of social influences on meal size among moderately obese and nonobese subjects. *Psychosomatic Medicine* 41: 19–26.

Kratochwill, T. R., and Brody, G. H. 1978. Single subject designs: A perspective on the controversy over employing statistical inference and implications for research and training in behavior modification. *Behavior Modification* 2: 291–307.

LaFrance, M., and Mayo, C. 1976. Racial differences in gaze behavior during conversations: Two systematic observational studies. *Journal of Personality and Social Psychology* 33: 547–552.

Landers, S. 1987a. CARE urges protection for animals and labs....*APA Monitor* (September): 28–29.

————. 1987b. Lab checks: Rigid or reciprocal? *APA Monitor* (December): 6–7.

————. 1988. Adolescent study presents dilemma. *APA Monitor* (September): 6.

Langer, E. J., and Piper, A. I. 1987. The prevention of mindlessness. *Journal of Personality and Social Psychology* 53: 280–287.

Langer, E. J., and Rodin, J. 1976. The effects of choice and enhanced personal responsibility for the aged: A field experiment in an institutional setting. *Journal of Personality and Social Psychology* 34: 191–198.

Larsen, C. C. 1982. Taub conviction revives centuries-old debate. *APA Monitor* (January): 1, 12–13.

Latané, B., and Darley, J. M. 1970. *The unresponsive bystander: Why doesn't he help?* New York: Appleton-Century-Crofts.

Lau, R. R., and Russell, D. 1980. Attributions in the sports pages. *Journal of Personality and Social Psychology* 39: 29–38.

Levin, J. R. 1982. Modifications of a regression-toward-the-mean demonstration. *Teaching of Psychology* 9: 237–238.

Levine, R. V.; West, L. J.; and Reis, H. T. 1980. Perceptions of time and punctuality in the United States and Brazil. *Journal of Personality and Social Psychology* 38: 541–550.

Lewin, R. 1981. Overblown reports distort obesity risks. *Science* 211: 258.

Lewis, L. K. 1986. Bibliographic computerized searching in psychology. *Teaching of Psychology* 13: 38–40.

Lippman, G. 1979. A vote for James: The "first" lab debate continues [letter to the editor]. *APA Monitor* (May): 3.

Locke, T. P.; Johnson, G. M.; Kirigin-Ramp, K.; Atwater, J. D.; and Gerrard, M. 1986. An evaluation of a juvenile education program in a state penitentiary. *Evaluation Review* 10: 281–298.

Loftus, E. F. 1979a. *Eyewitness testimony.* Cambridge, Mass.: Harvard University Press.

————. 1979b. The malleability of human memory. *American Scientist* 67: 312–320.

Loftus, E. F., and Burns, T. E. 1982. Mental shock can produce retrograde amnesia. *Memory & Cognition* 10: 318–323.

Lord, R. G., and Hohenfeld, J. A. 1979. Longitudinal field assessment of equity effects on the performance of major league baseball players. *Journal of Applied Psychology* 64: 19–26.

Lovaas, O. I.; Newsom, C.; and Hickman, C. 1987. Self-stimulatory behavior and perceptual reinforcement. *Journal of Applied Behavior Analysis* 20: 45–68.

Lubin, B.; Zuckerman, M.; Breytspraak, L. M.; Bull, N. C.; Gumbhir, A. K.; and Rinck, C. M. 1988. Affects, demographic variables, and health. *Journal of Clinical Psychology* 44: 131–141.

Luria, A. R. 1968. *The mind of a mnemonist.* New York: Basic Books.

McCain, L. J., and McCleary, R. 1979. The statistical analysis of the simple interrupted time-series quasi-experiment. In *Quasi-Experimentation: Design & analysis issues for field settings,* ed. T. D. Cook and D. T. Campbell, pp. 233–293. Chicago: Rand McNally.

McGrew, W. C. 1972. *An ethological study of children's behavior.* New York: Academic Press.

McGuigan, F. J. 1983. *Experimental psychology: Methods of research,* 4th ed. Englewood Cliffs, N.J.: Prentice-Hall.

McKinney, J. D.; Mason, J.; Perkerson, K.; and Clifford, M. 1975. Relationship between classroom behavior and academic achievement. *Journal of Educational Psychology* 67: 198–203.

McSweeney, A. J. 1978. Effects of response cost on the behavior of a million persons: Charging for directory assistance in Cincinnati. *Journal of Applied Behavior Analysis* 11: 47–51.

Maki, J. E.; Hoffman, D. M.; and Berk, R. A. 1978. A time series analysis of the impact of a water conservation campaign. *Evaluation Quarterly* 2: 107–118.

Marx, M. H. 1963. The general nature of theory construction. In *Theories in contemporary psychology,* ed. M. H. Marx, pp. 4–46. New York: Macmillan.

Maser, J. D., and Seligman, M. E. P., eds. 1977. *Psychopathology: Experimental models.* San Francisco: Freeman.

Melton, G. B., and Gray, J. N. 1988. Ethical dilemmas in AIDS research: Individual privacy and public health. *American Psychologist* 43: 60–64.

Melton, G. B.; Levine, R. J.; Koocher, G. P.; Rosenthal, R.; and Thompson, W. C. 1988. Community consultation in socially sensitive research. *American Psychologist* 43: 573–581.

Merritt, C. B., and Fowler, R. G. 1948. The pecuniary honesty of the public at large. *Journal of Abnormal and Social Psychology* 43: 90–93.

Metz, C. E. 1978. Basic principles of ROC analysis. *Seminars in nuclear medicine* 8: 283–298.

Milgram, S. 1977. Subject reaction: The neglected factor in the ethics of experimentation. Hastings Center Report, October.

Milgram, S.; Liberty, H. J.; Toledo, R.; and Wackenhut, J. 1986. Response to intrusion into waiting lines. *Journal of Personality and Social Psychology* 51: 683–689.

Miller, J. D. 1986, May. Some new measures of scientific illiteracy. Paper presented at the meeting of the American Association for the Advancement of Science, Philadelphia.

Miller, N. E. 1985. The value of behavioral research on animals. *American Psychologist* 40: 423–440.

Millon, T. 1969. *Modern psychopathology.* Philadelphia: Saunders.

Molcan, J.; Miller, T.; Dugoni, B.; and Heath, L. 1987 (November). Time series analyses of homocide data: The third day effect revisited. Paper presented at the meeting of the American Society of Criminology, Montreal, Quebec, Canada.

Mook, D. G. 1983. In defense of external invalidity. *American Psychologist* 38: 379–387.

Mooney, L. A., and Brabant, S. 1987. Deviance, deference, and demeanor: Birthday cards as ceremonial tokens. *Deviant Behavior* 8: 377–388.

Moore, B. R. and Stuttard, S. 1979. Dr. Guthrie and *Felis domesticus* or: Tripping over the cat. *Science* 205: 1031–1033.

Mulder, R. 1979. The effects of televised political ads in the 1975 Chicago mayoral election. *Journalism Quarterly* 56: 336–340.

Neisser, U. 1981. John Dean's memory: A case study. *Cognition* 9: 1–22.

Newcomb, T. M.; Koenig, K. E.; Flacks, R.; and Warwick, D. P. 1967. *Persistence and change: Bennington College and its students after twenty-five years.* New York: Wiley.

New town blues: HUD abandons a disaster. *Time*, October 16, 1978, p. 84.

Nowaczyk, R. H. 1984. The relationship of problem-solving ability and course performance among novice programmers. *International Journal of Man-Machine Studies* 21: 149–160.

O'Grady, K. E. 1982. Measures of explained variance: Cautions and limitations. *Psychological Bulletin* 92: 766–777.

O'Leary, K. D., and Borkovec, T. D. 1978. Conceptual, methodological, and ethical problems of placebo groups in psychotherapy research. *American Psychologist* 33: 821–830.

Oppenheim, A. N. 1966. *Questionnaire design and attitude measurement.* New York: Basic Books.

Orne, M. T. 1962. On the social psychology of the psychological experiment: With particular reference to demand characteristics and their implications. *American Psychologist* 17: 776–783.

Osgood, C. E., and Walker, E. G. 1959. Motivation and language behavior: A content analysis of suicide notes. *Journal of Abnormal and Social Psychology* 59: 58–67.

Palladino, J. J.; Carsrud, A. L.; Hulicka, I. M.; and Benjamin, L. T., Jr. 1982. Undergraduate research in psychology: Assessment and directions. *Teaching of Psychology* 9: 71–74.

Parr, V. H. 1979. Online information retrieval and the undergraduate. *Teaching of Psychology* 6:61–62.

Parry, H. J., and Crossley, H. M. 1950. Validity of responses to survey questions. *Public Opinion Quarterly* 14: 61–80.

Parsons, H. M. 1974. What happened at Hawthorne? *Science* 183: 922–932.

Patton, J. E.; Routh, D. K.; and Stinard, T. A. 1986. Where do children study? Behavioral observations. *Bulletin of the Psychonomic Society* 24: 439–440.

Peplau, L. A., and Gordon, S. L. 1985. Women and men in love: Gender differences in close heterosexual relationships. In *Women, gender, and social psychology,* ed. R. K. Unger and B. S. Wallston, pp. 257–291. Hillsdale, N.J.: Erlbaum.

Petzel, T. P.; Johnson, J. E.; and McKillip, J. 1973. Response bias in drug surveys. *Journal of Consulting and Clinical Psychology* 40: 437–439.

Phillips, D. P. 1977. Motor vehicle fatalities increase just after publicized suicide stories. *Science* 196: 1464–1465.

———. 1978. Airplane accident fatalities increase just after newspaper stories about murder and suicide. *Science* 201: 748–750.

———. 1983. The impact of mass media violence on U.S. homicides. *American Sociological Review* 48: 560–568.

Phillips, D. P., and Bollen, K. A. 1985. Same time, last year: Selective data dredging for negative findings. *American Sociological Review* 50: 364–371.

Piaget, J. 1965. *The child's conception of number.* New York: Norton.

Pishkin, V., and Shurley, J. T. 1983. Electrophysiological parameters in anxiety and failure: Evaluation of doxepin and hydroxyzine. *Bulletin of the Psychonomic Society* 21: 21–23.

Pitman, R. K.; Kolb, B.; Orr, S. P.; deJong, J.; Yadati, S.; and Singh, M. M. 1987. On the utility of ethological data in psychiatric research: The example of facial behavior in schizophrenia. *Ethology and Sociobiology* 8: 111S–116S.

Pollack, E. S., and Horm, J. W. 1980. Trends in cancer incidence and mortality in the United States, 1969–76. *Journal of the National Cancer Institute* 64: 1091–1103.

Polyson, J., and Levinson, M. 1982. Writing styles: A survey of psychology journal editors. *American Psychologist* 37: 335–338.

Posavac, E. J., and Carey, R. G. 1989. *Program evaluation,* 3d ed. Englewood Cliffs, N.J.: Prentice-Hall.

Posner, M. I. 1973. *Cognition: An introduction.* Glenview, Ill.: Scott, Foresman.

Poulton, E. C. 1973. Unwanted range effects from using within-subject experimental designs. *Psychological Bulletin* 80: 113–121.

————. 1975. Range effects in experiments on people. *American Journal of Psychology* 88: 3–32.

————. 1982. Influential companions. Effects of one strategy on another in the within-subjects designs of cognitive psychology. *Psychological Bulletin* 91: 673–690.

Poulton, E. C., and Freeman, P. R. 1966. Unwanted asymmetrical transfer effects with balanced experimental designs. *Psychological Bulletin* 66: 1–8.

Powell, D. A.; Milligan, W. L.; and Furchtgott, E. 1984. Interaction of physio-medical and psychosocial variables in age-related functional impairments. *International Journal of Aging and Human Development* 19: 235–252.

Reese, E. P. 1978. *Human behavior: Analysis and application,* 2d ed. Dubuque, Iowa: Wm. C. Brown.

Reimanis, G., and Green, R. F. 1971. Imminence of death and intellectual decrement in the aging. *Developmental Psychology* 5: 270–272.

Reynolds, G. S. 1968. *A primer of operant conditioning.* Glenview, Ill.: Scott, Foresman.

Riley, D. A. 1962. Memory for form. In *Psychology in the making,* ed. L. Postman, pp. 402–465. New York: Knopf.

Rimm, D. C., and Masters, J. C. 1979. *Behavior therapy: Techniques and empirical findings,* 2d ed. New York: Academic Press.

Rodman, J. L., and Burger, J. M. 1985. The influence of depression on the attribution of responsibility for an accident. *Cognitive Therapy and Research* 9: 651–657.

Roethlisberger, F. J. 1977. *The elusive phenomena: An autobiographical account of my work in the field of organized behavior at the Harvard Business School.* Cambridge, Mass.: Division of Research, Graduate School of Business Administration (distributed by Harvard University Press).

Rollin, B. E. 1985. The moral status of research animals in psychology. *American Psychologist* 40: 920–926.

Rosenfeld, A. 1981. Animal rights vs. human health. *Science* 81 (June): 18, 22.

Rosenhan, D. L. 1973. On being sane in insane places. *Science* 179: 250–258.

Rosenthal, R. 1963. On the social psychology of the psychological experiment: The experimenter's hypothesis as unintended determinant of experimental results. *American Scientist,* 51: 268–283.

————. 1966. *Experimenter effects in behavioral research.* New York: Appleton-Century-Crofts.

————. 1976. *Experimenter effects in behavioral research.* Enlarged ed. New York: Irvington.

Ross, A. S., and White, S. 1987. Shoplifting, impaired driving, and refusing the breathalyzer: On seeing one's name in a public place. *Evaluation Review* 11: 254–260.

Rotter, J. B. 1966. Generalized expectancies for internal versus external control of reinforcement. *Psychological Monographs* 80 (1, Whole No. 609): 1–28.

Rozin, P., and Jonides, J. 1977. Mass reaction time: Measurement of the speed of the nerve impulse and the duration of mental processes in class. *Teaching of Psychology* 4: 91–94.

Sackheim, H. A.; Gur, R. C.; and Saucy, M. C. 1978. Emotions are expressed more intensely on the left side of the face. *Science* 202: 434–436.

Salomon, G. 1987. Basic and applied research in psychology: Reciprocity between two worlds. *International Journal of Psychology* 22: 441–446.

Schaller, G. B. 1963. *The mountain gorilla.* Chicago: University of Chicago Press.

Schlosberg, H. 1965. Hints on presenting a paper at an APA convention. *American Psychologist* 20: 606–607.

Schnelle, J. F.; Kirchner, R. E.; Macrae, J. W.; McNees, M. P.; Eck, R. H.; Snodgrass, S.; Casey, J. D.; and Uselton, P. H., Jr. 1978. Police evaluation research: An experimental and cost-benefit analysis of a helicopter patrol in a high-crime area. *Journal of Applied Behavior Analysis* 11: 11–21.

Schoeneman, T. J., and Rubanowitz, D. E. 1985. Attributions in the advice columns: Actors and observers, causes and reasons. *Personality and Social Psychology Bulletin* 11: 315–325.

Schulz, R., and Bazerman, M. 1980. Ceremonial occasions and mortality: A second look. *American Psychologist* 35: 253–261.

Schuman, H.; Presser, S.; and Ludwig, J. 1981. Context effects on survey responses to questions about abortion. *Public Opinion Quarterly* 45: 216–233.

Schuman, H., and Scott, J. 1987. Problems in the use of survey questions to measure public opinion. *Science* 236: 957–959.

Schwartz, B., and Lacey, H. 1982. *Behaviorism, science, and human nature.* New York: Norton.

Scoville, W. B., and Milner, B. 1957. Loss of recent memory after bilateral hippocampal lesions. *Journal of Neurology, Neurosurgery, and Psychiatry* 20: 11–19.

Seligman, M. E. P. 1988 (August). Why is there so much depression today? The waxing of the individual and the waning of the commons. The G. Stanley Hall Lecture presented at the American Psychological Association, Atlanta.

Sharma, S., and Moskowitz, H. 1972. Effect of marijuana on the visual autokinetic phenomenon. *Perceptual and Motor Skills* 35: 891–894.

Sheldon, E. B., and Freeman, H. E. 1972. Notes on social indicators: Promise and potential. In *Evaluating action programs: Readings in social action and education,* ed. C. H. Weiss, 166–173. Boston: Allyn and Bacon.

Singer, B., and Benassi, V. A. 1981. Occult beliefs. *American Scientist* 69: 49–55.

Singer, M. 1982. Comparing memory for natural and laboratory reading. *Journal of Experimental Psychology: General* 111: 331–347.

Skinner, B. F. 1937. Two types of conditioned reflex: A reply to Konorski and Miller. *Journal of General Psychology* 16: 272–279.

———. 1951. How to teach animals. *Scientific American* 185: 26–29.

———. 1956. A case history in scientific method. *American Psychologist* 11: 221–233.

———. 1958. Teaching machines. *Science* 128: 969–977.

———. 1966. Operant behavior. In *Operant behavior: Areas of research and application,* ed. W. K. Honig, pp. 12–32. New York: Appleton-Century-Crofts.

———. 1967. B. F. Skinner...An autobiography. In *A history of psychology in autobiography,* ed. E. G. Boring and G. Lindzey, vol. 5, pp. 387–413. New York: Appleton-Century-Crofts.

Smith, P. K., and Lewis, K. 1985. Rough-and-tumble play, fighting, and chasing in nursery school children. *Ethology and Sociobiology* 6: 175–181.

Smith, R. J. 1977. Electroshock experiment at Albany violates ethics guidelines. *Science* 198: 383–386.

Smith, T. W. 1981. Qualifications to generalized absolutes: "Approval of hitting" questions on the GSS. *Public Opinion Quarterly* 45: 224–230.

Sommer, R. 1968. Hawthorne dogma. *Psychological Bulletin* 70: 592–595.

Spielberger, C. D. 1988. Report of the treasurer: 1987. *American Psychologist* 43: 499–505.

Spitz, R. A. 1965. *The first year of life.* New York: International Universities Press.

Sprague, R. L., and Sleator, E. K. 1977. Methylphenidate in hyperkinetic children: Differences in dose effects on learning and social behavior. *Science* 198: 1274–1276.

Stern, L. D. 1981. A review of theories of human amnesia. *Memory & Cognition* 9: 247–262.

Sternberg, R. J. 1982. Who's intelligent? *Psychology Today* (April): 30–39.

Stevens, S. S. 1951. Mathematics, measurement, and psychophysics. In *Handbook of experimental psychology*, ed. S. S. Stevens, pp. 1–49. New York: Wiley.

———. 1956. The direct estimation of sensory magnitude—loudness. *American Journal of Psychology* 69: 1–25.

Sun, M. 1981. Laetrile brush fire is out, scientists hope. *Science* 212: 758–759.

———. 1988. Debate rages over breast cancer study. *Science* 239: 17–18.

Swets, J. A. 1973. The relative operating characteristic in psychology. *Science* 182: 990–1000.

Swets, J. A.; Pickett, R. M.; Whitehead, S. F.; Getty, D. J.; Schnur, J. A.; Swets J. B.; and Freeman, B. A. 1979. Assessment of diagnostic technologies. *Science* 205: 753–759.

Taint of scholarly fraud. *Time*, December 6, 1976, p. 66.

Tedeschi, J. T.; Lindskold, S.; and Rosenfeld, P. 1985. *Introduction to social psychology*. St. Paul, Minn.: West.

Till, R. E. 1985. Verbatim and inferential memory in young and eldery adults. *Journal of Gerontology* 40: 316–323.

Trigg, G. L. 1979. In your own write. *Physical Review Letters* 42: 748.

Tversky, A., and Kahneman, D. 1971. Belief in the law of small numbers. *Psychological Bulletin* 76: 105–110.

———. 1974. Judgment under uncertainty: Heuristics and biases. *Science* 185: 1124–1131.

Underwood, B. J. 1949. *Experimental psychology*. New York: Appleton-Century-Crofts.

———. 1957. *Psychological research*. New York: Appleton-Century-Crofts.

Underwood, B. J., and Shaughnessy, J. J. 1975. *Experimentation in psychology*. New York: Wiley; Robert E. Krieger, 1983.

VanBiervliet, A.; Spangler, P. F.; and Marshall, A. M. 1981. An ecobehavioral examination of a simple strategy for increasing mealtime language in residential facilities. *Journal of Applied Behavior Analysis* 14: 295–305.

Van Nuys, D. 1975. On the phrasing of hypnotic suggestions: A brief case report. *Psychotherapy: Theory, Research and Practice* 12: 302–304.

Voss, J. F. 1987. Basic and applied research as problem solving: An analysis of constraints. *International Journal of Psychology* 22: 463–469.

Wade, N. 1976a. Animal rights: NIH cat sex study brings grief to New York museum. *Science* 194: 162–167.

———. 1976b. IQ and heredity: Suspicion of fraud beclouds classic experiment. *Science* 194: 916–919.

Wallace, W. P., and Underwood, B. J. 1964. Implicit responses and the role of intralist similarity in verbal learning by normal and retarded subjects. *Journal of Educational Psychology* 55: 362–370.

Wallraff, H. G., and Sinsch, U. 1988. The role of "outward-journey information" in homing experiments with pigeons: New data on ontogeny of navigation and general survey. *Ethology* 77: 10–27.

Ward, W. D., and Jenkins, H. M. 1965. The display of information and the judgment of contingency. *Canadian Journal of Psychology* 19: 231–241.

Warwick, D. P., and Lininger, C. A. 1975. *The sample survey: Theory and practice*. New York: McGraw-Hill.

Watson, J. B. 1913. Psychology as the behaviorist views it. *Psychological Review* 20: 158–177.

———. [1914] 1967. *Behavior: An introduction to comparative psychology*. New York: Holt, Rinehart and Winston.

Webb, E. J.; Campbell, D. T.; Schwartz, R. D.; Sechrest, L.; and Grove, J. B. 1981. *Nonreactive measures in the social sciences*, 2d ed. Boston: Houghton-Mifflin.

Weigel, R. H.; Loomis, J. W.; and Soja, M. J. 1980. Race relations on prime time television. *Journal of Personality and Social Psychology* 39: 884–893.

Weiss, J. M. 1977. Psychological and behavioral influences on gastrointestinal lesions in animal models. In *Psychopathology: Experimental models,* ed. J. D. Maser and M. E. P. Seligman, pp. 232–269. San Francisco: Freeman.

Wells, G. L.; Lindsay, R. C. L.; and Ferguson, T. J. 1979. Accuracy, confidence, and juror perceptions in eyewitness identification. *Journal of Applied Psychology* 64: 440–448.

Where the polls went wrong. *Time,* December 1, 1980, pp. 21–22.

Willems, E. P. 1969. Planning a rationale for naturalistic research. In *Naturalistic viewpoints in psychological research,* ed. E. P. Willems and H. L. Raush, pp. 44–71. New York: Holt, Rinehart and Winston.

Willems, E. P., and Raush, H. L., eds. 1969. *Naturalistic viewpoint in psychological research.* New York: Holt, Rinehart and Winston.

Willingham, W. W. 1974. Predicting success in graduate education. *Science* 183: 273–278.

Wilson, G. T. 1978. On the much discussed nature of the term "behavior therapy." *Behavior Therapy* 9: 89–98.

Wortman, C. B., and Loftus, E. F. 1981. *Psychology.* New York: Knopf.

Yankelovich, D. 1981. New rules in American life: Searching for self-fulfillment in a world turned upside down. *Psychology Today* (April): 35–91.

Yeaton, W. H., and Sechrest, L. 1981. Critical dimensions in the choice and maintenance of successful treatments: Strength, integrity, and effectiveness. *Journal of Consulting and Clinical Psychology* 49: 156–167.

———. 1986. Use and misuse of no-difference findings in eliminating threats to validity. *Evaluation Review* 10: 836–852.

Zechmeister, E. B., and Nyberg, S. E. 1982. *Human memory: An introduction to research and theory.* Monterey, Calif.: Brooks/Cole.

Subject Index

Author Index